Human Factors in Software Development and Design

Saqib Saeed
University of Dammam, Saudi Arabia

Imran Sarwar Bajwa
The Islamia University of Bahawalpur, Pakistan

Zaigham Mahmood
University of Derby, UK & North West University, South Africa

A volume in the Advances in Systems Analysis, Software Engineering, and High Performance Computing (ASASEHPC) Book Series

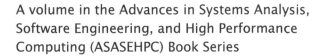

Information Science
REFERENCE
An Imprint of IGI Global

Managing Director:	Lindsay Johnston
Production Editor:	Christina Henning
Development Editor:	Erin O'Dea
Acquisitions Editor:	Kayla Wolfe
Typesetter:	John Crodian
Cover Design:	Jason Mull

Published in the United States of America by
Information Science Reference (an imprint of IGI Global)
701 E. Chocolate Avenue
Hershey PA, USA 17033
Tel: 717-533-8845
Fax: 717-533-8661
E-mail: cust@igi-global.com
Web site: http://www.igi-global.com

Library of Congress Cataloging-in-Publication Data

Human factors in software development and design / Saqib Saeed, Imran Sarwar
Bajwa, and Zaigham Mahmood, editors.
    pages cm
 Includes bibliographical references and index.
  ISBN 978-1-4666-6485-2 (hardcover) -- ISBN 978-1-4666-6486-9 (ebook) --
ISBN 978-1-4666-6488-3 (print & perpetual access) 1. Computer software--
Development. 2. Software architecture. I. Saeed, Saqib, 1970- II. Bajwa,
Imran Sarwar, 1979- III. Mahmood, Zaigham.
  QA76.76.D47H842 2015
  005.1--dc23
                        2014026480

This book is published in the IGI Global book series Advances in Systems Analysis, Software Engineering, and High Performance Computing (ASASEHPC) (ISSN: 2327-3453; eISSN: 2327-3461)

Advances in Systems Analysis, Software Engineering, and High Performance Computing (ASASEHPC) Book Series

Vijayan Sugumaran
Oakland University, USA

ISSN: 2327-3453
EISSN: 2327-3461

MISSION

The theory and practice of computing applications and distributed systems has emerged as one of the key areas of research driving innovations in business, engineering, and science. The fields of software engineering, systems analysis, and high performance computing offer a wide range of applications and solutions in solving computational problems for any modern organization.

The **Advances in Systems Analysis, Software Engineering, and High Performance Computing (ASASEHPC) Book Series** brings together research in the areas of distributed computing, systems and software engineering, high performance computing, and service science. This collection of publications is useful for academics, researchers, and practitioners seeking the latest practices and knowledge in this field.

COVERAGE

- Engineering Environments
- Metadata and Semantic Web
- Network Management
- Computer Graphics
- Storage Systems
- Performance Modelling
- Computer System Analysis
- Parallel Architectures
- Software Engineering
- Enterprise Information Systems

IGI Global is currently accepting manuscripts for publication within this series. To submit a proposal for a volume in this series, please contact our Acquisition Editors at Acquisitions@igi-global.com or visit: http://www.igi-global.com/publish/.

Titles in this Series

For a list of additional titles in this series, please visit: www.igi-global.com

Handbook of Research on Innovations in Systems and Software Engineering
Vicente García Díaz (University of Oviedo, Spain) Juan Manuel Cueva Lovelle (University of Oviedo, Spain) and B. Cristina Pelayo García-Bustelo (University of Oviedo, Spain)
Information Science Reference • copyright 2015 • 723pp • H/C (ISBN: 9781466663596) • US $515.00 (our price)

Handbook of Research on Architectural Trends in Service-Driven Computing
Raja Ramanathan (Independent Researcher, USA) and Kirtana Raja (IBM, USA)
Information Science Reference • copyright 2014 • 759pp • H/C (ISBN: 9781466661783) • US $515.00 (our price)

Handbook of Research on Embedded Systems Design
Alessandra Bagnato (Softeam R&D, France) Leandro Soares Indrusiak (University of York, UK) Imran Rafiq Quadri (Softeam R&D, France) and Matteo Rossi (Politecnico di Milano, Italy)
Information Science Reference • copyright 2014 • 520pp • H/C (ISBN: 9781466661943) • US $345.00 (our price)

Contemporary Advancements in Information Technology Development in Dynamic Environments
Mehdi Khosrow-Pour (Information Resources Management Association, USA)
Information Science Reference • copyright 2014 • 410pp • H/C (ISBN: 9781466662520) • US $205.00 (our price)

Systems and Software Development, Modeling, and Analysis New Perspectives and Methodologies
Mehdi Khosrow-Pour (Information Resources Management Association, USA)
Information Science Reference • copyright 2014 • 365pp • H/C (ISBN: 9781466660984) • US $215.00 (our price)

Handbook of Research on Emerging Advancements and Technologies in Software Engineering
Imran Ghani (Universiti Teknologi Malaysia, Malaysia) Wan Mohd Nasir Wan Kadir (Universiti Teknologi Malaysia, Malaysia) and Mohammad Nazir Ahmad (Universiti Teknologi Malaysia, Malaysia)
Engineering Science Reference • copyright 2014 • 686pp • H/C (ISBN: 9781466660267) • US $395.00 (our price)

Advancing Embedded Systems and Real-Time Communications with Emerging Technologies
Seppo Virtanen (University of Turku, Finland)
Information Science Reference • copyright 2014 • 502pp • H/C (ISBN: 9781466660342) • US $235.00 (our price)

Handbook of Research on High Performance and Cloud Computing in Scientific Research and Education
Marijana Despotović-Zrakić (University of Belgrade, Serbia) Veljko Milutinović (University of Belgrade, Serbia) and Aleksandar Belić (University of Belgrade, Serbia)
Information Science Reference • copyright 2014 • 476pp • H/C (ISBN: 9781466657847) • US $325.00 (our price)

www.igi-global.com

701 E. Chocolate Ave., Hershey, PA 17033
Order online at www.igi-global.com or call 717-533-8845 x100
To place a standing order for titles released in this series, contact: cust@igi-global.com
Mon-Fri 8:00 am - 5:00 pm (est) or fax 24 hours a day 717-533-8661

To My Sweet Daughters Rameen Saqib and Eshaal Saqib

Editorial Advisory Board

Table of Contents

Section 1
Introduction

Section 2
User-Centered Design

Section 3
Usability Engineering

Detailed Table of Contents

Section 1
Introduction

Chapter 1

Software engineering is largely concerned with the methodical, systematic production of quality software. Despite significant advances in technology over the last decade, software engineering still heavily relies on human efforts and human interaction to generate economic contributions. In more recent years, the question of software service complexity has become central to Global Software Development (GSD). However, few efforts have surfaced to challenge the complexity of the relational infrastructure of software teams that support the development of software architecture. This is important in order to sustain and support lean software development organisational structures particularly in an open service innovation environment. However, from a socio-economic perspective, there are few theoretical efforts that attempt to introduce new insights on how the human factors contribute towards a GSD value co-creation. The objective of this chapter is to examine the application of Social Network Analysis (SNA) and i* (i star) modelling techniques to examine how we could model the economic impact of software relational structures. The chapter explores how i* models leverage SNA concepts to model GSD. This chapter also offers a discussion on the theoretical development of the socio-economics of GSD in an "open innovation" context.

Chapter 2

Over the last two decades, public confidence and trust in government has declined visibly in several Western liberal democracies, owing to a distinct lack of opportunities for citizen participation in political processes, and has given way instead to disillusionment with current political institutions, actors, and practices. The rise of the Internet as a global communications medium has opened up huge opportunities and raised new challenges for government, with digital technology creating new forms of community, empowering citizens, and reforming existing power structures in a way that has rendered obsolete or inappropriate many of the tools and processes of traditional democratic politics. Through an analysis of the No. 10 Downing Street ePetitions Initiative based in the United Kingdom, this chapter seeks to engage with issues related to the innovative use of network technology by government to involve citizens in policy processes within existing democratic frameworks in order to improve administration, reform democratic processes, and renew citizen trust in institutions of governance.

This chapter presents an approach to the role of software engineering in developing solutions for new mobile technologies, like tablets. It discusses the importance of the new standards brought by emerging technologies such as engineering and how software must adapt to this new reality in order to identify the needs of data, information, integration, shares, and other issues that will contribute to the life cycle of these solutions. The chapter also discusses the contribution of users in the development process and improve these solutions. The research method is the case study conducted in industrial companies that use a digital catalog solution and sales force automation for tablets. This chapter presents a new approach based on commercial tablets which is supported by a platform of software and services called commercially Nimiam (www.nimiam.com.br).

Chapter 4

Much has been written about e-government within a growing stream of literature on ICT for development, generating countervailing perspectives where optimistic, technocratic approaches are countered by far more sceptical standpoints on technological innovation. This chapter seeks to, through the use of a case study, unravel the social dynamics shaping e-government projects used to reform public sector institutions. In particular, the research analyzes actor behaviour, motivations, and interactions surrounding the conception and maintenance of software platforms facilitating these transformations. The value of such an approach is based on a review of existing ICT and software development literature, which tends to be overly systems-rational in its approach and, as a consequence, often fails to recognise the degree to which project failure (viz. the general inability of the project design to meet stated goals and resolve both predicted and emerging problems) is symptomatic of a broader, much more complex set of interrelated inequalities, unresolved problems, and lopsided power-relationships both within the adopting organisation and in the surrounding environmental context.

Chapter 5

Whereas there are several instances of Open Source Software (OSS) projects that have achieved huge success in the market, a high failure rate has been reported for OSS projects. This study conducts a literature survey to gain insight into existing studies on the success of OSS projects. More specifically, this study seeks to extract the critical success factors for OSS projects. Based on the literature survey in this study, the authors found determinants of success in OSS projects and classified them into three broad categories of project traits, product traits, and network structure. These findings have important implications for both the OSS research community and OSS practitioners.

Section 2
User-Centered Design

Chapter 6

The user-centered design process among U.S. companies is commonly carried out by design teams. Groups of designers are commonly unable to create high quality work due to the need to first work out several issues. These issues include needing to get to know one another's capabilities while also learning how to effectively communicate through the many difficult decisions and deadlines common to software and Web design projects. This chapter describes the communication research that illuminates the process that groups go through before they can achieve high-quality results.

Chapter 7

This chapter describes how Situational Awareness (SA) can differ between roles in the design-use process. SA is not traditionally used to describe awareness between roles in the design-use process. However, SA between individuals or groups having various roles in the design-use process could be described, assessed, and used as a tool for improving a design process.

Chapter 8

Game design and development has already been discussed as a viable, motivating alternative to introduce Computer Science concepts to young students. In this sense, it would be useful to obtain a deeper understanding of which skills could be developed in these activities and how such skills could be useful in future careers. This chapter presents the design and evaluation of a Game Building Workshop aimed at introducing the fundamentals of structured programming to students. The games produced by students during 12 weeks were evaluated and the results confronted with students' questions and comments made along the workshop meetings and a final interview. The results indicate that students explored novel programming concepts in order to add features that were not initially planned for the proposed games. These additional features solve playability issues that are highly influential to the experience of the students as game players. Students also reused previously applied solutions to solve similar problems that appeared in subsequent activities. This is an indication that students developed or exercised analogy and abstraction skills during the workshop activities.

Chapter 9

Pankaj Kamthan, Concordia University, Canada

The movement towards agility is one of the most significant human-centered and socially oriented changes in industrial software engineering. In the practice of agile methodologies, there are different types of content (data, information, or knowledge) that are created, communicated, and consumed. It is imperative for an organization to manage such content, both during development and beyond deployment. This chapter proposes a conceptual model for understanding and exploring the use of Wiki as a vehicle for managing content in agile software development. In doing so, the parity between agile software development and Wiki is shown, human and social aspects of each are emphasized, the Social Web-Context of Wiki is demonstrated, illustrative examples are given, and the implications of committing to a Wiki are considered.

Chapter 10

Rosario Girardi, Federal University of Maranhão, Brazil
Adriana Leite, Federal University of Maranhão, Brazil

Automating software engineering tasks is crucial to achieve better productivity of software development and quality of software products. Knowledge engineering approaches this challenge by supporting the representation and reuse of knowledge of how and when to perform a development task. Therefore, knowledge tools for software engineering can turn more effective the software development process by automating and controlling consistency of modeling tasks and code generation. This chapter introduces the description of the domain and application design phases of MADAE-Pro, an ontology-driven process for agent-oriented development, along with how reuse is performed between these sub-processes. Two case studies have been conducted to evaluate MADAE-Pro from which some examples of the domain and application design phases have been extracted and presented in this chapter. The first case study assesses the Multi-Agent Domain Design sub-process of MADAE-Pro through the design of a multi-agent system family of recommender systems supporting alternative (collaborative, content-based, and hybrid) filtering techniques. The second one evaluates the Multi-Agent Application Design sub-process of MADAE-Pro through the design of InfoTrib, a Tax Law recommender system that provides recommendations based on new tax law information items using a content-based filtering technique.

Chapter 11

Zulaima Chiquin, Simón Bolívar University, Venezuela
Kenyer Domínguez, Simón Bolívar University, Venezuela
Luis E. Mendoza, Simón Bolívar University, Venezuela
Edumilis Méndez, Simón Bolívar University, Venezuela

This chapter presents a Model to Estimate the Human Factor Quality in Free/Libre Open Source Software (FLOSS) Development, or EHFQ-FLOSS. The model consists of three dimensions: Levels (individual, community, and foundation), Aspects (internal or contextual), and Forms of Evaluation (self-evaluation, co-evaluation, and hetero-evaluation). Furthermore, this model provides 145 metrics applicable to all three levels, as well as an algorithm that guides their proper application to estimate the systemic quality of human resources involved in the development of FLOSS, guide the decision-making process, and take possible corrective actions.

Chapter 12

Tariq Zaman, Universiti Malaysia Sarawak, Malaysia
Alvin W. Yeo, Universiti Malaysia Sarawak, Malaysia
Narayanan Kulathuramaiyer, Universiti Malaysia Sarawak, Malaysia

The existing frameworks and methodologies for software designing encompass technological aspects and needs of the urban settings. In software development, getting sufficient and correct requirements from the users is most important, because these requirements will determine the functionality of the system. In indigenous communities identifying the user needs and understanding the local context are always difficult tasks. This typical approach of designing indigenous knowledge management system generates the issues of indigenous knowledge governance, de-contextualisation, and data manipulation. Hence, the main research question this chapter addresses is, How can we introduce indigenous knowledge governance into ICT-based Indigenous Knowledge Management System (IKMS)? The study has been conducted in three phases with collaboration of two indigenous communities, Long Lamai and Bario of Sarawak, East Malaysia. The main outcome of the study is the methodology of conducting a multidisciplinary research and designing the Indigenous Knowledge Governance Framework (IKGF). The framework works as an analytical tool that can help in understanding the essential context in which indigenous knowledge management processes occur. The chapter argues that in order to design appropriate software tools for indigenous knowledge management, information technology professionals need to understand, model, and formalise the holistic indigenous knowledge management system and then use this understanding as a basis for technology design and approaches.

Section 3
Usability Engineering

Chapter 13

Ana Isabel Martins, University of Aveiro, Portugal
Alexandra Queirós, University of Aveiro, Portugal
Anabela G. Silva, University of Aveiro, Portugal
Nelson Pacheco Rocha, University of Aveiro, Portugal

This chapter aims to identify, analyze, and classify the methodologies and methods described in the literature for the usability evaluation of systems and services based on information and communication technologies. The methodology used was a systematic review of the literature. The studies included in the analysis were classified into empirical and analytical methodologies (test, inquiry, controlled experiment, or inspection). A total of 2116 studies were included, of which 1308 were classified. In terms of results, the inquiry methodology was the most frequent in this review, followed by test, inspection, and finally, the controlled experiment methodology. A combination of methodologies is relatively common, especially the combination of test and inquiry methodologies, probably because they assess different but complementary aspects of usability contributing to a more comprehensive assessment.

Chapter 14

Alexandra Queirós, University of Aveiro, Portugal
Margarida Cerqueira, University of Aveiro, Portugal
Ana Isabel Martins, University of Aveiro, Portugal
Anabela G. Silva, University of Aveiro, Portugal
Joaquim Alvarelhão, University of Aveiro, Portugal
Nelson Pacheco Rocha, University of Aveiro, Portugal

This chapter presents how the concepts of the International Classification of Functioning, Disability, and Health (ICF) can be used to optimize the role of personas and scenarios in the development and evaluation of Ambient Assisted Living (AAL) systems and services, especially in aspects related to human functioning and health conditions.

Chapter 15

Muhammad Ahmad Amin, Bahria University, Pakistan
Saqib Saeed, University of Dammam, Saudi Arabia

Amongst open-source e-learning systems, WebGoat, a progression of OWASP, provides some room for teaching the penetration testing techniques. Yet, it is a major concern of its learners as to whether the WebGoat interface is user-friendly enough to help them acquaint themselves of the desired Web application security knowledge. This chapter encompasses a heuristic evaluation of this application to acquire the usability of contemporary version of WebGoat. In this context of evaluation, the in-house formal lab testing of WebGoat was conducted by the authors. The results highlight some important issues and usability problems that frequently pop-up in the contemporary version. The research results would be pivotal to the embedding of an operational as well as user-friendly interface for its future version.

Preface

OVERVIEW

Software development is primarily a human activity. It is a process that requires the use of latest methodologies to develop a robust design and the use of the latest technologies to implement the design to construct the final software products that are fit for the intended consumption. Since the software is developed by people for the consumption of people, the consideration of human factors in an important element within the entire process. Appropriate implementation of such factors can help to ensure that the final product meets the desired requirements. Although newer tools and techniques for the development of software has resulted in increased productivity of developers and reduction in development costs, working in large teams, which is necessarily required for large software engineering projects, is still problematic. Although the time and cost estimation techniques have improved considerably, the influence of environmental factors and inherent complexity of large software development is still resulting in systems being over-budgeted and delivered late. Although consideration of human factors is involving newer management techniques, psychology of group dynamics, methods of team motivation, and systems of rewards, when dealing with highly skilled independent-minded professionals, interaction is not easy. Understanding of relevant human factors and correct implementation of these is therefore imperative to have the correct impact so that the software continues to be designed and constructed with embedded high quality that fully satisfies consumer requirements.

This book, *Human Factors in Software Development and Design*, is a reference text. It is a collection of 15 chapters, authored by 26 academics and practitioners from around the world. These contributions in this book aim to present practice reports, discussions, inherent issues, implementation strategies, latest research, as well as case studies from around the world focusing on the human factors aspect of software design and development.

BOOK OBJECTIVE

The aim of *Human Factors in Software Development and Design* is to publish high quality original research contributions on the specialized theme of human factors in software design and development processes. Specific objectives include the following:

- Reporting state of the art in the area of human factors with respect to software development.
- Disseminating the elements of good practices suggested and practices by researchers and practitioners in the field.
- Considering all relevant aspects of software development processes in relation to implications for human cognitive limits.
- Reporting and discussing strategies for improving software quality.
- Reporting case studies, best practices, and guidelines for technology design in this specialized area.

Readers, especially the software developers, researchers, and students of software engineering, will find it a useful text as it adds to the body of knowledge in the area of software user interface, human computer interaction, and human factors.

TARGET AUDIENCES

This volume is a reference text aimed at the following audiences:

- Software developers and computing practitioners interested in user interface design and related human factors
- Project managers interested in user involvement in the software engineering processes
- Researchers and students of human factors and user interface design interested in furthering their understanding of the subject.

BOOK ORGANIZATION

There are 15 chapters in this text. These are organized in three Sections as follows:

- **Introduction:** This consists of five chapters. The first chapter focuses on socio-economic factors relating to global software development, whereas the second chapter discusses innovations in the ICT as used in the public administration. The third contribution in this section is about the user involvement in the software production for tablet devices, and the next chapter presents a case study on e-government development. The final chapter looks into the success factors for open source projects.
- **User-Centered Design:** This section comprises seven chapters. The first chapter, which is Chapter 6 in the book, presents a case study on user-centered design processes, while the next chapter focuses on the management of situational awareness with respect to design-use processes of complex systems. The next two contributions provide a descriptive study of a games design workshop and the use of wikis for agile software development. The fifth contribution in this section discusses a semantic approach for multi-agent system design. In the next contribution, authors present a model to estimate human factor quality in open source development. The final chapter focuses on the challenges of designing knowledge-management systems.

- **Usability Engineering:** This section of the book has three contributions. The first chapter provides a review of the methods for usability evaluation, and the next chapter focuses on personas and scenarios for functioning and health conditions. The final contribution of this section, which is the last chapter in the book, presents a study on the role of usability in e-learning systems.

Brief Descriptions of the Chapters

Chapter 1 is titled "Open Innovation: Assessing the Socio-Economic Factors of Global Software Development" and authored by Noel Carroll. It looks into the socio-economic factors of global software development. The contribution discusses the current modelling techniques and examines the SNA (Social Network Analysis) and I Star (*) modelling techniques, in particular.

Chapter 2 is titled "Innovations in Information and Communication Technology Platforms for Public Administration: Consulting the British Public in the Digital Age." Authored by Shefali Virkar, this contribution presents an empirical study of an e-Petitions initiative in the UK and provides guidelines for developing citizen-centered e-government systems.

Chapter 3, titled "Software Engineering and New Emerging Technologies: The Involvement of Users for Development Applications for Tablets," is authored by Sergio Mazini. It is about user involvement for software development for tablet devices. This contribution discusses the mobile technologies and presents a case study of using the digital catalog solution and sales force automation for tablets.

Chapter 4, developed by Shefali Virkar, titled "The Games People Play: The Politics of Software Platform Development and ICT Project Design for Public Sector Administration Reform," presents a case study to unravel the social dynamics shaping e-government projects used to reform public-sector institutions. This contribution focuses on actor behavior, motivations, and interactions surrounding the conception and maintenance of software platforms facilitating these transformations.

Chapter 5, titled "Investigating the Success of OSS Software Projects" and authored by Amir Ghapanchi, presents a review of the existing literature to discuss and understand the success factors for developing open-source projects. A grouping of these factors in terms of project, product, and network classes is also discussed.

Chapter 6, developed by Laura Dahl and titled "Creating Effective Communication among User-Centered Technology Design," focuses on user-centered design processes with respect to software development and presents a case for effective communication between and across design teams. The current literature is surveyed and conclusions presented.

Chapter 7, contributed by Jens Alfredson, titled "Managing Differences in Situational Awareness Due to Roles in the Design-Use Process of Complex Systems," describes how Situational Awareness (SA) can differ between roles in the design-use process of complex software systems and explains how various roles in the design-use process can be more usefully employed in effective designs, focusing also on the management of related processes.

Chapter 8, developed by Barcelos et al. is titled "Improving Novice Programmers' Skills through Playability and Pattern Discovery: A Descriptive Study of a Game Building Workshop." It provides a descriptive study of a Game Design Workshop, aimed at introducing the fundamentals of structured programming to students, and illustrates how programming skills of novice software developers can be improved by dealing with playability issues and identifying relevant patterns.

Chapter 9, "Wiki for Agility," by Pankaj Kamthan, proposes the use of Wikis for managing different type of content with respect to agile software development. It discusses the parity between agile software development and Wikis, emphasizing human and social aspects in the Social Web-context of Wikis. Examples are also provided.

Chapter 10 is titled "A Semantic Approach for Multi-Agent System Design." Authored by Girardi and Leite, it emphasizes the need for automating software development processes. In this contribution, authors employ MADAE-Pro, an ontology-driven process model for the design processes of two different case studies. Based on their evaluation, the authors show how software artifacts produced are later reused.

Chapter 11, "Model to Estimate the Human Factor Quality in FLOSS Development," proposes a model for predicting human factor quality in open source projects. The authors consider level of project, aspects, and forms of evaluation as important parameters in their model. In order to quantitatively evaluate quality, 145 metrics are proposed as well.

Chapter 12 is contributed by Zaman et al. and titled "From Knowledge Management to Knowledge Governance: A System-Centred Methodology for Designing Indigenous Knowledge Management System." This contribution highlights the difficulties in designing knowledge management systems in indigenous communities. On the basis of two longitudinal studies, the authors present a systematic framework to understand the requirements of indigenous knowledge management processes.

Chapter 13 is titled "Usability Evaluation Methods: A Systematic Review." Discussing the concept and evaluation of usability evaluation, this chapter, authored by Martins et al., aims to analyze and classify the existing methodologies for the usability evaluation of products and services based on current ICTs. The contribution presents a review and results of a comparative study.

Chapter 14, titled "Personas and Scenarios Based on Functioning and Health Conditions," by Queiros et al., looks into the personas and various scenarios based on functioning and health conditions to first discuss the concepts of Int. Classification of Functioning, Disability, and Health (ICF) and then presents a framework for the evaluation of Ambient Assisted Living (AAL) systems and services.

Chapter 15, titled "Role of Usability in E-Learning Systems: An Empirical Study of OWASP Web-Goat," written by Amin and Saeed, focuses on e-learning systems, discussing the role of usability. The contribution presents an evaluation of a system based on OWASP to highlight usability problems and related issues. Important results are presented that are pivotal to the embedding of an operational as well as future user-friendly interfaces.

Zaigham Mahmood
University of Derby, UK & North West University, South Africa

Saqib Saeed
University of Dammam, Saudi Arabia
17 July 2014

Acknowledgment

The editors would like to thank the chapter authors who developed quality chapters for this book. Without their efforts, this publication would not have been possible. We would also like to thank Prof. Vijayan Sugumaran, the series editor of IGI Advances in Systems Analysis, Software Engineering, and High Performance Computing for accepting our book proposal. Special thanks are also due to IGI staff for their continuous support throughout the publication process of this text. Grateful thanks to the members of the advisory board and chapter reviewers for their efforts in reviewing the manuscripts and suggestions to improve the manuscripts.

Saqib Saeed
University of Dammam, Saudi Arabia

Imran Sarwar Bajwa
The Islamia University of Bahawalpur, Pakistan

Zaigham Mahmood
University of Derby, UK & North West University, South Africa

Section 1
Introduction

Chapter 1
Open Innovation:
Assessing the Socio-Economic Factors of Global Software Development

Noel Carroll
University of Limerick, Ireland

ABSTRACT

Software engineering is largely concerned with the methodical, systematic production of quality software. Despite significant advances in technology over the last decade, software engineering still heavily relies on human efforts and human interaction to generate economic contributions. In more recent years, the question of software service complexity has become central to Global Software Development (GSD). However, few efforts have surfaced to challenge the complexity of the relational infrastructure of software teams that support the development of software architecture. This is important in order to sustain and support lean software development organisational structures particularly in an open service innovation environment. However, from a socio-economic perspective, there are few theoretical efforts that attempt to introduce new insights on how the human factors contribute towards a GSD value co-creation. The objective of this chapter is to examine the application of Social Network Analysis (SNA) and i* (i star) modelling techniques to examine how we could model the economic impact of software relational structures. The chapter explores how i* models leverage SNA concepts to model GSD. This chapter also offers a discussion on the theoretical development of the socio-economics of GSD in an "open innovation" context.

INTRODUCTION

Open innovation is an emerging paradigm which exposes organisations to external or networked innovation to avail of newfound service capabilities (Chesbrough, 2003). While open innovation continues to receive increasing level of attention, it also highlights the importance of assessing the socio-economic contributory efforts of software teams developing software architecture. Nowadays, organisations are tasked with uncovering *"what is out there"* to combine external capabilities with internal innovation resources. Thus, over the past decade we witnessed two important key service developments: 1) increase in technology capability and accessibility, and 2) the emergence

DOI: 10.4018/978-1-4666-6485-2.ch001

of new business models. Similar to the growth in information technology (IT) throughout the 1990's, these developments opened up new opportunities to apply technological capabilities to address business needs. This is particularly evident within the field of software engineering (for example, Šmite et al. 2010) especially in global software development (GSD). Thus, uncovering what stabilises a GSD team is a critical element within the software system since it defines the structures and relations between them to develop software architecture. Software architecture is defined as *"the fundamental organisation of a system embodied in its components, their relationships to each other, and to the environment, and the principles guiding its design and evolution"* (IEEE, 2000). The relational properties are of significant interest as this chapter focuses on the need to understand how GSD can facilitate communication and interaction patterns to reuse software components for software architecture in an open innovation environment. This allows us to understand 'the system', organise its development process and plan for methods to reuse software components and support its evolution. At a most basic level, the software architecture will be specified using diagrams which have modelled subsystems, interfaces between them, components diagrams, classes, diverse descriptions, and the basic group of use cases. The architecture it typically validated by clients and developers to achieve the desired functionality. A service may be defined as *"a change in the condition of a person or a good belonging to some economic entity brought about as a result of the activity of some other economic entity, with the approval of the first person, or economic entity"* (Carroll, 2012). For the purpose of this chapter, the author is primarily interested in uncovering the socio-economic dynamics which contribute to the evolution of a GSD team. It examines how the relationship between stakeholders and decision-making influence the socio-economic dynamics of software development. This chapter offers a discussion on the need to apply social and economic considerations to software architectural development and decision-making tasks.

Research Focus

The modern service environment represents a paradigm shift away from technology as an organisational asset to technology enabled service. GSD is one such development which is becoming the normal practice in the software industry (Conchúir et al. 2009). GSD may be defined as software development process undertaken at geographically separated locations across national and organisational boundaries in a coordinated fashion involving real time (synchronous) and asynchronous interaction (Conchúir et al. 2009). Often the benefits of GSD described throughout literatures are summarised as follows:

1. To achieve cost benefits;
2. Reduced development costs;
3. To manage shortages in specific skills (larger and better-skilled developer pool);
4. Greater need of customer and market proximity;
5. Attraction of national legislations;
6. Greater time zone effectiveness;
7. Improved flexible resource capacity;
8. Availability of open source development;
9. Possibility of greater innovation;
10. Learning and transfer of best practices.

Thus, the modern software engineering field has become a more open, collaborative, and innovative global landscape which transfers valuable resources (such as knowledge and software resources) across a dynamic organisational relational structure. However, the openness and collaborative nature of international design structures is highly complex and not easily achieved. This chapter has identified how GSD shares similar opportunities to open innovation service environments which could reduce such complexities of GSD. Within service research, there has been increasing attention towards the relational structure which examines how a service environment is supported and stabilised from a socio-technical viewpoint (Carroll et al. 2010; Carroll et al. 2012). There have been significant developments in the field of software economics (for example, Boehm, 1984) and nowadays in software architecture and its economic contribution (for example, Boehm and Sullivan, 2000). However, despite the theoretical developments in open innovation and GSD, there are no efforts to bridge these developments and examine how their relational structure influences the socio-economic factors of software architec-

ture. While economies are typically associated with the notion of 'socio-economic' assessments, GSD environments may adopt a similar line of enquiry to examine the relationship between 'the social' and 'economic contribution'.

This chapter introduces the concept of social network analysis (SNA) (for example, Wasserman and Faust, 1994) and i* modelling (Yu, 2009) to examine how we could model the socio-economic impact of software relational structures (Figure 1). This chapter also offers a discussion on the theoretical development of the economics of GSD from an 'open innovation' viewpoint. In particular, this chapter presents a framework which explores the promise of open innovation in GSD. The central premise of this chapter is that to optimise GSD team efficiency in developing software architecture in an open innovation en-

Figure 1. Research overview. This indicates the overlap between open innovation, global software development and service relational structures. The core focus of this research is to examine how one can borrow relational mapping concepts to develop theoretical insights on the socio-economic factors of software development.

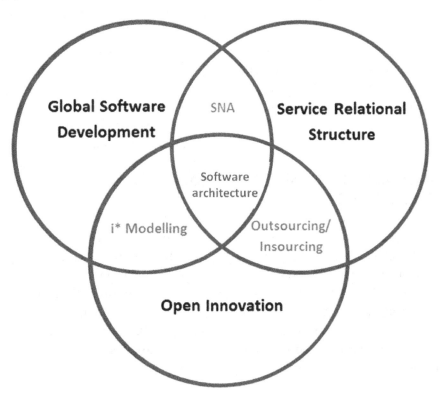

vironment, one should examine and understand the underlying relationships among social actors which ultimately contribute to economic activity.

Research Motivation

While examining the socio-economic factors of global software development, the author has identifies an imbalance between literature which focuses on the social factors and the economic factors. In short, much of the attention has been largely on economic modelling. For example, much of the research examines areas such as how business goals impact architecture decisions on cost, performance, security, modification, usability and ultimately their collective benefits (Asundi et al. 2001; Fichman and Kemerer, 2012). To add some balance to this research domain, this chapter sets out to examine whether we can develop an economic understanding of GSD based on social behaviour, for example, a groups relational structure, exchanging resources during decision-making, or matching social behaviour to economic output and developing insights as to how the reconfiguration of 'the social' may impact 'the economic' factors. The main premise of this research inquiry is to explore whether we can develop a different approach to model social behaviour of a software architecture development in a GSD environment and map this to economic behaviour.

THE GLOBAL LANDSCAPE OF SOFTWARE ENGINEERING

Software engineering is concerned with the application of methodologies to design, develop, operate, and maintain through the systematic production of software. To manage many of these processes, software engineering heavily relies on human efforts. To benefit from technical advances, software engineering organisations need to continuously redesign themselves appropriately, for example, software architecture, GSD and agile software development. Software architecture is the process of defining a structured solution which addresses both the technical and operational requirements. It is also concerned with optimising specific attributes through a number of decisions, all of which have a considerable impact on the quality, performance, and the overall success of the application. This adds to the complexity of software architecture development. We can describe this as a complex environment as it depends on the orchestration of several key socio-technical factors to deliver a software project. There are a number of key components of complex software architecture of GSD, for example:

1. Simple components (agents) relative to the whole system;
2. Non-linear interaction between components (i.e. "the whole is worth more than the sum of its parts");
3. Not controlled by any central executive and organised in a decentralised manner;
4. Emergent behaviours which focus on collective outcomes of the whole system, for example a hierarchical organisational structure, information processing, complex dynamics of GSD, and evolution and learning service system.

To illustrate the complexity and experience of a GSD environment at a high-level, one could suggest that its software architecture development relies on the four key factors (Figure 2):

1. **Dynamics:** Changing structure and behaviours of a GSD system;
2. **Information:** Representation, symbols, and communication to deliver software projects;
3. **Computation:** Processing information and acting on decisions;
4. **Evolution:** Adapting to a changing environment.

Figure 2. Key factors of software architecture development. This indicates the four main factors which interrelate to support the evolving nature of software architecture and which must be supported within a GSD environment.

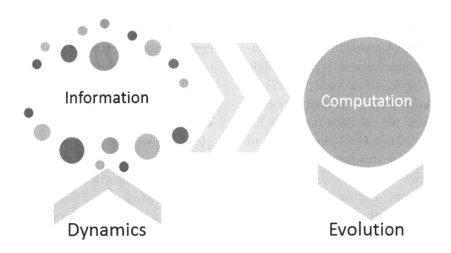

The key factors of software architecture development highlight the need to examine its complexity through a socio-economic lens in a GSD context. Software engineering relies on a systematic, disciplined, and quantifiable approach towards the software lifecycle and move from a conceptual solution to implementation. This transition implies that an economic change must take place. Software processes have received considerable attention in the software engineering field over the past decade and more recently on a global scale. Therefore, it is critical that we uncover the fundamental principles of the GSD ecological and its evolutionary service system which stabilises the software ecosystem. The author identifies the need to include social modelling for GSD in order to understand the dynamics and ultimately their economic contribution of these environments particularly within an open innovation environment. Software architecture shares similar characteristics to GSD. For example, both comprise of:

1. **Goals:** The complexity of software architecture is typically reduced by separating the overall design of the system and assigning specific elements to different stakeholders. This is normally outlined in the architecture documentation. Goals are a central characteristic within any software development project. Within a GSD environment, goals must be clear and concise to remove any ambiguity across different cultures and overcome any language barriers. In addition, it is worth noting that software engineers and architects are usually more concerned with tasks and user activities or actions performed in order to achieve the goals. This has also led to the development in goal-centered design.

2. **Multiple Stakeholders:** The development of a software system must involve (i.e. the development process) and cater for (i.e. users) a range of stakeholders from management, investors, developers, quality personnel and users. Stakeholders will have varying concerns and interests in the design and implementation of systems architecture. Stakeholders in a GSD environment are globally dispersed which calls for a clear mapping process of goals assigned to various

actors involved in the development of and decision-making tasks regarding software architecture.

3. **Recurring Styles:** Software architecture discipline had formulated certain standards which may be implemented to recurring concerns. For example, these styles may include architectural style, architectural pattern, and reference architecture. This is an important concept when we consider the need for recurring styles in a GSD environment to withhold software architecture consistency and standards.

4. **Quality-Driven:** The architecture of a software system is strongly associated with various quality attributes such as backward compatibility, reliability, security, and usability. The quality attributes are often the result of specific functional requirements. Considering the large challenge of managing multiple actors, with varying goals and styles, a quality-driven approach towards a GSD project is of vital importance to the control and ultimately the success of a project.

5. **Preserving Conceptual Integrity:** It is important that the architecture of a software system represents an overall vision of the project. It should align with the requirements and do what it was designed to do. This applies to a GSD context also where multiple stakeholders all try to serve individual interests or include additional functionalities which are not required. The quality-driven approach should support a project manager preserve the conceptual integrity of software architecture.

The points listed above provide an overview of the main characteristics of software architecture and how they share similar characteristics in a GSD environment. This is also applicable within a wider open innovation context.

OPEN INNOVATION IN GLOBAL SOFTWARE DEVELOPMENT

The concept of 'open innovation' captures the boundary-free view of the modern global service environment. Open innovation contributes towards organisations ability to harness innovation for competitive advantage (Chesbrough, 2003). In essence, organisations can now take advantage of existing innovations to propel internal technologies. This suggests that innovation is no longer an internal asset but rather an exchangeable entity which can be altered through service networks and customised to generate business value. However, it is a concern that much of the debate on open innovation is orchestrated by IT companies who focus on technical aspects which supposedly differentiates service delivery. While much of the effort still lies in understanding the benefits of its technical infrastructure, the fundamental concern comes down to whether a technology can add business value from open innovation. More importantly, one of the biggest challenges facing organisations engaged in GSD is developing a mechanism to assess the business value of software architecture. This would support organisations harness open innovation to avail of newfound capabilities while developing an understanding of the socio-economic contribution of software architecture.

Open innovation is considered to be a relatively new concept which examines the creation of value through the diffusion of innovation from external resources (Chesbrough, 2003). The funnelled approach of the open innovation model (Chesbrough, 2004) which combines external technologies with internal capabilities is one of the most documented approaches to understand the realignment of service provision for a targeted market opportunity. Thus, open innovation offers considerable promise for GSD environments. Chesbrough's (2004) model indicates the funnel effect of combining external capabilities with internal competencies to meet a specific market demand for new solutions.

Open innovation assumes that organisations ought to avail of external ideas and merge them with internal plans to advance specific technologies. In many cases, organisations will enter into a business relationship to combine specific competencies and capabilities in order to reach a certain goal and share a risk in doing so. This removes what was once considered to be boundary barriers and frees up the flow of innovation transferability between organisations to distribute knowledge. One of the key drivers of open innovation is the obvious cost savings required in an internally dedicated research team to develop new technologies. Nowadays, organisations often opt for licence agreements or joint ventures. Thus, open innovation has altered the concept of service capabilities from what was traditionally considered to an internal resource is now an external opportunity within the modern service environment. This is also true for GSD in the quest to optimise an organisation's software architecture. Considering that organisations can now avail of globally distributed knowledge, the service ecosystem is considered to be a 'flattened' (Friedman, 2006) global stage of innovation. This is what one may describe as the combination of servitization and open innovation. Organisations can therefore benefit from proven ('tried and tested') research or modular programming developments. While one might accept that the concept of open innovation has gathered increasing momentum across many research domains, there is also a correlation between the ability to facilitate an open innovation environment and the ability to in-source service capabilities. Now that the service ecosystem is considered to be a 'level playing field' (Friedman, 2006), the questions of how do organisations perform differently and how does an organisation compete by availing of widely available service capabilities remains unclear (Carr, 2004). These broad questions have stimulated the author's interests to delve into

understanding service open innovation within a GSD environment with particular focus on the software architecture. However, GSD introduces a number of challenges in relation to communication, coordination and control of the development process. These arise due to the distances involved in three dimensions – geographical, temporal, and socio-cultural (Conchúir et al. 2009). This draws our attention to examine the process of value co-creation within software architecture.

VALUE CO-CREATION: A SOCIO-ECONOMIC VIEW OF GSD

The concept of value co-creation implies that the customer plays a significant role to creating value within service systems (Spohrer et al. 2007; Carroll, 2012). Understanding the complexity of GSD network structures, process patterns, and methods is important to optimise the software architecture. Optimising software architecture focuses management attention on network performance and the critical success factors of service eco-system. Thus, the value creation process has changed in modern service environment as we move away from a 'chain' approach to a 'network' approach. In addition, Chesbrough (2011) provides an interesting argument in the need to move from a product-based view of service (such as Porters value chain) to a 'service value web'. Within the service value web, Chesbrough (2011) explains that there is no simple linear process of material inputs being transformed into outputs, but rather comprises of an iterative process that involves the customer in the whole process experience. This is also true in the case of software development. While the service value web undergoes a number of key phases, its relationships also creates value through external interactions with colleagues and customers across a GSD team.

Introducing new methods to model the socio-economic value of software architecture and service interactions is becoming increasingly important as many organisations particularly in GSD. Many of these software services were traditionally delivered through an inter-personal network collaborating together (Keast et al. 2004). There is continued interest in our ability to bridge the fields of service management and service computing and explore how both fields may support business relationships across complex service processes (Zhao et al. 2008). This is evident with the growth of Service Science (Carroll, 2012). Service Science promotes a new paradigm which acknowledges the need to systematically investigate how and why various entities (for example, organisations, people, technology) collaborate to create value without jeopardising quality standards. It also demonstrates the strong ties which exist between service system actors ('value co-creators') to deliver a service (for example, software development). Actors do not exist in isolation within a software development system. Rather, they exist in a shared software development environment whose interaction may provide us with behavioural analytics on software architecture decisions. The concept of value co-creation implies that the customer plays a significant role in creating value within services and view services as relational entities. Thus, this has ignited a curiosity in the author as to whether one can extend our understandings of GSD linkages or assemblages' (tracing actors behaviour) in the form of social interactions and convert this into economic metrics for greater service intelligence and analytics.

MODELLING THE SOCIO-ECONOMIC GSD ENVIRONMENT

This section briefly discusses two useful modelling techniques which have been explored for the purpose of this chapter:

1. i*
2. SNA

This section offers a discussion on the main benefits of each technique and how they may be used to support the analysis of the socio-economic factors in GSD. For additional reading on the techniques and methodologies employed for these techniques, readers are advised to review the referenced material.

i* (i Star)

i* is a modelling technique which is typically implemented to gain a better understanding of the problem domain, for example, requirements analysis. It offers users the opportunity to compare situation "*as-is*" and "*ought-to-be*" to support some reasoning logic on the organisational ecosystems and examines actors use of IT to achieve specific goals (Yu, 1997; Santander and Castro, 2002; Yu, 2009; Yu et al. 2011). Therefore, it probes for questions such as who achieves a specific objective and why a function was achieved in a certain manner. While i* is typically used to understand requirements by examining why a proposed system is needed, who is involved, and what relationships exist among various actors, one can also employ i* to examine the foundation of GSD relationships. However, it is worth noting that i* does not offer much insight into what *was* achieved. Thus, the technique allows us to examine any dependencies between actors using four key factors:

1. **Goal**: Strategic goals can be mapped to attributes to explore the viability of achieving economic objectives. One may also tweak goals to meet predefined economic targets;
2. **Soft Goal**: Soft goals can be mapped to attributes to examine the competence and capabilities of actors in their attempt to achieve economic objectives. In addition, this provides managers with an opportunity to identify any shortfalls in skills and capabilities to achieve specific goals;

3. **Task**: Tasks can be mapped to class operations to identify actors responsible for a specific contribution. One can also identify which team members may work best together to optimise software development efficiencies;

4. **Resources**: Resources can be mapped as classes to determine what ought to be invested to achieve a specific goal. This also provides managers with the opportunity to explore whether certain goals are feasible when compared with the economic return-on-investment.

The four factors provide further intelligence on intents, reasons, motivations, and economic factors resulting in specific behaviour within software development environments. All of these factors have economic attributes attached to their distributed intentionality to meet specific objectives as in the case of GSD. These factors support our ability to examine how actors serve self-interests by restructuring intentional relationships within a working environment. It can also offer insight on how decisions regarding software development are influenced. Thus, i* provides us with a lens to describe and analyse social relationships. One of the key benefits of i* is that we can examine the social structure in an early stage of GSD (for example, requirements analysis) and access how the social structure and information systems may be reconfigured to improve economic opportunities. In addition, i* allows management to examine key factors across a GSD architecture such as workability, believability, connectivity, cohesion, ability and viability. This may be achieved through two main modelling components of i* (Yu, 2009):

1. **Strategic Dependency Model (SDM)**: Describes the network of dependency relationships among various actors in an organisational context and indicates who an actor is and who depends on the productivity of another actor.

2. **Strategic Rationale Model (SRM)**: Model the reasons associated with each actor and their dependencies. It provides information about how actors achieve their goals and soft goals which impact the decisions and ultimately the project outcome.

This section briefly discusses the benefits of i* to model and analyse the relationships among stakeholders within software architecture. It indicates how i* may be used to examine how social actors relate to each other in terms of goals to be achieved, task performance and resources utilisation. While i* provides us with an abstraction of how a GSD environment can exploit existing relationships, we can also incorporate the power of SNA to examine the behavioural interaction properties of GSD.

Social Network Analysis (SNA)

SNA is an approach and set of techniques which supports the study of resource exchanges (for example, information) among actors (Carroll, 2012). There is a large body of literature which suggests that SNA can present us with a unique method to model and monitor the contributory value of actors and infrastructure within many network environments (for example, Berkowitz, 1982; Wellman and Berkowitz, 1988; Scott, 1991; Wasserman and Faust, 1994; Tichy, et al. 1979; Hansen, 1999; Watts, 2004; Hassan, 2009; Carroll et al. 2010; Carroll, 2012). It is claimed that managers have ignored the 'dynamic characteristics of networks and the ways that dynamic qualities of networks affect organisations' flexibility and change' (Cross and Parker, 2004; p. 133). This has unavoidably led to organisations failing to capture the 'health' of their service networks performance (for example, behavioural, functional, compositional, and structural) and the overall contributory value of service linkages (i.e., relational structures). Table 1 provides an overview of the principles of

Table 1. General principles of a network (extracted from Carroll, 2012)

Characteristic	Description
Structure	A collection of nodes and links that have a distinct format or topology which suggests that function follows form.
Emergence	Network properties are emergent as a consequence of a dynamic network achieving stability.
Dynamism	Dynamic behaviour is often the result of emergence or a series of small evolutionary steps leading to a fixed-point final state of the system.
Autonomy	A network forms by the autonomous and spontaneous action of interdependent nodes that "volunteer" to come together (link), rather than central control or central planning.
Bottom-up Evolution	Networks grow from the bottom or local level up to the top or global level. They are not designed and implemented from the top down.
Topology	The architecture or topology of a network is a property that emerges over time as a consequence of distributed – and often subtle – forces or autonomous behaviours of its nodes.
Power	The power of a node is proportional to its degree (number of links connecting to the network), influence (link values), and betweenness or closeness; the power of a network is proportional to the number and strengths of its nodes and links.
Stability	A dynamic network is stable if the rate of change in the state of its nodes/links or its topology either diminishes as time passes or is bounded by dampened alternations within finite limits.

a network which are important to assessment of GSD environments and their interactions.

SNA is a technique which can therefore assists us to examine the relational structures of a GSD environment. It can provide us with a lens to examine the socio-technical entities and allows us to examine whether we can convert the results into economic values (for example, Carroll, 2012). Thus, the application of SNA is appropriate as Wasserman et al. (2005) discusses how we can identify the formal representation and modelling of networks. This approach also compliments what Spohrer and Maglio (2009) describes as the importance of implementing new modelling methods in modern service environments. However, there are many difficulties in modelling the intertwining complexity and dynamic configuration (IfM & IBM, 2008) of people, knowledge, activities, interactions, and intentions which creates and delivers value. Thus, SNA presents us with a suitable technique to develop socio-economic analytics of software architecture.

SOCIO-ECONOMICS OF AN OPEN INNOVATION ENVIRONMENT

This section proposes the suitability of combining i* and SNA within a GSD open innovation environment. While the i* modelling framework provides a semi-formal agent-oriented conceptual modelling language, SNA allows us to visualise resource being exchanged within a network. Thus, one needs a coherent framework and analytical methods to capture both emergent process patterns between a specific set of linkages and their properties among a defined set of actors. Tichy et al. (1979) provides an overview of network concepts and network properties as summarised in Table 2. These are considered fundamental to service network dynamics while examining the socio-economic factors of an open innovation GSD environment. The properties of a network may be examined in three broad categories: transactional, nature of links, and structural characteristics. The transactional content explores what is exchanged by actors (e.g. information) during the formation of a GSD team. Thus, we can elaborate on these properties to establish metrics on GSD performance (Carroll et al. 2012) to inform management on how economic factors are influenced by social behaviour and decision-making.

The nature of the links considers the strength and qualitative nature of the relation between two or more nodes. The structural characteristics examine the overall pattern of relationships between the actors, for example, clustering, network density, and special nodes on the network are all structural characteristics. Watts and Strogatz (1998), report that real-world networks are neither completely ordered nor completely random, but rather exhibit properties of both. In addition, they claim that the structure of network can have dramatic implications for the collective dynamics of a system, whose connectivity the network represents, and that large changes in dynamic behaviour could be driven by even subtle modifications to the network structure. Therefore, the orchestration of structural relations (emergent property of the connection, e.g. the exchange process) or attributes (intrinsic characteristics, e.g. value of an exchange) become a central concept to analyse a networks structural properties. This complements what one might describe as dynamic GSD behaviour which contributes towards economic activity, i.e. performance.

SNA can be employed as a technique to graphically represent and visualise service relational structures. More importantly, SNA is an approach and set of techniques which can assist in to study the exchange of resources and competencies (for example, information) among actors in a GSD team. SNA is a technique which can therefore assists us to examine the relational structures of the socio-economic entities. The application of SNA is appropriate as Wasserman et al. (2005)

Table 2. Social network analysis concepts and network properties (Carroll, 2012)

Property	Explanation
Transactional Content	Four types of exchanges: 5. Expression of effect (e.g. initiate a transaction) 6. Influence attempt (e.g. negotiating software requirements) 7. Exchange of information (e.g. terms and conditions) 8. Exchange of goods and services (e.g. payment)
Nature of links 5. Intensity 6. Reciprocity 7. Clarity of Expression 8. Multiplexity	The strength of the relations between individuals (i.e. intensity of service interactions) The degree to which a relation is commonly perceived and agreed on by all parties to the relation (i.e. the degree of symmetry) The degree to which every pair of individuals have clearly defined expectations about each other's behaviour in the relation, i.e. they agree about appropriate behaviour between one another (i.e. project contributions) The degree to which pairs of individuals are linked by multiple relations. Multiple roles of each member (e.g. consumer, supplier, negotiator, etc.) and identifies how individuals are linked by multiple roles (the more roles, the stronger the link).
Structural Characteristics 13. Size 14. Density (Correctedness) 15. Clustering 16. Openness 17. Stability 18. Reachability 19. Centrality 20. Star 21. Liaison 22. Bridge 23. Gatekeeper 24. Isolate	The number of individuals participating in the network (i.e. GSD eco-system) The number of actual links in the network as a ratio of the number of possible links The number of dense regions in the network (i.e. network positioning or structural holes) The number of actual external links of a social unit as a ratio of the number possible external links The degree to which a network pattern changes over time (i.e. level of innovation) The average number of links between any two individuals in the network. The degree to which relations are guided by the formal hierarchy The service with the highest number of nominations (staff performance) A service which is not a member of a cluster but links two or more clusters A service which is a member of multiple clusters in the network (i.e. a linking pin) A star who also links the social unit with external domains (i.e. knowledge diffusion) A service which has uncoupled from the network.

discusses how we can identify the formal representation and modelling of networks through SNA. It allows us to implement new modelling methods in GSD to uncover the correlation between social behaviour, dynamics and the outcome of economic performance. However, there are many difficulties in modelling the intertwining complexity and dynamic configuration (IfM & IBM, 2008) of people, knowledge, activities, interactions, and intentions which creates and delivers value. Marsden (2005) explains that, as a technique, SNA data collection practices throughout literature typically involve survey methods.

A common method in analysis has been on implicit or explicit snowball sampling. To develop an understanding of social networks, one must undertake a rigorous description of the relationship patterns of the research population as the starting point of analysis. Investigating the relationships which exist within a social network is a tedious task, for example, data gathering, analysis, manipulation, and calculation using matrices to record data. SNA software is vital to support these tasks and to provide a visualisation which represents the relational descriptions (for example UCINET). This allows us to mathematically represent the network data and learn of structural characteristics of the service network environment. The majority of social network studies apply either "whole-network" (set of interrelated actors which are considered for analytical purposes) or "egocentric" (focus on a focal actor and the relationships in their loyalty) research designs (Marsden, 2005). Freeman (1989) defines how whole-network

data in set-theoretic, graph-theoretic, and matrix terms. In matrix terms, a study may examine one set of actors which are linked through one set of relationships at a specific period of time which provides a sociomatrix (i.e., one-mode data) (for example, see Table 3). Data which examines more than one set of relationships at various periods of time (i.e. to examine change) is described as two-mode (Wasserman and Faust, 1994). Therefore it is important to gain a sufficient sample size to examine the service network.

SNA and i* assumes that actors are interconnected, with real consequences for behaviour and dynamics which can provide insight on how they impact on economic performance. Structures may be altered to optimise the networks outcomes which present an opportunity to develop service network analytics.

Establishing GSD Socio-Economic Metrics

Throughout management science literature, there has been an increase in the level of attention given to service analytics, for example, 'big data'. Collecting data on human activity is a very valuable resource. The collection techniques and is considered a valuable tool to assess organisational capabilities, hence the rise in data mining research. Data mining fosters a greater sense of learning within a GSD open innovation environment. In essence, data mining is a process of discovering patterns within large datasets to extract information

Table 3. Example of a simple sociomatrix demonstrating the relationship between a group of four staff members (1 represents a 'connection', 0 represents 'no connection')

Person	John	Mary	Joe	Susan
John		1	0	1
Mary	1		1	0
Joe	1	0		0
Susan	1	1	0	

and transform it into an understandable structure for improved service intelligence.

In many cases, the introduction of new technologies has introduced novel approaches to analyses data which has previously been unseen spatial and temporal insights. This is exciting from a socio-economic data mining viewpoint. For example, it supports a GSD project to uncover new insights on the socio-economic nature of software architecture development and the dynamic behaviour of a team. It also allows managers to map economic stability and identify where weaknesses may exist. New technologies have improved managers' ability to monitor real-time data to determine the stability of the open innovation environment. For example, streaming data can provide real-time analytics on software development tasks which are completed within a global team against compliance issues raised. Thus, techniques for online monitoring and analysis of GSD environments can present us with improved online control of software quality and team cohesion.

Assessing how socio-economic impacts GSD environments require both quantitative and qualitative measurements of a software team. The indicators may be used to assess the socio-economic impacts of behaviour on performance, for example:

1. Changes in staffing demographics;
2. Alterations to the social network dynamics of a team;
3. Results of software development market analyses;
4. Cost activity of software development;
5. Demand for software services;
6. Level of trust among members to cooperate on achieving objectives;
7. Level of productivity among actors, clusters, regions and the overall team cohesion, lines of code, unit test failures, unit test coverage, number of bugs found in their code, number of bugs fixed, code review comments, test coverage and completeness of tests;
8. Time to complete a task against completion estimate time;
9. Level of exchange of information/ideas to support software development amongst a team;
10. Changes in the rules and regulations of team participation or employment;
11. Changes in employment terms and conditions which impact on goals;
12. Agility, responsiveness, and delivery timeliness.

While quantitative measurements of such factors listed above are important for the socio-economic assessment process, qualitative measurements also add greater clarity to the findings, for example 'the story' behind the data mining process. Gaining an understanding of GSD values and concerns is an important first step in conducting a socio-economic impact assessment. Any changes to a GSD relational infrastructure allows us to examine real, measurable and often significant effects on the human relational structure and how it impacts or influences economic metrics. This provides a significant insight on the dynamics of software architecture open innovation within a GSD environment. For example, we can assess how the market dynamics influence the internal technology base and alter the software development process by external technology insourcing (i.e. open innovation) to meet the needs of a current market (Figure 3).

There are a number of factors which ought to be considered (see Figure 3.) in the establishment of socio-economic metrics of a GSD open innovation environment. There are three main categories of assessment which are explored for the purpose of this chapter namely social, technology and economic metrics. Each of these sets of metric categories should examine its impact on the market, the GSD team, insourcing innovations, and the overall GSD performance. If we take one of the factors, for example 'social' (illustrated in Figure 3), we can investigate the

Figure 3. Establishing socio-economic metrics. This indicates the need to develop a cyclical assessment strategy for a number of factors including social, technology and economic to examine opportunities in a particular market, team, level of innovation and its possible contribution to performance.

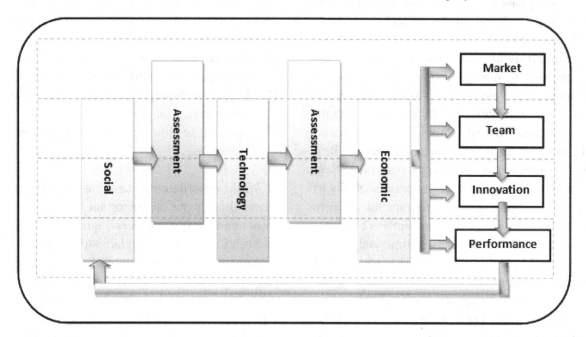

development of specific metrics. We can delve a little deeper into the network model of a GSD open innovation environment (see Figure 4) to which we can visualise the level of interaction and examine actor dependencies. Figure 4 illustrates how we can map actor interaction within a GSD environment and therefore allow us to visualise the configuration of team relational structures. Understanding these relational structures provide valuable information on how teams are socially interacting to deliver economic performance. While we develop and understanding on the social structures, we can also examine whether the alteration of the team dynamic structures impact on economic performance. In addition, Table 4 examines the social factors and its GSD economic contribution which is described as actor analytics. It outlines how each modelling technique can lend certain capabilities towards our investigation of socio-economic exploration.

For demonstrative purposes, we can presume that the differently shaded (coloured) nodes represent a specific function of a GSD team. From a management perspective, one may wish to analyse their team formation to determine the most efficient way to orchestrate a GSD actors. Additionally, when one examines the individual actors, one may also want to determine any dependencies between actors (using i*). Table 4 demonstrates how we could approach our exploration of service metrics for a GSD open innovation environment and how it enables or inhibits economic performance. The network characteristics are drawn from Table 1 and the example of analysis was drawn from Table 2 to identify how one could approach and inquiry on whether network structures within a GSD environment can impact on the economic performance.

Table 4 provides an overview of the actor analysis which supports our understanding of a GSD open innovation environment. There are

Figure 4. Example of SNA mapping of a GSD environment. This indicates how we can model the level of interaction among GSD actors and identify patterns of behaviour which is described in this chapter as GSD actor analytics and their economic contribution. By altering the pattering of interaction, managers may be able to improve economic performance.

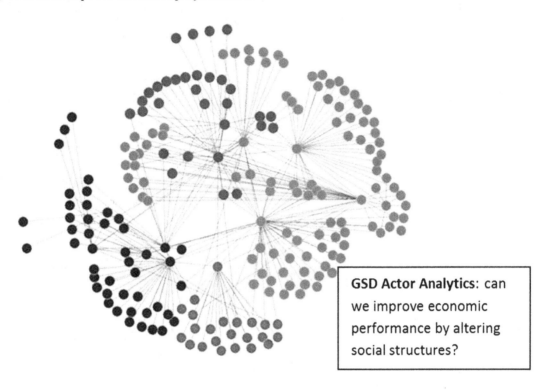

GSD Actor Analytics: can we improve economic performance by altering social structures?

two main macro categories considered which are 'social' and 'economic' (which can be extended to include technical analysis). Within each of the categories, one can examine the network characteristics. These characteristics become a focal point on which one may develop specific metrics to draw correlations between changes in network structures and economic contributions.

These measures allow a GSD team to benefit from monitoring the impact of change in the network structure on software economics. The results may provide greater intelligence on how value is increased through the interaction of certain actors and where opportunities may exist for greater efficiency or economic growth. Identifying and implementing a metrics system will vary between organisations. Therefore, it is important to listen to customers and employees

requirements to optimise software architecture processes and their interrelationships.

Modelling GSD Socio-Economic Environments

As discussed throughout this chapter, SNA and i* are ideal and complementary techniques for GSD. The express insights on actors, actor interaction, tasks and their dependencies upon other tasks, resources allocation and resource exchanges, and examines how hard goals and/or soft goals are achieved. There is a significant and valuable overlap between i* and SNA which can provide a useful strategic lens on socio-economic environments. The i* framework proposes an agent-oriented approach to examine requirements engineering which focuses on the intentional characteristics of agents

Table 4. GSD open innovation: Example of GSD actor analytics

Lens	Network Characteristic	Suitability of Techniques		Example of Analysis (Software Architecture Development)
		i*	SNA	
Social	Structure		X	• Intensity • Reciprocity • Bridge
	Emergence	X		• Network reliability • Clarity of expression • Goals
	Dynamism	X	X	• Openness • Gatekeeper • Isolate
	Autonomy	X	X	• Trust • Reachability
Economic	Bottom-up Evolution	X	X	• Stability • Multiplexity • Goals
	Topology		X	• Size • Transactional content • Level of complexity
	Power		X	• Density • Centrality • Liaison • Resources • ■ Time to market
	Stability	X	X	• Clustering • Star • Soft goals • ■ Risk mitigation
	Software productivity	X	X	• Cost • Design complexity • Labour and capital costs • Code and documentation costs • Development and rework costs • Staffing
	Software support	X	X	• Distribution costs • Software/Tools • Flexibility • Cost and risk reduction • Evolvability

(Yu et al. 2011). The various agent attributes and their intentional properties discussed within this chapter (i.e., goals, beliefs, abilities, etc.) are the basis for strategic relationships (see Figure 5). To model these relationships on a macro level drew the author's attention towards the SNA approach. Combined, both techniques can demonstrates where bottlenecks exist in the network and allow us to drill-down to discover whether there may be intentional discrepancies on a micro level or indeed any opportunities for configurations of dependencies or relational structures to improve economic performance.

Open Organisational Modelling Environment[1] (OpenOME) is an excellent open-source goal-modeling tool which is widely used to

Figure 5. Overlap between modelling techniques. This indicates the interrelationship between i*, SNA and economic views to examine GSD actor analytics and their economic contribution.

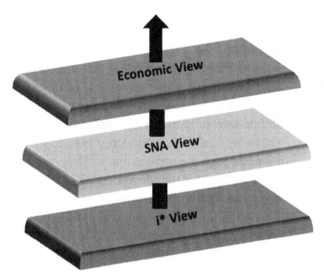

Economic view (how can we reconfigure the GSD relational structure and/or intentional properties to improve economic performance?)

Social Network Analysis (how does the relational infrastructure impact on economic performance?)

i*(which agent attributes and intentional properties are the basis for strategic relationships?)

model agents' attributes and their intentional properties. OME provides an excellent graphical interface to develop models through computer-aided analysis which links information between requirements, specification and architectural design phases of development. This lends itself to improved insights on business process (re) engineering. Thus, i* models are particularly useful to gather information on shifting requirements within a GSD environment, allowing us to examine "*what if?*" questions. In addition, we can examine the quality of the model by making trade-offs between requirements alternatives and economic requirements. SNA provides a bridge between the requirements view and the economic view. SNA demonstrated how interactions are achieved to sustain economic activity. UCINET is an excellent tool to conduct SNA (Borgatti et al. 2002) – there are also several others. UCINET is a comprehensive software package to support the analysis of social network data. IT is capable of examining up to 32,767 nodes. As discussed earlier in this chapter, SNA methods can allow us to examine key concepts such as centrality measures, subgroup identification, role analysis,

elementary graph theory, and permutation-based statistical analysis. UCINET presents users with excellent matrix analysis routines, such as matrix algebra and multivariate statistics. Combined, i* and SNA can offer us insight on how actor properties and social interactions contribute to economic activity. As part of the future research strategy, the author is linking i* and SNA to a business process modelling tool which generates a business intelligence dashboard to present economic activity. This will support our ability to demonstrate the relationship of key performance indicators between social activity and economic performance.

DISCUSSION

This chapter explores the notion of merging the benefits of i* and SNA modelling techniques to gain a better understanding of software architecture dynamics which contribute to GSD economic performance. In reviewing the literature of the GSD social world, the notion of economic metrics may be considered simplistic. However, the author recognises the need to refine and further explore the connection between these concepts and their network properties. In addition, within the field of economic, there may be considerable promise in game theory in the formation of these GSD metrics. Game theory can provide us with more "*mathematical models of conflict and cooperation between intelligent rational decision-makers*" (Myerson, 1991) as in the case of GSD. From the formation of these metrics we can learn of 'solution concepts' in actor autonomy and examine how intentional properties are altered by network properties and contribute towards economic activity. This will be realised through the introduction of a business intelligence tool. This is important as the concept of open innovation grows in research interest and becomes more applicable to software engineering. Furthermore, empirical evidence of these new approaches will offer valuable insights through case studies to produce analytical models of software architecture. From this point, the author will build on this work and be in a position to incorporate both qualitative quantitative reasoning to model a GSD open innovation environment. This chapter argues that socio-economic metrics ought to be the heart of GSD, from inception, composition, evaluation, implementation and deployment, maintenance and evolution of software development environments.

CONCLUSION

Software engineering innovations are not merely technical in nature, but are deeply social, with hidden assumptions about human knowledge and skills and learning. New economic models and techniques must be introduced alongside software developments to assess the business value of technical advances. More importantly, we need to incorporate the social and knowledge transfer factors in these assessments. One approach to this is using SNA and i*-like modelling techniques. GSD components may be viewed

as autonomous agents who interact and request services from each other. Thus, the relationships among components can provide us with critical socio-economic analytics which provide metrics and semantic characterisations of interconnections and their functionalities. While this chapter discusses how i* provides a representation of social and intentional relationships within a network, it offers a suitable approach to examine the internal behaviours to address actor dependencies. In addition, through the application of SNA one can model the impact of such dependencies on the GSD ecology and its impact on economic performance. The contribution of this chapter offers a discussion on the need for alternative methods to model the socio-economic dynamics of software development. This chapter presents a comprehensive discussion on the first attempts to introduce new approaches to model the socio-economic factors of software architecture in a GSD ecosystem and open innovation environment. This can also provide us with a logical-level design view of the GSD environment. Ultimately, understanding the economic impact at various management levels of network structural decisions will also support the architectural design of GSD. Thus, architectural design decisions will to be driven by ways that are more connected to open innovation value co-creation. As part of the future work, the next step is to conduct a comprehensive case study to identify specific metrics and semantics of a GSD environment. In addition, it would be interesting to see how social structure influences the requirements engineering processes (e.g., how various actors should be interviewed to elicit requirements, or how the negotiation could be performed to arrive at consensus regarding features and their values) and also the distribution of deployment tasks (how development could be assigned to optimise performance, even how software modules could be deployed to optimise operation costs, etc.). In addition to these techniques, more emphasis will be placed on data mining to offer a real-time analytics insight on GSD through a business intelligence tool. Ultimately, the goal is to optimise both the socio-technical and socio-economic opportunities that exist within GSD environments to guide managers decision-making tasks.

REFERENCES

Asundi, J., Kazman, R., & Klein, M. H. (2001). Economic Modeling of Software Architectures. *News at SEI*. Retrieved from Website: http://www.sei.cmu.edu/library/abstracts/news-at-sei/architect3q01.cfm

Berkowitz, S. D. (1982). *An introduction to structural analysis: The network approach to social research*. Toronto: Butterworth.

Boehm, B. (1984). *Software Engineering Economics*. Englewood Cliffs, NJ: Prentice-Hall.

Boehm, B. W., & Sullivan, K. J. (2000). Software economics: A roadmap. In *Proceedings of the conference on The future of Software engineering* (pp. 319-343). ACM.

Borgatti, S. P., Everett, M. G., & Freeman, L. C. (2002). *Ucinet for Windows: Software for Social Network Analysis*. Cambridge, MA: Analytic Technologies.

Carr, N. (2004). *Does IT Matter? Information Technology and the Corrosion of Competitive Advantage*. Boston: Harvard Business School Press.

Carroll, N. (2012). *Service science: An empirical study on the socio-technical dynamics of public sector service network innovation*. (PhD Thesis). University of Limerick, Limerick, Ireland.

Carroll, N., Richardson, I., & Whelan, E. (2012). Service Science: Exploring Complex Agile Service Networks through Organisational Network Analysis. In Agile and Lean Service-Oriented Development: Foundations, Theory and Practice. Hershey, PA: IGI Global.

Carroll, N., Whelan, E., & Richardson, I. (2010). Applying social network analysis to discover service innovation within agile service networks. *Service Science, 2*(4), 225–244. doi:10.1287/serv.2.4.225

Chesbrough, H. (2003). *Open Innovation: The New Imperative for Creating and Profiting from Technology*. Boston: Harvard Business School Press.

Chesbrough, H. (2011). Bringing Open Innovation to Services. *MIT Sloan Management Review, 52*(2), 85–90.

Chesbrough, H. (2004). *UC Berkeley, Open Innovation: Renewing Growth from Industrial R&D*. Paper presented at the 10th Annual Innovation Convergence. Minneapolis, MN.

Conchúir, Ó. (2009). Benefits of global software development: Exploring the unexplored. *Software Process Improvement and Practice, 14*(4), 201–212. doi:10.1002/spip.417

Cross, R. L., & Parker, A. (2004). *The Hidden Power of Social Networks: Understanding how Work Really Gets Done in Organizations*. Boston, MA: Harvard Business School Press.

Fichman, R. G., & Kemerer, C. F. (2012). Adoption of software engineering process innovations: The case of object-orientation. *Sloan Management Review, 34*(2).

Freeman, L. C. (1989). Social Networks and the Structure Experiment. In Research Methods in Social Network Analysis. George Mason University Press.

Friedman, T. L. (2006). *The world is flat*. New York: Penguin Books.

Hansen, M. (1999). The search-transfer problem: The role of weak ties in sharing knowledge across organization subunits. *Administrative Science Quarterly, 44*(1), 82–111. doi:10.2307/2667032

Hassan, N. R. (2009). Using Social Network Analysis to Measure IT-Enabled Business Process Performance. *Information Systems Management*, *26*(1), 61–76. doi:10.1080/10580530802557762

IEEE. (2000). *Std 1471-2000, IEEE Recommended Practice for Architectural Description of Software Intensive Systems*. Retrieved from Website: http://standards.ieee.org/catalog/software4.html#1471-200

Ifm and IBM. (2008). *Succeeding through Service Innovation: A Service Perspective for Education, Research, Business and Government*. Cambridge, UK: University of Cambridge Institute for Manufacturing.

Keast, R., Mandell, M. P., Brown, K., & Woolcock, G. (2004). Network Structures: Working Differently and Changing Expectations. *Public Administration Review*, *64*(3), 363–371. doi:10.1111/j.1540-6210.2004.00380.x

Marsden, P. V. (2005). Recent Developments in Network Measurement. In P. J. Carrington, J. Scott, & S. Wasserman (Eds.), *Models and methods in social network analysis* (pp. 8–30). New York: Cambridge University Press. doi:10.1017/CBO9780511811395.002

Myerson, R. B. (1991). Game Theory: Analysis of Conflict. Harvard University Press.

Santander, V. F. A., & Castro, J. F. B. (2002). Deriving Use Cases from Organizational Modeling. In *Proceedings of IEEE Int. Conf. Requirements Eng.* doi:10.1109/ICRE.2002.1048503

Scott, J. (1991). *Social Network Analysis: A Handbook*. London: Sage.

Šmite, D., Wohlin, C., Gorschek, T., & Feldt, R. (2010). Empirical evidence in global software engineering: A systematic review. *Empirical Software Engineering*, *15*(1), 91–118. doi:10.1007/s10664-009-9123-y

Spohrer, J., & Maglio, P. P. (2009). Service Science: Toward a Smarter Planet. In Service Engineering. Wiley.

Spohrer, J., Maglio, P. P., Bailey, J., & Gruhl, D. (2007). Steps Toward a Science of Service Systems. *IEEE Computer*, *40*(1), 71–77. doi:10.1109/MC.2007.33

Tichy, N. M., Tushman, M. L., & Frombrun, C. (1979). Social Network Analysis for Organizations. *Academy of Management Review*, *4*, 507–519.

Wasserman, S., & Faust, K. (1994). *Social network analysis: Methods and applications*. Cambridge, UK: Cambridge University Press. doi:10.1017/CBO9780511815478

Wasserman, S., Scott, J., & Carrington, P. J. (2005). Introduction. In P. J. Carrington, J. Scott, & S. Wasserman (Eds.), *Models and methods in social network analysis* (pp. 1–7). New York: Cambridge University Press. doi:10.1017/CBO9780511811395.001

Watts, D. J. (2004). The "New" Science of Networks. *Annual Review of Sociology*, *30*(1), 243–270. doi:10.1146/annurev.soc.30.020404.104342

Watts, D. J., & Strogatz, S. H. (1998). Collective Dynamics of 'Small-World' Networks. *Nature*, *393*(6684), 440–442. doi:10.1038/30918 PMID:9623998

Wellman, B., & Berkowitz, S. D. (1988). *Social Structures: A Network Approach*. Greenwich, CT: JAI Press.

Yu, E. (2009). Social Modeling and i. In A. T. Borgida, V. Chaudhri, P. Giorgini, & E. S. Yu (Eds.), *Conceptual Modeling: Foundations and Applications - Essays in Honor of John Mylopoulos (LNCS)* (Vol. 5600). Springer.

Yu, E. (1997). Towards Modelling and Reasoning Support for Early-Phase Requirement Engineering. In *Proceedings of IEEE Int. Symp. Requirements Eng.* (pp. 226-235). IEEE. doi:10.1109/ISRE.1997.566873

Yu, E., Giorgini, P., Maiden, N., & Mylopoulos, J. (2011). *Social Modeling for Requirements Engineering*. Cambridge, MA: MIT Press.

Zhao, J. L., Hsu, C., Jain, H. K., Spohrer, J. C., & Tanniru, M. (2008). ICIS 2007 panel report: bridging service computing and service management: How MIS contributes to service orientation. *Communications of the Association for Information Systems, 22*, 413–428.

ADDITIONAL READING

Beecham, S., Carroll, N., & Noll, J. A decision support system for global team management: expert evaluation. In Global Software Engineering Workshops (ICGSEW), IEEE Seventh International Conference on Global Software Engineering Workshops (ICGSEW 2012) 27-30 August, Porto Alegre, Rio Grande do Sul, Brazil. pp. 12-17. (2012). doi:10.1109/ICGSEW.2012.14

Carroll, N. Towards the Development of a Cloud Service Capability Assessment Framework, Book Chapter in Zaigham Mahmood (Ed). Chapter 12, Continued Rise of the Cloud: Advances and Trends in Cloud Computing. Springer London (2014) pp. 289-336

Carroll, N., & Helfert, M. (2014). (forthcoming). Service Capabilities within Open Innovation - Revisiting the Applicability of Capability Maturity Models. *Journal of Enterprise Information Management*.

Carroll, N., & Wang, Y. Service Networks Performance Analytics: A Literature Review. *Cloud Computing and Service Science Conference (CLOSER 2011)*, Noordwijkerhout, Netherlands (2011)

Carroll, N., Whelan, E. and Richardson, I.: Application of Social Network Analysis to Service Networks Performance Analytics: A Literature Review. Lero Technical Report (Lero-TR-2010-06), University of Limerick, December (2010)

Felin, T., Foss, N. J., Heimeriks, K. H., & Madsen, T. (2012). Microfoundations of routines and capabilities: Individuals, processes, and structure. *Journal of Management Studies, 49*(8), 1351–1374. doi:10.1111/j.1467-6486.2012.01052.x

Fiol, M. (2001). Revisiting an identity-based view of sustainable competitive advantage. *Journal of Management, 6*(6), 691–699. doi:10.1177/014920630102700606

Ghoshal, S., & Moran, P. (1996). Bad for practice: A critique of the transaction cost theory. *Academy of Management Review*, 13–47.

Gregor, S. (2006). The Nature of Theory in Information Systems. *Management Information Systems Quarterly, 3*(30), 611–642.

Helfat, C. E., & Peteraf, M. A. (2003). The dynamic resource-based view: Capability lifecycles. *Strategic Management Journal, 24*(10), 997–1010. doi:10.1002/smj.332

Normann, R. Reframing business: when the map changes the landscape. Chichester, New Sussex: Wiley (2001)

Schumpeter, J. A. (1934). *The Theory of Economic Development*. Cambridge, MA: Harvard University Press.

Spohrer, J., Maglio, P. P., Bailey, J., & Gruhl, D. (2007). Steps Toward a Science of Service Systems. *IEEE Computer*, *40*(1), 71–77. doi:10.1109/MC.2007.33

Tapscott, D. (1999). *Creating Value in the Network Economy*. Boston, MA: Harvard Business School Press.

Weill, P., Subramani, M., & Broadbent, M. (2002). Building IT infrastructure for strategic agility. *Sloan Management Review*, *44*(1), 57–65.

KEY TERMS AND DEFINITIONS

Global Software Development: Is the process of moving centralised software development at 'home' to dispersed teams and/or external organisations in remote locations and would always involve staff based in at least two different countries.

i* (i Star): Is a modelling technique which is typically implemented to gain a better understanding of the problem domain, for example, requirements analysis.

Open Innovation: Is an emerging paradigm which exposes organisations to external or networked innovation to avail of newfound service capabilities.

Software Engineering: Is the study and application of engineering to the design, development, and maintenance of software.

Socio-Economic: Is generally concerned with a social science study of how economic activity affects social processes or indeed how social factors impact on economic performance.

Social Network Analysis (SNA): An approach and set of techniques which examines the exchange of resources (for example, information) among actors. SNA also demonstrates the value of ties and relationships between each node to provide a visual and mathematical representation of interaction and exchanges which influence behaviour.

Value Co-Creation: Is the process of enhancing organisational knowledge by involving the customer as an active partner in the creation and meaning and value.

ENDNOTES

[1] https://se.cs.toronto.edu/trac/ome

Chapter 2

Innovations in Information and Communication Technology Platforms for Public Administration:
Consulting the British Public in the Digital Age

Shefali Virkar
University of Oxford, UK

ABSTRACT

Over the last two decades, public confidence and trust in government has declined visibly in several Western liberal democracies, owing to a distinct lack of opportunities for citizen participation in political processes, and has given way instead to disillusionment with current political institutions, actors, and practices. The rise of the Internet as a global communications medium has opened up huge opportunities and raised new challenges for government, with digital technology creating new forms of community, empowering citizens, and reforming existing power structures in a way that has rendered obsolete or inappropriate many of the tools and processes of traditional democratic politics. Through an analysis of the No. 10 Downing Street ePetitions Initiative based in the United Kingdom, this chapter seeks to engage with issues related to the innovative use of network technology by government to involve citizens in policy processes within existing democratic frameworks in order to improve administration, reform democratic processes, and renew citizen trust in institutions of governance.

INTRODUCTION

During the last two decades, there has been increased questioning of traditional democratic politics in Western liberal democracies, largely

due to a decline in and a lack of opportunity for public participation in these processes. Such concerns are largely thought to be embodied in (amongst other phenomena) low voter turnout during elections; a trend particularly noticeable

DOI: 10.4018/978-1-4666-6485-2.ch002

amongst young people where only half of those eligible to vote actually do so (The Electoral Commission Report, 2005). This is especially worrying and problematic for governments, as it speaks of growing political apathy and a broader, more general disillusionment with current political institutions, actors and practices. Whilst it is impossible to comprehensively untangle all the reasons for the decline in civic participation in these countries, there is little doubt that many citizens feel distanced from any sense of political relevance or power, often under the impression that not only will their votes and individual voices be drowned out in the clamour of the crowd, but that the rules which govern their daily lives are drawn up by politicians and bureaucrats whom they will never meet and who are usually extremely difficult to contact (Eggers, 2005).

Leading commentators have described the political processes and institutions integral to Western democracies as undergoing what has been variously described as 'a crisis of legitimacy', a 'credibility crisis' or a 'crisis of democracy' (cf. Habermas, 1985, Archibugi & Held, 1995), and are fast reaching agreement that the fundamental flaw lies in traditional decision-making practices which are, in their current form, often democratically inadequate as they fail to provide extensive and relatively equal opportunities for citizens, communities and groups to contribute towards the shaping of decision-making agendas (Sclove 1995). The focus of discourse and scholarly activity, both in academic and policy circles, has thus gradually shifted away from a more centralised, top-down conception of 'government' – those formal institutions and processes which operate at the level of the nation state to maintain public order and facilitate collective action (Stoker, 1998) – towards the notions of 'governance', an idea which, while traditionally a synonym for government, has been captured in recent theoretical work as signifying 'a change in the meaning of government referring to a new process of governing; or a changed condition of ordered rule; or

the new method by which society is governed' (Rhodes, 1996: 652).

Governance is thus seen to be ultimately concerned with crafting the conditions for ordered rule and collective action, or 'the creation of a structure or an order which cannot be externally imposed, but which is the result of the interaction of a multiplicity of governing and each other influencing actors' (Kooiman & Van Vliet, 1993: 64), and is thus a conceptual way of capturing shifts in the character of political rule which has been stretched to encompass a range of different transformations including an emphasis on drawing citizens and communities into the process of collaborative participation in political processes and the creation of new forms of governable subjects (Newman, 2005).

DIS(CONNECTED) CITIZENSHIP? AN EXPLORATION OF KEY CONCEPTS

The idea of governance, and by extension e-Governance, may therefore be said to comprise of two distinct but complementary elements: that of e-Government – which encompasses all the formal institutional and legal structures of a country, and e-Democracy – which can be said to refer to the participative and deliberative processes which operate within those structures (Virkar, 2007). Broadly speaking, on the one hand, e-Government itself may be divided into two distinct areas: (1) e-Administration, which refers to the improvement of government processes and to the streamlining of the internal workings of the public sector often using ICT-based information systems, and (2) e-Services, which refers to the improved delivery of public services to citizens through multiple electronic platforms (Virkar, 2011). On the other, the concept of e-Democracy may be further subdivided into two distinct areas: e-Engagement (or e-Participation), which emphasises opportunities for greater consultation and dialogue between government and citizens, and e-Voting, the expression of fundamental democratic rights and duties online (Virkar, 2007).

e-Engagement as a policy, if defined by an express intent to increase the participation of citizens in decision-making through the use of digital media, would consequently involve the institutionalised provision of resources to facilitate the responsible and collaborative decision making involved ultimately in institutional and social change. Whilst the earliest speculations about the Internet and Democracy emphasised the potential for direct, unmediated participation (OECD 2001) and the transformative nature of the process of public engagement, this chapter follows the view of scholars such as Coleman and Gotze (2001) that whilst e-Democracy is incompatible with a political culture of élitism, it is not about replacing what has evolved so far but instead, rather than seeking to radically transform governance along any particular ideological line, it aims to complement the institutions and processes of representative democracy.

In this view, facilitating the involvement of different sections of society in the process of government is now seen as a democratic prerequisite in many advanced liberal democracies, with some commentators such as Fishkin (1995) highlighting the need for 'mass deliberation', and emphasising the need for people and their representatives to be brought together to collaborate on issues of mutual interest. The recent exponential growth in access to new Information and Communication Technologies (ICTs), and the expansion of a newly-created digital environment wherein people shop, talk, and otherwise spend large parts of their lives in online spaces, has opened up a plethora of new opportunities for interaction between power elites and the various constituent elements of civil society. At the same time, their rapid proliferation has raised important questions and triggered debates as to who is able to participate and to what extent they may do so, as well as the types of participation such technologies make possible at

different levels of government and their impact on different government institutions and democratic processes (Virkar, 2011).

This chapter aims to assess, through the use of a relevant exploratory case study, whether the innovative use of network technology (in particular the Internet and its associated applications) in the Government 2.0 era to involve citizens in policy processes within existing democratic frameworks would eventually lead to radical transformations in government functioning and policy or merely to modest political reform. In doing so, it seeks to explore the factors, particularly those rooted in a country's legal and institutional foundations, that might hinder or enable the successful implementation of e-consultation projects at different levels of government and develop a set of recommendations for overcoming any barriers encountered. The main idea behind Government 2.0 is participation by citizens, through the use of Web 2.0 Technologies, a term referring to the collection of social media through which individuals are active participants in creating, organizing, editing, combining, sharing, commenting, and rating Web content as well as forming a social network through interacting and linking to each other.

Technologies used include blogs, wikis, social networking hubs, (such as Facebook and MySpace), Web- based communication modes like chatting and online chat groups, photo-sharing tools such as Flickr and Picasa, video casting and sharing platforms like YouTube, audio-sharing media such as Podcasts, mashups, widgets, virtual worlds, microblogs like Twitter, and the social annotation and bookmarking of Web sites (Ferguson, 2006). Through these social media individuals act as active agents in creating, organizing, combining and sharing information. The emphasis is on an outside-in wisdom of crowds approach, where data and information are created by a network of users outside of an organizational boundary in a collaborative manner. This is different from the inside-out authoritative know-all approach typical to the Web 1.0 era, where an organization or apex body is the key creator and organizer of the content and the people are considered passive mere consumers of information (Chun et.al, 2010).

GOVERNANCE, ICTs, AND PUBLIC ENGAGEMENT IN THE EUROPEAN UNION

Whilst early speculations about the Internet and democracy emphasised the potential for direct, unmediated debate and discussion and stressed the radically transformative nature of the process of public engagement in a manner that led some scholars to go as far as to predict the end of the nation-state in favour of direct democracy (Margolis, 2007), this chapter follows the view of those who believe that whilst e-democracy in its purest sense may be altogether incompatible with a political culture of elitism (often unavoidable within the framework of a representative democracy), it is in practice sometimes neither feasible nor indeed desirable to replace what has evolved so far. Both theorists and practitioners talk of creating a 'civic commons in cyberspace' that would elicit and coordinate citizen comments and reactions to problems facing public institutions in order 'to create a link between e-government and e-democracy – to transcend the one-way model of service delivery and exploit for democratic purposes the feedback paths that are inherent to digital media' (Coleman, 2011).

The emergence of the European Union (E.U.), and its evolution as a policymaking and legislative body, particularly over the last 20 years, has, raised several questions regarding the extent to which Europe constitutes a transnational public sphere in which citizens can debate and participate (Scharpf, 1999), particularly as the process of European integration over the last decade and a half has initiated a profound restructuring of the region's 'public space'; within member-state polities, at the European level and in a complex interplay between European, national, regional and local levels (Koopmans & Statham, 2000). This intricate arrangement is clearly illustrated by the fact that whilst policy decisions in Europe are increasingly taken at the supranational and international levels, the nation-state has remained the primary focus for collective identities; with public debates and citizen participation in policy processes both still primarily situated at the national level and generally directed by national or local authorities.

Trust in European institutions and support for the integration process has steadily declined since the early 1990s (Thomassen & Schmitt, 1999), and many scholars point to a democratic deficit at the core of existing legitimacy problems within the E.U. which they attribute mainly to, on the one hand, a dichotomy resulting from the development of Europe's institutions and their increasing competencies and influence on European citizens' conditions of life (Bicking & Wimmer, 2010) and, on the other, inherent flaws present in those same institutions resulting in a limited 'Europeanisation' of public discourse across the European Body Politic in comparison with the emphasis placed on the national political space as an arena for public debates and a source for collective identification and notions of citizenship (Peters et. al., 2005). It is fast being recognised that in order to promote greater inclusiveness, efforts must be made to better connect citizens to the people and institutions that represent them, and better embed these links within the networks of government (Kies & Wojcik, 2010).

RESEARCH METHODOLOGY

Case study research consists of a detailed investigation of phenomena within a given context, often with data being collected over a period of time, the aim of which is to provide an analysis of the surrounding environment and processes to throw light on the theoretical issues being investigated

(Eisenhardt, 1989). The phenomenon under examination is thus not isolated from its context, rather it is of interest precisely because the aim is to observe and understand actor behaviour and/or organisational processes and their interplay with the surrounding environment. The use of a case study itself is therefore not as much a method as it is a research strategy, where the context is deliberately included as part of the overall design. Today, case studies are widely used in organisational research across the social sciences, indicating growing confidence in the approach as a rigorous research strategy in its own right (Hartley, 2005). As research done by adopting this strategy is typically done in the field, the presence of too many observations and uncontrollable 'variables' makes the application of standard experimental or survey approaches infeasible.

Further, information tends to be scattered and generally cannot be picked up using one single method. Case studies thus typically combine a number of data collection methods such as participant observation, direct observation, interviews, focus groups, ethnography, document analysis, questionnaires etc., where evidence may be quantitative or qualitative depending on the research issues at hand. The approach is consequently flexible, allowing for new methods to be incorporated as new sources of data and new actors present themselves. The case study approach may thus be and has been used for various purposes – to provide a descriptive narrative, to generate new theory, or to test existing theory through the triangulation of data (Virkar, 2011).

From the above discussion, it follows that the use of a case study for this chapter is particularly apt for two reasons. Firstly, the approach is particularly useful for examining research issues that require a detailed understanding of socio-political, economic, or organisational processes through the collection and analysis of rich data. Secondly, as discussed above, case study research design is

also more flexible than other frameworks such as laboratory-based or survey-based approaches, in that it is able to reconcile different research methods and harness the evidence gathered to generate novel theory from any creative insights that might ensue from the juxtaposition of data at various points in the analysis.

The choice of case study aims to fill the gaps in the existing literature on ICTs and public participation in the European Union, firstly by focusing on the factors arising from the political dynamics and organisational culture within the context of online political participation on the Prime Minister's e-Petitions Gateway, and examining how these in turn influenced élite and non-élite political actor perspectives as circumscribed by the relationships between actor perspectives, organisational reform, and institutional change. It was felt that the case study method would be best suited to this exploratory study given the multiplicity of sources of evidence available, and the reliability and validity of conclusions drawn would benefit from a convergence or 'triangulation' of data collected from these sources.

The empirical study presented in this chapter has one key limitation, which is that the discussed findings and their implications are obtained from a single case study that examined a particular mode of e-participation using an experimental technological platform targeting a specific user group. Thus, although the findings throw light on some of the non-technical factors influencing the outcome of e-consultation projects, indeed e-participation initiatives, worldwide, caution needs to be taken when generalizing these findings and discussion to other technologies, groups, or governments. That said, despite this threat to the validity of the case at hand, the use of mixed method data triangulation has ensured that study fully captures the key elements of and challenges to the development of innovative e-participation technologies based on old forms of citizen engagement.

E-CONSULTATION: TWO-WAY GOVERNANCE IN THE DIGITAL AGE?

The shift in thinking about e-governance[1] from being a technology-driven process to one that is more citizen-focused, and the recognition of the need to promote greater inclusiveness in decision-making processes, may be clearly seen in the emergence of concrete policies for e-democracy (in addition to those dealing with e-government) in many European countries over the last decade. This is most notably so in the United Kingdom, where several e-democracy projects are publicly funded, and both Parliament and the Government have over the years outlined sets of policy principles on the subject. One such set of guidelines, a consultation paper issued by the UK government in July 2002 (HM Government, 2002), which sets out a clear policy agenda for e-democracy and contains a detailed but useful division of the concept into two distinct areas: e-voting (or the use of technology in elections and associated structures and processes), and e-engagement (or e-participation, which emphasises opportunities for greater consultation and dialogue between government and citizens).

A long-established way of engaging citizens in dialogue with policy makers is that of Consultation, where citizens are given the opportunity to provide feedback to government on matters of public importance and participate in the shaping of issues relevant to them (OECD, 2001). Whilst there is a need for dialogue at several different stages during the policy process, the process of consultation has traditionally involved discussion based around a pre-determined policy issue defined by the government during its initial formative stages, on which citizen's views and opinions are then sought (Rosen, 2001). The government sets the questions and manages the process, often laying down the parameters within which the consultation is to take place. Only in rare cases are citizens invited to suggest issues for discussion that they,

as private individuals, might consider particularly important. At the heart of the consultative process, therefore, lies the provision of information and the establishment and maintenance of channels of communication between government and its citizens.

The use of ICTs in consultative processes is catching on as their potential for allowing policymakers to interact directly with the users of the services, to target the opinions of those at whom a policy is aimed, and to seek general citizen input on matters of national importance is gradually being recognised (Virkar, 2013b). The speed and immediacy of ICT networks allow people to communicate, give feedback, ask questions, complain, exchange information effectively and build relationships with their representatives; and governments too may benefit from any information they obtain by using it to enhance the quality of policymaking and general administrative functions. Broad guidelines for 'conventional' written consultation by more traditional means are already in place in most of the Western world, and these are now being used as a basis for e-consultation (OECD, 2003), with this type of e-democracy thus encompassing what may be referred to as 'a continuum of consultation', ranging from low level information gathering and aggregation towards a fuller quasi-deliberative level of interaction.

Despite contrary claims from scholars such as Rash (1997) and Bimber (1998), the consultative model is not without its problems as it is sometimes presented as facilitating direct, unmediated access to government for special interest groups of a sort that may distort opinion on particular issues. Information gathered from the consultative process is usually regarded as a passive resource, largely due to the fact that communication by direct question-asking is based on the need to generate quantifiable and comparable responses to particular policy innovations. The result is that the consultative model may only allow for inputs that fit within parameters already set down by policy makers, with a marked danger that opinions which question the necessity or legitimacy of a policy or otherwise be outside the ambit of pre-defined issues, are deliberately marginalised or excluded altogether, particularly if discussions are 'moderated' (Whyte & Macintosh, 2003). In order to further the analysis of issues affecting the impact of ICTs on existing democratic frameworks, this chapter sets out a three-fold categorisation of noteworthy cases across Europe along different axes depending on their duration, the level of the participating government organisation, and from whom feedback is sought. Three categories of e-consultation initiatives in Europe may be derived from this author's research, and are set out in Table 1.

- **Duration**: Projects when classified according to duration may be examined under three sub-categories – long term, short term, and one-off consultations – depending on the length of time that they lasted for.
- **Long Term Consultations**: Include those e-consultation initiatives which are either specifically set up as long-lasting initiatives or which become permanent initiatives after an initial trial period. Projects such as these tend to provide permanent platforms to solicit continual citizen participation and feedback on highly topical issues as and when they arise, and are not

bound around a particular political event or related to a particular occurrence.
- **Short Term Consultations:** include those initiatives that seek to obtain citizen opinions around specific political events or during a designated fixed period of time. These initiatives are intentionally short-term, are focused on getting citizen input for a specific purpose, and come to a close once the event or time period is at an end.
- **One-Off Consultations:** Are highly specialised issue-based e-consultations, generally held on an ad hoc basis for a fixed period of time. Such consultations tend to be used by government as a means of gathering information from a well-defined target group on a specific, often on a pressing issue and, of the three types of consultation discussed so far, are the most likely to have a visible impact on government policy.
- **Level of Government:** Case studies may also be classified according to the level of government at which they are implemented; more specifically as projects implemented by local government agencies, at the level of national government and at the inter-governmental or pan-European level.
- **Local Government Consultations:** Refer to e-consultation projects of note initiated at the level of local government within the E.U.

Table 1. Categorisation of innovative examples of e-consultation initiatives

	Local Initiatives	**National Initiatives**	**European Initiatives**
SHORT TERM CONSULTATIONS	• Madrid Participa (Spain) • Iperbole (Italy) • Bristol City Council (UK)	• The No. 10 Downing Street ePetitions Website (UK) • Tana Otsustan Mina (Estonia) • The Scottish Parliamentary Initiative (UK)	• Your Voice in Europe (the European Commission)
LONG TERM CONSULTATIONS	• The City of Esslingen (Germany)	• Digital Administration Programme: the Democracy Project (Denmark) • Energy Technology Futures (Canada)	• Toute l'Europe (based in France)
ONE-OFF CONSULTATIONS	• The City Planning Commission of Kalix (Sweden)	• Online Parliamentary Inquiry into Domestic Violence (UK) • FloodForum.net (UK)	• The Future of Food (Germany / the Netherlands)

- **National Government Level Consultations:** Include all e-consultation initiatives begun within national government ministries and associated institutions.
- **Inter-Governmental or Pan-European Initiatives:** Are those projects initiated at the regional and pan-European level, generally as supranational agreements between different European government.
- **Nature of the Target Audience:** Projects may also be categorised and discussed according to their target audience or in terms of the section of the population from whom feedback is sought. Whilst most initiatives are generally concerned with obtaining feedback from the general public on a variety of issues, a small number seek to obtain specific information from a carefully targeted, often specially selected group.

In building on the categorisation discussed above, and attempting to compile a rich and informative inventory of issues that are or can become significant to the implementation of e-consultation projects, this chapter will look briefly at the No. 10 Downing Street e-Petitions Website as a pioneering effort by a national government department to harness digital technology to recast and reinvigorate democratic processes within its respective spheres of influence.

UNDERSTANDING POLITICAL PARTICIPATION ONLINE

The design and implementation of complex computer systems, such as those that support e-consultation platforms, requires a better understanding in practitioner circles of the users of such networks and the settings in which they work. Part of the problem resides in the implicit treatment of ordinary people as unskilled, non-specialist users of technology and their networks comprising of elementary processes or factors that can be studied in isolation in a field laboratory setting (Bannon, 1991). Although psychology has a long tradition of contributing to computer systems design and implementation, it has been a neglected discipline in scholarly circles and key issues such as those relating to the underlying values of the people involved in large-scale system design and their motivation in the work setting have been missed out in recent computer science-based scholarly analysis (Salvendy, 2012). Conceptualising and understanding people as actors in situations, on the other hand, with a set of skills and shared practices based on work experiences with others, requires a reorientation in the way in which the relationship between key elements of computer system design, namely people, technology, work requirements, and organisational constraints in work settings, is negotiated (Kuutti, 1996).

The use of the terms 'human factors' and 'human actors' give us a clue as to how people in system design clusters are approached (Virkar, 2011). More particularly, the terms highlight difference in how people and their contributions are perceived, the former connoting a passive, fragmented, depersonalised, somewhat automatic human contribution to the systems environment; the latter an active, controlling, involved one (Carayon et. al, 2012). More precisely, within the human factor approach, the human element is more often than not reduced to being another system component with certain characteristics that need to be factored into the design equation for the overall human-machine system (Czaja & Nair, 2012). In doing so, the approach de-emphasises certain important elements of work design: the goals, values, and beliefs which technologists and system-users hold about life and work (Jacko et. al., 2012). By using the term human actor, emphasis is placed on users and developers as autonomous agents possessing the capacity to control, regulate, and coordinate their behaviour, rather than them being on par and analysed as mere information processing automatons (Proctor & Vu, 2012).

The study of actor interactions is key to e-consultation initiatives, as it is important determine the impact that actor motivations have on the consultative process and subsequently on policy outcomes. One approach to understanding behaviour is to look at the composition of individual actors, rather than the system as a whole. This is largely because political actors are driven by a combination of organisational and institutional roles and duties and calculated self-interest, with political interaction being organised around the construction and interpretation of meaning as well as the making of choices (Virkar, 2013). The main actors in electronic consultation process may be placed into two groups:

- **Internal Actors:** Comprise chiefly of those institutional actors responsible for the maintenance, upkeep and running of a project, including (a) officers of the assembly who are responsible for the operation of the system such as IT specialists and forum moderators, and (b) elected representatives (and their support staff) who respond to petitions individually and collectively.

- **External Actors:** Comprise of two distinct categories including (a) participants or the person (or group) who initiates an online interaction after identifying an issue and follows its progress through from submission to final feedback and outcome and (b) citizens: those individuals who may or may not be entitled to participate but who will invariably impact the outcome of a policy process through their ability to shape public opinion.

The central issue that needs to be understood whilst studying the development of ICT platforms and their implementation in public sector organisations through an analysis of actor interactions is thus: Why do people do what they do? One approach to understanding behaviour is to look at the rationality of individual actors, rather than at

human factors or at the computer system network as a whole. This is largely because human actors are driven by a combination of organisational and institutional roles and duties and calculated self-interest, with political, social, and economic interactions being organised around the construction and interpretation of meaning as well as the making of choices.

One approach to the study of political e-participation begins by defining and examining the motives and goals that prompt actors to interact and participate in decision- and policy making processes online. All behaviour is motivated in some way and individuals will engage in a particular behaviour in order to achieve a desired end (Atkinson & Birch, 1970). Political actors, in particular, have a complex set of goals including power, income, prestige, security, convenience, loyalty (to an idea, an institution or the nation), pride in work well done, and a desire to serve the public interest (as the individual actor conceives it). Added to this, individuals and private citizens tend to participate in politics for altruistic or conformist reasons, to boost their self-esteem, to self-enhance, and to achieve self-efficacy (Cruickshank, et. al., 2010). Actors range from being purely self-interested 'climbers' or 'conservers' motivated entirely by goals which benefit themselves and their status quo rather than their organizations or the society at large, to having mixed motives as 'zealots', 'advocates' and 'statesmen' motivated by goals which combine self interest and altruistic loyalty with larger values (Downs, 1964).

For citizens and users of the e-participation application, the motivation to use the system may be either intrinsic or extrinsic (Cruickshank et. al., 2010). Intrinsic motives include the desire to feel competent and self-determining, to show altruism, or to seek to increase the welfare of others. On the other hand, extrinsic motives are usually associated with some sort of external reward in the social, economic, or political sphere. Both these manifest themselves in conditional co-operation, social pressure, thresholds and the bandwagon effect (Margetts et. al., 2012). Different motives and goals may underlie the same surface behavior, with the social and psychological consequences of participation may be different for different users (i.e. some participate to gain information or support, others to communicate), resulting in a set of nested, interrelated interactions with the framework of a large meta-game or playing field (Virkar, 2011). Consequently, the motivations and goals for using the online resources will determine how they will they be used, by whom, and when.

An in-depth analysis of the ICT for development literature by this researcher identified five actor groups involved in games relating to the implementation of e-government projects:

1. **Politicians:** The first group identified comprises of elected representatives of various hues, guided and influenced chiefly by electoral imperatives and a need to maintain their public image, and are therefore concerned with directing both key economic policy issues as well as issues of public service delivery.

2. **Administrators/Civil Servants:** This group of actors is guided by their perceptions of existing institutional 'culture' and practices and their positive (or negative) attitudes towards internal bureaucratic reforms such as concerns about the down-sizing of administrative services to promote 'efficiency' and a sense of being policed by elected government through the introduction of ICTs.

3. **Organisations Dealing with Technical Designing of IT and ICT Systems:** The approach private IT suppliers take to e-government might be considerably different to what the adopting government agency actually needs or wants from a system.

4. **Citizens:** This is another particularly interesting group of actors as one is never quite sure what their reaction to the implementation of e-government will be. Whilst in theory citizens should welcome the introduction of a system that simplifies administrative processes, in practice it is equally possible that some citizens might not be very happy if a more efficient system was put into place.

5. **International Donors:** This final actor group controls the purse-strings and oftentimes comes to the table with 'higher' ideals coloured by ideas prevalent in international politics (such as the desire to see a particular brand of 'good governance' in the developing world).

The empirical study of the No. 10 Downing Street ePetitions Initiative presented in this chapter has one key limitation, which is that the discussed findings and their implications are obtained from a single case study that examined a particular mode of e-government using an experimental technological platform targeting a specific user group to solicit electronic feedback on key issues of politics and policy. Therefore, although the findings throw light on most of the key factors influencing the behaviour of actors and actor groups involved with the development of e-consultation platforms, indeed e-governance initiatives, worldwide, care needs to be taken to avoid over-generalizing these findings and conclusions whilst examining other technologies, groups, or governments. That said, despite this potential threat to the validity of the case at hand, the use of mixed method data triangulation as a research strategy ensures that study fully captures the key elements of and challenges to and the motives and machinations prevalent behind the development of innovative e-government technologies based on old forms of democracy, citizen participation, and engagement.

PUBLIC ADMINISTRATION AND ICT POLICY IN THE UNITED KINGDOM

e-Governance policy in the United Kingdom in its most recent form began to take shape in the late-1990s, with the central overarching issue for almost all government-based ICT projects initiated during that period and after being to attempt to improve the democratic character of public decision-making and delivering greater legitimacy by involving the public directly (Harrison & Mort, 1998). Whilst there have been huge changes in public administration, particularly over the last couple of decades with the State seeking greater administrative efficiency through the computerisation and the digital storage of data, scholars are divided as to how effective these policy changes have really been in furthering public participation (Ward, Gibson, & Lusoli, 2003). To date much of what has been achieved in terms of practical e-democracy in the UK appears to centre more around information provision about the government and its activities and in ensuring that government services are available on the Web (i.e. electronic service provision), rather than on the other, more interactive side of e-democracy whereby feedback from the public is actively sought on issues relevant to their everyday lives (Dutton & di Gennaro, 2006).

In the UK, the actual mechanisms by which the public can communicate with government appear to have remained essentially unchanged; with some studies, for example, showing that interaction with elected representatives has not really moved on from where it was a few decades ago compared to the pace of change in other Western liberal democracies such as the United States, largely as a consequence of European integration (Pleace, 2007). In this vein, whilst local, national, and central government agencies within the UK today publish a vast amount of material online, their websites should not be taken simply as mere repositories of information, but instead fulfil a dual role of both informing and connecting with the public (Pleace, 2007). A good example of this two-fold role played by government websites is The No.10 Downing Street Website, gateway to the Office of the Prime Minister and host to the Prime Minister's e-Petitions Gateway, which on the one hand serves to inform the public about the role and functions of the Prime Minister, and on

the other is uniquely placed to provide the crucial link for interaction between the Prime Minister and the public.

THE NO.10 DOWNING STREET E-PETITIONS INITIATIVE

One method by which members of the public have traditionally placed their views before government is by the submission of petitions, formal issue-based requests to a higher authority such as a Head of State or Parliament, which are signed by one or a number of citizens (Macintosh, Malina & Farrell, 2002). In the United Kingdom, the practice of petitioning is a long established one – reputed to be even older than that of voting – wherein paper-based petitions consisting of a bundle of sheets bearing the names and signatures of the petitioners were (and still are) usually presented to the Prime Minister at the door of his official residence of No.10 Downing Street. In November 2006, the humble petition received a 21st Century makeover when the Prime Minister's Office in partnership with mySociety, a project associated with the charity UK Citizens Online Democracy[2], launched an electronic petitioning service on its website to provide citizens with a modern, more convenient parallel: the electronic or e-Petition. The No.10 Downing Street ePetitions System was brought firmly into the spotlight soon after its launch by a petition submitted to the website against the Government's proposed Vehicle Tracking and Road Pricing Policy which, between the time it began collecting signatures in December 2006 and its closure in February 2007, was widely publicised and attracted over 1.8 million signatories – a protest seen by some commentators as the 'biggest protest against government policy since the anti-war demonstrations of 2003' (Wheeler, 2007).

Simply defined, an e-Petition is a form of petition posted on a website (Pleace, 2007). e-Petitions may be created easily by an individual or group, posted on the host website for anyone to read and, by adding their details such as an email address to verify their authenticity, may be 'signed' by any visitor to the site. Whilst in theory there is little difference between a paper petition and an electronic petition, except for the way in which signatures are collected and delivered and for the fact that the system has built into it the opportunity for partial communication between government and petitioner, in practice, the introduction of the e-petitions section on the Prime Minister's website has opened up the possibility of a new channel by which groups and individual citizens may put across their viewpoint to the Prime Minister's Office directly without going through traditional media conduits and thereby potentially being able to influence the direction or nature of current political debate.

In combining traditional access to politics with technology, e-petitions are a powerful way of making politicians and decision-makers aware of those hidden issues which are currently important to a small group of people but which might in the future become important issues pertinent to larger sections of society. The key questions are, however, what in the long-term would be the impact of the No.10 e-Petitions Initiative on democratic processes within the UK and how might it contribute towards re-engaging the public?

RECONFIGURING GOVERNMENT-CITIZEN RELATIONS THROUGH E-PETITIONS

Any analysis must keep in mind that to begin with, the e-Petitions system is an almost-direct replica of the traditional petitions model, whereby citizens may petition the government electronically and receive partial feedback on their opinions (Virkar, 2007). The system does not, however, engage citizens further than this nor use their comments within a full-scale e-consultation forum. In addition, it must be remembered that e-petitions (much like their traditional counterparts) are not meant to be representative of a country's opinion as, say, an opinion poll might be. Instead, they simply indicate what one group of people think on a subject, with accepted wisdom stating that only the most vocal citizens who feel most strongly about an issue and who are comfortable with using the Internet as a medium of communication will sign up to them. For those citizens who are either usually satisfied with most proposals or for whom political participation (particularly online) is generally not a top-of-mind consideration, there is little compulsion to participate.

Whilst e-petitions are thus, in one sense, not a radically new democratic tool whereby the voice of the majority would translate directly into a legal change; there do remain a number of advantages to e-petitioning (Lindner & Riehm, 2009). In the first instance, citizens may obtain background information on an issue, make comments, sign petitions online, and receive feedback on the progress of their petition: a process which, at least in theory, would make for a more informed petitioner and an overall better quality of participation, as citizens may take their time to research the finer points of a particular issue before they decide whether or not to support it. From a government perspective, popular petitions and their associated comments may be used during the policy process, with extremely high-profile petitions serving to highlight issues and uncover underlying discontents which have not as yet been picked up by the mainstream media (Virkar, *forthcoming* 2013c).

There is, however, no formal obligation for the Government to actively pursue views raised once the initial communication has been established with the citizen, there is no guarantee that this new form of voter engagement would necessarily lead to concrete changes in policy. Questions may be asked as to how seriously both citizens and government officials would take this form of interaction should there be no popular or extremely topical issue to keep the mainstream media interested. Additionally, when it comes to designing and deriving policy, the Government is faced with the challenge of balancing and sustaining the overarching democratic requirements of openness, accessibility, and participation with the need to stay within legally stipulated Data Protection standards (Macintosh, Malina, & Farrell, 2002). Similarly, given how easy it is to start and sign up to a petition – over 3,313 people, for example, supported a call for Tony Blair to stand on his head and juggle ice-cream– there is a good chance that more genuine petitions may get mixed up or overlooked if a fair and unbiased process is not put in place to identify and sift out more 'pertinent' views from 'less important' ones (Geoghegan, 2007).

Keeping these considerations in mind it is, first and foremost, necessary for those administering a system to ensure that the more mundane but equally pressing issues that do not have either the media hype or numbers to support them get noticed and dealt with. There is also a further need for the Government to recognise and take into account the presence of a silent, but possibly far larger proportion of the population who may hold moderate but equally pertinent views on an issue. One way in which both concerns may be dealt with would be to frame a comprehensive set of general guidelines from existing policy surrounding electronic interactions which would allow views gathered from the website to feed into a much wider policymaking context such as an interactive consultation, whereby they may be discussed and deliberated upon by a wider section of the Body Politic representing different sides of the debate.

DESIGNING PUBLIC POLICY FOR E-DEMOCRACY IN THE UK

The case of the Prime Minister's e-Petitions illustrates that devising public policy for digital democracy may sound contradictory and in many cases an unnecessary waste of government resources.

This is because, on the one hand, traditional notions of democracy intrinsically imply a limitation of State power in favour of its citizens through a bottom-up process where individuals initiate action and individual freedoms are protected. On the other, the implementation and development of the information superhighway and its associated infrastructure has been a market- and not state-led process which is said to attenuate the power of the State in favour of other forces in local, national, and world politics.

Particularly affected are those ideas dealing with access to public information, through the introduction into the political system of new ways of conceptualising 'old' values such as transparency and new styles of public administration which draw on a mixture of corporate management principles and Weberian models of bureaucratic ordering and functioning. With the current generation of citizens being not only information-consumers, but increasingly acting as *producers* of web content, the innovative use of Information and Communication Technologies offers up the possibility of new consultation spaces and the potential to increase the breadth and depth of citizen participation in the public sphere (Ferguson, 2006). Representative democracy in its most traditional form is thus being increasingly challenged as the Internet and its associated technologies make the logistical distribution of public information much easier and less costly, with citizens demanding greater participation in public affairs and the adoption of new forms of accountability and control of government.

The increasing sophistication of technology often runs contrary to legalities relating privacy, anonymity, identity management, and privacy-enhancing tools if, through increasingly complex technology, the government is able to control and monitor citizens and in doing so encroach on basic fundamental rights (Dutton & Peltu, 2007). Such security concerns are generally manifested in discussions of risks posed by technology to citizens' anonymity and privacy, and the collection and storage of sensitive data, as the development of online government services opens up new possibilities of intrusion by third parties into government databanks and exchanges of information between different departments (Hiller & Bélanger, 2001). In addition, questions arise as to whether the responsibility for the accuracy and security of personal data should reside with government, given that it alone has the manpower and financial resources capable of handling such a task, or whether personal data should – as in the case of the Downing Street ePetitions system – be entrusted to an independent third-party (Irani, Elliman, & Jackson, 2007).

Government has a privileged *sui generis* position in the fabric of society, especially in terms of access to information. In recognising this, however, little attention has so far been paid to the *kind* of information and content necessary to promote digital citizenship and engender trust. It has been argued that ideally, digital democracy should provide both government and citizen with a diversity of content and quality information that has a high cultural value, notions of which are not easy to define (Bishop & Anderson, 2004). In this respect, Freedom of Information acts and ordinances which set out to define the ways in which 'information' and 'data' are perceived and dealt with within a country's legal framework often come in useful, as they set boundaries on the degree to which government may store and use citizen data that it has collected for specific, often publicly-stated purposes (Hiller & Bélanger, 2001). At the same time, the potential of Web 2.0 technologies to empower modalities necessary to functionalise the relationship between government and individual members of the public are also further enhance.

There also exists in the literature a well-documented record of cases in the UK where the reality of online public engagement or electronic service provision initiatives has often fallen short of initial – both government and citizen – expectations (Pleace, 2007). This often happens when those using the technology anticipate that its intro- duction will result in an increased simplification of government processes, and are disappointed when the complexity of those processes remains at best unchanged, or becomes even more complex (Virkar, 2011). Government officials and civil servants also are often apprehensive about using unfamiliar or innovative technology and are cautious about participating in initiatives that might either bind them to a course of action which in the long term could both damage the government and prove detrimental to their own public image or which, in the short term, could open them up to attack from the citizenry without there being adequate legal protection.

CONCLUSION

From a discussion of the themes and issues brought out in this chapter, the key to successful e-participation projects appears to be the presence of clearly spelled-out goals, adequate planning and preparation of the initiative, the presence of a disaster management plan in case a contingency should arise, and the innovative combination of technology and policy to reach out to as many citizens as possible: in short, the ability of government to combine not only the creative use of new technologies with a balanced understanding of the Internet and of what actually works online, but also to successfully understand both citizens and government servants and their motivations and be able to anticipate and tackle the (often unrealistic) expectations of technology held by them.

Currently practiced *laissez-faire* regulation is, however, usually based on the assumption that not only are users aware that their information is being monitored and being used in particular ways by those collecting it, but that there do exist ways and means by which they might guard against unnecessary intrusions and fraud. Issues surrounding user authentication and information security thus have the potential to impact the ability of a process to generate trust and increase participation by determining access to information, the protection of citizen identity, and the prevention of abuse of government systems.

ICT-based public engagement may not, in the long-term, wholly replace conventional, more personalised methods of government-citizen interaction, but can definitely be used to complement them so as to overcome their shortcomings and provide government with new methods and innovative ways in which it might reach out, communicate, and interact with its citizens. The relationship between technology and trust thus needs to be explored and dealt with thoroughly if a meaningful and sustained two-way interaction between external and internal actors is to be developed and maintained whilst simultaneously balancing existing notions of privacy, data protection, and grappling with new and emerging variants of digital fundamental rights and duties.

In conclusion, this author would suggest that, for any government which chooses to use ICTs to increase citizen participation in decision-making processes, the ultimate idea would be to neither use online public engagement to completely supplant the offline decision-making processes of elected representatives (as techno-enthusiasts might argue) nor altogether reject online public engagement (as Net-sceptics would prefer), but instead use the Internet and its associated technologies and applications to help elected representatives strengthen their democratic mandate and develop more informed, publicly-supported policy proposals to further strengthen State institutions and processes.

REFERENCES

Bannon, L. J. (1991). From Human Factors to Human Actors: The Role of Psychology and Human Computer Interaction Studies in System Design. In J. Greenbaum, & M. Kyng (Eds.), *Design At Work: Cooperative Design of Computer Systems* (pp. 25–44). Lawrence Erlbaum Associates, Inc. Publishers.

Barber, B. R. (1984). *Strong Democracy: Participatory Politics for a New Age*. Berkley, CA: University of California Press.

Bellamy, C., & Taylor, J. A. (1998). *Governing in the Information Age*. Maidenhead, UK: Open University Press.

Bicking, M., & Wimmer, M. A. (2010). Tools and Technologies in eParticipation: Insights from Project Evaluation. In F. De Cindio, A. Machintosh, & C. Peraboni (Eds.), *Online Deliberation: Proceedings of the Fourth International Conference* (pp. 75 – 86). OD2010.

Bimber, B. (1998). The Internet and Political Transformation: Populism, Community and Accelerated Pluralism. *Polity*, *31*(1), 133–160. doi:10.2307/3235370

Bishop, P., & Anderson, L. (2004). *E-Government to E-Democracy: 'High-Tech' Solutions to 'No Tech' Problems*. Paper presented to the Australian Electronic Governance Conference. Melbourne, Australia.

Blumler, J. C., & Coleman, S. (2001). Realising Democracy Online: A Civic Commons in Cyberspace (IPPR Citizens Online Research Publication No.2). London, UK: IPPR.

Carayon, P., Hoonakker, P., & Smith, M. J. (2012). Human Factors in Organizational Design and Management. In G. Salvendy (Ed.), *Handbook of Human Factors and Ergonomics* – (4th ed., pp. 534–552). John Wiley and Sons. doi:10.1002/9781118131350.ch18

Catinat, M., & Vedel, T. (2000). Public Policies for Digital Democracy. In K. L. Hacker, & J. van Dijk (Eds.), *Digital Democracy: Issues of Theory and Practice* (pp. 184–208). London: Sage Publications.

Chun, S., Shulman, S., Sandoval, R., & Hovy, E. (2010). Government 2.0: Making Connections Between Citizens, Data and Government. *Information Polity Journal*, *15*(1-2), 1–9.

Coleman, S. (2011). The Wisdom of Which Crowd? On the Pathology of a Listening Government. *The Political Quarterly, 82*(3), 355–364.

Coleman, S., & Gotze, J. (2001). *Bowling Together: Online Public Engagement in Policy Deliberation.* London: Hansard Society.

Cruickshank, P., Edelmann, N., & Smith, C. (2010). Signing an e-Petition as a Transition from Lurking to Participation. In H. J. Scholl, & M. Janssen (Eds.), *Electronic Government and Electronic Participation: Joint Proceedings of Ongoing Research and Projects of IFIP EGOV and IFIP ePart 2010* (pp. 275–282). Linz, Austria: Trauner Verlag.

Czaja, S. J., & Nair, S. N. (2012). Human Factors Engineering and Systems Design. In G. Salvendy (Ed.), *Handbook of Human Factors and Ergonomics* (4th ed., pp. 38–56). John Wiley and Sons. doi:10.1002/9781118131350.ch2

di Gennaro, C., & Dutton, W. H. (2006). The Internet and the Public: Online and Offline Political Participation in the UK. *Parliamentary Affairs, 59*(2), 299–313. doi:10.1093/pa/gsl004

Dutton, W. H., & Peltu, M. (2007). *Reconfiguring Government Public Engagements: Enhancing the Communicative Power of Citizens* (Oxford Internet Institute Forum Discussion Paper No. 9). Oxford Internet Institute.

Eggers, W. D. (2005). *Government 2.0: Using Technology to Improve Education, Cut Red Tape, Reduce Gridlock and Enhance Democracy.* Lanham, MD: Rowman and Littlefield Publishers Inc.

Eisenhardt, K. M. (1989). Building Theories from Case Study Research. *Academy of Management Review, 14*(4), 532–550.

Ferguson, R. (2006). *Digital Dialogues: Interim Report, December 2005 – August 2006.* London: The Hansard Society.

Fieldhouse, E., Tranmer, M., & Russel, A. (2007). Something about Young People or Something about Elections? Electoral Participation of Young People in Europe: Evidence from a Multilevel Analysis of the European Social Survey. *European Journal of Political Research, 46*(6), 797–822. doi:10.1111/j.1475-6765.2007.00713.x

Fishkin, J. S. (1995). *The Voice of the People: Public Opinion and Democracy.* New York: Yale University Press.

Geoghegan, T. (2007). The Petition, the 'Prat' and the Political Ideal, *BBC News – Magazine: February 13, 2007.* Available at: http://news.bbc.co.uk/1/hi/magazine/6354735.stm

Goodhart, M. (2007). Europe's Democratic Deficits through the Looking Glass: The European Union as a Challenge for Democracy. *Perspectives on Politics, 5*(3), 567–584. doi:10.1017/S1537592707071551

Hoff, J. (2006). The Shaping of Digital Political Communication – Creating e-Democracy in a Danish Municipality: Intentions and Realities. In H. K. Hansen, & J. Hoff (Eds.), *Digital Governance://Networked Societies. Creating Authority, Community and Identity in a Globalized World* (pp. 261–299). Copenhagen: Samfundslitteratur Press/NORDICOM.

Jacko, J. A., Yi, J. S., Sainfort, F., & McClellan, M. (2012). Human Factors and Ergonomic Methods. In G. Salvendy (Ed.), *Handbook of Human Factors and Ergonomics –* (4th ed., pp. 289–329). John Wiley and Sons. doi:10.1002/9781118131350.ch10

Janssen, D., & Kies, R. (2004). Online Forums and Deliberative Democracy: Hypotheses, Variables and Methodologies. *e-Democracy Centre e-Working Papers No. 1.*

Karwowski, W. (2012). The Discipline of Human Factors and Ergonomics. In G. Salvendy (Ed.), *Handbook of Human Factors and Ergonomics* – (4th ed., pp. 3–37). John Wiley and Sons. doi:10.1002/9781118131350.ch1

Kies, R., & Wojcik, S. (2010). European Web-Deliberation: Lessons from the European Citizens Consultation. In F. De Cindio, A. Machintosh, & C. Peraboni (Eds.), *Online Deliberation: Proceedings of the Fourth International Conference* (pp. 198 – 211). OD2010.

Kuutti, K. (1996). Activity Theory as a Potential Framework for Human Computer Interaction Research. In B. A. Nardi (Ed.), Context and Consciousness: Activity Theory and Human Computer Interaction (pp. 17 – 44). Boston, MA: MIT Press.

Loukis, E., & Wimmer, M. A. (2010). Analysing Different Models of Structured Electronic Consultation on Legislation Under Formation. In F. De Cindio, A. Macintosh, & C. Peraboni (Eds.), *Online Deliberation: Proceedings of the Fourth International Conference* (pp. 14 – 26). OD2010.

Macintosh, A., Malina, A., & Farrell, S. (2002). Digital Democracy through Electronic Petitioning. In W. J. McIver Jr, & A. K. Elmagarmid (Eds.), *Advances in Digital Government: Technology, Human Factors and Policy* (pp. 137–162). Dordrecht: Kluwer Academic Publishing. doi:10.1007/0-306-47374-7_8

Proctor, R. W., & Vu, K.-P. L. (2012). Selection and Control of Action. In G. Salvendy (Ed.), *Handbook of Human Factors and Ergonomics* (4th ed., pp. 95–116). John Wiley and Sons. doi:10.1002/9781118131350.ch4

Salvendy, G. (2012). *Handbook of Human Factors and Ergonomics* (4th ed.). John Wiley and Sons. doi:10.1002/9781118131350

Thomassen, J., & Schmitt, H. (1999). Introduction: Political Representation and Legitimacy in the European Union. In H. Schmitt, & J. Thomassen (Eds.), *Political Representation and Legitimacy in the European Union* (pp. 3–21). Oxford, UK: Oxford University Press. doi:10.1093/0198296614.003.0001

Virkar, S. (2007). *(Dis) Connected Citizenship? Exploring Barriers to eConsultation in Europe. Report to the European Commission for the The Breaking Barriers to eGovernment: Overcoming Obstacles to Improving European Public Services.* Project.

Virkar, S. (2011). *The Politics of Implementing e-Government for Development: The Ecology of Games Shaping Property Tax Administration in Bangalore City.* (Unpublished Doctoral Thesis). Oxford, UK: University of Oxford

Virkar, S. (2013a). Designing and Implementing e-Government Projects: Actors, Influences, and Fields of Play. In S. Saeed & C. G. Reddick (Eds.), Human-Centered Design for Electronic Government. Hershey, PA: IGI Global.

Virkar, S. (2013b). What's in a Game? The Politics of Shaping Property Tax Administration in Bangalore, India. In J. Bishop, & A. M. G. Solo (Eds.), *Politics in the Information Age.* London: Springer Inc.

Virkar, S. (2013c). Re-engaging the Public in the Digital Age: e-Consultation Initiatives in the Government 2.0 Landscape. In Encyclopedia of Information Science and Technology (3rd ed.). Hershey, PA: IGI Global.

ADDITIONAL READING

Hacker, K. L., & van Dijk, J. (2000). Introduction: What is Digital Democracy? In K. L. Hacker, & J. van Dijk (Eds.), *Digital Democracy: Issues of Theory and Practice* (pp. 1–9). London: Sage Publications.

Hagen, M. (2000). Digital Democracy and Political Systems. In K. L. Hacker, & J. van Dijk (Eds.), *Digital Democracy: Issues of Theory and Practice* (pp. 54–69). London: Sage Publications.

Hartley, J. (2005). Case Study Research. In C. Cassell, & G. Symon (Eds.), *Essential Guide to Qualitative Methods in Organisational Research* (pp. 323–333). London: Sage Publications.

Heeks, R. (2000). The Approach of Senior Public Officials to Information-Technology Related Reform: Lessons from India. *Public Administration and Development,20*(3), 197–205. doi:10.1002/1099-162X(200008)20:3<197::AID-PAD109>3.0.CO;2-6

Heeks, R. (2003). Most eGovernment-for-Development Projects Fail: How Can the Risks be Reduced? *iGovernment Working Paper Series – Paper No. 14*, University of Manchester (UK).

Held, D. (1996). *Models of Democracy*. Cambridge: Blackwell Publishers.

Hiller, J.S., & Bélanger, F. (2001). Privacy Strategies for Electronic Government. *The PriceWaterHouseCoopers E-Government Series*, January 2001

H.M.Government. (2002). *In the Service of Democracy – A Consultation Paper on a Policy for Electronic Democracy. Published by the Office of the e-Envoy*. London, United Kingdom: The Cabinet Office.

Irani, Z., Elliman, T., & Jackson, P. (2007). Electronic Transformation of Government in the UK: Research Agenda. *European Journal of Information Systems, 16*(4), 327–335. doi:10.1057/palgrave.ejis.3000698

Jankowski, N., & van Selm, M. (2000). The Promise and Practice of Public Debate in Cyberspace. In K. L. Hacker, & J. van Dijk (Eds.), *Digital Democracy: Issues of Theory and Practice* (pp. 149–165). London: Sage Publications. doi:10.4135/9781446218891.n9

Jenkins, H., & Thorburn, D. (2004). Introduction: The Digital Revolution, The Informed Citizen and the Culture of Democracy. In H. Jenkins & D. Thorburn (Eds.) Democracy and New Media (pp. 1-20). Cambridge, M.A.: M.I.T. Press.

Kooiman, J., & van Vliet, M. (1993). Introduction: Governance and Public Management. In K. A. Eliassen, & J. Kooiman (Eds.), *Managing Public Organisations: Lessons from Contemporary European Experience* (2nd ed., pp. 1–7). London: Sage Publications.

Koopmans, R., & Statham, P. (2002). The Transformation of Political Mobilisation and Communication in the European Public Spheres: A Research Outline. *Report to the European Commission dated 18th February 2002*.

Lindner, R., & Riehm, U. (2009). Electronic Petitions and Institutional Modernisation. *eJournal of eDemocracy and Open Government*, 1(1), 1 - 11

Lorenz, J., Rauhut, H., Schweitzer, F., & Helbing, D. (2011). How Social Influence Can Undermine the Wisdom of Crowd Effect. *Proceedings of the National Academy of Sciences of the United States of America, 108*(22), 9020–9025. doi:10.1073/pnas.1008636108 PMID:21576485

Lowndes, V., Pratchett, L., & Stoker, G. (2001). Trends in Local Government: Part 1 – Local Government Perspectives. *Public Administration, 79*(1), 205–222. doi:10.1111/1467-9299.00253

Margolis, M. (2007). E-Government and Democratic Politics. In P. G. Nixon, & V. N. Koutrakou (Eds.), *E-Government in Europe: Rebooting the State* (pp. 1–18). London: Routledge.

National Audit Office (2002). *Better Public Services through eGovernment: Academic Article in Support of Better Public Services through eGovernment*. Report by the Comptroller and Auditor General, April 2002.

Newman, J. (2005). *Remaking Governance: Peoples Politics and the Public Sphere*. Bristol: The Policy Press.

OECD. (2001). *Citizens as Partners: Information, Consultation and Public Participation in Policymaking*. Paris: OECD Press.

OECD. (2003). *Promise and Problems of E-Democracy: Challenges of Online Citizen Engagement*. Paris: OECD Press.

Peters, B., Sifft, S., Bruggmann, M., & Konigslow, K. (2005). National and Transnational Public Spheres: The Case of the EU. In S. Liebfried, & M. Zurn (Eds.), *Transformations of the State?* (pp. 139–160). Cambridge: Cambridge University Press. doi:10.1017/CBO9780511752193.007

Pleace, N. (2007). E-Government in the United Kingdom. In P. G. Nixon, & V. N. Koutrakou (Eds.), *E-Government in Europe: Rebooting the State* (pp. 61–74). London: Routledge.

Rhodes, R. A. W. (1996). The New Governance: Governing without Government. *Political Studies*, *44*(4), 652–667. doi:10.1111/j.1467-9248.1996.tb01747.x

Rosen, T. (2001) E-Democracy in Practice: Swedish Experience of New Political Tool, Available at www.svenkom.se/skvad/e-democracy-en.pdf

Scharpf, F. W. (1999). *Governing in Europe: Effective and Democratic?* Oxford: Oxford University Press.

Sclove, R. (1995). *Democracy and Technology*. New York: Guilford Press.

Stoker, G. (1998). Governance as Theory: Five Propositions. *International Social Science Journal*, *50*(155), 17–28. doi:10.1111/1468-2451.00106

The Electoral Commission. (2005). *Election 2005: Engaging the Public in Great Britain – an Analysis of Campaigns and Media Coverage*. London: The Electoral Commission.

The Royal Academy of Engineering. (2007). *Dilemmas of Privacy and Surveillance: Challenges of Technological Change*. Report available at: www.raeng,org.uk/policy/reports/default.htm

West, D. M. (2004). E-Government and the Transformation of Services and Citizen Attitudes. *Public Administration Review*, *64*(1), 15–27. doi:10.1111/j.1540-6210.2004.00343.x

Whyte, A., & Macintosh, A. (2003). Analysis and Evaluation of E-Consultations. *e-Service Journal*, *2*(1), 9–34. doi:10.2979/ESJ.2002.2.1.9

KEY TERMS AND DEFINITIONS

Actors: The individuals, groups or other entities whose interactions shape the direction and nature of a particular game being considered.

Actor Goals and Motivations: The aims that key actors seek to attain and maintain from interacting with other players, encompassing both broader long-term achievements as well as more short- to medium-term rewards.

Actor Perceptions: Include the preferences and opinions of key institutional players that help determine the disjoint between project design and current ground realities, together with the nature and direction of organisational reform and institutional change.

Country Context Gap: Refers to the gap that arises when a system designed in theory for one country is transferred into the reality of another.

Design-Actuality Gap Model or Framework: Is a framework for project evaluation which contends that the major factor determining project outcome is the degree of mismatch between the current ground realities of a situation ('where are we now'), and the models, conceptions, and assumptions built into a project's design (the 'where the project wants to get us').

E-Administration: Refers to the improvement of government processes and to the streamlining of the internal workings of the public sector often using ICT-based information systems.

E-Consultation: Refers to the process whereby citizens are given the opportunity to provide feedback to government online on matters of public importance and participate in the shaping of issues relevant to them via the new digital media.

E-Democracy: May be defined by the express intent to increase the participation of citizens in decision-making through the use of digital media and the application of Information and Communication Technologies to political processes. e-Democracy may be subdivided into e-Engagement (or e-Participation), e-Voting, e-Consultation.

E-Engagement: Refers to the overall enhancement of opportunities for greater consultation and dialogue between government and its citizens through the encouragement of online citizen action and citizen participation in political processes electronically.

E-Governance: Refers to the use of ICTs by government, civil society, and political institutions to engage citizens in political processes and to the promote greater participation of citizens in the public sphere.

E-Government: Refers to the use of Information and Communication Technologies by government departments and agencies to improve internal functioning and public service provision. Broadly speaking, e-government may be divided into 2 distinct areas: e-Administration and e-Services.

E-Services: Which refers to the improved delivery of public services to citizens through multiple electronic platforms.

E-Voting: May be defined broadly as the expression and exercise of fundamental democratic rights and duties online through specially developed digital platforms.

Games: Arena(s) of competition and cooperation structured by a set of rules and assumptions about how to act in order for actors to achieve a particular set of objectives.

Hard-Soft Gap: Refers to the difference between the *actual, rational design* of a technology (hard) adopted within a project and the *actuality of the social context*, namely people, culture, politics, etc., within which the system operates (soft).

Managerial Variables: Are those institutional variables relating to project management and other *soft* variables of project design and implementation, which include the efficiency and effectiveness of a supply chain, the characteristics of an agency's culture, and the capacity of an adopting agency to adapt to and to manage change.

Moves: May be defined as actions, decisions and other plays made by key actors taken to arrive at key goals, usually if not always based on their strategy of choice.

Partial Failure: Of an initiative is a situation in which major goals are unattained or where there are significant undesirable outcomes.

Political Variables: Are those *soft* institutional variables relating to the perceptions and impressions that public servants have regarding potential labour cuts, administrative turnover, and changes in executive direction generated by the development of e-government.

Private-Public Gap: Refers to the mismatch that results when technology meant for private organisations is used in the public sector without being adapted to suit the role and aims of the adopting public organisation.

Project Outcome: Or the sum total of the interaction between organisational and institutional realities and the project design carried out within the constraints of the current organisational and institutional set-up.

Rules: The written or unwritten codes of conduct that shape actor moves and choices during a game.

Strategies: Include tactics, ruses, and ploys adopted by key actors during the course of a game to keep the balance of the engagement in their favour.

Success: Of an initiative is a situation in which most actor groups attain their major goals and do not experience significant undesirable outcomes.

Technological Variables: Are those institutional variables relating to technology and other *hard* elements of project design and implementation, which include the ability of a user-population to access ICTs, the quality of the user population's Internet use, the availability of an internal technological infrastructure, and the provision of technical skills to the government workforce.

Total Failure: Of an initiative is a situation where a project is either never implemented or in which a new system is implemented but is almost immediately abandoned.

ENDNOTES

[1] Otherwise called Electronic Governance, this term refers to the use of technology to enhance the structural (institutional and legal) frameworks and processes of governance. Based on discussions in earlier sections of this paper, the notion of eGovernance may be conceptually divided into eGovernment (which is concerned with electronic public service delivery) and eDemocracy (where technology is used to impact the quality and nature of democratic processes).

[2] UK Citizens Online Democracy was a project which began life by setting up a website to discuss the Freedom of Information Act proposed by the Blair Administration in 1999/2000.

Chapter 3
Software Engineering and New Emerging Technologies:
The Involvement of Users for Development Applications for Tablets

Sergio Ricardo Mazini
University Center Toledo Araçatuba (UNITOLEDO), Brazil

ABSTRACT

This chapter presents an approach to the role of software engineering in developing solutions for new mobile technologies, like tablets. It discusses the importance of the new standards brought by emerging technologies such as engineering and how software must adapt to this new reality in order to identify the needs of data, information, integration, shares, and other issues that will contribute to the life cycle of these solutions. The chapter also discusses the contribution of users in the development process and improve these solutions. The research method is the case study conducted in industrial companies that use a digital catalog solution and sales force automation for tablets. This chapter presents a new approach based on commercial tablets which is supported by a platform of software and services called commercially Nimiam (www.nimiam.com.br).

INTRODUCTION

In the current globalization and competitive scenario, now-a-days the organizational structures in manufacturing companies are objects of big changes, aiming to become closer to the customer needs and even to expand its services offers, whether these services are connected to tangible goods or not. In such state of affairs, new available technologies appear as a partner for the offer of products and services, whether for manufacturing industries that add services to products or simply for services companies.

With the advent of tablets, specifically the iPad Apple, there is a creation of a new category of intermediate mobile devices from notebooks to smartphones. Sato (2011) comments that these new portable devices with touch screens make the connectivity and access easier to multimedia content, like: videos, photos, text, email, etc., thus transforming the way we deal with and seek information. In this context, software solutions

DOI: 10.4018/978-1-4666-6485-2.ch003

available for computers and notebooks have to be rethought and redesigned to utilize the full potential of tablets. According to an article by Gartner (2012), tablets feature a wide variety of business opportunities and a new design paradigm that requires new policies, technologies and skills.

As per the research carried out by Strategy and Analytics (2012), the global market for tablets reached 25 million units in the second quarter of 2012. Apple increased its shares holding to 68 percent, reaching its highest level in nearly two years. The Microsoft tablets remained a niche solution, but future may see changes with the attention focused on the upcoming release of Windows 8.

In a world of stiff competition, commoditization and constant search for new and contemporary brands tend to create associations related to cutting edge innovation. The advertising aesthetics constantly seek to associate their brands atmosphere to modernity that involves tablets, especially the iPad by Sato (2011). In this time of rapid changes in social practices, political and economic environment, technology plays a key role to create new opportunities and ways of doing business.

A customer is getting less and less of time at the moment of buying a product. In other words, customer has limited time at the time of making purchase. That is why the information of products and comparison between companies must be shown with agility and must also create curiosity and enchantment. Currently many salesmen, even with the use of traditional solutions of Sales Force Automation (SFA), still take orders manually in front of a client and type it later on the computer system. Motivated by these phenomenon and ideas, a full commercial software platform is created which is based on tablets (called Nimiam) and presented in this chapter.

The chapter aims to present a new commercial approach based on new technologies demonstrating its contribution to the innovation process for sales and marketing and also for providing allied services to the products offered by companies manufacturing goods.

After the bibliographic research of the most important themes connected to the subject, that is: services characteristics, innovation, the contribution of information technology, the following research questions are addressed, which will be the key to the development of this research based chapter.

- What is Nimiam solution?
- How to identify the importance of software engineering in developing solutions for new technologies and identify the need and contribution of users in the development process and improve these solutions?

The research is carried out considering two companies, one from the Brazilian footwear market and the other from Brazilian linen market, and has the aim of analysing the use of emergent technologies; that is tablets, with the innovative approach of sales and marketing to offer new services. In the case studies, a solution named 'Nimiam' of digital catalogues will be presented and its effect on strength of sales through tablets will be analyzed.

BACKGROUND

Software Engineering and Mobile Application Development

A software engineering as a process by which an individual or team organizes and manages the creation of a software-intensive system, from concept through one or more formal releases (Wasserman, 2010).

Also according to the Wasserman (2010), software engineering for the development of mobile applications is similar to other devices, but applications for mobile devices require additional requirements, such as:

- **Potential Interaction with Other Applications:** Most embedded devices only have factory-installed software, but mobile devices may have numerous applications from varied sources, with the possibility of interactions among them;
- **Sensor Handling:** Most modern mobile devices, e.g., "smartphones", include an accelerometer that responds to device movement, a touch screen that responds to numerous gestures, along with real and/or virtual keyboards, a global positioning system, a microphone usable by applications other than voice calls, one or more cameras, and multiple networking protocols;
- **Native and Hybrid (Mobile Web) Applications:** Most embedded devices use only software installed directly on the device, but mobile devices often include applications that invoke services over the telephone network or the Internet via a web browser and affect data and displays on the device;
- **Families of Hardware and Software Platforms:** Most embedded devices execute code that is custom-built for the properties of that device, but mobile devices may have to support applications that were written for all of the varied devices supporting the operating system, and also for different versions of the operating system. An Android developer, for example, must decide whether to build a single application or multiple versions to run on the broad range of Android devices and operating system releases
- **Security:** Most embedded devices are "closed", in the sense that there is no straightforward way to attack the embedded software and affect its operation, but mobile platforms are open, allowing the installation of new "malware" applications that can affect the overall operation of the device, including the surreptitious

transmission of local data by such an application.

- **User Interfaces:** With a custom-built embedded application, the developer can control all aspects of the user experience, but a mobile application must share common elements of the user interface with other applications and must adhere to externally developed user interface guidelines, many of which are implemented in the software development kits (SDKs) that are part of the platform.
- **Complexity of Testing:** While native applications can be tested in a traditional manner or via a PC-based emulator, mobile web applications are particularly challenging to test. Not only do they have many of the same issues found in testing web applications, but they have the added issues associated with transmission through gateways and the telephone network.
- **Power Consumption:** Many aspects of an application affect its use of the device's power and thus the battery life of the device. Dedicated devices can be optimized for maximum battery life, but mobile applications may inadvertently make extensive use of battery-draining resources.

Innovation through New Emerging Technologies

Innovation has become one of the key differentiators of economic position of organizations, with impacts on their level of development, growth rates and dynamism. Innovation stands out and is largely responsible for the gains for countries and companies in competitive scenario by Arruda and Rossi (2009). Therefore, for a need of innovation in the contemporary economy, whether in manufacturing companies and service companies, there is consensus among all actors involved in the competitive process: firms, strategic partners, government, customers and universities.

Sundbo (1997) brings out the discussions about the innovation process in services companies and inquires whether these companies innovate constantly and how the innovation activities are organized and managed. These questions are analyzed based on the traditional theories relevant in industrial companies. The importance of the innovation process which is widely known in the academic and empirical area, as well has a role by service activities in producing systems are becoming more important, combine themselves to make the innovation of the services a matter of big importance by Gallouj and Weinstein (1997).

Innovation takes many different forms, but it can be summarized in four different dimensions of change, or the 4Ps of innovation by Francis and Bessant (2005):

- Product innovation: changes in the products / services that a company offers.
- Process innovation: changes in the way products / services are created and submitted or offered to the consumer.
- Position Innovation: changes in the context in which products / services are introduced.
- Paradigm Innovation: changes in basic mental models that guide what a company does.

External sources of knowledge and information are among the greatest number of resources for innovation activities in enterprises. Open innovation has become a concept to provide comprehensive search of external resources. The concept introduced by Chesbrough (2003) discusses a new path to innovation through collaboration of various actors in the value chain for the pursuit of new knowledge and technologies. It is a relatively new concept, which has attracted the attention of a large number of researchers and companies (Ryzhkova, 2009).

This new paradigm innovation enables a broad discussion about various organizational aspects, notably: business model, reduction of time and cost, and risk dilution mainly expanding limits of performance of organizations in the creation and capture of value through possible gains in terms of innovation and competitiveness (Rossi, 2009). In this context, companies can seek partnerships and involvement of other sources of information that can contribute to the innovation process, among which customers stand out. The identification and involvement of customers at the right time can contribute to the innovation process and help companies sustain a long-term competitive advantage (Lettl et al., 2006).

In the era of open innovation, which absorbs external knowledge, organization can become an important factor in the creation of successful innovations. Researchers have wondered about a more active engagement from customers to develop new products than traditional market research method. According to Fuller and Matzler (2007), customers can virtually be integrated into the business process innovation through new interactive tools that allow companies to obtain valuable input from customers via the Internet.

In this context, new technologies such as tablets and virtual environments also increase the speed and persistence of customer engagement and increase the company's ability to explore the social dimension of customer knowledge, enabling the creation of virtual communities of consumption.

The direct involvement of customers through new tools and technologies for managing marketing allows creation and distribution of value (Tretyak & Sloev, 2013). Thus, the effect of tangible and intangible resources in the relationship of customers and suppliers is being responsible for mutual benefits in the creation of value and shared values (Coley et al., 2012). With this industrial companies are currently subject to major changes, many of today's organizations have changed its organizational structure to initiate being responsive to customer needs or to expand its service sector to customers (Gebauer & Kowalkowski, 2012).

Aungst and Wilson (2005) describe that mobile computing and wireless can add value to specific business processes and define four areas of opportunity for the use of these technologies:

- Customer Relationship Management (CRM), with the ability of customers to access their orders and current status of the same;
- Sales Force Automation (SFA), with the ability of sellers to send customer orders to their companies, from anywhere, anytime;
- Field Service Automation (FSA), with the possibility of providing services by airlines;
- Mobile Messaging Service (MMS), with the possibility of monitoring products such as refrigerators and air conditioners, to request preventive maintenance services;

Currently, mobile and wireless technology are no longer a novelty and can be used both internally and in inter-organizational relationships, facilitating and contributing to the exchange of information and knowledge about the company, its brands, products and promotions. Salo (2012) describes

the impact of the use of mobile technologies, both for internal use and in use for coordination between business partners, as illustrated in Figure 1.

The cell 1 of Figure 1 demonstrates that the impact of mobile technology on internal coordination is greater than the impact on inter-organizational coordination, as an example there are some wood-processing industries which use Radio Frequency Identification (RFID) technology in its manufacturing process. The cell 2 shows the situation in which the impact of mobile technology on internal coordination as well as on inter-organizational relationship is high, as an example the functionality of ERP systems that connect buyers and suppliers, exchanging information on products and applications. The cell 3 demonstrates low impact of mobile technology on internal coordination as well as low impact on inter-organizational coordination, as an example those companies that have not invested in mobile technologies or do it on demand. The cell 4 demonstrates the low impact of mobile technology on the internal coordination and high impact on inter-organizational coordination, as an example

Figure 1. Impacts of mobile technology on the coordination in the buyer-seller relationship (Salo, 2012)

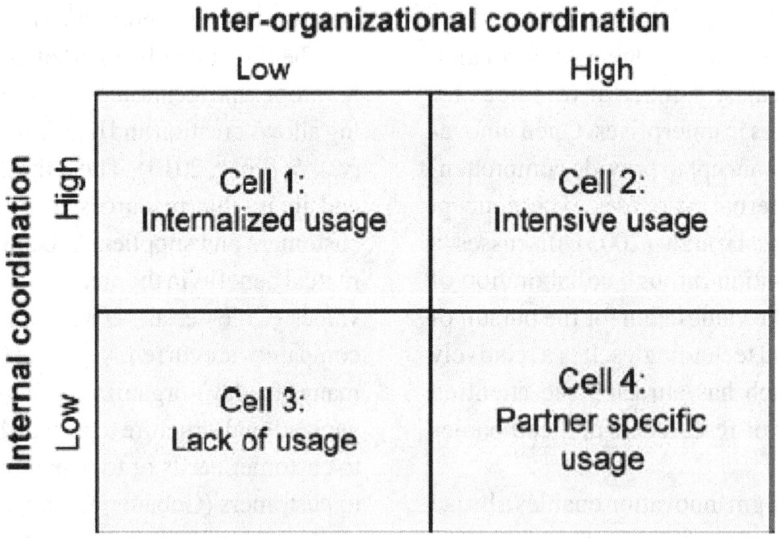

those companies that use these technologies in the automation of its sales force (Salo, 2012).

The solution Nimiam, next presented in this chapter fits as an example for cell 2 in Figure 1, where it is the high use of mobile technologies internally in the organization as well as for inter-organizational coordination; that is both for sales force automation and for providing coordination new services to customers.

MAIN FOCUS OF THE CHAPTER

The main focus of this chapter is to present Nimiam - a new commercial approach, based for new technologies, demonstrating its contribution on the innovation of sale and marketing process and also to offer services accompanying tangible products offered by the companies. Search also present the contribution of end users in the development and innovation of the solution presented in chapter. Next now, we have presented the Nimiam solution and two case studies of companies that use this solution and try to innovate the offer of services to customers.

What Nimiam Is? Solution to Digital Catalogue and Digital Requests for Tablet

The aim of this tool (Nimiam) is to make available some commercially innovate solution of Digital Catalogue, Sale Strengths and Business Intelligence (BI) for the use of tablets specially iPad from Apple, which allows sales staff to take and gain more information about their products at the time of sale. The aim of this solution is to provide a different buying experience where the customer can go deep and explore on the options from the commercial catalogue of the company. The project proposes to reach the following results:

- Create, organize and publish a digital catalogue of products that allow acccss and crossing of different multimedia contents, as: information about new products, videos of the product and technology, social nets contents and many other options and ways of seeing the products.
- Use some useful resources available on the iPad Apple platform to make a differentiated experience to the customer at the moment of testing and choosing the products.
- Sales force can integrate in a quick and consistent way as a commercial web reward and with the own management system of the company;
- Provide relevant information to sales staff through a BI commercial that allows the increase of "intelligence" of commercial/sales actions and enhance the performance to the customer.
- Take the final customer to all marketing actions and concepts of products that make the company brands stronger.

With regard to the previous sales practices used by companies, as a printed catalogue and the sale strength that sale paper blocks printed in graphics; the solution Nimiam provides the possibility of different innovative practices, for example:

- Updating of recent commercial tools, getting the best of the technology on the Apple platform;
- Optimization of information for the commercial staff, taking more information with the aim of potential sales;
- Having autonomy to create and to make available digital catalogues, getting the market and sale opportunities closer;
- Improve the communication with the sale staff;

- Showing that the company brands are in constant innovation.

Modules from Nimiam

Below there is a detailed table of the modules that make part of the platform, as shown in Table 1.

Innovation on the Sales and Marketing Process by Nimiam

The approach proposed by Nimiam is made in four steps: Edit the catalogue, integrate commercial rules, distribute contents and collect requests and information, as illustrated in Figure 2.

Table 1. Nimiam modules (developed by Authors, 2013)

Commercial Rearguard   Module is responsible for integration of Sales Force Automation (SFA) with ERP of company, exporting product information and trade policy, creation of multimedia content for the application on iPad and importing sales made on iPad to company ERP system. The entire configuration Digital Catalog is done through the Commercial Rearguard on Web
Digital Catalog iPad   Module is responsible for providing information about availability and selection of products in a Digital Catalog that allows detailed view of products as well as informs the end customer on all marketing activities of the company. It collects important and relevant information about customers.
Sales Force iPad   Module is responsible for collecting Request Orders with all details of color, finish and size. It also allows the queries regarding inventory of finished applications ready for delivery to the customer, as well as collecting some important and relevant information about customers.

Figure 2. Approach of new experiences of sales based in tablets (developed by the authors, 2013)

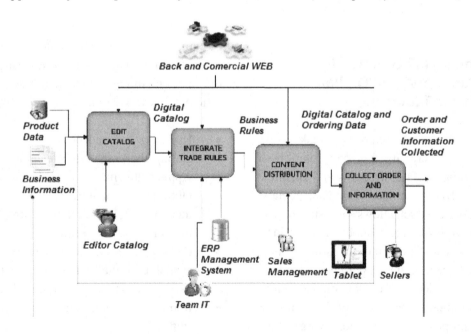

Edit Catalog

In this first step, based on the information available from company about marketing, the editor of the catalog initially upload resources on web at the commercial rearguard to make catalog: photos, videos, PDFs, etc.. After the catalogs are created, define the pages and its respective layouts, as well as the best way to navigate between pages. Product information: code, description, color, size, specification, are imported from company ERP system or registered in their own back catalog by the editor. Generally a company has several types of catalogs: a specific line or group of products, marketing catalog, prompt delivery catalog or prompt service, conceptual catalog, among others. At the end of this step, company's catalogs are editorialized and made available on web at the commercial rearguard platform.

Integrate Commercial Rules

In this step the IT (Information Technology) team - provides information about the company's business rules so the sales orders/ requests can be collected. Among the information that is integrated into the commercial rearguard onweb include: salesmen, customers of each salesman, price table, payment terms, transport facility, discounts policy, etc. This information is exported directly from management ERP system to the commercial rearguardand will be further useful to start initial sales requests collected on the tablet.

Distribute Content

With the created catalogue and information of commercial rules available on the rearguard of the commercial platform, now it is possible to release this content through the web to salesmen of tablets in the area. This allows the subsequent use of solutions on an off-line way, that is, without internet connection. This is made by the administration sales staff, after a set of internal tests to ensure consistency of information and quality of the catalogue. As a result of this step, all salesmen of tablets have the catalogues of ready products to be used at the moment of sale.

Collect Requests and Information

Finally, as the last step of the approach, salesmen show their customers the product catalog products and marketing information of company that reinforce the brand and its differences from other pr. Customers, in turn, make a selection of products in a shopping cart which will later be transformed into one or more applications already validated with the commercial rules of the company. At the time of sale, if the seller has an Internet connection the application is automatically sent to the company and the customer can receive an email with a copy of one's request/ requirement, including photos of products.

By contact with the customer, this last step will provide important feedback to the previous steps of the approach thus generating an evolutionary cycle of improvements in navigation of the catalog, in the form of collecting applications, and provide a time where it is possible to collect information regarding the knowledge sharing between the company and its customers.

Innovation Driven by Customers

Among the suggestions and innovations requested by client users of the solution can be highlighted:

- The separation of the items in the shopping cart list, allowing typing after several sales orders are generated at once.
- Show the price of the products identified icon below the figures of these products.
- Show the changing colors of products in images with thumbnail format, just above the main image of every product.
- Show additional information for each product by clicking on it.

To illustrate the use of some tools of Nimiam solution, two real case studies are presented where the customers have already used the solution.

Research Method

With the aim of taking information about new sales experiences/ expectations based on tablets, an exploratory research was carried out through a qualitative/ case study approach. The exploratory character of research is justified, because even with the existence of publications about service innovation (Barras, 1986; Gallouj, 1997, Sundbo, 1997) and guided innovation in manufacturing companies (Gebauer *et al.,* 2012; Rubalcaba *et al.,* 2012), there is the lack of research that considers the service innovation in manufacturing companies provided by the use of new technologies like tablets which can afford some innovation on the sales process, marketing and provided services. Further it is more relevant when it is straightly connected to the Brazilian scenery and other emergent markets.

The qualitative research was used, as this approach makes possible the comprehension of people's opinions about the phenomenon studied, which promotes the study of an exploratory research. The survey unit for the qualitative study/ case research was companies and customers that have been using the solution, Nimiam, based on tablets as a way of creating new sales experiences with the customer. To collect the information, primary data sources were used that according to Yin (2005) allows the researcher to dedicate a huge diversity of questions, such as: historical, behavioral and attitudinal.

The collection of primary information from companies and customers was made through interviews:

- **Interviews with Company Personnel:** Interviews were conducted with the commercial managers and salesmen of companies that were using the Nimiam solu-

tion. Interviews were not structured ones and conducted with a set of questions (that was recorded to raise the reliability on the study). Interviews collected the data about the origins, necessities, structures and variables that influenced the use of Nimiam. A non-structured interview was also conducted (that was recorded to raise the reliability on the study) with the persons responsible for Information Technology area of user companies and data was collected about the organizational structure of the project, the organizational process and the implementation of variable that influences the project.

- **Interviews with Customers:** Information was collected from some customers who have used the solution. Information was about which content, facilities and agility on the service offered by the salesperson.

On the stage of analyzing information, interviews were transcribed and the relevant information, as per aim of the research, was organized in a way to get all the main references to the Nimiam project. There was also a confrontation with the theory and the analysis of the case study according to the Nimiam solution. The construct validity of the research happened through the using of multiple sources of information and the interaction with the involved constructs since the literature.

Case Study 1

Democrata Footwear

Democrata Footwear, www.democrata.com.br, is a traditional male footwear company from Franca-SP, Brazil. In November 2011 they launched the challenge to automate the sales strength and substitute the printed catalogue by digital ones for the Exhibition 'Couromodas 2012', that would take place in two months. It demonstrates the agility on the process of implementation of tools.

Figure 3. Case study Democrata (developed by the authors, 2013)

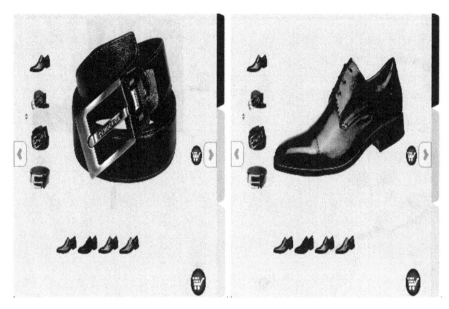

Democrata Footwear had developed previously a web module for submitting requests that were made on the representation offices and not in front of the customer. Nowadays Democrata uses the module of Commercial Rearguard method and Digital Catalogue iPad that substituted the printed catalogue and the Sale Strength of Nimiam totally integrated to its ERP system. Figure 3 illustrates the screen of the products catalogue from Democrata with a selection option to buy where it can be noticed that other products are also showen that can also be considered with the principal one. The suggestion of other products offered as an additional service to clients, informing them about the fashion trend and accessories combination, which help companies to create differentiation during the sale and add some important value to the clients.

Democrata Footwear, through the technological resources available on the Nimiam solution, tends to disseminate information and knowledge towards the products. For this the company makes available some videos that explain the manufacturing process of its products and the technology used.

Case Study 2

Teka: Bed, Table, and Bath Linen

Teka - Bed, Table and Bath Linen, www.teka.com.br, is one of the biggest clothing industries from Brazil, located in Blumenau – SC, Brazil. In April 2012 they decided to substitute its sale printed catalogue, that used to be distributed to a staff of 150 salesmen, for digital catalogue. Teka owns many catalogues for the different areas of products: children products, professional, decoration, among others. Initially a catalogue was made and distributed and tested by nine salesmen. Then, this catalogue was revised and released to the rest of the staff. Figure 4 shows the screen of Teka products catalogues, on the left side there is the vertical sight of the tablet and on the right side is the horizontal sight that show more options of the same products or product combinations.

Teka - Bed, Table and Bath Linen through the technological available resources on the Nimiam solution, tends to disseminate information and knowledge regarding the companies, their products, projects and promotions. So the company

Figure 4. Case study Teka (developed by the authors, 2013)

makes available some catalogues in which there is a little about its history, its concerns about sustainability projects and social responsibilities.

Analysis of the Results

The reported case studies show that the Nimiam is not a specific application for a niche market but also flexible enough to meet diverse business segments and can show various types of products.

The solution of digital catalog and collection requests in tablets is relatively new, just 2 years old since its conception. Today, there are about 20 companies using the solution, most of them being major brands of Brazilian industry, and have more than 300 salesmen in the field and another 150 in the stage of implementation. It shows the technical and commercial viability of this solution.

Prior to the use of digital catalogues, the salesmen had to carry printed catalogues that used to take a longer time to describe to a customer. With the use of digital module catalogue of Nimiam solution with tablet, information sharing has become easier with the customer. There is improvement of the images shown to the customers making it possible for fruitful interactions with enthusiasm at the moment of sale. This adds some value to the sales experience towards customers. Further, the Nimiam solution has made possible the offer of suggestions of products combination to customers, which could not happen earlier. It also helps to advertise marketing actions, promotions and more information about the brand and its products.

As the customer's time is increasingly becoming scarce, the speed at the time of sale is essential success key. Besides the agility, customers need to feel comfortable with the new solution is important. The great challenge of the module catalog is to be as simple and intuitive so that a customer feels comfortable to flip through it, as used to do with the printed catalog.

The salesmen also need to notice the benefits of the solution otherwise they will not use it in their daily routine, as it happened in many other cases of implementation of AFV solutions. For it, the big challenge of the module is to collect the request and ask the salesmen to get the request on the tablet – where salesmen can see that it is quicker than it would be on the printed blocks written by hand.

Through the results of the research, it was found that the initial acceptance of using tablets does not depend on the people's age, as customers or salesmen, but depends on the predisposition to innovation, curiosity and lack of fear of new technologies. The tablet helps a lot on breaking prejudices by its friendly differentials, like touchscreen, weight, mobility and wide screen. The application must correspond properly and be intuitive enough so that someone, even without further explanation, could be able to use it and also feel comfortable during the process. By the reports that we got on the researches, after the third attempt that someone makes and cannot do a certain operation, they just give up.

It was also reported that the changes between horizontal and vertical views of the tablet by rotating the device did not work very well in practice. Now-a-days it is possible to get some more information about a particular product simply by turning the tablet horizontally, but it had not happened in earlier cases, so the costumer or salesmen used to end up using only one way of visualizing the product from the beginning to the end of the commercial process. The cover of the tablet can determine the choice of the position.

There were some reports of the commercial staff from Teka about the enchantment of customers when seeing the products through the tablet, allowing some bigger detailing about the technical information of the products, where it is possible to share information and knowledge between a company and a customer. There are also reports of the commercial staff from Democrata about the agility and the increase of sales due to the possibility of showing customers more products in a shorter period of time.

The benefits brought from these new technologies contribute to the innovation process in the area of sales and marketing, and also provide some favorable atmosphere for the creation, organization, publicity, information and knowledge sharing between the companies and the customers, creating effective results for both of them. It also allows companies previously focused on the manufacturing and sales of products, to take facilitating services to their customers, adding some value to the sale.

The solution is being expanded to collect information in the field by extending its functionalities to CRM (Customer Relationship Management) and collecting even more valuable information from customers and prospects (Brambilla, 2009). Also under consideration is a new search module for a selling point for use on tablet by commercial providers to collect information at the point of sale, such as: product status and its competitors in market, prices, photo showcase, among others. The characteristics of tablets, specifically the iPad with the quality of the retina screen, photo and video, will make all new experiences and new ways of use for future innovations. This is already happening today in a natural way as virtual current costumer is getting more involved on the use and benefits of this platform.

RELATED WORK

Over the years, with the development of information technology, the methods and techniques employed in software development through software engineering have also had to evolve. The active involvement of end-users, from the earliest stages of the development process, are necessary to ensure important issues such as: usability, functionality and business requirements.

The involvement of users is already known in the literature: Chesbrough (2003), Lettl et al. (2006) and among other authors. The contribution of this chapter comes against exemplify practical case of involving users in the development and improvement of a solution made for use in mobile devices such as tablets.

FUTURE RESEARCH DIRECTIONS

An innovation in the services of industrial companies is the trend on the services marketing and practice available in some companies. With the arrival of mobile devices, themes like mobile marketing have also become an interesting subject for practical as well as for academic arena. This chapter contributes on this direction, but some suggestions are summarized below for further research considerations:

- Researches focused on the innovation area of service.
- Researches focused on the mobile marketing and on the use of new technologies.
- Researches focused on the customer involvement in those processes are important and urgent.

CONCLUSION

The systematic application of this approach would allow corporate customers especially in the fashion and furniture sector, which is also the initial focus of the Nimiam solution, to link their respective brands with the atmosphere of innovation and cutting edge solution offered by Nimiam.

In line with current policies of Sustainability and Governance which has been adopted by a company in general, the Nimiam allows an immediate reduction in costs of catalog printing and paper consumption. Through research with existing customers the cost of printing is either same or less than the current cost of Nimiam solution. However, this will be neutralized on long term basis. Another benefit is the reduction in the number of physical samples due to the vast variety and options of photos and multimedia content of the same product that are available in the digital catalog. The limited samples will be required to present to the final costumer to notice the resistance, weight and quality of the material by physical contact.

Currently the biggest success challenge of this commercial platform is to achieve scalability of the solution, that is, with a substantial increase in the number of users, without losing the agility and proximity achieved with current clients.

As reported by Agner (2012), migration from printed magazines, newspapers and books to tablets is relatively new and there is not enough research to prove the benefits of its implementation and to ensure that concepts of ergonomics and semiotics are being met by the design of interfaces for tablets solutions., However, for the proposed solution to maintain an open channel of communication from business to customers, it is a notable contribution by this process for the creation, organization, advertising, and sharing of information and knowledge. Thus, it generates results and competitive advantage for these companies.

The presented use of Nimiam solution supported by case studies indicates that innovation of facilitating services for sales and marketing processes can be achieved by companies through information technology interface. In a developing country like Brazil or some other emerging economies, a solution like Nimiam, presented in this chapter, can provide competitive advantages to companies with the increase in number of sales, number of serviced and loyal customers, once they notice that being served by a company which carefully offers the best products and new services on an innovating way.

Resuming the research questions proposed, was identified through the analysis of case studies, literature review and the solution used by companies, that software engineering should suit the existing emerging technologies, such as tablet, and that the involvement of the users who are customers of the solution is an extremely important factor for the development and improvement of application.

REFERENCES

Agner, L. (2012). *Usability of journalism to tablets: A review of the interaction by gestures at a news app. In 12o ErgoDesign*. Natal, Brazil: USIHC.

Arruda, C., & Rossi, A. (2009). Creating the conditions for innovation. *Dom. The Journal of the Dom Cabral Foundation, 8*, 37–43.

Aungst, S. G., & Wilson, D. T. (2005). A primer for navigating the shoals of applying wireless technology to marketing problems. *Journal of Business and Industrial Marketing, 20*(2), 59–69. doi:10.1108/08858620510583650

Barras, R. (1986). Towards a Theory of Innovation in Services. *Research Policy, 15*(4), 161–173. doi:10.1016/0048-7333(86)90012-0

Bessant, J., & Tidd, J. (2009). *Innovation and Entrepreneurship*. Porto Alegre: Bookman.

Brambilla, F. R. (2009). Sales Force Automation (SFA) como ferramenta de vendas em aplicação do Customer Relationship Management (CRM). In SIMPOI. São Paulo, Brazil: Academic Press.

Chesbrough, H. W. (2003). The era of open innovation. *MIT Sloan Management Review, 44*(3), 35–41.

Coley, L. S., Lindemann, E., & Wagner, S. M. (2012). Tangible and intangible resource inequity in customer-supplier relationships. *Journal of Business and Industrial Marketing, 27*(8), 611–622. doi:10.1108/08858621211273565

Francis, D., & Bessant, J. (2005). Targeting innovation and implications for capability development. *Technovation, 25*(3), 171–183. doi:10.1016/j.technovation.2004.03.004

Füller, J., & Matzler, K. (2007). Virtual Product experience and customer participation – A chance for customer-centered, really new products. *Technovation, 27*(6-7), 378–387. doi:10.1016/j.technovation.2006.09.005

Gallouj, F., & Weinstein, O. (1997). Innovation in Services. *Research Policy, 26*(4-5), 537–556. doi:10.1016/S0048-7333(97)00030-9

Gartner Research. (2011). *Ipad and Beyond: The Media Tablet in Business*. Retrieved August 10, 2012, from http://www.gartner.com/technology/research/ipad-media-tablet/

Gebauer, H., & Kowalkowski, C. (2012). Customer-focused and service-focused orientation in organizational structures. *Journal of Business and Industrial Marketing, 27*(7), 527–537. doi:10.1108/08858621211257293

Gebauer, H., Ren, G., Valtakoski, A., & Reynoso, J. (2012). Service-driven manufacturing: Provision, evolution and financial impact of services in industrial firms. *Journal of Service Management, 23*(1), 120–136. doi:10.1108/09564231211209005

Grove, S. J., Fisk, R. P., & Jonh, J. (2003). The future of services marketing: Forecasts from ten services experts. *Journal of Services Marketing, 17*(2), 107–121. doi:10.1108/08876040310467899

Kotler, P. (1993). *Administração de Marketing: análise, planejamento, implementação e controle*. São Paulo: Atlas.

Lettl, C., Herstatt, C., & Gemuenden, H. G. (2006). Learning from users for radical innovation. *International Journal of Technology Management, 33*(1), 25. doi:10.1504/IJTM.2006.008190

Rossi, A. (2009). *The open innovation as a source of value creation for organizations*. Retrieved August 15, 2010, from http://www.fdc.org.br/pt/pesquisa/inovacao/Documents/artigos_blog/inovacao_aberta.pdf

Rubalcaba, L., Michel, S., Sundbo, J., Brow, S., & Reynoso, J. (2012). Shaping, organizing, and rethinking service innovation: A multidimesional framework. *Journal of Service Management, 23*(5), 696–715. doi:10.1108/09564231211269847

Ryzhkova, N. (2009). *The contribution of the user innovation methods to open innovation*. Blekinge, Sweden: Blekinge Institute of Technology.

Salo, J. (2012). The role of mobile technology in a buyer-supplier relationship: A case study from the steel industry. *Journal of Business and Industrial Marketing, 27*(7), 554–563. doi:10.1108/08858621211257329

Sato, S.K. (2011). The advertising aesthetic innovation: Smartphones and tablets. *Thought and Reality Magazine, 26* (3).

Strategy Analytcs. (2012). *Apple iPad Captures 68 Percent Share of 25 Million Global Tablet Shipments in Q2 2012*. Retrieved August 10, 2012, from http://blogs.strategyanalytics.com/TTS/post/2012/07/25/Apple-iPad-Captures-68-Percent-Share-of-25-Million-Global-Tablet-Shipments-in-Q2-2012.aspx

Sundbo, S. (1997). Management Innovation in Services. *Service Industries Journal, 17*(3), 432–455. doi:10.1080/02642069700000028

Tretyak, O., & Sloev, I. (2013). Customer flow: Evaluating the long-term impact of marketing on value creation. *Journal of Business and Industrial Marketing, 28*(3), 221–228. doi:10.1108/08858621311302877

Wasserman, A. I. (2010). Software Engineering Issues for Mobile Application Development. *FoSER, 2010*(November), 7–8.

Yin, R. K. (2005). Case study: Planning and methods (3rd ed.). Porto Alegre: Bookman.

ADDITIONAL READING

Antikainen, M., Mäkipää, M., & Ahonen, M. (2010). Motivating and Supporting Collaboration in Open Innovation. *European Journal of Innovation Management, 13*(1), 100–119. doi:10.1108/14601061011013258

Augusto, M., & Coelho, F. (2009). Market orientation and new-to-the-world products: Exploring the moderating effects of innovativeness, competitive strength, and environmental forces. *Industrial Marketing Management, 38*(1), 94–108. doi:10.1016/j.indmarman.2007.09.007

Aungst, S. G., & Wilson, D. T. (2005). A primer for navigating the shoals of applying wireless technology to marketing problems. *Journal of Business and Industrial Marketing, 20*(2), 59–69. doi:10.1108/08858620510583650

Babío, N. C., & Rodríguez, R. G. (2010). Talent management in professional services firms: A HR issue? *The International Journal of Organizational Analysis, 18*(4), 392–411. doi:10.1108/19348831011081877

Beal, A. (2008). *Strategic information management: how to transform information and information technology in growth factors and high performance in organizations*. São Paulo: Atlas.

Bennett, R. C., & Cooper, R. G. (1981). Beyond the marketing concept. *Business Horizons, 22*(3), 76–83. doi:10.1016/0007-6813(79)90088-0

Bernoff, J., & Li, C. (2008). Harnessing the Power of the Oh-So-Social Web. *MIT Sloan Management Review, 49*(3), 36–42.

Bodin, P., & Wiman, B. (2004). Resilience and other stability concepts in ecology: Notes on their origin, validity, and usefulness. *ESS Bulletin, 2*(2), 33–43.

Bonabeau, E. (2009). Decisions 2.0: The Power of Collective Intelligence. Winter 2009. *MIT Sloan Management Review, 50*(2), 45–52.

Bonner, J. M., & Walker, O. C. Jr. (2004). Selecting influential business-to-business customers in new product development: Relational embeddedness and knowledge heterogeneity considerations. *Journal of Product Innovation Management, 21*(3), 55–69. doi:10.1111/j.0737-6782.2004.00067.x

Boudreau, K., & Lakhani, K. R. (2009). How to Manage Outside Innovation. *MIT Sloan Management Review, 50*(4).

Boyatzis, R. E., & Kolb, D. A. (1995). From learning styles to learning skills: The executive skills profile. *Journal of Managerial Psychology, 10*(5), 3–17. doi:10.1108/02683949510085938

Braun, V., & Herstatt, C. (2008). The Freedom-Fighters: How incumbent corporations are attempting to control user-innovation. *International Journal of Innovation Management, 12*(3), 543–572. doi:10.1142/S1363919608002059

Bretschneider, U., Huber, M., Leimeister, J. M., & Krcmar, H. (2008). Community for innovations: developing an integrated concept for open innovation. In: *Proceedings of the IFIP 8.6 Conference*, Madrid, Spain. doi:10.1007/978-0-387-87503-3_28

Brockhoff, K. (2003). Customers' perspectives of involvement in new product development. *International Journal of Technology Management, 26*(5/6), 464–481. doi:10.1504/IJTM.2003.003418

Bruneau, M., Chang, S. E., Eguchi, R. T., Lee, G. C., O'Rourke, T. D., & Reinhorn, A. M. et al. (2003). A framework to quantitatively assess and enhance the seismic resilience of communities. *Earthquake Spectra, 19*(4), 733–752. doi:10.1193/1.1623497

Bunduchi, R., Weisshaar, C., & Smart, A. U. (2011). Mapping the benefits and costs associated with process innovation: The case of RFID adoption. *Technovation, 31*(9), 505–521. doi:10.1016/j.technovation.2011.04.001

Chesbrough, H., & Crowther, A. K. (2006). Beyond high-tech: Early adopters of open innovation in other industries. *R & D Management, 36*(3), 229–236. doi:10.1111/j.1467-9310.2006.00428.x

Chesbrough, H. W. (2003). The era of open innovation. *MIT Sloan Management Review, 44*(3), 35–41.

Chiaroni, D., Chiesa, V., & Frattini, F. (2011). The Open Innovation Journey: How firms dynamically implement the emerging innovation management paradigm. *Technovation, 31*(1), 34–43. doi:10.1016/j.technovation.2009.08.007

Christensen, C. M. (1997). *The Innovators Dilemma: When New Technologies Cause Great Firms to Fail*. Cambridge, MA: Harvard Business School Press.

Christensen, C. M., & Bower, J. L. (1996). Customer power, strategic investment, and the failure of leading firms. *Strategic Management Journal, 17*(3), 197–218. doi:10.1002/(SICI)1097-0266(199603)17:3<197::AID-SMJ804>3.0.CO;2-U

Christensen, J. F., Olesen, M. H., & Kjaer, J. S. (2005). The industrial dynamics of Open Innovation: Evidence from the transformation of consumer electronics. *Research Policy, 34*(10), 1533–1549. doi:10.1016/j.respol.2005.07.002

Cunningham, P., & Wilkins, J. A. (2009). A Walk in the Cloud. *Information Management Journal, 43*(1), 22–30.

Dahan, E. (2002). The Virtual Customer. *Journal of Product Innovation Management, 19*(5), 332–353. doi:10.1016/S0737-6782(02)00151-0

Dahlander, L. (2006). Managing beyond firm boundaries: Leveraging user innovation networks. Department of Technology Management and Economics, Gothenburg: Chalmers University of Technology.

Daniels, S. (1998). The strategic use of information systems. *Work Study*, *47*(5), 167–171. doi:10.1108/00438029810229309

Dibrell, C., Davis, P. S., & Craig, J. B. (2009). The performance implications of temporal orientation and information technology in organization-environment synergy. *Journal of Strategy and Management*, *2*(2), 145–162. doi:10.1108/17554250910965308

Dogson, M., Gann, D., & Salter, A. (2006). The role of technology in the shift towards open innovation: The case of Procter & Gamble. *R & D Management*, *36*(3), 333–346. doi:10.1111/j.1467-9310.2006.00429.x

Dörner, N., Gassmann, O., & Gebauer, H. (2011). Service innovation: Why is it so difficult to accomplish? *The Journal of Business Strategy*, *32*(3), 37–46. doi:10.1108/02756661111121983

Edvardsson, B. (1996). Making service-quality improvement work. *Managing Service Quality*, *6*(1), 49–52. doi:10.1108/09604529610108153

Enkel, E., Kausch, C., & Gassmann, O. (2005). Managing the risk of customer integration. *European Management Journal*, *23*(2), 203–213. doi:10.1016/j.emj.2005.02.005

Franke, N. (2009). How can users' creativity be implemented in new products and services? *European Conference on Innovation*. Lund University.

Franke, N., & Schreier, M. (2002). Entrepreneurial opportunities with toolkits for user innovation and design. *International Journal on Media Management*, *4*(4), 225–234. doi:10.1080/14241270209390004

Fredberg, T., Elmquist, M., & Ollila, S. (2008). *Managing Open Innovation – Present Findings and Future Directions.* VINNOVA Report VR 2008, n.02, VINNOVA - Verket för Innovationssystem/Swedish Governmental Agency for Innovation Systems.

Füller, J., & Matzler, K. (2007). Virtual Product experience and customer participation – A chance for customer-centered, really new products. *Technovation*, *27*(6-7), 378–387. doi:10.1016/j.technovation.2006.09.005

Gallouj, F. (2002). Innovation in services and the attendant old and new myths. *Journal of Socio-Economics*, *31*(2), 137–154. doi:10.1016/S1053-5357(01)00126-3

Gartner Research. (2011). Ipad and Beyond: The Media Tablet in Business. Retrieved August 10, 2012, from http://www.gartner.com/technology/research/ipad-media-tablet/

Gassmann, O. (2006). Opening up the innovation process: Towards an agenda. *R & D Management*, *36*(3), 223–228. doi:10.1111/j.1467-9310.2006.00437.x

Gebauer, H., Krempl, R., Fleisch, E., & Friedli, T. (2008). Innovation of product-related services. *Managing Service Quality*, *18*(4), 387–404. doi:10.1108/09604520810885626

Gladwell, M. (2010). A small change: why the revolution will not be tweeted. *The New Yorker*, Annals of Innovation. Available in: <http://www.newyorker.com/reporting/2010/10/04/101004fa_fact_gladwell?currentPage=all>. Access in: October 8th, 2010.

Grunert, K. G., Jensen, B. B., Sonne, A. M., Brunsø, K., Byrne, D. V., & Clausen, C. et al. (2008). User-oriented innovation in the food sector: Relevant streams of research and an agenda for future work. *Trends in Food Science & Technology*, *19*(11), 590–602. doi:10.1016/j.tifs.2008.03.008

Hennala, L., Parjanen, S., & Uotila, T. (2011). Challenges of multi-actor involvement in the public sector front-end innovation processes. Constructing an open innovation model for developing well-being services. *European Journal of Innovation Management, 14*(3), 364–387. doi:10.1108/14601061111148843

Hertog, P., Aa, W., & Jong, M. W. (2010). Capabilities for managing service innovation: Towards a conceptual framework. *Journal of Service Management, 21*(4), 490–514. doi:10.1108/09564231011066123

Ho, C.-F. (1996). Information technology implementation strategies for manufacturing organizations: A strategic alignment approach. *International Journal of Operations & Production Management, 16*(7), 77–100. doi:10.1108/01443579610119171

Hung, C. L., Chou, J. C.-L., & Shu, K. Y. (2008). Searching for Lead Users in the Context of Web 2.0. In: *Proceedings of the 2008 IEEE ICMIT*, 344-349. doi:10.1109/ICMIT.2008.4654388

Ifinedo, P. (2007). An empirical study of ERP success evaluations by business and IT managers. *Information Management & Computer Security, 15*(4), 270–282. doi:10.1108/09685220710817798

Inauen, M., & Wicki, S. A. (2011). The impact of outside-in open innovation on innovation performance. *European Journal of Innovation Management, 14*(4), 496–520. doi:10.1108/14601061111174934

Jain, P.JAIN. (2005). A comparative analysis of strategic human resource management (SHRM) issues in an organizational context. *Library Review, 54*(3), 166–179. doi:10.1108/00242530510588926

Janzik, L., & Herstatt, C. (2008). Innovation Communities: Motivation and Incentives for Community Members to contribute. In: *Proceedings of the 2008 IEEE ICMIT*, 350-355. doi:10.1109/ICMIT.2008.4654389

Jiménez-Jiménez, D., & Sanz-Valle, R. (2005). Innovation-human resource management fit: An empirical study. *International Journal of Manpower, 26*(4), 364–381. doi:10.1108/01437720510609555

Johne, A., & Storey, C. (1998). New service development: A review of the literature and annotated bibliography. *European Journal of Marketing, 32*(3/4), 184–251. doi:10.1108/03090569810204526

Katz, R. L. (1974). Skills of an effective administrator. *Harvard Business Review*, (52): 90–102.

Kelly, D., & Storey, C. (2000). New service development: Initiation strategies. *International Journal of Service Industry Management, 11*(1), 45–63. doi:10.1108/09564230010310286

Klouwenberg, M. K., Koo, W. J. D., & Schaik, J. A. M. (1995). Establishing business strategy with information technology. *Information Management & Computer Security, 3*(5), 8–20. doi:10.1108/09685229510104945

Lai, L. S. L., & Turban, E. (2008). Groups Formation and Operations in the Web 2.0 Environment and Social Networks. *Group Decision and Negotiation, 17*(5), 387–402. doi:10.1007/s10726-008-9113-2

Laursen, K., & Salter, S. (2006). Open for innovation: The role of openness in explaining innovation performance among UK manufacturing firms. *Strategic Management Journal, 27*(2), 131–150. doi:10.1002/smj.507

Lazzarotti, V., & Manzini, R. (2009). Different modes of open innovation: A theoretical framework and an empirical study. *International Journal of Innovation Management, 13*(4), 615–636. doi:10.1142/S1363919609002443

Lettl, C. (2007). User involvement competence for radical innovation. *Journal of Engineering and Technology Management, 24*(1-2), 53–75. doi:10.1016/j.jengtecman.2007.01.004

Lettl, C., Herstatt, C., & Gemuenden, H. G. (2006). Learning from users for radical innovation. *International Journal of Technology Management*, *33*(1), 25. doi:10.1504/IJTM.2006.008190

Lilien, G. L., Morrison, P. D., Searls, K., Sonnack, M., & Von Hippel, E. (2002). Performance assessment of the lead user idea-generation process for new product development. *Management Science*, *48*(8), 1042–1059. doi:10.1287/mnsc.48.8.1042.171

Lusch, R. F. (2007). Marketing's evolving identify: defining our future. American Marketing Association, 26(2).

Lüthje, C., & Herstatt, C. (2004). The Lead User Method: An outline of empirical findings and issues for future research. *R & D Management*, *34*(5), 553–568. doi:10.1111/j.1467-9310.2004.00362.x

Marnewick, C., & Labuschagne, L. (2005). A conceptual model for enterprise resource planning (ERP). *Information Management & Computer Security*, *13*(2), 144–155. doi:10.1108/09685220510589325

Matthing, J., Sandén, B., & Edvardsson, B. (2004). New service development: Learning from and with customers. *International Journal of Service Industry Management*, *15*(5), 479–498. doi:10.1108/09564230410564948

Mattos, C. A., & Laurindo, F. J. B. (2008). The role of the web in improving customer input to the service/product development process: Brazilian cases. *Product: Management & Development*, *6*(1).

Meirelles. D. S. (2003). The service sector and economic infrastructure services. Thesis (PhD in Industrial Economics and Technology) - Federal University of Rio de Janeiro, Rio de Janeiro.

Moore, G. A. (1991). *Crossing the Chasm: marketing and selling high-tech products to mainstream customers*. New York: Harper Business Essentials.

Morcillo. P. (1997). De la Dirección Estratégica Tecnologia e Innovación. Un enfoque de Competencias, Madrid: Civitas.

Morris, M., Bessant, J., & Barnes, J. (2006). Using learning networks to enable industrial development: Case studies from South Africa. *International Journal of Operations & Production Management*, *26*(5), 532–557. doi:10.1108/01443570610659892

Muller, A., Hutchins, N., & Pinto, M. C. (2012). Applying open innovation where your company needs it most. *Strategy and Leadership*, *40*(2), 35–42. doi:10.1108/10878571211209332

Nalebuff, B., & Ayres, I. (2003). *Why Not? How to Use Everyday Ingenuity to Solve Problems Big and Small*. Boston: Harvard Business School Press.

Nambisan, S. (2002). Designing virtual customer environments for new product development. *Academy of Management Review*, (27): 392–413.

Olson, E., & Bakke, G. (2001). Implementing the lead user method in a high technology firm: A longitudinal study of intentions versus actions. *Journal of Product Innovation Management*, *18*(2), 388–395. doi:10.1016/S0737-6782(01)00111-4

Ong, M. (2009). *Fiat Mio: Bringing crowdsourcing to the automotive industry*. Available in: <http://www.headlightblog.com/2009/10/fiat-miobringing-crowdsourcing-to-the-automotive-industry/>. Access in: October 2009.

Petty. N., J; Thomson, O, P; Stew, G. (2012). Ready for a paradigm shift? Part 1: Introducing the philosophy of qualitative research. *Manual Therapy*.

Piller, F. T., & Ihl, C. (2009). *Open innovation with customers. Technology and Innovation Management group*. RWTH Aachen University.

Piller, F. T., & Walcher, D. (2006). Toolkits for idea competitions: A novel method to integrate users in new product development. *R & D Management*, *36*(3), 307–318. doi:10.1111/j.1467-9310.2006.00432.x

Prandelli, E., Verona, G., & Raccagni, D. (2006). Diffusion of Web-Based Product Innovation. California Management Review, University of California, 48(4).

Rossi, A. (2009). Open innovation as a source of value creation for organizations. http://www.fdc.org.br/pt/pesquisa/inovacao/Documents/artigos_blog/inovacao_aberta.pdf Access in: January, 2011.

Ryzhkova, N. (2009). *The contribution of the user innovation methods to open innovation*. School of Management, Blekinge Institute of Technology.

Santos, C. R., & Brasil, V. S. (2010). Consumer involvement in processes product development: a qualitative study with consumer goods companies. *Revista de Administração de Empresas (RAE), 50*(3).

Sawhney, M., & Prandelli, E. (2000). Communities of Creation: Managing Distributed Innovation in Turbulent Markets. *California Management Review*, *42*(4), 24–54. doi:10.2307/41166052

Sawhney, M., Verona, G., & Prandelli, E. (2005). Collaborating to Create: The Internet as a Platform for Customer Engagement in Product Innovation. *Journal of Interactive Marketing*, *19*(4), 4–17. doi:10.1002/dir.20046

Schiuma, G., & Lerro, A.Schiuma. (2008). Knowledge-based capital in building regional innovation capacity. *Journal of Knowledge Management*, *12*(5), 121–136. doi:10.1108/13673270810902984

Schumpeter. J. A. (1934). A Teoria do Desenvolvimento Econômico: Uma Investigação sobre Lucros, Capital Credito, Juros e do ciclo de negócios, Harvard University Press, Cambridge, MA.

Shah, S. K., & Franke, N. (2003). How Communities Support Innovative Activities: An Exploration of Assistance and Sharing Among End-Users. *Research Policy*, (32): 157–178.

Shapiro, A. L. (2000). *The Control Revolution: how the internet is putting individuals in charge and changing the world we know*. New York, NY: Public Affairs.

Sundbo, J.Sundbo. (1999). Empowerment of employees in small and medium-sized service firms. *Employee Relations*, *21*(2), 105–127. doi:10.1108/01425459910266385

Terwiesch, C., & Xu, Y. (2008). Innovation Contests, Open Innovation, and Multiagent Problem Solving. *Management Science*, *54*(9), 1529–1543. doi:10.1287/mnsc.1080.0884

Thomas, M. A.Thomas. (1996). What is a human resources strategy? *Health Manpower Management*, *22*(2), 4–11. doi:10.1108/09552069610791668 PMID:10158774

Tietz, R., Füller, J., & Herstatt, C. (2006). Signalling: an innovative approach to identify lead users in online communities. In T. Blecker, & G. Friedrich (Eds.), *Customer Interaction and Customer Integration* (pp. 453–467). Berlin: GITO-Verlag.

Toubia, O., & Florès, L. (2007). Adaptive Idea Screening Using Consumers. *Marketing Science*, *26*(3), 342–360. doi:10.1287/mksc.1070.0273

Van De Meer, H. (2007). Open Innovation - the Dutch treat: Challenges in thinking in business models. *Creativity and Innovation Management*, *6*(2), 192–202. doi:10.1111/j.1467-8691.2007.00433.x

Vanhaverbeke, W. (2006). The interorganisational context of Open Innovation. In Chesbrough, H., Vanhaverbeke, W. & West, J. (eds.), Open Innovation: Researching a New Paradigm. Oxford University Press.

Von Hippel, E. (1986). Lead Users: A source of novel products concepts. *Management Science, 32*(7), 791–805. doi:10.1287/mnsc.32.7.791

Von Hippel, E. (1988). *The Sources of Innovation.* New York: Oxford University Press.

Von Hippel, E. (1998). Economics of product development by users: The impact of 'Sticky' local information. *Management Science, 44*(5), 629–644. doi:10.1287/mnsc.44.5.629

Von Hippel, E. (2002, June). Horizontal innovation networks: by and for users. *MIT Sloan School of Management Working Paper*, No. 4366-02.

Von Hippel, E. (2005). *Democratizing Innovation.* Cambridge, MA: MIT Press.

Von Hippel, E. (2007). Horizontal innovation networks: By and for users. *Industrial and Corporate Change, 16*(2), 293–315. doi:10.1093/icc/dtm005

Von Hippel, E., & Katz, R. (2002). Shifting innovation to users via toolkits. *Management Science, 48*(7), 821–833. doi:10.1287/mnsc.48.7.821.2817

Wentz, L. (2010). At Fiat in Brazil, Vehicle Design Is No Longer By Fiat: Automaker is Relying on Consumers and Social Media for a 2010 Concept Car. 2010. http://adage.com/results? endeca=1&return=endeca&search_offset=0&search_order_by=score&x=0&y=0&search_phr ase=At+Fia t+in+Brazil%2C+Vehicle+Design+Is+No+Lo nger+By+Fiat. Access in October 2010.

West, J., & Gallagher, S. (2006). Challenges of open innovation: The paradox of firm investment in open-source software. *R & D Management, 36*(3), 319–331. doi:10.1111/j.1467-9310.2006.00436.x

KEY TERMS AND DEFINITIONS

Business Intelligence: Business Intelligence is a set of theories, methodologies, processes, architectures, and technologies that transform raw data into meaningful and useful information for business purposes. BI can handle large amounts of information to help identify and develop new opportunities. Making use of new opportunities and implementing an effective strategy can provide a competitive market advantage and long-term stability.

Creativity: Is a phenomenon whereby something new and valuable is created (such as an idea, a joke, a literary work, a painting or musical composition, a solution, an invention etc.).

Computer Integrated Manufacturing: The aim of CIM is to produce the required amount of the product of acceptable quality at the right time.

Digital Catalog: Digital Catalog is a software that allows the creation, editing and release of product catalogs, allowing for the inclusion of videos, banners and sounds as the goal of promoting a company, its brand and products.

Enterprise Resource Planning: ERP is a software-driven business management system that integrates all facets of the business, including planning, manufacturing, sales, and marketing. ERP systems can be used to manage operational business information for corporate resource planning.

Information Systems: Are defined as a set of interrelated components that collect (retrieve), process, store and distribute information to support decision making and organizational control.

Information Technology: Technological resources and computational generation and use of information. Its main components are: hardware, software, telecommunications and data management.

Innovation: Innovation is the development of new values through solutions that meet new requirements, needs, or needs customer and market needs in value adding new ways. This is accomplished through more effective products, processes, services, technologies, or ideas that are readily available to markets, governments, and society.

iPad: iPad is a device shaped tablet produced by Apple Inc. The device was announced on January 27, 2010, at a press conference at the Yerba Buena Center for the Arts in San Francisco. The iPad has been touted as a device situated halfway between a MacBook and an iPhone. The device uses the same operating system as the iPhone, iOS.

Human Resources: Is the set of individuals who make up the workforce of an organization, business sector, or economy. "Human capital" is sometimes used synonymously with human resources, although human capital typically refers to a more narrow view (i.e., the knowledge the individuals embody and can contribute to an organization). Likewise, other terms sometimes used include "manpower", "talent", "labor", or simply "people".

Learning Organization: Is the term given to a company that facilitates the learning of its members and continuously transforms itself. Learning organizations develop as a result of the pressures facing modern organizations and enables them to remain competitive in the business environment.

Mobile Devices: Mobile device is a mini device that allows people to do computing activities such as accessing data and sending information to others. In this chapter, mobile device refers to tablet than can be used with the Nimiam solution.

Motivation: Is a *psychological* feature that arouses an organism to act towards a desired *goal* and elicits, controls, and sustains certain goal-directed behaviors. It can be considered a driving force; a psychological one that compels or reinforces an action toward a desired goal.

Organizational Culture: Is the behavior of humans who are part of an organization and the meanings that the people attach to their actions. Culture includes the organization values, visions, norms, working language, systems, symbols, beliefs and habits. It is also the pattern of such collective behaviors and assumptions that are taught to new organizational members as a way of perceiving, and even thinking and feeling.

Organizational Resilience: It is the ability that an organization has to respond quickly and effectively to a change that was scheduled. The organizational resilience can lead to the development of organizations that conserve classic and localized to delocalized structures and people-centered structures, enabling them work anytime anywhere. All organizations that aims to succeed in challenging times, uncertainties and pressures economic, social and technological changes need to be resilient.

Organizational Strategy: The basic action is structured and developed by the company to achieve adequately and preferentially differentiated objectives envisioned for the future, to better position the company towards its environment and strategic planning is a process of formulating organizational strategies in which one seeks the inclusion of the organization and its mission in the environment in which it is acting.

Manufacturing Resources Planning: Are the systems of administration of large production which has been used by companies and have as main objective to calculate the needs of productive resources in order to care for delivery of customer orders, with minimal inventory building, planning purchases and production of components for items that occur only at such times and quantities required.

Mobile Devices: Mobile device is a mini device that allows people to do computing activities such as accessing data and sending information to others. In this chapter, mobile device refers to tablet than can be used with the Nimiam solution.

Motivation: Is a *psychological* feature that arouses an organism to act towards a desired *goal* and elicits, controls, and sustains certain goal-directed behaviors. It can be considered a driving force; a psychological one that compels or reinforces an action toward a desired goal.

Sales Force Automation: Sales Force Automation (SFA) is a technique of using software to automate the business tasks of sales, including order processing, contact management, information sharing, inventory monitoring and control, order tracking, customer management, sales forecast analysis and employee performance evaluation.

Services: A type of *economic activity* that is intangible, is not stored and does not *result* in *ownership*. A service is consumed at the *point of sale*. Services are one of the two key components of *economics*, the other being *goods*.

Tablet: Tablet is a personal device in clipboard format that can be used for Internet access, personal organization, viewing photos, videos, reading books, newspapers and magazines and entertainment with games. Features a touch screen (touchscreen) which is the primary input device. The fingertip or pen drives its functionality. It is a new concept: should not be equated with a complete computer or a smartphone, although it has features of both.

Chapter 4
The Games People Play:
The Politics of Software Platform Development and ICT Project Design for Public Sector Administration Reform

Shefali Virkar
University of Oxford, UK

ABSTRACT

Much has been written about e-government within a growing stream of literature on ICT for development, generating countervailing perspectives where optimistic, technocratic approaches are countered by far more sceptical standpoints on technological innovation. This chapter seeks to, through the use of a case study, unravel the social dynamics shaping e-government projects used to reform public sector institutions. In particular, the research analyzes actor behaviour, motivations, and interactions surrounding the conception and maintenance of software platforms facilitating these transformations. The value of such an approach is based on a review of existing ICT and software development literature, which tends to be overly systems-rational in its approach and, as a consequence, often fails to recognise the degree to which project failure (viz. the general inability of the project design to meet stated goals and resolve both predicted and emerging problems) is symptomatic of a broader, much more complex set of inter-related inequalities, unresolved problems, and lopsided power-relationships both within the adopting organisation and in the surrounding environmental context.

INTRODUCTION

Over the course of the last two decades, globalisation and Information Technology have been rapidly dismantling traditional barriers to trade, travel and communication, fuelling great promise for progress towards greater global equity and prosperity. Attracted by the 'hype and hope' of

Information and Communication Technologies (ICTs), development actors across the world have adopted computer-based systems and related ICTs for use in government as a means reforming the inefficiencies in public service provision. Whilst a number of these electronic government or 'e-government' projects have achieved significant results, evidence from the field indicates that

DOI: 10.4018/978-1-4666-6485-2.ch004

despite the reported success stories, the rate of project failure remains particularly high.

Much as been written about e-government within a growing stream of literature on ICT hardware and software platform development, generating countervailing perspectives where optimistic, technocratic approaches are countered by far more sceptical standpoints on technological innovation. However, in trying to analyse both their potential and real value, there has been a tendency for scholars to see e-government applications as isolated technical artefacts, analysed solely as a collection of hardware and software. Far less work is based on empirical field research, and models put forward by scholars and practitioners alike often neglect the actual attitudes, choices, and behaviour of the wide array of actors involved in the implementation and use of new technology in real organisations, as well as the way in which the application shapes and is shaped by existing social, organisational, and environmental contexts.

This chapter seeks to, through the use of a case study, unravel the social dynamics shaping e-government projects used to reform public sector institutions. In particular, the research analyses actor behaviour, motivations, and interactions surrounding the conception and maintenance of e-government software platforms facilitating these transformations. The value of such an approach is based on a review of existing ICT and development literature which tends to be overly systems-rational in its approach and, as a consequence, often fails to recognise the degree to which project failure (viz. the general inability of the project design to meet stated goals and resolve both predicted and emerging problems) is symptomatic of a broader, much more complex set of interrelated inequalities, unresolved problems, and lopsided power-relationships both within the adopting organisation and in the surrounding environmental context.

The main goal of this chapter is thus to examine the issues thrown up by the organisational and institutional transformations that occur in public administration through the conception and application of ICT platforms therein from a multidisciplinary perspective, through the use of a single central case study. The case study from which this chapter is drawn focused on a project aimed at digitising property tax records and administrative processes within the Revenue Department of the Greater Bangalore City Municipal Corporation. In recognising the need to turn property tax into a viable revenue instrument that delivers high tax yields without compromising on citizen acceptance, the Bangalore City Corporation sought to improve its property tax administration system through the introduction of a computerised database and digital mapping techniques used to track compliance and to check evasion.

RESEARCH METHODOLOGY

The ultimate aim of this chapter is thus to contribute to the development of a conceptual framework that is relevant to policy discussions of e-government software platform design and maintenance within not only an Indian, but also a broader global context. In order to augment theoretical discussions of administrative reform in a digitised world, this chapter uses a case study to explore its central research issues, within which a mixed methods approach using a combination of qualitative and quantitative data was selected in order to inform and strengthen the understanding of the relationships between the actors, inputs, and project outputs. The aim of the study was, therefore, to evolve ideas that could be generalised across similar situations and the research was consequently developed in the following steps:

- In-depth review of existing theoretical perspectives and literature surrounding corruption and tax evasion, ICTs and public administration, and property tax reform.
- Qualitative analysis of official documents
- Collection and analysis of quantitative data relevant to the case

- Developing case studies through in-depth personal interviews
- Data analysis and interpretation
- Preparation of conclusions and their validation
- Recommendations for the future

The use of mixed-method case study research is becoming increasingly popular in the social sciences, and is fast being recognised as a successful approach for investigating contemporary phenomena in a real-life context when the boundaries between phenomenon and context are not evident and where multiple sources of evidence present themselves (Yin, 2003). It was thus felt to be a particularly apt way of studying the nature and impact of actor actions, motivations and behaviours on e-government software platform conception and design, where the aim is not simply to judge whether the project at hand represents a success or failure, but is to understand the qualities inherent in the architecture that have made it so.

More precisely, case study research consists of a detailed investigation of phenomena within a given context, often with data being collected over a period of time. The aim of this approach is thus to provide the researcher with an all-round analysis of the surrounding environment and processes, in order that they might throw light on the theoretical issues being investigated (Eisenhardt, 1989). The phenomenon under examination is thus not isolated from its context, rather it is of interest precisely because the aim is to observe and understand actor behaviour and/or organisational processes and their interplay with the surrounding environment. The use of a case study itself is therefore not as much a method as it is a *research strategy*, where the context is deliberately included as part of the overall design. Today, case studies are widely used in organisational research across the social sciences, indicating growing confidence in the approach as a rigorous research strategy in its own right (Hartley, 2005).

As research conducted by adopting this strategy is typically done in the field, the presence of too many observations and uncontrollable 'variables' makes the application of standard experimental or survey approaches infeasible. Further, information tends to be scattered and generally cannot be picked up using one single method. Case studies thus typically combine a number of data collection methods such as participant observation, direct observation, interviews, focus groups, ethnography, document analysis, questionnaires etc., where evidence may be quantitative or qualitative depending on the research issues at hand. The approach is consequently flexible, allowing for new methods to be incorporated as new sources of data and new actors present themselves. The case study approach may thus be and has been used for various purposes – to provide a descriptive narrative, to generate new theory, or to test existing theory through the triangulation of data (Virkar, 2011).

The theoretical framework adopted by this research will emphasise three issues: first, the politics involved in the conception, innovation, and governance of software platforms for public administration, which is related to the set of institutions and rules that set the limits on, and the incentives that result in, the constitution and working of interdependent networks of actors within the industry and within government; second, the concept of electronic government itself as circumscribed by socio-political and economic development; and finally, the relationship and interrelationships between technology, organisation, and institutional change. To do this, the chapter will ground its case study in three major complementary strands of literature:

1. A conceptual discussion of the role and interactions of a multiplicity of actors with diverse motivations and strategies conceptualized as an 'ecology of games', within the umbrella of New Institutionalism, and their role in shaping political organisations

and institutions, with special reference to the success or failure of e-government projects.

2. The literature which deals with public administration reform and the role of Information and Communication Technologies in improving the functioning of public administration and reducing corruption in a developing country context.

3. A discussion of the importance of the ICT hardware and software industry, with special reference to software platform design for e-government and politico-economic development in India.

Conclusions will be reached through the concurrent use of three dimensions – theoretically on the basis of existing literature, descriptively on the basis of a case study, and analytically using the concept of the Ecology of Games.

For the larger study from which this chapter is drawn, 40 personal interviews were conducted over a 24-month period. The interviewees can be roughly divided into four groups based on their relationship to the case: Senior Civil Servants involved with the planning and implementation of the project, including current and former BBMP Commissioners, Deputy Commissioners for Revenue, and Revenue Officers, Revenue and Tax Officials, primarily Assistant Revenue Officers (AROs) responsible for the in-the-field collection and administration of property tax in the city, Software Developers involved in the conception, design, and implementation of the project, and Miscellaneous Actors including journalists and external consultants.

Twenty-seven subjects agreed to full-length interviews and to have their comments recorded. This included all six members of the project planning committee, one senior official involved with the implementation of the GIS, and twenty senior revenue officers involved with the system's application in the field. Additional informal interviews conducted face-to-face or over the email were also used to close gaps in knowledge or to follow up new information and anchor the interpretation of events

and motives in the perceptions of participants. In addition to the recorded interviews, this chapter uses information and quotes obtained informally from people related to the project who did not wish to be interviewed formally or have their comments recorded, in order to obtain a cross-hierarchical view of the impact of process re-engineering on the organisational culture and practical issues on the ground. Out of the 13 people in this category, 10 were junior revenue officials (Station Managers, Tax Inspectors and Accountants) working under the AROs interviewed, 2 were Revenue Officers supervising the overall administration of the Revenue Offices and one person was a local correspondent from a leading national daily.

From the above discussion, it follows that the use of a case study for this chapter is particularly apt for two reasons. Firstly, the approach is particularly useful for examining research issues that require a detailed understanding of socio-political, economic, or organisational processes through the collection and analysis of rich data. Secondly, as discussed above, case study research design is also more flexible than other frameworks such as laboratory-based or survey-based approaches, in that it is able to reconcile different research methods and harness the evidence gathered to generate novel theory from any creative insights that might ensue from the juxtaposition of data at various points in the analysis. This, despite the truism which states that a single case study cannot always provide an answer to these questions globally; for even the examination of a single case can suggest significant ways of addressing issues that could, through application, be relevant to a wider variety of cases across disciplines.

E-GOVERNMENT: DEFINITION AND SCOPE

Simultaneous with the shift towards a more inclusive process of participation in political decision-making and public sector reform has been an increased interest in the new digital Information and Communication Technologies (ICTs) and the ways in which they may be used to effectively complement and reform existing political processes. Developments in communication technologies have historically resulted in changes in the way in which governments function, often challenging them to find new ways in which to communicate and interact with their citizens, and ICTs today are seen to possess the potential to change institutions as well as the mechanisms of service delivery, bringing about a fundamental change in the way government operates and a transformation in the dynamic between government and its citizens (Misra, 2005). The work of the public sector has traditionally been highly information-intensive; government has been, and still remains, the single largest collector, user, holder and producer of information (Heeks, 2000), and is considered to be a central resource 'in pursuing democratic/political processes, in managing resources, executing functions, measuring performance, and in service delivery' (Isaac-Henry, 1997).

e-Government has today become an influential concept for scholars concerned with public administration reform and better overall governance. In developed countries, large-scale projects at the local level have typically concentrated on the creation of virtual or digital town-halls through the automation and distribution of well-structured administrative services (Dutton, 1999). However, while online e-government service initiatives have become common in many countries, and in a variety of contexts, such applications are characteristically built with a primary focus on administration-citizen interaction, rather than on explicitly supporting plans for strategic organisational development. Further, although considerable attention has been paid to how e-government can help public bodies improve their services, there are relatively few studies that focus on the long term sustainability of such initiatives, particularly in the developing world. In contrast to most literature in the canon, therefore, this project focused on in this study seeks to illustrate that

the potential for improved government-citizen interactions and private-public collaborations for the development of e-government platforms and public sector reform programmes may be realised through not only the development of a 'virtual front office' but also through the enhancement of their positive influence on back-office organisation and culture. In defining e-Government as the use of Information and Communication Technologies (such as Wide Area Networks, the Internet, and mobile computing) by government agencies to transform relations with citizens, businesses, and other arms of government, almost all conceptions of e-government indicate three critical transformational areas in which ICTs have an impact (Ndou, 2004):

- **The Internal Arena:** Where Information and Communication Technologies are used to enhance the efficiency and effectiveness of internal government functions and processes by intermediating between employees, public managers, departments, and agencies.
- **The External Arena:** Where ICTs open up new possibilities for governments to be more transparent to citizens and businesses by providing multiple channels that allow them improved access to a greater range of government information.
- **The Relational Sphere:** Where ICT adoption has the potential to bring about fundamental changes in the relationships between government employees and their managers, citizens and the state, and between nation states; with implications for the democratic process and the structures of government.

Thus, although the term e-government is primarily used to refer to the usage of ICTs to improve administrative efficiency, it arguably produces other effects that would give rise to increased transparency and accountability, reflect on the relationship between government and citizens, and help build new spaces for citizens to participate in their overall development (Gascó, 2003).

E-GOVERNMENT DELIVERY MODELS

e-Government applications tend to develop in two stages (Virkar, 2011). Initially, a back-office system is set up within the adopting agency to handle online processes and information about services provided by the agency is published on a website. The second step involves the setting up of the 'front-office': the use of ICTs in the actual delivery of a service, where citizens can interact with the site to download application forms and information sheets for a variety of services such as filing a tax return or renewing a license, with more sophisticated applications being able to process online payments.

A key three-stage strategy used by actors in games related to the design and development of e-government systems and technology policy, particularly those in developing countries who wish to radically transform public administration by moving government services from manual processes to online systems, is to adopt different models of service delivery at different stages of the development process. The first move generally involves the automation of basic work processes and the online provision of information and services by government departments from computers based within the departmental premises (Bhatnagar, 2003).

Citizens interact with a designated government employee or private computer operator who accesses data and processes transactions on their behalf. Locating online terminals within agency premises tends to result in greater ownership of the system by government staff, reducing resistance to technology and facilitating easier acceptance of change. However, the downside of this mode of delivery is that citizens are still required to visit different government departments to avail of different public services, all within their fixed hours of work. In addition, the dependence of an entire agency office on a single person (or small group of people) to operate the system may cause friction.

The second stage in the evolution of service delivery is the use of conveniently located citizen kiosks or service centres in public places, again manned by public or privately hired operators (Basu, 2004). This mode of delivery scores over the previous one as multiple services – municipal, state or federal – may be offered at each location. Kiosks also generally stay open longer than government offices, both before and after regular office hours, maximising system coverage by allowing working individuals to access services at times more convenient to them. In recent years, citizen service centres have become popular, particularly in countries where Internet penetration is low.

The final platform of e-government service delivery, popular in countries where Internet penetration and skills are high, is the one-stop shop online portal from where citizens with a computer and an Internet connection may, at any time of day, access a whole range of public information and services themselves without having to visit a kiosk or depend on a computer operator (West, 2004). However, for such a mode of delivery to become ubiquitous, a number of conditions need to be in place – citizens must have the technological hardware and skills to access the system, the back-end of the government agency must be fully computerised, government staff must be trained on the new technology, security and privacy loopholes must be closed, and trust in online transactions must be built up.

The step-by-step strategy outlined above is generally adopted by key political and administrative actors involved with the implementation of e-government projects, and if followed may reduce political tensions and controversies that might arise as the result of change by not only ensuring maximum citizen access to services, but also an increased acceptance of the technology by agency staff (Bhatnagar, 2003).

UNDERSTANDING ACTOR BEHAVIOUR

The central issue that needs to be understood whilst studying the development of ICT platforms and their implementation in public sector organisations through an analysis of actor interactions is thus: *Why do people do what they do?* One approach to understanding behaviour is to look at the rationality of individual actors, rather than the system as a whole. This is largely because political actors are driven by a combination of organisational and institutional roles and duties and calculated self-interest, with political interaction being organised around the construction and interpretation of meaning as well as the making of choices.

Political actors, in general, have a complex set of goals including power, income, prestige, security, convenience, loyalty (to an idea, an institution or the nation), pride in work well done, and a desire to serve the public interest (as the individual actor conceives it). According to Downs (1964) actors range from being purely self-interested ('climbers' or 'conservers' motivated entirely by goals which benefit themselves and their status quo rather than their organizations or the society at large) to having mixed motives ('zealots', 'advocates' and 'statesmen' motivated by goals which combine self interest and altruistic loyalty with larger values). An in-depth analysis of the ICT for development literature by this researcher identified five actor groups involved in games relating to the implementation of e-government projects:

1. **Politicians:** The first group identified comprises of elected representatives of various hues, guided and influenced chiefly by electoral imperatives and a need to maintain their public image, and are therefore concerned with directing both key economic policy issues as well as issues of public service delivery.

2. **Administrators / Civil Servants:** This group of actors is guided by their perceptions of existing institutional 'culture' and practices and their positive (or negative) attitudes towards internal bureaucratic reforms such as concerns about the down-sizing of administrative services to promote 'efficiency' and a sense of being policed by elected government through the introduction of ICTs.

3. **Organisations Dealing with Technical Designing of IT Systems for Tax Collection:** The approach private IT suppliers take to e-government might be considerably different to what the adopting government agency actually needs or wants from a system.

4. **Citizens:** This is another particularly interesting group of actors as one is never quite sure what their reaction to the implementation of e-government will be. Whilst in theory citizens should welcome the introduction of a system that simplifies administrative processes, in practice it is equally possible that some citizens might not be very happy if a more efficient system was put into place.

5. **International Donors:** This final actor group controls the purse-strings and oftentimes comes to the table with 'higher' ideals coloured by ideas prevalent in international politics (such as the desire to see a particular brand of 'good governance' in the developing world).

Introducing e-government initiatives into public bodies is a tricky game to play, as computerisation alters the work-load, work profile and content of the average public sector employee; impacting accountability, reducing the opportunities for exercising discretion, making performance more visible and flattening the hierarchy (Bhatnagar, 2004), and often forcing the need for retraining and retooling and sometimes creating redundancy. Many projects tend to face internal resistance from staff – particularly from the middle to lower levels of the civil service – with moves made to reengineer processes and effect back-end computerisation having a profound effect on the way civil servants perform their duties and perceive their jobs. Very often in developing countries, it is the fear of the unknown that drives this resistance, especially if the introduction of new technology results in a change of procedures and the need for new skills. Further, in corrupt service delivery departments, there may be pressure to slow down or delay the introduction of technology-led reforms due to the impending loss of additional income.

FROM HUMAN FACTORS TO HUMAN ACTORS: THE PSYCHOLOGY BEHIND COMPUTER SYSTEM DESIGN

The design and implementation of complex computer systems requires a better understanding in practitioner circles of the users of such networks and the settings in which they work. Part of the problem resides in the implicit treatment of ordinary people as unskilled, non-specialist users of technology and their networks comprising of elementary processes or *factors* that can be studied in isolation in a field laboratory setting (Bannon, 1991).

Although psychology has a long tradition of contributing to computer systems design and implementation, it has been a neglected discipline in scholarly circles and key issues such as those relating to the underlying values of the people involved in large-scale system design and their motivation in the work setting have been missed out in recent computer science-based scholarly analysis (Salvendy, 2012).

Conceptualising and understanding people as *actors* in situations, on the other hand, with a set of skills and shared practices based on work experiences with others, requires a reorientation in the way in which the relationship between key

elements of computer system design, namely people, technology, work requirements, and organisational constraints in work settings, is negotiated (Kuutti, 1996).

The terms 'human factors' and 'human actors ' give a clue as to how people in system design clusters are approached (Virkar, 2011). More particularly, the terms highlight difference in how people and their contributions are perceived, the former connotating a passive, fragmented, depersonalised, somewhat automatic human contribution; the latter an active, controlling, involved one (Carayon et. al, 2012).

More precisely, within the Human Factor approach, the human element is more often than not reduced to being another system component with certain characteristics that need to be factored into the design equation for the overall human-machine system (Czaja & Nair, 2012). In doing so, the approach de-emphasises certain important elements of work design: the goals, values, and beliefs which technologists and system-users hold about life and work (Jacko et. al., 2012).

By using the term *human actors*, emphasis is placed on users and developers as autonomous agents possessing the capacity to control, regulate, and coordinate their behaviour, rather than them being on par and analysed as mere information processing automatons (Proctor & Vu, 2012).

ANALYTICAL FRAMEWORK: THE ECOLOGY OF GAMES

From the turn of the century to the present, there has been a progressive movement away from the view that governance is the outcome of rational calculation to achieve specific goals by a unitary governmental actor, and in that context metaphors based on games have been extremely useful in developing new ways to think about the policy process. A look through the literature reveals that although political games have been described by scholars within a range of differing contexts, from electoral politics to administrative functioning, no comprehensive description of the public organization as a system of these various interactions actually exists (Virkar, 2013).

The use of Game Theory and most other game metaphors (although differing widely in their orientation) have had, according to scholars, one major limitation for clarifying policy processes: they focus squarely on a single arena or field of action; be it a school, a county, a legislature, etc. Yet, by their very nature, policy making and implementation cut across these separate arenas, in both their development and impact (Firestone, 1989). In e-government projects for instance, systems built by both public and private enterprises for use by government employees and citizens across different political constituencies must be enforced by legislative acts created and interpreted by national branches of government. In addition, actors at different levels of the policy system encounter divergent problems posed by the system in question and their actions are influenced by varied motives. What is needed, therefore, is a framework that goes beyond single games in order to focus on how games 'mesh or miss' each other to influence governance and policy decisions. One of the few efforts to look at this interaction and interdependence was Norton Long's (1958) discussion of "The Local Community as an Ecology of Games."

The Ecology of Games framework, as first laid out by Long in the late 1950s offers a New Institutionalist perspective on organisational and institutional analysis. As with most theories of new institutionalism, it recognises that political institutions are not simple echoes of social forces, and that routines, rules and forms within organisations and institutions evolve through historically interdependent processes that do not reliably and quickly reach equilibrium (March & Olsen, 1989). Long developed the idea of the ecology of games as a way of reconciling existing debates about who governed local communities as he believed they had significant flaws. The crucial insight in Long's

theory however, was not the idea of games *per se* which, as has been discussed earlier, was already well developed, but his linking of that notion to the metaphor of an ecology (Firestone, 1989). Ecology as a concept relates to the interrelationships of species in their environment, allowing for numerous relationships amongst entities, and has been used to understand the relationships among individuals and more complex social systems. Most obviously, co-existence within a common space results in competition for resources and power between different actors, and can result in unique modes of operation as means of achieving ones aims. This in turn may lead to either mutual non-involvement in the same space, or active co-operation between different actors and the development of symbiotic relationships. All this speaks of a singular interdependence between different actors within a given territory. Although there may be other relationships as well, what is significantly missing is a single, rational, coordinating presence.

Games themselves are social constructs that vary over time and across social contexts (Crozier & Friedberg, 1980). Similar types of games might recur within similar social settings, but all games tend to be uniquely situated in place and time, and any typology of games that might emerge across a cumulative body of studies is likely to remain quite abstract. Despite this, Dutton (1992) has identified several key attributes that all games may share. First, every game has a set of goals, purposes, or objectives, with some actors within certain games having multiple aims. For example, a civil servant within the software development game might need to meet efficiency targets set by his department through the taking of decisions regarding the procurement of technology and choice of supplier that conform to stringent budgetary requirements. Similarly, software developers may choose to advertise the quality of their products and maintain their stranglehold over niche markets by quoting top-end prices at the outset of negotiations.

Second, a game has a set of prizes, which may vary widely from profit to authority to recognition, and are distinct from the objectives of the players. For instance, the same civil servant seeking to increase the efficiency of his department and conform to its budget might expect to get a promotion, an honour, or earn a better public reputation outside of the workplace. Software sales personnel may likewise expect to earn bonuses or larger commissions. Third, games have rules that govern the strategies or moves open to players depending on the organisational or institutional settings within which they are played. Any large-scale regulatory game incorporates bureaucrats, legislators, regulated firms, and oft-times entire industries; but also may include the public, the media, the courts, and other actors willing and able to become involved. Rules need not be public or fair (depending on whether public or private interests are involved), may change over time, and may or may not need consensus to be accepted. Finally, a game has a set of players, defined by the fact that they interact – compete or cooperate – with another in pursuing the game's objectives.

For Long, territories (or fields of play) were defined quite literally by being local communities. The notion of an 'ecology' of games underlines not only the degree to which not all players in any given territory are involved in the same game, but also the fact that different players within that territory are likely to be involved in a variety of games (Dutton & Guthrie, 1991). Games can thus be interrelated in several ways. Some actors ('players') might be simultaneously participating in different games, and some players might transfer from one game to another[1]. Plays (i.e. moves or actions) made in one game can affect the play of others. Also, the outcome of one game might affect the rules or play of another. However, although individuals may play a number of games, their major preoccupation for the most part is with one, central game (Long, 1958). A researcher might be able to anticipate a range of strategies open to individuals or organizations if we know what role they play in the game(s) most central to them. Conversely, when the actions of players appear irrational to an observer, it is likely that the observer does not know the games in which players are most centrally involved; the players' moves in one game might be constrained by their moves within other games.

Moved from the community context to the world of e-government platform design, adoption, and implementation, territories may be diverse – from the inner circle of the project design team, through to the adopting organisation, the nation and finally the international policy arena – but the idea of each stage being a political community or a collection of actors whose actions have political implications is still very much applicable. The ecology of games metaphor thus provides us with a useful way to think about how the various players interact in making and carrying out administration and developing policy.

ASSESSING PROJECT OUTCOME: THE DESIGN-ACTUALITY GAP MODEL

Like all political interactions, the behaviour of actors related to the design and uptake of e-government projects is circumscribed by the organisations and institutions within which they are played out, and by the range of actors taken from the individuals and groups directly and indirectly involved with the process of governance. The outcome of an e-government project therefore does not depend on a single project entity alone, and instead depends on the interaction between different actors in the process and the nature of the relationships between them. Gaps in project design and implementation can in reality be seen as expressions of differences arising from the interaction between different (often conflicting) actor moves and strategies, determined to a large extent by actor perceptions, and played out within the context of set circumstances.

Heeks (2003) concluded that the major factor determining project outcome was the degree of mismatch between the current realities of a situation (the 'where are we now') and the models, conceptions, and assumptions built into a project's design (the 'where the e-government project wants to get us'). From this perspective, e-government success and failure depends largely on the size of this *'design-actuality gap'*: the larger gap, the greater the risk of e-government failure, the smaller the gap, the greater the chance of project success. By examining numerous case studies related to ICTs and e-government failure in developing countries, Heeks (2002) identified three dominant categories of reported outcome: *total failure*, *partial failure*, and *success*.

- The first possible outcome is *total failure*, where a project is either never implemented or in which a new system is implemented but is almost immediately abandoned.
- A second possible outcome is the *partial failure* of an initiative, in which major goals are unattained or where there are significant undesirable outcomes. Cases range from straightforward underachievement to more complex "sustainability failures" of an initiative.
- Finally, one may see the *success* of an initiative, in which most actor groups attain their major goals and do not experience significant undesirable outcomes.

Heeks also identified three so-called 'archetypes of failure', situations when a large design-actuality gap, and consequently project failure, is likely to emerge: *Hard-Soft Gaps* (the difference between the actual, rational design of the technology and the actuality of the social context within which it operates), *Public-Private Gaps* (the mismatch that results when technology meant for private organisations is used in the public sector without being adequately adapted to the adopting organisation) and *Country Context Gaps* (the gap that arises when a system designed for one country is transferred unaltered into the reality of another).

The above discussion reveals that although the strength of the Ecology of Games lies in its ability to identify and analyse the interrelationships between the different actors involved in the process of e-government system design and adoption, when taken alone it provides no insight into the consequences of this behaviour and its impact on project outcome. Similarly, the Design-Actuality Gap model is able to analyse structural weaknesses in a project's design but doesn't on its own provide an adequate explanation of the decision-making processes that led to such structural deficiencies in the first place. The results and analysis of this chapter will, therefore, rely on the two frameworks being used in combination to arrive at prescribed solutions and examples of best practice within the case study at hand. The advantage of using such an approach is that it allows the researcher to not only identify and analyse patterns of behaviour within the case under study, but also link decisions and actions to specific project outcomes.

DIGITISING PROPERTY TAX RECORDS IN BANGALORE, INDIA: EXAMINING ACTOR ATTITUDES AND PERCEPTIONS

Against the background of technological innovation in Karnataka state, project planners from the Greater Bangalore City Corporation (BBMP) felt that the manual system of property tax administration was archaic, opaque, and inefficient. All the members of the core project group believed that property tax collections under the manual system had suffered from poor record keeping and bad information management practices, slow processing times, and overcomplicated assessment and payment procedures. These had, in turn, created frustration amongst taxpayers and resulted in low levels of compliance. The computerised property tax system was thus borne out of a need to reform the manual system of property tax administration in Bangalore and improve tax revenues and compliance through the improvement of back-office efficiency, the simplification of tax collection, and the reduction of money lost through malpractice through the effective detection and deterrence of tax evasion – spurred on by the need to enhance power, authority and reputations.

Having identified senior state revenue officials, municipal tax administrators, and local tax collectors as the target users of the system, the ultimate aim of the project designers was to create an Internet-based 'back-office' database which could be used to monitor all aspects of property taxation: in essence property identification, tax dues assessment, revenue collection, and tax compliance monitoring. The application was put together using an Oracle database on an open-source software platform, with the architects using J2E and Java technology to construct the back-end application servers. Personal Digital Assistant (PDA) devices were integrated into the system so that revenue officers could go out in the field to collect taxes, and then use them to upload data back in real time. It was envisaged that citizens would in time also become users of the system, and would be able to have unrestricted access to their property records (and those of the entire city) online. The system's single-most unique feature was to be its eventual use of Geographic Information Systems (GIS) or online virtual mapping tools, to visually aid the revamping of the addressing system and to improve tax coverage through more comprehensive property identification and stricter monitoring (Virkar, 2011).

Interviews with tax officials revealed that most felt that there had been serious problems with the manual system of tax administration. They claimed that the biggest hurdles to the efficient administration of tax that they encountered prior to the introduction of the computerised database were poor and haphazard recordkeeping and large amounts of paperwork that needed to be done manually. Information was scattered and the process of calculating tax due, administering collections and checking up on defaulters was extremely unsystematic. While, as expected, none of the revenue officials interviewed mentioned government employee corruption as being serious problem, many interviewees spoke of the difficulties they faced in identifying and catching tax evaders. Most officials interviewed felt that the introduction of technology had greatly impacted old work processes and had helped alleviate the difficulties they faced under the manual system. They believed that the centralisation of data, the ease with which citizens could access their tax information, and the setting up of tax collection points across the city had all helped in bringing more properties into the tax net and contributed significantly towards improving tax payer compliance. All the officials interviewed felt that their interactions with the public had significantly decreased since the introduction of the computerised system, and a little over half them believed their overall relationship with citizens had improved as a result.

However, while acknowledging that the use of digitised records, computer printouts and online databases had had a positive impact on their work, some interviewees were quick to point out that technology had been used simply to automate existing processes, and that old infrastructural problems (such as poor electricity supply and old computers) and problems related to a lack of skills and training on the computerised system had not been resolved. Only a small percentage of revenue officials reported that they had been consulted during the design stage of the project. Further, there appeared to be no mechanism in place to solicit user feedback once the initial system had been developed. Almost all the officials interviewed said they felt disconnected from system. Most professed a high degree of unfamiliarity with the system, and were completely unaware of its key features. For instance, only one tax official mentioned the introduction of GIS mapping techniques as being useful to his work and that of his staff, a worrying fact given that the core project team had placed much store by the GIS maps as a tool to track property tax payments and identify defaulters. These are not good signs, as effective system implementation requires employees to fully accept and adopt the technology in the belief that it will do them some well-defined good.

Further, none of the officials interviewed knew how to operate even its most basic features. With no scheme in place to give them any formal training on the system, all the interviewees reported to be completely dependent on a private computer operator to feed in, change and retrieve electronic property tax data. This, the researcher feels, created a new problem within revenue offices and limited the effectiveness of the system, as it resulted in a shift in the balance of power within the workplace to the disadvantage of revenue officials and consequently hardened their attitude towards computerisation. Senior officers, once enthusiastic about the system, spoke about the frustration they felt at being unable to fulfil their supervisory role and at being put at the mercy of a junior employee. Junior tax officials, already slightly sceptical of the system, feared that their skill levels would put them at a disadvantage within the office and could eventually result in redundancy.

Opinions were divided about whether or not computerisation of the system that had led to improved tax yields. Most tax officials felt that while the introduction of the computerised system had positively impacted tax collections to some extent, there were many other reasons as to why tax yields had improved. For others, the introduction of the Self Assessment Scheme as a means of shifting the responsibility of tax payments onto the shoulders of the citizens and reducing the workload of revenue staff was almost as (if not more) important as the introduction of technology into the workplace. It may be concluded from the interviews that general citizen apathy towards property tax is to a large extent a consequence of poor public awareness about the benefits of pay-

ing property tax, a lack of enforcement measures and a general dislike of cumbersome processes – problems which cannot be solved through the introduction of technology alone.

IDENTIFYING GAMES THAT IMPACT THE PLANNING AND UPTAKE OF ICTs IN BUREAUCRACIES

An examination of the interviews and other data collected during field research reveals that the eventual outcome of the revenue department project can be interpreted as the consequence of a number of players making moves within a number of separate but interrelated games related to the project's design, implementation and adoption. At least six kinds of games appear to have influenced the impact the system has had on tax administration in Bangalore city. They include expertise games, power and influence games, policy games, turf struggles, games of persuasion and business games. Within each game, the following elements may be identified from the case at hand to help the researcher arrive at an in-depth analysis of the impact that various interactions have on the outcome of the project under study. They are:

1. **Key Actors:** the individuals, groups or other entities whose interactions shape the particular game being considered.
2. **Game Rules:** the written or unwritten codes of conduct that shape actor moves and choices during a game.
3. **Actor Goals and Motivations:** the aims that key actors seek to attain and maintain from interacting with other players, both broader long-term achievements as well as more short- to medium-term rewards.
4. **Key Strategies:** tactics, ruses, and ploys adopted by key actors during the course of a game to keep the balance of the engagement in their favour.

5. **Key Moves:** decisions and other plays made by key actors to arrive at key goals, usually if not always based on their strategy of choice.

From the games identified during the course of this author's research, a four-fold taxonomy has been developed which classifies and analyses behaviour depending on the level of actor interactions along four different axes: the field of play, the key actors involved, the main objective(s) of the game under study and the nature and/or spirit in which the game has been played. The four categories are elaborated on below:

1. **Arena or Field of Play:** Actor interactions may be classified according to the arena within which they are played out. In other words, this classification – which has its roots in initial work done by Vedel (1989) and Dutton (1992) – focuses on the reach and influence of actors within a given context, and the impact of their actions (both direct and indirect) on project outcomes.

   a. **Project-Specific Games:** Are generally played by individuals and groups of actors directly involved with the case under study. Such interactions usually occur during the planning and execution of a project and impact.

   b. **Organisation-Specific Games:** Are played out within the department or organisation within which the case study is based, involving not only actors directly concerned with the case study but also others within the institution whose moves come to bear influence on the project at hand.

   c. **City or Regional Level Games:** Include those interactions between actors whose power or reach extends to the level of the city or region within which the project is based, and who are playing power games for relatively high stakes. The goals, moves and strategies chosen by actors at this level may or

may not have a direct link to the case study, however they come to bear either a direct or indirect influence on its eventual outcome.

   d. **National Level Games:** Involve players who have their eye on attaining some sort of national prestige or who are influenced by other actors or discourses operating at the national level. Here again, actors may or may not be directly attached to the project or organisation under study.

   e. **International Level Games:** Are played chiefly by actors or groups of actors possessing international clout and/or aspirations. Games played at this level usually do not have a direct bearing on the project under study, however, actors might indirectly influence outcomes by attempting to gain power/prestige through adhering to popular trends, binding project planners to third-party conditonalities or merely by subscribing to certain schools of thought.

2. **Key Actors Involved:** Games may also be classified according to the key actors involved in each interaction studied. This axis thus aims to study interactions within the context of the key players – who they are and who they interact with.

   a. **Interactions Internal to the Project Planning/Core Group:** Includes any games being played exclusively between constituent elements of the project planning committee or the core group responsible for the design and execution of the project under study.

   b. **Core Project Group vs. Other Members of Implementing Department:** Cover games played between members of the core project committee and other individuals and/or groups within the implementing department who are otherwise not directly involved on the project at hand.

c. **Games within the Implementing Organisation:** Are played out between groups and individual actors who are members of the implementing organisation. Such interactions may or may not be directly related to the ICT4D project, but their outcome would have an impact on its eventual success or failure.

d. **Department/Organisation vs. External Players:** Cover interactions between the implementing department/organisation acting in a unified, institutional capacity and other external players such as the media, citizens and civil society organisations.

e. **Games Played by External Actors:** Which have little or no direct connection to the current project, but which nonetheless have a significant impact on its eventual success or failure.

3. **Actor Goals:** A third way of classifying actor interactions is based on the goals that different actor groups seek to attain by engaging with other players. Actors within each game are bound to have multiple goals that motivate them to act in certain ways, and thus it is important when applying this classification to identify the primary motivating factor behind each move.

a. **Games of Power and Prestige:** Involve moves to enable actors to gain or shore up their individual power and prestige or those of their group.

b. **Games to Maintain Status Quo:** Are those interactions whereby players seek to maintain the status quo. These games are generally played when actors perceive a threat to their current position or status, and thus act to preserve their current standing in the hierarchy.

c. **Games to Achieve Change:** Are those interactions that attempt to change a current situation or process within a department or organisation, primarily through the attainment of project goals and objectives.

d. **Games to Achieve Political and Policy Aims:** Are those moves and strategies played by actors to achieve certain political or policy aims which may or may not have a direct relationship or bearing on the project under study.

e. **Games to Further Ideology and/or Discourse:** Comprise chiefly those games played by actors who are generally driven by a particular ideology or discourse and wish to use their political influence to impose their ideas on either the implementing organisation or on the project planners themselves.

4. **Nature of Game Play:** The final axis against which games may be classified analyses the nature of the political dynamic between the key actors within which the project was conceived and implemented. In other words, this axis differentiates between positive and negative actors and the impact of their actions on their sphere of influence.

a. **Constructive Game Play:** Includes altruistic and other positive moves, where competition is seen to be constructive and controlled/restrained rivalry brings about positive results. Such games are therefore win-win situations, and include all those moves that have a positive impact on the adoption of new technologies within a development context

b. **Destructive Game Play:** Involves fierce rivalries and negative competition, resulting in zero-sum games where actors act purposefully to win at the cost of their so-called 'opponents', thereby creating a negative project environment and often resulting in a large wastage of time and resources.

PUBLIC SECTOR REFORM GAMES: PROCESS RE-ENGINEERING AND E-GOVERNMENT

Information and communication technologies bring about rapid changes in management patterns, such as the breakdown of traditional administration hierarchies and the streamlining of decision-making within and across agencies. Steps to adopt and use ICTs in government are thus generally taken as part of a broader reform or change-management agenda driven by actors from different levels, where new technology is introduced to solve existing administrative problems. The re-engineering of administrative processes is possibly the most important step in implementing an application, as it requires that an agency undertakes substantial reform of its organisational structure (Bhatnagar, 2004). This is particularly true as using ICTs with out-dated or inappropriate processes can increase corruption and other forms of poor governance by providing opportunities for officials to perform dishonest activities faster and still avoid detection (Pathak & Prasad, 2005).

Re-engineering processes often involves playing games to change the mind-sets and culture of an organisation's workforce, including using strategies that recognise the need to train employees, improve skill sets, and deploy appropriate supporting infrastructure to enable online processes that are useful to both the user and the implementing organisation. A common strategy in a successful implementation game is to map existing methods and procedures, usually followed by the simplification of these procedures in such a way that the overall task can be completed in as few steps as possible (Misra, 2005).

The looked-for outcome of such an exercise is that of mutual cooperation; where all the players in the game accept the modification of processes that result in fewer steps, any eventual reduction in the number of people needed to perform tasks, and the automation of certain operations that result in eventual back-end computerisation. However, this is not always the case, and re-engineering games may get stymied in conflicting moves made by different key players. This thesis argues, therefore, that the use of ICTs alone will not guarantee the success of a project in achieving its objectives and reaching its full potential. Successful e-government systems and re-engineered processes standardise rules and procedures, but it is the well thought-out games played by project designers and implementers which ultimately bring down resistance and fear, reduce opportunities for exercising discretion, and create an environment conducive to the adoption of the new technology.

Related to this, project managers whilst implementing a project have to decide whether they will adopt a top-down approach to decision-making, or whether they will select a more participatory style. Whilst a top-down approach to project management does yield a number of benefits – including the speeding up of decisions that might otherwise be difficult to make (particularly true for cases like the one under study, where employees might attempt to resist the introduction of technology when faced with dramatic changes) – such an approach means that during the planning of a system, priority goes to those features and aspects which are seen as important by a select, centralised group of planners. There is a danger that some of the priorities of the main users, the staff on the ground, may be overlooked and any mismatch between design and user needs may result in employees rejecting the system. To add to this, most of the literature on organisational change in the private sector stresses the importance of employee participation in the planning of change-inducing projects (Lefebvre & Lefebvre, 1996), particularly to enhance staff morale, an idea that is fast catching on in public sector management and e-government circles (Heeks, 2006).

EXPLORING THE CASE OF THE GREATER BANGALORE CITY MUNICIPAL CORPORATION (BBMP)

The State of Karnataka is particularly interesting when studying the various games and interactions related to the use of Information Technology for public service reform within Indian government departments, as ongoing processes of change within different government agencies in the state have had the use of ICTs deeply implicated in them, and many government and quasi-government bodies have entered into partnerships with private and non-profit organisations. In recent years, there has been growing pressure placed by citizen groups, international agencies, and the local media on both city corporations and the state government to rationalise existing revenue collection structures and improve the collection of property tax in the field, both within cities and across the State at large.

In view of the need to turn property tax in to a productive tax instrument, the Greater Bangalore Municipal Corporation (BBMP) teamed up with a series of private and not-for-profit technology firms in partnerships which aimed to improve property tax collections across Bangalore city using computerised revenue records and Geographical Information Systems (GIS)-based property mapping. Against the background of technological innovation in the State, project planners decided to do away with the manual, paper-based system of property tax administration considering it to be increasingly archaic, opaque, and inefficient. In particular, members of the core project group felt that property tax collections under the manual system had over the years suffered consistently from poor recordkeeping and bad information management practices, slow processing times, and overcomplicated assessment and payment procedures. This had, in turn, created frustration amongst taxpayers and resulted in increasingly low levels of tax compliance. The computerised property tax system was thus borne out of an ever-growing need to reform the old system of property tax administration in Bangalore city and to improve tax revenues and compliance through the improvement of back-office efficiency, the simplification of tax collection, and the reduction of money lost as a result of malpractice through the effective detection and deterrence of tax evasion. Concurrently planners were also spurred on by the need to enhance their own power, authority, and reputations with their respective spheres of influence and beyond.

Interviews with key people involved with the design and implementation of the project, conducted between 2005 and 2009, brought to light a number of games or interactions operating at different levels or 'arenas', all of which had an impact – direct or indirect – on the effectiveness of the system and its eventual performance. These are outlined below:

1. **Project Planning Committee Games:** See Table 1.
2. **BBMP Revenue Department Games:** See Table 2.
3. **Bangalore City Games:** See Table 3.
4. **National-Level Games:** See Table 4.

WHAT'S IN A GAME? DISCUSSING E-GOVERNMENT SUCCESS AND FAILURE

This chapter sought to unravel the social dynamics shaping e-government projects used to reform public sector institutions. In particular, its chief aim was to analyse actor behaviour, motivations, and interactions surrounding the conception, development and maintenance of e-government software platforms facilitating these transformations. The principal approach of this research to the issues thrown up by these cross-sectoral interactions was the use of an empirical case study dealing with the design, implementation, and subsequent use of an electronic property tax system based in the

Table 1. Project planning committee games

Games	Key Players	Key Objectives	Nature of Moves
e-Government Movement	Various current senior BBMP officials, software providers.	Encourage BBMP departmental reform through the use of technology.	Positive Game Play
System Conception and Design c) Formation of the Core Project Planning Group d) Initial Design and Conception of the System	Various current senior BBMP officials, software providers. BBMP officials on the project planning committee, eGovernments Foundation representatives.	Take credit for the initial design idea and design process. Design and launch a successful system.	Negative Game Play Altruistic Game Play
Digital Democracy	Senior BBMP officials and eGovernments Foundation members.	Seek to influence the design of the PTIS to support their conception of democracy.	Negative Game Play

(Source: *Author Analysis, 2010*)

Table 2. BBMP revenue department games

Games	Key Players	Key Objectives	Nature of Moves
System Acceptance Games	Project planning group (Senior BBMP officials, software providers, external consultants), senior and junior revenue officials.	Get officials on the ground to accept and adopt the system.	Positive Game Play
Efficiency Games	Senior BBMP officials, Assistant Revenue Officers, and junior revenue staff.	Hold down costs and increase tax revenues by improving efficiency.	Positive Game Play
Management Control	Senior BBMP officials, Revenue officials.	Expand power and decisional control.	Negative Game Play
Game to Control Petty Corruption	Senior BBMP officials, Revenue officials.	Reduce revenue losses from petty corruption.	Negative Game Play
Revenue Office Politics	Revenue Officials, Assistant Revenue Officers, Station Managers, junior revenue staff.	Assert 'superior' status, retain power and authority within the field office.	Negative Game Play

(Source: *Author Analysis, 2010*)

Table 3. Bangalore city games

Games	Key Players	Key Objectives	Nature of Moves
Image Building Game	BBMP officials, the media, citizens.	Improve image of the BBMP as an accountable, modern and responsive government agency.	Positive Game Play
Tax Compliance Game	BBMP officials, the media, citizens.	Encourage citizens to pay taxes through a mixture of carrot and stick initiatives.	Largely Positive Game Play

(Source: *Author Analysis, 2010*)

Table 4. National-level games

Games	Key Players	Key Objectives	Nature of Moves
Image Building Game	BBMP officials, the media, citizens.	Improve image of the BBMP as an accountable, modern and responsive government agency.	Positive Game Play
Tax Compliance Game	BBMP officials, the media, citizens.	Encourage citizens to pay taxes through a mixture of carrot and stick initiatives.	Largely Positive Game Play

(Source: *Author Analysis, 2010*)

Revenue Department of the Greater Bangalore Municipal Corporation (BBMP).

The overarching aim of the computerised system was to improve tax revenues and tax compliance through the streamlining of tax administration processes by increasing back-office efficiency, simplifying methods of tax payment, reducing the amount of money lost through petty corruption, and improving tax yields and citizen compliance through the speedy detection of tax evasion. Designers of the project sought to use automation and digitisation to improve data management in the revenue offices, reduce the use of discretion by government officials in revenue-related decisions, and make property tax collection processes more transparent. In particular, the system sought to increase revenues from property tax through better quality data, quicker evaluations, greater computational accuracy, and positive psychological reinforcement; whilst at the same time reducing losses in revenue occurred as a result of back-office inefficiencies and fraudulent practices through the use of digital databases and GIS maps. However, as illustrated by the case study, the underlying motivations for the individual partners and actors within each of the participating organisations turned out in some instances to be widely divergent, resulting in several highly divisive and negative outcomes within the context of the project under study.

As the analysis in previous sections has shown, certain key games with local impacts get played out in different arenas between actors influenced by not only local but also national and interna-tional factors. An examination of interview data and other documents brought to light a number of games in different arenas, each involving key actors related to the project, whose interplay had a bearing on the project's eventual outcome. No single game can account for the ultimate outcome of the Revenue Department project at the time of writing, and instead the impact that the system has had on property tax administration can be best understood as an 'interacting set' or 'ecology' of games – as discussed in previous sections. Games that shaped the development and adoption of the system appear to have be layered or 'nested', with some contained within others.

Key games found to have significantly shaped the outcome of the system appear to have been played during the initial stages of the process, either during the time of its conception (in the form of positive and negative interactions between members of the project planning committee) or at the stage of internal implementation and adoption (in the form of friction between the core project team and the intended end-users such as the field officers), corroborating the findings of the quantitative data analysis set out in the previous section of this chapter. The only city-level game that had any significant impact on the project appeared to be the Tax Compliance game, played between the BBMP and the taxpayers of Bangalore. Other games at the city and national levels were primarily found to be ideological games and games centred around the interplay of market forces, thus having little direct bearing on the tax administration system and its eventual fate.

Questions remained, however, as to whether conflicting motivations and interests could be aligned to ensure win-win situations for all actors concerned and to promote the long-term sustainability of the project at hand. The discussion of the case study in previous sections also reveals that at the heart of each game lay a design-actuality gap, usually brought about from a power struggle stemming from a deep-seated mistrust between different actor groups. In particular, the case study demonstrates that gaps arise because those with the power and authority to take design or implementation decisions at different key stages of the process are usually unwilling to allow any initiative to go ahead that would give the other actor group(s) in the game more autonomy over the system or more control over their actions. Design-actuality gaps also arise when key actors refuse to acknowledge the impact that external, tangential factors and circumstances have on the shaping of decisions and government policy.

In recognising that design-actuality gaps open up and give way to unfavourable project outcomes if designers and top managers assume that localised outcomes result only from direct local influences, discounting the impact of other factors external to the project at hand, preliminary findings suggest that the project may at the time of writing be classed as a *partial failure* under Heeks' threefold categorisation. However, as evidenced by the discussion, this so-called 'failure' is neither a straightforward case of the outright inability of project managers to achieve stated objectives nor is it a so-called 'sustainability failure'. Causes of failure to meet stated aims appear to be two-fold: manifested through Hard-Soft gaps, stemming from competitive and divisive moves made by actors in key games relating to the system's design and implementation that generated conflict and disharmony in later attempts by users to adopt the system, and Private-Public gaps, rooted in fierce competition and oftentimes rivalry between key executive members on both sides of the profit-non profit divide that stemmed from their differing values, work cultures, and agendas.

CONCLUSION

Rapidly evolving economic and social contexts mean that political institutions and the people who constitute them cannot afford to get bogged down in traditional work practices or be impervious or resistant to change themselves. Whilst this does not necessarily mean a wholesale rejection of what has gone before, it does mean that there needs to be a constant assessment and reassessment of workplace values and current practices, eliminating those which result in behaviours that are detrimental to the functioning of the organisation and encouraging those that promote positive interactions.

Organisations and institutions, particularly those which form the political core of a society, cannot afford to be seen to have been left behind, as the people within those institutions are generally looked to as political trendsetters and role models in addition to being responsible for societal welfare. Software platform development for e-government thus needs to be able to respond to swiftly and appropriately to these changes, and the growing demand for cost-effective high-quality programming has resulted in several collaborative cross-sectoral partnerships between software developers and government organisations globally. However, as illustrated by the case study, the underlying motivations for the individual partners and actors within these partnerships can be widely divergent, and may result in highly divisive and negative outcomes.

The discussion put forward in this chapter reveals that at the heart of a political game usually lies a power struggle, brought about through a deep-seated mistrust between different actor groups. This holds particularly true for the process of software conception and design where, the case study put forward demonstrates, gaps in quality and overall technical applicability arise because those with the power and authority to take design or implementation decisions are usually unwilling to allow any initiative to go ahead that would give the other actor group(s) in the game more autonomy over the process or system. Further, certain key games with local impacts get played out in different arenas between actors influenced by not only local but also national and international factors. Problems arise if designers and top managers assume that localised outcomes result only from direct local influences, discounting the impact of other factors external to the project at hand.

Added to this, there is a tendency for power élites to lose touch with ground realities when devising projects for their organisations as well as for their citizens, especially when planners comprise the higher echelons of government and operate within a top-down command-and-control system of management. There is also a danger that high-level project planners will, in looking at macro-outcomes, ignore outliers and how these may precipitate unexpected turns of events. This holds particularly true when existing patterns of communication and information exchange fail to be flexible or unable to adapt to changing situations.

In modern times, people and their governments have struggled to find easy, cheap, and effective ways to run countries. ICT-based applications have the potential to revolutionise patterns of communication between authority and citizenry, radically restructuring politics and governance at all levels by making systems more integrated, transparent, and efficient. However critics of e-government, and more particularly of its introduction into developing country contexts, contend that administrative reform is not an important enough issue to justify exposing cash-strapped governments to the risks and opportunity costs associated with ICT projects.

Whilst it is widely recognised that ICTs are strategically important to a country, and the need for investment in e-government is generally well-accepted, questions related to the balancing of investment in ICTs with the need to give priority to other basic infrastructural requirements still need to be answered, and there is apprehension in some quarters that money used for e-government will absorb scarce developmental resources whilst not delivering on potential benefits. Further, it is still unclear whether administrative reforms stimulated by e-government will in the long run feed into a country's other economic, societal, and development goals, or simply divert resources away from areas where they are needed into already cash-rich sectors and industries such as those related to software design and development. Only time and further research will be able to tell.

REFERENCES

Bannon, L. J. (1991). From Human Factors to Human Actors: The Role of Psychology and Human Computer Interaction Studies in System Design. In J. Greenbaum, & M. Kyng (Eds.), *Design At Work: Cooperative Design of Computer Systems* (pp. 25–44). Lawerence Erlbaum Associates, Inc. Publishers.

Bhatnagar, S. (2004). *E-Government: From Vision to Implementation*. New Delhi: Sage Publications.

Carayon, P., Hoonakker, P., & Smith, M. J. (2012). Human Factors in Organizational Design and Management. In G. Salvendy (Ed.), *Handbook of Human Factors and Ergonomics* – (4th ed., pp. 534–552). John Wiley and Sons. doi:10.1002/9781118131350.ch18

Crozier, M., & Friedberg, E. (1980). *Actors and Systems*. University of Chicago Press.

Czaja, S. J., & Nair, S. N. (2012). Human Factors Engineering and Systems Design. In G. Salvendy (Ed.), *Handbook of Human Factors and Ergonomics* (4th ed., pp. 38–56). John Wiley and Sons. doi:10.1002/9781118131350.ch2

Dada, D. (2006). The Failure of E-Government in Developing Countries: A Literature Review. *The Electronic Journal on Information Systems in Developing Countries, 26*(7), 1–10.

Downs, A. (1964). *Inside Bureaucracy*. Boston: Little Brown.

Dutton, W. H. (1992). The Ecology of Games Shaping Telecommunications Policy. *Communication Theory, 2*(4), 303–324. doi:10.1111/j.1468-2885.1992.tb00046.x

Firestone, W. A. (1989). Educational Policy as an Ecology of Games. *Educational Researcher, 18*(7), 18–24. doi:10.2307/1177165

Heeks, R. (2003). *Most eGovernment-for-Development Projects Fail: How Can the Risks be Reduced?* (i-Government Working Paper Series, Paper No. 14). Manchester, UK: IDPM.

Jacko, J. A., Yi, J. S., Sainfort, F., & McClellan, M. (2012). Human Factors and Ergonomic Methods. In G. Salvendy (Ed.), *Handbook of Human Factors and Ergonomics –* (4th ed., pp. 289–329). John Wiley and Sons. doi:10.1002/9781118131350. ch10

Jick, T. D. (1979). Mixing Qualitative and Quantitative Methods: Triangulation in Action. *Administrative Science Quarterly, 24*(4), 602–611. doi:10.2307/2392366

Karwowski, W. (2012). The Discipline of Human Factors and Ergonomics. In G. Salvendy (Ed.), *Handbook of Human Factors and Ergonomics* (4th ed., pp. 3–37). John Wiley and Sons. doi:10.1002/9781118131350.ch1

Kuutti, K. (1996). Activity Theory as a Potential Framework for Human Computer Interaction Research. In B. A. Nardi (Ed.), *Context and Consciousness: Activity Theory and Human Computer Interaction* (pp. 17–44). Boston: MIT Press.

Lewis, A. (1982). *The Psychology of Taxation*. Oxford, UK: Martin Robertson & Company.

National Institute of Urban Affairs. (2004). *Reforming the Property Tax System (Research Study Series no. 94)*. New Delhi: NIUA Press.

Proctor, R. W., & Vu, K.-P. L. (2012). Selection and Control of Action. In G. Salvendy (Ed.), *Handbook of Human Factors and Ergonomics* (4th ed., pp. 95–116). John Wiley and Sons. doi:10.1002/9781118131350.ch4

Salvendy, G. (2012). *Handbook of Human Factors and Ergonomics* (4th ed.). John Wiley and Sons. doi:10.1002/9781118131350

Scharpf, F. W. (1997). *Games Real Actors Play: Actor-Centered Institutionalism in Policy Research*. Oxford, UK: Westview Press.

Vedel, T. (1989). Télématique et configurations d'acteurs: Une perspective européenne. *Reseaux, 7*(37), 9–28.

Virkar, S. (2011). *The Politics of Implementing e-Government for Development: The Ecology of Games Shaping Property Tax Administration in Bangalore City*. (Unpublished Doctoral Thesis). University of Oxford, Oxford, UK.

West, D. A. (2004). E-government and the Transformation of Service Delivery and Citizen Attitudes. *Public Administration Review, 64*(1), 15–27. doi:10.1111/j.1540-6210.2004.00343.x

Yin, R. K. (2003). *Case Study Research: Design and Methods (vol. 5)*. London: Sage Publications.

ADDITIONAL READING

Asquith, A. (1998). Non-elite Employees' Perceptions of Organizational Change in English Local Government. *International Journal of Public Sector Management, 11*(4), 262–280. doi:10.1108/09513559810225825

Basu, S. (2004). E-Government and Developing Countries: An Overview. *International Review of Law Computers & Technology, 18*(1), 109–132. doi:10.1080/13600860410001674779

Beinhocker, E. D. (2006). *The Origin of Wealth: Evolution, Complexity and the Radical Remaking of Economics*. Boston, MA: Harvard Business School Press.

Bhatnagar, S. (2003). E-Government: Building a SMART Administration for India's States. In S. Howes, A. Lahiri, & N. Stern (Eds.), *State-level Reform in India: Towards More Effective Government* (pp. 257–267). New Delhi: Macmillan India Ltd.

Bruhat Bangalore Mahanagara Palike (2000). *Property Tax Self-Assessment Scheme: Golden Jubilee Year 2000*. Mahanagara Palike Council Resolution No. 194/99-2000, Bangalore, 2000 [Handbook].

Bruhat Bangalore Mahanagara Palike (2008). *Assessment and Calculation of Property Tax Under the Capital Value System (New SAS): 2007- 2008*. Bangalore, 2007 [Unpublished Handbook].

De', R. (2007). Antecedents of Corruption and the Role of E-Government Systems in Developing Countries. In the Electronic Government 6th International Conference, EGOV 2007, *Proceedings of Ongoing Research*, Regensburg, Germany, September 3-7, Available at: http://www.iimb. ernet.in/~rahulde/CorruptionPaperEgov07_RDe. pdf (Accessed on: 5th December 2013)

Dutton, W. H. (1999). *Society on the Line: Information Politics in the Digital Age*. Oxford: Oxford University Press.

Heeks, R. (2000). The Approach of Senior Public Officials to Information Technology Related Reform: Lessons from India. *Public Administration and Development*, *20*(3), 97–205. doi:10.1002/1099-162X(200008)20:3<197::AID-PAD109>3.0.CO;2-6

Heeks, R. (2006). *Implementing and Managing eGovernment – An International Text*. New Delhi: Vistar Publications.

Isaac-Henry, K. (1997). Development and Change in the Public Sector. In K. Isaac-Henry, C. Painter, & C. Barnes (Eds.), *Management in the Public Sector: Challenge and Change* (pp. 1–25). London: International Thomson Business Press.

Jha, S. N., & Mathur, P. C. (1999). *Decentralization and Local Politics*. New Delhi: Sage Publications.

Misra, S. (2005). eGovernance: Responsive and Transparent Service Delivery Mechanism. In A. Singh (Ed.) Administrative Reforms: Towards Sustainable Practices (pp. 283-302). New Delhi: Sage Publications.

Ronaghan, S. A. (2002). Benchmarking E-Government: A Global Perspective. The United Nations Division for Public Economics and Public Administration (DPEPA) Report. http://unpan1. un.org/intradoc/groups/public/documents/un/ unpan021547.pdf

Sinha, K. P. (1981). *Property Taxation in a Developing Economy*. New Delhi: Puja Publications.

KEY TERMS AND DEFINITIONS

Actor: The individuals, groups or other entities whose interactions shape the direction and nature of a particular game being considered.

Actor Goals and Motivations: The aims that key actors seek to attain and maintain from interacting with other players, encompassing both broader long-term achievements as well as more short- to medium-term rewards.

Actor Perceptions: Include the preferences and opinions of key institutional players that help determine the disjoint between project design and current ground realities, together with the nature and direction of organisational reform and institutional change.

Country Context Gap: Refers to the gap that arises when a system designed in theory for one country is transferred into the reality of another.

Design-Actuality Gap Model or Framework: Is a framework for project evaluation which contends that the major factor determining project outcome is the degree of mismatch between the current ground realities of a situation ('where are we now'), and the models, conceptions, and assumptions built into a project's design (the 'where the project wants to get us').

E-Administration: Refers to the improvement of government processes and to the streamlining of the internal workings of the public sector often using ICT-based information systems.

E-Consultation: Refers to the process whereby citizens are given the opportunity to provide feedback to government online on matters of public importance and participate in the shaping of issues relevant to them via the new digital media.

E-Democracy: May be defined by the express intent to increase the participation of citizens in decision-making through the use of digital media and the application of Information and Communication Technologies to political processes. e-Democracy may be subdivided into e-Engagement (or e-Participation), e-Voting, e-Consultation.

E-Engagement: Refers to the overall enhancement of opportunities for greater consultation and dialogue between government and its citizens through the encouragement of online citizen action and citizen participation in political processes electronically.

E-Governance: Refers to the use of ICTs by government, civil society, and political institutions to engage citizens in political processes and to the promote greater participation of citizens in the public sphere.

E-Government: Refers to the use of Information and Communication Technologies by government departments and agencies to improve internal functioning and public service provision. Broadly speaking, e-government may be divided into 2 distinct areas: e-Administration and e-Services.

E-Services: Refers to the improved delivery of public services to citizens through multiple electronic platforms.

E-Voting: May be defined broadly as the expression and exercise of fundamental democratic rights and duties online through specially developed digital platforms.

Games: Arena(s) of competition and cooperation structured by a set of rules and assumptions about how to act in order for actors to achieve a particular set of objectives.

Hard-Soft Gap: Refers to the difference between the *actual, rational design* of a technology (hard) adopted within a project and the *actuality of the social context*, namely people, culture, politics, etc., within which the system operates (soft).

Managerial Variables: Are those institutional variables relating to project management and other *soft* variables of project design and implementation, which include the efficiency and effectiveness of a supply chain, the characteristics of an agency's culture, and the capacity of an adopting agency to adapt to and to manage change.

Moves: May be defined as actions, decisions and other plays made by key actors taken to arrive at key goals, usually if not always based on their strategy of choice.

Partial Failure: of an initiative is a situation in which major goals are unattained or where there are significant undesirable outcomes.

Political Variables: Are those *soft* institutional variables relating to the perceptions and impressions that public servants have regarding potential labour cuts, administrative turnover, and changes in executive direction generated by the development of e-government.

Private-Public Gap: Refers to the mismatch that results when technology meant for private organisations is used in the public sector without being adapted to suit the role and aims of the adopting public organisation.

Project Outcome: Or the sum total of the interaction between organisational and institutional realities and the project design carried out within the constraints of the current organisational and institutional set-up.

Rules: The written or unwritten codes of conduct that shape actor moves and choices during a game.

Strategies: Include tactics, ruses, and ploys adopted by key actors during the course of a game to keep the balance of the engagement in their favour.

Success: Of an initiative is a situation in which most actor groups attain their major goals and do not experience significant undesirable outcomes.

Technological Variables: Are those institutional variables relating to technology and other *hard* elements of project design and implementation, which include the ability of a user-population to access ICTs, the quality of the user population's Internet use, the availability of an internal technological infrastructure, and the provision of technical skills to the government workforce.

Total Failure: Of an initiative is a situation where a project is either never implemented or in which a new system is implemented but is almost immediately abandoned.

ENDNOTES

[1]   Long, 'The Local Community as an Ecology of Games', p. 253.

Chapter 5
Investigating the Success of OSS Software Projects

Amir Hossein Ghapanchi
Griffith University, Australia

ABSTRACT

Whereas there are several instances of Open Source Software (OSS) projects that have achieved huge success in the market, a high failure rate has been reported for OSS projects. This study conducts a literature survey to gain insight into existing studies on the success of OSS projects. More specifically, this study seeks to extract the critical success factors for OSS projects. Based on the literature survey in this study, the authors found determinants of success in OSS projects and classified them into three broad categories of project traits, product traits, and network structure. These findings have important implications for both the OSS research community and OSS practitioners.

1. INTRODUCTION

Although there are several successful instances of open source projects that have achieved a huge success in the market, it has been observed that most OSS projects are abandoned after a while and experience failure (Colazo & Fang 2009; Chengalur-Smith & Sidorova 2003). Addressing the current situation of a high failure rate amongst OSS projects, the focus of the present study is on helping OSS projects become aware of the factors that impact their success.

In response to the current situation of a high failure rate amongst OSS projects, our focus herein is on helping OSS projects increase their chance of success by informing them of the factors that may impact their success.

This paper provides an overview of current state-of-the-art research in OSS "success" literature. The aim of this research is to help OSS projects succeed by developing a framework that represents antecedents of "success" in OSS projects according to the literature. Moreover, in order to make more sense of the list of antecedents, this paper aims to bundle the antecedents into meaningful categories. Hence the research question guiding this study is as below:

RQ: What factors impact success in OSS projects, and how can we group them?

DOI: 10.4018/978-1-4666-6485-2.ch005

Given the current situation regarding the high failure rate of OSS projects and also the proliferating reliance of firms on OSS applications (Sen 2007), seeking answers for this question is important. The answers to this question can inform many OSS practitioners including OSS project managers, potential OSS adopters, and potential OSS sponsors of the factors that determine the future success of an OSS project.

This paper is organized as follows. Section 2 contains a literature review on OSS success. Section 3 presents the research methodology. Section 4 presents the results of the research, i.e. a framework for antecedents to success in OSS projects. Section 5 presents the concluding remarks.

2. LITERATURE REVIEW

2.1 Open Source Software

Utilising novel intellectual property laws, a new software development and distribution paradigm has emerged over last two decades, which in February 1998 was termed open source software development (Midha 2007). Unlike proprietary software in which the program's source code is a trade secret and is protected by law, in OSS the source code is publicly available for anyone who would like to see it. OSS products are developed under an open source licence that permits their users to observe, modify and redistribute the program's source code (Open Source Initiative 2005).

A typical OSS project starts with what (Raymond 1999) calls "scratching a developer's personal itch". An OSS project initiator who has a software idea starts writing the code. Since the community is intended to be able to see the software, it is released under a license that allows the community to see the source code and use the software. The developers in the community can contact the project administrator(s) and join the development team. Moreover, the community users can communicate with the project team and ask

for help, or request new features or report a bug in the system, or even contribute to the development. As a result of this evolution, OSS is said to meet user needs better than traditional closed-source software (Loshin 2005). Being involved with development process, users may be more satisfied with open source software (Midha 2007).

Unlike closed source software (CSS) in which the program's source code is a trade secret and is protected by law, in OSS, the source code is publicly available for anyone who would like to see it. However, this cannot fully define OSS because even though access to source code is normally open in OSS applications, there may be some exceptions like software developed under Microsoft's share source initiative. Normally OSS applications are developed by volunteers rather than paid developers, but there are some contradictory cases like Linux which is developed by volunteers as well as paid developers. Hence, "a software which is developed by volunteer developers" can also not completely define OSS. Open Source Initiative (OSI) defines OSS as software released under a license approved by OSI (Open Source Initiative 2005). Researchers agree on the definition of OSS proposed by OSI. OSS could be free or commercial; but, the focus of this study will be on free OSS.

OSS development has been an important area of research because of the large number of OSS applications that have been highly successful and are being used by millions of users. Apache, Mozilla Firefox, Linux, Unix and Perl are examples of such software. Table 1 shows some application areas of OSS along with examples of popular open source packages in each area.

2.2 OSS History

OSS originated in the early 1960s, when key foundations of Internet were being constructed in academic settings like MIT and Berkeley. That was probably of early attempts to share software source code by developers. OSS was then termed

Table 1. Examples of OSS packages

Applications	Popular Open Source Packages
Web server	Apache, NetMax, WebServer
Office suites	StarOffice, KOffice, IOffice2000
Browsers	Mozilla, Opera, Netscape Communicator
Database	MySQL, DBMaker, PostGreSQL
Multimedia	XMovie, MPEG TV
Interpreters	Java, Perl, Python
Development platform	Gnome, KDE, GNUstep

in February 1998 by a group of "free software" proponents (e.g. Tim O'Reilly).

Emergence of Unix operating system as well as the "C" programming language (both developed in Bell labs) in 1970s was the next step towards the evolution of OSS. Other institutions adopted Unix freely or at a cheap price, and made further improvements that were shared with others. In addition, taking benefit from Internet as a facilitator, computer programmers could contribute to the software by their innovative ideas. However, these cooperative software development activities were being carried out informally and no effort was being done to restrict reuse of the software. This made the owner of Bell labs (AT&T) to put copy right over Unix. As a result, in 1980s a process started to formalize these collaborative software development activities.

In 1983, Free Software Foundation (FSF) was created by MIT artificial intelligence lab, aiming at development and distribution of software at zero cost. To do so, FSF provided a formal licensing procedure namely "General Public License (GPL)" that prevented claiming of property rights over collaboratively developed software. GPL forced software users neither to impose licensing restrictions on others nor on any additions to the source code.

Expansion of Internet in 1990s led to acceleration of OSS activities (Moody 2002). A large number of contributors devoted a huge amount of contribution to OSS projects, and numerous OSS applications emerged, most notably Linux (an operating system developed in 1991).

Moody (2002) believes that the most important milestone in OSS has been initiating the development of Linux operating system in 1991 by Linus Torvalds, an undergraduate student at the University of Finland. Linus liked to have a Unix-like operating system on his 386 computer so started writing a new operating system. Linus had two motivations for his act: first, felt guilty whenever he was using a shareware for not paying the fees; and second, he did not like to pay for Minix, a UNIX compatible operating system (Moody 2002). Therefore, Linus made the software freely available through File transfer Protocol (FTP). Although, Linus Torvalds released early versions of Linux under his own licensing terms, which implied any redistribution to be free of charge, for later versions (0.1.2) FSF's GPL was adopted.

Another innovation was growing alternative approaches to licensing OSS applications. Although during 1980s, the GPL was the dominant OSS license, this situation changed in 1990s. Most importantly Debian, an institution which was founded to spread Linux, introduced "Debian Free Software Guidelines" in 1995 that became the Open Source Definition. These guidelines let licensee bundle cooperatively developed software with proprietary software source code.

2.3 OSS vs. CSS

Open source software is best understood in contrast with closed source software (CSS). In closed-source software development (CSSD), software source code is neither accessible by users during the project nor after development, but in open-source software development (OSSD), it is publicly available to everyone during as well as after development.

In spite of having some similarities, OSSD and CSSD are different in many ways. For example, CSS projects hire developers and pay them to develop software and try to sell it, while OSS projects seek to attract volunteer programmers to develop a software under the terms of a license that eventually lets everybody have the outcome of the work and even use its source code. As another example, contrary to CSSD, in OSSD, project team size changes frequently over time. Furthermore, unlike CSSD, in OSSD, users can highly involve in development process and even contribute to development activities. In OSSD, the lifecycle is usually longer than CSSD because the program's codes are continuously updated (Tirole & Lerner 2002).

2.4 OSS Development Model

Raymond (1999) was the first significant study to explain OSS development process and methodology. Raymond proposed the metaphor of the 'cathedral' and the 'bazaar' to compare traditional closed source software development with the OSS development. Raymond compared developing a CSS to a cathedral. 'Cathedral' metaphor indicates to a limited number of developers who develop software in isolation from the community. On the other hand, OSS was likened to a bazaar as it is an unorganized place in which everyone could participate (Raymond 1999). This approach encourages the community to participate in and contribute to the open source project in different ways like submitting bugs or doing code review. OSS relies mainly on "rapid prototyping" which means iteratively development by community contributors based on their requirements. Here, simultaneous development and bug fixing lead to high levels of quality.

Although Raymond (1999) model has been cited very frequently in OSS literature as an explanation for OSS development, it has also been criticized by several researchers. Feller et al. (2005) also criticized Raymond's terminology of "cathedral and bazaar" because "bazaar" traditionally refers to distribution of products and services rather than production.

There are three clusters of reason for initiating a new OSS, namely technological reasons, socio-political reasons and economic reasons (Schweik & Semenov 2003). The first category contains technological reasons such as to work with the leading edge of technology, to leverage the OSS community for R&D, or to meet developers' computing needs. The second class comprises socio-political reasons such as to fulfil some need for a sense of belonging to a community, to satisfy an intrinsic motivation to do the work, to help overcome the global software digital divide, or to fulfil a wish to involve in altruistic work. The third cluster is composed of economic reasons such as to gain future job opportunities, to benefit from indirect revenues (e.g. selling related products and services), to benefit from free or low cost software, or to build or enhance programming skills.

A typical OSS project starts when one developer has an idea and is sufficiently motivated to put it into practice. An OSS project initiator(s) who has an idea for software starts writing the code and releases the first version of the software. Raymond (2001) calls this a programmer "scratching a personal itch". For instance, Torvalds initially developed the kernel of the Linux operating system. Then, he publicized the source code on the Internet and asked other developers to contribute it (Learmonth 1997). The software is then released under a license that allows the community to both examine the source code and use the software. Making software publically available on the Internet provides developers from all around the world with the opportunity to contribute to the project by adding to and improving the code, reporting and resolving defects, suggesting and implementing software features, providing feedback, testing and documenting the software, and providing community support. In response to such feedbacks, the core project developers integrate the changes into the software and release a new version.

2.5 OSS Project Lifecycle

The life cycle of software is a period of time starting from the conception of the application until the moment that the software no longer operates the functions it is supposed to perform. The lifecycle of the conventional CSS development projects is composed of sequential phases from requirement elicitation to software maintenance. The most generic life cycle for a typical traditional CSS project has four phases of planning, analysis, design, and implementation (Fitzgerald 2006). OSS projects do not follow such sequential, rigid steps. Rather, an OSS project evolves through various development phases as it moves towards a mature application. A typical OSS project passes through various phases of: (1) planning, (2) pre-alpha, (3) alpha, (4) beta, (5) stable, and (6) mature respectively. These phases are called "development status". In what follows, each development status is described in the Glossary section at the end of the chapter (some of the definitions are adopted from Rothfuss 2002). It should be noted that these definitions are for OSS projects hosted in Sourceforge.net, the major OSS host in the world. These definitions may not completely be identical for other OSS.

2.6 OSS Success

Simply put, success is defined as the achievement of something that is desired (Midha, 2007). Measuring success for OSS can be difficult because it is subjective. Crowston et al. (2006) states "… these measures [OSS success measures] are hard to define for regular I/S [closed source software] projects and doubly hard for FLOSS [Free/Libre OSS] projects, because of the problems defining the intended user base and expected outcomes".

That is why there are different perspectives in the literature on OSS success.

It has been observed that more than 80% of OSS projects become abandoned (Colazo & Fang 2009; Chengalur-Smith & Sidorova 2003). This is because they cannot maintain a healthy level of activity or cannot attract the participation of, and contributions from, individual developers (Fang & Neufeld 2009; Colazo & Fang 2009). On the other hand, there are many successful examples of open source projects that have achieved a huge success in the market. Mozilla Firefox, Apache, Open office and Linux operating system are examples of such projects.

3. RESEARCH METHOD

This paper employed a literature survey approached in which we searched certain key words on variety of academic journals in the field of Information Systems (IS) and Information Technology (IT). Depending on the search services offered by the search engine, the titles, abstracts, keywords, and in some cases full text of the journal articles and conference proceedings in the included electronic databases were searched using the following search terms:

("Open source software" OR "OSS" OR "Open
    source project")
AND
("Success" OR "Failure")

We then reviewed the publications extracted (e.g. journal papers, conference proceedings, and dissertations) and filtered based on reading their titles, abstracts, or full text. This process resulted in a final list of papers which explored antecedents to OSS projects' success. Having reviewed the extracted papers, we identified factors affecting Oss success. In order to make our analysis more informative, we next sought to categorize them into meaningful clusters. Thus, we went through our source of studies in the literature, and looked for appropriate labels for each set of factors. It helped us to bundle most of the factors.

4. RESULTS

We identified 3 main categories, including project traits, product traits, and network structure. Figure 1 shows our taxonomy of antecedents to success in OSS projects. As mentioned, we uncovered that in the existing literature, there were investigations of three broad categories of antecedent to OSS success. One is project traits, such as project topic, programming language, project audience and licence restrictiveness (Stewart et al. 2006; Subramaniam et al. 2009; Crowston & Scozzi 2002). Another category is product traits, such as software modularity, complexity, degree of decomposition, degree of coupling and software quality (Liu 2008; Colazo 2007; Midha 2007). The third category includes factors that are related

to network structure, such as the structure within which core developers collaborate, core/periphery fitness and network embeddedness (Grewal et al. 2006; Y. Long 2006). In what follows, each category of factors will be briefly introduced.

4.1 Project Traits

This category incorporates various traits of the project. Some of the factors in this category are the ones which are defined by project initiators (e.g. programming language, project topic or project audience), and the others relate to the resources that the project possesses (e.g. stock of developers or having highly-ranked administrators).

The factors in this category whose impact on OSS project success have been examined in the current literature include (but are not limited to) the following: Project type: the type of the project (e.g. application development tool); Project topic: OSS repositories (e.g. Sourceforge) classify OSS projects into different topic categories (e.g. Graphics);

Figure 1. Classification of OSS success factors in the literature

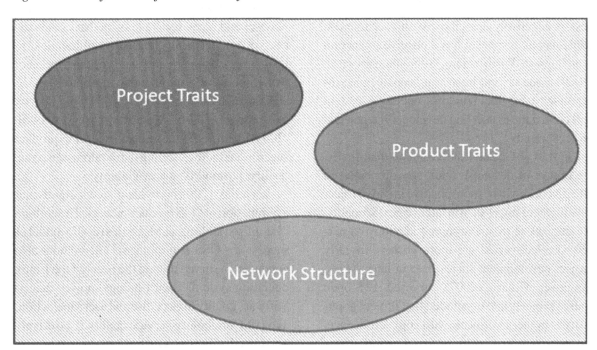

Licence: shows which of the open source licences the project is holding; Sponsorship: whether the project is sponsored by a company; Using common programming languages: whether the project uses a common programming language (e.g. "C"); Audience: whether the project is user-targeted or developer-targeted; Project lifespan: how long has the project existed; Number of developers: the number of developers registered on a project's website; Number of administrators: the number of people who manage the project; Administrator rank: the rank of a project's administrators as ranked by their peers; and Developers' experience: how experienced the project developers are in terms of the time span they have been writing programs.

Prior research on the impact of project traits on OSS success has resulted in interesting findings. One of the first attempts in this regard was the research by Crowston & Scozzi (2002) in which the authors showed that using more common programming languages, having more developers and more highly-ranked or top-rated project administrators influence project success defined by activity, development status and use. Stewart et al. (2006) demonstrated that licence restrictiveness is negatively associated with user interest, while having a sponsor has a positive impact on user interest. Furthermore, Subramaniam et al. (2009) made several interesting conclusions; for example, using the Windows operating system will contribute to user and developer interest and project activity.

Stewart & Gosain (2006b) found that, firstly, the impact of developer team size on perceived effectiveness will be more positive in early project development stages than in later stages. Secondly, the impacts of trust and shared ideology on perceived effectiveness are more positive in early project development stages than in later stages. Moreover, Colazo (2007) surveyed 121 open source projects and concluded that project popularity is higher in projects with copy left licence.

4.2 Product Traits

This category refers to software traits which have been studied to examine their impact on OSS success. The factors in this category whose impact on OSS project success have been examined in the current literature include (but are not limited to): Software modularity (Conley 2008; Midha 2007); Software complexity (Midha et al. 2010; Liu 2008); Degree of decomposition (Liu 2008); Degree of coupling (Liu 2008); and Software quality (Lee et al. 2009; Fang & Colazo 2010; Colazo 2007; Conley 2008). In what follows, some key findings from papers in this category are provided.

Fang & Colazo (2010) demonstrated that software complexity is positively associated with the number of defects in the software. Midha et al. (2010) found that the cognitive complexity of software is positively associated with the probability of having defects in the source code. The authors also concluded that the cognitive complexity of software negatively relates to developers' contribution to the project. Further, Liu (2008) uncovered that the degree of product coupling is negatively related to product quality.

Conley (2008) examined 203 OSS product releases and made the conclusion that certain aspects of product quality (e.g. software complexity) influence software quality, and certain aspects of work process (e.g. number of contributors) mediates the relationship between product modularity and product quality. Moreover, Crowston et al. (2003) identified some indicators for OSS product success, including meeting the requirements, code quality, portability and availability.

Lee et al. (2009) provide a recent significant examination of OSS product success. The authors customised DeLone & McLean's (2003) model of success for OSS environment. The authors also conducted a survey among the users of the Linux operating system. Their findings showed that (i) Software quality impacts use and user satisfaction, and (ii) Community service quality is positively associated with user satisfaction.

4.3 Network Structure

A pile of network structure related factors have been examined in the literature for their impact on OSS success. Researchers working on this area usually apply network analysis of OSS projects through project mailing lists, forums and so forth. The factors in this category whose influence on OSS project success have been investigated in the current literature include (but are not limited to): Collaboration structure of core developers (Colazo 2007); Centrality (Liu 2008); Core/periphery fitness (Y. Long 2006); Network embeddedness (Grewal et al. 2006); Community level structure (Colazo 2007); and Structural holes (Liu 2008). The following will present some key results from studies in this category.

Liu (2008) found that developer team centrality is positively related to product success. Another key finding of Liu (2008) was that the average number of structural holes spanned by developers is positively associated with product quality. Grewal et al. (2006) introduced "OSS project technical success" and discovered that some aspects of network embeddedness have powerful but subtle effects on project success. Furthermore, Colazo (2007) surveyed 121 OSS projects and concluded that project popularity is less in the projects with higher boundary spanning activities. Another key finding of Colazo (2007) was that boundary spanning activity negatively impacts product quality.

Y. Long (2006) is another interesting study that took network structure into account and made the following important conclusions: (i) network structure (centralisation and core/periphery fitness) positively impacts project performance; (ii) network structure (centralisation and core/periphery fitness) is positively associated with quantity of knowledge sharing; and (iii) quantity of knowledge sharing mediates the relationship between network structure (centralisation and core/periphery fitness) and project performance.

5. CONCLUSION

This paper conducted a literature survey and identified that in the extant literature and found that there are examinations of three broad categories of antecedents to OSS project success in the literature. One is product traits, such as software modularity, complexity, degree of decomposition, degree of coupling and software quality (Liu 2008; Colazo 2007; Midha 2007). The second category includes factors that relate to network structure, such as the structure within which core developers collaborate, core/periphery fitness and network embeddedness (Grewal et al. 2006; Y. Long 2006). Another category is project traits, such as project topic, sponsorship, project audience and licence restrictiveness (Stewart et al. 2006; Subramaniam et al. 2009; Crowston & Scozzi 2002).

REFERENCES

Carillo, K. & Okoli, chitu. (2008). The Open Source Movement: A Revolution In Software Development. *Journal of Computer Information Systems*, *49*(2), 1–9.

Chengalur-Smith, S., & Sidorova, A. (2003). *Survival of open-source projects: A population ecology perspective*. Paper presented at the 24th International Conference of Information Systems. Atlanta, GA.

Colazo, J. (2007). *Innovation success: An empirical study of software development projects in the context of the open source paradigm*. The University of Western Ontario.

Colazo, J., & Fang, Y. (2009). Impact of license choice on Open Source Software development activity. *Journal of the American Society for Information Science and Technology*, *60*(5), 997–1011. doi:10.1002/asi.21039

Crowston, K., Annabi, H., & Howison, J. (2003). *Defining open source software project success.* Paper presented at the 24th International Conference on Information Systems. Seattle, WA.

Crowston, K., Howison, J., & Annabi, H. (2006). Information systems success in free and open source software development: Theory and measures. *Software Process Improvement and Practice, 11*(2), 123–148. doi:10.1002/spip.259

Crowston, K., & Scozzi, B. (2002). Open source software projects as virtual organisations: Competency rallying for software development. *IEE Software Proceedings, 149*(1), 3–17. doi:10.1049/ip-sen:20020197

Davis, F. D., Bagozzi, R. P., & Warshaw, P. R. (1989). User Acceptance of Computer Technology: A Comparison of Two Theoretical Models. *Management Science, 35*(8), 982–1003. doi:10.1287/mnsc.35.8.982

DeLone, W. H., & McLean, E. R. (2003). The DeLone and McLean Model of Information Systems Success: A Ten-Year Update. *Journal of Management Information Systems, 19*(4), 9–30.

Fang, Y., & Neufeld, D. (2009). Understanding Sustained Participation in Open Source Software Projects. *Journal of Management Information Systems, 25*(4), 9–50. doi:10.2753/MIS0742-1222250401

Feller, J. et al. (2005). *Perspectives on Free and Open Source Software.* Cambridge, MA: MIT Press.

Fitzgerald, B. (2006). The transformation of open source software. *Management Information Systems Quarterly, 30*(3), 587–598.

Grewal, R., Lilien, G. L., & Mallapragada, G. (2006). Location, location, location: How network embeddedness affects project success in open source systems. *Management Science, 52*(7), 1043–1056. doi:10.1287/mnsc.1060.0550

Haenlein, M., & Kaplan, A. M. (2004). A Beginner's Guide to Partial LeastSquares Analysis. *Understanding Statistics, 3*(4), 283–297. doi:10.1207/s15328031us0304_4

Koch, S., & Schneider, G. (2002). Effort, cooperation and co-ordination in an open source software project: GNOME. *Information Systems Journal, 12*(1), 27–42. doi:10.1046/j.1365-2575.2002.00110.x

Learmonth, M. (1997). *Giving It All Away.* Available at: http://metroactive.com /papers/metro/05.08.97/cover/linus-9719.html

Liu, X. (2008). *Design architecture, developer networks and performance of open source software projects.* Boston: Boston University.

Long, J. (2004). *Understanding the creation and adoption of information technology innovations: The case of Open Source software development and the diffusion of mobile commerce.* The University of Texas at Austin.

Long, J. (2006). Understanding the Role of Core Developers in Open Source Software Development. *Journal of Information, Information Technology, and Organizations, 1*, 75–85.

Loshin, P. (2005). Something for Everyone! Open Source Isn't Just For Linux Users. *Computer Power User, 5*(5), 66–71.

Midha, V. (2007). *Antecedent to the success of open source software.* The University of North Carolina at Greensboro.

Midha, V. et al. (2010). Improving Open Source Software Maintenance. *Journal of Computer Information Systems, 50*(3), 81–90.

Mockus, A., Fielding, R. T., & Herbsleb, J. D. (2002). Two case studies of open source software development: Apache and Mozilla. *ACM Transactions on Software Engineering and Methodology, 11*(3), 309–346. doi:10.1145/567793.567795

Moody, G. (2002). *Rebel code: Linux and the open source revolution*. London: Penguin.

Netcraft. (2007, February). *Web Server Survey*. Available at: http://news.netcraft.com/archives/web_server_survey.Html

Open Source Initiative. (2005). Available at http://www.opensource.org

Paulson, J. W., Succi, G., & Eberlein, A. (2004). An Empirical Study of Open-Source and Closed-Source Software Products. *IEEE Transactions on Software Engineering*, 30(4), 246–256. doi:10.1109/TSE.2004.1274044

Qureshi, I., & Fang, Y. (2011). Socialization in Open Source Software Projects: A Growth Mixture Modeling Approach. *Organizational Research Methods*, 14(1), 208–238. doi:10.1177/1094428110375002

Raymond, E. S. (1999). The Cathedral and the Bazaar. *First Monday*, 3(3).

Raymond, E. S. (2001). *The Cathedral and the Bazaar: Musings on Linux and Open Source by an Accidental Revolutionary* (Rev. ed.). Sebastopol, CA: O'Reilly.

Rehman, R. U. (2006). *Factors that contribute to open source software project success*. (Master thesis). Carleton University.

Rothfuss, G. J. A. (2002). *A Framework for Open Source Projects*. (M.S. Thesis). University of Zurich.

Schadler, T. (2004). *Open Source Moves into the Mainstream*. Cambridge, MA: Forrester Research.

Schermelleh-Engel, K., Moosbrugger, H., & Müller, H. (2003). Evaluating the Fit of Structural Equation Models: Tests of Significance and Descriptive Goodness-of-Fit Measures. *Methods of Psychological Research*, 8(2), 23–74.

Schweik, C., & Semenov, A. (2003). The Institutional Design of Open Source Programming: Implications for Addressing Complex Public Policy and Management Problems. *First Monday*, 8(1). doi:10.5210/fm.v8i1.1019

Sen, R. (2007). A Strategic Analysis of Competition Between Open Source and Proprietary Software. *Journal of Management Information Systems*, 24(1), 233–257. doi:10.2753/MIS0742-1222240107

Stewart, K. J., Ammeter, A. P., & Maruping, L. M. (2006). Impacts of License Choice and Organizational Sponsorship on User Interest and Development Activity in Open Source Software Projects. *Information Systems Research*, 17(2), 126–144. doi:10.1287/isre.1060.0082

Stewart, K. J., & Gosain, S. (2006). The impact of ideology on effectiveness in open source software development teams. *Management Information Systems Quarterly*, 30(2), 291–314.

Subramaniam, C., Sen, R., & Nelson, M. L. (2009). Determinants of open source software project success: A longitudinal study. *Decision Support Systems*, 46(2), 576–585. doi:10.1016/j.dss.2008.10.005

Tirole, J., & Lerner, J. (2002). Some Simple Economics of Open Source. *The Journal of Industrial Economics*, 50(2), 197–234.

Tirole, J., & Lerner, J. (2005). The Scope of Open Source Licensing. *Journal of Law Economics and Organization*, 21(1), 20–56. doi:10.1093/jleo/ewi002

Uchida, S. et al. (2005). Software analysis by code clones in open source software. *Journal of Computer Information Systems*, 45(3), 1–11.

KEY TERMS AND DEFINITIONS

Alpha Development Status: The source code works at least some of the time, and starts to form. The developers expand the functionality of the application by adding software features and test the intended functionality. As soon as the project starts to publish serious releases of the application, the OSS project enters the beta phase.

Beta Development Status: In the phases anterior to beta (planning, pre-alpha, and alpha), the project team's focus is on designing, constructing, and basic testing of the planned functionality. In the beta, the project begins to release serious versions of the application. In the beta stage, the source code retains faults that are gradually removed leading to a more reliable software. In this stage, the project continues to receive features suggests from users.

Mature Development Status: Little or no development happens because the software application performs its intended functionality reliably. If any change is deemed to apply, the project team do it with caution. The OSS project might stay in the mature phase for several years before it becomes obsolete, or is replaced by a better application.

Open Source Software: Utilising novel intellectual property laws, a new software development and distribution paradigm has emerged over last two decades, which in February 1998 was termed open source software development (Midha 2007). Unlike proprietary software in which the program's source code is a trade secret and is protected by law, in OSS the source code is publicly available for anyone who would like to see it. OSS products are developed under an open source licence that permits their users to observe, modify and redistribute the program's source code (Open Source Initiative 2005).

Planning Development Status: The project is just an idea and no source code has been written. Immediately after a source code is committed, the project gets into the pre-alpha phase.

Pre-Alpha: The project team releases a preliminary code, but the source code does not compile or run. It is hard for the users to understand the meaning of the source code. Promptly after the source code finds its eventual direction, the OSS project enters alpha phase.

Stable Development Status: By improving the quality of the software, the project enters from beta phase to stable phase. In this stage, the remaining software defects are weeded out and the missing features are incorporated. If no significant alternation occurs over a long period of time, the OSS project moves into the mature phase. It should be noted that in Sourceforge.net, there is no clear boundary between beta and stable phases. It is a subjective decision to choose between these two because project development status is set by project administrators and they have different perception of project quality. However, it is commonly agreed that the majority of development activities happen in beta and stable phases of an OSS project.

Section 2
User–Centered Design

Chapter 6
Creating Effective Communication among User-Centered Technology Design Groups

Laura B. Dahl
University of Utah, USA

ABSTRACT

The user-centered design process among U.S. companies is commonly carried out by design teams. Groups of designers are commonly unable to create high quality work due to the need to first work out several issues. These issues include needing to get to know one another's capabilities while also learning how to effectively communicate through the many difficult decisions and deadlines common to software and Web design projects. This chapter describes the communication research that illuminates the process that groups go through before they can achieve high-quality results.

INTRODUCTION

The user-centered design process among U.S. companies is commonly accomplished as a team project. Technology design and development has become so complex that multiple individuals are needed to meet the needs of engineering, graphics, and user-centered design. For example, one enterprise website update might require several engineers who each specialize in one of many potential coding languages. Several user-centered design specialists might also be required, including one to deal with the information architecture and another who researches and creates effective user experience designs. Because many user-centered technology projects involve collaboration and cooperation of a group of experts, each team much learn to work together by communicating effectively.

Such a diverse group of people needs to devote time and energy in order to become an effective team. Research from small group communication and technology education can help explain the process and difficulties that may arise before a group becomes effective enough to create high quality output. This research illuminates the idea

DOI: 10.4018/978-1-4666-6485-2.ch006

that effective user-centered design is much more complex than simply putting experts together. Instead, effective teamwork requires time and development of several communication behaviors, including identity formation, helping, negotiating, and group process. This chapter will describe research relevant to technology design teams as they attempt to navigate the opportunities and challenges that face them as they meet the needs and expectations given them.

The Nature of Communication

The approach to communication for this chapter is one that takes into account the context in which it takes place. This is a stance where one must know who the speaker and the hearer are and when and where the communication takes place. This idea is unlike the ways people make contact over the telephone, or radio and television. This view emphasizes the channels for transmitting and receiving messages. However, I am using a description of communication that also means interaction, and communication and interaction are used interchangeably in this chapter.

When a speaker utters a phrase that has some message value and does so in a particular social situation and at a point in the stream of a conversation, the speaker is both communicating and interacting (Ellis & Fisher, 1994). She is communicating because the words carry meaning and content and interacting because the meanings function to express social relationships. It is impossible to one during group communication without the other.

Yet, design team members have their autonomy and often choose to engage in some communication behaviors and not in others during certain situations. Each member is capable of free will and choice. This choice is not random; instead, each member chooses to behave on what is considered appropriate in a given situation. Often, choice to participate is limited in the sense that many alternatives are eliminated based on past

exchanges. Team members may not be aware of these constraints, but they submit to them anyway. For example, they speak in a way common to the design team using the specific rules of syntax and meaning that conforms to those rules, even though they may not be aware of the rules that constrain their choices.

Because members of a design team are professionals wishing to find success in their work, they often honor the constraints placed upon their communicative acts. Design team managers would be wise to consider this reality, and should create a space of open and honest communication that allows for a developing interaction that promotes creativity.

HISTORY OF COMMUNICATION RESEARCH ON TEAM PROCESS

Groups go through stages of development and abilities before they can make effective decisions and accomplish high quality tasks. Communication scholars have long studied the characteristics involved with successful group work. Much of this work was in line with a positivist viewpoint emphasizing control and precision while favoring the laboratory experiment over naturalistic data collection strategies. However, this important research did find that group work and collaboration does not come easy. Rather, it requires time and development of several communication behaviors before high quality decisions and task outcomes become apparent.

Group process is the term used to describe the stages that teams go through before achieving high quality output. Several early pundits identified stages of group development from the vast small group communication research during the first half of the twentieth century. For example, Charrier (1974), an employee of Proctor and Gamble, wrote a summary of group development based on earlier laboratory work. The original document was written to help group managers at his company better understand the dynamics of teamwork. Tuckman (1965; 1977) used a meta-analytical method to contrast and combine results from the previous thirty years of controlled, laboratory studies of small groups. Both Charrier and Tuckman described similar and distinct stages that groups must go through in a linear fashion to achieve maximum effectiveness, including (1) formation and orientation (politeness), (2) catharsis and learning how to work together (hostility and confrontation), (3) normalizing (focus, action, and testing), (4) performing (purposive and efficient), and (5) adjourning. Although this work helped to explain what happens within teams, it viewed group process as simple, isolated, and static.

In contrast to the linear sequence models, McGrath (1991) articulated a theory of groups based on years of his own and colleagues' empirical research. This research was a response to the laboratory-driven studies that assumed groups exist in isolation, while ignoring the physical, temporal, and social context of the environment. He argued that groups are embedded within larger social communities, organization, neighborhoods, and departments. Rarely do these groups work on simple tasks; instead, he argued that most groups are engaged in tasks and goal directed activities that often result in project completion. By observing short-term groups in their social context, he determined that groups engage in four modes of group activity, including inception, technical problem solving, conflict resolution, and project completion. These modes are potential, not required, forms of activity and groups are always involved in one or another of these modes. For example, the modes of inception and completion are involved in all group goals and tasks, but technical problem solving and conflict resolution may or may not be necessary for any specific group activity.

Similarly, Poole et al.'s (Poole, 1996; Poole & Roth, 1989) group process model was a response to the idea that group decisions develop in a single, universal set of stages. Instead, groups may evolve along any of several alternative sequences. Consistent through all these studies was the observation of short-term, face-to-face groups embedded within their social context during decision tasks. The researchers carefully devised complex tasks, such as "formulating federal regulatory rules to setting dormitory policies to analyzing a management case study" (Poole et al., 1993). The theoretical construct that developed out of several years of researching short-term decision-making groups was named the Multiple-Sequence Model of Group Development. This modern and widely accepted model argues that groups work concurrently on three interlocking activity tracks that are necessary for team development: (1) task-process activity (used to manage the task), (2) relational activities (used to manage interpersonal relationships), and (3) topical focus (issues of concern to a group). A group may be working primarily on one of these activity tracks at any given time, and group life is sometimes interrupted by "breakpoints" or changes in conversation that mark the shift to a new track. However an individual design team communicates, all tracks, including relationship building, are necessary to the success of a team. Poole's model is widely accepted and helps to explain the process that groups go through before they can achieve high quality success. More recent research has described other factors that influence group process including changing group membership, learning how to communicate effectively, and even conflict.

CONTEMPORARY RESEARCH INTO GROUP PROCESS

New Groups

Groups are new when either first formed or when a new member joins. These groups begin a phase characterized by lack of unity and unfamiliarity with each member's skills and potential to contribute. Although some members may already be familiar with others' skills and expertise, not all members are aware of the knowledge, norms, and performance expectations of a group (D. M. Brown, 2013). Each member comes with their own preconceived ideas and norms, and this exhibits as individualism that is contrary to the goals and needs of the group. This period is usually marked by introductions and small talk, so it takes time for people in a group to develop relationships that contribute to each member's ability to have enough empathy and rapport to get through negotiations and effective decision making for high quality output. At this point, decision-making and task output is only as good as the best group member.

Key to creating a shared meaning for the group is communication behaviors that promote good interpersonal relationships (Barge, 1996). For example, self-disclosure—sharing of personal information—is critical at this stage for learning about one another. The communication acts that people use during this stage quickly become the norms by which groups operate, so open sharing and discussion are essential to the future success. An effective tool for making norms and expectations explicit is to develop a team charter or set of goals. Such a tool is a first step in setting group expectations and deadlines. Hillier (2012) described the use of written goals as a tool for conflict resolution. For example, a group member attempting to mediate an awkward conversation may begin by stating, "we talked about this in the charter and all agreed that…" This early agreement can also act as an instrument throughout the life of the group as it develops new norms to ensure appropriate team functioning.

Developing Groups

Group Identity

Critical to getting past the initial stage and through the life of a group is continued communication for building and maintaining relationships, discussing relevant project topics, and accomplishing tasks (Barge, 1996; Hirokawa & Poole, 1996). Yet, effective collaboration among design teams only occurs once each member identifies with his/her group (Wenger, 1998; Wenger, McDermott, & Snyder, 2002). Group identification is defined by in-group favoritism and discrimination against out-groups (Tajfel & Turner, 1986). Design team members identify with the group when they see themselves as belonging to the same social category, share some emotional involvement, and achieve some consensus about the team and their membership in it. Yet, a shared social identity often develops through the individuality and heterogeneity of group members (Postmes, Spears, Lee, & Novak, 2005). For example, the wide variety of backgrounds and skills within a design team has the potential to develop a strong solidarity.

Triandis (1995) reported group identity could be influenced by diverse cultures, due to unique communication styles. Such disparate social patterns can impact the communication behaviors leading toward group identity. Because many software and Web design teams are now international and multicultural, it is important to understand that members may come to a group with different understandings of how to communicate effectively. For example, the social patterns of individualism and collectivism regard social harmony differently. Individualism is characterized by loosely linked individuals who view themselves as independent of collectives and who give priority to their own goals over others. Collectivism is a social pattern consisting of closely linked individuals who see themselves as part of one or more collectives (work group, family, tribe, nation).

Comparatively, members of collective cultures view themselves with a "we" identity, while those in an individualistic culture draw on an "I" identity. Members of collectivistic cultures are concerned with maintaining relational harmony, which can sometimes lead to groupthink. Such a problem state occurs when a group makes faulty decisions in an attempt to maintain cohesiveness. Janis (1971) and Rosander (1998) argue that such groups do take advantage of the mental efficiency of many and fail to reality test. In contrast, members of individualistic cultures emphasize self-realization and individuality (Hirokawa, 2003), often leading to conflict and difficulty in collaborative agreement. Individualism and collectivism are two uncommon extremes when looking at the complete makeup of many design teams. Although members can differ in their incoming social patterns, over time a group develops its own social norms through relationship building and discussion about tasks (Poole & DeSanctis, 1989). The resulting group identity and cohesion can mitigate the problems associated with individualism and collectivism.

Although it is clear through the literature and group research that group identity is an important component of effective communication, group identity in professional design groups may not appear easily or be a priority. Further research is needed of real groups to ascertain how identity plays a role in working task completion and decision making. However, continued and prolong communication often promotes group identity, and the following sections describe behaviors that often helps individuals identify with group members.

Continued and Prolonged Communication Develops Group Identity

According to Johnson et al. (1991), five overarching elements promote coordinated efforts among members to develop group identity: individual accountability, frequent interaction, social skills, group processing discussion, and positive interdependence.

Individual Accountability

Individual accountability is defined as both the individual and other group members are aware of a member's performance toward a task. The purpose of cooperative groups is to make each member stronger, and accountability is the key

to ensuring that all group members are, in fact, strengthened.

Individual accountability results in members knowing they cannot "free loaf" on the work of others. Lack of follow through can be an issue when it is difficult to identify each members' offered work, when contributions are redundant, and when individuals do not feel responsible for the final outcome (Whitworth & Biddle, 2007). Instead, each member should be assigned a task and become accountable to its completion, as is common within most design teams. This personal responsibility involves contributing his or her efforts toward accomplishing the group's goals and helping other group members do likewise. The greater the cohesion and group identity among a design team, the more members will feel personally responsible for contributing their efforts toward accomplishing the collective goals.

Whitworth and Biddle (2007) interviewed 22 individuals on software design teams about their experience collaborating with Agile practices. They found that by regularly communicating as a group to assign small chunks of action, design teams developed a high level of social support and accountability. Such is the result of constant feedback to individuals through daily and weekly team meetings, where awareness of group activity and commitment to shared goals is communicated. Interviewees viewed sharing knowledge and receiving feedback mutually as common knowledge, which could then be used as a basis for action that is approved by the entire team.

Consequences within these cohesive teams for poor quality or incomplete work were highly social rather than disciplinary. Instead, accountability was seen to result from frequent questioning or joking about individual action (or inaction) during a clear and public expression of the need to follow through on the task. Sometimes, members expressed disappointment or disapproval in front of the group, but when responses were elicited that explained difficulties or problems completing a task, the team replied with understanding and support. Such group acceptance and awareness resulted in an increased sense of individual responsibility and self-worth regarding project assignments.

Positive Interdependence

Positive interdependence involves the collective feeling of "we" instead of "me." Group members have to know that they either sink or swim together. It is positive interdependence that requires group members to work together to accomplish something beyond individual success. Once it is well understood, interdependence highlights that each group member's efforts are required and indispensable, while each person has a unique contribution to make because of his or her own unique knowledge and resources.

Yet, interdependence is a matter of trust among design team members. Trust is characterized by the belief that colleagues within the team possess the knowledge, confidence, and integrity to complete their assigned tasks. This trust is enhanced among professional teams when members help each other (Mayer & Davis, 1995). Conversely, trust declines when individuals see others on the team not fulfilling their obligations or see them as incongruent to accepted norms (Piccoli & Ives, 2003).

McHugh et al. (2012) observed and documented three software design teams using highly collaborative practice. Over six-months, they interviewed and observed the practices of designers, business analysts, developers, scrum masters, product owners, and quality assurance personnel. Each team held a daily "standup" meeting in which transparency and visibility was provided on the day-to-day task progression. Individual accountability manifested through reporting of task advancement and potential delays. These reviews and summaries provided the transparency and visibility needed to quickly seek clarification when delays occurred. Immediate discussion was then carried out to improve work processes. All these communicative behaviors resulted in trust among their members; trust was augmented by an increase in transparency, accountability, communication, knowledge sharing, and feedback.

Regular and Frequent Interaction Practices

The discipline of cooperation includes ensuring that group members meet to work together to discuss tasks and promote each other's success. Collaborative design practices, such as those found in Agile teams, promote regular planned and unplanned interactions. To achieve group identity, members need to do real work together, while interacting and discussing the activities. Suck "promotive interaction" exists when people encourage and facilitate each other's attempts to complete tasks meant to meet group goals. Through promoting each other's success, group members build a personal support system for one another. Johnson et al. (1991) recommended three steps to encourage and promote this interaction among defined groups: (1) scheduled time for the group to meet, (2) highlight interdependence that requires members to work together to achieve the group's goals, and (3) promote encouragement and facilitation of each other's efforts.

Ultimately, promotive interaction over long-term may have greatest effect on high-quality outcomes. Enacting positive interdependence powerfully influences efforts to achieve, caring and committed relationships, and social competence. Such promotive interaction is characterized by members providing each other with efficient and effective help and assistance, while doing the varied work of exchanging needed resources, discussing information efficiently and effectively, providing each other with feedback to improve subsequent performance, challenging one another's conclusions and reasoning to promote higher-quality decision-making, and being motivated to strive for mutual benefit. Groups developing an identity do real work together.

Brown, Lindgaard, and Robert (2011) studied collaborative events and interaction designers and developers at four companies. All the design teams were jointly motivated by project goals and project-specific outcomes. Collaborative work and interactions served to clarify project aims; it regularly shifted and realigned individual activity, because it was intertwined with other team members. For example, design ideas were presented that enhanced, eliminated, or constrained something from the software interface. Questions would then be posed that reflected on or changed how a design idea might be an assumption, gap, or capability.

Social Skills Development

In cooperative design teams, members are required to successfully discuss subject matter while also using interpersonal and small group skills required to function as part of a group. When good teamwork skills are not used, task work will tend to be substandard. However, better teamwork skills usually result in higher quality and quantity of project outcomes. Several communication behaviors are characteristic of high quality teamwork skills and should be practiced and used as design teams work together. These skills generally include communication behaviors including functioning, formulating and fermenting.

- **Functioning**: Functioning skills are those needed to manage the group's activities and completing the task and maintaining effective working relationships. All members need to be able to share their ideas and materials. Individuals need to ask questions to get others to share their ideas and thinking processes. By asking for facts and reasoning, group members can then understand, discuss, and correct each other's thinking. Continued discussion should in-

clude helping the group move ahead rather than staying stalled for lack of direction. All members should be encouraged to participate. For example, other members can be asked to share what they are thinking or what their ideas are, because individuals begin to feel that their ideas are valued. Furthermore, essential to building relationships among design team members is the expressing of support and acceptance. Support can be expressed both verbally and nonverbally. Nonverbal support begins as eye contact, nodding, and a look of interest. Verbal support could include praising and seeking others' ideas and conclusions.

- **Formulating**: Formulating skills are those necessary for providing the conceptual structures needed to build deeper levels of understanding and stimulating the use of higher quality reasoning strategies. These skills include: summarizing out loud what has been discussed, seeking accuracy by asking for clarifications and pointing out relevant ideas or facts, and asking that all members vocalize their implicit reasoning processes thereby making ideas and information open to correction and discussion.

- **Fermenting**: Fermenting skills are those needed to stimulate reconceptualization of ideas, cognitive conflicts, the search for more information, and communication of the rationale behind one's conclusions. These skills are aimed at causing group members to dig deeper into the material, and they sometimes involve challenging other group members by criticizing ideas while communicating respect for them.

Design teams can think more divergently about an issue by finding out how other members think about it. Once all opinions are compared and contrasted, ideas can be synthesized and integrated into one position that everyone can agree on. This step can sometimes involve conflict, yet continued discussion and negotiation can move members beyond disagreement to the state of agreement. As members understand that argument does not equate with conflict, they may feel comfortable negotiating and disagreeing with other group members. Such negotiation has the potential to create high-quality decisions critical for user-centered design.

Because technology creation groups are often characterized by diverse experts, tasks are usually divided according to expertise. This results in varying viewpoints that require negotiation. Such negotiation will not become effective until a group has developed to the point where members understand how to work through difficult communication. As a group works towards consensus, members of differing opinions can be asked to justify their stance based on facts and reasoning. Any valid ideas should be valued and considered when synthesizing and making final decisions. For example, Whitworth (2008) interviewed members of highly collaborative software development teams who exhibited well-developed social skills enabling them to work together better. She found that these teams were often associated with a positive collaborative climate that can contribute to high performance. Daily meetings among the teams gave a constant immersion and engagement of members, as well as the development of norms and rituals surrounding team activity. Such regular interaction encouraged members to feel closer to the project team and identify with it. This identification increased feelings of belonging, security, comfort, and willingness to cooperate in the team. Such feelings create a safe place for members to practice their functional, formulating, and fermenting skills. For instance, several fermenting skills were evident when daily meetings had a mediating and balancing effect on project activity. Requests for task completion were negotiated regarding feasibility and time constraints during team discussion involved realistic goal setting.

Group Decision Making

Ellis and Fisher (1994) described a heuristic for group decision making based on a standard set of steps meant to create a space of good decision making. This prescriptive decision making is based on the "ideal" process, based on a rational approach to problem solving. The steps in this model are useful and can be applied in many situations.

Generating Ideas

Design is largely a difficult and messy interaction (Cooper & Cronin, 2007). Designers are often asked to imagine and define something that has never been seen before, while creating technology on an ambition timeline. Each team must develop a sophisticated understanding of complexity, while balancing priorities and understanding limitations and opportunities. As a design team faces the need to find solutions is this stressful space, it may be even more critical to follow a prescriptive method for decision making.

All groups must first generate information and ideas that members can use. It is a mistake to think that ideas and creativity can simply emerge. Each design group must make a concentrated effort to increase its supply of useable information.

Comparative Analysis

This technique is meant to draw inspiration from other technology designs. The idea here is not to copy another design in such a way that can lead to copyright infringement. Instead, a comparative analysis is meant to make comparisons across many different resources while each gives inspiration that adds to creativity.

To effectively do a comparative analysis, each team member should call out inspiration from another source, even if it is the smallest idea. One group member should be responsible for recording the ideas on a large and visible pad. After members have contributed many ideas, the group should go back to the list and begin paring it down and evaluating how these new ideas can contribute to the design.

Brainstorming

This technique is meant to stimulate the group's creativity, while eliminating some of the communicative constraints, especially criticism and evaluation. The essential technique for brainstorming is to disallow any criticism or evaluation of an idea presented by any group member, until the session's conclusion. This is crucial during brainstorming because fear of criticism often stifles creativity. As group members realize they will not be criticized for their ideas, they often relax and increase in ideas as they begin to flow forth.

The group should record every idea so it is available to everyone. Writing the ideas on a large pad or whiteboard makes this feasible. Do not spend too much time on brainstorming for ideas. A few hours should be sufficient for getting all they ideas out to the open. If you find your ideas getting repetitious, it is a good idea to stop. After group members have produced many ideas, they can return to the list and begin paring it down to the best ideas, while applying critical thinking techniques so as to eliminate weak or unworkable ideas and focus on the best ones.

Decision Making Strategies

After a group generates ideas and information, it must begin making decisions. Although the decision making approach described here is no guarantee to quality decisions, using an orderly approach to decision making usually improves the likelihood the group will be successful (Hirokawa & Poole, 1996). The model described here is the Rational Reflection Model (Siebold, 1992), based in part on Dewey's (1916) reflective model but containing major additions from current research.

In the Rational Reflection approach, design group members work through a series of steps designed to help them reflect on dimensions of a problem in a rational manner. The group is meant to proceed through each step and communication is limited to characteristics of the problem under consideration.

Define and limit the problem: The group begins by defining and setting boundaries on the problem. By determining the problem's scope early on, the group is better able to also limit the discussion required for finding a final solution. Ideally, each member of the group should have input and agree upon what the problem includes and does not include.

Ellis and Fisher (1994) recommend several tips for proceeding through the discussion about defining the problem:

1. Define the problem specifically by phrasing it as a question.
2. Determine the importance of the problem to the group.
3. Discuss group goals related to the problem.
4. Identify resources available to the group related to the issue.
5. Clarify all constraints, including meeting times and due date.

Analyze the problem and gather information: This is the primary essence of the decision-making process. Successful groups do not jump quickly into the solution phase; instead, they spend time on the step before suggesting solutions (Hirokawa & Poole, 1996). The purpose of this step is to collect information and evidence, helping the group explore and clarify the problem. The following are important issues for the problem analysis stage:

1. Review information about your audience and persona(s).
2. Research the history and causes of the problem.
3. Discuss how the problem relates to other issues.

4. Collect information relevant to the problem and discuss this information.
5. Challenge the facts and assumptions to make sure they stand the test of scrutiny.
6. Finally, make sure you have enough information

Establish decision criteria: At this stage, the group decides what criteria meet an acceptable decision. The group should come to a consensus on specific criteria, and these should provide methods of evaluation. If the decision criteria are properly developed, they will help the design team recognized acceptable decision proposals while rejecting inappropriate ones.

During this stage the group's discussion should focus on what an ideal decision would look like, what it would include and exclude. They should decide what is reasonable as a final decision, even one less than ideal because it may not be possible to reach an ideal decision. Finally, the group should consider what would be valid and feasible about the decision.

Discuss possible solutions: Now is the time to discuss the most useful solutions. It is important to wait until this stage because premature discussion of solutions is often associated with poor decision-making (Ellis & Fisher, 1994). Now that the group has gone through the previous stages, it is now in a much better position to examine solutions.

The goal of this stage is to come up with as many ideas as possible. Seek quantity before quality. Do not be afraid to propose as many alternatives as possible, while recording every suggestion regardless of how absurd it might be. Before finishing this phase, consider the following questions:

1. Have all possible solutions been considered?
2. What evidence is in support of each alternative?
3. Has the group use brainstorming techniques to produce ideas?

Determine the best solution: This stage is the point where the group agrees on a final solution. A design team does this by testing the possible solutions against the decision criteria it established earlier. The goal is to find the best solution to your discussion in light of the decision criteria, including feasibility and desirability. The team should discard any unsatisfactory solutions, while concentrating its discussion on the remaining alternatives and making sure the discussion includes minimizing the problem, making it workable, and comparing its advantages to disadvantages.

Determine how to implement the final solution: Once a final decision has been reached, the group must then implement a solution. This discussion should include assignment to individuals for the various tasks.

Effective group work is influenced by the success of how well the group functions. As a result, group members should take time to examine the process by which they are making decisions and completing tasks. Group members should take time to review feedback while analyzing and reflecting upon it. Each group should then work to improve the quality of its task work and teamwork by setting improvement goals. Groups should also celebrate the successes of both teamwork and task work.

Brown (2013), a co-owner of a user experience design firm, argued for the need to educate design team members so they are better prepared to use effective collaboration and productive conflict. Productive conflict among design team members is not necessarily divisive and turbulent; it is a process for arriving at a shared understanding. Negotiation and disagreements help to clarify and refine decisions about a project. Through conflict and shared ideas and knowledge, design teams align in their comprehension of the project's direction, approach, and outcome. Conflict should be addressed and resolved through conversation and decision-making. Sometimes, conflict can be made evident through misunderstandings, egos, and disinterest. Brown maintained that designers must learn how to work with the diverse people on their team through frequent interaction. They must take time to cultivate rapport and empathy for team members mitigate the muddy characteristics that can plague them.

CHARACTERISTICS OF AN EFFECTIVE TEAM

The literature on small group communication has demonstrated a number of group interaction characteristics that are clearly different in newly formed as compared to longer-term designed grips. These characteristics have implications for the kind of give-and-take discussion that is essential to group identity and team effectiveness, regardless of the setting.

A highly effective team is able to design technology projects at a much higher quality than an individual. Such an outcome occurs through group maturity resulting in identity that improves the quality and effectiveness of group member participation. A number of characteristics have been observed among such highly effective teams. These groups have greater solidarity (Postmes, Spears, & Cihangir, 2001). Group members are highly motivated to do well (Brandon & Hollingshead, 1999). These groups have better interpersonal relationships that allow them greater freedom to talk and share openly. Members of these groups find greater satisfaction, effective decision-making, and orientation to the task. They are better able to form social-emotional roles with others in the group, and this allows them to better deliberate through negotiation (Edwards & Harwood, 2003; Wang, 1994). Members are more willing to help each other. They have a greater awareness as each other's skills and abilities. Group members have a greater ability to share information effectively. They also have a willingness to disagree, and may have discovered a preferred method for resolving conflict. Because they have learned how to collaborate and work together, they experience an improved ability to complete difficult intellectual tasks.

All members of a mature and effective team have developed a common system of goals and needs. Members of these groups exhibit the strongest task and goal interdependence. This period of interaction is at its most complex as each member strives towards common goals. All sources of the team combine to make this a condition of greatest potential. Such a state is a potential because in every situation you cannot be assured that all individuals are willing and able to carry out the tasks very for high quality output. However, a design team that is already stacked with the necessary roles to complete a task has a greater chance of meeting high quality expectations.

IMPLICATIONS FOR USER-CENTERED DESIGN TEAMS

Give groups time and experiences (meetings or otherwise) together to give them the opportunity to get to know one another, including their expertise and skill set. Once a group gets to know one another, they need many opportunities to interact and work out how to work together well. This type of communication does not come easy, but it is necessary so that team members understand how to communicate effectively when working through difficult decisions and tasks.

Group members must be willing to participate in team project meetings and relational building times. The success of team negotiation and decision-making hinges on members' willingness to participate in sometimes difficult communication behaviors, including conflict. Among U.S. design teams, conflicts are normal. Productive conflict and negotiation are important skills to making a team effective resulting in high-quality output. However, negative conflict can damage a group's ability to work, so it should be dealt with.

Group identity matters. Creating a group identity is more than having a team name. Such an identity is built through frequent interaction where members learn how to effectively work together. Group maturity and identity are the necessary ingredients for effective, high-quality output. Group identity through extensive interaction results in individual accountability, interdependence, willingness to share information and use promotive interaction, increased social skills, and ability to improve group work. These are all characteristics that make a highly effective design team that is capable of great work that benefits users.

REFERENCES

Barge, J. K. (1996). Leadership Skills and the Dialectics of Leadership in Group Decision Making. In *Communication and group decision making* (2nd ed., pp. 301–342). Thousand Oaks, CA: Sage Publications.

Brandon, D. P., & Hollingshead, A. B. (1999). Collaborative Learning and Computer-Supported Group. *Communication Education*, *48*(2), 1–19. doi:10.1080/03634529909379159

Brown, D. M. (2013). *Designing Together*. San Francisco, CA: New Riders Press.

Brown, J. M., Lindgaard, G., & Biddle, R. (2011). Collaborative Events and Shared Artifacts: Agile Interaction Designers and Developers Working Toward Common Aims. In *Proceedings of 2011 AGILE Conference*. IEEE. doi:10.1109/AGILE.2011.45

Charrier, G. (1974). Cog's ladder: a model of group development. In J. E. Jones (Ed.), *The 1974 Annual Handbook for Group Facilitators* (pp. 142–145). Hoboken, NJ: John Wiley & Sons.

Cooper, A., & Cronin, R. R. D. (2007). *About Face 3: The Essentials of Interaction Design*. Indianapolis, IN: John Wiley & Sons.

Dewey, J. (1916). *Democracy and Education*. Mineola, NY: Dover Publications, Inc.

Dunn-Jensen, L. M. (2014). Groups Meet... Teams Improve: Building Teams That Learn. *Academy of Management Learning & Education*, *13*(1), 151–153.

Edwards, C., & Harwood, J. (2003). Social Identity in the Classroom: An Examination of Age Identification Between Students and Instructors. *Communication Education*, *52*(1), 60–65. doi:10.1080/03634520302463

Ellis, D. G., & Fisher, B. A. (1994). *Small Group Decision Making: Communication and the Group Process*. New York: McGraw-Hill.

Hirokawa, R. Y. (2003). Communication and Group Decision-Making Efficacy. In *Small Group Communication: Theory & Practice* (pp. 125–133). Los Angeles, CA: Rosbury Publishing Co.

Hirokawa, R. Y., & Poole, M. S. (1996). *Communication and Group Decision Making*. Thousand Oaks, CA: SAGE Publications.

Janis, I. L. (1971). Groupthink. *Psychology Today*, *5*(6), 43–46.

Johnson, D., & Johnson, R. (1991). *Cooperative learning: Increasing college faculty instructional productivity*. Indianapolis, IN: Jossey-Bass.

Mayer, R. C., Davis, J. H., & Schoorman, F. D. (1995). An Integrative Model of Organization Trust. *Academy of Management Review*, *20*(3), 709–734.

Mcgrath, J. E. (1991). Time, Interaction, and Performance (TIP): A Theory of Groups. *Small Group Research*, *22*(2), 147–174. doi:10.1177/1046496491222001

McHugh, O., Conboy, K., & Lang, M. (2012). Agile Practices: The Impact on Trust in Software Project Teams. *IEEE Software*, *29*(3), 71–76. doi:10.1109/MS.2011.118

Piccoli, G., & Ives, B. (2003). Trust and the Unintended Effects of Behavior Control in Virtual Teams. *Management Information Systems Quarterly*, *27*(3), 365–395.

Poole, M. S. (1996). Group communication and the structuring process. In Small Group Communication: Theory & Practice (7th ed., pp. 85–95). Madison, WI: Brown & Benchmark.

Poole, M. S., & DeSanctis, G. (1989). *Use of Group Decision Support Systems as an Appropriation Process*. Paper presented at the System Sciences. Kailua-Kona, HI.

Poole, M. S., & Roth, J. (1989). Decision Development in Small Groups V Test of a Contingency Model. *Human Communication Research*, *15*(4), 549–589. doi:10.1111/j.1468-2958.1989.tb00199.x

Postmes, T., Spears, R., & Cihangir, S. (2001). Quality of Decision Making and Group Norms. *Journal of Personality and Social Psychology*, *80*(6), 918–930. doi:10.1037/0022-3514.80.6.918 PMID:11414374

Postmes, T., Spears, R., Lee, A. T., & Novak, R. J. (2005). Individuality and Social Influence in Groups: Inductive and Deductive Routes to Group Identity. *Journal of Personality and Social Psychology*, *89*(5), 747–763. doi:10.1037/0022-3514.89.5.747 PMID:16351366

Rosander, M., Stiwne, D., & Granstrom, K. (1998). "Bipolar groupthink": Assessing groupthink tendencies in authentic work groups. *Scandinavian Journal of Psychology*, *39*(2), 81–92. doi:10.1111/1467-9450.00060 PMID:9676161

Seibold, D. R. (1979). Making Meetings More Successful: Plans, Formats, and Procedures for Group Problem-Solving. *Journal of Business Communication*, *16*(4), 3–20. doi:10.1177/002194367901600401

Tajfel, H., & Turner, J. C. (1986). The Social Identity Theory of Intergroup Behavior. In *Psychology of Intergroup Relations* (pp. 1–19). Chicago: Nelson-Hall Publishers.

Triandis, H. C. (1995). *Individualism & Collectivism*. Boulder, CO: Westview Press.

Tuckman, B. W. (1965). Developmental sequence in small groups. *Psychological Bulletin*, *63*(6), 384–399. doi:10.1037/h0022100 PMID:14314073

Tuckman, B. W., & Jensen, M. A. C. (1977). Stages of Small-Group Development Revisited. *Group & Organization Management*, *2*(4), 419–427. doi:10.1177/105960117700200404

Wang, A. Y. (1994). Pride and Prejudice in High School Gang Members. *Adolescence*, *29*(114), 279–291. Retrieved from http://web.a.ebscohost.com.ezproxy.lib.utah.edu/ehost/detail?sid=b9dfc377-8d27-4165-8dd9-ca51192b63c0%40sessionmgr4001&vid=2&hid=4101&bdata=JnNpdGU9ZWhvc3QtbGl2ZQ%3d%3d#db=s3h&AN=9408150252 PMID:8085481

Wenger, E. (1998). *Communities of Practice*. Cambridge, UK: Cambridge University Press. doi:10.1017/CBO9780511803932

Wenger, E., McDermott, R., & Snyder, W. (2002). *Cultivating Communities of Practice*. Boston, MA: Harvard Business School Press.

Whitworth, E. (2008). Experience Report: The Social Nature of Agile Teams (pp. 429–435). In *Proceedings of Agile 2008 Conference*. IEEE. doi:10.1109/Agile.2008.53

Whitworth, E., & Biddle, R. (2007). *The Social Nature of Agile Teams*. Paper presented at the AGILE. Washington, DC.

KEY TERMS AND DEFINITIONS

Agile: Agile software design is based on iterative and incremental development, where requirements and solutions evolve through collaboration between self-organizing and cross-functional teams. This process promotes adaptive planning, creative development and delivery, a time-boxed iterative approach, while encouraging rapid and flexible response to change. For example, many agile teams meet daily to discuss and collaborate on current development issues.

Consensus: Consensus is the extent of group loyalty (identity) felt by group members toward a decision. A group may be fully committed to a decision, while not necessarily agreeing with it. They have chosen to commit to a majority decision of the group, so group members work to put it into effect without ever fully agreeing to it.

Conflict: Because a design task involves discussion of how to accomplish it, a group must negotiate who must be accountable for which components, where they will find information to accomplish the task, and what the final product will look like. Discussion and negotiation works best when people have competing goals, and this can create communication that is more aggressive or competitive. Negotiation and productive conflict allow design groups to improve decision quality while avoiding premature and potentially erroneous consensus. Conflict and negotiation allows group members to work through a proposal by accepting it, modifying it, or developing a completely new idea based on a more complete understanding of the original proposal's shortcomings.

Decision Making: A group reaches a decision when its members achieve consensus on a proposal, based on all choices available to them. Consensual decision-making means that group goals have either been met or are overshadowed by group goals.

Group Identity: Group identification is defined by in-group favoritism and discrimination against the out-group. Some degree of compatible group interests must exist for cohesion to occur among members.

Group Process: Groups require successive communication behaviors to proceed from a low-performing, introductory group to one outputting high-quality work because members experience high cohesion. Group process takes time and development of group identity and ability to communicate well.

Negotiation: Negotiation describes decision-making when all members of the group do not share common goals or cannot reach agreement. An appropriate negotiation is carried out when a group attempts to satisfy the task requirements by: (1) showing a correct understanding of the issue, (2) determining the minimal characteristics any alternative must possess, (3) identifying relevant and realistic set of alternatives, and (4) carefully examining the alternatives in relation to each previously agreed upon choice.

Chapter 7
Managing Differences in Situational Awareness Due to Roles in the Design-Use Process of Complex Systems

Jens Alfredson
Saab Aeronautics, Sweden

ABSTRACT

This chapter describes how Situational Awareness (SA) can differ between roles in the design-use process. SA is not traditionally used to describe awareness between roles in the design-use process. However, SA between individuals or groups having various roles in the design-use process could be described, assessed, and used as a tool for improving a design process.

INTRODUCTION

Complex systems are in themselves costly and their rational is that they provide high values in the settings that they are used in. If the system fails to function or functions suboptimal the consequences for this could be costly, severe or even devastating. A specific problem is when a situation could not be managed, due to lack of SA.

This chapter explains SA as a concept and how the SA concept could be used to describe the design-use process. The chapter also describes how various roles in the design-use process affect the design and thereby also future situations where the end product is to be used. Later in the

chapter, the focus is on how to manage the actual design process, given the premises explained in the earlier part of the chapter.

SITUATIONAL AWARENESS

SA is a frequently used term in Human Factors (HF) literature. It is a term used by users, researchers, developers and more. What SA is about is to know what is going on in the past, present and the future. SA is a central concept for complex systems with human in the loop, partly due to its positive correlation to performance. Therefore, it is important to regard SA already in the develop-

DOI: 10.4018/978-1-4666-6485-2.ch007

ment of complex systems, to understand what it is, what dimensions it has, and how to manage those insights for development purposes.

In the late 80's and early 90's there were a healthy and fruitful debate in the research community about SA, what it was, and how or if it should be defined. Even though not all questions that arose in that debate has been answered, more recent work has to a large extent focused on using the concept in various domains, and less focused on questions on definitions.

SA is a concept that has been proved to be useful first, within the aviation domain, and later in a wide area of domains. The wide recognition and frequent use of the concept indicates that it fills a need. SA has been defined and re-defined several times. It is difficult to clarify statements about high or low SA without explicit reference points. Also, the SA concept could be positioned to other concepts to help understand the concept.

First, the issue of SA is related to decision making in dynamic systems, where speed and accuracy of operator response is critical. As automation and task complexity increase, an operator is at greater risk of becoming lost in a system. This tendency is especially common in multimodal systems, where a specific display unit can, at different times, represent quite different physical states of the world. Accordingly, system failures due to mode errors have become more common. The SA concept has proved to be a fruitful framework for categorising operator errors, for instance, pilot errors in civil aviation (Endsley, 1995b, Jones & Endsley, 1996), or errors associated with offshore drill crews (Sneddon, Mearns, & Flin, 2006).

Second, SA is closely related to established concepts in the information-processing paradigm, predominately in human factors research. SA is often regarded as being principally in the cognitive domain (Hartman & Secrist, 1991). One SA model in mainstream HF research that includes information processing comprises three levels. Endsley's (1988), definition of SA seems to have attracted most adherents; "the perception of the elements

in the environment within a volume of time and space, the comprehension of their meaning, and the projection of their status in the near future" (p. 792). Based on this definition Endsley (1988; 1995b) has developed a SA model that comprises three levels:

- Level 1, perception of task relevant elements. For instance, a pilot has to perceive task elements such as other aircraft, display meters, enunciators, and radio messages.
- Level 2, interpretation of task elements. On this level, a synthesis is made that go beyond the characteristics of the perceived elements. Information is interpreted in terms of its relation to pertinent goals. A fighter pilot, for instance, should be able to assess the intentions of enemy aircraft on the basis of their number, distance, speed and formation. Equally true is that a civilian pilot must assess intent of other aircraft such as in a busy air corridor.
- Level 3, projection of future states. This represents the highest level of SA, where the operator predicts the unfolding of events which, in turn, provide a basis for decision making. A fighter pilot realising an enemy attack predicts its speed and direction and then chooses the optimal alternative - counter attack, evasion action or retreat. Heavy air traffic over a civilian airport has comparable prediction requirements.

Each of these levels contains identifiable cognitive processes and attendant performance deficits. Lack of SA at level 1 may be caused by a range of factors that include vigilance decrements, discrimination failures and non-optimal sampling strategies in supervision. Errors at level 2 are related to mismatches between system characteristics and an operator's mental model. Level 3 errors may occur in spite of accurate perception and interpretation of task relevant information, as projection of future states is an extremely complex cognitive task. Taxing on working memory and attentional resources, mental simulations require good mental models. Focusing on errors, however, is not necessarily fruitful for reaching higher level goals, such as increased safety, since it is hard to determine what an error is, how to classify it, how to add its effects to other errors, and what the effects are to safety (Dekker, 2003; 2005; 2007).

Normally we know in behavioural sciences what to measure and how to measure it, since we usually are interested in the assessment of presence of something. In the case of SA, focus is on assessment of absence of it, which is a paradox that complicates measurement. In general, it is an easier task to measure the occurrence or prevalence of something. In measuring the lack of something, the expected outcome might be a result of inappropriate methods, unreliable instruments, invalid procedures, and so forth, as well as a true omission/lack of data. Literature seldom is concerned with perceiving and discussing SA in normal (colloquial) situations. Literature is usually concerned about situations where, for instance, a pilot is lacking SA. To appropriately measure something that is missing it is necessary to identify what should have been present. Normative models of (high) SA are seldom at hand in a particular context. Often a lack of SA is related to a subjective feeling of the constituents of high SA.

The increased interest in SA might be explained both in empirical and theoretical terms. Some empirical circumstances contributing to increased interest are incidents and severe accidents that might be attributable to user faults. Intuitively, we realise that the risk that users become lost in systems increases with the higher degree of automation present in dynamic systems.

Not only the system that the user is attempting to control may change rapidly, but also the representation of the system may change frequently, along with the means for monitoring and steering. With today's multimode systems, information and the means of presentation are further complicated.

Along with more sophisticated technology interfaces become more complex. Increased complexity is usually contradictory to user friendliness.

Theoretically, a comprehensive SA model integrates a number of specific cognitive processes, which have been identified as relevant to the tasks to be fulfilled by a user. In this context, user thinking represents an advanced form of information processing. A minimum of five components making up SA were identified in a review of literature, depending of the resolution that is useful for a deeper understanding of SA. These components are descriptions that can be used to understand the concept of SA, by linking it to other theories of human behaviour. The components, however, are not discrete parts of SA in the sense that they divide SA into sub-SA terms to be measured instead of measuring SA. The rationale behind the use of SA is that the phenomenon is not covered by other terms and is to be viewed as a whole. Further, the components cannot be interpreted as a linear information flow. As Neisser (1976) described the perceptual cycle, human perception is far from being linear. Neisser's cycle has been used to spread some light on the dim theoretical surroundings of SA by, for instance, Smith and Hancock (1995) as well as Adams, Tenney, and Pew (1995). Each component is integrated with a variety of feedback loops. At a specific point in time, SA is highly dependent on previously experienced states of SA, reflecting only a snapshot of the ongoing dynamics. Below, five components are identified:

- **Attention (Vigilance, Decoding, etc.):** The first component concerns attentional resources that are allocated to the processing of relevant task specific information. Vigilance (user's ability to detect gradual or discrete changes of stimuli), may be necessary for survival in some scenarios. Vigilance is to a large extent determined by physiological prerequisites and less prone to training. Decoding of data depends on both modality specific attributes and prior knowledge. A lack of SA at this level might be about simple misreading of instruments or digital data, weak signals/stimuli that are not detected, non-optimal mental resource allocation, and so forth.

- **Perception (Active Search, Identification, etc.):** The second component embraces perceptual processes, active search processes, which result in identification of information/objects. Users are sometimes exposed to such a high number of stressors that their perceptual abilities are impeded. A lack of SA on this level implies indulgence, fatigue or stress reactions (for instance, distortion of normal search patterns); deficient selective processes leading to "freezing behaviour" or "confusion". In extreme environments, for instance, in a fighter aircraft the pilots are sometimes exposed to high G forces, high level of stress and a high speed. The result could be, for instance, a loss of peripheral perception of information or a loss of or detrimental colour perception.

- **Memory (Encoding, Storage, Retrieval, Meta-Information Capabilities, etc.):** The third component is often divided into encoding, storage and retrieval of information. The encoding process generally requires rehearsal and elaboration of information to be efficient. Short-term storage of information is limited and easily lost among surrounding noise or information. Working memory capacity has been found to be a predictor for flight SA (Sohn & Doane, 2004). Long term storage is more robust, permanent and, in some sense, unlimited. Still the retrieval of information can be the crucial bottleneck in remembering relevant information. Learning sufficient retrieval cues during training is important. Providing users with realistic contextual cues influence retrieval.

Another pertinent memory quality may be individual differences in meta-information capabilities. This may be one of the most neglected determinants of SA. A lack of SA at this level might be about a too high mental workload; preventing efficient encoding or elaboration of information. Accordingly, users may lose important information, lose temporal or spatial cues relevant to their tasks, get lost in a multi-mode environment, and so forth. Obsolete metacognitive structures may not be applicable in a new context, resulting in, for instance, misjudgement of their own ability to solve upcoming problems.

- **Interpretation (Mental Model, Meaning, Inference, Decision, etc.):** The fourth component is about interpretation of the attended, perceived and memorised information. Usually the information has meaning defined by task or mission. While primary components, in an aviation context, take care of the detection and identification of aircraft in the vicinity or enemy aircraft, this component could be about interpretation of intentions of surrounding pilots based on behaviour and manoeuvres. Drawing upon previous experiences, pilots make inferences and decisions about current events. Faults at this level may stem from premature or undeveloped mental models of others' behaviour, inappropriate prerequisites for interpretations in a particular context, or wrong decision rules. Humans are also subjected to a wide range of biases in their judgements.

- **Prediction (Mental Simulation, Forecast, Prophecy, etc.):** The fifth component concerns prediction of future events as a ground for decisions. This is a demanding cognitive task that requires a superior ability of mental simulation. Using available information, a pilot must weigh different information and make a short term forecast. Experience increases users' ability to make long term projections about future events that they may encounter. A lack of SA at this level may have detrimental effects on planning and long term survival. Concrete behaviour might be misdirected and even jeopardising lives.

Failures in these components may affect SA negatively. Endsley, Bolté, and Jones, (2003) described factors that work to undermine SA as SA demons, and exemplified with: Attentional tunneling, Requisite memory trap, WAFOS (Workload, Anxiety, Fatigue, and Other Stressors), Data overload, Misplaced salience, Complexity creep, Errant mental models, and Out-of-the-loop syndrome. . However, factors that undermine SA could be controlled to some extent by understanding their potential effects. For instance, when evaluating what to automate system designers could chose a specific type of automation well suited for a task with known demands on the user cognitive resources, to achieve better performance (Taylor, Reinerman-Jones, Szalma, Mouloua, & Hancock, 2013). Also, for car drivers it is important to regard context for adaptable driver automation, and what people need and want different information in different contexts (Davidsson & Alm, 2014).

Good SA is not necessarily an ability that the user possesses in the same sense that he/she possesses good calculus ability or a good pitch perception. SA consists of a conglomerate of human abilities and interaction with task, colleagues, organisation, environment and technique. A user's task can easily be changed according to the current situation. Hence, it is possible that a user is in full control one moment with a high level of SA, and in an adjacent sequence of actions is out of control with a drastically reduced SA. This phenomenon reflects the rapid dynamic changes that can occur in a hyper dynamic environment, such as an aircraft.

One of the reasons why the concept of SA has been able to win ground, although missing a well based theoretical foundation, is that it seems that almost everybody has something to relate to as SA. Even though there are a variety of definitions of SA, and the theoretical problems of SA remains, most people (and even researchers) tend to agree that they have something to relate to as SA in their experience.

It is far from easy to reach the same consensus on that the mental concept of SA is applicable on machines. Machines are without the intelligence of the human mind, and without conscious awareness. It could be taken as an incentive to improve a SA model if it is applicable to a machine and thereby might be missing what makes SA characteristic to humans.

In a study by Mulgund, Rinkus, Illgen, Zacharias, and Friskie (1997) the three levels in Endsley's model of SA have been compared to a model of data fusion (DF) processes:

The Joint Directors of Laboratories (JDL) Data Fusion Subpanel have identified three levels of fusion processing products (Waltz & Llinas, 1990; White & Cohen, 1980):

Level 1 DF: Fused position and identity estimates
Level 2 DF: Friendly or hostile military situation assessments
Level 3 DF: Hostile force threat assessments. (p. 2)

The study points out the similarities and even fuses the two models into one four-level model consisting of the first level of DF followed by Endsley's three levels. The model was then the base of a prototype demonstrating how an online SA processor could be used (Mulgund et al., 1997). Demonstrating that this is possible, also demonstrates that the SA model used are very mechanistic in its structure. Maybe it is less surprising that a SA model that are influenced by sequential mechanical processes, are used to explain the SA of computers, than it is that such a model is used to understand human cognition.

By applying Endsley's SA levels it is possible to assess a machine's SA, comparing internal representation in a computer with the external truth. The SA of one computerised pilot model has been measured by the use of a reference computerised pilot model (Zacharias, Miao, Illgen, Yara, & Siouris, 1996). The basis of the comparison is Endsley's SA model. As Endsley suggests that SA can be measured by objective questions, for instance, using SAGAT (Situation Awareness Global Assessment Technique) (Endsley, 1988; 1995a; 2000; Jones & Kaber, 2005), testing SA at level 1-3 by comparing a statement with an objective truth, this could be applied to computers as well as humans, although the human subjectivity makes it hard to argue that these kind of judgements are really objective (e.g. Annett, 2002; Walker, Stanton, & Young, 2006).

One of the ideas behind the study by Zacharias et al. (1996), was that one computerised pilot model was not provided with all the information about the external situation, while another pilot model was. The SA of the computerised pilot model could thereby be measured by comparing the objective truth in one of the pilot models, with the incomplete representation in the measured pilot model.

Applying the same SA model on humans, as on groups of humans and on machines, or even a design process, implies that the SA of a person is to be comparable to the SA of a non-human entity (e.g. group or a machine). By doing so, the risk is that some aspects of human cognition that are important to grasp the situation are neglected. Also the view proposed in this dissertation could be extended to incorporate machines or groups of agents. However, it is important to regard the importance of the fundamental difference between the human conscious awareness, and a non-conscious awareness.

A strong rationale for using the theoretical concept of SA, is its positive practical implications, such as how useful it is in the process of developing complex systems. Therefore it is also important to regard practical aspects such as take into consideration what is possible to measure, and not be overly abstract.

The definition suggested below therefore focuses on awareness and what is related to that, rather than a purely theoretical abstraction of SA. To illustrate SA and to help the reader with a visual representation, Venn diagrams will be presented in a series of figures. This type of Venn diagrams have been used before to visualise SA (Alfredson, et al., 1996; Alfredson, 2001; 2007; Dekker & Lützhöft, 2004). The metacognitive component is stressed in the proposed definition. Considering the criteria of the definition, the following definition is proposed (see also, Alfredson, 2001; 2007):

High SA is when someone is fully aware of a high relative awareness

RELATIVE AWARENESS

If someone is not aware of a situation he/she does not have SA, because of an absence of knowing what is happening. Relative awareness is a combination of actual awareness and required awareness (see Figure 1) and thus takes into account that SA relate to performance. Good performance is dependent upon personal awareness of the elements that require awareness. If actual awareness is not as high as required awareness there is a lack of SA (see Figure 2, 3 and 4).

AWARENESS OF RELATIVE AWARENESS

If someone is not aware of that he/she has high relative awareness of a situation he/she does not have SA, because, with a bit of bad luck, he/she might just as easily has lost it without knowing. This part of the definition addresses how SA relates to metacognition. If experienced relative awareness is not the same as actual relative awareness there is a lack of SA. For instance, if a subject

Figure 1. The figure illustrates the relationships between different information areas in a dynamic situation. Each information area contains information about current state, past states, future states and relationships between states of a dynamic situation. A = Situation: This area symbolises all information that concerns a dynamic situation. B = Awareness: This area symbolises information about a dynamic situation of which a person is aware. C = Required awareness: This area symbolises information about a dynamic situation that is required to be fully aware of what is relevant in a situation. D = Actual awareness: This area symbolises information about a dynamic situation that is both in a person's awareness and also required for the person to be aware of what is relevant in a situation. D/C = Relative awareness: The relative awareness is not an information area, but a quotient of two areas; the area of actual awareness and the area of required awareness.

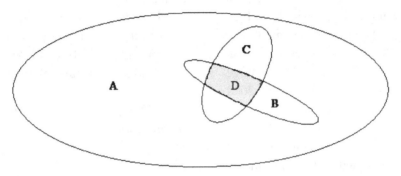

Figure 2. High SA. When a person has high SA the areas C and D become the same area, since the person is aware of all that is important in the situation. B is larger than C and incorporates C.

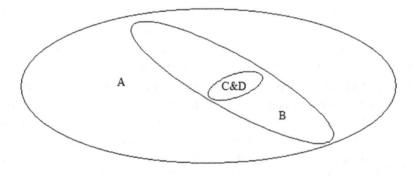

thinks that his/her relative awareness is high, when it actually is low, or he/she thinks that it is low when it is high then the level of awareness of relative awareness is low (see Table 1).

Table 1 illustrates the relationship between *awareness of relative awareness* (metacognitive ability) and *relative awareness*, by showing the possible outcome of SA depending on four possible combinations of relative awareness and awareness of relative awareness. A high relative awareness accompanying a high awareness of relative awareness describes an ideal scenario with high SA. A high awareness of relative awareness, when relative awareness is low implies low SA. A risk for underestimation of a person's SA is present with low awareness of relative awareness together with high relative awareness. Perhaps the most devastating scenario is when low awareness of

Figure 3. Low SA. A person has got low SA when he/she is not very much aware, even if he/she is aware of the right things. B is smaller than C. This could also be the case when the situation is hard to grasp, because of high demands, that is, C is too large to be aware of. Now B and D becomes the same area in the diagram.

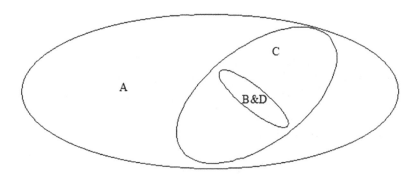

Figure 4. Aware of something unreal. The figure visualises an example of when a person is aware of something that is not a part of the situation at hand. This could be the case when someone is misperceiving, remember the wrong thing, or even hallucinating. Another possibility for this configuration to occur is that the situation A has become smaller. Since the situation is dynamically changing, it cannot only undergo qualitative changes, but also quantitative changes.

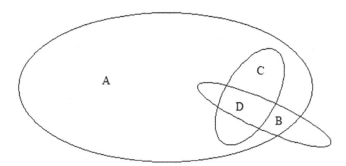

relative awareness is combined with low relative awareness.

It is not farfetched that a person that is not aware of the required information in a situation might not either be the best assessor at the meta-level of assessing that there are incorrectness's in that respect. Walker, Stanton, and Young (2006) found, in a study on car drivers, that drivers demonstrated little self-awareness of diminished SA.

Or, as expressed by McGuinness (2004, p. 5): "In terms of situational awareness, a well-calibrated individual is one who has a high level of actual SA *and* correctly perceives this to be the case in his or her perceived SA."

However, a task may be well performed even if the individual cannot express how in it is done. Rasmussen (1983, 1986) distinguishes between skill based, rule based and knowledge based behaviour. A very familiar task that has become a skill is often performed without conscious reflection.

The awareness of relative awareness is a metacognitive aspect of SA. Flavell (1976) expresses

Table 1. The relationship between "Awareness of Relative Awareness" and "Relative Awareness"

	Low Awareness of Relative Awareness	**High Awareness of Relative Awareness**
High relative awareness	-(Underestimation)	+
Low relative awareness	--(Overestimation)	-

metacognition as "one's knowledge concerning one's own cognitive processes and products or anything related to them" (p. 232). Metacognition refers to one's knowledge and active regulation of one's own cognitive processes and products, or, in less technical terms; thinking about thinking (Brown, 1987; Flavell, 1976).

Metacognition is an important aspect of cognition, in understanding how people form their understanding of the world, or fails to form a correct understanding, which we are still learning to understand (Chambres, Izaute, & Marescaux, 2002). Perkins (1989) highlights the "metacognitive shortfall", in his theory of shortcomings in everyday reasoning, and suggests various contributing factors: People may not be aware of how badly biased their situation model is; They may not be aware of how easy it is to extend a situation model. They may not reconsider a conclusion after obtaining new information about the situation.

Experts however, are often regarded as superior decision-makers in the literature, partly because they possess better metacognitive skills. For instance, as expressed by Proctor and Dutta (1995) "One attribute of skilled problem solvers is that they are better able to monitor their own cognitive processing" (p. 216), or Means, Salas, Crandall, and Jacobs (1993) *"Metacognitive skills* may well constitute the best candidates for generalizable skills that will aid decision making across domains" (p. 324) and later in the same text "Better performers employ metacognitive strategies, and teaching the strategies to poor performers leads to improvement on the task" (p. 324).

It is not hard to find examples of situations where a user's understanding of the situation is totally dependent on his/her metacognition. For instance, if a user is to decide whether to engage a certain automatic system or not, may depend on how the user judges his/her own current ability to manually perform the corresponding task, considering his/her own understanding of the situation and the own workload, and relating the own abilities to the automations abilities.

Since modern systems continuously are becoming more complex and more highly automated, this problem increases in relevance. Interaction between human and the technical system is not only about interaction on the surface, but about a deep interaction between the agents. That is, interaction is not only about how to perceive elements and understand what they are going to do, but also being aware of the level of awareness that the agents possesses respectively, including yourself.

Other situations where the user has to use metacognition, is in collaboration and communication with other persons. It is not only machine agents that the user has to relate his/her own understanding of the situation to. In fact the user continuously has to assess his/her own mental state, as part of the overall situation assessment.

Since metacognition is important to form an understanding of what is going on in the world, it is easy to see its relevance for building SA. McGuinness (1995) adds two components to the three levels of SA that were proposed by Endsley (1988). The components are *metacognition* and *response selection*. McGuinness (1995) points to metacognition as relevant for both *SA knowledge contents* and *SA-related processes*.

By comparing assessments on SA obtained by SAGAT with confidence ratings about the response, the metacognitive aspect of how well calibrated a subject is in his/her SA assessment, has been investigated in military command and control (Lichacz & Farrell, 2005) and air traffic control (Lichacz, Cain, & Patel, 2003).

When Stanton et al. (2006) proposed a theory for distributed SA (DSA) the system level was described as a meta level for individual SA: "Moreover, there are then two aspects of SA at any given node: individual SA of one's own task, and a 'meta-SA' of the whole system's DSA" (p. 1308).

Disregarding the metacognitive aspects of SA, will lead to less valuable interpretations of data collected as measure of SA. Often data from various kinds of SA measures differs in their interpretation. If the data itself is valid, the differences in interpretation might be due to weaknesses in the model of SA. For instance, it is possible that some of the differences between pilots' rating of own SA and observers ratings of pilot's SA could be explained in terms of metacognition. Walker, Stanton, and Young (2006) reported that car drivers' self-awareness of SA was very low in a study on vehicle feedback. In a study of experienced road cyclists Knez and Ham (2006) found that fatigued participants underestimated their ability to maintain SA.

One way of extending the SA theory is to include the meta-situation in which the situation is present. Any situation is present in a context or meta-situation, which in turn is present in yet another meta-situation, and so forth, as visualised in Figure 5. Woltjer (2009) studied how "the performance of complex socio-technical systems is shaped by constraints, and the actions of complex socio-technical systems shape constraints in order to manage constraints". There are often several reasons for studying a situation. It might be that the situation is studied as part of a study of user behaviour or interface evaluation, of a complex system. The study might also have several restrictions like timeframes, financial restrictions, and technical expectations. The researchers conducting the study, their background and expectations might even be considered to be included in the meta-situation. The study might be conducted with the ambition to be published in a scientific journal, or perhaps with the ambition to cut down on future development costs of a studied artefact. Both the situation and the meta-situation change dynamically, but perhaps at different paces. Still, both the situation and meta-situation might change drastically, because of an unexpected event. It is therefore necessary for anybody who is studying SA to be aware of the situation, the meta-situation, and their fluctuations, to come to the right conclusions. If they are, they can adapt to the changes. An example of a meta-situation could be the design-use process for a complex system used in the situation. Adapting to the dynamics of the situation and meta-situation requires four steps:

Figure 5. Meta-situation. When studying a situation (A), it always exists in a context or meta-situation (M).

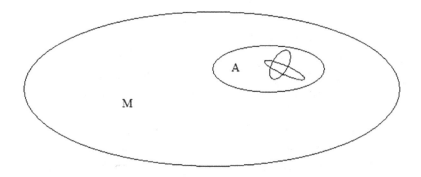

- Monitoring the changes.
- Understanding the meaning of the changes.
- Predicting the future impact on the study.
- Deciding and taking action.

The reader can now recognise the parallel between the first three steps and the three levels of SA proposed by Endsley (1988). What is referred to is the researcher's SA. Flach (1995) stated that: "It might also be argued that science is a complex, dynamic work environment (although the time constants are much longer than even process control). If this is true, then it might be useful to recursively apply the question of situation awareness to the science of situation awareness." (p. 25).

The meta-situation is a relevant part of a developer's SA. As the meta-situation changes the decisions and actions that are the most suitable also change. The methods and models used might then also change.

SITUATIONAL AWARENESS IN THE DESIGN-USE PROCESS

The differences in SA due to roles in the design-use process, refers to the notions of SA that is formed by actors in various roles, such as the user, the designer, the researcher, the manager, and so forth. The roles could due to different information provided to them, different experience and training background, different tasks and other role-specific perspectives differ in their notion of both the concept of SA, as such, and the notion of a specific person's, team's or role's (such as a group of users) SA.

To create good design, information about the design criteria is needed. To achieve good design it is useful to focus on a set of sub-goals in the process towards the good design. Examples of such sub-goals are, to reach a good level of pilot mental workload or to help forming good SA. Good SA is the foundation for effective decision making (Endsley, 1995b). Endsley, Bolstad, Jones, and

Riley (2003) as well as Endsley, Bolté, and Jones (2003) describe SA oriented design as comprised by three components: SA requirements analysis, SA-oriented design principles, and SA measurement and validation.

It is essential to know what individuals are aware of in a situation, and to understand why they are acting the way they are. Design is about making choices and it is therefore particularly relevant to focus on the differences in SA, since the differences could guide the design choices. If we learn how to manage differences in SA in the development of complex systems, the value of the systems in use will increase. Complex systems appear in many sectors of our society and the applicability of knowledge on their development therefore has great potential. Managing differences in SA in the development of complex systems are increasingly important since there is an increase in complexity of large socio-technical systems of today. Methods and techniques for designing and developing large socio-technical systems are increasingly important to produce efficient and usable solutions. In later years, attempts have been made to address this matter, through a variety of approaches, such as user-centred design, usability engineering, ecological interface design, user experience, and many others. For instance, Cajander (2010) examined what happens when user-centred system design approaches are applied to organisations.

There are other means to manage the SA than those of the person or group experiencing the SA. For instance, a designer of a system used in the situation or a manager for the person, influences the possibilities for the person to perceive, understand and predict, which strongly affects the situational awareness. It is important to regard both design and management, the SA thereby can be enhanced. The affecting factor might be distant in time and space, but still affecting the situation and control of those factors could contribute to the management of the situation. It is important to include both the end users at the "sharp end"

(Reason, 1990), right where the action is with all sorts of constraints, such as constraints, as well as persons at the "blunt end". Reason (1997) explains how organizational accidents have become an increasing concern in modern complex systems where people at different levels of an organisation interact with technology, forming a system. Rankin, Lundberg, Woltjer, Rollenhagen, and Hollnagel (2014) has provided a framework for analyzing adaptations in high-risk work, includitng means to describe strategies and blunt-end/sharp-end interactions. In the design process of complex systems it is important to understand how strategies and interactions at the blunt-end affect the sharp-end performance. Also, the safety culture of the organisation, reflecting individuals' attitudes, beliefs, perceptions and values in the organisation is important to manage safe operations, which is an important aspect varying between organisations (Ek, 2006). To analyse, understand and prevent organizational accidents it is not enough to focus only on the SA of an individual or team, although those concerns may be important contributing factors. At each level, within and outside, an organisation there are individuals and teams trying to cope with a situation and forming SA. It is important to recognise that the levels affect each other, as the goal shifts form optimising SA or striving to share SA, to managing the situation.

The focus on the situation, meta-situation, is particularly relevant from the view of developing complex systems including efforts in design and development. It is important to be aware of what will affect the situation to be able to perform an adequate analysis of how to, if not control the situation, so at least influence the situation with acts from various agents. By assessing the impact from each agent and potentially from any act of any agent and comparing those to each other, differences will appear that could influence concrete design efforts, as well as, broader considerations regarding, for instance, development efforts.

One of the major reasons for using the concept of SA in the development of complex systems is pragmatic: Applying the concept to the design might help creating good design. Since SA is used to evaluate human-machine interfaces, the concept should enhance the design process, and increase the benefits of the result of the improved design process. The concept of SA can be used for at least three purposes in the design process:

- Enhancing the design process, by providing rationale sub-goals created from an understanding of SA.
- Enhancing the actual design by helping the designer to understand the design criteria, and there relative importance.
- Ensuring that the design is satisfying, by testing the design in relation to SA.

Design recommendations, based on Endsley's three level model of SA (Endsley, 1988) have been presented to help designers to make a better design (Endsley, 1995b; Endsley, Bolstad, Jones, & Riley, 2003; Endsley, Bolté, & Jones, 2003). Jones, Endsley, Bolstad and Estes (2004) even developed a designer's situation awareness toolkit (DeSAT) to provide support to the designer through tutorials and application specific tools.

SA could very well enhance both the design process as well as the design itself. However, by broadening the use of the SA concept within the field of design it might be possible to find even better applications to enhance the design and the design process, for instance, making the design more sensitive to the characteristics of a specific context, and explicitly regarding the differences in SA due to roles in the design-use process.

ROLES IN THE DESIGN-USE PROCESS

There could be differences in SA between individuals or groups having various roles in the design-use process. There are many roles in the design-use process. One possible relationship between roles in a fictive example of a design-use process would be that one researcher is developing design methodology, another develops SA theory and assessment methodology and a third is perhaps evaluating end user behaviour. There might be several designers adopting the research findings, in their work after that they, for instance, have red a book or attended a course. The designers are then interacting with managers, marketing people, production people and more, trying to find an acceptable design solution. Even though the designers are working at different companies and with different subsystems, it might be that their design efforts are consumed by several end users, trying to manage a current task, in their organisation. During the life-cycle of a complex system various types of maintenance personal will also interact with and modify the system, and they in turn will utilize user information as part of the support system (Candell, 2009).

All these people might have too little time to optimally perform their tasks, and are all trying to obtain an acceptable result of their efforts. For instance, many decisions are to be made under extreme time pressure, in a hyper dynamic setting with high stakes, which all are characteristics of a typical context, where naturalistic decision making is applicable (Klein, Orasanu, Calderwood, & Zsambok, 1993). Although this fictive example is an extreme simplification of a real equivalent, it yet gives a sense of the multi-facetted situation of the chain of a development process. To achieve good SA for a single end user or team, there has to be valuable contributions from many parts of this chain. A researcher might contribute with design-oriented research, and a developer with research-oriented design (Albinsson, 2004; Fällman, 2003). It is not enough for an end user to have perfect individual properties, to form good SA, there has to be assistance from other roles in the design-use process. For instance, the design will affect the SA. Attempts have been made to influence the SA by providing design principles

(i.e. principles of design for SA) to be used by designers (Endsley, Bolté, & Jones, 2003).

Together, the user and a technical system form a Joint Cognitive System – JCS (Hollnagel & Woods, 1983; 2005; Woods & Hollnagel, 2006). The interdependence between the two parts of the JCS, to be able to fulfil the tasks of the JCS, is often prominent. By an accurate interaction between the two parts of the JCS, information can be exchanged in order to make the JCS act as one unit, with the desired behaviour. However, also the designer could be regarded as a part of the JCS, even though the interaction from the designer (i.e. the design) is located earlier in time, than the user's interaction. Reason (1988) addresses the role of design regarding errors by explaining how passive failures, such as errors in design, create latent conditions, or *resident pathogens*. The latent failures are therefore failures that are made far from the point in time and space where it occurs, so it is not the person who is handling the situation at the time of the incident/accident that are the main reason, or at least not the only reason, to the incident/accident.

Handley (2014) has provided a network model for human interoperability, including the human view (Handley & Smillie, 2008) composed of seven aspects (concept, constraints, tasks, roles, human network, training, and metrics), to be able to define and evaluate human interoperability in networked environments, which is central for many design processes of complex systems. Another approach supporting function allocation design challenges focusing on five key requirements for effective function allocation was presented by Feigh and Pritchett (2014), that can be regarded in a model of human-automation function allocation (Pritchett, Kim, & Feigh, 2014b). Also, the same requirements have been suggested to be measured by eight metrics to assess function allocation in the design process (Pritchett, Kim, & Feigh, 2014a). Defense Science Board (2012), suggests to "abandon the debate over definitions of levels of autonomy and embrace a three-facet (cognitive echelon, mission timelines, human-machine system trade spaces) autonomous systems framework…" (p. 2). It is not only the function allocation between the agents in the real-time environment that has to be performed, but also the distribution of tasks between the roles in the design-use process has to be function allocated, see Table 2. Otherwise, the risk is that tasks will not be performed, or be badly performed, which may affect the SA at the sharp end.

Whichever strategy for function allocation is selected, it is far from obvious that all designers use it. Papantonopoulos (2004) found some variations between strategies for the design of cognitive task allocation between ten studied system designers. In the same study, a common design strategy for task allocation was found: To apply a selected automation technology before or concurrent to task analysis, which is not the sequence that would be found in typical design literature (Papantonopoulos, 2004). A person reading the design literature would certainly risk getting the wrong impression of how designers work compared to the reported empirical findings. It has been showed that shared knowledge among engineers that design a system is related to the technical design and that, for instance system development time is affected by shared knowledge in engineering design teams (Avnet & Weigel, 2013).

Users are often considered as one of the subsystems of the global device by designer, and occasionally modelled through basic design principles or elements of an imagined scenario, dependent on what type of meetings are held through the design process (Darses & Wolff, 2006). Not only the type of meetings, but also the

design perspectives adopted by the designers in the design work affects the design outcome (Hult, Irestig, & Lundberg, 2006).

Similar to an architect who is designing a building, an organisation could be designed as well (Simons, 2005). Also the design-use process can in itself be designed. The technological design (e.g. component, relations, etc.) and the institutional design (e.g. responsibilities, allocation of costs, etc.) can both be formed by the higher level process design (i.e. designing the design process) (Koppenjan & Groenewegen, 2005).

If the design process is properly designed to manage situations, future users of products from the design process could indirectly benefit from this through increased SA.

The role of the usability designer is important for successful systems development, and it is important that the actual design solutions are directly influenced by the usability designer (Boivie, Gulliksen, & Göransson, 2006; Gulliksen, Boivie, & Göransson, 2006). Usable systems can support user SA. Depending on how a situation is represented, different means for interpretations and solutions emerge. Novel techniques supplies new opportunities to knowledge representation.

The role of the designer is important and valuable in the development of complex systems. Even if an end user could express a need it is the task of the designer to create a design solution. It is a simple solution, to let the user make all the choices, but is it the best solution? Does the user really want to make all the choices? Maybe there are too many choices? Do you really want to make the recipe yourself when you go to a restaurant? Is it not better if the professional food-designers

Table 2. The roles of function allocation affecting SA in development of complex systems

	Static	**Dynamic**
Between agents	Static function allocation between agents in a JCS	Dynamic function allocation between agents in a JCS
Between roles	Static function allocation between roles in the design-use process	Dynamic function allocation between roles in the design-use process

in the kitchen make some of the choices? It may also be that the efforts of making the choices are too heavy for the user's preferences.

All choices take mental effort to do. It is possible that we will have to develop a better understanding of the cost and benefit of choice, to be able to find the optimal level of choice. Even a trained designer does not possess all the HF related knowledge that may be beneficial, how is it then possible to expect the user to know that? Maybe the user knows what he/she wants, on a low level, but not on a higher level. Designing for the user demands design knowledge and especially design knowledge regarding HF. By just transferring design work to the user, the risk is that the user could not perform the design due to lack of competence or lack of time to make the effort, and the risk is also that other tasks of the user become worse performed due to the added workload imposed by added design tasks.

Also, performance and team SA will risk negative effects in an unrestricted environment with a lot of options. In a micro world setting with geographically distributed decision-makers acting as a team to control a dynamic system Brehmer and Svenmarck (1995) demonstrated better performance for decision-makers in a restricted hierarchical information structure than for those who, were fully connected so that they all could communicate with each other. Also, in a study of military command and control at battalion level Artman (2000) demonstrated how a technological implementation with fewer restrictions on information spreading seams to increase the efforts needed for the team to establish team SA.

Personalization of functions and user interfaces is no guarantee for implementing true user requirements. Sometimes the effectiveness of an organization will become superordinated personal preferences and individual attitudes. Additionally, personal preferences are not always considering optimal design solutions from an information presentation point of view. Interview data are not always reflecting users' desires, but could well be influenced by commercials and technical

capabilities. Sometimes it is a large discrepancy between what people are claming they are doing and what they actually are doing. Therefore, the outcome of a feasibility analysis provides measures of people's opinions, but does not necessarily reflect their future behaviour.

In many modern contexts the development has not ended when the product leaves the factory where it has been produced. A complementary approach to letting the user make the final design is to build in capability into the technical systems to assess the situation and adapt its behaviour accordingly. Fredriksson (2004) presents a method and approach toward establishment of open computational systems called online engineering, that focuses on the continuous refinement of behaviour and qualities, according to temporary concerns and individual aspects of cognitive agent, both human and machines. The process of creating SA is present in the running system, as well as in the preceding technical development process. To be able to aid SA the roles in the design process have to complement each other and therefore have to, at some level, share an understanding of each other's roles and contributions to this process.

The designers' contexts shape their understanding of their situation and thereby their SA. Although the end user is at the sharp end, designers and researchers are at the sharp end too, just another end. Who is not? What human being is not constrained by reality? SA is a matter for everybody. We have to manage our situation, whatever the situational context, or meta-situation, may be. However, by assessing SA in various contexts the development process of complex systems will be provided with valuable input.

MANAGING THE DESIGN-USE PROCESS

If something fails or work suboptimal, the reason for that could be found either in the technical part or in the human part or in the interaction between the two. Somewhat simplified the humans and the technical parts, are all part of the same system. Therefore, it is necessary from a development perspective to regard both of these parts of the total system simultaneously. The consequence of this is that the human contribution has to be regarded together with the technical. This is why it is necessary to include knowledge about human decision making into an iterative development process with a holistic approach to evaluations of the future system.

When managing differences in SA in the development of complex systems it is central to regard that empirical results, however valid, comes from the past and design is about the future. It is important to get a good description about the future context, for instance, by means of task analysis, including cognitive task analysis, and various user inputs. Singer (2002) demonstrated the use of including final users early in the development process when studying methods for validating cockpit design. A later example of when collecting users' opinions early in the design phase could enhance the situational awareness of a future complex system by regarding this in a development process is Barchéus and Mårtensson (2006) that reported on the views of air traffic controllers on future technology in air traffic management.

Many complex systems also have long life-cycles (e.g. Alfredson & Andersson, 2012). Considerations to regard is, for instance, that it is important that design solutions are not only relevant for today's technical solutions, but also comply with general interaction principles (Alfredson, Holmberg, Andersson, & Wikforss, 2011) that are more likely to be valid in a future context. However, it is impossible to foresee all consequences of a suggested design of a future system. This calls for an iterative development process. Only if we can test ideas and implementations in an iterative process, will we be able to avoid the pitfalls of bad human-system interaction. We need to use state-of-the-art methods, simulations and scenarios explicitly suited for iterative development of human-system interaction.

It is not possible to develop a system guaranteeing to generate SA, since the SA is context dependent. When developing a system, however, it is important to try to estimate a future context in which the system are likely to be used. When designing a future system we will encounter the envisioned world problem, where we as developers have to envision a world that does not yet exist, and try to figure out what is important there (Dekker, 1996; Dekker & Woods, 1999; Woods & Dekker, 2001). Often developers tend to focus on the technological advances and do not put as much effort into understanding the new conditions that humans in the envisioned world will experience. When some technology is changing, peoples understanding of the domain and their tasks change as well. In the evaluation of future system/product features or total performance, it is important to consider alternative design solutions and not only make comparisons with current systems/products, since work procedures, interaction dialogues, tasks, and organisation may be changed due to the implementation of the new technology.

Being aware of the own SA as well as of other agents' SA is mentally demanding. Even though the long term memory is practically infinite, the conscious awareness may not be aware of all the other agents SA simultaneously because of cognitive limitations, for instance, in short term memory and attention (Miller, 1956). The consciousness has to process information from the external world, through the senses, as well as memories and internal representations, such as mental models. Working memory specifically relates to higher levels of SA, such as projection (Gutzwiller & Clegg, 2013).

Differences within a team could be used for assessing the team SA, since it is important to have a reciprocal awareness between decision makers of SA aspects, to form a shared understanding of the situation at hand. Degree of agreement is therefore an important aspect of shared SA and thereby also of team SA. If agents differ in their understanding of the situation (or task) they have more difficult supporting each other. Further, if agents differ in their understanding of each other's SA or in their understanding of the team SA, they also have more difficult supporting each other. The equivalent approach could be used also for large organisations (i.e. groups of teams), systems of systems and roles in the design-use process.

The differences at the level of a team could be assessment of the situation by the individual versus assessment of the situation by a team member (situation-oriented degree of agreement), assessed individual SA by the individual versus assessed individual SA by a team member (team-oriented degree of agreement), or team SA assessed by the individual versus team SA assessed by a team member (also, team-oriented degree of agreement), to assess team SA.

The differences at the level of roles in the design-use process could be the design-use process as it is perceived by one role versus the design-use process as it is perceived by another role (process-oriented degree of agreement), or the role as it is actually manifested in reality versus the role as it is perceived by an other role (role-oriented degree of agreement), to assess common understanding or SA between the roles in the design-use process. Extrapolating this approach, differences between agents on any level could be analysed, such as, at the level of SA for systems of systems or why not intergalactic SA, dependent on the question at hand.

CONCLUSION

This paper has highlighted key aspects of managing differences in situational awareness due to roles in the design-use process of complex systems.

To conclude, it is important to be aware of both the impact the design process has on the end user SA as well as being aware of that designers and other contributors to the design process themselves has to consume design process properties that form their SA (of a meta-situation), indirectly having

an effect on the end user situation through the design. SA between individuals or groups having various roles in the design-use process could therefore be described, assessed and used as a tool for improving a design process.

ACKNOWLEDGMENT

This research has been supported by the Swedish Governmental Agency for Innovation Systems (Vinnova) through the National Aviation Engineering Research Program. This paper presents a selected revision and update to Alfredson (2007).

REFERENCES

Adams, M. J., Tenney, Y. J., & Pew, R. W. (1995). Situation awareness and the cognitive management of complex systems. *Human Factors*, *37*(1), 85–104. doi:10.1518/001872095779049462

Albinsson, P.-A. (2004). *Interacting with command and control systems: Tools for operators and designers.* Licentiate thesis (No. 1132). Linköping, Sweden: Linköping University.

Alfredson, J. (2001). *Aspects of situational awareness and its measures in an aircraft simulation context.* Licentiate thesis (No. 865). Linköping, Sweden: Linköping University.

Alfredson, J. (2007). *Differences in situational awareness and how to manage them in development of complex systems.* Doctoral dissertation (No. 1132). Linköping, Sweden: Linköping University.

Alfredson, J., & Andersson, R. (2012). Managing human factors in the development of fighter aircraft. In E. Abu-Taieh, A. El Sheikh, & M. Jafari (Eds.), *Technology Engineering and Management in Aviation: Advancements and Discoveries* (pp. 101–116). IGI Global.

Alfredson, J., Angelborg-Thanderz, M., Danielsson, M., Farkin, B., Farmer, E., Hadley, B., et al. (1996). *Human awareness criteria* (Tech. Rep. No. VINTHEC-WP1-TR01). Amsterdam: National Aerospace Laboratory NLR.

Alfredson, J., Holmberg, J., Andersson, R., & Wikforss, M. (2011). Applied cognitive ergonomics design principles for fighter aircraft. In HarrisD. (Ed.) *Proceedings of the 9th International Conference on Engineering Psychology and Cognitive Ergonomics (EPCE 2011)* (pp. 473–483). Springer-Verlag. doi:10.1007/978-3-642-21741-8_50

Annett, J. (2002). Subjective rating scales: Science or art? *Ergonomics*, *45*(14), 966–987. doi:10.1080/00140130210166951 PMID:12569049

Artman, H. (2000). Team situation assessment and information distribution. *Ergonomics*, *43*(8), 1111–1128. doi:10.1080/00140130050084905 PMID:10975176

Avnet, M. S., & Weigel, A. L. (2013). The structural approach to shared knowledge: An application to engineering design teams. *Human Factors*, *55*(3), 581–594. doi:10.1177/0018720812462388 PMID:23829032

Barchéus, F., & Mårtensson, L. (2006). Air traffic management and future technology: The views of the controllers. *Human Factors and Aerospace Safety*, *6*(1), 1–16.

Boivie, I., Gulliksen, J., & Göransson, B. (2006). The lonesome cowboy: A study of the usability designer role in systems development. *Interacting with Computers*, *18*(4), 601–634. doi:10.1016/j.intcom.2005.10.003

Brehmer, B., & Svenmarck, P. (1995). Distributed decision making in dynamic environments: Time scales and architectures of decision making. In J.-P. Caverni, M. Bar-Hillel, F. H. Barron, & H. Jungermann (Eds.), *Contributions to decision making - I* (pp. 155–174). Amsterdam: Elsevier.

Brown, A. (1987). Metacognition, executive control, self regulation, and other more mysterious mechanisms. In F. E. Weinert, & R. H. Kluwe (Eds.), *Metacognition, motivation and understanding* (pp. 65–116). Hillsdale, NJ: Erlbaum.

Cajander, Å. (2010). *Usability - Who Cares? The Introduction of User-Centred Systems Design in Organisations*. Doctoral thesis, Uppsala University, Sweden. Uppsala: Acta Universitatis Upsaliensis.

Candell, O. (2009). *Development of Information Support Solutions for Complex Technical Systems using eMaintenance*. Doctoral dissertation. Luleå, Sweden: Luleå University of Technology.

Chambres, P., Izaute, M., & Marescaux, P.-J. (Eds.). (2002). *Metacognition: Process, function and use*. Boston: Kluwer Academic Publishers. doi:10.1007/978-1-4615-1099-4

Darses, F., & Wolff, M. (2006). How do designers represent to themselves the users' needs? *Applied Ergonomics*, *37*(6), 757–764. doi:10.1016/j.apergo.2005.11.004 PMID:16442493

Davidsson, S., & Alm, H. (2014). *Context adaptable driver information – Or, what do whom need and want when?* Applied Cognitive Ergonomics.

Defense Science Board (2012). *The role of autonomy in DoD systems*. Washington, DC: Undersecretary of Defense.

Dekker, S. W. A. (1996). Cognitive complexity in management by exception: Deriving early human factors requirements for an envisioned air traffic management world. In D. Harris (Ed.), Engineering psychology and cognitive ergonomics, volume I: Transportation systems (pp. 201-210). Aldershot, UK: Ashgate.

Dekker, S. W. A. (2003). Illusions of explanation: A critical essay on error classification. *The International Journal of Aviation Psychology*, *13*(2), 95–106. doi:10.1207/S15327108IJAP1302_01

Dekker, S. W. A. (2005). *Ten questions about human error: A new view of human factors and systems safety*. Mahwah, NJ: Erlbaum.

Dekker, S. W. A. (2007). Doctors are more dangerous than gun owners: A rejoinder to error counting. *Human Factors*, *49*(2), 177–184. doi:10.1518/001872007X312423 PMID:17447661

Dekker, S. W. A., & Lützhöft, M. (2004). Correspondence, cognition and sensemaking: A radical empiricist view of situation awareness. In S. Banbury, & S. Tremblay (Eds.), *A cognitive approach to situation awareness: Theory and application* (pp. 22–41). Aldershot, UK: Ashgate.

Dekker, S. W. A., & Woods, D. D. (1999). Extracting data from the future: Assessment and certification of envisioned systems. In S. Dekker, & E. Hollnagel (Eds.), *Coping with computers in the cockpit* (pp. 131–143). Aldershot, UK: Ashgate.

Ek, Å. (2006). *Safety culture in sea and aviation transport*. Doctoral dissertation. Lund, Sweden: Lund University.

Endsley, M. R. (1988). Situation awareness global assessment technique (SAGAT). In *Proceedings of the IEEE National Aerospace and Electronics Conference* (pp. 789-795). New York: IEEE.

Endsley, M. R. (1995a). Measurement of situation awareness in dynamic systems. *Human Factors*, *37*(1), 65–84. doi:10.1518/001872095779049499

Endsley, M. R. (1995b). Toward a theory of situation awareness in dynamic systems. *Human Factors*, *37*(1), 32–64. doi:10.1518/001872095779049543

Endsley, M. R. (2000). Direct measurement of situation awareness: Validity and use of SAGAT. In M. R. Endsley, & D. J. Garland (Eds.), *Situation awareness analysis and measurement* (pp. 147–173). Mahwah, NJ: Erlbaum.

Endsley, M. R., Bolstad, C. A., Jones, D. G., & Riley, J. M. (2003). Situation awareness oriented design: From user's cognitive requirements to creating effective supporting technologies. In *Proceedings of the Human Factors and Ergonomics Society 47th Annual Meeting* (pp. 268-272). Santa Monica, CA: Human Factors and Ergonomics Society.

Endsley, M. R., Bolté, B., & Jones, D. G. (2003). *Designing for situation awareness: An approach to user-centered design*. London: Taylor & Francis. doi:10.1201/9780203485088

Fällman, D. (2003). *In romance with the materials of mobile interaction: A phenomenological approach to the design of mobile information technology*. Doctoral dissertation. Umeå, Sweden: University of Umeå.

Feigh, K. M., & Pritchett, A. R. (2014). Requirements for effective function allocation: A critical review. *Journal of Cognititve Engineering and Decision Making*, *8*(1), 23–32. doi:10.1177/1555343413490945

Flach, J. M. (1995). Maintaining situation awareness when stalking cognition in the wild. In D. J. Garland & M. R. Endsley (Eds.), *Proceedings of an International Conference on Experimental Analysis and Measurement of Situation Awareness* (pp. 25-34). Daytona Beach, FL: Embry-Riddle Aeronautical University Press.

Flavell, J. H. (1976). Metacognitive aspects of problem solving. In L. B. Resnick (Ed.), *The Nature of Intelligence* (pp. 231–235). Hillsdale, NJ: Erlbaum.

Fredriksson, M. (2004). *Online engineering: On the nature of open computational systems.* Doctoral dissertation (No. 2004:05). Karlskrona, Sweden: Blekinge Institute of Technology.

Gulliksen, J., Boivie, I., & Göransson, B. (2006). Usability professionals: Current practices and future development. *Interacting with Computers, 18*(4), 568–600. doi:10.1016/j.intcom.2005.10.005

Gutzwiller, R. S., & Clegg, B. A. (2013). The role of working memory in levels of situation awareness. *Journal of Cognitive Engineering and Decision Making, 7*(2), 141–154. doi:10.1177/1555343412451749

Handley, H., & Smillie, R. (2008). Architecture framework human view: The NATO approach. *Systems Engineering, 11*(2), 156–164. doi:10.1002/sys.20093

Handley, H. A. H. (2014). A network model for human interoperability. *Human Factors, 56*(2), 349–360. doi:10.1177/0018720813493640 PMID:24689253

Hartman, B. O., & Secrist, G. E. (1991). Situational awareness is more than exceptional vision. *Aviation, Space, and Environmental Medicine, 62*, 1084–1089. PMID:1741725

Hollnagel, E., & Woods, D. D. (1983). Cognitive systems engineering: New wine in new bottles. *International Journal of Man-Machine Studies, 18*(6), 583–600. doi:10.1016/S0020-7373(83)80034-0

Hollnagel, E., & Woods, D. D. (2005). *Joint cognitive systems: Foundations of cognitive systems engineering.* Boca Raton, FL: Taylor & Francis. doi:10.1201/9781420038194

Hult, L., Irestig, M., & Lundberg, J. (2006). Design perspectives. *Human-Computer Interaction, 21*(1), 5–48. doi:10.1207/s15327051hci2101_2

Jones, D. G., & Endsley, M. R. (1996). Sources of situation awareness errors in aviation. *Aviation, Space, and Environmental Medicine, 67*(6), 507–512. PMID:8827130

Jones, D. G., Endsley, M. R., Bolstad, M., & Estes, G. (2004). The designer's situation awareness toolkit: Support for user-centered design. In *Proceedings of the Human Factors Society 48th Annual Meeting* (pp. 653-657). Santa Monica, CA: Human Factors Society.

Jones, D. G., & Kaber, D. B. (2005). Situation awareness measurement and the situation awareness global assessment technique. In N. Stanton, A. Hedge, K. Brookhuis, E. Salas, & H. Hendrick (Eds.), *Handbook of human factors and ergonomics methods* (pp. 42.1–42.7). Boca Raton, FL: CRC Press.

Klein, G., Orasanu, J., Calderwood, R., & Zsambok, C. (Eds.). (1993). *Decision making in action: Models and methods.* Norwood, NJ: Ablex.

Knez, W. L., & Ham, D. J. (2006). A comparison of the effects of fatigue on subjective and objective assessment of situation awareness in cycling. *Journal of Sports Science & Medicine, 5*(1), 89–96. PMID:24198685

Koppenjan, J., & Groenewegen, J. (2005). Istitutional design for complex technological systems. *International Journal of Technology. Policy and Management, 5*(3), 40–257.

Lichacz, F. M. J., Cain, B., & Patel, S. (2003). Calibration of confidence in situation awareness queries. In *Proceedings of the Human Factors and Ergonomics Society 47th Annual Meeting* (pp. 222-226). Santa Monica, CA: Human Factors and Ergonomics Society. doi:10.1177/154193120304700147

Lichacz, F. M. J., & Farrell, P. S. E. (2005). The calibration of situation awareness and confidence within a multinational operational net assessment. *Military Psychology*, *17*(4), 247–268. doi:10.1207/s15327876mp1704_1

McGuinness, B. (1995). Situational awareness measurement in cockpit evaluation trials. In Situation Awareness: Limitations and Enhancement in the Aviation Environment (AGARD-CP-575, pp. 7.1-7.8). Neuilly-Sur-Seine, France: NATO Research and Technology Organization.

McGuinness, B. (2004). Quantitative analysis of situational awareness (QUASA): Applying signal detection theory to true/false probes and self-ratings. In *Proceedings of 9th International Command and Control Research and Technology Symposium* (pp. 159-178). Washington, DC: US Department of Defence Command and Control Research Program.

Means, B., Salas, E., Crandall, B., & Jacobs, T. O. (1993). Training decision makers for the real world. In G. A. Klein, J. Orasanu, R. Calderwood, & C. E. Zsambok (Eds.), *Decision making in action: Models and methods* (pp. 306–326). Norwood, NJ: Ablex.

Miller, G. A. (1956). The magical number seven, plus or minus two: Some limits on our capacity for processing information. *Psychological Review*, *63*(2), 81–97. doi:10.1037/h0043158 PMID:13310704

Mulgund, S., Rinkus, G., Illgen, C., Zacharias, G., & Friskie, J. (1997). OLIPSA: On-line intelligent processor for situation assessment. In K. Garner (Ed.), *Second Annual Symposium and Exhibition on Situational Awareness in the Tactical Air Environment*. Patuxent River, MD: Naval Air Warfare Center Aircraft Division.

Neisser, U. (1976). *Cognition and reality principles and implications of cognitive psychology*. San Francisco: Freeman.

Papantonopoulos, S. (2004). How system designers think: A study of design thinking in human factors engineering. *Ergonomics*, *47*(14), 1528–1548. doi:10.1080/0014013041233129091 6 PMID:15697068

Perkins, D. N. (1989). Reasoning as it is and could be: An empirical perspective. In D. M. Topping, D. C. Crowell, & V. N. Kobayashi (Eds.), *The 3rd International Conference on Thinking* (pp. 175-194). Hillsdale, NJ: Erlbaum.

Pritchett, A. R., Kim, S. Y., & Feigh, K. M. (2014a). Measuring human-automation function allocation. *Journal of Cognititve Engineering and Decision Making*, *8*(1), 52–77. doi:10.1177/1555343413490166

Pritchett, A. R., Kim, S. Y., & Feigh, K. M. (2014b). Modeling human-automation function allocation. *Journal of Cognititve Engineering and Decision Making*, *8*(1), 33–51. doi:10.1177/1555343413490944

Proctor, R. W., & Dutta, A. (1995). *Skill acquisition and human performance*. London: SAGE.

Rankin, A., Lundberg, J., Woltjer, R., Rollenhagen, C., & Hollnagel, E. (2014). Resilience in everyday operations: A framework for analyzing adaptations in high-risk work. *Journal of Cognititve Engineering and Decision Making*, *8*(1), 78–97. doi:10.1177/1555343413498753

Rasmussen, J. (1983). Skills, rules, and knowledge: Signals, signs, and symbols, and other distinction in human performance models. *IEEE Transactions on Systems, Man, and Cybernetics*, *13*(3), 257–266. doi:10.1109/TSMC.1983.6313160

Rasmussen, J. (1986). *Information processing and human-machine interaction: An approach to cognitive engineering*. New York: North-Holland.

Reason, J. (1988). Cognitive aids in process environments: Prostheses or tools? In E. Hollnagel, G. Mancini, & D. D. Woods (Eds.), *Cognitive engineering in complex dynamic worlds* (pp. 7–14). London: Academic Press.

Reason, J. (1990). *Human error*. Cambridge, UK: Cambridge University Press. doi:10.1017/CBO9781139062367

Reason, J. (1997). *Managing the risks of organizational accidents*. Aldershot, UK: Ashgate.

Simons, R. (2005). *Levers of organization design: How managers use accountability systems for greater performance and commitment*. Boston: Harvard Business School Press.

Singer, G. (2002). *Methods for validating cockpit design: The best tool for the task*. Doctoral dissertation. Stockholm: Royal Institute of Technology.

Smith, K., & Hancock, P. A. (1995). Situation awareness is adaptive, externally directed consciousness. *Human Factors*, *37*(1), 137–148. doi:10.1518/001872095779049444

Sneddon, A., Mearns, K., & Flin, R. (2006). Situation awareness and safety in offshore drill crews. *Cognition Technology and Work*, *8*(4), 255–267. doi:10.1007/s10111-006-0040-1

Sohn, Y. W., & Doane, S. M. (2004). Memory processes of flight situation awareness: Interactive roles of working memory capacity, long-term working memory, and expertise. *Human Factors*, *46*(3), 461–475. doi:10.1518/hfes.46.3.461.50392 PMID:15573546

Stanton, N. A., Stewart, R., Harris, D., Houghton, R. J., Baber, C., & McMaster, R. et al. (2006). Distributed situation awareness in dynamic systems: Theoretical development and application of an ergonomics methodology. *Ergonomics*, *49*(12-13), 1288–1311. doi:10.1080/00140130600612762 PMID:17008257

Taylor, G. S., Reinerman-Jones, L. E., Szalma, J. L., Mouloua, M., & Hancock, P. A. (2013). What to automate: Addressing the multidimensionality of cognitive resources through systems design. *Journal of Cognitive Engineering and Decision Making*, *7*(4), 311–329. doi:10.1177/1555343413495396

Walker, G. H., Stanton, N. A., & Young, M. S. (2006). The ironies of vehicle feedback in car design. *Ergonomics*, *49*(2), 161–179. doi:10.1080/00140130500448085 PMID:16484143

Waltz, E., & Llinas, J. (1990). *Multisensor data fusion*. Norwood, MA: Artech House.

White, L. J., & Cohen, E. I. (1980). A domain strategy for computer program testing. *IEEE Transactions on Software Engineering*, *6*(3), 247–257. doi:10.1109/TSE.1980.234486

Woltjer, R. (2009). *Functional modeling of constraint management in aviation safety and command and control*. Doctoral dissertation (No.1249). Linköping, Sweden: Linköping University.

Woods, D. D., & Dekker, S. W. A. (2001). Anticipating the effects of technology change: A new era of dynamics for ergonomics. *Theoretical Issues in Ergonomics Science*, *1*(3), 272–282. doi:10.1080/14639220110037452

Woods, D. D., & Hollnagel, E. (2006). *Joint cognitive systems: Patterns in cognitive systems engineering*. Boca Raton, FL: Taylor & Francis. doi:10.1201/9781420005684

Zacharias, G. L., Miao, A. X., Illgen, C. X., Yara, J. M., & Siouris, G. M. (1996). SAMPLE: Situation awareness model for pilot in-the-loop evaluation. In *Proceedings of the First Annual Symposium on Situational Awareness in the Tactical Air Environment*. Patuxent River, MD: Naval Air Warfare Center Aircraft Division.

KEY TERMS AND DEFINITIONS

Complex Systems: Many different and inter-related parts.

Design: Forming ideas for realization.

Design-Use Process: The life-cycle and context from design to use.

Function Allocation: Deciding who should do what.

Human Factors: Ergonomics, including human-machine interaction and its consequences.

Roles in the Design-Use Process: The designer, the user, the manager etcetera.

Situational Awareness: Being aware of what is going on.

Chapter 8
Improving Novice Programmers' Skills through Playability and Pattern Discovery:
A Descriptive Study of a Game Building Workshop

Thiago Schumacher Barcelos
Instituto Federal de Educação, Ciência e Tecnologia de São Paulo, Brazil & Universidade Cruzeiro do Sul, Brazil

Roberto Muñoz Soto
Universidad de Valparaíso – Escuela de Ingeniería Civil Informática, Chile

Ismar Frango Silveira
Universidade Cruzeiro do Sul, Brazil & Universidade Presbiteriana Mackenzie, Brazil

ABSTRACT

Game design and development has already been discussed as a viable, motivating alternative to introduce Computer Science concepts to young students. In this sense, it would be useful to obtain a deeper understanding of which skills could be developed in these activities and how such skills could be useful in future careers. This chapter presents the design and evaluation of a Game Building Workshop aimed at introducing the fundamentals of structured programming to students. The games produced by students during 12 weeks were evaluated and the results confronted with students' questions and comments made along the workshop meetings and a final interview. The results indicate that students explored novel programming concepts in order to add features that were not initially planned for the proposed games. These additional features solve playability issues that are highly influential to the experience of the students as game players. Students also reused previously applied solutions to solve similar problems that appeared in subsequent activities. This is an indication that students developed or exercised analogy and abstraction skills during the workshop activities.

DOI: 10.4018/978-1-4666-6485-2.ch008

INTRODUCTION

Along the last decade, students' enrollment rates in undergraduate courses related to Computer Science (CS) and Information Technology (IT) have been decreasing in various countries. Muratet et al. (2009) identified a 25% decrease in the number of students enrolled in Computer Science careers in a French university between 2005 and 2009. Crenshaw et al. (2008) reported that the interest of North American students for CS courses declined by 50% during the '00 decade. Hernandez et al. (2010) compared the student enrollment rate in CS courses of a top Brazilian university to the same rate in a university in the United States and found that the same tendency for a diminishing interest appears in both countries.

It has been argued (Hernandez et al., 2010) that student enrollment in computing courses is historically related to the spread of technological advances, such as the personal computer and the Internet. Based on this argument, it would be surprising to witness a lack of students' interest for the field of computing nowadays, given the high degree of technological achievements in the past few years, besides of their pervasiveness. After all, children and teenagers deal with a growing variety of interactive computational devices, such as tablets, cell phones and portable videogames. However, the increasing exposure to such gadgets does not seem to stimulate students to pursue technology-related careers. One possible reason that has been pointed out is that students are not properly exposed to Computer Science concepts during the basic educational levels, since CS is not considered as a Basic Science in any curricula (Barcelos & Silveira, 2012; Carter, 2006). High dropout rates in introductory courses may also be related to the lack of motivating didactic strategies (Rizvi, Humphries, Major, Jones, & Lauzun, 2011).

On the other hand, the presence of some skills in specific knowledge areas may contribute to the academic success of CS and IT students. Skills related to Mathematics are often mentioned to have an influence in student achievement in CS/IT. Such studies are not new; Campbell and McCabe (1984) analyzed a sample of 256 freshmen of an north American university to conclude that SAT scores in Math, high school rank and average grade high school grades in Math are predictors for the group of students who continued in the course after two semesters. More recently, Wilson e Shrock (2001) found a similar correlation between the number of Math disciplines taken by students during high school and their performance in an introductory CS discipline. Beaubouef (2002) presents an extensive discussion about the importance of Math topics that are related to many subjects studied in CS. It may be convenient, though, to identify which are the high-level skills related to Math that should be mastered by students in order to improve their academic performance in CS/IT. As a consequence, college education would be able to deliver better professionals to the labor market.

Abstraction is, for instance, a relevant skill that is present in the field of Mathematics and that is equally important to Computing. A discussion about this topic is presented by Kramer (2007), who argues that building and understanding abstract models is crucial to object-oriented design and programming; also, selecting the most important aspects of a given real situation and leaving out unnecessary details is important to the activities of a requirements engineer. On the other hand, the process of problem solving in Math involves skills related to abstraction, such as analogy, generalization and specialization (Polya, 2004).

This chapter presents the design of a Game Building Workshop aimed at teaching the fundamentals of programming to students enrolled in Computing-related courses. The workshop was designed based on previous evidence (Bayliss & Strout, 2006; Leutenegger, 2006) that the domain of game design and construction might have a relevant impact on students' motivation. Besides that, our objective was also to understand how students might develop higher-order skills, such as abstraction, by dealing with tasks related to game design, which are presented at progressive levels of complexity. The workshop structure and its activities are presented, also discussing its pedagogical foundations. In order to analyze its impacts, an experimental evaluation of the workshop activities was conducted in the first semester of 2013. Based on the observation of lab activities and analysis of the games produced by students, the role of students' motivation is discussed, as well as how traces of pattern recognition skills could be identified on students' works.

BACKGROUND

Game Design as a Teaching Strategy

Building games has been advocated as a teaching strategy to develop skills in fields such as computational thinking (Settle, 2011), logic reasoning (Souza & Dias, 2012) and programming fundamentals (Hernandez et al., 2010). Games are often seen as a motivating resource for students of the new generations, defined by Prensky (2004) as *digital natives*. These students, born after the 1990 decade, usually grew up dealing with several interactive devices such as cell phones, videogames and computers. Hence, games are one kind of digital media that students are very familiar with, supposedly bringing a unlimited potential for its use in educational activities. Peppler and Kafai (2009) argue that games are so integrated into modern culture that students should develop a *fluency* in games, that is, a deeper understanding of its mechanics and how they are built. In addition to that, Salen (2007, p. 302) states that digital games are "entry points for many young people into digital literacy, social communities, and tech-savvy identities".

It is important to point out that, in a general sense, digital games are no more than interactive systems with special requirements related to the way the interaction with its user takes place. The interaction with the player must provide increasing challenges and unpredictable outcomes, but also allow the player to feel "in control" in order to explore the world of the game (Barcelos, Carvalho, Schimiguel, & Silveira, 2011). In their classic work about user interface development, Hix & Hartson (1993) argue that a regular user perceives the system interface as the whole system; there lies the importance of good user interface design. Clearly, this also applies to the design of digital games. Salen (2007) has already mentioned that digital game design is a process of "reflection-in-action", as discussed by Schön & Bennett (1996): the designer must take into consideration the possibilities and constraints that emerge during the design process. According to these authors, this process may only take place when the designer actively deals with the materials. In the case of software design, the "materials" are not tangible; in this case, prototyping must be used to identify and reflect about the design possibilities.

Several authoring and programming environments were developed in the last years to facilitate the process of creating games. These environments include Scratch (MIT Media Lab, 2012), Alice (Carnegie Mellon University, 2013), GameMaker (YoYo Games, Ltd., 2014) and Kodu Game Lab (Microsoft Research, 2014), among others. These environments allow children and teenagers to create their own games in a less complex way than what was possible with traditional programming languages. Some research works describe the learning outcomes obtained by young students who are introduced to these game creation environments. Maloney et al. (2008) analyze 536 projects made in Scratch by children and teenagers in an after-school computer clubhouse to conclude that the participants successfully incorporated in their project concepts of user interaction, loops and message synchronization, among others. Participants were not explicitly instructed to use Scratch and frequently opted to use this environment, despite the fact there were other activities available. The authors argue that the simplified programming mechanics and the immediate feedback may have stimulated the participants to use Scratch. Stolee and Fristoe (2011) analyze games developed with Kodu Game Lab that were made available at an online community. Concepts such as variables, control flow, Boolean logic and rudimentary instantiation of objects could be identified in the games. Hernandez et al. (2010) describe a didactic experience with freshman in an introductory discipline of an Information Technology undergraduate course. Students built games using GameMaker environment and applied the concepts of variables, event handling and loops. The approval rate of students and the number of delivered exercises both increased after this experience, which may be an indicative that students were more motivated to learn introductory programming concepts by building games.

Experiences like the one described by Hernandez et al. (2010) indicate that undergraduate students may also benefit from didactic strategies that incorporate game building. Malan & Leitner (2007) describe a programming fundamentals course that was modified to present the basic programming structures to students using Scratch; afterwards, Java syntax and structures were introduced. Most students perceived that this approach helped them to deal with the complexity of the Java syntax, especially those that had no previous programming experience. According to the authors of such study, Scratch environment allowed students to focus almost exclusively on the logical aspects of the developed projects. The code in Scratch is made out of blocks that only "snap" together in syntactically correct ways; hence, students do not have to deal with syntax issues when they start coding. Other experiences where digital game creation was incorporated into introductory programming courses at the undergraduate level are described by Rizvi et al. (2011), Leutenegger (2006) and Bayliss & Strout (2006). The evaluation of such initiatives is usually based on the improvement of overall grades or the self-perception of students about their motivation

with the course. However, few studies have dealt with the question of specific skills and contents that might have been learned by students. These studies are mostly focused on Computer Science outreach programs (Franklin et al., 2013; Adams & Webster, 2012; Denner, Werner, & Ortiz, 2012) and include some kind of assessment of programming skills acquisition. However, little attention has been given to how higher-level cognitive skills related to these programming activities would be useful to students that will continue their studies in CS or IT.

Programming-Related Skills

Several authors have researched about skills differences between novice and expert programmers. These studies often have a cognitivist basis and have been developed since the late 1970's. For example, according to McKeithen et al. (1981), the differences between novice and expert programmers do not lie only in their capacity to process large quantities of significant information. This has been demonstrated in other domains than programming, such as chess (Waters, Gobet, & Leyden, 2002), web navigation (Chen, Fan, & Macredie, 2006), music (Colley, Banton, Down, & Pither, 1992) or physics (Chi, Feltovich, & Glaser, 1981; Larkin, McDermott, Simon, & Simon, 1980). Apart from information processing skills, there is evidence that the differences may reside in the way novices and experts gather and organize information (Lister, Simon, Thompson, Whalley, & Prasad, 2006). Although it is expected that experts possess more knowledge than novices, Bateson et al. (1987) indicate that experts also have a more sophisticate and flexible knowledge organization. A representative example from an experiment in the domain of chess is described by Chase & Simon (1973): expert chess players have better information recall when pieces are associated to a strategy; however, their recalling is much worse when pieces are randomly distributed on the board, because the known abstract models of attack and defense are no longer present. This example is revisited by Bateson et al. (1987) and Lister et al. (2006), who argue that expert programmers tend to organize and recall their knowledge using higher-order strategies.

A similar argument is made by Weiser & Shertz (1983), who state that expert programmers are no different from experienced physics as far as their problem-solving skills are considered. The authors argue that both professionals represent a given problem in terms of general principles that do not appear in the general statement of the problem. Also, they identified that programming skills were related to the time necessary to write a new program in order to make it functional, to the number of times a program is submitted before completion, the number of known languages, and the familiarity to some programming concepts. On the other hand, skills were not related to the time needed to debug, modify or understand a new program.

The previous findings are related to those reported by Shneiderman & Mayer (1979), who argue about differences between novice and expert programmers and about the differences between the syntactic and semantic memories in the domain of computer programming. Semantic memory is relatively independent from the syntactic rules of some programming language, and semantic knowledge can be constructed by constantly engaging in problem-solving activities (Bateson et al., 1987). Besides that, semantic knowledge is stored as general and meaningful sets of information (Shneiderman & Mayer, 1979). Bateson et al. (1987) indicate that expert programmers use the syntactic memory and a high-level knowledge plan to guide their programming activities. Previously, Shneiderman (1976) had already identified that expert programmers can perform better than novices on recalling structured programs, although the former ones may introduce syntactic mistakes that do not compromise the output of the program (in other words, its semantic aspect).

Soloway et al. (1982) suggest that expert programmers use more than syntactic and semantic knowledge when writing code to solve a problem; they would also rely on a high level plan based on previous knowledge and reflection. According to these authors, a plan is a procedure or set of activities in which the key elements of the process have been summarized and represented in an explicit form. When faced with a new problem, an expert retrieves from her knowledge base the possible plans that were useful in similar situations and incorporates those plans into the solution. Possible plans are classified in three categories (Soloway et al., 1982): (a) strategic plans, that specify a global strategy to define an algorithm; (b) tactical plans, that specify a local strategy to solve a problem; (c) execution plans, that rely on characteristics of a specific programming language to implement tactical and strategic plans.

Based on the previous findings about the way experts solve problems, it would be useful for educators to have a systematic way to "communicate" these skills to novices, perhaps through a set of patterns. For instance, software patterns have been proven to be a powerful tool to represent knowledge about best practices used by experts in the area of software design and development (Muller, Haberman, & Averbuch, 2004). One of main advantages of patterns is the possibility to reuse and adapt them to solve new problems, as long as the pattern matches the relevant characteristics of previous problems for which it has been proven to be useful. According to East et al. (1996), students must develop and apply two skills in order to properly use patterns. The first skill is being able to choose the most appropriate model or schema among similar ones. The second one is being able to adapt and modify patterns to suit the solution to the problem that is being currently solved.

Both of these skills are related to aspects of abstraction. Polya (2004) defined that aspects related to abstraction (analogy, generalization and specialization) are crucial for a Math student to succeed in problem-solving tasks. A similar definition in the context of programming skills acquisition is presented by Haberman & Muller (2008), who defined abstraction by the following features: (a) generalization of specific examples; (b) identification, extraction, and isolation of essential components, and (c) ignoring or holding back irrelevant details. Abstraction skills related to pattern identification and usage must be obtained through various experiences, similar to the development of semantic memory (Bateson et al., 1987); also, adequate teacher support may be necessary to help students identify which might be the relevant aspects of some problem (Haberman & Muller, 2008; Clancy & Linn, 1999).

Hence, game design activities have already been used to motivate and engage students; previous results show that students may successfully deal with fundamental programming concepts through some game engine and afterwards make a "smoother" transition to conventional programming languages. On the other hand, based on previous research (Bateson et al., 1987; Soloway et al., 1982; Shneiderman & Mayer, 1979) it is expected that a novice programmer will increasingly rely on higher-order semantic plans when he/she becomes more experienced. These plans may be defined by using analogy and abstraction (Polya, 2004; East et al., 1996); in this chapter, this particular hypothesis is tested in the context of digital game building activities. Considering that most students that take part in such activities may be classified as digital natives, as stated by Prensky (2004), it will also analyzed how their previous experience with digital games, if any, may influence their programming skills development.

GAME BUILDING WORKSHOP

Structure

The Game Building Workshop was designed to be incorporated into a introductory course on fundamentals of programming to freshmen in a professional education career in Informatics offered by the São Paulo Federal Institute of Education, Science and Technology, Brazil. This type of career is offered in Brazil to students that are enrolled at the same time in regular high school or that have already completed this educational level. It is a 3-semester long course aimed at preparing students to the job market in a short time. Learning the fundamentals of programming and the syntax of a first programming language is usually a significant hurdle to students; hence, the issues with high failure and dropout rates mentioned before are also present in this course. The Game Building Workshop was initially designed as a strategy to deal with these issues. At the same time, a secondary goal for the workshop was that its activities were partially compliant to curriculum guidelines related to the development of computational thinking skills. The CSTA (Computer Science Teachers Association) Standards for Computer Science Education at the K-12 level (CSTA, 2011) define that students should be exposed to the principles of construction of algorithms; also, they should be able to use some fundamental programming structures (looping behavior, conditional statements, logic, expressions, variables and functions) between the last years of middle school and the first years of high school. This way, the workshop activities should be flexible enough to be also offered in the future to students that are enrolled only in regular high school education.

The workshop activities are distributed along 12 weeks; each weekly meeting lasts about 2.5 hours, when students explore concepts related to game design (sprite animation, collision detection, keyboard and mouse control, for instance) and also to programming fundamentals (e. g., variables, conditional and loop structures, messages). Each activity is related to the construction of interaction mechanisms that are present in a digital game. Scratch was the tool used to develop the games due to the similarity of its programming structures to those used by traditional, structured programming languages.

In the first meetings of the workshop, students are introduced to the Scratch environment, to the concept of variables and to basic conditional and looping structures. Starting in the fourth meeting, students begin to implement full-featured games. The implemented games are: a digital version of the Rock-Paper-Scissors hand game, a war simulation game (named *Point-and-Shoot* from now on) and clones of the famous games Breakout and Pacman. In Rock-Paper-Scissors game, students define keystrokes for each one of the three possible actions of both players and define how the outcomes of the game will be displayed. In Point-and-Shoot game, students build an algorithm that defines a linear trajectory for a bullet, triggered by a keypress, and the possible conditions for the bullet to explode (hitting an enemy target or a wall). Breakout rules also involve defining a linear trajectory, but now of a

ball, with the additional rule that it has to bounce when it hits a brick or a player-controlled paddle. In Pacman students must implement controls for main character's movements, constrained by the paths of a maze, and also define the movements of two ghost enemies. One of the ghosts should chase the Pacman and the other one should follow a fixed path inside the maze. This last game is the Workshop's final project and its results are part of students' evaluation (Figure 1).

The workshop follows a Problem-Based-Learning (PBL) perspective. According to Merril (2002), PBL is a student-centered strategy; they should work in a collaborative way to find a solution to a problem proposed by the teacher. The teacher's role is to help students to mobilize their own previous knowledge and then build new knowledge in order to solve the problem. This new knowledge is gradually built, based on empirical experimentation. In each Workshop meeting, teacher is meant to present a previously

Figure 1. Examples of games produced during the Game Building Workshop

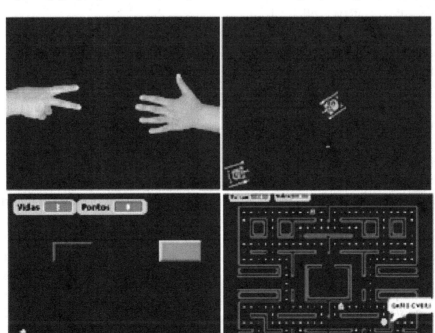

implemented version of the game to illustrate the features that should be implemented by the students. Then, students begin to work and the teacher may intervene when asked by them.

In order to define Workshop activities and their organization according to the schedule of the meetings, four guidelines were defined, presented and justified as follow:

1. *The motivation for all workshop activities is the implementation of some game's features:* This guideline is grounded on the game fluency development advocated by Peppler and Kafai (2009), who argue that digital games are a cultural artifact for the new generations; hence, when students are engaged in game building activities, these activities may provide opportunities for critical thinking and meaningful learning;

2. *The sequence of activities must propel students to building full-featured games:* This guideline is based on the Use – Modify – Create framework introduced by Lee *et al.* (2011). In many of the activities, students are initially asked to interact with small programs. Once students are familiarized with the programming structures used, they are invited to introduce some modifications to the original features of the programs. Eventually, students will be confident enough to create their own games from scratch using skills they have acquired on previous activities. One should notice that this strategy is not entirely "linear": a student may be a "creator" at some stage and then be a "user" in a following activity in order to understand a novel concept. Nevertheless, the structure of Workshop activities is designed to allow students to be "creators" more and more often in subsequent activities.

3. *Activities must progressively require that students explore new concepts and, at the same time, reuse concepts that were previously explored by them:* As students must

learn new concepts in order to accomplish new tasks and also use concepts that were previously learned, it is expected that the activities present a challenging level that is always proportional to the students' skills. This guideline is based on the flow theory, discussed by Nakamura & Csikszentmihalyi (2009). According to the authors, flow is a state of deep concentration and engagement in a given activity, when higher productivity levels could be reached; when one's skill level matches the level of challenge required by a given activity, he/she is said to be in the flow state. This is applicable when students are working autonomously; however, teacher support is still needed when a student is not able to accomplish a task otherwise. These situations are defined by Vygotsky (1978) as representing the Zone of Proximal Development (ZPD) of an individual. While some activities demand that students reuse simple concepts on their own, other activities will require the help of the teacher, since students would be probably working at their ZPD.

4. *Game mechanics should be simple and bring references to the world of "real" games that are meaningful to students:* This guideline is also grounded on the game fluency (Peppler & Kafai, 2009) that students should develop. Besides this, building game elements that are simple are crucial to manage students' expectations, as it would not be viable to ask students to build complex games (including 3D elements or complex algorithms, for instance). Also, when students are challenged to build a known game element, this might help them to engage in a "reflection-in-action" process (Schön & Bennett, 1996) as their previous experience with a similar game may be a reference for the quality level desired for the given element.

In each meeting of the Workshop, students have to deal with a new programming concept. At the same time, concepts introduced in previous meetings should be necessary again in subsequent activities to allow students to identify some key situations and apply the concepts accordingly. This organizing strategy is compliant to the third guideline presented before.

The activity scheduling for the Game Building Workshop is presented in Table 1 each activity is presented together with the new concepts that are introduced with it.

It must be noted that even the fundamental concepts of programming are introduced in the first four weeks through the implementation of the mechanics of small games. Variables and iteration structures are implemented in a fishing game (2nd week), in which the player must perform mouse clicks on sprites that represent fishes in order to get points. The conditional execution of statements is introduced through a guessing game (3rd week): the player has a limited number of attempts to guess a number that was randomly chosen by the game. In this occasion, the computer generation of random numbers is also discussed with the students due to its importance to the game mechanics that they will build in the following meetings.

Due to the adoption of the PBL perspective, a computer laboratory is the preferred environment to the Workshop activities. Students are encouraged to work in pairs using the computer in order to stimulate discussions and exchange of ideas. As expected, the domain of digital games naturally brings a motivational appeal to students, as well as it is also expected that they would share and compare their results with their peers.

Experimental Design

The Game Building Workshop experiment was first offered during the first semester of 2013 to a group of 40 freshmen of São Paulo Federal Institute. The types of problems to be solved by students, as described in the previous section, would be quite different from those usually found in a programming fundamentals course. Besides that, one could expect that the domain of digital games is familiar to students, considering the age range that typically enroll in the course (usually students from 15 to 20 years old). Hence, building digital games could be an intrinsically motivating activity to these students. If this hypothesis is correct, students' motivation would be observed on their attitudes towards the activities or on the artifacts produced by them. Based on these

Table 1. Activity schedule for the Game Building Workshop

Week	Activity	Novel Concepts Introduced
1	Control two sprites with the keyboard and identify their collision	Algorithm, statement, simple conditional structure (IF), logical conditions
2	Fishing game	Variables and operations Iteration structures – "infinite loop"
3	Guess the number	Iteration structures with logical conditions Relational conditions and expressions
4	Rock-Paper-Scissors	Synchronization through message broadcasting
5-6	Point-and-Shoot	OR Boolean operator IF…ELSE conditional structure
7-8	Breakout	--
9-11	Pacman	AND Boolean operator
12	Final projects presentation	--

perceptions, the experimental design was defined according to a qualitative perspective; thus, three research questions guided its definition:

1. *Which strategies are used to implement the features proposed by the teacher?* The identification of possible common strategies used by students is relevant to understand how they may improve their expertise in programming by solving problems that gradually demand some previous knowledge.
2. *Which quality aspects of digital games are valued by students?* Considering that students probably had some previous experiences with digital games, this question tries to identify which game features are most appreciated by students. Although the Workshop activities were initially not designed to incorporate these characteristics, the main intention was to verify if students' motivation – or the games implemented by them – would be affected in any way by their preferences as gamers.
3. *Do students implement additional features that were not required by the activities?* This question was added as a complement to Question 2, after a preliminary analysis of the implemented games showing that a high number of students added extra features to their games. An in-depth analysis of these extra features and the strategies used to implement them could clarify the role of the game mechanics on students' learning process.

Initially, students answered a survey to allow the identification of their previous experience with digital games. They also identified through a 5-point Likert scale how 19 quality aspects for digital games influenced their user experience. The quality aspects are derived from the playability heuristics described by Barcelos et al. (2011) and were presented in a non-technical language. The original list of heuristics is presented in Table 2.

All games implemented by students during the workshop were collected for analysis. In order to identify how gameplay issues possibly affected the students' implementation strategies, games were separated in two categories: (i) games that incorporated only the minimum features required in the activity; (ii) games that incorporated extra features. This separation was possible because game design activities were part of the regular program of the course and, as such, students always had to complete a minimum set of features in order to get credits for each activity. Then, a heuristic evaluation of all extra features was performed. Heuristic evaluation was originally defined by Nielsen and Molich (1990) as a method to identify usability issues in an interface by means of a systematic inspection, based on a set of quality criteria – the usability heuristics. However, in this context, the method was adapted to allow the identification of playability criteria associated to the extra features incorporated to games by students. Two of the authors of this paper independently analyzed the games, associating at least one of the 19 playability heuristics to each extra feature. Finally, the results of the analysis were checked against each other to identify discrepancies; the combined results were then compared to the answers given by students in the survey.

All activities of the workshop took place in a computer laboratory. The observation of the class activity was conducted as an educational ethnography. Goetz & LeCompte (1984) indicate that, in this research modality, researcher should bear in mind some important aspects of the group that will be observed, such as: individual profiles, the place where the group meets, their interactions and the motivation for them. In order to facilitate the latter analysis of the observed events, audio recordings of all workshop meetings were captured with previous consent of the participants. The objective was to identify students' doubts and comments about each activity and their interactions with the teacher and with each other. The analysis was conducted using the audio recordings' transcripts . During

Table 2. Playability heuristics extracted from Barcelos et al. (2011)

H1	Game controls must be clear, customizable and physically comfortable; their response time must be immediate.
H2	The player must be able to customize video and audio settings.
H3	The player must easily find information about the game status and score.
H4	The game must allow the player to develop skills that should be necessary later on in the gameplay.
H5	The game must provide a clear tutorial.
H6	All visual features must be understandable to the player.
H7	The player must be able to save the current state of the game to continue playing later on.
H8	Visual layout and menus must be intuitive and organized to allow the player to focus only on gameplay.
H9	The game story must be rich and engaging.
H10	The graphics and sound track must spark the player's interest.
H11	The digital characters and the environment must look realistic and consistent.
H12	The main goal of the game must be immediately clear to the player.
H13	The game must propose secondary additional goals along with its main goal.
H14	The game must present many challenges and allow different strategies.
H15	Design of the game pace must consider the player's fatigue and attention levels.
H16	The challenge must be adjustable to the player's skill.
H17	The player must be rewarded for his/her achievements in a clear and immediate way.
H18	Artificial intelligence (AI) must provide unexpected challenges and surprises to the player.
H19	The game must provide hints, but not too many.

the Workshop's last meeting, students presented their Pacman final projects to the teacher and were interviewed, based on the following questions: (i) which strategies were used to implement the game characters; (ii) which features were harder to implement; (iii) which features students would like to add to the game, if they continued to develop them. The interviews were also recorded and transcribed for later analysis.

It must be pointed out that specific providences should be taken in order to assure the validity of a qualitative research. Creswell & Miller (2000) present nine different validation procedures that could be used depending on the audience of the study, the availability of individuals to perform additional verifications, and the costs of using them. The option of this work was to use the triangulation of methods, defined as the comparison between data obtained by different sources. In the case of this study, students' profile, obtained by the

initial survey, the analysis of the games produced by students, the observation of class activities and the final interview are the data sources included in the triangulation.

Results

Students' Profile

Thirty students answered the initial survey. Most of them (23 students) are 15, 16 or 17-year old and are regularly enrolled in High School. The remaining ones are older students who are able to enroll in professional education courses. Seventy-seven percent of students declared to be regular gamers (47% claim to spend from 1 to 5 hours a week playing games and another 27% claim to spend from 5 to 15 hours a week with this activity; 3% of them spend less than an hour a week playing). The group has a relative experience playing games: 66% of them have played games for three of more years.

The quality criteria most often cited by students as highly influential to their user experience (i.e. rated 4 or 5 in the Likert scale) are shown in Figure 2. They are related to saving the game state (H7 – 92.9%), the presence of clear visual features (H6 – 89.3%), the quality of the game story (H9 – 85.7%), variety of challenges and strategies (H14), challenges provided by AI (H18 – 78.6%), comfort and response time of controls (H1 – 75%) and graphics and sound quality (H10 – 75%).

Additional Features in Games and Association to Playability Criteria

During the workshop, students developed 29 Rock-Paper-Scissors games, 22 Point-and-shoot games, 29 Breakout games and 21 Pacman games. The number of games had some variation from activity to activity due to the absence of students in some meetings; besides, some students opted to work in pairs in some activities and alone in

others. opted to look for extra features only in these games, which were the Workshop's last four activities; the mechanics of the first games were very simplified, since they targeted to introducing students to programming fundamentals. It was found out that many students spontaneously added more features to the games than the ones that were explicitly proposed in the activities. We could observe that students made frequent comments during the activities about their intention to improve the mechanics and visual aspects of the games to suit their preferences. The first references to this intention could be observed in the second activity (Fishing game), when a student indicates that the displayed fish should change its position in a quicker way (the student's speech is translated to English, as the original transcript is in Brazilian Portuguese):

The fish should become quicker when the player gets less points, 20 [points] is too much... I think I should try to lower this [the points limit] from 20 to 10

Figure 2. Distribution of answers to the question: "How relevant are the following criteria for you to enjoy a game?"

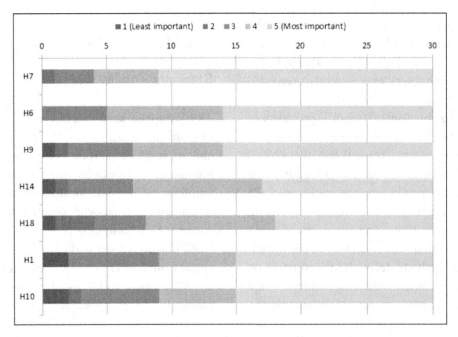

In the original description of the activity, students were asked to implement a fish that changes its position in the screen. The player should perform mouse clicks on the fish to get points, and when the player gets 20 points, the fish would change its position in a quicker way. That student considered that it took too long for the game to get "harder" and identified that lowering the limit that defined a quicker repositioning of the fish would be the solution.

Another representative example was identified when students were building the Rock-Paper-Scissors. A limitation of the Scratch environment was identified by one student:

There will be a playability problem here. Look at this: the first player can make his move, and the second one can just wait for a little while to make his move... So, it's possible to cheat! Isn't there a way to solve this?

This student identified that, initially, the actions of both players in the game were not synchronized in any way; in order to add this feature, students were required to use the message broadcasting and synchronization mechanisms provided by Scratch. However, students would only be introduced to these features in the following meetings. This example is representative of a tendency that could be identified in other episodes: some game features were very relevant to students, even though they required the use of more advances programming techniques.

Consonant with the PBL methodology, the students were encouraged to experiment with new programming structures and with the Scratch environment to implement the desired extra features. In addition, they tended to add more extra features to games during subsequent meetings. Figure 3 shows the proportion of games with minimum features and extra features in each activity.

Two of the extra features that were more often found in each game are presented in Table 3. Additionally, the playability heuristics that were associated to each extra feature during the heuristic evaluation are also presented. It is noteworthy that most extra features are associated to the presentation of visual features (H6), often associated to the

Figure 3. Proportion of games with minimum and extra features

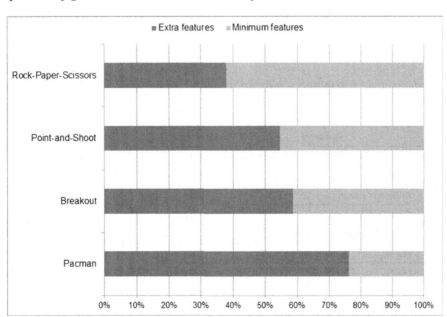

game status and score (H3), but some features are also associated to the response time of controls (H1) and presence of graphical and sound effects that would spark the player's interest (H10). In the last column, the programming concepts that should be used to implement each extra feature are presented.

The most implemented extra feature in Rock-Paper-Scissors game was a message shown in screen background that indicated which player won the match or if there was a draw – 9 from 29 games (31%) presented this feature. Although the activity actually required that students implemented the message, the most straightforward method would be to use a Scratch's "say" command, linked to one of the sprites. Each element that is displayed on the screen (named in Scratch as the "stage") is a sprite, and every command must be attached to a sprite or to the stage. If the code is associated to the stage, for the purpose of this feature it must continuously verify the state of other sprites; this is an additional challenge to students, as it will be discussed later. The most implemented extra feature in the Point-and-Shoot game (10 from 22 games, near the half part) was allowing the player to immediately shoot again while the last shot bullet was still heading towards the opposite side of the screen. This feature overcomes a limitation of Scratch that will also be discussed in the fol-

lowing section. In the Breakout game, the most frequent extra feature (9 from 29 games) was an animation that shows the paddle fading out when it misses the ball. In Figure 4 an example of the extra features in Rock-Paper-Scissors and Breakout are presented.

In Pacman, the most implemented extra feature (8 from 21 games, more than a third part) was an indication of the number of remaining lives and sound effects (7 games) for events such: the beginning of the game, the moment when Pacman "eats" a yellow dot, and the collision of Pacman with a ghost. It is important to point out that students were not expected to create their own sound effects and graphics during the workshop; hence, the same set of images and sounds was made available to them, even though its use was not required in every activity. Students had Internet access during the activities and were allowed to search for additional items as they desired.

The transcription of the final interviews with students reveal their intentions to improve the mechanics and visual aspects of the Pacman games they developed if they had more time to work on them. A content analysis was performed on the students' speech as defined by Bardin (1977) in order to identify their intentions. A few representative examples are pointed out:

Table 3. Most implemented extra features, playability heuristics associated and programming concept(s) needed

Game	Feature	Heuristics	Programming concept(s) needed
Rock-Paper-Scissors	Win / draw message in screen background	H3; H6	Busy loop or Message broadcast
	Score	H3; H6	Variables
Point-and-Shoot	Allow new shot	H1	Message broadcast
	Game Over Screen	H3; H6	Message broadcast
Breakout	Fade out of paddle when losing ball	H6; H10	Loop with defined number of iterations
	More bricks to be destroyed	H14	None (sprite duplication is sufficient)
Pacman	Display number of lives	H3; H6	Variables or Busy loop or Message broadcast
	Sound effects	H10	None (only correct usage of "play sound" command)

Figure 4. Example of extra features added to Rock-Paper-Scissors and Breakout

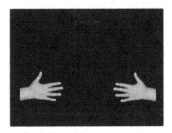   

As the game level rises, I would make it more difficult, I would add more ghosts

Oh, I would add that 'little power' so that it [the Pacman] could defeat its opponents

I would make it [the game] harder by making them [the ghosts] move faster

The categories defined from the content analysis are presented in Table 4, in decreasing order of the number of occurrences in students' speech. During the process of determining these categories, each one of them was associated to the playability heuristics that most closely expressed the meaning of the extra features suggested by students.

The first category, "More difficulty levels", was associated to the students' ideas related to making Pacman or the ghosts faster as the player successfully eats all the white dots on the maze. The second category, "Give more powers to Pacman", mostly grouped the students' references to a feature that is present in the original game: the

"power pills" that, when eaten by Pacman, causes the ghosts to move in a slower pace and allows the Pacman to eat the ghosts to get extra points. In the final interview, one student even mentioned his failed attempt to actually implement this feature:

I managed to make it [the power pill], when the Pacman touched it, the ghosts started to glow... But then I had to change a lot of things, I erased it and had to start all over again [...] But it worked like this: when he ate the pill, he started to glow... But then he would not change back.

Students also wished that the enemies has more powers, such as "faster movements", or simply that the game had more enemies (as the students were asked to implement only two ghosts, due to time limitations). Finally, the fourth category, "Add rewards", grouped references to additional rewards that should be added to the game in the students' opinion. In this case, another feature of the real game was frequently mentioned: the fruit that appear near to the center of the maze at specific time intervals, allowing the player to

Table 4. Students' intention to add features to Pacman and associated heuristics

Number of Occurrences	Categories	Heuristics
8	More difficulty levels	H14 / H16
7	Give more powers to Pacman	H14 / H16
7	Give more powers to enemies	H14 / H16
5	Add rewards	H17

get extra points. Apart from being mentioned in the students' intentions, this feature was actually added in two of the games built by the students.

Twenty-two excerpts of the students' speeches were associated to heuristic H14 (the game must present many challenges and allow different strategies). These excerpts were related to adding more levels to the game or adding more powers to the main character or its enemies. The same occurrences could also be associated to heuristic H16 (challenge must be adjustable to the player's skill); should more levels and more skillful enemies be added to the game, it would demand additional skills from the player. Besides that, five excerpts were associated to heuristic H17 (The player must be rewarded for his/her achievements in a clear and immediate way) when students mention that the game should provide bonus features, such as the little bonus fruit that are available in the original Pacman game when the player reaches a given score.

Problem-Solving Strategies and Patterns

In order to analyze the possible recognition and usage of patterns by students to solve problems, it was necessary to identify the strategy used to implement each of the subtasks demanded in each game. In the scope of this analysis, a subtask is the most atomic goal that should be accomplished by students in order to add a new functionality to the game. For example, in Point-and-Shoot, making the bullet fire in a linear trajectory when a key is pressed is considered as a subtask; detecting the

collision of the bullet with an enemy target and implementing an animation that shows the target "exploding" is another subtask. As mentioned before, students were required to complete a given number of subtasks in each meeting to get credit for the activity.

The workshop activities required the completion of a total of 38 subtasks; 12 of them were related to the preliminary activities of the workshop, 5 to Rock-Paper-Scissors, 8 to Point-and-Shoot, 5 to Breakout and 8 to Pacman. It is reasonable to expect that the students' skills would be more consolidated in the last weeks of the workshop; so, the identification of patterns is focused on the subtasks of the last two games, Breakout and Pacman. The analysis of these games allowed to identify that the usage of sprites to calculate distances and positioning of game elements appears to be a strategy widely recognized and used by students.

A subtask related to the positioning of game elements is present in Breakout: whenever the ball cannot be reached by the paddle anymore, the player must lose one life and the ball must be repositioned over the paddle for a new turn. The strategies used by students to implement this subtask are presented in Table 5. Most students opted to create a new, "artificial" sprite that covers the bottom of the screen, and the collision of the ball with this sprite is used to identify that it cannot be reached by the paddle (Figure 5). Checking the y-coordinate of the ball would be a more straightforward strategy, as it did not require the creation of an additional sprite, but surprisingly it was adopted by a smaller number of students.

Table 5. Strategies to implement the subtask "detect when the paddle misses the ball" in Breakout

Strategy	Number of Games	% of Games
Collision with "artificial" sprite	17	58.6%
Verification of y-coordinate	5	17.2%
Subtask not implemented	7	24.1%
Total	29	100.0%

Figure 5. Example of sprite used to detect the position of the ball

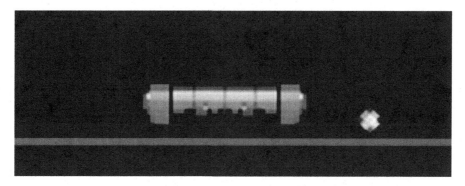

In Pacman a similar strategy was used by most students to detect when the main character of the game or an enemy ghost reached the end of the side tunnels that are present in the middle of the maze. One subtask requested that students implemented the classic rule stating that the Pacman shall appear at the opposite side of the maze when it reaches the end of each tunnel (Figure 6). Again, most students opted to create an additional sprite and detect the collision of the Pacman with this sprite instead of checking the x and y coordinates of the Pacman sprite. The statistics for this subtask are displayed in Table 6.

Another subtask in Pacman is related to the implementation of the ghost that should follow a fixed path inside the maze. In this case, a prevailing strategy could not be identified; however, the three most used strategies all rely on programming features previously experienced by students. The first strategy used an atomic command of Scratch, named *glide*. It requires a pair of (x, y) coordinates and an interval in seconds as parameters and, when executed, moves the sprite to the specified position, in a linear trajectory whose duration is specified by the given time interval. Using this command is very convenient to solve this subtask; however, in previous similar situations, students

Figure 6. Example of sprite used to detect the position of Pacman

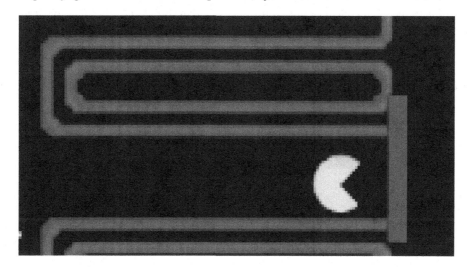

Table 6. Strategies to implement the strategy "detect when Pacman reaches the end of the tunnel"

Strategy	Number of Games	% of Games
Collision with "artificial" sprite	14	66.7%
Verification of x and y coordinates	3	14.3%
Range verification of x-coordinate	2	9.5%
Subtask not implemented	2	9.5%
Total	21	100.0%

had trouble using it, especially when it was necessary to interrupt the movement of the sprite due to its collision to other sprite (refer to the Discussion section for further details). This might be a possible explanation for the existence of the other two strategies. They are both similar because they are based on a loop with a stop condition: reaching a position given by a pair of coordinates, or reaching an "artificial" target sprite, identical to the one used in the previously described strategies. The loop step moves the sprite a few steps ahead at a time. Some coding options are shown for each of the three strategies in Figure 7. Table 7 shows the statistics for this subtask, where it is possible to notice that the three strategies were equally present in the implemented games.

Discussion

The motivation of students to implement additional features in games seemed to be closely linked to playability aspects. Many students implemented

similar features, and a possible explanation to this fact is the social nature of the activity: students naturally interacted with each other in the computer laboratory and compared the functionalities of the games they implemented. In the audio transcripts of the workshop activities it was possible to identify several moments when students questioned some of the interaction mechanisms that restrained gameplay and tried to improve them on their own. These events were more frequent when the activities started to involve the implementation of game mechanics that were reasonably more complete, that is, since students started to implement Rock-Paper-Scissors.

It is possible to infer, based on the heuristic evaluation of extra features and the survey answered by students, that most features were associated to quality aspects that students also consider as absolutely relevant to their own experience as game players. The additional features were often associated to the display of visual features (H6), mostly related to the game status and score

Figure 7. Strategies to implement the subtask "implement the ghost that follows a fixed path inside the maze"

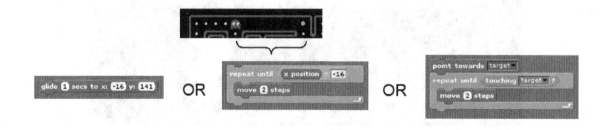

Table 7. Strategies to implement the subtask "implement the ghost that follows a fixed path inside the maze"

Strategy	Number of Games	% of Games
Use of *glide* command	6	28.6%
Use of loop – stop condition with coordinate	6	28.6%
Use of loop – stop condition with sprite collision	6	28.6%
Other	1	4.8%
Subtask not implemented	2	9.5%
Total	21	100.0%

(H3), but features related to the response time of game controls (H1) and presence of graphic and sound effects (H10) were also identified. This is an indication that the "quality" of the proposed activities, in terms of its interactive features, has an impact in the students' motivation to engage in such activities.

In spite of that, when the features students would like to add to Pacman (if they continued to develop the game) were analyzed, it was noticed that students did not necessarily restrained their intentions to the quality aspects that were initially cited in the survey. By interpreting the students' speech in the final interviews, it is possible to associate heuristics H16 and H17 to their intention to add new difficulty levels, bonus items and additional powers to Pacman and its enemies. These heuristics were not frequently cited in the survey: they were, respectively, 16th and 17th in the decreasing order of the relevant heuristics in the students' opinion. On the other hand, heuristic H14, which is related to the presence of several challenges and different strategies, can also be associated to most features suggested by students, and this heuristic was the fourth most cited in the survey. These discrepancies indicate that, initially, students may not have realized the importance of making the game harder when the player improves her skills (expressed by H16) or the importance of providing clear and immediate rewards (expressed by H17). However, after being involved with several game design issues

for several weeks, it seems that students begin to consider these particular issues as relevant. It is important to point out that, as a whole, heuristics H14 (that was already cited in the initial survey), H16 and H17 can be associated to level design, which is a crucial feature of game design (Juul, 2005). The practical experiences during the workshop seemed to make the students more aware of how growing levels of difficulty could be implemented in the game.

While students seemed to have expanded their own conceptions about quality in games, it is also true that most additional features found in the games built by students are similar to features that can be found in "real" games. It is the case of full-screen "game over" and "win" messages, sprite animations, score and lives control, previously mentioned in the heuristic evaluation of the games. In final interview, students also revealed their intention to add features of the real Pacman game in their projects. Based on this information, it could be argued that students were not engaged in a truly creative design process, but they could have copied known features instead. Nevertheless, this strategy is valid, considering that the main objective of the workshop was to help students develop programming skills, and not to develop an original design for a game. The critical reflection of students about the features that seemed to be "missing" in the games they were developing is consonant with the game fluency introduced by Peppler & Kafai (2009) and with the fourth guideline for the definition of the workshop activities ("*The game mechanics should be simple and yet bring references to the world of "real" games that are meaningful to students*"). Based on their previous gaming experience, students not only identify that "something is missing" in the game design, but also develop strategies to incorporate the desired functionalities. Sometimes these strategies even demanded that students dealt with programming concepts that were relatively new to them at the time they were needed.

Other aspect that emerged after several meetings was the reuse of some programming structures to solve problems similar to those that were already present in previous meetings. The problems were basically related to sprite animation and collision detection. The students produced some solutions that can be considered as "unusual" when they are seen from the point of view of conventional programming languages that do not provide an interactive authoring environment, such as Scratch. Nevertheless, it is possible to identify the influence of some particular functionalities of Scratch in the unconventional solutions provided. It could be argued that, motivated by desire to create better games, students sometimes had to deal with new concepts to implement additional features; at other times, they had to identify when solutions previously known by them were applicable, either empirically – engaging in a "reflection-in-action" process (Schön & Bennett, 1996) – or with the help of the teacher, working at their Zone of Proximal

Development (Vygotsky, 1978). The occurrences of both situations will be discussed in the following subsections.

Exploring New Programming Structures to Add New Features

An analysis of the games' most frequent extra features reveals that students in fact had to deal with and understand novel abstract concepts in order to implement them. In Table 3, programming concepts that were necessary to implement these additional features have already been presented. This section will discuss how students dealt with those concepts. In order to implement the win/draw message displayed in the screen background of Rock-Paper-Scissors, students had to use either a busy wait loop to continuously verify the game state or a message broadcast mechanism. Scratch provides a *forever* loop that allows the implementation of busy wait loops in a fairly easy way. Figure 8 presents an example of such a loop to check the number of the *costume* (i.e., the graphical depiction) currently displayed by the sprite that represents each player in the game. It is interesting to point out that this strategy has not been used or presented to students before, although they have used the *forever* and *if* structures separately in previous activities.

In Point-and-Shoot game, students had to overcome a limitation of the Scratch environment to allow the player to immediately shoot again. In

Figure 8. Busy wait loop implemented by a student in Rock-Paper-Scissors. "Jogador" is a Portuguese word for "player"

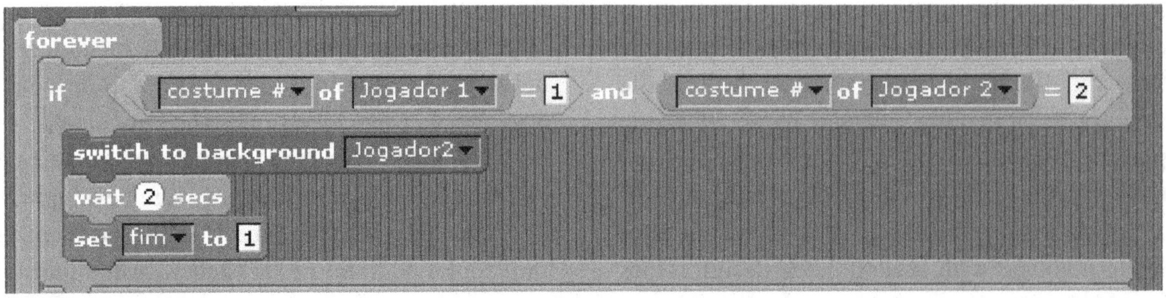

this case, the most straightforward implementation is to associate the loop that defines the trajectory of the bullet to a key press event. However, this strategy prevents the player from shooting again while the bullet has not yet collided with the wall or the enemy. Some students identified that this might be a huge disadvantage to the player if a shot is missed. In addition to that, the bullet is represented by a single sprite to simplify the implementation; so, two or more bullets cannot be presented at the same time, introducing a large latency time between shots. Considering the simple strategy mentioned above, a new key press event cannot be detected while the current loop is still executing; technically speaking, each block of commands in Scratch is executed as a separate thread, whose execution cannot be interrupted by other threads. However, there is one exception to this behavior: a thread can be interrupted when its trigger event is a message. This exception was identified by many students that solved the issue by associating the loop that defines the trajectory of the bullet to a "message received" event. This way, the loop execution can be immediately interrupted when a new message is received, thus allowing a new shot. The message broadcast mechanism was also used to implement a "game over" screen: a message is sent to the screen background (which has the same behavior as a sprite) to change its depiction to the desired message. The concept of message synchronization had been presented to students one week earlier, and these extra features seem to indicate that students were confident enough to explore the new concept.

Identifying Patterns to Solve Similar Problems

In two situations, students had to deal with similar problems in order to implement game features: identifying the position of a given sprite on the screen – in Arkanoid, when the ball is positioned at the same height or lower than the paddle, and in Pacman, when the main character of the game

reaches the end of the tunnel. Scratch provides special variables that store the value of the x and y coordinates of a sprite at all times; however, a significant parcel of students preferred to rely on the strategy of positioning a new sprite at the position to be detected, and check for the collision of this new sprite with the desired sprite.

Why would students rather reuse a more laborious solution? One possible explanation is that positioning a sprite on a desired position of the screen is predominantly a visual operation that does not demand a higher-order abstraction about the Cartesian coordinates of the sprite. In the scope of Mathematics Education, the visual level is the first and less sophisticated level of geometrical reasoning, according to the van Hiele model (Jones, 2002). As mentioned before, most students that attended the workshop are enrolled in the second or third year of Brazilian high school education. Usually, topics of Analytic Geometry are first covered in the third and last year of High School (Brasil, 2002); hence, it could either be assumed that many students had limited experience with Analytic Geometry concepts or that these students were not confident enough to explore the programming structures provided by Scratch to identify the positioning of sprites on Cartesian plane.

In either case, it is possible to identify that operations related to the creation of new sprites and collision detection were extensively used in the previous activities. Indirectly, this is a consequence of the second guideline for the workshop activities ("*Activities must progressively require that students explore new concepts and, at the same time, reuse concepts that were previously explored by them*"). Figure 9 presents a block diagram depicting the relationship between all subtasks that involve the concept of sprite collision. It is possible to notice that this concept was necessary in three subtasks in Point-and-Shoot, which may have influenced the students to use collisions to overcome their limitations with Geometry concepts in the following activities.

Figure 9. Relationship between subtasks involving the concept of collision. Subtasks in blue explicitly involved collision; subtasks in green were solved by students using collision.

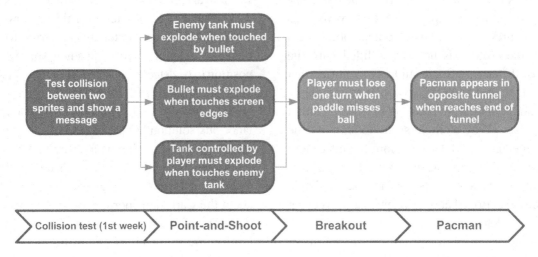

During the process of game building, it is often necessary to move sprites in a step-by-step fashion to allow collision detection with other moving sprites. This need led students to recognize possible uses for iterative structures with stop conditions. The first occasion when this structure was absolutely necessary was in Point-and-Shoot. A loop that defines the trajectory of the bullet and the enemy tank must be interrupted only when a collision with another sprite is detected, so it is not possible to initially define the number of loop iterations. At this point, the availability of Scratch's "glide" command was confusing for several students. This happened because, although it is possible to define a linear trajectory with a single *glide* command, its execution cannot be stopped. In this case, a feature of Scratch was a

hurdle to solving the problem, in contrast to the last situation, when the concept of sprite collision allowed students to overcome their difficulties. Here, students are required to understand and apply a loop structure similar to the one shown in Figure 10.

A similar strategy could be used in Breakout to move the ball and detect its collision to the paddle and the blocks. At this moment, the ball must bounce off the obstacle. In this occasion, an example of loop usage to move the ball was presented to all students at the beginning of the activity, so no disparate solutions were identified. Then, in Pacman, students must define a fixed path inside the maze for one of the ghosts. Students did not follow a single strategy in this case. As presented in Table 7, in twelve games

Figure 10. Example of a loop structure with a stop condition based on collision

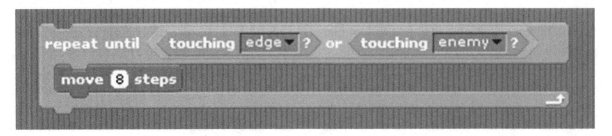

students reused the strategy of using a loop with a stop condition. This may indicate that students identified a similarity to the problems previously solved in Point-and-Shoot and Breakout. This hypothesis is confirmed by one of the students in the final interview. When questioned about how he implemented the ghost, his answer was:

I did just like we have done before with the tank game [Point-and-shoot]... He [the ghost] moves some steps forward until he reaches the right position, and then he turns... down, left, right, wherever he must go

In six of the games where this strategy was applied, the coordinates of the position where the ghost should change his direction were used in the stop condition. However, in the other six games, sprites were used to define the positions between which the ghost should move; this is additional evidence to the difficulties of students to deal with Cartesian coordinates. In other six games, students preferred to use Scratch's "glide" command – in this case, the collision is detected by the Pacman sprite and not the ghost sprite, so the strategy turns out to be effective.

Figure 11 shows that moving sprites by using loops with collision detection was also a frequent strategy in previous activities, particularly in Point-and-Shoot. In 12 out of 21 Pacman games,

students reused a previous strategy using loops to detect collisions. However, several students still chose a strategy that did not require implementing a loop. This is consonant to the findings of Ginat (2004), who identified that novice programmers tend to find it difficult to identify the boundaries for a loop; as mentioned before, this difficulty seems to have been circumvented by some students by using a "artificial" sprite to indicate the loop boundary (Figure 12).

FUTURE RESEARCH DIRECTIONS

It is important to point out that the features identified in the students' games do not necessarily indicate that students understood all of the programming concepts that were applied to implement them. Hence, in future works it is necessary to evaluate how students' knowledge about key concepts has evolved during the workshop. This could be accomplished by assessing students with pre and posttests related to programming knowledge; however, it is often the case that students have no previous knowledge about programming when they begin their studies. Further works will analyze the performance of the students who attended the workshop in the following disciplines related to programming in comparison to those students who have not attended the workshop, that

Figure 11. Relationship between subtasks involving the concept of loop. In grey subtasks, simpler loops are used. Blue subtasks demand loops with stop conditions. Students reused previous strategies to solve the green subtask.

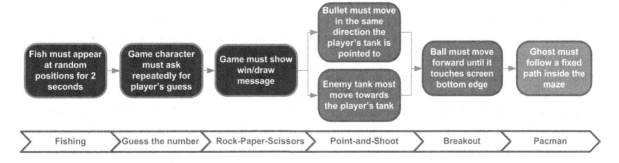

Figure 12. Strategy used by a student to implement the ghost that follows a fixed path. The red dots are sprites, used to define the stop condition of the loop used to move the ghost.

is, who took part in a programming fundamentals course with traditional activities.

Although it was not feasible to evaluate students' previous knowledge about programming in this case, all students should have developed higher-order problem solving skills in Mathematics classes. Hence, a test has been developed based on the Brazilian official Math examinations in order to evaluate problem solving skills of students who start the workshop. The goal of such test was to verify if the skills that students appear to have developed or exercised during the workshop, such as analogy and generalization, could be transferred to the Math domain. Such skills are also crucial to the study of Software Engineering (Kramer, 2007) in undergraduate CS/IT courses, so it would be relevant to apply the workshop to freshman of undergraduate courses to identify if the workshop activities may incentive students to further study topics that appeared in their first projects, even in an incipient way, such as encapsulation, successive refining and process synchronization.

Some Math topics were also used during the workshop activities. For instance, students had to deal with inequalities, arithmetical operations and positioning of sprites on the Cartesian plane. One could expect that students with a greater knowledge of these topics would be more resourceful in the workshop activities; on the other hand, the workshop activities may create opportunities for students to learn these Math topics in a meaningful way. Further works are necessary to assess the impact of the workshop activities on the students' knowledge of Math topics.

CONCLUSION

Digital games are a part of everyday life of many prospective CS or IT students. Therefore, it would be natural that these students expect to build games as a part of their activities in the course. Unfortunately, the initial activities in the course are often not motivating, and this may discourage students to continue studying in the area. Game design and construction have already been discussed as a viable and motivating alternative to introduce Computer Science concepts to students. However, it is important to understand which skills students may acquire through building games and how these skills can be useful as they continue their studies.

In order to investigate this issue, a Game Building Workshop was designed to be offered to students of a professional education course in Brazil. The definition of the Workshop activities was conducted by four guidelines, based on previous research results. Hence, the activities were heavily based on the construction of digital games that were similar to "real" games. Besides this, the activities required that students explored the same programming concepts several times. The selection and organization of activities seem to have influenced the students' motivation and attitude towards some of the proposed tasks. All the games produced by students were evaluated in a period of 12 weeks and the results confronted with the students' questions and comments during the workshop meetings and during a final interview. Thus, the present investigation produced three main contributions:

- Students tended to implement additional features in the games in order to overcome limitations identified by them. These limitations were related to playability aspects that were previously classified by students as very relevant to their experience as game players. This indicates that the motivation of students led them to explore new topics to implement these additional features.
- Students reused solutions for previously solved problems in similar contexts that appeared in subsequent activities. The sequence of the workshop activities was designed to make students recall and use previously seen concepts, although students were not explicitly instructed to search for patterns. Based on the previous contribution, it could be argued that the domain of game design and the features of the programming environment may have contributed to make students exercise higher-order skills that are important for a CS/IT professional.
- The impact of the workshop activities on the students' motivation to solve quite complex problems indicates that the used guidelines have a potential to direct the definition of game building workshops oriented towards different target audiences and aimed at developing different skills.

In regular introductory courses, abstraction skills are also exercised; however, they may be initially neglected because of the limited scope of the activities. Game design may stimulate students to deal with bigger problems right from the start and, most important, develop skills to cope with them. After all, a "fun reward" awaits for those who succeed.

REFERENCES

Adams, J. C., & Webster, A. R. (2012). What do students learn about programming from game, music video, and storytelling projects? In *Proceedings of the 43rd ACM technical symposium on Computer Science Education* (pp. 643–648). New York: ACM. doi:10.1145/2157136.2157319

Barcelos, T. S., Carvalho, T., Schimiguel, J., & Silveira, I. F. (2011). Análise comparativa de heurísticas para avaliação de jogos digitais. In *Proc. IHC+CLIHC 2011* (pp. 187–196). Pernambuco, Brazil: SBC.

Barcelos, T. S., & Silveira, I. F. (2012). Teaching computational thinking in initial series. In *Proceedings of CLEI 2012*. Medellín: Centro Latinoamericano de Estudios en Informática.

Bardin, L. (1977). *Content analysis*. Lisbon: Edições 70.

Bateson, A. G., Alexander, R. A., & Murphy, M. D. (1987). Cognitive processing differences between novice and expert computer programmers. *International Journal of Man-Machine Studies*, *26*(6), 649–660. doi:10.1016/S0020-7373(87)80058-5

Bayliss, J. D., & Strout, S. (2006). Games as a "flavor" of CS1. *SIGCSE Bulletin*, *38*(1), 500–504. doi:10.1145/1124706.1121498

Beaubouef, T. (2002). Why computer science students need math. *SIGCSE Bulletin*, *34*(4), 57–59. doi:10.1145/820127.820166

Brasil. Ministério da Educação. (2002). *PCN+ Ensino Médio: Orientações Curriculares Complementares aos Parâmetros Curriculares Nacionais*. Brasília: MEC/SEB.

Campbell, P. F., & McCabe, G. P. (1984). Predicting the success of freshmen in a computer science major. *Communications of the ACM, 27*(11), 1108–1113. http://doi.acm.org/10.1145/1968.358288

Carnegie Mellon University. (2013). *Alice - An educational software that teaches students computer programming in a 3D environment*. Retrieved August 15, 2013, from http://www.alice.org

Carter, L. (2006). Why students with an apparent aptitude for computer science don't choose to major in computer science. *SIGCSE Bulletin*, *38*(1), 27–31. doi:10.1145/1124706.1121352

Chase, W. G., & Simon, H. A. (1973). Perception in chess. *Cognitive Psychology*, *4*(1), 55–81. doi:10.1016/0010-0285(73)90004-2

Chen, S. Y., Fan, J.-P., & Macredie, R. D. (2006). Navigation in hypermedia learning systems: Experts vs. novices. *Computers in Human Behavior*, *22*(2), 251–266. doi:10.1016/j.chb.2004.06.004

Chi, M. T. H., Feltovich, P. J., & Glaser, R. (1981). Categorization and representation of physics problems by experts and novices. *Cognitive Science*, *5*(2), 121–152. doi:10.1207/s15516709cog0502_2

Clancy, M. J., & Linn, M. C. (1999). Patterns and pedagogy. *SIGCSE Bulletin*, *31*(1), 37–42. doi:10.1145/384266.299673

Colley, A., Banton, L., Down, J., & Pither, A. (1992). An Expert-Novice Comparison in Musical Composition. *Psychology of Music*, *20*(2), 124–137. doi:10.1177/0305735692202003

Crenshaw, T. L., Chambers, E. W., Metcalf, H., & Thakkar, U. (2008). A case study of retention practices at the University of Illinois at Urbana-Champaign. In *Proc. SIGCSE 2008* (pp. 412–416). New York: ACM. doi:10.1145/1352135.1352276

Creswell, J. W., & Miller, D. L. (2000). Determining validity in qualitative inquiry. *Theory into Practice*, *39*(3), 124–130. doi:10.1207/s15430421tip3903_2

Denner, J., Werner, L., & Ortiz, E. (2012). Computer games created by middle school girls: Can they be used to measure understanding of computer science concepts? *Computers & Education, 58*(1), 240–249. doi:10.1016/j.compedu.2011.08.006

East, J. P., Thomas, S. R., Wallingford, E., Beck, W., & Drake, J. (1996). Pattern-based programming instruction. In *Proceedings of the ASEE Annual Conference and Exposition*. Washington, DC: ASEE.

Franklin, D., Conrad, P., Boe, B., Nilsen, K., Hill, C., & Len, M., … Waite, R. (2013). Assessment of computer science learning in a scratch-based outreach program. In *Proceeding of the 44th ACM technical symposium on Computer science education* (pp. 371–376). New York, NY: ACM. doi:10.1145/2445196.2445304

Ginat, D. (2004). On Novice Loop Boundaries and Range Conceptions. *Computer Science Education*, *14*(3), 165–181. doi:10.1080/0899340042000302709

Goetz, J. P., & LeCompte, M. D. (1984). *Ethnography and qualitative design in educational research*. Orlando, FL: Academic Press.

Haberman, B., & Muller, O. (2008). *Teaching abstraction to novices: Pattern-based and ADT-based problem-solving processes*. IEEE. doi:10.1109/FIE.2008.4720415

Hernandez, C. C., Silva, L., Segura, R. A., Schimiguel, J., Ledon, M. F. P., Bezerra, L. N. M., & Silveira, I. F. (2010). Teaching Programming Principles through a Game Engine. *CLEI Electronic Journal*, 1–8.

Hix, D., & Hartson, H. (1993). Developing user interfaces: ensuring usability through product and process. New York: John Wiley & Sons, Inc.

Jones, K. (2002). Issues in the Teaching and Learning of Geometry. In *Aspects of Teaching Secondary Mathematics: perspectives on practice* (pp. 121–139). London: Routledge.

Juul, J. (2005). *Half-real: Video Games between Real Rules and Fictional Worlds*. MIT Press.

Kramer, J. (2007). Is abstraction the key to computing? *Communications of the ACM*, *50*(4), 36–42. doi:10.1145/1232743.1232745

Larkin, J., McDermott, J., Simon, D. P., & Simon, H. A. (1980). Expert and Novice Performance in Solving Physics Problems. *Science*, *208*(4450), 1335–1342. doi:10.1126/science.208.4450.1335 PMID:17775709

Lee, I., Martin, F., Denner, J., Coulter, B., Allan, W., & Erickson, J. et al. (2011). Computational thinking for youth in practice. *ACM Inroads*, *2*(1), 32–37. doi:10.1145/1929887.1929902

Leutenegger, S. T. (2006). A CS1 to CS2 bridge class using 2D game programming. *Journal of Computing Sciences in Colleges*, *21*(5), 76–83.

Lister, R., Simon, B., Thompson, E., Whalley, J. L., & Prasad, C. (2006). Not seeing the forest for the trees: novice programmers and the SOLO taxonomy. In *Proceedings of the 11th annual SIGCSE conference on Innovation and technology in computer science education* (pp. 118–122). New York, NY: ACM. doi:10.1145/1140124.1140157

Malan, D. J., & Leitner, H. H. (2007). Scratch for budding computer scientists. *SIGCSE Bulletin*, *39*(1), 223–227. doi:10.1145/1227504.1227388

Maloney, J. H., Peppler, K., Kafai, Y., Resnick, M., & Rusk, N. (2008). Programming by choice: urban youth learning programming with scratch. In *Proceedings of the 39th SIGCSE technical symposium on Computer science education* (pp. 367–371). New York, NY: ACM. doi:10.1145/1352135.1352260

McKeithen, K. B., Reitman, J. S., Rueter, H. H., & Hirtle, S. C. (1981). Knowledge organization and skill differences in computer programmers. *Cognitive Psychology*, *13*(3), 307–325. doi:10.1016/0010-0285(81)90012-8

MIT Media Lab & the Lifelong Kindergarten Group. (2012). Scratch. *Scratch*. Retrieved April 27, 2012, from http://scratch.mit.edu

Merril, D. (2002). A Pebble-in-the-Pond Model For Instructional Design. *Performance Improvement*, *41*(7), 41–46. doi:10.1002/pfi.4140410709

Microsoft Research. (2014). *Kodu Game Lab Community*. Retrieved January 16, 2014, from http://www.kodugamelab.com/

Muller, O., Haberman, B., & Averbuch, H. (2004). (An almost) pedagogical pattern for pattern-based problem-solving instruction. *ACM SIGCSE Bulletin*, *36*(3), 102. doi:10.1145/1026487.1008025

Muratet, M., Torguet, P., Jessel, J.-P., & Viallet, F. (2009). Towards a serious game to help students learn computer programming. *International Journal of Computer Games Technology*, 3:1–3:12. doi:10.1155/2009/470590

Nakamura, J., & Csikszentmihalyi, M. (2009). Flow theory and research. In *Oxford Handbook of Positive Psychology* (2nd ed., pp. 195–206). Oxford, UK: Oxford University Press.

Nielsen, J., & Molich, R. (1990). Heuristic evaluation of user interfaces. In *CHI '90: Proceedings of the SIGCHI conference on Human factors in computing systems* (pp. 249–256). New York: ACM. http://doi.acm.org/10.1145/97243.97281

Peppler, K., & Kafai, Y. (2009). Gaming Fluencies: Pathways into Participatory Culture in a Community Design Studio. *International Journal of Learning and Media*, *1*(4), 45–58. doi:10.1162/ijlm_a_00032

Polya, G. (2004). *How to solve it: a new aspect of mathematical method*. Princeton, NJ: Princeton University Press.

Prensky, M. (2004). *Digital Game-Based Learning*. Washington, DC: McGraw-Hill Pub. Co.

Rizvi, M., Humphries, T., Major, D., Jones, M., & Lauzun, H. (2011). A CS0 course using Scratch. *Journal of Computing Sciences in Colleges*, *26*(3), 19–27.

Salen, K. (2007). Gaming literacies: A game design study in action. *Journal of Educational Multimedia and Hypermedia*, *16*(3), 301–322.

Schön, D., & Bennett, J. (1996). Reflective conversations with materials. In T. Winograd, J. Bennett, L. De Young, & B. Hartfield (Eds.), *Bringing design to software*. New York: ACM Press.

Settle, A. (2011). Computational thinking in a game design course. In *Proceedings of the 2011 conference on Information technology education* (pp. 61–66). New York, NY: ACM. doi:10.1145/2047594.2047612

Shneiderman, B. (1976). Exploratory experiments in programmer behavior. *International Journal of Computer & Information Sciences*, *5*(2), 123–143. doi:10.1007/BF00975629

Shneiderman, B., & Mayer, R. (1979). Syntactic/semantic interactions in programmer behavior: A model and experimental results. *International Journal of Computer & Information Sciences*, *8*(3), 219–238. doi:10.1007/BF00977789

Soloway, E., Bonar, J., & Ehrlich, K. (1982). What do novices know about programming? In *Directions in Human-Computer Interaction* (pp. 87–122). New York: Ablex.

Souza, P. R. de A., & Dias, L. R. (2012). Kodu Game Labs: Estimulando o Raciocínio Lógico através de Jogos. In *Anais do 23º Simpósio Brasileiro de Informática na Educação*. Rio de Janeiro: SBC. Retrieved from http://br-ie.org/pub/index.php/sbie/article/view/1733

Stolee, K. T., & Fristoe, T. (2011). Expressing computer science concepts through Kodu game lab. In *Proceedings of the 42nd ACM technical symposium on Computer science education* (pp. 99–104). New York: ACM. doi:10.1145/1953163.1953197

The CSTA Standards Task Force. (2011). *CSTA K-12 Computer Science Standards*. New York: ACM Computer Science Teachers Association. Retrieved from http://csta.acm.org/Curriculum/sub/CurrFiles/CSTA_K-12_CSS.pdf

Vygotsky, L. S. (1978). Zone of Proximal Development. In *Mind in society: The development of higher psychological processes* (pp. 52–91). Oxford, UK: Harvard University Press.

Waters, A. J., Gobet, F., & Leyden, G. (2002). Visuospatial abilities of chess players. *British Journal of Psychology*, *93*(4), 557–565. doi:10.1348/000712602761381402 PMID:12519534

Weiser, M., & Shertz, J. (1983). Programming problem representation in novice and expert programmers. *International Journal of Man-Machine Studies*, *19*(4), 391–398. doi:10.1016/S0020-7373(83)80061-3

Wilson, B. C., & Shrock, S. (2001). Contributing to success in an introductory computer science course: a study of twelve factors. In *Proceedings of the thirty-second SIGCSE technical symposium on Computer Science Education* (pp. 184–188). New York: ACM. doi:10.1145/364447.364581

YoYo Games, Ltd. (2014). *GameMaker: Studio*. Retrieved January 16, 2014, from https://www.yoyogames.com/studio

ADDITIONAL READING

Adams, J. C., & Webster, A. R. (2012). What do students learn about programming from game, music video, and storytelling projects? In *Proceedings of the 43rd ACM technical symposium on Computer Science Education* (pp. 643–648). New York: ACM. doi:10.1145/2157136.2157319

Avraamidou, A., Monaghan, J., & Walker, A. (2012). Abstraction Through Game Play. *Technology. Knowledge and Learning*, *17*(1-2), 1–21. doi:10.1007/s10758-012-9189-2

Barcelos, T. S., Costa, G. C., Muñoz, R., & Silveira, I. F. (2014). Informal HCI: Fixing Playability Issues As A Strategy To Improve The Skills Of Novice Programmers. *IEEE Latin American Transactions*, *12*(1), 29–35. doi:10.1109/TLA.2014.6716489

Barr, V., & Stephenson, C. (2011). Bringing computational thinking to K-12: What is Involved and what is the role of the computer science education community? *ACM Inroads*, *2*(1), 48–54. doi:10.1145/1929887.1929905

Basawapatna, A., Koh, K. H., Repenning, A., Webb, D. C., & Marshall, K. S. (2011). Recognizing computational thinking patterns. In *Proceedings of the 42nd ACM technical symposium on Computer science education* (pp. 245–250). Presented at the SIGCSE 2011, New York: ACM.

Basawapatna, A. R., Koh, K. H., & Repenning, A. (2010). Using scalable game design to teach computer science from middle school to graduate school. In *Proceedings of the fifteenth annual conference on Innovation and technology in computer science education* (pp. 224–228). New York, NY, USA: ACM. doi:10.1145/1822090.1822154

Basawapatna, A. R., Repenning, A., Koh, K. H., & Nickerson, H. (2013). The Zones of Proximal Flow: Guiding Students Through a Space of Computational Thinking Skills and Challenges. In *Proceedings of the Ninth Annual International ACM Conference on International Computing Education Research* (pp. 67–74). New York: ACM. doi:10.1145/2493394.2493404

Bayliss, J. D., & Strout, S. (2006). Games as a "flavor" of CS1. *SIGCSE Bulletin*, *38*(1), 500–504. doi:10.1145/1124706.1121498

Bourgonjon, J., Valcke, M., Soetaert, R., & Schellens, T. (2010). Students' perceptions about the use of video games in the classroom. *Computers & Education*, *54*(4), 1145–1156. doi:10.1016/j.compedu.2009.10.022

Brennan, K., & Resnick, M. (2012). New frameworks for studying and assessing the development of computational thinking. In *Proceedings of the 2012 annual meeting of the American Educational Research Association*. Vancouver: American Educational Research Association.

De Souza, C. S., Garcia, A. C. B., Slaviero, C., Pinto, H., & Repenning, A. (2011). Semiotic traces of computational thinking acquisition. In *Proceedings of the Third international conference on End-user development* (pp. 155–170). Heidelberg: Springer-Verlag.

Denner, J., Werner, L., & Ortiz, E. (2012). Computer games created by middle school girls: Can they be used to measure understanding of computer science concepts? *Computers & Education*, *58*(1), 240–249. doi:10.1016/j.compedu.2011.08.006

Desuvire, H., & Wiberg, C. (2009). Game Usability Heuristics (PLAY) for Evaluating and Designing Better Games: The Next Iteration. In A. A. Ozok, & P. Zaphiris (Eds.), *Online Communities, LTCS 5621* (pp. 557–566). Springer-Verlag.

Eckerdal, A. (2009). *Novice Programming Students' Learning of Concepts and Practise* (PhD Thesis). Uppsala University, Sweden.

Febretti, A., & Garzotto, F. (2009). Usability, playability, and long-term engagement in computer games. In *Proc. CHI '09* (pp. 4063–4068). New York, NY, USA: ACM. doi:10.1145/1520340.1520618

Federoff, M. (2002). *Heuristics and usability guidelines for the creation and evaluation of fun in video games* (Master's Dissertation). Indiana University.

Franklin, D., Conrad, P., Boe, B., Nilsen, K., Hill, C., & Len, M., … Waite, R. (2013). Assessment of computer science learning in a Scratch-based outreach program. In *Proceeding of the 44th ACM technical symposium on Computer science education* (pp. 371–376). New York, NY, USA: ACM. doi:10.1145/2445196.2445304

Goldberg, M. (2007, August 9). A complete history of Breakout. *Classic Gaming*. Retrieved October 10, 2013, from http://classicgaming.gamespy.com/View.php?view=Articles.Detail&id=395

Gorriz, C. M., & Medina, C. (2000). Engaging girls with computers through software games. *Communications of the ACM*, *43*(1), 42–49. doi:10.1145/323830.323843

Harel, I. (1991). *Children Designers: Interdisciplinary constructions for learning and knowing mathematics in a computer-rich school*. New Jersey: Ablex Publishing.

Henderson, P. B. (2011). MATH COUNTS: Mathematical reasoning in computing education. *ACM Inroads*, *1*(3), 22–23. doi:10.1145/1835428.1835438

Hu, C. (2011). Computational thinking: what it might mean and what we might do about it. In *Proceedings of the 16th annual joint conference on Innovation and technology in computer science education* (pp. 223–227). New York, NY, USA: ACM. doi:10.1145/1999747.1999811

Kafai, Y. (2006). Playing and making games for learning: Instructionist and Constructionist Perspectives for Game Studies. *Games and Culture*, *1*(1), 36–40. doi:10.1177/1555412005281767

Kafai, Y. B., Franke, M. L., Ching, C. C., & Shih, J. C. (1998). Game Design as an Interactive Learning Environment for Fostering Students' and Teachers' Mathematical Inquiry. *International Journal of Computers for Mathematical Learning*, *3*(2), 149–184. doi:10.1023/A:1009777905226

Kuruvada, P., Asamoah, D. A., Dalal, N., & Kak, S. (2010). Learning Computational Thinking from Rapid Digital Game Creation. In *Proceedings of 2nd Annual Conference on Theoretical and Applied Computer Science* (pp. 31–35). Stillwater, OK, USA.

Malone, T. W. (1980). What makes things fun to learn? Heuristics for designing instructional computer games. In *Proceedings of the 3rd ACM SIGSMALL symposium and the first SIGPC symposium on Small systems* (pp. 162–169). New York, NY, USA: ACM. doi:10.1145/800088.802839

McMaster, K., Rague, B., & Anderson, N. (2010). Integrating Mathematical Thinking, Abstract Thinking, and Computational Thinking. In *Frontiers in Education Conference (FIE) 2010* (pp. S3G–1–S3G–6). doi:10.1109/FIE.2010.5673139

Muller, O. (2005). Pattern oriented instruction and the enhancement of analogical reasoning. In *Proceedings of the first international workshop on Computing education research* (pp. 57–67). New York: ACM. doi:10.1145/1089786.1089792

Mustaro, P. N., Silva, L., & Silveira, I. F. (2011). Using games to teach design patterns and computer graphics. *Instructional Design: Concepts, Methodologies. Tools and Applications.*, *1*(1), 173.

Papert, S. (1980). *Mindstorms: children, computers and powerful ideas*. New York: Basic Books.

Papert, S. (1993). *The children's machine: rethinking school in the age of the computer*. New York: Basic Books.

Pinelle, D., Wong, N., & Stach, T. (2008). Heuristic evaluation for games: usability principles for video game design. In *CHI '08: Proceeding of the twenty-sixth annual SIGCHI conference on Human factors in computing systems* (pp. 1453–1462). New York, NY, USA: ACM. doi:10.1145/1357054.1357282

Pittman, J. (2011). The Pac-Man Dossier. Retrieved December 15, 2012, from http://home.comcast.net/~jpittman2/pacman/pacmandossier.html

Prensky, M. (2001). Digital natives, digital immigrants. *On the Horizon*, *9*(5), 1–6. doi:10.1108/10748120110424816

Resnick, M., Maloney, J., Monroy-Hernández, A., Rusk, N., Eastmond, E., & Brennan, K. et al. (2009). Scratch: Programming for all. *Communications of the ACM*, *52*(11), 60–67. doi:10.1145/1592761.1592779

Salen, K., & Zimmerman, E. (2003). *Rules of Play: Game Design Fundamentals*. Massachusetts: The MIT Press.

Schell, J. (2008). *The art of game design: a book of lenses*. Burlington, MA: Elsevier.

Selwyn, N. (2009). The digital native - myth and reality. *Aslib Proceedings*, *61*(4), 364–379. doi:10.1108/00012530910973776

Settle, A. (2011). Computational thinking in a game design course. In *Proceedings of the 2011 conference on Information technology education* (pp. 61–66). New York, NY, USA: ACM. doi:10.1145/2047594.2047612

Shneiderman, B. (2004). Designing for fun: How can we design user interfaces to be more fun? *Interaction*, *11*(5), 48–50. doi:10.1145/1015530.1015552

Soloway, E. (1986). Learning to program = learning to construct mechanisms and explanations. *Communications of the ACM*, *29*(9), 850–858. doi:10.1145/6592.6594

Wing, J. M. (2006). Computational thinking. *Communications of the ACM*, *49*(3), 33–35. doi:10.1145/1118178.1118215

Wu, M. L., & Richards, K. (2011). Facilitating computational thinking through game design. In *Proceedings of the 6th international conference on E-learning and games, edutainment technologies* (pp. 220–227). Berlin, Heidelberg: Springer-Verlag.

KEY TERMS AND DEFINITIONS

Analogy: According to Polya (2004), a problem-solving skill related to the identification of similarities between situations or objects. It is informally used even in everyday situations, but it can also be systematically used to solve problems. For instance, a strategy to solve a mathematical problem would be to find an analogous instance of the problem, with simpler constraints, for which a solution can be found.

Breakout: A popular arcade game initially developed by Atari in 1976. It consists of a ball that travels across the screen and bounces off the top and side walls of the screen. A line of bricks is presented on the upper side of the screen; when the ball hits a brick, it is destroyed. The ball must not touch the bottom of the screen. To prevent this from happening, the player controls a moving paddle to bounce the ball upwards.

Busy Wait Loop: It is the simplest form of process synchronization. A loop that continuously verify if some Boolean condition is fulfilled; when the condition is true, the code inside the loop is executed.

Pacman: A game developed by Nanco Ltd. and first released in 1980. The player controls Pacman through a maze, eating yellow dots. When all the yellow dots are eaten, Pac-Man is taken to the next stage. Four ghosts chase Pacman, each of them following a particular strategy. If an enemy touches Pac-Man, a life is lost and the Pacman itself withers and dies.

Pattern: In the context of software development, a pattern is a previously defined solution for a class of known problems. A software developer who is able to identify the main characteristics of the pattern in a given problem instance may reuse the solution specified in the pattern definition. Analogy skills are required to successfully use patterns.

Problem-Based Learning (PBL): A pedagogical perspective where learning takes place through the experience of problem-solving. Students should work in groups to identify what they already know, what they need to know, and how to access new information that may lead to resolution of the problem. The role of the teacher in a PBL environment is to facilitate learning by guiding and monitoring the learning process.

Sprite: From the latin *spiritus*. In computer graphics, a sprite is originally a 2D image that can be quickly drawn repeated times, leaving no traces of its previous appearances (hence the analogy with "spirit"). Sprite drawing was usually supported by several hardware and software optimizations in the first personal computers and videogame consoles. In Scratch, any object that can be individually manipulated on the screen is called a sprite.

Chapter 9
Wiki for Agility

Pankaj Kamthan
Concordia University, Canada

ABSTRACT

The movement towards agility is one of the most significant human-centered and socially oriented changes in industrial software engineering. In the practice of agile methodologies, there are different types of content (data, information, or knowledge) that are created, communicated, and consumed. It is imperative for an organization to manage such content, both during development and beyond deployment. This chapter proposes a conceptual model for understanding and exploring the use of Wiki as a vehicle for managing content in agile software development. In doing so, the parity between agile software development and Wiki is shown, human and social aspects of each are emphasized, the Social Web-Context of Wiki is demonstrated, illustrative examples are given, and the implications of committing to a Wiki are considered.

INTRODUCTION

For the past half century, software has played an integral role in the advancement of many sectors of society. The increasing significance of and dependence on software of the society underscores its development and evolution. There are multiple viewpoints of a software system, one of which is engineering. The discipline of *software engineering* advocates a systematic and disciplined approach towards the development and evolution of software systems.

In the past decade, there have been a number of significant changes in industrial software engineering, including the movement towards agility. The agile methodologies are part of a shift from predictive to adaptive approach towards software development (Highsmith, 2009). It has been shown in a number of studies that agile methodologies are being increasingly deployed in many organizations of different sizes, for a variety of application domains, for software projects with teams that are geographically-collocated or, more recently, geographically-dispersed (Smite, Moe, & Ågerfalk, 2010; Brown, 2012).

The ability to manage content has been considered important for an organization (Schneider, 2009), and doing so can be a critical difference between success and failure of a software project (Perkins, 2006). It is also known that a number of human and social factors need to be considered in managing content effectively (Thomas, Kellogg, & Erickson, 2001). The emphasis on the people

DOI: 10.4018/978-1-4666-6485-2.ch009

involved in software development is among the hallmarks of agility. It is therefore crucial to understand and explore means that can effectively accommodate the human and social dimensions of managing content in agile software development.

In the past decade, one technological means, namely that of the *Social Web* (O'Reilly, 2005), has gained acceptance and prominence. There are a number of noteworthy applications within the Social Web environment, including *Wiki* (Leuf & Cunningham, 2001). The purpose of this chapter is to understand and explore the use of Wiki for managing the content that is created, communicated, and consumed in agile software development, from the perspectives of human-centered and socially-oriented software engineering, as well as that of the Social Web.

The rest of the chapter is organized as follows. First, background and previous work relating agile methodologies, content management, and Wiki is considered. This is followed by introduction of a conceptual model for integrating Wiki in agile software development for the purpose of managing content systematically, discussion of salient aspects of the conceptual model, and presentation of representative examples illustrating the conceptual model. Next, directions for future research are highlighted. Finally, concluding remarks are given.

BACKGROUND

This section provides relevant background on agile software development and Wiki, and discusses previous work relating agile software development, content management, and Wiki.

Understanding Agility

The origins of the basic ideas behind agility date back to the 1950s (Larman & Basili, 2003), although they resurfaced and became prominent only after large-scale commoditization of software. In the 1990s, a number of limitations of rigidity in approaches for the development of certain types of software systems were realized. The drive to cope with these limitations led to the inception of agility in industrial software development.

The *Agile Manifesto* characterizes the term "agile" and provides a vision for agile software development. It is motivated by the need for organizations to adequately respond to variability in the market, and to improve the relationship between technical and non-technical stakeholders, thereby reducing risk and increasing the likelihood of success of software projects.

For the sake of this chapter, an *agile methodology* is a software development methodology based on the Agile Manifesto. The other terms can be derived similarly. An agile methodology is usually equipped with a process that outlines how the development of software should proceed over time.

Characteristics of an Agile Methodology

There are a number of discernible human-centered and socially-oriented characteristics of an agile methodology, including the following:

- **People Orientation:** The agile methodologies place a strong emphasis on communication between people. Indeed, one of the stated values in the Agile Manifesto is "People over Process". This is realized in several ways, such as usually having a collocated team of a small number of people that frequently meet face-to-face, informality of agile project artifacts, and collectively sharing responsibilities pertaining to development and delivery. The agile methodologies also embrace collaboration in many ways (Tabaka, 2006), as implied by two values of the Agile Manifesto, namely "Individuals and Interactions over Processes and Tools" and "Customer Collaboration over Contract Negotiation".

- **Community Validation:** Initially, the agile methodologies were isolated and, in some cases, were individual efforts. However, that has changed in the last few years. The awareness of agile methodologies in industry has improved, and they are being increasingly adopted for software development. They have garnered support in national and international standards, such as the ISO/IEC/IEEE 26511 Standard, the ISO/IEC/IEEE 26515 Standard, and the ISO/IEC/IEEE 29148 Standard. The adoption of agile methodologies in the industry has also motivated academia in using these methodologies in software engineering-related programs, in order to prepare students accordingly (Devedžić & Milenković, 2011; Mahnic, 2012; Fancott, Kamthan, & Shahmir, 2012).

- **Risk Alleviation:** There are a number of risks in any software project (Galorath & Evans, 2006), including lack of knowledge or imperfect knowledge of the application domain, especially if it is unfamiliar to the agile team; understanding of users, especially if they are remotely located and belong to a culture that is unfamiliar to the agile team; uncertainty in the market; and changes in implementation technology, especially if they arrive close to the time when the product is scheduled for release. The agile methodologies, by virtue of their construction, have the ability to endure the impact of such risks better than certain other software development methodologies.

- **Green Alignment:** There is substantial consumption of energy during the development and use of software, the consequences of which are well-known to environmentalists. As members of society, it is a moral and ethical imperative upon software engineers to take measures towards minimizing consumption of energy. From the perspective of lean production in soft-

ware development (Coplien & Bjørnvig, 2010), the agile methodologies aim to reduce, or even prevent, waste. They do so by optimizing the use of resources as early as possible, namely during agile requirements engineering (Sillitti & Succi, 2005), and producing artifacts (documents and/or models) only if necessary. This aligns agile methodologies with the principles of *sustainable software development*, commonly referred to as *Green IT* (Taina, 2011).

Deciding Upon an Agile Methodology

The Agile Manifesto constitutes the basis for a number of agile methodologies, including *Crystal Clear*, *Dynamic Systems Development Method* (DSDM), *Extreme Programming* (XP), *Feature-Driven Development* (FDD), *Open Unified Process* (OpenUP), and *Scrum*. It has been concluded regularly by many surveys that XP and Scrum are among the agile methodologies currently in common use.

The trends in the awareness of "agility" as per software development could be examined using utilities such as *Alexa* (http://www.alexa.com) and *Google Trends* (http://www.google.ca/trends). Figure 1 shows the results of searching for the term "Agile Scrum" in Google Trends.

The agile methodologies have evolved in the past few years, and continue to evolve, individually as well as collectively. This evolution has been driven by the experience of agile methodologies in industrial settings and increasing confluence of agile methodologies and user experience design methodologies. For example, there are significant changes in the specifications of both XP and Scrum, there are usability-related extensions of both XP and Scrum, and there are hybrid agile methodologies that include elements of multiple agile methodologies. Indeed, these initiatives have led to variants, such as *Agile Experience Design* (AXD), *U-Scrum, User-Centered Agile Process*

Figure 1. A snapshot of search trends for the term "Agile Scrum" between 2004 and 2013

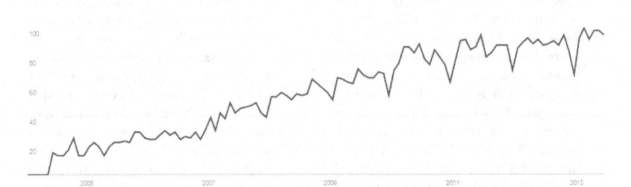

(UCAP), and *XPnUE*, of established agile methodologies, such as XP and Scrum.

For those responsible for managing an organization, the selection of, or a transition to, an appropriate agile methodology is a crucial issue from the standpoint of strategic management (Moreira, 2013). However, addressing this crucial issue in detail is beyond the scope of this chapter.

Understanding Wiki

The origins of the basic ideas behind Wiki date back to the 1940s (Bush, 1945), although they came to fruition only after the birth of the Internet and the pressing need for content management in organizations. In the 1990s, the use of patterns in software engineering (Appleton, 1997) was gaining acceptance; however, existence of a means to collaboratively author and globally disseminate patterns continued to be a challenge. This changed with the advent of the Web, followed by the introduction of technologies that could support server-side programming for a client-side delivery, and led to the inception of Wiki.

Characteristics of a Wiki

There are a number of discernible human-centered and socially-oriented characteristics of a Wiki

(Leuf & Cunningham, 2001; Ebersbach et al., 2008), including the following:

- **Collectiveness:** A Wiki is inspired by the need of an environment for collaborative work by a decentralized, usually geographically dispersed, group of people (Tapscott & Williams, 2006). A resource on a Wiki can be submitted or edited by anybody with appropriate permissions, at any time, using only the interface of a Web user agent, on different kinds of devices. From a software engineering perspective, Wiki is an example of end-user software engineering.

- **Creativeness:** A Wiki serves as platform for exploration and evaluation. In doing so, a Wiki supports a four-stage framework for creativity (Shneiderman, 2000): *Collect, Relate, Create,* and *Donate.* For example, a Wiki can be used as a medium for 'playing' games involving customers, as well as others, to inspire innovation (Hohmann, 2006). These games include *Spider Web, Product Box, Buy a Feature, Show and Tell, Start Your Day,* and *Speed Boat.*

- **Perspectiveness:** A Wiki is holistic, as the whole is greater than the sum of its parts (namely, individual resources). A single resource may solve only a small, simple, problem. However, it is the thematically-related and topically-organized collective of resources on a Wiki that aims to solve a bigger, more complex, problem. This architectural aspect of Wiki has been inspired by the notion of a *pattern language* (Alexander, Ishikawa, & Silverstein, 1977).

- **Openness:** A Wiki embraces the notions of open source, as well as open content. A Wiki system is usually based on a compendium of technologies and tools that are available as *open source software* (OSS). A resource on a Wiki is available to all those with appropriate rights. This aids setting up an inexpensive software development infrastructure with low technical barrier for usage, both of which are important for small-and-medium sized enterprises (SMEs) that, conventionally, have been one of the main adopters of agile methodologies. It could be noted that openness of Wiki does not automatically imply that it is uncontrolled.

Deciding Upon a Wiki

There are a number of technologies and tools responsible for a Wiki, of which the most significant is a Wiki system. For the sake of this chapter, a Wiki system can be viewed as a distributed content management system. The Wiki systems have evolved over the years, and currently there are a number of contenders in the market. For example, *MediaWiki* and *TWiki* are among the Wiki systems currently in common use. The software architecture of Wiki systems vary. A Wiki system may provide a number of different templates for different purposes. For example, a Wiki system may provide templates for creating articles, bibliographic entries, or blog items. A Wiki system may be installed locally or remotely (as a Wiki hosting service). If preferred otherwise, there are also Wiki hosting services (or Wiki 'farms'). For example, *Wikia* and *Wikispaces* are among the Wiki hosting services currently in common use.

There are also certain agile project management systems, such as *OnTime*, *PBwiki*, and *ThoughtWorks Mingle*, which provide native support for Wiki via in-built Wiki system engines.

To ensure that a deployment of a Wiki system reaches its desired potential, the selection of (or a transition to) a Wiki system appropriate for an agile project is crucial. However, given the increasing number of Wiki systems available, the selection of a suitable Wiki system has also become somewhat non-trivial. There are both patterns and anti-patterns for Wiki adoption (Mader, 2008). It is also possible to use a sequence of these adoption patterns to steer and guide new users of Wiki. There are also tools such as *WikiMatrix* (http://www.wikimatrix.org/) that provide a regularly updated list of Wiki systems. It also provides interactive means to compare Wiki systems, and a wizard that recommends (and, therefore, helps choose) a Wiki system based on the answers to a set of questions.

Related Work

There have been relatively few noteworthy initiatives, in academia as well as in industry, towards the use of Wiki in software engineering, in general, and agile software development, in particular. In the rest of this section, these efforts are discussed chronologically.

Planning Game is one of XP's core practices, and provides necessary guidance for product delivery. In one of the earliest works on the use of Wiki in agile software development, the details of *XPSwiki*, a tool based on *Swiki* for supporting Planning Game, are described (Pinna et al., 2003). However, XPSWiki is currently not available for public use.

In 2006, the *Wikis for Software Engineering* (Wiki4SE) series of workshops, as part of the *International Symposium on Wikis and Open Collaboration* (WikiSym), were introduced. In the same year, connection between Wiki and agile software development was drawn (Cunningham,

2006). Ever since, there has been a notable increase in the use of Wiki in software engineering, in general, and agile software development, in particular.

The uses of Wiki as a placeholder for meeting agenda and minutes, and for linking documentation and source code, have been highlighted (Louridas, 2006). There are a number of patterns for computer-mediated communication (Schümmer & Lukosch, 2007), and Wiki is an example of SHARED BROWSING and CENTRALIZED OBJECTS patterns. The potential for interplay between agility and Wiki is apparent in the AGILE LIFECYCLE pattern (Mader, 2008). The usability of Wikis in managing software requirements in course projects has been evaluated, and the results are mixed (Minocha, Petre, & Roberts, 2008). The relevancy of a number of Social Web Applications (including Wiki) to project management, requirements engineering, design, and programming has been asserted (Ras, Rech, & Weber, 2009). The arguments are then used as a basis to formulate hypothesis and derive research questions for a survey. Using a Wiki has been listed among the 97 essential things that a software project manager should consider (Davis, 2009). The article lists a number of benefits of using a Wiki for software project stakeholders, but the coverage is not organized and is seemingly one-sided. The development and use of *SoftWiki*, a Semantic Wiki for social requirements engineering, has been described (Lohmann et al., 2009). SoftWiki allows export to Requirements Interchange Format (RIF). However, the use of RIF is not prevalent in the current practice of agile methodologies. There are a number of patterns that characterize Web 2.0 (Governor, Hinchcliffe, & Nickull, 2009), and Wiki is cited as an example of SOFTWARE AS A SERVICE, PARTICIPATION-COLLABORATION, RICH USER EXPERIENCE, THE SYNCHRONIZED WEB, and COLLABORATIVE TAGGING patterns. The reasons for and uses of Wiki in helping people from different disciplines collaborate during software development have been highlighted

(Phuwanartnurak, 2009). Using a survey as an instrument, the relevance of Wiki for collaborative knowledge management has been assessed and the characteristics of Wiki users have been given (Hester, 2010). The uses of Wiki for user story (Cohn, 2004) education, both inside and outside a classroom, have been given (Fancott, Kamthan, & Shahmir, 2012). Finally, using an integrated knowledge management life cycle (Dalkir, 2005), a starting point for the confluence of agile software development, knowledge management, and Wiki has been outlined (Kamthan, 2013).

To summarize, in the studies on the use of Wiki for different aspects of software development so far, there is, in general, more emphasis on the process and product, and less on people. Furthermore, only few characteristics of Wiki have been deemed relevant for software development. Finally, there is inadequate attention towards a systematic integration of Wiki in a software project, as well as towards exploring the implications, both positive and negative, in a commitment to Wiki for managing content in agile software development.

UNDERSTANDING AND EXPLORING THE USE OF WIKI FOR MANAGING CONTENT IN AGILE SOFTWARE DEVELOPMENT

In this section, the notion of Wiki is associated with agile software development. In doing so, the perspective is that of content management, and the transition is from abstraction to concretization.

Agile Software Development and Content

There is creation, communication, and consumption of content in any engineering endeavor. In software engineering, in general, and in agile software development, in particular, content is created during the execution of a software process, and is communicated and consumed by the members of a software project team and beyond.

There are different kinds of content at different stages of a software project, from its inception to its conclusion. This content can have several notable properties: it can be of different types (such as, data, information, or knowledge), can exist in different forms (such as, physical or digital), can be in different modalities (such as, visual or aural), and can be in different states (such as, static or dynamic).

For the sake of this chapter, data, information, and knowledge are pairwise different, but related: knowledge is a kind of information (or is metainformation, that is, information about information), and information is a kind of data, but the converse in each case is not necessarily true. For example, a string of characters is data; however, if it is not meaningful, then it is not information, and, if it is not truthful, it is not knowledge.

There are different ways of classifying knowledge (Dalkir, 2005). From the perspective of articulation, knowledge can be classified into the following categories: (1) *Tacit* (knowledge that can not be articulated), (2) *Implicit* (knowledge that can be, but has not been, articulated), and (3) *Explicit* (knowledge that has been articulated). In Table 1, examples of these types of knowledge, as they relate to agile software development, are given.

An agile methodology consists of a number of activities, and principles and practices that govern those activities. The execution of an activity may lead to an artifact. There can be a number of artifacts in an agile project, including agile requirements, user interface design prototypes, and snippets of source code. In certain cases, an artifact can be a form of explicit knowledge.

A proper management of content is necessary for it to remain current and relevant. For the rest of the chapter, the attention is on information management, and, to a certain extent, on knowledge management, unless otherwise stated.

Table 1. A collection of aspects related to Agile Software Development and their corresponding knowledge types

Knowledge Type	Agile Software Development
Tacit	Modeling Skill
Implicit	Rationale for Selecting a Use Case Format
Explicit	Use Case Model

Agile Software Development and Wiki

For a systematic integration of Wiki in agile software development, a conceptual model, as shown in Figure 2, is proposed (Kamthan, 2013).

The aim of this conceptual model is to provide an understanding of the salient elements of agile software development that can serve as entry points in such integration. These elements along with their interrelationships are inspired by the different viewpoints of software engineering given by the *IEEE Software and Systems Engineering Standards Committee*. An agile project is usually supported by a variety of resources, including *computer-aided software engineering* (CASE) tools. It follows from Figure 2 that Wiki is perceived as a kind of resource that assists other elements of agile software development.

It can be expected that an agile team that adopts the aforementioned conceptual model belongs to the present generation that is aware of current technical developments. Indeed, in the context of this chapter, such an agile team lies in the intersection of the classes of people identified as *Digital Natives*, *Agile Project Stakeholders*, and *Wiki Users*, as shown in Figure 3 (Kamthan, 2013).

The designated roles and corresponding responsibilities of members in an agile team depend on the type of agile methodology. For example, the roles and responsibilities of members in an XP team are different from that of a Scrum team. This, evidently, affects how a Wiki is administered and used by an agile team.

Figure 2. *A conceptual model for integrating Wiki in agile software development*

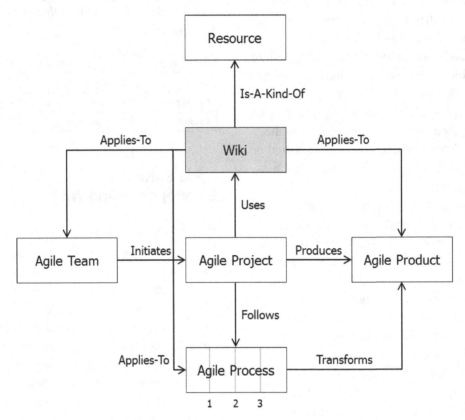

Figure 3. *An agile team composed of digital natives that are interested in software development and are committed users of Wiki*

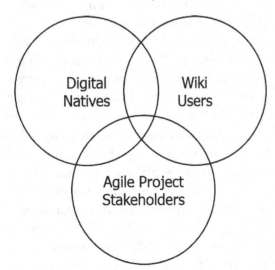

In pursuing an agile project, an agile team can use a Wiki, for a number of purposes, throughout an agile process, to arrive at an agile product: for collective awareness, for communicating, for collaborating, for brainstorming, for documenting, for organizing (classifying), for reflecting, for annotating, for versioning, for hyperlinking, for archiving and retrieving, for preserving, for disseminating, for publishing, and so on. The thread that binds these human-centered and socially-oriented activities is the management of content.

Scenarios of Using Wiki for Managing Content in Agile Software Development

In this section, representative cases on the interrelated topics of conception, extension, and reflection are given.

Conception: Agile Project Artifacts and Wiki

A Wiki can help make implicit knowledge explicit, and can help an agile team create, syndicate, and digest such explicit knowledge. Furthermore, such a Wiki need not be isolated. For example, a Wiki can act as a placeholder for an agile requirement description, and this description can be annotated with information included or transcluded, as necessary, from other Social Web Applications (http://www.go2web20.net/), as illustrated in Figure 4.

There are a number of candidates for metainformation, including author information, application domain knowledge, and status information. The information and metainformation can be mutually related in a number of ways, including hyperlinking.

Extension: Beyond a Single Agile Project

The organization responsible for the agile project may use Wiki for a variety of reasons beyond, but not unrelated to, software development. For example, it is known that an organizational chart can serve as a useful starting point for the identification and classification of stakeholders, a carefully crafted and collated collection of Frequently Asked Questions (FAQs) can assist new members of an agile team, and information on past projects can be useful for process improvement, conceptual reuse, and cost estimation. A Wiki could be used to maintain an organizational chart, collection of FAQs, or a list of past projects.

In sociology, a *boundary object* describes information used in different ways, by different communities. There are a number of characteristics

Figure 4. A social web application is a source for metainformation associated with an agile requirement description

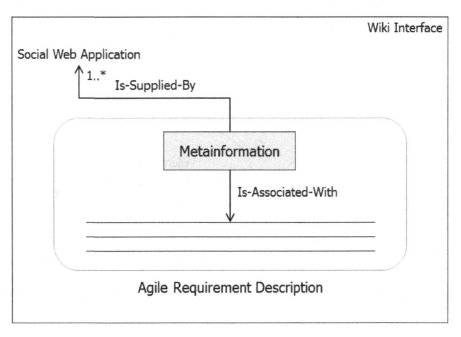

desirable of artifacts to act as boundary objects (Wenger, 1998; Star & Griesemer, 1989; Efimova, 2009): *Modularization, Abstraction, Accommodation*, and *Standardization*. From a sociological perspective, agile project artifacts, equipped with the metainformation garnered from Social Web Applications supporting a Wiki system, act as boundary objects. For example, these artifacts could be used for purposes that are related to but beyond software development, such as analytics and retrospectives, during or after the closure of the agile project (Moreira, 2013).

Extension: Beyond a Single Wiki

There are a growing number of projects under the auspices of the *Wikimedia Foundation* that can complement the content of a locally or remotely installed Wiki system. Furthermore, Wikis that are internal or external to the organization can complement the ones meant for the agile project. The resulting architecture of knowledge from the perspective of Wiki is shown in Figure 5.

For example, *Wikipedia* is among the major projects of the Wikimedia Foundation, and can serve an agile project in many different ways. It is known that Wikipedia is a community-wide voluntary effort towards a multilingual encyclopedia that is free for all (in the sense of access, participation, and cost), and for the past decade has served as an exemplar of large-scale collaboration and documentation (Reagle Jr., 2010; O'Sullivan, 2012). For an agile team, Wikipedia could serve as an informative source for definitions and a reference for examples. For newcomers to Wiki, mature sections of Wikipedia could serve as an example of organization and presentation of content. Wikipedia relies on a number of tools to provide a dependable service: it uses MediaWiki as its Wiki system, and deploys an *Article Feedback Tool* (AFT) to solicit and collate feedback on its articles. The use of AFT can help improve the quality of information that is input indirectly into an agile process. In fact, by contributing to Wikipedia, the members of an agile team can indirectly help their own projects. There are also

Figure 5. A Wiki 'universe' consisting of agile project artifacts and more

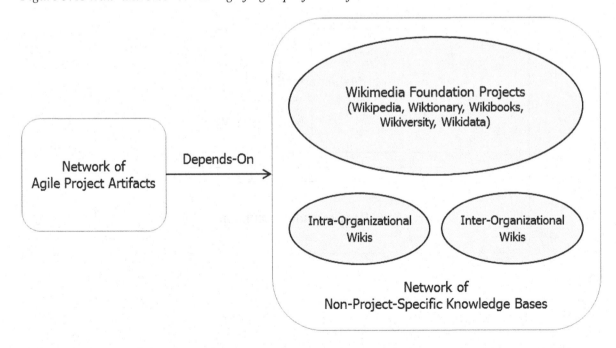

tools such as the *WikiMindMap* (http://wikimind-map.com/) that can automatically create a mind map of a given Wikipedia article with its title as the central concept, and thereby aid a Wikipedia article reader.

Reflection: Feedback and Wiki

The agile process, as depicted in Figure 2, is iterative as well as incremental. It is the solicitation and accommodation of feedback that makes an agile process iterative, and contributes to the quality of agile project artifacts. There can be different kinds of feedback (Lohmann et al., 2009), say, due to *commenting*, *rating*, and *voting*.

A Wiki can serve as a means for soliciting feedback from agile project stakeholders. A Wiki template may allow support for a fill-out form embedded in a document. In Wiki markup, a form, upon rendering, appears as a two-dimensional text field. A form can be used for commenting on (for example, the information contained in)

the document. A comment after submission (and, possibly, approval) may be available publicly. This comment may have the details of its author, date, and time, and may be appended to the document, thereby *extending* the original document, as shown in Figure 6.

For example, commenting can be useful for providing feedback during a review of an agile project artifact, such as an agile requirement description, a task description, or a low-fidelity prototype description. The comments could subsequently be used for revising and/or recommending the corresponding agile project artifact.

The organization and presentation of content is relevant to the consumer of that content. The different types of metainformation may need to, upon rendering, be positioned differently with respect to information. For example, a tag cloud could be placed anywhere in the vicinity of information, but feedback must, logically, follow information. In certain Wiki systems, such organization and presentation can be done automatically.

Figure 6. An abstract organization and presentation of information, and its reflection, in a Wiki

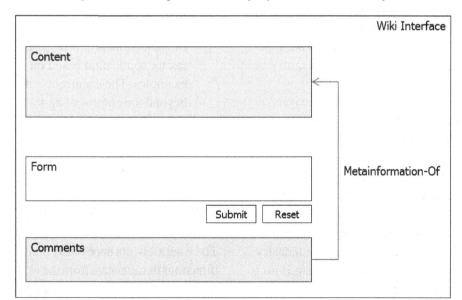

Limitations of Wiki for Managing Content in Agile Software Development

The perceived benefits of Wiki come with their associated costs. In some cases, the costs are ephemeral; in other cases, they are essential. There are different kinds of limitations of the use of Wiki for managing content in agile (and even in non-agile) software development, including the following:

- **Trustworthiness:** There is no inherent support by Wiki for assessing the quality of content, such as relevance or recency of feedback, on a Wiki. Furthermore, automated or exhaustive testing of certain quality attributes, such as credibility and usability, is difficult. The trustworthiness of publicly accessible and editable Wikis, such as Wikipedia (Denning et al., 2005), has been questioned over the years. The primary concerns have been the legitimacy of information, the potential for vandalism, and unauthorized, automatic, manipulation by bots, although undesirable changes can be reverted. Therefore, certain degree of monitoring and control of a Wiki, especially if it permits external access, may be inevitable.
- **Preparedness:** Using Wiki effectively as a means for managing content requires in-depth understanding of a number of areas, including information architecture, interaction design, and hypermedia design. However, these topics are currently not part of the curriculum of many current software engineering programs in academia or training programs in industry. Therefore, or even otherwise, there is no a priori guarantee that an agile team is adequately prepared in these areas. It is known that acceptance of a technology by its users is not automatic (Venkatesh et al., 2003). Indeed, an effective use of Wiki may require scaffolding (Díaz & Puente, 2011) or training (Rettich, 2011).
- **Innovativeness:** The creation of agile project artifacts requires the availability and support for certain technologies. It is possible to embed a variety of different kinds of media in Wiki markup (similar to that in HTML/XHTML markup). For example, a UML Use Case Diagram could be saved in an appropriate image format and included in Wiki markup. However, in itself, a Wiki system does not have native support for conceptual modeling. In general, it is currently not possible to use Wiki as a development platform to create non-textual media.
- **Persistence:** Wiki does not exist in isolation and, like many other electronic products, is not immune to the changes in its ecosystem. There is no a priori guarantee that a Wiki engine, a Wiki hosting service, or a Wiki application, will persist and continue to provide anticipated support for the entire duration of an agile project. The suspension in the development of Swiki and the discontinuation of *Luminotes* (a note-taking application based on Wiki) serve as examples. The occurrence of such events is beyond the control of agile software development, and an agile project may or may not be able to sustain the ramifications of such disruptive events.

FUTURE RESEARCH DIRECTIONS

There are a few, not necessarily mutually exclusive, directions that emanate from the work presented in this chapter. These avenues are discussed briefly in the following.

Empirical Support for Wiki Scenarios

The scenarios presented in this chapter are for the purpose of illustration. They are by no means exhaustive or exclusive, and their depth and breadth are limited by considerations of space. Indeed, formulation of other scenarios, based on further observations and analysis of agile projects in industry as well as in academia, can be useful, and is therefore of research interest.

For example, a survey supervised by the author in Winter 2013, of about 30 undergraduate students in their capstone projects that deployed agile methodologies, revealed that (1) the students with industrial experience were significantly more likely to be familiar with and embrace the use of Wiki, and (2) the students preferred the use of a Wiki hosting service over the use of a Wiki system.

Agile Social Network Studies

There are different kinds of social community types in software development, each with different technological needs (Tamburri, Lago, & van Vliet, 2013). Identifying social community types in distributed agile software development, classifying them according to the proneness for use of Wiki for managing content, and subsequently performing a *social network analysis* (SNA) of each social community type (Golbeck, 2013) are of research interest.

For example, in SNA, *centrality* refers to a collection of distribution metrics that aim to quantify the "importance" or "influence" (in some sense) of a particular node (or a set of nodes) within a social network. The identification of the most central actors in an agile social network is of research interest as it can aid in a number of ways, including (1) help examine the extent of correlation between prominence of stakeholders and the success (or quality) of agile projects, and (2) help examine the extent of correlation between the nature of information flow among stakeholders and the success (or quality) of agile projects.

Software Engineering Education and Human-Computer Interaction Education

The inclusion of agile methodologies is becoming increasingly relevant to software engineering curriculum. It is known that Wiki, like many other Social Web Applications, has implications towards education (Frydenberg, 2008), and that a number of *perceived affordances* and *signifiers* (Norman, 2013) of Wiki are aligned with the theories of learning based on *connectivism, constructivism,* and *navigationism* (Lee & McLoughlin, 2011). Therefore, it can be useful to investigate the extent to which Wiki can help the teaching and learning of concepts from, say, agile project management or agile user experience (Brown, 2013), help towards content reuse, help instilling behavioral competencies (including 'soft skills' such as accountability and collaborativeness), and so on.

For example, using Wikis for software engineering or human-computer interaction, connection(s) between seemingly disparate concepts in these disciplines can be shown to or can be 'discovered' by students by scanning through the articles or by using WikiMindMap. This is important in the light of the fact that software engineering and human-computer interaction evolved initially as independent disciplines, and agile software development has played a significant role in their convergence, opening new vistas of synergy between software engineering and human-computer interaction. This trend is likely to continue, and it is in the interest of the students to remain informed.

CONCLUSION

There is presence of essential or ephemeral content in each phase of an agile process. This content, by its inherent nature, is usually developing, dynamic, and distributed, and can occur as information or metainformation. The ability to manage content that is created, communicated, or consumed during development is a necessary imperative for an organization, in general, and for the success of an agile project, in particular.

To do that, there is need for cost-effective, sustainable information and communication technology (ICT), and Wiki, although not specifically designed for agile software development, serves as a suitable candidate in many different ways. The conceptual model presented in this chapter provides an initial step in the direction of understanding the use of Wiki for managing content in agile software development.

The co-evolution of agility and Wiki contributes uniquely to the effort of managing content in agile software development, in a variety of different ways, in different stages of development. Furthermore, doing so can suggest a promising starting point for managing such content in a larger context, namely that of the Social Web, as shown by various examples given in this chapter.

For a realization of the potential of incorporating an ICT in agile software development, it is crucial that the ICT be aligned with the corresponding organization's enterprise architecture, the principles of the Agile Manifesto, and the expectations of the stakeholders involved. The bottom-line is that the use of the ICT should help, not hinder, the people, the process, and the product of an agile project.

Even so, the prospects of using an ICT usually come with its share of concerns, and Wiki is no exception. The integration of Wiki in agile software development, as with other Social Web Applications (Bauerlein, 2011), comes with its share of adverse side-effects and associated costs that must be considered.

REFERENCES

Alexander, C., Ishikawa, S., & Silverstein, M. (1977). *A pattern language: towns, buildings, construction.* Oxford, UK: Oxford University Press.

Appleton, B. (1997). Patterns and software: Essential concepts and terminology. *Object Magazine Online, 3*(5), 20–25.

Bauerlein, M. (2011). *The digital divide: arguments for and against Facebook, Google, texting, and the age of social networking.* London: Penguin.

Brown, A. W. (2012). *Enterprise software delivery: bringing agility and efficiency to the global software supply chain.* Boston, MA: Addison-Wesley.

Brown, D. (Ed.). (2012). *Agile user experience design: a practitioner's guide to making it work.* Oxford, UK: Newnes.

Bush, V. (1945). As we may think. *Atlantic Monthly, 176*(1), 101–108.

Cohn, M. (2004). *User stories applied: for agile software development.* Boston, MA: Addison-Wesley.

Coplien, J. O., & Bjørnvig, G. (2011). *Lean architecture: for agile software development.* Hoboken, NJ: John Wiley & Sons.

Cunningham, W. (2006, August). Design principles of wiki: how can so little do so much? In *International Symposium on Wikis* (pp. 13-14), Odense, Denmark. doi:10.1145/1149453.1149459

Dalkir, K. (2005). *Knowledge management in theory and practice.* Burlington, MA: Elsevier Butterworth-Heinemann.

Davis, B. (2009). *97 things every project manager should know: collective wisdom from the experts.* Sebastopol, CA: O'Reilly Media.

Denning, P., Horning, J., Parnas, D., & Weinstein, L. (2005). Wikipedia risks. *Communications of the ACM, 48*(12), 152–152. doi:10.1145/1101779.1101804

Devedžić, V., & Milenković, S. A. R. (2011). Teaching agile software development: A case study. *Education. IEEE Transactions on, 54*(2), 273–278.

Díaz, O., & Puente, G. (2011, October). Wiki scaffolding: helping organizations to set up wikis. In *Proceedings of the 7th International Symposium on Wikis and Open Collaboration* (pp. 154-162). New York, NY: ACM. doi:10.1145/2038558.2038583

Ebersbach, A., Adelung, A., Dueck, G., Glaser, M., Heigl, R., & Warta, A. (2008). *Wiki: web collaboration*. New York, NY: Springer.

Efimova, L. A. (2009). *Passion at work: blogging practices of knowledge workers. Novay PhD Research Series, 24*. Enschede, The Netherlands: Novay.

Fancott, T., Kamthan, P., & Shahmir, N. (2012). Implications of the Social Web Environment for User Story Education. *Electronic Journal of e-Learning, 10*(1).

Ferreira, D., & da Silva, A. R. (2008, September). Wiki supported collaborative requirements engineering. In Proceedings of Wikis4SE 2008 Workshop. Porto, Portugal: Academic Press.

Frydenberg, M. (2008). Wikis as a tool for collaborative course management. *MERLOT Journal of Online Learning and Teaching, 4*(2), 169–181.

Galorath, D. D., & Evans, M. W. (2006). *Software sizing, estimation, and risk management: when performance is measured performance improves*. Boca Raton, FL: CRC Press. doi:10.1201/9781420013122

Golbeck, J. (2013). *Analyzing the social web*. Oxford, UK: Newnes.

Governor, J., Hinchcliffe, D., & Nickull, D. (2009). *Web 2.0 architectures: what entrepreneurs and information architects need to know*. Sebastopol, CA: O'Reilly Media.

Hester, A. J. (2010, May). Increasing collaborative knowledge management in your organization: characteristics of wiki technology and wiki users. In *Proceedings of the 2010 Special Interest Group on Management Information System's 48th annual conference on Computer personnel research on Computer personnel research* (pp. 158-164). New York, NY: ACM. doi:10.1145/1796900.1796961

Highsmith, J. (2009). *Agile project management: creating innovative products*. Upper Saddle River, NJ: Pearson Education.

Hoda, R., Noble, J., & Marshall, S. (2012). Documentation strategies on agile software development projects. *International Journal of Agile and Extreme Software Development, 1*(1), 23–37. doi:10.1504/IJAESD.2012.048308

Hohmann, L. (2006). *Innovation games: creating breakthrough products through collaborative play*. Upper Saddle River, NJ: Pearson Education.

Kamthan, P. (2013, May). On the role of wiki for managing knowledge in agile software development. In *Collaboration Technologies and Systems (CTS), 2013 International Conference on* (pp. 622-623). New York, NY: IEEE. doi:10.1109/CTS.2013.6567299

Larman, C., & Basili, V. R. (2003). Iterative and Incremental Development: A Brief History. *Computer, 36*(6), 47–56. doi:10.1109/MC.2003.1204375

Lee, M. J., & McLoughlin, C. (2011). *Web 2.0-based e-learning: applying social informatics for tertiary teaching*. Hershey, PA: Information Science Reference.

Leuf, B., & Cunningham, W. (2001). *The wiki way: quick collaboration on the web*. Boston, MA: Addison-Wesley.

Lohmann, S., Dietzold, S., Heim, P., & Heino, N. (2009, March). A Web Platform for Social Requirements Engineering. In *Software Engineering* (Vol. 150, pp. 309–315). Workshops.

Louridas, P. (2006). Using wikis in software development. *Software, IEEE*, *23*(2), 88–91. doi:10.1109/MS.2006.62

Mader, S. (2008). *Wikipatterns: a practical guide to improving productivity and collaboration in your organization*. Hoboken, NJ: John Wiley & Sons.

Mahnic, V. (2012). A capstone course on agile software development using Scrum. *Education. IEEE Transactions on*, *55*(1), 99–106.

Minocha, S., Petre, M., & Roberts, D. (2008). Using wikis to simulate distributed requirements development in a software engineering course. *International Journal of Engineering Education*, *24*(4), 689–704.

Moreira, M. (2013). *Being agile: your roadmap to successful adoption of agile*. New York, NY: Apress. doi:10.1007/978-1-4302-5840-7

Norman, D. A. (2013). *The design of everyday things: revised and expanded edition*. New York, NY: Basic Books.

O'Reilly, T. (2005). What is web 2.0: design patterns and business models for the next generation of software. Sebastopol, CA: O'Reilly Network.

O'Sullivan, M. D. (2012). *Wikipedia: A New Community of Practice?* London: Ashgate Publishing.

Perkins, T. K. (2006, June). *Knowledge: the core problem of project failure. CrossTalk*.

Phuwanartnurak, A. J. (2009, May). Interdisciplinary collaboration through wikis in software development. In *Wikis for Software Engineering, 2009. WIKIS4SE'09. ICSE Workshop on* (pp. 82-90). New York, NY: IEEE. doi:10.1109/WIKIS4SE.2009.5070000

Pinna, S., Mauri, S., Lorrai, P., Marchesi, M., & Serra, N. (2003). XPSwiki: an agile tool supporting the planning game. In *Extreme Programming and Agile Processes in Software Engineering* (pp. 104–113). New York, NY: Springer. doi:10.1007/3-540-44870-5_14

Ras, E., Rech, J., & Weber, S. (2009). Investigating the suitability of web X.Y. features for software engineering-towards an empirical survey. In *Software Engineering* (pp. 285–296). Workshops.

Reagle, J. M. (2010). *Good faith collaboration: The culture of Wikipedia*. Cambridge, MA: MIT Press.

Rettich, K. (2011, October). Using the wiki to deliver paperless software documentation. In *Professional Communication Conference (IPCC), 2011 IEEE International* (pp. 1-8). New York, NY: IEEE. doi:10.1109/IPCC.2011.6087219

Schneider, K. (2009). *Experience and knowledge management in software engineering* (pp. 99–109). New York, NY: Springer. doi:10.1007/978-3-540-95880-2_4

Schummer, T., & Lukosch, S. (2007). *Patterns for computer-mediated interaction* (Vol. 11). Hoboken, NJ: John Wiley & Sons.

Shneiderman, B. (2000). Creating creativity: User interfaces for supporting innovation. *ACM Transactions on Computer-Human Interaction*, *7*(1), 114–138. doi:10.1145/344949.345077

Sillitti, A., & Succi, G. (2005). Requirements engineering for agile methods. In *Engineering and Managing Software Requirements* (pp. 309–326). New York, NY: Springer. doi:10.1007/3-540-28244-0_14

Šmite, D., Moe, N. B., & Ågerfalk, P. J. (2010). *Agility across time and space: implementing agile methods in global software projects*. New York, NY: Springer. doi:10.1007/978-3-642-12442-6

Star, S. L., & Griesemer, J. R. (1989). Institutional ecology, 'translations' and boundary objects: Amateurs and professionals in Berkeley's museum of vertebrate zoology, 1907-39. *Social Studies of Science, 19*(3), 387–420. doi:10.1177/030631289019003001

Tabaka, J. (2006). *Collaboration explained: facilitation skills for software project leaders*. Upper Saddle River, NJ: Pearson Education.

Taina, J. (2011). Good, Bad, and Beautiful Software-In Search of Green Software Quality Factors. *CEPIS UPGRADE, 12*(4), 22–27.

Tamburri, D. A., Lago, P., & van Vliet, H. (2013). Uncovering latent social communities in software development. *Software, IEEE, 30*(1), 29–36. doi:10.1109/MS.2012.170

Tapscott, D., & Williams, A. D. (2008). *Wikinomics: how mass collaboration changes everything*. London: Penguin.

Thomas, J. C., Kellogg, W. A., & Erickson, T. (2001). The knowledge management puzzle: Human and social factors in knowledge management. *IBM Systems Journal, 40*(4), 863–884. doi:10.1147/sj.404.0863

Venkatesh, V., Morris, M. G., Davis, G. B., & Davis, F. D. (2003). User acceptance of information technology: Toward a unified view. *Management Information Systems Quarterly, 27*(3).

Wenger, E. (1998). *Communities of practice: learning, meaning, and identity*. Cambridge, UK: Cambridge University Press. doi:10.1017/CBO9780511803932

ADDITIONAL READING

Ambler, S. (2002). *Agile modeling: effective practices for extreme programming and the unified process*. Hoboken, NJ: John Wiley & Sons.

Boehm, B., & Turner, R. (2003). *Balancing agility and discipline: a guide for the perplexed*. Boston, MA: Addison-Wesley.

Bunse, C., Feldmann, R. L., & Dörr, J. (2004). Agile methods in software engineering education. In *Extreme Programming and Agile Processes in Software Engineering* (pp. 284–293). New York, NY: Springer. doi:10.1007/978-3-540-24853-8_43

Coplien, J. O., & Harrison, N. B. (2005). *Organizational patterns of agile software development*. Upper Saddle River, NJ: Prentice-Hall.

Dingsøyr, T., Nerur, S., Balijepally, V., & Moe, N. B. (2012). A decade of agile methodologies: Towards explaining agile software development. *Journal of Systems and Software, 85*(6), 1213–1221. doi:10.1016/j.jss.2012.02.033

Ghezzi, C., Jazayeri, M., & Mandrioli, D. (2003). *Fundamentals of software engineering*. Upper Saddle River, NJ: Prentice-Hall.

Gothelf, J., & Seiden, J. (2013). *Lean UX: Applying lean principles to improve user experience*. Sebastopol, CA: O'Reilly Media.

Hibbs, C., Jewett, S., & Sullivan, M. (2009). *The art of lean software development: a practical and incremental approach*. Sebastopol, CA: O'Reilly Media.

Kamthan, P. (2009). A methodology for integrating the social web environment in software engineering education. *International Journal of Information and Communication Technology Education, 5*(2), 21–35. doi:10.4018/jicte.2009040103

Kamthan, P. (2011). An exploration of the social web environment for collaborative software engineering education. *International Journal of Web-Based Learning and Teaching Technologies, 6*(2), 18–39. doi:10.4018/jwltt.2011040102

Kniberg, H. (2011). *Lean from the Trenches: Managing Large-Scale Projects with Kanban.* Sebastopol, CA: Pragmatic Bookshelf.

Kovitz, B. (2003). Hidden skills that support phased and agile requirements engineering. *Requirements Engineering*, 8(2), 135–141. doi:10.1007/s00766-002-0162-9

Larman, C. (2004). *Agile and iterative development: a manager's guide.* Boston, MA: Addison-Wesley.

Larman, C., & Vodde, B. (2008). *Scaling lean & agile development: thinking and organizational tools for large-scale Scrum.* Upper Saddle River, NJ: Pearson Education.

Mens, T., Serebrenik, A., & Cleve, A. (Eds.). (2014). *Evolving Software Systems.* New York, NY: Springer. doi:10.1007/978-3-642-45398-4

Messerschmitt, D. G., & Szyperski, C. (2005). *Software ecosystem: understanding an indispensable technology and industry.* Cambridge, MA: MIT Press.

Mohammadi, S., Nikkhahan, B., & Sohrabi, S. (2009). Challenges of user involvement in extreme programming projects. *International Journal of Software Engineering and Its Applications*, 3(1), 19–32.

Nonaka, I. (1995). *The knowledge-creating company: how Japanese companies create the dynamics of innovation.* Oxford, England: Oxford University Press.

Poppendieck, M., & Poppendieck, T. (2007). *Implementing lean software development: from concept to cash.* Upper Saddle River, NJ: Pearson Education.

Rich, N. (Ed.). (2006). *Lean evolution: lessons from the workplace.* Cambridge, England: Cambridge University Press. doi:10.1017/CBO9780511541223

Rubin, E., & Rubin, H. (2011). Supporting agile software development through active documentation. *Requirements Engineering*, 16(2), 117–132. doi:10.1007/s00766-010-0113-9

Rüping, A. (2003). *Agile documentation: a pattern guide to producing lightweight documents for software projects.* Hoboken, NJ: John Wiley & Sons.

Séguin, N., Tremblay, G., & Bagane, H. (2012). Agile principles as software engineering principles: an analysis. In *Agile Processes in Software Engineering and Extreme Programming* (pp. 1–15). New York, NY: Springer. doi:10.1007/978-3-642-30350-0_1

Selwyn, N. (2003). Apart from technology: Understanding people's non-use of information and communication technologies in everyday life. *Technology in society*, 25(1), 99–116. doi:10.1016/S0160-791X(02)00062-3

Shuhud, M. I. M., Richter, A., & Ahmad, A. (2013). Supporting requirements elicitation practices. In *Collaboration and Technology* (pp. 306–321). New York, NY: Springer. doi:10.1007/978-3-642-41347-6_22

Weller, K. (2010). *Knowledge representation in the social semantic web.* Berlin, Germany: Walter de Gruyter. doi:10.1515/9783598441585

KEY TERMS AND DEFINITIONS

Affordance: A property, or multiple properties, of an object that provides some indication to a user of how to interact with that object or with a feature of that object.

Agile Methodology: A software development methodology based on the Agile Manifesto.

Artifact: A document or a model produced during software development.

Digital Native: A person who was born at the time digital technologies were taking shape and/or has grown up with digital technologies.

Social Web: The perceived evolution of the Web in a direction that is driven by 'collective intelligence,' realized by information technology, and characterized by user participation, openness, and network effects.

Use Case: A sequence of actions performed by a system, which yields an observable result of value to an actor of that system.

User: An individual who interacts with the software system usually, but not always, with a specific goal.

User Experience: A person's perception and responses that result from the use and/or anticipated use of a product or service.

User Story: A high-level requirement statement that contains minimally sufficient information to produce a reasonable estimate of the effort to implement it.

Wiki: A Web Application developed cooperatively by a community of users, allowing any user to add, delete, or modify information.

Chapter 10
A Semantic Approach for Multi-Agent System Design

Rosario Girardi
Federal University of Maranhão, Brazil

Adriana Leite
Federal University of Maranhão, Brazil

ABSTRACT

Automating software engineering tasks is crucial to achieve better productivity of software development and quality of software products. Knowledge engineering approaches this challenge by supporting the representation and reuse of knowledge of how and when to perform a development task. Therefore, knowledge tools for software engineering can turn more effective the software development process by automating and controlling consistency of modeling tasks and code generation. This chapter introduces the description of the domain and application design phases of MADAE-Pro, an ontology-driven process for agent-oriented development, along with how reuse is performed between these sub-processes. Two case studies have been conducted to evaluate MADAE-Pro from which some examples of the domain and application design phases have been extracted and presented in this chapter. The first case study assesses the Multi-Agent Domain Design sub-process of MADAE-Pro through the design of a multi-agent system family of recommender systems supporting alternative (collaborative, content-based, and hybrid) filtering techniques. The second one evaluates the Multi-Agent Application Design sub-process of MADAE-Pro through the design of InfoTrib, a Tax Law recommender system that provides recommendations based on new tax law information items using a content-based filtering technique.

1. INTRODUCTION

Knowledge systems have evolved from expert systems to agent-oriented or multi-agent systems. A software agent is an entity that perceives its environment through sensors and acts upon that environment through actuators (Russel, & Nor-

vig, 2009). Having the properties of autonomy, sociability and learning ability, software agents are a very useful software abstraction to the understanding, engineering and use of both complex software problems and solutions like distributed and open systems and to support the decision making process (Leite, Girardi, Cavalcante, 2008b)

DOI: 10.4018/978-1-4666-6485-2.ch010

(Newton, & Girardi, 2007). Agent attributes allow approaching the complexity of software development through appropriate mechanisms for software decomposition, abstraction and flexible interactions between components (Wooldridge, Jennings, & Kinny, 2000).

On the other hand, automating software engineering tasks is crucial to achieve better productivity of software development and quality of software products. Knowledge engineering approaches this challenge by supporting the representation and reuse of knowledge of how and when to perform a development task. Therefore, knowledge tools for software engineering can turn more effective the software development process by automating and controlling consistency of modeling tasks and code generation.

In the last years, many efforts have been devoted to the research on agent-oriented software engineering. The proposals have evolved from simple techniques for modeling specific applications to methodologies and software processes for supporting reuse in agent-oriented development. Earlier phases of agent-oriented development have been extensively explored in the literature. There is a different situation on medium development phases like architectural and detailed multi-agent design where several research topics are still open, between them the lack of systematic approaches for modeling architectures of software agents and multi-agent systems. This article contributes with concrete solutions to this challenge by formalizing a knowledge-based approach to the architectural and detailed design of families of multi-agent systems. A family of software systems (Pohl, Bockle, Linden, 2005) is defined as a set of systems sharing some commonalities but also having particular features.

Knowledge representation formalisms, like ontologies (Gruber, 1995), are used by modern knowledge systems, to represent and share the knowledge of an application domain. Supporting semantic processing, they allow for more precise information interpretation. Thus, knowledge systems can provide greater usability and effectiveness than traditional information systems. This is particularly the case of knowledge systems for software engineering.

MADAE-Pro ("Multi-agent Domain and Application Engineering Process") (Girardi, & Leite, 2011) (Leite, Girardi, 2009) is a process for the development and reuse of families of multi-agent software systems, which consists of two complementary sub-processes: Multi-agent Domain Engineering and Multi-agent Application Engineering. Multi-agent Domain Engineering is a process for the development of a family of multi-agent software systems in a problem domain, by applying MADEM ("Multi-agent Domain Engineering Methodology") (Girardi, & Leite, 2008); and Multi-agent Application Engineering, the one for constructing a specific agent-oriented application by reusing one or more of those families (Drumond, & Girardi, 2008), using MAAEM ("Multi-agent Application Engineering Methodology") (Drumond, & Girardi, 2008) (Leite, Girardi, & Cavalcante, 2008b). The process consolidates a long term research effort on techniques, methodologies and tools for promoting reuse on agent-oriented software development (Girardi, & Leite, 2008) (Leite, Girardi, & Cavalcante, 2008a) (Leite, Girardi, Cavalcante, 2008b).

Besides providing support for reuse in multi-agent software development, through the integration of concepts of Domain Engineering and Application Engineering, MADAE-Pro is an ontology-driven process where models of requirements, agents and frameworks are represented as instances of the ONTORMAS ("ONTOlogy driven tool for the Reuse of Multi-Agent Systems") ontology (Leite, Girardi, Cavalcante, 2008a). Thus, concepts are semantically related allowing effective searches and inferences, facilitating the understanding and reuse of software models during the development of specific applications in a domain. Also, the models can be easily documented, adapted and integrated.

This work introduces the description of the domain and application design phases of MADAE-Pro, illustrating how software artifacts produced from the first phase are reused in the last one. Examples are extracted from two case studies we have conducted to evaluate MADAE-Pro. The first case study evaluates the Multi-Agent Domain Design sub-process of MADAE-Pro through the development of ONTOSERS ("ONTOlogy-based SEmantic web Recommender Systems") (Mariano, 2008) (Mariano, Girardi, Leite, Drumond, & Maranhão, 2008), a multi-agent system family of recommender systems supporting alternative (collaborative, content-based and hybrid) filtering techniques. The second one, evaluates the Multi-Agent Application Design (Girardi, 1992) sub-process of MADAE-Pro through the reuse of ONTOSERS for the development of InfoTrib. InfoTrib (Mariano, 2008) is a tax law recommender system in which, based on a user profile specifying his/her interests in the diverse types of taxes, the system provides recommendations based on new tax law information items using a content-based filtering technique.

The paper is organized as follows. Section 2 gives an overview of the MADAE-Pro software development process, introducing its lifecycle, a general description of the supporting methodologies and the ONTORMAS tool. Section 3 details the particular tasks of the Multi-agent Domain Design and Multi-agent Application Design Engineering phases of MADAE-Pro along with the guidelines provided by these methodologies to carry out those tasks. Examples from case studies on the evaluation of these phases are also described. Section 4 references related work discussing its similarities and differences with MADAE-Pro. Finally, section 5 concludes the paper with some considerations on ongoing work.

2. AN OVERVIEW OF MADAE-PRO

MADAE-Pro is an ontology-driven process model which integrates an iterative, incremental and goal-driven life cycle (section 2.1) along with the MADEM and MAAEM methodologies for Multi-agent Domain Engineering and Multi-agent Application Engineering, respectively. Its phases, tasks and products are conceptualized in the ONTORMAS ontology and both, specific or multi-agent system families are represented as instances of this knowledge base (section 2.2).

Main modeling concepts and tasks of MADEM and MAAEM are based both on techniques for Domain and Application Engineering (Arango, 1988) (Czarnecki, & Eisenecker, 2000) (Harsu, 2002) and of multi-agent system development (Cossentino, 2002) (Dileo,Jacobs, & Deloach, 2002) (Odell, Parunak, & Bauer, 2000) (Silva, & Lucena, 2007). For the specification of a problem to be solved, both methodologies focus on modeling goals, roles and interactions of entities of an organization, representing the requirements of either a multi-agent system family or a specific multi-agent application from the point of view of the organization stakeholders. Entities have knowledge and use it to exhibit autonomous behavior. An organization is composed of entities with general and specific goals that establish what the organization intends to reach. The achievement of specific goals allows reaching the general goal of the organization. For instance, an information system can have the general goal of "satisfying the information needs of an organization" and the specific goals of "satisfying dynamic or long term information needs". Specific goals are reached through the performance of responsibilities in charge of particular roles with a certain degree of autonomy. Pre-conditions and post-conditions may need to be satisfied for/after the execution of a responsibility. Knowledge can be consumed and produced through the execution of a responsibility. For instance, an entity can play the role of "retriever" with the responsibility of executing the responsibility of satisfying the dynamic information needs of an organization. Another entity can play the role of "filter", in charge of the responsibility of satisfying the long-term information needs of the organization. Sometimes, entities have to communicate with other internal or external entities (like stakeholders) to cooperate in the execution of a responsibility. For instance, the entity playing the role of "filter" may need to interact with a stakeholder to observe his/her behavior in order to infer his/her profile of information interests.

For the specification of a design solution, roles are assigned to reactive or deliberative agents structured and organized into a particular multi-agent architectural solution according to non-functional requirements. Agents have skills related to one or a set of computational techniques that support the execution of responsibilities in an effective way. According to the previous examples, skills can be, for instance, the rules of the organization to access and structure its information sources.

For implementation, agent design models are mapped to agents, behaviors and communication acts, concepts involved in the JADE (Bellifemine, Caire, & Greenwood, 2007) and JESS framework (Friedman-Hill, 2003), which is the adopted implementation platform.

Variability modeling is a main concern on the construction of multi-agent system families. In MADAE-Pro, it is carried out in parallel with all MADEM phases to determine the common and variable parts of a family. This is done by identifying the "Variation Points" and its correspondent "Variants". A variation point is the representation of a concept subjected to variation. A variant represents the alternative or optional variations of such a concept.

2.1 The MADAE-Pro Lifecycle

Figure 1 illustrates the MADAE-Pro process life cycle using the SPEM ("Software Process Engineering Metamodel") notation (Object

Management Group, 2013). The cycle is iterative, incremental and goal-driven. Iterations can occur between the phases for refining modeling products. Techniques are associated to each development phase to guide the modeling tasks. Figure 1 also shows the consumed and generated products of each phase. MADAE-Pro consists of six development phases: domain analysis (Leite, Girardi, Cavalcante, 2008a), domain design and domain implementation, supported by the MA-DEM methodology and application requirements engineering (Leite, Girardi, Cavalcante, 2008a), application design and application implementation, supported by the MAAEM methodology.

The domain analysis phase of MADEM approaches the construction of a domain model specifying the current and future requirements of a family of applications in a domain by considering domain knowledge and development experiences extracted from domain specialists and applications already developed in the domain, including products of the Multi-agent Application Engineering sub-process. This phase consists of the following modeling tasks: modeling of domain concepts, goal modeling, role modeling, role interaction modeling and user interface prototyping. The product of this phase, a domain model, is obtained through the composition of the products constructed through these tasks: a concept model, a goal model, a role model, a set of role interaction models, one for each specific goal in the goal model and a prototype of the user interface.

The domain design phase of MADEM approaches the architectural and detailed design of multi-agent frameworks providing a solution to the requirements of a family of multi-agent software systems specified in a domain model. This phase consists of two sub-phases: the architectural design sub-phase which establishes an architectural model of the multi-agent society including the knowledge shared by all agents in their communication and their coordination and cooperation mechanisms; and the agent design sub-phase which defines the

Figure 1. The MADAE-pro lifecycle

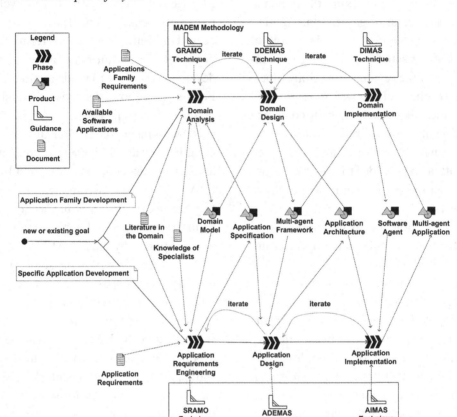

internal design of each reactive or deliberative agent, by modeling its structure and behavior. A multi-agent framework model of the multi-agent society is constructed as a product of this phase, composed of an architectural model and a set of agent models.

The domain implementation phase of MA-DEM approaches the mapping of design models to agents, behaviors and communication acts, concepts involved in the JADE (Bellifemine, Caire, & Greenwood, 2007) and JESS framework (Friedman-Hill, 2003), which is the adopted implementation platform of MADAE-Pro. An implementation model of the multi-agent society is constructed as a product of this phase, composed of a model of agents and behaviors and a model of communication acts.

MAAEM is a methodology for requirement analysis, design and implementation of multi-agent applications through compositional reuse of software artifacts such as domain models, multi-agent frameworks, pattern systems and software agents previously developed in the MADEM Domain Engineering process.

The requirements analysis phase of MAAEM looks for identifying and specifying the requirements of a particular application by reusing requirements already specified in domain models. This phase follows a set of modeling tasks consistently uniform with the ones of the MADEM domain analysis phase, for producing a set of models composing the multi-agent application specification. The MAAEM requirements analysis phase is performed through the following modeling tasks: concept modeling, goal modeling, role modeling, role interaction modeling and user interface prototyping. The product of this phase, an application specification, is obtained through the composition of the products constructed through these tasks: a concept model, a goal model, a role model, a set of role interaction models, one for each specific goal in the goal model and a prototype of the user interface.

In the application design phase, developers reuse design solutions of a family of applications and adapt them to the specific requirements of the application under development. A set of models composing the multi-agent application architecture are produced by following a set of modeling tasks consistently uniform with the ones of the MADEM domain design phase. This phase consists of two sub-phases: the architectural design sub-phase aiming at constructing a multi-agent society architectural model and the agent design sub-phase, which defines the internal structure of each reactive or deliberative agent in the society. The architectural design sub-phase consists of four tasks: multi-agent society knowledge modeling, multi-agent society modeling, agent interaction modeling, and coordination and cooperation modeling. The agent design sub-phase consists of two tasks: agent knowledge modeling and agent action modeling.

In the application implementation phase, agent behaviors and interactions are identified and specified in a particular language/platform for agent development. a behaviors model and communication acts model are generated in this development phase.

Along all MAAEM phases, reuse is carried out by identifying variation points in MADEM products and selecting appropriate variants.

2.2 The ONTORMAS Tool

ONTORMAS (Leite, Girardi, & Cavalcante, 2008a) is a knowledge based-system whose knowledge base is an ontology which conceptualizes the MADAE-Pro methodologies. It guides the modeling tasks and representation of their generated products as instances of its class hierarchy.

The ONTORMAS ontology consists of a set of classes organized hierarchically, with the main super classes: "Variable Concepts" (Figure 2), "Modeling Concepts" (Figure 2), "Modeling Tasks" and "Modeling Products". The super class "Variable Concepts" and corresponding subclasses are used to specify the variability of a multi-agent system family.

This is accomplished through the definition of "Variation Points" and "Variants." A variation point represents a variable concept. A variant represents the alternative or optional variations of such concept. The super class "Modeling Concepts" specifies the modeling concepts of the MADEM and MAAEM methodologies. In the super class "Modeling Tasks" and corresponding subclasses are defined the MADEM and MAAEM modeling tasks.

As an example, Figure 3 illustrates the representation of the tasks performed in the phases of Domain Design and Application Design. These tasks consist of the "Domain Engineering Tasks", which subtasks are related to the MADEM methodology and the "Application Engineering Tasks", related to the MAAEM methodology. In the super class "Modeling Products" and corresponding subclasses define the MADEM and MAAEM products. Products can be simple or composed of sub-products. For instance, Figure 4 illustrates the classes and instances of the multi-agent society model produced by both MADEM and MAAEM.

The products of MADEM and MAAEM are represented as instances of the corresponding concepts in the ONTORMAS class hierarchy, having each modeling concept a particular graphical notation. This facilitates not only the instantiation process but also contributes for reducing the complexity of the modeling tasks allowing the visualization, decomposition and refinement of the modeling products.

Figure 2. Semantic network with main modeling concepts of MADEM and MAAEM

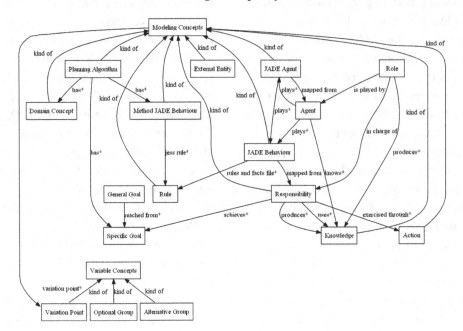

3. THE DOMAIN DESIGN AND APPLICATION DESIGN TASKS

This section details the Domain Design and Application Design tasks of MADAE-Pro showing how software artifacts of the ONTOSERS architectural model (Mariano, 2008) (Mariano, Girardi, Leite, Drumond, & Maranhão, 2008) are produced and reused on the design of the InfoTrib multi-agent recommender system (Mariano, Girardi, Leite, Drumond, & Maranhão, 2008). ONTOSERS-DM is an application family that specifies the common and variable requirements of recommender systems based on the ontology technology of the Semantic Web, using three information filtering approaches: content-based (CBF), where an item is recommended in terms of its similarity with other items that the user evaluated positively in the past, collaborative (CF), where an item is recommended according to the last preferences of other users with similar interests, and hybrid filtering (HF), where the two previous filtering approaches are combined (Mariano, 2008) (Mariano, Girardi, Leite, Drumond, & Maranhão, 2008). InfoTrib is

a tax law recommender system in which, based on a user profile specifying his/her interests in the diverse species of taxes, the system provides recommendations based on new tax law information items. InfoTrib supports collaborative and content based filtering.

Figure 5 shows a refinement of the MADAE-Pro lifecycle, previously illustrated in Figure 1, detailing the tasks and products of the Domain Design and Application Design phases.

3.1 The Domain Design Tasks

Domain Design approaches the architectural and detailed design of multi-agent frameworks providing a solution to the requirements of a family of multi-agent software systems specified in a domain model. It consists of two sub-phases: the Architectural Design sub-phase, establishes an architectural model of the multi-agent society including the knowledge shared by all agents in their communication and their coordination and cooperation mechanisms; and the Agent Design

Figure 3. Semantic network of the tasks and subtasks of the design phase of MADEM and MAAEM

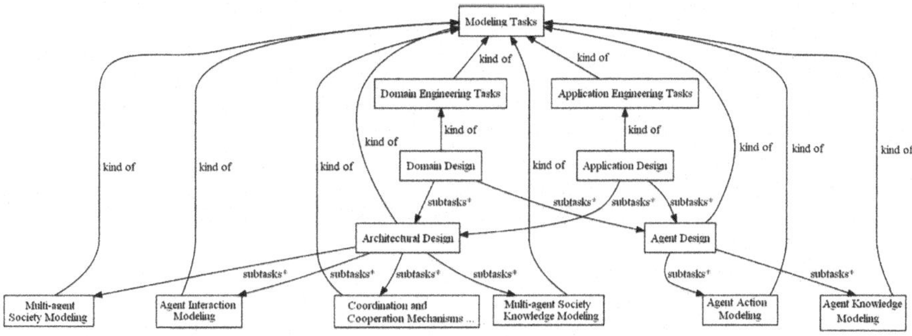

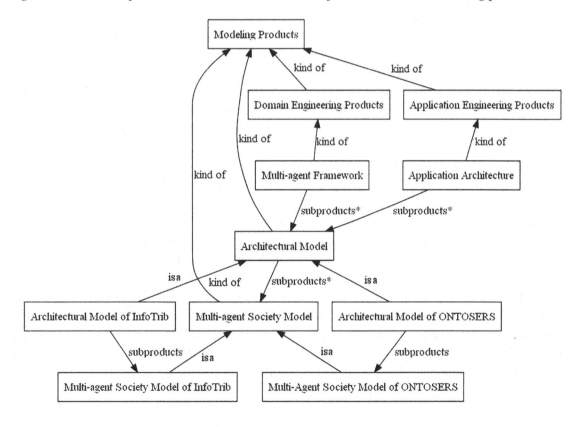

sub-phase, that defines the internal design of each agent, modeling its structure and behavior.

The Architectural Design sub-phase is performed through the following modeling tasks: multi-agent knowledge society modeling, multi-agent society modeling, agent interaction modeling and coordination and cooperation mechanisms modeling. An architectural model is the product of this sub-phase and it is composed of each one of these sub-products: multi-agent knowledge society model, multi-agent society model, agent interaction model and coordination and cooperation mechanisms model, respectively. The purpose of the design sub-phase is to perform the detailed design of each agent in the application, resulting in a set of agent models, each one composed of a

Figure 4. Relationships between classes and instances of the MADAE-Pro modeling products

Figure 5. The domain design and application design phases of MADAE-Pro

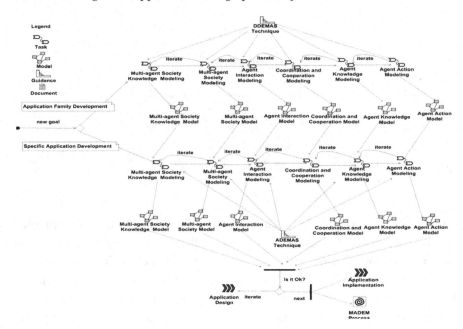

set of agent knowledge models and a set of agent action models.

The purpose of the multi-agent knowledge society modeling task is to represent the concepts shared by all agents in their communication. This is done through the construction of a model of the multi-agent society knowledge, represented in a semantic network. It was developed based on the role interaction model of the ONTOSERS domain model (Mariano, Girardi, Leite, Drumond, & Maranhão, 2008).

Part of the multi-agent society knowledge model of ONTOSERS is shown in Figure 6. In ONTOSERS, the main concept is the personalized recommendation, which is based on the user model and on the filtered items. Filtered items are information items whose similarity with a user model was assessed. The user model represents the user profile, which is composed by the user identification and interests. The information filtering agents exchange information filtering communicative knowledge between them.

In the multi-agent society modeling task, the roles identified in the domain analysis phase are assigned to agents. An agent can play one or more roles according to the affinity between their responsibilities, number of interactions between them or functional cohesion criteria. The variable part of this model is specified by defining variation points for variant responsibilities and similarity, variation points for variant skills.

The Multi-agent Society Model of ONTOSERS is shown in Figure 7. It was built based on the Role Model of the ONTOSERS domain model (Mariano, Girardi, Leite, Drumond, & Maranhão, 2008). The key difference between this model and the role model (Domain Analysis phase) is that, in the multi-agent society model, the main abstraction is an agent and not a role. All roles that interact with the User external entity were assigned to the "User Interface" agent, as shown in Figure 7. The "User Interface" agent is in charge of the following responsibilities: Explicit profile acquisition (Input interface role), Implicit profile acquisition (User Monitor role), Ontology instance user model creation and update (User modeler role), Personalized recommendation production

Figure 6. Part of the ONTOSERS multi-agent society knowledge model

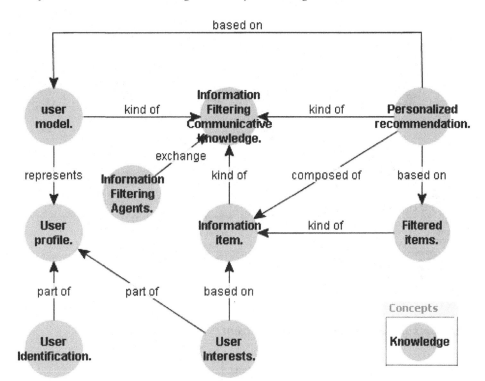

(Selector role) and Delivery of personalized recommendation (Output interface role).

Figure 8 shows the variability part of the "User Interface" agent organized in three groups of alternative responsibilities: "Explicit profile acquisition", where the applications of the family acquire a user profile just as explicit specify by a user through a form, "Implicit profile acquisition", where the user profile is inferred from his/her behavior and the "Explicit and Implicit profile acquisition", where both methods are used by the family applications.

The interactions between the agents, modeled in the agent interaction modeling task, can take place in the form of messages exchanged by agents or as notifications of an external event. Messages are specified following the FIPA-ACL guidelines (Shujun, & Kokar, 2013) and are represented by the performative, written in uppercase letters, and their respective content between parentheses.

The agent interaction model depicted in Figure 9 was built based on the role interactions model of the ONTOSERS domain model (Mariano, Girardi, Leite, Drumond, & Maranhão, 2008). First of all, the "User Interface" agent captures the user navigational behavior of the user and their interests. After that, the "User Interface" agent sends the user model to the "Filter" agent through the INFORM(ontology-based user model) message. The latter also perceives new information items from the Ontology based information source external entity and suggests the new item to the "User Interface" agents through the PROPOSE(New Information Items) message. The "User Interface" agents that accept this suggestion answer it with an ACCEPT_PROPOSAL (Model of the current user) message. After performing the similarity analysis, the "Filter" agent sends the INFORM_REF(Filtered Items) to the agents that accepted its proposal. Then the "User Interface"

Figure 7. Part of the ONTOSERS multi-agent society model showing the "user interface" agent

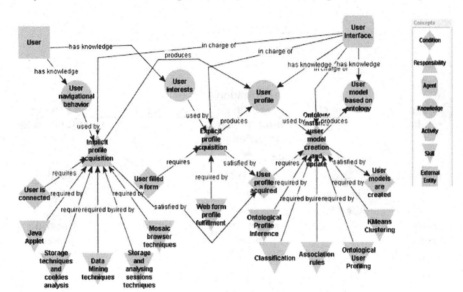

Figure 8. Variation point in the "user interface" agent

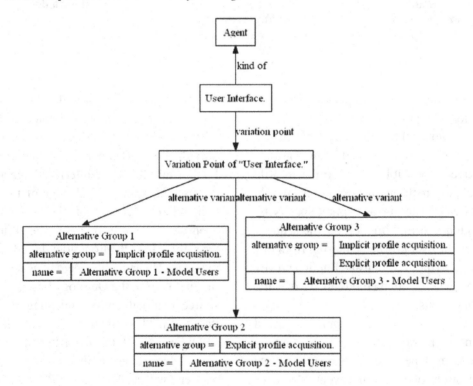

Figure 9. ONTOSERS agent interaction model

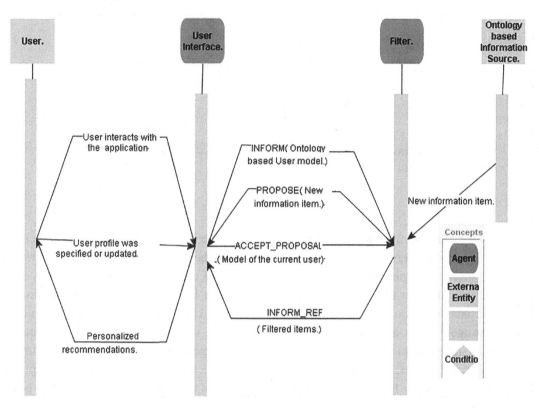

Figure 10. ONTOSERS coordination and cooperation model

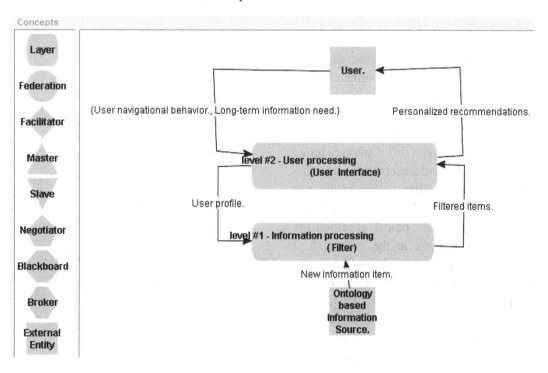

Figure 11. Part of the ONTOSERS agent knowledge model for "user interface" agent

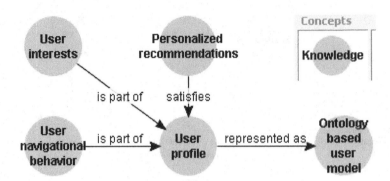

agents present the "Personalized Recommendations" to their respective users.

The coordination and cooperation mechanisms modeling task aims at either reusing or creating appropriate mechanisms of coordination and cooperation between agents to produce a coordination and cooperation mechanisms model satisfying non-functional requirements. Architectural patterns and design rules such as functional cohesion are also taken into account in the architectural design task.

The ONTOSERS framework is structured in a two layer multi-agent architecture as in Figure 10. The agents in the "User processing" layer interact with the user monitoring their navigational behavior, interests and delivering the recommendations, constructed using the filtered items provided by the "Information processing" layer. The Information processing layer is composed by a "Filter" agent, which interacts with the "Ontology based information source" in order to obtain the information items that are filtered according to the user models, obtained from the "User Processing" layer.

The agent knowledge model specifies the knowledge of each agent in the society. It is built based on the agent knowledge previously specified on the multi-agent society knowledge model. In terms of the "User Interface" agent, the required knowledge is the user interests and the user navigational behavior, which are part of the "User profile", represented as an "Ontology based

user model". The personalized recommendations satisfy the user profile. Part of the knowledge model of the "User Interface" agent is depicted in Figure 11. Thus, a variation point was created for the "User profile" knowledge having as an optional variant "User navigational behavior" knowledge (Figure 13) this optional variant could be selected for the construction of applications aiming at automatically acquiring user profiles.

Figure 12. Variation point of the user profile knowledge

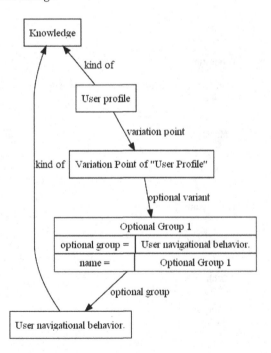

Figure 13. ONTOSERS agent action model showing the "filter" agent

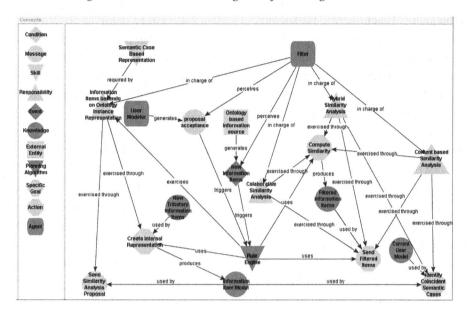

The last task of the Domain Design phase looks for constructing an Agent Action Model, representing the action that an agent will perform in this environment according to its responsibilities. In this model, the agent perceptions of its environment are represented: an event or the possible messages it can receive from other agents or external entities.

There are two ways of mapping perceptions to actions. The first one is when a perception is directly mapped to an action. In this case, the agent is considered of reactive type. The other one is when there is a plan, and then, by reasoning, the appropriate action to achieve a goal is chosen according to the perception of the agent. In this case, the agent is considered of deliberative type. To perform actions, agents must have skills to carry out their responsibilities and also meet a certain pre-condition.

In the ONTOSERS Agent Action Model illustrated in Figure 13 when the "Filter" agent is started it performs the information source monitoring. Once the information source is updated (new information items), the representation of new information items as ontology instances is

executed. Then the "Filter" agent proposes the "User Interface" agents to measure the similarity between the new information item and their respective user models. Each "User Interface" agent performs the evaluate new information item proposal. For each accepted proposal the "Filter" agent performs the "Similarity Analysis" responsibility. The "Hybrid Similarity Analysis" responsibility considers the results of both content based and collaborative methods to produce the "Filtered information items".

3.2 The Application Design Tasks

In the Application Design phase developers, reuse design solutions of a family of applications and adapt them to the specific requirements of the application under development. Otherwise, they design a multi-agent architecture from scratch, providing a solution to the requirements of the multi-agent application specified in the Requirement Analysis Phase.

This phase consists of two sub-phases: the architectural design phase aiming at constructing a multi-agent society architectural model and the agent design phase, which defines the internal structure and behavior of each agent in the society. The architectural design phase consists of five tasks: multi-agent society knowledge modeling, multi-agent society modeling, agent interaction modeling, and coordination and cooperation modeling. The detailed design phase has two tasks: agent knowledge modeling and agent action modeling.

The purpose of the multi-agent society knowledge modeling subtask is to represent the meaning of concepts that agents of the society need to understand in order to communicate with each other. This is done through the construction of a model of the multi-agent society knowledge, represented in a semantic network. Part of the Multi-agent Knowledge Society Model of InfoTrib is depicted in Figure 15. This model was developed from the ONTOSERS Multi-agent Knowledge Society model (Figure 7). In this model some knowledge was specialized from the Tax domain as, for example, the "Tributary normative instrument", "Tributary elements" and "Taxes" knowledge.

In the multi-agent society modeling task, the roles identified in the application analysis phase are assigned to agents. An agent can play one or more roles according to the affinity between their responsibilities, number of interactions between them or functional cohesion criteria.

Agents defined in the Multi-agent Society model are associated with one or more roles of the Role Model through the "plays" relationship. By searching ONTORMAS for agents associated with the roles previously reused in the Application Requirements Engineering phase, a Multi-agent society model can be selected for reuse.

An advanced search can be expressed through the JESS Tab (Figure 15). In this example, it was performed a search in the ONTORMAS knowledge base looking for Multi-agent Society models to reuse. For this, they were used as search arguments, the "User modeler" and "Input interface" roles. The search result was the ONTOSERS Multi-agent Society Model. Then, it was selected the variable part of the family according to the InfoTrib requirements. From the Multi-agent Society model of ONTOSERS (Figure 7), it was

Figure 14. InfoTrib multi-agent knowledge society model

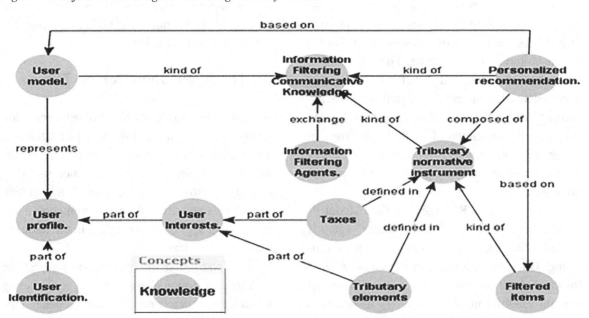

Figure 15. Advanced query through JESS Tab

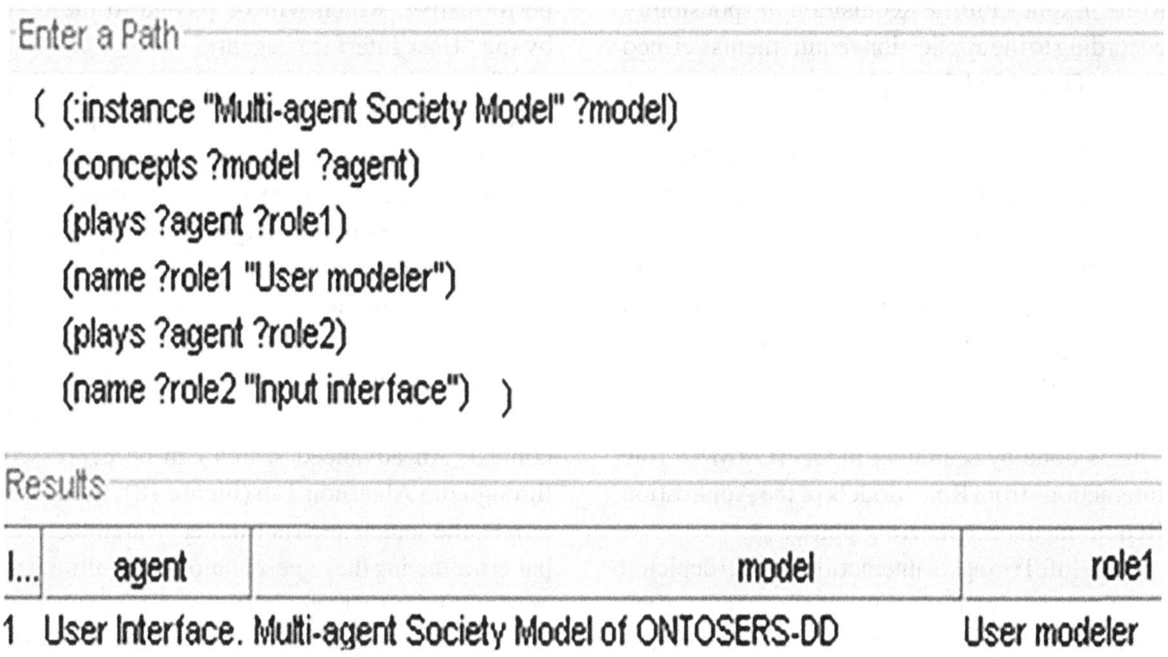

Enter a Path

```
(  (:instance "Multi-agent Society Model" ?model)
   (concepts ?model  ?agent)
   (plays ?agent ?role1)
   (name ?role1 "User modeler")
   (plays ?agent ?role2)
   (name ?role2 "Input interface")   )
```

Results

I...	agent	model	role1
1	User Interface.	Multi-agent Society Model of ONTOSERS-DD	User modeler

Figure 16. Part of the InfoTrib multi-agent society model showing the "user interface" agent

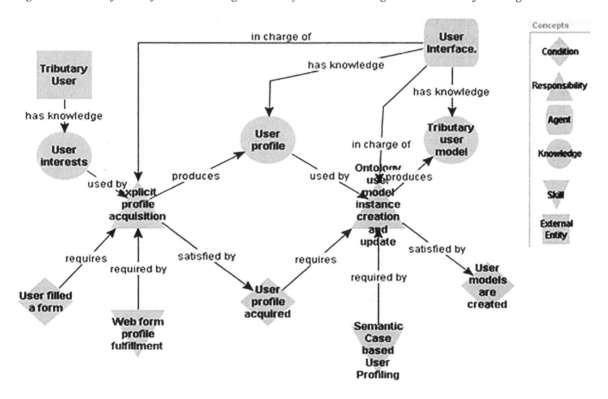

selected the variant "Alternative Group 2" related to the "Explicit Profile Acquisition" responsibility according to the application requirements defined in the Goal Model (Application Requirements Engineering phase). Figure 16 illustrates part of InfoTrib Multi-agent Society model, built by reusing the ONTOSERS Multi-agent Society model (Figure 7).

In the Agent Interaction Modeling sub-task, the interactions between the agents are specified following the FIPA-ACL guidelines (Shujun, & Kokar, 2013). The first step in this task should looks for a reusable interaction agent model. This is done by searching in ONTORMAS role interactions from Role Models of the Application Requirements Engineering phase.

The InfoTrib agent interactions model depicted in Figure 17 was built reusing the ONTOSERS agent interactions model (Figure 9). First of all, the "Filter" agent perceives a new information item, it will propose to the "User Interface" agent, through a PROPOSE performative, the similarity analysis between the new information item and the user model. If accepted, the agent will return with an ACCEPT performative. The filtered

items are delivered through an INFORM_REF performative, which will be passed to the user by the "User Interface" agent).

The Coordination and Cooperation modeling task aims at either reusing or creating appropriate mechanisms of coordination and cooperation between agents to produce a coordination and cooperation model satisfying non-functional requirements.

The selection of architectural patterns is performed in ONTORMAS. Therefore, the description of the application goal is compared with the problem described in each pattern and application context. An advanced search can be expressed through the Algernon Tab (Figure 18). In the example, the search aims at finding an architectural pattern allowing the representation of a multi-agent architecture in different levels of abstraction. The query was made with the terms "multi-agent" and "abstraction level" in the "context" and "problem" slots over instances of the "Architectural Pattern" class, obtaining as result the "Multi-agent Layer" architectural pattern.

The InfoTrib Coordination and Cooperation Model (Figure 19) was built by adapting the ON-

Figure 17. InfoTrib agent interaction model

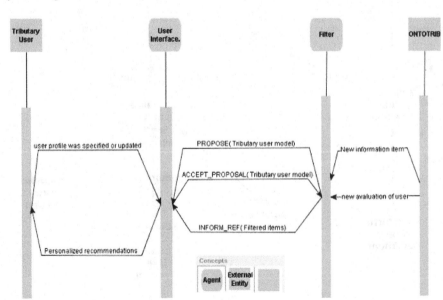

Figure 18. Advanced query through Algernon Tab

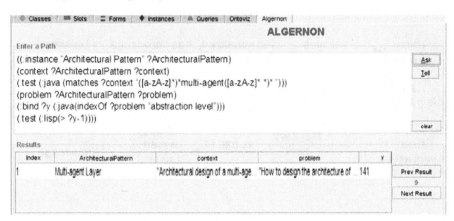

TOSERS Coordination and Cooperation Model (Figure 10). So they have similarities but also differences. For example, the "User processing" layer receives only the "User interests" knowledge and the information from ONTOTRIB is specifically for Tributary Law.

In the Knowledge Agent Model, the knowledge of each agent in the society is defined. The InfoTrib Knowledge Agent Model is illustrated in Figure 20. It was built from the ONTOSERS

Knowledge Agent Model (Figure 12), the "User navigational behavior" optional variant was not selected because it does not apply to the explicit modeling requirements of InfoTrib. Furthermore, some new and specific tributary concepts like "Tributary user model" were added.

The last developed model in the design phase of the application is the Agent-Based Model. This model represents the agent actions on the environment in accordance with the responsibilities that

Figure 19. Coordination and cooperation model

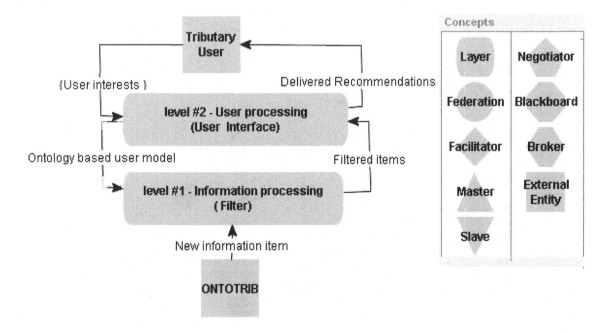

Figure 20. InfoTrib knowledge agent model for "user interface" agent

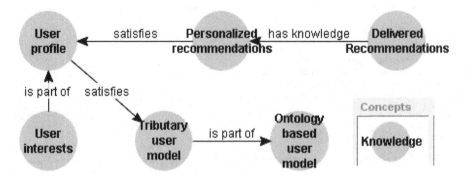

have been assigned, these ones being related to a particular specific goal. In this model are also represented agent's perceptions from the environment: an event or the possible messages that it may receive from other agents or external entities that will trigger his actions. In Figure 21 is shows the INFOTRIB Action Model.

4. RELATED WORK

Several approaches for agent-oriented software development, like GAIA (Handerson-Sellers, 2005)

(Wooldridge, Jennings, & Kinny, 2000) (Zambonelli, Jennings, & Wooldridge,2003), PASSI (Cossentino, 2002) (Handerson-Sellers, 2005) TROPOS (Bresciani et al., 2004) (Handerson-Sellers, 2005) (Silva, Castro, Tedesco, Araújo, Moreira, & Mylopoulos, 2006) (Mylopoulos, Castro, & Kolp, 2013) and domain engineering processes (Nunes, Kulesza, Nunes, & Lucena, 2009), have been already developed to increase the productivity of the software development process, the reusability of the generated products, and the effectiveness of project management.

Figure 21. InfoTrib agent action model showing the "filter" agent

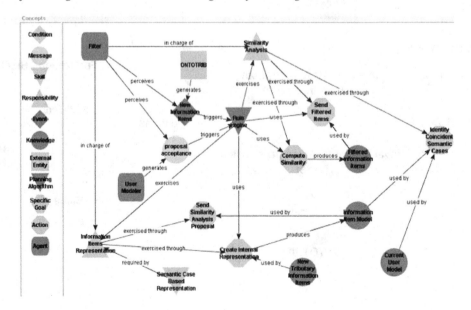

GAIA is a methodology based in human organization concepts. It supports the analysis and design phases for multi-agent system development. Tropos is an agent-oriented software development methodology supporting the complete multi-agent development process. It is based on the i* organizational modeling framework. PASSI is a process for multi-agent development integrating concepts from object-oriented software engineering and artificial intelligence approaches. It allows the development of multi-agents systems for special purposes as mobiles and robotics agents and uses an UML-based notation. A domain engineering process is described in (Nunes, Kulesza, Nunes, & Lucena, 2009) which focuses on system families including domain scoping and variability modeling. This process integrates a UML-based method, the PASSI methodology and a modeling language for developing multi-agent system product lines.

Table 1 summarizes and compares some characteristics of GAIA, PASSI, TROPOS, MADAE-Pro and the domain engineering process described above. All the approaches propose an iterative life cycle, where a software product goes through several refinements during the development process. With the exception of GAIA, in all other approaches, the life cycle is also incremental, where a software product is represented in several models to facilitate its understanding.

For the supported development phases, all these approaches cover analysis and design while PASSI, TROPOS and MADAE-Pro also support the implementation phase. The domain engineering process described above covers the domain engineering phases of early and late requirements, domain design and domain implementation. To our knowledge, only MADAE-Pro provides support for both domain and application engineering.

For the available development tools, PASSI is supported by PTK, a Rational Rose plug-in allowing modeling in AUML and code generation. The application of TROPOS is assisted by the TAOM-Tool (Perini, Susi, 2004), an Eclipse plug-in allowing system modeling with the i* framework. The MADAE-Pro process is supported by the ONTORMAS tool that allows modeling and storage of individual applications and families of multi-agent applications as instances of the ONTORMAS ontology. To our knowledge, GAIA does not have a tool support yet.

For reuse activities, GAIA and TROPOS allow the reuse of models and code in an informal way. PASSI permits the reuse of source code from class and activity diagrams. The domain engineering process described in (Nunes, Kulesza, Nunes, &

Table 1. A simple comparison of agent-oriented software development approaches

Features	Gaia	Passi	Tropos	Domain Engineering Process	Madae-pro
Lifecycle	Iterative within each phase, but sequential between phases	Iterative across and within all phases and incremental	Iterative and Incremental	Iterative and Incremental	Iterativ e and Incremental
Coverage of the lifecycle	Analysis and design	Analysis, design and implementation	Analysis, design and implementation	Analysis, design and implementation of system families	Analysis, design and implementation of system families and specific applications
Tool Support	No	Yes	Yes	Yes	Yes
Reuse Support	Informal	Informal	Informal	Systematic (partially)	Systematic
Variability Modeling Support	No	No	No	Yes	Yes

Lucena, 2009) is based on the concept of features, a system property relevant to some stakeholder, used to capture commonalities and to discriminate products in software product lines. However, this process does not offer guidelines for the selection, adaptation and integration of software artifacts. MADAE-Pro allows reuse of both models and source code of software products giving support for their selection, adaptation and integration.

For the variability modeling support, only MADAE-Pro and the domain engineering process described in (Nunes, Kulesza, Nunes, & Lucena, 2009) support it. This approach uses an extension of UML for modeling variability (Goma, 2005) while MADAE-Pro uses MADAE-ML, an ontology-driven modeling language.

Two main features distinguish MADAE-Pro from other existing approaches. First, it provides support for reuse in multi-agent software development, through the integration of the concepts of Domain Engineering and Application Engineering. Second, it is a knowledge-based process where models of agents and frameworks are represented as instances of the ONTORMAS ontology. Thus, concepts are semantically related allowing effective searches and inferences thus facilitating the understanding and reuse of the models during the development of specific applications in a domain. Also, the ontology-driven models of MADAE-Pro can be easily documented, adapted and integrated.

Table 2 summarizes and compares some design features of GAIA, PASSI, TROPOS, Domain Engineering Process and MADAE-Pro according to the following comparison criteria: supporting the specification of the global multi-agent system architecture, including the interaction of agents with the environment; enabling the specification of the architecture of each agent in the society, representing both the agent structure and behavior; using of a specific protocol in agent interactions and adopting ontologies for software agent knowledge bases and/or knowledge shared by the agent in the society.

For the specification of the architecture of a multi-agent system, the GAIA methodology proposes three models: an agent model that identifies the types of agents that will be part of the society, a service model defining the agent services and an acquaintance model representing the communication between different agents. PASSI specifies the architectural solution of the multi-agent system as a set of class and sequence diagrams. In the TROPOS methodology, the multi-agent system architecture is defined in terms of subsystems (actors) and their dependencies in an actor diagram. In this stage, architectural styles are selected to guide the definition of the multi-agent system architecture. The Domain Engineering Process in (Nunes, Kulesza, Nunes, & Lucena, 2009) defines a multi-agent system architecture in two stages. The first stage is static modeling, which determines how agents are structured. The second step is dynamic modeling that defines the interactions between agents, objects and roles. This task produces some UML

Table 2. A simple comparison of design phases in agent-oriented software development approaches

Features	Gaia	Passi	Tropos	Domain Engineering Process	Madae-pro
System Architecture	Yes	Yes	Yes	Yes	Yes
Agent Architecture	No	Yes	Yes	Yes	Yes
Interaction Protocols	No	FIPA-ACL	FIPA-ACL	No	FIPA-ACL
Support for Ontology	No	Yes	No	No	Yes

activity diagrams extended for the agent paradigm. As introduced in previous sections, the MADAE-Pro multi-agent system architecture is developed through four models: a Multi-Agent Knowledge Society model, representing knowledge shared by all agents of the multi-agent society; a Multi-Agent Society model, where agents of the society are organized according to their knowledge, skills and responsibilities; a Coordination and Cooperation model representing appropriate mechanisms of coordination and cooperation between agents satisfying non-functional requirements and an Interaction Agent Model, where the interactions between the agents are represented.

For the specification of the architecture of each agent in the society, the GAIA methodology does not specify the agents in a detailed level. In the Domain Engineering Process in (Nunes, Kulesza, Nunes, & Lucena, 2009), agents are individually defined in terms of their capabilities in a task specification diagram (an extension of the UML sequence diagram). The TROPOS methodology defines the detailed design of agents adding details to architectural components. In the PASSI methodology, each agent detailed design is specified in a structure definition diagram. This diagram is very similar to a UML class diagram and shows the agents of the society and their tasks. In MADAE-Pro, an Agent Action model represents the actions of each agent and the Agent Knowledge Model specifies the particular knowledge of each agent.

For the protocol used in agent interactions, there is not a specific protocol in the GAIA methodology and in the Domain Engineering Process in (Nunes, Kulesza, Nunes, & Lucena, 2009). PASSI, TROPOS and MADAE-Pro adopt the FIPA-ACL protocol.

Finally, for the adoption of ontologies as software agent knowledge bases the PASSI methodology defines ontology adoption in agent society model. It is represented in UML class diagrams and OCL constraints. The Domain Engineering Process in (Nunes, Kulesza, Nunes, & Lucena, 2009) and the TROPOS methodology

does not explicitly propose the use of ontologies. In MADAE-Pro, the knowledge shared by the agent in the society is represented in the Multi-agent Knowledge Model in the architectural design phase. Also the knowledge of each agent in the society is represented in an Agent Knowledge Model. Both the Multi-agent Knowledge Model and the Agent Knowledge Model are mapped to OWL ontologies.

From the characteristics summarized in Table 2, it can be seen that the approaches have many similarities. For example, in all approaches, except the GAIA methodology, the design phase is divided into two main steps that are the architecture design and the detailed design, which probably must have been influenced by other paradigms, such as object orientation, that treats the system design in this way. Another common feature in several of the approaches is the use of the FIPA-ACL protocol to represent the communication acts of agents and the use of UML sequence diagrams adapted. There are some differences between the approaches we can also mention besides the very definition of agents, tasks, resources, and others that have some conceptual differences, the use of ontologies and the modeling language. Among the approaches that differ from the others that use diagrams AUML to build the models, the TROPOS methodology uses the framework i * and MADAE-Pro, that uses a language based on ontologies called MADAE-ML. The use of ontologies is a differential of PASSI and MADAE-Pro approaches.

5. CONCLUSION AND FURTHER WORK

This work described the domain design and application design phases of MADAE-Pro, a knowledge-based process model, showing how software artifacts produced on the first phase are reused in the last one.

The SPEM process modeling language has been used to formalize the process, thus providing a standard, documented and ambiguity free representation of MADAE-Pro. The formalization of MADAE-Pro has allowed the systematic application of its life cycle and MADEM and MAAEM methodologies for the construction of multi-agent system families and specific multi-agent applications as well. Also, this formal model provides a basic framework for automating the MADAE-Pro development tasks.

The software artifacts produced by MADAE-Pro are represented as instances of the ONTORMAS tool, which serves as a repository of the reusable software artifacts and is a knowledge-based tool supporting application development.

MADAE-Pro has been evaluated with case studies approaching both the development of application families (Girardi, & Leite, 2008) (Mariano, Girardi, Leite, Drumond, & Maranhão, 2008) and specific applications (Drumond, & Girardi, 2008) (Newton, & Girardi, 2007).

The proposed software process is part of a project for the improvement of multi-agent development techniques, methodologies and tools. With the knowledge base provided by ONTORMAS, an integrated development environment is being developed as an expert system, aiming at automating various tasks of both MADEM and MAAEM, through a set of production rules that explores the semantic representation of modeling products in its knowledge base which are used for reasoning about the creation and transformation of models of families or specific multi-agent applications, following the different abstraction levels of the MADAE-Pro modeling tasks. Thus, fast application development and partial code generation will be provided.

MADAE-Pro currently supports compositional reuse, based on the selection, adaptation and composition of software artifacts. A generative approach for reuse has been explored with the specification of the GENMADEM methodology (Jansen, & Girardi, 2006) and the ONTOGEN-MADEM tool (Jansen, & Girardi, 2006). ONTO-GENMADEM provides support for the creation of Domain Specific Languages to be used on the generation of a family of applications in a domain. Further work will extend ONTORMAS for supporting ONTOGENMADEM allowing generative reuse in Multi-agent Application Engineering.

ACKNOWLEDGMENT

This work is supported by CAPES, CNPq, and FAPEMA research funding agencies of the Brazilian government.

REFERENCES

Arango, G. F. (1988). *Domain engineering for software reuse* (Doctoral dissertation). Retrieved from ProQuest Dissertations and Theses. (UMI No. 8827979).

Bellifemine, F., Caire, G., & Greenwood, D. (2007). *Developing Multi-Agent Systems with JADE*. Chichester, UK: John Wiley & Sons. doi:10.1002/9780470058411

Cossentino, M. (2005). From Requirements to Code with PASSI Methodology. In B. Henderson-Sellers, & P. Giorgini (Eds.), *Agent-Oriented Methodologies* (pp. 79–106). Hershey, PA: Idea Group Publishing; doi:10.4018/978-1-59140-581-8.ch004

Czarnecki, K., & Eisenecker, U. W. (2000). *Generative Programming: Methods, Tools, and Applications*. New York, NY: ACM Press/ Addison-Wesley Publishing Co..

Dileo, J., Jacobs, T., & Deloach, S. (2002). Integrating Ontologies into Multi-Agent Systems Engineering. *Proceedings of 4th International Bi-Conference Workshop on Agent Oriented Information Systems (AOIS 2002)*. Bologna, Italy.

Drumond, L., & Girardi, R. (2008). A Multi-agent Legal Recommender System. *Journal of Artificial Intelligence and Law*, 16(2), 175–207. doi:10.1007/s10506-008-9062-8

Friedman-Hill, E. (2003). *Jess in action: rule-based systems in java*. Greenwich, UK: Manning Publications Co.

Girardi, R. (1992). In O. Frameworks (Ed.), *Application Engineering: Putting Reuse to Work. Dennis Tsichritzis* (pp. 137–149). Geneva, Switzerland: University of Geneva.

Girardi, R., & Leite, A. (2008). A Knowledge-based Tool for Multi-Agent Domain Engineering. *Knowledge-Based Systems*, 21(7), 604–611. doi:10.1016/j.knosys.2008.03.036

Girardi, R., & Leite, A. (2011). Knowledge Engineering Support for Agent-Oriented Software Reuse. In M. Ramachandran (Ed.), *Knowledge Engineering for Software Development Life Cycles: Support Technologies and Applications* (pp. 177–195). Hershey, PA: IGI Global; doi:10.4018/978-1-60960-509-4.ch010

Goma, H. (2005). *Designing Software Product Lines with UML: From Use Cases to pattern-based Software Architectures*. Boston, MA: Addison-Wesley. doi:10.1109/SEW.2005.5

Gruber, T. R. (1995). Toward Principles for the Design of Ontologies used for Knowledge Sharing. *International Journal of Human-Computer Studies*, 43(5-6), 907–928. doi:10.1006/ijhc.1995.1081

Handerson-Sellers, B., & Giorgini, P. (2005). *Agent-Oriented Methodologies*. Hershey, PA: IDEA Group Publishing. doi:10.4018/978-1-59140-581-8

Harsu, M. (2002). *A Survey of Domain Engineering*. Tampere, Finland: Tampere University of Technology.

Jansen, M., & Girardi, R. (2006). GENMADEM: A Methodology for Generative Multi-agent Domain Engineering. In MorisioMaurizio (Ed.), *Proceedings of the 9th International Conference on Software Reuse (LNCS)*, (Vol. 4039, pp. 399-402). New York, NY: Springer. doi:10.1007/11763864_32

Leite, A., & Girardi, R. (2009). A Process for Multi-Agent Domain and Application Engineering: the Domain Analysis and Application Requirements Engineering Phases. In *Proceedings of the 11th International Conference on Enterprise Information Systems (ICEIS'09)*. Milan, Italy: INSTICC.

Leite, A., Girardi, R., & Cavalcante, U. (2008). An Ontology for Multi-Agent Domain and Application Engineering. In *Proceedings of the 2008 IEEE International Conference on Information Reuse and Integration (IEEE IRI-08)*. Piscataway, NJ: IEEE Press. doi:10.1109/IRI.2008.4583012

Leite, A., Girardi, R., & Cavalcante, U. (2008). MAAEM: A Multi-agent Application Engineering Methodology. In *Proceedings of the 20th International Conference on Software Engineering and Knowledge Engineering (SEKE'08)*. Skokie, IL: Knowledge Systems Institute.

Mariano, R. (2008). *Development of a Family of Recommender Systems based on the Semantic Web Technology and its Reuse on the Recommendation of Legal Tax Information Items*. (Unpublished Master's dissertation). Federal University of Maranhão, Brazil.

Mariano, R., Girardi, R., Leite, A., Drumond, L., & Maranhão, D. (2008). A Case Study on Domain Analysis of Semantic Web Multi-agent Recommender Systems. *Proceedings 3th International Conference on Software and Data Technologies (ICSOFT'08)*. New York, NY: SciTePress.

Mylopoulos, J., Castro, J., & Kolp, M. (2013). The Evolution of Tropos. In J. Bubenko, J. Krogstie, O. Pastor, B. Pernici, C. Rolland, & A. Sølvberg (Eds.), *Seminal Contributions to Information Systems Engineering* (pp. 281–287). New York, NY: Springer; doi:10.1007/978-3-642-36926-1_22

Newton, E., & Girardi, R. (2007) PROPOST: A knowledge-based tool for supporting Project Portfolio Management. *Proceedings of the International Conference on Systems Engineering and Modeling (ICSEM 2007).* Piscataway, NJ: IEEE Press doi:10.1109/ICSEM.2007.373328

Nunes, I., Kulesza, U., Nunes, C., & Lucena, C. A. (2009). A Domain Engineering Process for Developing Multi-Agent Systems Product Lines. In *Proceedings of the 8th International Conference of Autonomous Agents and Multiagent Systems(AAMAS'12).* Liverpool, England: IFAAMAS.

Object Management Group. (2013). *Software Process Engineering Metamodel Specification.* Needham, MA: OMG Press.

Odell, J., Parunak, H. V., & Bauer, B. (2000). Extending UML for Agents. In *Proceedings of the Agent-Oriented Information Systems Workshop at the 17th National Conference on Artificial Intelligence (AAI'00).* Palo Alto, CA: AAAI Press.

Perini, A., & Susi, A. (2004). Developing Tools for Agent-Oriented Visual Modeling. In G. Lindemann, J. Denzinger, I. J. Timm, & R. Unland (Eds.), *Multi-agent System Technologies.* . New York, NY: Springer. doi:10.1007/978-3-540-30082-3_13

Pohl, K., Bockle, G., & Linden, F. (2005). *Software Product Line Engineering: Foundations, Principles and Techniques.* New York, NY: Springer. doi:10.1007/3-540-28901-1

Russel, S., & Norvig, P. (2009). *Artificial Intelligence: A Modern Approach* (3rd ed.). Upper Saddle River, NJ: Prentice-Hall.

Shujun, L., & Kokar, M. (2013). Agent Communication Language. In I. Mohammed, & S. Mohamad (Eds.), *Flexible Adaptation in Cognitive Radios* (pp. 37–44). New York, NY: Springer.

Silva, C., Castro, J., Tedesco, P., Araújo, J., Moreira, A., & Mylopoulos, J. (2006). Improving the Architectural Detailed Design of Multi-Agent Systems: The Tropos Case. In *Proceedings of the 5th International Workshop on Software Engineering for Large Scale Systems (SELMAS'06).* New York, NY: ACM Press.

Silva, V., & Lucena, C. (2007). Modeling Multi-Agent Systems. *Communications of the ACM, 50*(5), 103–108. doi:10.1145/1230819.1241671

Wooldridge, M., Jennings, N. R., & Kinny, D. (2000). The Gaia Methodology for Agent-Oriented Analysis and Design. *Journal of Autonomous Agents and Multi-Agent Systems, 3*(3), 285–312. doi:10.1023/A:1010071910869

Zambonelli, F., Jennings, N., & Wooldridge, M. (2003). Developing multi-agent systems: The Gaia methodology. *ACM Transactions on Software Engineering and Methodology, 12*(3), 317–370. doi:10.1145/958961.958963

ADDITIONAL READING

Brenner, W., Zarnekow, R., & Wittig, H. (2012). *Intelligent software agents: foundations and applications.* New York, NY: Springer.

Ferber, J. (1999). *Multi-agent systems: an introduction to distributed artificial intelligence.* Boston, MA: Addison-Wesley.

Gabbay, D. M., Hogger, C. J., & Robinson, J. A. (Eds.). (1998). *Handbook of logic in artificial intelligence and logic programming.* Oxford, England: Clarendon Press.

Gerhard, W. (2013). *Multiagent Systems* (2nd ed.). Cambridge, England: MIT Press.

Girardi, R. (2010). Guiding Ontology Learning and Population by Knowledge System Goals. In *Proceedings of the International Conference on Knowledge Engineering and Ontology Development (KEOD'14)*. Lisbon, Portugal: INSTICC.

Jain, V., & Singh, M. (2013). Ontology Development and Query Retrieval using Protégé Tool. [IJISA]. *International Journal of Intelligent Systems and Applications*, 5(9), 67–77. doi:10.5815/ijisa.2013.09.08

Kossiakoff, A., Sweet, W. N., Seymour, S., & Biemer, S. M. (2011). *Systems engineering principles and practice*. Chichester, England: John Wiley & Sons. doi:10.1002/9781118001028

Krueger, C., & Clements, P. (2013). Systems and Software Product Line Engineering with BigLever Software Gears. In *Proceedings of the 17th International Software Product Line Conference*. New York, NY: ACM. doi:10.1145/2491627.2493905

Krueger, C. W. (1992). Software reuse. *ACM Computing Surveys*, 24(2), 131–183. doi:10.1145/130844.130856

Krueger, C. W. (2006). New methods in software product line practice. *Communications of the ACM*, 49(12), 37–40. doi:10.1145/1183236.1183262

Langley, P., Laird, J., & Rogers, S. (2009). Cognitive architectures: Research issues and challenges. *Cognitive Systems Research*, 10(2), 141–160. doi:10.1016/j.cogsys.2006.07.004

Luger, G. F. (2005). *Artificial intelligence: Structures and strategies for complex problem solving*. Boston: Addison-Wesley.

Mujumdar, A., Masiwal, G., & Chawan, P. M. (2012). Analysis of various software process models. [IJERA]. *International Journal of Engineering Research and Applications*, 2(3), 2015–2021.

Müller, J. P., Wooldridge, M. J., & Jennings, N. (1997). Agent Theories, Architectures, and Languages. In *Proceedings of the ECAI'97 Workshop (ATAL)*. Amsterdam, Netherlands: IOS Press.

Nwana, H. S., Lee, L. C., & Jennings, N. R. (1996). Coordination in software agent systems. *British Telecom Technical Journal*, 14(4), 79–88.

Pohl, K. (2010). *Requirements engineering: fundamentals, principles, and techniques*. New York, NY: Springer. doi:10.1007/978-3-642-12578-2

Pokahr, A., Braubach, L., & Lamersdorf, W. (2005). A flexible BDI architecture supporting extensibility. *Proceeding of the Intelligent Agent Technology, IEEE/WIC/ACM International Conference*. Piscataway, NJ: IEEE Press doi:10.1109/IAT.2005.9

Shaw, M., & Garlan, D. (1996). *Software architecture: perspectives on an emerging discipline*. Englewood Cliffs, NJ: Prentice Hall.

Smith, B. L., Tamma, V., & Wooldridge, M. (2011). An ontology for coordination. Applied Artificial Intelligence Journal, 25(3), 235-265.

Sommerville, I. (2010). *Software Engineering* (9th ed.). Boston, MA: Addison Wesley.

Staab, S., & Studer, R. (2010). *Handbook on ontologies*. New York, MA: Springer.

Studer, R., Benjamins, V. R., & Fensel, D. (1998). Knowledge engineering: principles and methods. *Data & Knowledge Engineering Journal*, 25(2), 161-197.

Van der Hoek, W., & Wooldridge, M. (2012). Logics for Multiagent Systems. *AI Magazine*, 33(3), 92–105.

Vivekanandan, K., & Rama, D. (2013). Analysing the Scope for Testing in PASSI Methodology. *International Journal of Advanced Research in Computer Science and Software Engineering*, 3(1), 420–426.

Wooldridge, M. (2009). *An Introduction to Multiagent Systems* (2nd ed.). Chichester, UK: John Wiley & Sons.

KEY TERMS AND DEFINITIONS

Architectural Design: A software design phase of a software development process that establishes an architectural model of the application, defining the component modules and their coordination and cooperation mechanisms.

Domain and Application Engineering: Domain Engineering is a process for the development of a reusable application family in a particular domain problem, and Application Engineering, the one for the construction of a specific application based on the reuse of software artifacts in the application family previously produced in the Domain Engineering process.

Multi-Agent System: A system composed of several agents interacting in their environment to accomplish tasks that are beyond their individual capabilities in order to achieve the overall goal of the system.

Ontologies: Ontologies are knowledge representation structures capable of expressing a set of entities in a given domain, their relationships and axioms, being used by modern knowledge-based systems as knowledge bases to represent and share knowledge of a particular application domain.

Software Agent: An autonomous software entity that perceives its environment through sensors and acts upon that environment through actuators.

Software Architecture: A software computational solution to a problem showing how the component parts of a system interact, thus providing an overview of the system structure.

Software Design: A software development phase that approaches the architectural and detailed design of software applications providing a solution to the requirements specified in the requirements engineering phase.

Software Reuse: Software reuse is a task of creating software systems from already existing software in order to construct software at lower cost, with better quality, and in less time.

Chapter 11
Model to Estimate the Human Factor Quality in FLOSS Development

Zulaima Chiquin
Simón Bolívar University, Venezuela

Kenyer Domínguez
Simón Bolívar University, Venezuela

Luis E. Mendoza
Simón Bolívar University, Venezuela

Edumilis Méndez
Simón Bolívar University, Venezuela

ABSTRACT

This chapter presents a Model to Estimate the Human Factor Quality in Free/Libre Open Source Software (FLOSS) Development, or EHFQ-FLOSS. The model consists of three dimensions: Levels (individual, community, and foundation), Aspects (internal or contextual), and Forms of Evaluation (self-evaluation, co-evaluation, and hetero-evaluation). Furthermore, this model provides 145 metrics applicable to all three levels, as well as an algorithm that guides their proper application to estimate the systemic quality of human resources involved in the development of FLOSS, guide the decision-making process, and take possible corrective actions.

INTRODUCTION

The success of an organization almost always depends on the skills of the people working towards performing their tasks and attaining the organization's strategic goals. Communities related to Free/Libre Open Source Software (FLOSS) do not escape from this reality. These communities are formed by volunteers, who, in some cases, do not receive any financial compensation. Volunteers contribute based on an intrinsic motivation, a personal necessity and/or an expectation of future profitability.

DOI: 10.4018/978-1-4666-6485-2.ch011

In this work, human factors involved in FLOSS development are analyzed and a Model to Estimate the Human Factor Quality in the FLOSS Development (EHFQ-FLOSS) is proposed. Through 145 metrics, this model aims to estimate quality of individuals, communities and foundations related to the development and design of FLOSS.

The methodology used in this research consisted on an adaptation of the definition of its metrics of the Systemic Methodological Framework for Research of Information Systems, including the Goal Question Metric (GQM) approach, Basili(1994). This framework is based on the action-research approach and includes the DESMET methodology to evaluate the solutions generated (Pérez et al., 2004). The model provides a guide for FLOSS developers, communities, and foundations, who are willing to manage and improve quality of their human capital. This model was defined based on a compilation made by different authors and defined below.

This chapter, in addition to the Introduction, presents the background for the next section and the proposed model, followed by the metrics that allow its operationalization and the algorithm that allows the application of the model proposed, and finally, the conclusions and future work.

BACKGROUND

The Human Perspective of the Systemic Quality Model (Pérez, et al., 2006) was used as a reference. This Model, takes into account the fundamentals of best practices of Personal Software Process (PSP), Team Software Process (TSP) and People-Capability Maturity Model (P-CMM). This is a quality model that contemplates three perspectives: product, process and human and its structure has 4 levels:

- **Level 0- Dimensions:** Defined by internal aspects and contextual aspects of the product, the process and the people.

- **Level 1- Categories:** Defined in the human aspect are: individual, team and organization.

- **Level 2- Characteristics:** Each category has specific characteristics associated with it. The individual has seven characteristics associated with it. The team has four characteristics and organization has four characteristics.

- **Level 3- Metrics:** The human perspective proposes 128 metrics to estimate its quality.

Contributions by various authors are also included and aspects that software developers should have have been classified as individual and teamwork-related. Individual aspects that software developers should have include voluntary work and motivation, according to Somerville (2006), and labor skills according to Marelli (2000). In teamwork-related aspects, the mechanisms proposed by Crowston (2010) to coordinate FLOSS development were taken into account. These mechanisms highlight the presence and skills of a leader, communication as analyzed by Pressman (2006), and evaluation of human behavior based on ethics according to Montuschi (2002). Ethical values presented by Himanen (2004), which are present in the hacker's behavior, are also underscored.

The first area of the model, which is the Personal Software Process (PSP) is a framework used to provide a structured and disciplined focus in the development of software applied to process control and management at a personal level (Humprey, 2000). It highlights the developers' skills and habits such as, individual work planning, use of well-defined processes and error prevention for managing quality in their projects. Humprey (2000) adds that developers need to understand well the work to be done as well as know, select and use the best methods in order to do extraordinary work. And that only highly motivated developers build superior software.

The second area of the model is Team Software Process (TSP), a framework to build self-directed project teams that make high quality software (SEI, 2010). Self-directed teams have the following characteristics: Understanding of goals, defined roles and responsibilities of each team member, record of project data such as productivity and quality, a process and strategy appropriate for the project, defined standards applicable to the software, risk evaluation and records, management and report of the project's status.

And the third area of the model is the People-Capability Maturity Model (P-CMM). The P-CMM establishes the best practices followed by organizations in their human talent management (Curtis et al., 2009). The basic principles of P-CMM are:

- In mature organizations, the workforce's capability is related to the business' revenue.
- The capability of the workforce should be defined in relation to strategic business' goals
- This capability can be measured and improved at multiple levels in the organization, including individuals, work groups, workforce and the organization as a whole.
- The organization must invest in improving key business competencies.
- Workforce improvement can be carried on as an integrated process of proven practices and processes.
- The organization is responsible for providing improvement opportunities for their workforce and individuals are responsible for seizing them.

Because technology and organizational forms evolve quickly, organizations must also continuously improve their workforce practices and develop new competencies including those focused on dealing with the human aspects in the development of a project, but are mainly based on a privative business approach.

As a consequence of this, it is necessary to review from the standpoint of the FLOSS movement, where Elliott and Scacchi (2008) show that the ideological basis mobilized people to unite and contribute to the development of FLOSS. Additionally, the same authors state that successful FLOSS projects are based on the combination of concerted control and Web communication. As to the management of the development of open code, Xu et al. (2011) report three effective control models in a FLOSS community: result, clan, and self-control. This Model is intended to take the features present in corporation-oriented quality models and add them to the elements present in FLOSS that have been successful.

EHFQ-FLOSS QUALITY MODEL

Figure 1 summarizes the notions associated with each one of the features presented by different authors by means of a conceptual model linked to the EHFQ-FLOSS Quality Model. It can be seen that the model consists of 4 significant topics. The first topic is FLOSS, highlighting its main features and specially those of the community. The second topic is related to human aspects that are present in individuals and in their relationships to other people, such as teamwork. The third topic is associated with software quality, analyzing quality models that evaluate human aspects in an individual manner, in the development team, and in organizations. Finally, the fourth topic describes the types of evaluations that can be applied to people and communities. Taking into account all features already mentioned, the four topics are presented in an integrated conceptual model.

The EHFQ-FLOSS Quality Model we have devised is tridimensional (see Figure 2), with the first dimension representing the evaluation methods; the second consisting of the levels and the third composed of the aspects. The Evaluation

Figure 1. Conceptual model for EHFQ-FLOSS

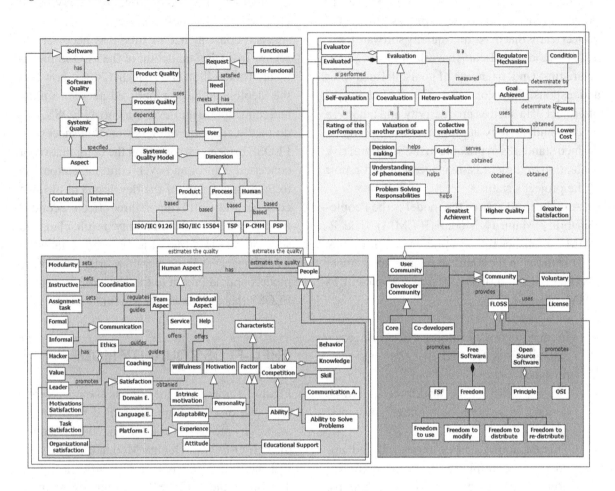

Methods dimension refers to the type of evaluation to be characterized based on the roles that will be played by evaluators and those evaluated. This dimension is divided into Self-eval(self-evaluation), Co-eval(co-evaluation) and External Eval (external or hetero-evaluation). The other dimension, i.e., Levels, consists of divisions determined by the forms of collaboration with the development of free software, including Ind (individual), Com (community) and Foun (foundations). The last dimension is Aspects, which estimates the quality of Internal Aspects and Contextual Aspects for each level, based on the evaluation form. Each dimension of the model is described below.

Evaluation Methods Dimension

The evaluation methods refer to the way in which an individual, community or foundation is evaluated based on the different roles they fulfill, including in the evaluation process both evaluators and the evaluated party. When the different roles are included in the evaluation process, three forms of participation were considered: self-evaluation, co-evaluation and hetero-evaluation. Evaluation methods dimension include:

- **Self-Evaluation:** Ability of the Individual, the Community and Foundations to recognize their own achievements and progress. As well as having a critical and reflection

Figure 2. EHFQ-FLOSS quality model

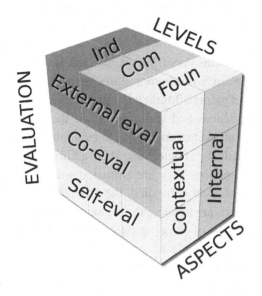

attitude to recognize their own limitations; it also serves to determine the factors that have influenced their performance, and to adopt the corrective measures that will help move formation process forward. Communities and Foundations may be self-evaluated through a SWOT analysis (Strengths, Weaknesses, Opportunities and Threats).

- **Co-Evaluation:** A form of reciprocal evaluation among entities at the same level (among Individuals, Communities or Foundations), in which activities and achievements are assessed, assuming critical stances vis-à-vis the others (No entiendo que quiere decir esta oracion con este Others aqui.) and bolstering social values like coexistence, solidarity, socialization and mutual respect. It is aimed at perfecting the results of self-evaluations in terms of their educational character.

- **Hetero-Evaluation or External Evaluation:** Is the reflection process to evaluate achievements, wise decisions and limitations, in which the evaluator is

an entity external to the Community or the Foundation and is at a higher level than that of the evaluated and uses corrective methods to strengthen performance development.

Hetero-evaluation allows tuning and counteracting the results of self-evaluation and co-evaluation. By applying the different forms of evaluation as per Onetti (2011), more reliable results can be obtained.

Levels Dimension

The Levels are divisions determined by different forms of collaboration in FLOSS development. The levels are classified into Individual, Community and Foundation, considering human factors that are present in persons both in terms of individuals and groups, as in the case of teamwork, but based on the environment of a Community and a Foundation.

Individual Level

Features that prevail in individuals to work in FLOSS development are detailed below. Sommerville (2005) refers to factors that have to be present in the development staff. Those factors include experience, skills, adaptability, attitude, educational support and communicational skills. Marelli (2000) states that workers require knowledge and skills for the organization to reach its goals and purposes. Martín et al (2009) point out that Intrinsic Motivation is used by non-profit entities to support the process of self-selection and to attract committed individuals. Another expectation of FLOSS developers, which has been demonstrated by Ghosh (2002), is learning and sharing knowledge with other developers. In FLOSS, volunteers that develop their own products prevail. Moreover, volunteers assist the community without expecting any profit or any economic reward for their work, just to feel satisfied with tasks, motivations or organizations. Himanen (2004) mentions the following 7 ethical values, passion, freedom, social value, accessibility, activity, responsibility and creativity, which are all present in the behavior of a hacker. In this regard, Stallman (2004) defines a hacker as someone who loves programming and enjoys exploring new possibilities intended for the common good, which are features that prevail in volunteers developing FLOSS. In summary, a total of 9 features are obtained for this level, to-wit:

IND.1: *Experience*: Empiric knowledge measured in time, determined by the number of years/months the individual has been working, and based on his/her mastering of a problem, using a particular platform or a programming language.

IND.2: *Skill*: Ability of the individual to solve problems, use tools, programs or communicate with other individuals.

IND.3: *Adaptability*: Flexibility of the individual to adjust to the working methods and ideals of the community.

IND.4: *Attitude*: Behavior of the individual under different adverse circumstances.

IND.5: *Knowledge*: Result of learning based on experience or education. "Knowing" how to apply techniques, methods, use tools or program in a specific language.

IND.6: *Exchange*: Contributing, donating and receiving contributions and/or knowledge related to the development of FLOSS.

IND.7: *Voluntariness:* Willingness of an individual to offer a service for the community to perform any non-profit activity.

IND.8: *Ethic*: Actions taken by human beings in a conscious manner, based on judgment and morals. Values defined in the hacker's ethics include: passion, freedom, social value, accessibility, activity with responsibility and creativity as indicated preoviously.

IND.9: *Intrinsic motivation*: Interest of the individual while performing an activity for plea-sure and without any external motivation, from which the individual feels a sensation of self-improvement, pleasure or success.

Features vary from one individual to another; some can have common skills, but in the end, each one of them builds their knowledge based on their experiences and learning; this is the reason an evaluation instrument has to be applied to these individuals to determine their abilities to fulfill the functions they are entrusted with. For each feature of an individual, the different evaluation methods are applied, depending on the case, and the result of crossing these both dimensions is defined in Table 1.

It is worth highlighting that in Table 1, self-evaluation is applied to all features of the individual level, unlike co-evaluation and external evaluation, which are not applied to IND.1 and IND.9, because these features are identified by the own individual and not by his/her peers or an external evaluator.

When a team to work on FLOSS is to be set up, individuals are grouped to constitute the community; and for this community to be successful in terms of its own project certain criteria have to be fulfilled.

Community Level

In this context, the community under study is the Community of FLOSS Development. According to Stallman (2004), the community is a group of people that cooperate with each other, following the ideals of freedom, with the aim of developing and promoting FLOSS. This work is not oriented toward the communities of users, since the evaluation criteria could be fully different. At this level, features typical of the community are explained below as taken from different authors. McGuines (2008) states that the leader has the ability to focus the team, communicate a vision, and inspire and stimulate the development of others. The leader is another member of the team and the main function

Table 1. Features of the individual, community and foundation level vs. evaluation methods

Level	Features	Evaluation Methods		
		Self-Evaluation	Co-Evaluation	External Evaluation
Individual	IND.1	✓	✗	✗
	IND.2	✓	✓	✓
	IND.3	✓	✓	✓
	IND.4	✓	✓	✓
	IND.5	✓	✓	✓
	IND.6	✓	✓	✓
	IND.7	✓	✓	✓
	IND.8	✓	✓	✓
	IND.9	✓	✗	✗
Community	COM.1	✓	✗	✗
	COM.2	✓	✗	✓
	COM.3	✓	✗	✗
	COM.4	✓	✗	✗
	COM.5	✓	✗	✗
	COM.6	✓	✗	✗
	COM.7	✓	✗	✓
	COM.8	✓	✗	✗
	COM.9	✓	✗	✗
Foundation	FOUN.1	✓	✗	✗
	FOUN.2	✓	✗	✗
	FOUN.3	✓	✗	✓
	FOUN.4	✓	✗	✗

of the leader consists of coordinating the operation of the tasks and keeping the team together. The leader must coordinate the work and support team members. Furthermore, Pressman (2006) points out that a software engineering team has to establish efficient methods to coordinate the staff performing the work. To attain this goal, a communication mechanism has to be established among the members of the team. According to Stallman (2004), cooperation of the members of the community makes it possible to build FLOSS, developing pieces of codes, notifying errors, sending codes on how to overcome failures, among other things. From this situation, improvement ideas are developed among the different programmers to obtain the software. These programmers are usually registered in a community. To exchange work and ideas, they use several tools, including: coordination, control and communication. Meanwhile, Humphrey (1998) quoted by Pressman (2006), refers to Team Software Personal (TSP), and speaks about building self-directed teams that plan and follow up their works, set goals and develop their own processes and plans, thus obtaining a total of 9 features, as follows:

COM.1: *Leadership:* Ability to focus the team, communicate a view and inspire and stimulate the development of others.

COM.2: *Coordination:* Action related to planning, organizing and controlling the different tasks and entrusting the members of the community with said tasks, with a view to obtaining, improving and/or distributing FLOSS.

COM.3: *Control:* Checking that the goal has been reached based on the tasks volunteers in the community have been entrusted with.

COM.4: *Communication:* Exchange of information among the members of the community.

COM.5: *Cooperation:* Joint contribution of the volunteers in the community for the development of FLOSS, providing different activities performed using common methods.

COM.6: *Self-directed team:* Group of people that are organized in the community based on the independence to set their goals, general objectives, functions, responsibilities for each one of their members, identify a process and the appropriate strategy for the project, define standards, evaluate risks and reactions and register, manage and report the status of the project.

COM.7: *Activity of the community:* Quantity and quality of actions performed by the community within a determined period of time.

COM.8: *Identity:* Features of the community, based on what it is, where it comes from and where it goes to, creating their own plans and commitments.

COM.9: *Use of tools:* Checking if communities use tools to coordinate, control and communicate their activities related to FLOSS.

Table 1 presents the intersection of features of the dimensions of the Community level with evaluation methods, highlighting that self-evaluation is applied to all features of the Community level.

It is worth reviewing the working method of communities, analyzing their structure and functioning. When a community executes a project following a predefined order, it can obtain better results. Some communities are supported by foundations for their organization and these foundations promote the projects of the communities based on their ideals of freedom.

Foundation Level

According to the Free Software Foundation (1991), the Linux Foundation (2011) and the Mozilla Foundation (2011), foundations are non-profit organizations, which follow the FLOSS ideology. At this level, the prevailing features are based on the mission of this type of organizations and on the best practices of the People Capability Maturity Model (P-CMM) to line up motivation of individuals with motivation of organizations and retain human assets (people with relevant skills and knowledge) within the organization. A summary of the proposed features are presented below.

FOUN.1: *Human Capital management:* Strategy to win, organize and retain volunteers and/or permanent staff.

FOUN.2: *Ideological basis:* Set of ideas defining the cultural basis of the foundation. Toward the outside, it expresses a resource that identifies the foundation and toward the inside, it is a statement which is adhered to by the members of the foundation. In FLOSS, the following principles are defined: anti-monopolistic, solidarity-based and free.

FOUN.3: *Sponsorship:* Public or private contribution to execute the FLOSS projects or activities related to the promotion or dissemination of FLOSS.

FOUN.4: *Techniques and practices for their overall task:* Set of techniques and/or guidelines to be followed by the foundation to attain its objectives.

It is worth analyzing the features of foundations because they are mainly entrusted with disseminating the ideals of the community and seeking contribution from entities that may collaborate with the projects.

Table 1 presents the intersection of features of the dimensions of the Foundation level with evaluation methods, highlighting that self-evaluation is applied to all features of the Community level; in the case of external evaluation, it is only applied in FOUN.3.

After having proposed evaluation methods and levels, the third phase of the proposed model is described below: Internal and external Aspects.

Aspects Dimension

The Aspects help divide evaluation from two different points of view: internal and contextual. Internal aspects are those that are not visible to other people and contextual are those that can be observed from the outside. These evaluation methods are defined below:

- **Internal Aspects in Individuals:** These aspects are determined by the skills and knowledge of the individuals, and include: Experience, Skills, Attitude, Knowledge, Voluntariness and Intrinsic Motivation.
- **Internal Aspects in Communities and Foundations:** These aspects are determined by the internal structure and functioning of communities and foundations. The internal aspects of Communities include: Coordination, Control, Self-led Teams and Identity; and in the case of Foundations, Human Capital Management.
- **Contextual Aspects in Individuals:** These aspects are determined by the ability of individuals to relate to their environment, and include Adaptability, Exchange and Ethics.
- **Contextual Aspects in Communities and Foundations:** Determined by the overall

features of Communities and Foundations, they also establish a comparison of objectives proposed to actual performance. Contextual aspects of Communities are: Coordination, Control, Self-led Teams and Identity; and those of Foundations include: Ideological Basis, Sponsorship and Techniques and Practices for their overall task.

Internal Aspects of individuals are features typical of each individual based on his/her skills, knowledge and experiences. On the other side, from an organizational approach, Daft (2007) relates Internal Aspects in communities and foundations to their structure, specifically to formalization in documents, task specialization, centralized decision-making, professionalism and authority hierarchy.

Contextual Aspects study the circumstances external to the system, such as necessities, pressures, rules, opportunities and resources; they also make a comparison between the proposed goals and actual performance. In individuals, a dynamic interaction exists between people and their environment. In the organizational area, Daft (2007) states that these aspects can be conceived as a set of interrelated elements that underpin the structure of an organization and its working processes, and which are specifically based on the culture, environment, goals and strategies, number of people comprising the organization and technology. According to Daft (2007), to understand and evaluate organization, it is necessary to examine the contextual and structural aspects.

METRICS FOR EHFQ-FLOSS QUALITY MODEL

A total of 145 metrics were specified for this model. 58 metrics were obtained for the Individual Level, 50 were obtained for the Community Level and 37 for the Foundation Level. Specific questions and metrics were developed using the GQM approach based on the set of human factors defined in each dimension, Basili (1994). Questions, in turn, were formulated to be answered by different participants in the FLOSS development process, including representatives of foundations, communities and the own individuals, all of which somehow contribute with project development.

Goal, Questions and Metrics are specified for each one of the features defined for the Individual, Community and Foundation levels. Table 2 shows the application of GQM approach to the formulation of the metrics of the model for the following features: Intrinsic Motivation (Individual Level), Community Activity and Foundation Sponsorship.

Algorithm to Apply the EHFQ-FLOSS Quality Model

The algorithm is divided into three large sections that can be selected based on the evaluator's needs. The first section consists of estimating the Individuals' human quality; the second estimates human quality in Communities and the third estimates human quality in Foundations, regardless of the order. The possible results of the quality levels are: NULL, INITIAL, IN PROCESS, CONSOLIDATED, and ADVANCED. In this sense, the steps to be taken to measure human quality in FLOSS development through the proposed model are graphically explained in the algorithm. According to the acceptance standard followed by the Laboratory of Information Systems Research of the Simón Bolívar University (LISI-USB), at least 75% of the proposed features should be met for the evaluation, because a lower percentage would compromise the evaluation quality.

The algorithm (Figure 3) allows each level to be evaluated separately, obtaining application results for one, two or three levels, without it being necessary to evaluate all 3 levels. In case that the evaluator desires to obtain a systemic evaluation, the 3 levels have to be evaluated, regardless of the application order.

Evaluation of the EHFQ-FLOSS Quality Model

By means of DESMET methodology (Kitchenham,1996), a reliable and impartial model, which helped to validate the EHFQ-FLOSS Quality Model, was identified. DESMET proposes a set of practical and technical criteria to select an evaluation method that allows methods and/or tools in the Software Engineering field to be evaluated. DESMET application, the most appropriated method to evaluate the EHFQ-FLOSS Quality Model was the feature analysis – survey. This evaluation method resorts to a group of experts in the area under study, in this case FLOSS, to validate the suitability of the model.

Evaluation Planning

The explanation of the steps proposed for the feature analysis – survey and how they were applied for the case of the EHFQ-FLOSS Quality Model are found below.

1. **Scope:** All metrics for the model were evaluated using the feature analysis – survey method, with experienced professionals in FLOSS that verified the suitability of the Model and the ranges of values suggested for the metrics.
2. **Evaluation Bases:** To efficiently evaluate the model and their metrics, two lists of definition of features must be developed: one for the evaluation of the general features of the model and another for the evaluation of the specific features of the model. These features are presented in Table 3.

Roles and Responsibilities

The definition of roles and responsibilities applied in the evaluation is as follows:

Table 2. Example of metrics of the EHFQ-FLOSS quality model

Evaluation Method	Level	Feature	Goal	Question	Metric	Formulation
Self-evaluation	Individual	Intrinsic motivation	Evaluate personal growth	Is personal growth a factor influencing personal motivation of individuals?	Determination of personal growth as a factor influencing personal motivation.	5=Very frequently 4=Frequently 3=Sometimes 2=Few times 1=Never 0=Doesn't know 0=Not applicable
					Determination to enforce the own individual's purposes	
			Evaluate operational autonomy	Is operational autonomy a factor influencing personal motivation of individuals?	Determination of operational autonomy as a factor influencing personal motivation	5=Very frequently 4=Frequently 3=Sometimes 2=Few times 1=Never 0=Doesn't know 0=Not applicable
Self-evaluation and external evaluation	Community	Activity	Identify successful projects obtained	Has the community produced successful projects over the two last years?	Determination of the percentage of successful projects based on projects completed.	5=Between 91 and 100 4=Between 76 and 90 3=Between 51 and 75 2=Between 26 and 50 1=Between 0 and 25 0=Doesn't know 0=Not applicable
					Existence of successful projects over the 2 past years	5=yes 1=No 0=Doesn't know 0=Not applicable
Self-evaluation and external evaluation	Foundation	Sponsorship	Evaluate processes of the organization	Does the organization use advertising media to request for sponsorship?	Existence of advertising to gain sponsors	5=yes 1=No 0=Doesn't know 0=Not applicable
					Amount of advertising media to gain sponsors	5= More than 6 4=Between 5 and 6 3=Between 3 and 4 2=Between 1 and 2 1=None 0=Doesn't know 0=Not applicable

- **Promoters:** The LISI-USB and the authors.
- **Evaluators:** The authors of this research, which were responsible for conducting the evaluation and analyze the results.

- **Counselors:** The counselors were the experts that directly participated in the evaluation. Then, two experts in FLOSS were chosen; these experts evaluated the model.

Figure 3. Algorithm of the application of the EHFQ-FLOSS quality model

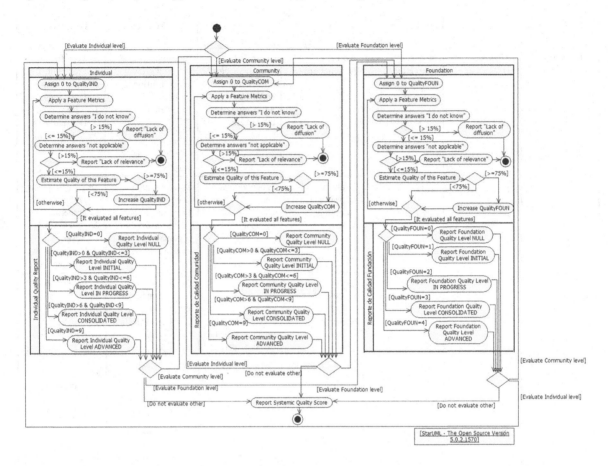

- **Expert 1:** FLOSS activist. GNU Project Director in Venezuela. Expert in organization of FLOSS communities. Representative of the National Free Software Congress (CNSL) in Venezuela.
- **Expert 2:** FLOSS activist. Responsible for the community of Mozilla users in Venezuela.

Evaluation Procedure

To perform the evaluation, the following steps were taken:

1. A questionnaire was sent to each one of the experts to evaluate the features, both for the general and specific features as well as for their metrics. Answers to questions on a feature or its metrics were based on the scales defined in Table 3.

2. The results from the experts were taken for each feature, for both the general features and the percentage of positive answers; that is, those that obtained a value of 1, were calculated.

3. For each feature, both the general features and metrics, an acceptable level was defined as seventy five percent (75%) of positive answers from the experts (value 1).

4. Based on the previous criteria, the acceptance percentages were obtained for each one of the features defined, for both the general features and each metric.

Table 3. General and specific features for the evaluation of the model and its metrics, respectively

	Feature	Description	Scale
General	Model pertinence	Refers to the suitability of the EHFQ-FLOSS Quality Model within the context.	1: means that the Model is pertinent. 0: means that the Model is not pertinent.
	Completeness of categories involved	Refers to whether the model offers total coverage to specified human quality of FLOSS.	1: means that the Model is complete in terms of categories used. 0: means that according to the context, there are some categories that the Model has to consider.
	Suitability for the context	Refers to whether the quality specification of the Model is suitable for the evaluation context.	1: means that the Model is suitable for the evaluation context. 0: means that the Model is not suitable for the evaluation context.
	Accuracy	Refers to whether the quality level specified by the Model to measure human quality in FLOSS is accurate.	1: means that the quality level specified is accurate. 0: means that the quality level specified is not accurate.
	Understandability in the application of the model	Refers to whether the application of the model through the algorithm is easy to understand.	1: means that the algorithm is understandable. 0: means that the algorithm is not understandable.
	Completeness in the tool	Refers to whether the algorithm covers all the steps specified in the human aspects of FLOSS.	1: means that the algorithm is complete in terms of categories used. 0: means that according to the context, categories exist that the algorithm has to consider.
Specific	Metric pertinence	Refers to whether a metric is suitable to measure the existence of a related feature.	1: means that the metric is pertinent. 0: means that the metric is not pertinent.
	Metric feasibility	Refers to whether measuring the proposed feature through the metric is feasible or not.	1: means that the metric is feasible. 0: means that the metric is not feasible.
	Depth level	Refers to whether the metric description has the detail level suitable to understand its content.	1: means that the metric has the suitable depth level. 0: means that the metric does not have the suitable depth level.
	Metric scale	Refers to whether the proposed scale is suitable to measure the metric.	1: means that the scale is suitable. 0: means that the scale is not suitable.

(Source: Adapted from Sosa, 2005)

5. A model is considered acceptable, according to the six defined features (pertinent, completeness, suitability for the context, accuracy, understandability in a model application, completeness in the tool) if the following conditions are fulfilled: *The average of acceptance percentages of the six features must be higher than the acceptance level defined (75%).*

6. A metric is considered acceptable, according to the four defined features (pertinent; feasible, depth level and metric scale), if the following conditions are fulfilled:

a. It must be pertinent and feasible. Due to their condition of metrics, the fact that their measurement is feasible must be a necessary condition.

b. The average of acceptance percentages of the five features must be higher than the acceptance level defined (75%).

Analysis and Discussion of Results

The experts evaluated a model by the general features as shown in Table 3. The overall result obtained is that the EAH-DSL model is pertinent, suitable for the context, accurate, complete accord-

Figure 4. Results of the application process of the feature analysis: Survey, general evaluation of the EHFQ-FLOSS quality model

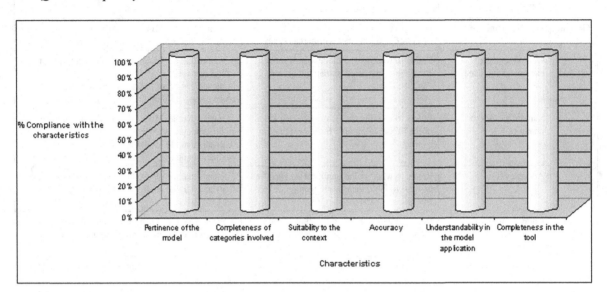

ing to the categories involved and understandable and complete in terms of the algorithm. Figure 4 shows the result of the evaluation of a model's general features, obtaining 100% in all features defined.

Subsequently, the Level dimension of the model was evaluated with all specific features presented in Table 3. Figure 5 shows the results of the evaluation performed by experts in the following features: Experience, Skills and Adaptability. It can be observed that Expert1 rated the metric below 75%, which suggests that scales of metrics defined for experience should be changed, because generally, FLOSS developers tend to have years of experience instead of months as the EHFQ-FLOSS Quality Model proposes. And Expert2 proposed to change scale in 3 metrics defined for the skill feature. In relation to the adaptability feature, evaluator1 considers that one of the metrics is a little ambiguous. However, the average rating of metrics defined for experience, skills and adaptability of both evaluators is higher than the 75% defined by the estimated quality index.

In the Community level, experts evaluated the model through the specific features as defined in Table 3; the results were classified based on the evaluation methods; which include self-evaluation, i.e. the community evaluates itself, examines its ideals, the way it is coordinated and controlled; and also external evaluation. According to these two evaluation methods, experts assessed the metrics of each feature, obtaining that all features evaluated by experts have 100% acceptance in terms of pertinence, feasibility, depth and scale.

In the Foundation level, experts also assessed the model through the specific features defined in Table 3: the results were classified based on the evaluation methods, which include self-evaluation, i.e. the Foundation evaluates itself, examines its management of human capital, its ideological basis, its techniques and general practices and sponsorship; and external evaluation in which the Foundation reviews its sponsorship. According to these two evaluation methods, experts evaluated the metrics of each feature and reported the result of the self-evaluation in terms of pertinence, feasibility, depth and scale of the metrics associated with the features of human capital management, ideological basis, techniques and practices for their general work and sponsorship. For all features,

Figure 5. Application process of a feature analysis: Survey; evaluation of experience, skills and adaptability applied in the individual level – Self-evaluation

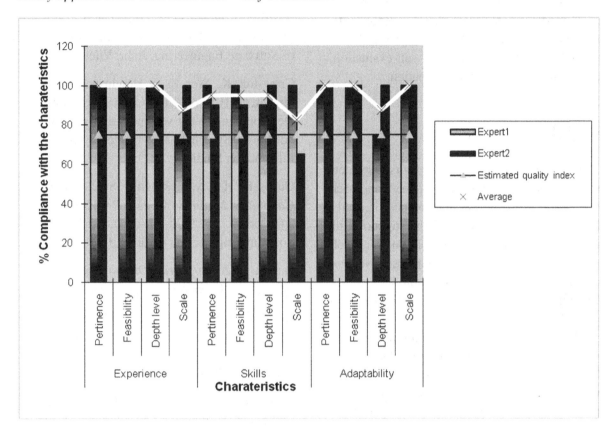

100% acceptance was obtained. Likewise, the external evaluation process reviewed pertinence, feasibility, depth level and scale of metrics associated with the features of sponsorship, obtaining 100% acceptance for all features.

These results showed that the estimated quality index in its three levels, i.e. Individual, Community, and Foundation, is higher than the quality estimation index proposed.

FUTURE WORK

In a future work, a model will be applied to a Community and a Foundation that have successfully implemented their projects, so as to be able to evaluate performance and potentiality of the model and, at the same time, validate the set of human factors defining it.

Likewise, it is recommended to have a comprehensive model that considers product, process and human aspect (proposed in this model) for the development of Free Software (FS). It is also suggested to strengthen and study existing relations in the aforementioned dimensions in order to create an even broader model. Also, it is recommended to incorporate Free Software development not only through communities but also through private and government companies.

Individuals and their organization around communities to create Free Software are without a doubt two of the elements that have propelled this movement worldwide. Nevertheless, it was not found in the literature any article evaluating the number of people involved in the development of FS. As main goal achieved during this essay, there is the relationship that exists among the mentioned characteristics related to individuals, communities and foundations to the different evaluation methods identified: self-evaluation, co-evaluation and external evaluation.

CONCLUSION

The methodology implemented to pursue an internal investigation allowed for a systematic approach to each one of the phases that compose it, establishing a conceptual framework that supported the proposal. Knowing previous work on FS as well as disciplined time-management, improvement in personal, team and organization productivity will allow the identification of weaknesses in individuals, communities and foundations.

Based on the human factors present in the development of FLOSS, the EHFQ-FLOSS Quality Model was developed to estimate quality of Individuals, Communities and Foundations involved in the development of this type of software. This model was defined based on three dimensions: Levels, Evaluation methods and Aspects, so as to evaluate human aspects in FLOSS development. The respective features were defined for each dimension and 145 metrics were developed using the GQM approach. These metrics, together with the algorithm to apply a model, rendered operationalization of the model possible.

Finally, this investigation contributes to the development of the body of knowledge of Quality Assurance and Free Software since this new model seeks to benefit development communities by providing them with the first version of an evaluated, objective and complete instrument;

REFERENCES

Basili, V., Caldeira, G., & Rombach, H. D. (1994). Goal Question Metric Paradigm. In Encyclopedia of Software Engineering. John Wiley & Sons.

Crowston, K., Wei, K., & Howinson, J. & Wiggins, A. (2010). Free/Libre Open Source Software Development: What we know and what we do not know. Syracuse, NY: University School of Information Studies.

Curtis, B., Hefley, B., & Miller, S. (2009). *People Capability Maturity Model (P-CMM) Version 2.0* (2nd ed., pp. 2009–TR-003). Pittsburgh, PA: Software Engineering Institute. CMU/SEI.

Daft, R. L. (2007). *Teoría y Diseño Organizacional (9ᵗʰ ed.)*. DF, México: Cengage Learning Editores.

Elliot, M., & Scacchi, W. (2008). Mobilization of software developers: The free software movement. *Information Technology & People*, *21*(1), 4–33. doi:10.1108/09593840810860315

Ghosh, R., Glott, R., Krieger, B., & Robles, G. (2002). Free/Libre and Open Source Software: Survey and Study (Technical Report). Netherlands: International Institute of Infonomics, University of Maastricht. Retrieved from http://www.math.unipd.it/~bellio/FLOSS%20Final%20Report%20-%20Part%204%20-%20Survey%20of%20Developers.pdf

Himanen, P. (2004). *La ética del hacker y el espíritu de la era de la información*. Barcelona: Destino libro.

Humprey, W. (2000). *The personal software process (PSP)*. Pittsburgh, PA: Software Engineering Institute. CMU/SEI.

Humprey, W. (2009). *The Watts New? Collection: Columns by the SEI's Watts Humphrey*. Pittsburgh, PA: Software Engineering Institute. CMU/SEI.

Kitchenham, B. (1996). *DESMET: A method for evaluating Software Engineering methods and tools* (Technical Report TR96-09). Department of Computer Science, University of Keele.

Linux Foundation. (n.d.). *About Us*. Retrieved January 5, 2011 from: http://www.linuxfoundation.org/about

Marelli, A. (2000). *Introducción al análisis y desarrollo de modelos de competencias*. Montevideo: Boletín Cinterfor/OIT. N° 149.

Martín, N., Martín, V., & Trevilla, C. (2009). *Influencia de la motivación intrínseca y extrínseca sobre la transmisión de conocimiento: El caso de una organización sin fines de lucro*. CIRIEC-España, revista de economía pública, social y cooperativa.

McGuinness, M. (2008). *Creative Management for Creative Teams, Business Coaching and Creative Business*. Retrieved from: http://media.lateralaction.com/creativemanagement.pdf

Montuschi, L. (2004). *Ética y razonamiento moral, Dilemas morales y comportamiento ético en las organizaciones*. Buenos Aires: Serie Documentos de Trabajo Universidad del CEMA. Retrieved from http://www.ucema.edu.ar/publicaciones/download/documentos/219.pdf

Mozilla Foundation. (2011). *The Mozilla Foundation*. Retrieved from http://www.mozilla.org/foundation/

Onetti, V. (2011). *La Evaluación, Innovación y experiencias educativas*. ISSN 1988-6047, 39. Retrieved February 2011 from: http://www.csi-csif.es/andalucia/modules/mod_ense/revista/pdf/Numero_39/VANESSA_ONETTI_ONETTI_1.pdf

Pérez, M., Domínguez, K., Mendoza, L., & Grimán, A. (2006). *Human Perspective in System Development Quality*. Acapulco, México: AMCIS.

Perez, M., Grimán, A., Mendoza, L., & Rojas, T. (2004). A Systemic Methodological Framework for IS Research. New York: *AMCIS*.

Pressman, R. (2006). *Ingeniería del Software, Un enfoque práctico. 6ª edición*. DF, México: McGrawHill.

Ramírez, Y. (2004). El perfil de competencias y la evaluación cualitativa del aprendizaje en la I y II etapas de educación básica. *Educere*, *8*(25), 159–166.

Software Engineering Institute (SEI). (2010). *Team Software Process*. Retrieved from http://www.sei.cmu.edu/tsp/

Sommerville, I. (2005). *Ingeniería del Software*. Madrid: Pearson Educación.

Sosa, J. (2005). *Perspectiva Humana en la Calidad Sistémica de los Sistemas de Información*. (Master Degree Thesis). Universidad Simón Bolívar, Venezuela.

Stallman, R. M. (2004). *Software libre para una sociedad libre*. Madrid: Traficantes de Sueños.

Xu, B., Xu, Y., & Lin, Z. (2011). A Study of Open Source Software Development from Control Perspective. University of Nebraska.

KEY TERMS AND DEFINITIONS

Co-Evaluation: Refers to a reciprocal evaluation between beings of the same level where activities, group and individual achievements are valued and critical positions are assumed. Through co-evaluation social values such as cohabitation, solidarity, socialization and mutual respect are enhanced with the purpose of allowing maximum improvement of results.

Evaluation: A regulation mechanism that measures the achievement of goals compared to the initial proposal and that incorporates the individual evaluated and the evaluator as well as their context in order to take corrective measures.

FLOSS Communities: A group of people who cooperate among each other fulfilling the freedom ideal. (Stallman, 2004).

FLOSS Foundations: Non-profit organizations who are independently managed and in charge of constantly producing new free Software.

Free Open Source Software (FLOSS): Refers to a work philosophy that integrate FS with open code. The FS movement and the open code movement are different and have different philosophies but share common practices. (Howison et al, 2006).

Heteroevaluation: It is the process of reflecting to collectively measure the effort and achievements of the individuals or teams involved in order to strengthen performance.

Intrinsic Motivation: The interest for the tasks developed and the identification with the organization's mission that allows the individual visualize his/her professional development with more autonomy within a work environment and in alignment with ethical and moral values.

Self-Evaluation: Is the capacity human beings have to recognizing their own achievements and advances as well as reflecting and a having a critical attitude towards their own limitations. This capacity determines the factors that influence their behavior and, lastly, take corrective measures that will help in the development process.

Software Quality: Is the degree to which the implicit and explicit user and client requirements are met through a standardized process performed and elaborated by skilled workers or teams.

Systemic Quality: It refers to the total quality in all its dimensions and not partial quality in each dimension. Dimensions are basically formed in two perspectives: Product and Process. By combining these two dimensions with effectiveness and efficiency we obtain four additional dimensions (product and process efficiency and product and process effectiveness), which we combine to client and user point of view. (Callaos y Callaos, 1996).

Chapter 12

From Knowledge Management to Knowledge Governance:
A System-Centred Methodology for Designing Indigenous Knowledge Management System

Tariq Zaman
Universiti Malaysia Sarawak, Malaysia

Alvin W. Yeo
Universiti Malaysia Sarawak, Malaysia

Narayanan Kulathuramaiyer
Universiti Malaysia Sarawak, Malaysia

ABSTRACT

The existing frameworks and methodologies for software designing encompass technological aspects and needs of the urban settings. In software development, getting sufficient and correct requirements from the users is most important, because these requirements will determine the functionality of the system. In indigenous communities identifying the user needs and understanding the local context are always difficult tasks. This typical approach of designing indigenous knowledge management system generates the issues of indigenous knowledge governance, de-contextualisation, and data manipulation. Hence, the main research question this chapter addresses is, How can we introduce indigenous knowledge governance into ICT-based Indigenous Knowledge Management System (IKMS)? The study has been conducted in three phases with collaboration of two indigenous communities, Long Lamai and Bario of Sarawak, East Malaysia. The main outcome of the study is the methodology of conducting a multidisciplinary research and designing the Indigenous Knowledge Governance Framework (IKGF). The framework works as an analytical tool that can help in understanding the essential context in which indigenous knowledge management processes occur. The chapter argues that in order to design appropriate software tools for indigenous knowledge management, information technology professionals need to understand, model, and formalise the holistic indigenous knowledge management system and then use this understanding as a basis for technology design and approaches.

DOI: 10.4018/978-1-4666-6485-2.ch012

INTRODUCTION

Understanding user requirements is a critical step in the development of usable software systems. In conventional software development methodologies, the end-users and beneficiaries of the system are considered well aware, skilled and motivated to adopt the software solutions. Normally, the end-users define its need in an abstract written form to help software engineers in understanding their requirements. But this may not be the case for designing software for rural and indigenous communities. The end-users in these communities may never have used technologies, have less or no skills of information and communication technologies (ICT) and may never thought about having an ICT solution for their problem. Hence, understanding the user requirement in these communities and for indigenous knowledge management systems, which fundamentally differ so far from technology supported systems represent particular challenges.

A wide range of digital tools have been developed and cultural heritage institutions are exploring the use of ICTs for preservation and improving access to Indigenous Knowledge (IK). However, ICTs for indigenous knowledge management (IKM) have been designed using the conventional approach of creating and manipulating databases of knowledge (Velden, 2010). Early efforts in IKM focused on developing digital technologies to store, capture, and distribute knowledge (Agrawal, 2002). The focus at present has shifted, however, to make explicit the tacit and implicit knowledge. The current approaches tend to overlook the community's creative expressions, practices of innovation and instead consider IK to be a static resource frozen in time and place. These typical approaches of IK databases design thus fail to a large extent in serving the needs of indigenous communities, as it tend to alienate IK from the essential context such as social, cultural and governance framework (Velden, 2010; Winschiers-Theophilus, Jensen, & Rodil, 2012).

The prime objective of this research is to develop a holistic framework for IKM that projects the ontological structure of the wider social cultural and governance system in which IKM processes occur. The investigation was done in three phases; firstly, we explored the theoretical gaps and the inherent structure of IKMS in communities. Secondly, we addressed the gaps by modelling IKMS in communities and designing a structured indigenous knowledge governance framework. Thirdly, we used the framework to model an existing IKMS and for designing, developing and implementation of ICT-based IKMS. The designed framework helps researchers and ICT professionals to understand the unique structure of IKM and accommodate it in the design and development of ICT-based IKMS.

The remainder of this chapter is structured as follows. The first part of the paper presents background of the research field and introduction of the sites and communities where research has been conducted. Second part illustrates the research framework and each phase of the study in detail. The last part, concluding section, presents reflection of the study.

BACKGROUND

Unique Features of IKMS

Current technological trends and developments have hardly been informed by indigenous and rural knowledge systems (Kapuire & Blake, 2011), which is different from non-indigenous knowledge systems in many ways. The unique features of IKMS are based on two basic system perspectives: "holistic" and "living".

Holistic System

We define "holistic" as a "whole" system where all aspects of life – both tangible (such as oral traditions and activities) and intangible (such as governance systems and spiritual values) – are assimilated and interconnected and cannot be separated from one another. According to Velden (2002), IK is a highly contextualised body of knowledge that is linked to location, situation and cultural, social and historical context. IKMS is a complex structure that cannot be understood by only examining the parts (processes, technology, people, economic, social and ideological aspects). It must also take into account how the parts interact to make a whole system.

Living System

In Western epistemologies, IK is generally interpreted as a static and archaic form of knowledge while the indigenous researchers interpret IK as;

- A way of life (McGregor, 2004)
- A way of knowing (Aikenhead & Ogawa, 2007) and
- Adaptable and creative system (Macchi & Oviedo, 2008).

The indigenous perspective is not just "knowledge" per se (a thing, an object) but also a way of life that includes dynamic practices such as oral traditions, listening to stories, singing songs, reciting prayers, dancing at celebrations, and participating in ceremonies; all of which are passed on from generation to generation.

In the conventional approaches of IKM, knowledge is de-contextualised by extracting it from the living and holistic system of IK and storing it as data in databases. IKM is a long process and complex system of activities that deals with the multidimensional challenges such as digital technologies, intellectual property rights and the complex social, cultural and belief system of the communities. The current ICT-based IKMS and the frameworks provide a product-view of IKM and mainly satisfy the Western conception of knowledge management, in which knowledge is stored as abstract entities in digital forms. Hence,

a well-formulated holistic framework is needed to provide real-time modelling of the living IKMS assimilated with the structure and use of ICT tools.

Data and Information Governance Frameworks

In this section, we present an analysis on selected frameworks of data, information and knowledge governance.

Khatri and Brown's Data Governance Framework

Khatri and Brown presented a data governance framework that includes five interrelated decision domains: Data principles; Data quality; Metadata; Data access; and Data lifecycle (Khatri & Brown, 2010).

The framework is designed for practitioners to help them develop a data governance strategy for managing data as an organisational asset. The scope of the framework is limited to knowledge assets and related control mechanisms concerning mainly explicit forms of data representation.

Data Governance Institute's Framework for Data Governance

Another framework by DGI, focuses on one or more related data-areas describing 10 inter-related components: mission, goals, governance metrics, data rules, decision rights, accountabilities, controls, data stakeholders, data governance office and data stewards (Thomas, 2006). The framework recommends establishing "universal objectives" to enable better decision-making and to ensure transparency of the data management process.

The framework is useful for data protection and managing data capture, storage and usage in the right context. However, the framework considers the role of management and organisational structure as outside components in the data governance lifecycle.

IBM's Information Governance Framework

IBM's framework for information governance assesses the current state of information system and the desired future state of maturity (Soares, Deutsch, Hanna, & Malik, 2012). The framework relates information governance to high-level business processes where data is considered one part of the business system. The framework is composed of 11 disciplines of governance across four distinct focus layers.

The review of the literature has shown that no framework exists that addresses shortcomings listed above; that is, no available framework to model IKM processes and structure within the context of indigenous knowledge governance. Existing organisational KM frameworks mainly address the issue of managing explicit knowledge (data and information) while overlooking the unique features of IKMS that are based on implicit and tacit knowledge. In addition, we note that previous knowledge management research has focused on the design and development of conceptual models, and not implementation of these models.

Limited attention has been directed at how the frameworks and models are implemented and validated, such as in the case of World Bank's Framework for Action and Virtual Repatriation programme. The same has been reported by Zent (2009).

Research Problem

Development organisations acknowledge and recognise the role of IK as a solution to local problems. A wide range of ICT tools has been developed for management of this highly valued resource. However, several researchers highlighted the challenges that the technology can raise in managing IK (Oppenneer, 2008). IK takes predominantly tacit and implicit forms, locked in the community's activities and governed by social and cultural frameworks. The use of ICTs for IKM can cause problems when IK is de-contextualised, extracted from living and holistic local systems, and stored as data.

In addition, Western cultural values, which tend to be embedded within the technology, can dominate the values, social and cultural systems and communicative preferences of indigenous peoples (Winschiers-Theophilus et al., 2012). Hence, technology and database management should only be seen as supportive elements or mechanisms in a wider system of IK governance that includes the application of customary laws, institutional authority and structures, and collaborative activity mechanisms in the community where technology is deployed. In order to design appropriate ICT tools for IKM, ICT professionals need to understand the holistic indigenous knowledge management system and then use this understanding as a basis for ICT-based IKMS' design and approaches.

The Research Sites

The study was conducted in two remote sites of Sarawak in East Malaysia: Long Lamai, a Penan settlement, and Bario, a Kelabit settlement. Sarawak is situated on the northwest of the island of Borneo. Indigenous peoples – collectively known a *Dayaks* - comprise two-thirds of Sarawak's population (Ngidang, 2005). Many, distinct ethnic groups exist in Sarawak, including the Penan and Kelabits. These two sites were chosen largely because Universiti Malaysia Sarawak (UNIMAS) maintains a research collaboration and development partnership with Bario and Long Lamai communities.

Research Methodology

The research methodology and operationalisation process (Figure 1) is divided into three phases. In Phase 1, we conducted a literature review and collected the empirical data to discover exist-

Figure 1. Research operationalization

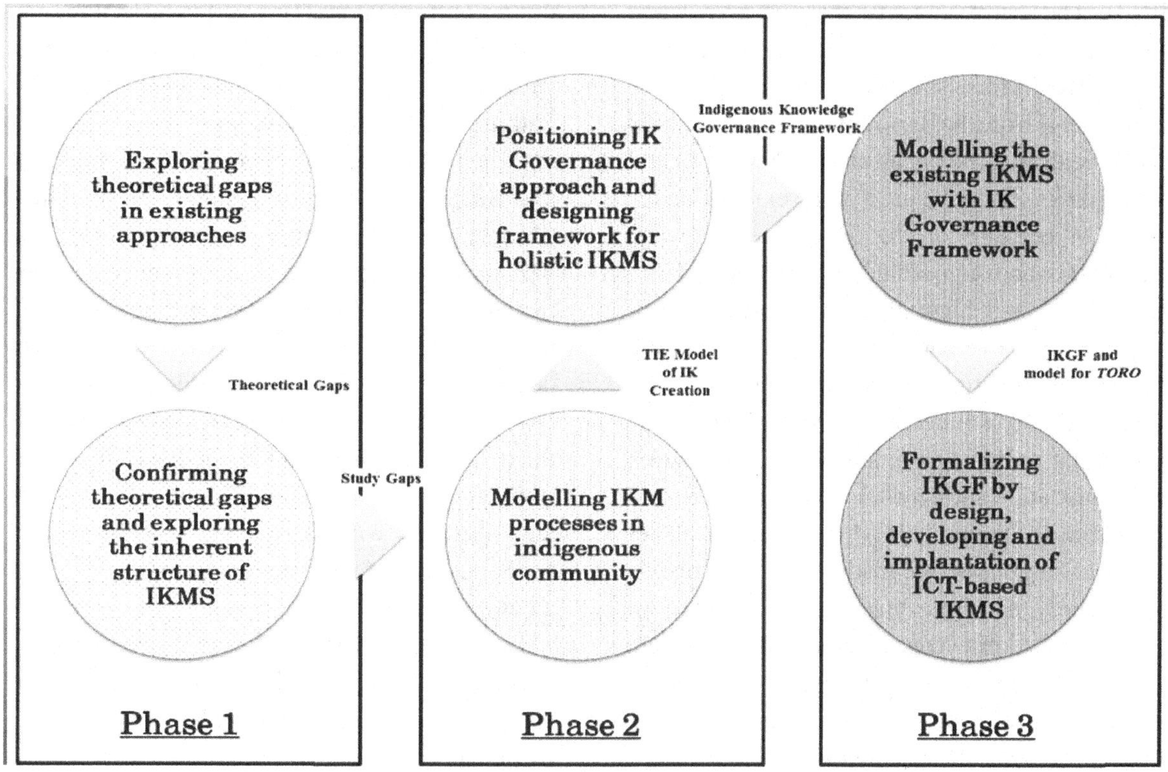

Phase 1   Phase 2   Phase 3

ing theoretical gaps among studies of IKMS. In Phase 2, we addressed the gaps by designing and modelling the indigenous knowledge management processes and the indigenous knowledge governance system. In Phase 3, we used the framework to model an existing community IKMS and then formalised the framework by using it as a base for the design, development and implementation of ICT-based IKMS.

Phase 1: Exploring Theoretical Gaps

The Phase 1 comprises of through literature review and field study to explore the research and study gaps. In this phase, literature review has been conducted to explore the theoretical gaps in existing literature. The review found a gap at epistemological level in defining IKM. The current definitions tends to de-emphasise the comprehensive process oriented IKM and mainly focuses on the processes of "capturing" and "distribution"

while undermining IK creation process (Yeo, Zaman, & Kulathuramaiyer, 2013). The approaches also reflected in the digital technology designs. As noted by Agrawal (2002) the main aim of the IKM databases is to "collect" and "distribute" available information.

Based on the Burtis (2009); Ngulube (2002) and Velden (2010), we identified the influencing factors that's should be considered and addressed by the researchers and softwareware engineers while developing a digital solution for IKM. The focus of software system for IKM should be extended to incorporate complex issues of IK ownership, intellectual property rights legislation, cultural protocols and technical issues in the form of choice of media and access at the project planning level.

The second part of the first phase explores the study gaps by observing a case study from the field and to develop a methodological approach to reveal the inherent structure of IKMS in indigenous community of Bario (Yeo, et al., 2013). The study confirms that the knowledge creation process is arguably the most important step in IKM processes. It is highly rated by the respondents from the Bario community. The study also reveals that the organisation's KM tools and frameworks cannot be used in the existing shape for IKM because of the differences between indigenous and non-indigenous knowledge domains. The study highlights the important role of community's governance structure in information dissemination, resources allocation and coordinating community's collective activities. The results reveal that in Bario community, the information communication and access is closely linked with the relationship and role of information seeker in the local governance institutions. The results of the study also argue that there is a need to incorporate the knowledge of modern legal system with access to expertise of indigenous customary, statutory and religious systems of governance. The study highlights the features that are not taken into account in the conventional approaches of designing ICT tools and frameworks for IKM. These features include the indigenous governance system, organisational structure, the protection of IK and resource management, and collective community activities.

Phase 2: Positioning Indigenous Knowledge Governance

As explored in Phase 1 of the study, the recent wave of research undermines the knowledge creation process in indigenous communities which is an important and well established area of research and development in organisations. The ultimate effect is that software engineers focus on the "dissemination" and "storage" processes while neglecting the "living" characteristic of IK. In this phase first, we delineate in more detail the knowledge creation process in indigenous communities and present it as a "living system". A living system is one that constantly creates new knowledge, closely connected to day-to-day activities and social systems and is reflected upon before acceptance and assimilation. Furthermore, we outlined the community's engagement process with new information and know-how and present Tacit, Implicit and Explicit (TIE) model of knowledge creation in indigenous communities (Zaman, Yeo, & Kulathuramaiyer, 2011a). The TIE model emphasises on community's activities as part of IKMS process and highlights the need to address it in ICT-based IKMS project design. The concept of embedding ICT-based IKMS as part of the existing IKMS will enhance the relationship between knowledge forms (tacit, implicit and explicit) and community activities and ultimately will address the problems related to IK de-contextualisation and storage of IK as a cultural fossil.

In second part of the Phase 2, we expanded the scope of indigenous knowledge management with notion of indigenous knowledge governance. In indigenous way of life, communities govern their knowledge by coordinating activities that are influenced and controlled by social and cultural systems. In this context, IK represents a critical resource that needs to be focused towards specific processes and governance activities. From our literature review, we found the definition of indigenous data and information governance and we explored the lack of definition for indigenous knowledge governance. To address this gap, we presented the definition of indigenous knowledge governance (IKG) as the system of governance comprises of people, processes and technology used to formally manage and protect structured and unstructured indigenous knowledge assets to guarantee commonly understood, correct, complete, trusted, secure and findable information throughout the indigenous community.

IKG concept covers the governance of both structured and unstructured knowledge assets simultaneously. The structured assets include data and information while unstructured assets include activities and the social and cultural context. After defining IKG, we modelled the IKM processes and structure within the context of indigenous knowledge governance and presented indigenous knowledge governance framework as a holistic model of indigenous knowledge management (Zaman, Yeo, & Kulathuramaiyer, 2011b).

The standard IKGF (Figure 2) is an abstract model of IKM system contains the set of cooperating components that are grouped into seven layers Capital Layer; IK Governance Layer; Activity Layer; KM Layer; Data Repository Layer; Community Engagement Layer; and Cross-Cutting External Environment Layer.

The holistic nature of the framework is reflected in inter-linked and inter-dependent connection of the various layers of the model. Main layer of the framework is governance layer which comprises of three components; stakeholders, social system and coordination mechanism. The second layer is activity layer. The activities on communal and family level are the key drivers of indigenous knowledge management in these communities. While performing these activities the community exercises different knowledge management processes i.e. singing songs or telling stories are the normal activities of the community celebrations. While singing song or telling stories they do exercise the knowledge management processes (knowledge management layer). The data repository layer represents the community repository of experiences, poems, stories, folklores and songs. The community engagement layer indicates the

Figure 2. The logical architecture view of a layered IKGF (Zaman, et al., 2011b)

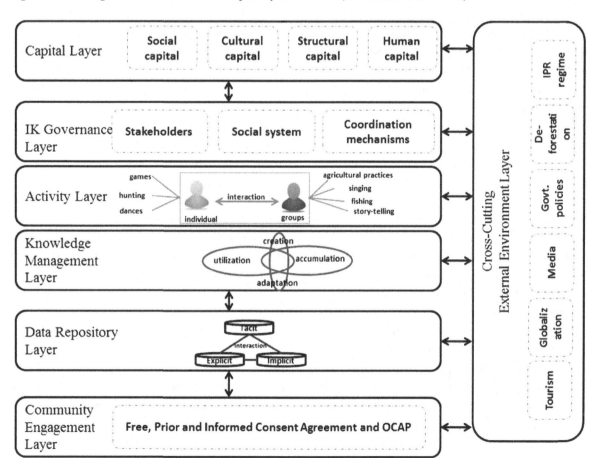

principles of data and information governance i.e ownership, control, access and possession (OCAP) (First Nations Centre, 2007) and free, prior and informed consent (FP&IC) (HREOC, 2009). The capital layer in the framework represents the outcome of the indigenous knowledge management system. The external environment layers highlights the external factors that effects on all or many components of the indigenous knowledge management system.

The model (Figure 2) explains the relationship between different components of indigenous knowledge management system and then structures the associated components in layers so researchers can better understand the complex IKMS.

Phase 3: Validating and Formalising IKGF

In this phase of the research, first we presented an explanatory case study of using IKGF as an analytical tool. In order to illustrate how IKGF can be used to represent the holistic IKMS model, we apply it to model Toro, a complex indigenous knowledge management system of the Penan community of Long Lamai in upper Baram of Sarawak.

Toro is a joint activity of a Penan family and also works as an activity-based knowledge sharing and mentoring journey in the forest that links community elders to members of the younger generations in grooming future guardians of the rainforest. Mentoring includes lessons on livelihood combined with a notion of stewardship, incorporating concepts of conservation ethics and ownership. Depicting the complex structure of Toro in IKGF layers model helps in understanding the holistic context of Penan's IKMS.

In second part of this phase, we formalise the framework by using it for designing, developing and implementing the eToro platform (Siew, Yeo, & Zaman, 2013). The eToro platform is a combination of software (for fata collection and content management system) and community activities

to support the Indigenous Botanical Knowledge (IBK) of the Penan community of Long Lamai. The proposed framework has helped in developing a common understanding of software developers and community members (end-users) for planning, designing, developing and implementing ICT-based IKMS. From the researchers' perspective, a series of formalised methodology were identified. These are: (1) Designing Process Flow Diagrams in order to understand processes, roles, actions & rights of stakeholders; (2) Developing Cultural Protocols for community, researchers and data engagement; (3) Designing Data Instruments for eliciting community needs and acquisition of eToro; (4) Developing Prototypes for digital data collection and indigenous content management and (5) Capacity Building Program for participatory digital data collection and processing (Zaman, Yeo, & Kulathuramaiyer, 2013). It is always difficult to translate social and the cultural aspects into ICT-based IKMS because of the complex context parameters and the difficulty of communicating the community perspective. To address this limitation, the IKGF can help in three important aspects: first, to identify the relation between the community coordination mechanism, governance system and activities. Second, to distinguish the parameters of social, cultural and governance context that sustains the overall IKMS. Finally, to develop the thorough understanding of community members (end-users) and researcher's perspectives of IKMS, focus on the broader outcomes and explore the relationship with external environment.

CONCLUSION

Based on the results of this research, IKM is a complex system that cannot be understood by examining individual parts (processes, data, activities, people, economic etc.) only. It is also about how these parts interact and combine to make a whole system. Whereas a wide range of digital IKM tools have been developed, special attention has been given to use ICT for the management of this highly valuable resource. IK takes predominantly tacit and implicit forms, locked in the community's activities and governed by local social and cultural frameworks. The use of ICT for IKM, will create the problem of knowledge de-contextualisation by extracting IK from the living and holistic system and storing it as raw data. Furthermore, ICTs alone cannot provide all the answers or solutions to IKM, but it can be a part of the solution. In order to design an adequate ICT-based IKMS, a holistic approach needs to be adopted that accommodates the community communication pattern, social and cultural systems and governance mechanism.

ACKNOWLEDGMENT

The authors wish to thank Garen Jengan, Wilson Bian Bilare, and the elders of Long Lamai and Bario communities for their support, guidance, and taking part in this research. The authors also wish to provide acknowledgement of funding from the Universiti Malaysia Sarawak under Zamalah Pascasiswazah and Dana Principal Investigator (DPI) Fund.

REFERENCES

Agrawal, A. (2002). Indigenous knowledge and the politics of classification. *International Social Science Journal*, *54*(173), 287–297. doi:10.1111/1468-2451.00382

Aikenhead, G., & Ogawa, M. (2007). Indigenous knowledge and science revisited. *Cultural Studies of Science Education*, *2*(3), 539–620. doi:10.1007/s11422-007-9067-8

Berkes, F. (2008). *Sacred ecology*. Routledge.

Burtis, A. T. (2009). Managing Indigenous Knowledge And Traditional Cultural Expressions: Is Technology The Solution? *Articles*, *33*, 10.

First Nations Centre. (2007). *OCAP: Ownership, Control, Access and Possession. Ottawa*, Canada: First Nations Information Governance Committee, Assembly of First Nations Ottawa.

Gnaniah, J., Yeo, A., Songan, P., Zen, H., & Hamid, K. A. (2004). *A Comparison on the Implementation Approaches for the e-Bario and e-Bedian Projects*. Paper presented at the 7th International Conference on Work With Computing Systems (WWCS). Kuala Lumpur.

Hall, B. L., Dei, G. J. S., & Rosenberg, D. G. (2000). *Indigenous knowledges in global contexts: Multiple readings of our world*. University of Toronto press.

Harris, R., Bala, P., Songan, P., Lien, E. K. G., & Trang, T. (2001). Challenges and opportunities in introducing information and communication technologies to the Kelabit community of North Central Borneo. *New Media & Society*, *3*(3), 270–295. doi:10.1177/14614440122226092

Hawley, A. W. L., Sherry, E. E., & Johnson, C. J. (2004). A biologists' perspective on amalgamating traditional environmental knowledge and resource management. *British Columbia Journal of Ecosystems and Management*, *5*, 36–50.

HREOC. (2009). *Native Title Report 2008 Human Rights and Equal Opportunity Commission, Sydney*. Sydney: Native Title Unit Australian Human Rights Commission.

Kapuire, G. K., & Blake, E. (2011). *An attempt to merge local and technological paradigms in the digital representation of indigenous knowledge*. Paper presented at the Indigenous Knowledge Technology Conference 2011. Namibia.

Khatri, V., & Brown, C. V. (2010). Designing data governance. *Communications of the ACM, 53*(1), 148–152. doi:10.1145/1629175.1629210

Macchi, M., & Oviedo, G. (2008). *Indigenous and traditional peoples and climate change: Issues Paper*. International Union for Conservation of Nature.

Mathias, E. (1996). *Recording and Using Indigenous Knowledge: A Manual*. International Institute for Rural Reconstruction, Silang, Cavite, Philippines.

Mazzocchi, F. (2009). *Analyzing Knowledge as Part of a Cultural Framework: The Case of Traditional Ecological Knowledge* (Vol. 36). Academic Press.

McGregor, D. (2004). Coming full circle: Indigenous knowledge, environment, and our future. *American Indian Quarterly, 28*(3/4), 385–410. doi:10.1353/aiq.2004.0101

Nakashima, D., & Roué, M. (2002). Indigenous knowledge, peoples and sustainable practice. Encyclopedia of Global Environmental Change, 5, 314-324.

Ngidang, D. (2005). Deconstruction and reconstruction of Native Customary Land tenure in Sarawak. 東南アジア研究, *43*(1), 47-75.

Ngulube, P. (2002). Managing and preserving indigenous knowledge in the knowledge management era: challenges and opportunities for information professionals. *Information Development, 18*(2), 95-102.

Oppenneer, M. (2008). *A Value Sensitive Design Approach to Indigenous Knowledge Management Systems*. Retrieved 11 Oct, 2012, from http://www.ethnosproject.org/site/wp-trackback.php?p=71

Siew, S.-T., Yeo, A. W., & Zaman, T. (2013). *Participatory Action Research in Software Development: Indigenous Knowledge Management Systems Case Study. In Human-Computer Interaction. Human-Centred Design Approaches, Methods, Tools, and Environments* (pp. 470–479). Berlin: Springer.

Soares, S., Deutsch, T., Hanna, S., & Malik, P. (2012). *Big Data Governance: A Framework to Assess Maturity. IBM Data Magazine*.

Thomas, G. (2006). *The DGI data governance framework*. Orlando, FL: The Data Governance Institute.

Velden, M. V. D. (2002). Knowledge facts, knowledge fiction: The role of ICTs in knowledge management for development. *Journal of International Development, 14*(1), 25–37. doi:10.1002/jid.862

Velden, M. V. D. (2010). *Design for the contact zone*. Paper presented at the Seventh International Conference on Cultural Attitudes Towards Communications and Technology. Vancouver, Canada.

Winschiers-Theophilus, H., Jensen, K., & Rodil, K. (2012). *Locally situated digital representation of indigenous knowledge*. Paper presented at the Cultural Attitudes Towards Technology and Communication. Australia.

Yeo, A. W., Zaman, T., & Kulathuramaiyer, N. (2013). Indigenous Knowledge Management in the Kelabit community in Eastern Malaysia: Insights and reflections for contemporary KM design. *International Journal of Sociotechnology and Knowledge Development, 5*(1), 23–36. doi:10.4018/jskd.2013010103

Zaman, T., Yeo, A. W., & Kulathuramaiyer, N. (2011a). *Harnessing community's creative expression and indigenous wisdom to create value*. Paper presented at the Indigenous Knowledge Technology Conference 2011 (IKTC2011): Embracing Indigenous Knowledge Systems in a New Technology Design Paradigm. Windhoek, Namibia.

Zaman, T., Yeo, A. W., & Kulathuramaiyer, N. (2011b). *Indigenous Knowledge Governance Framework (IKGF): A holistic model for indigenous knowledge management.* Paper presented at the Second International Conference on User Science and Engineering (i-USEr2011) Doctoral Consortium. Kualalumpur.

Zaman, T., Yeo, A. W., & Kulathuramaiyer, N. (2013). Augmenting Indigenous Knowledge Management with Information and Communication Technology. *International Journal of Services Technology and Management, 19*(1/2/3), 12.

Zent, S. (2009). *A genealogy of scientific representations of indigenous knowledge. In Landscape, process, and power: Re-evaluating traditional environmental knowledge. Studies in environmental anthropology and ethnobiology* (pp. 19–67). Oxford, UK: Berghan Books.

ADDITIONAL READING

Dyson, L. E., Hendriks, M., & Grant, S. (2007). *Information technology and indigenous people.* Information Science Pub.

Kapuire, G. K., & Blake, E. (2011). *An attempt to merge local and technological paradigms in the digital representation of indigenous knowledge.* Paper presented at the Proceedings of the Indigenous Knowledge Technology Conference 2011, Namibia.

Martin, K., & Mirraboopa, B. (2003). Ways of knowing, being and doing: A theoretical framework and methods for indigenous and indigenist re-search. *Journal of Australian Studies, 27*(76), 203–214. doi:10.1080/14443050309387838

Mit, E., Shiang, C. W., Khairuddin, M. A., & Borhan, N. H. (2011). *Integrate cultures and beliefs into genealogy software for remote communities in Borneo.* Paper presented at the User Science and Engineering (i-USEr), 2011 International Conference on. doi:10.1109/iUSEr.2011.6150570

Siew, S. T., & Yeo, A. W. (2011, 4-8 July). *Employing participatory action research to augment software development for rural communities.* Paper presented at the Proceedings of the 25th British Computer Society Conference on Human-Computer Interaction., Newcastle Upon Tyne, UK.

Siew, S. T., & Yeo, A. W. (2012). *Adapting PRISMA for software development in rural areas: A mobile-based healthcare application case study.* Paper presented at the Second International Conference of the Southeast Asian Network of Ergonomics Societies Conference (SEANES '12), Langkawi, Malaysia.

Smith, D. (2005). *Researching Australian Indigenous governance: a methodological and conceptual framework.* Centre for Aboriginal Economic Policy Research.

Velden, M. V. D. (2002). Knowledge facts, knowledge fiction: The role of ICTs in knowledge management for development. *Journal of International Development, 14*(1), 25–37. doi:10.1002/jid.862

Velden, M. V. D. (2010). *Design for the contact zone.* Paper presented at the Proceedings of the Seventh International Conference on Cultural Attitudes Towards Communications and Technology, Vancouver

Winschiers-Theophilus, H., Bidwell, N. J., Chivuno-Kuria, S., & Kapuire, G. K. (2010). *Determining requirements within an indigenous knowledge system of African rural communities.* Paper presented at the Annual Research Conference of the South African Institute of Computer Scientists and Information Technologists. doi:10.1145/1899503.1899540

Winschiers-Theophilus, H., Winschiers-Goagoses, N., Rodil, K., Blake, E., Zaman, T., Kapuire, G. K., & Kamukuenjandje, R. (2013). Moving away from Erindi-roukambe: Transferability of a rural community-based co-design. *WG 9.4: Social Implications of Computers in Developing Countries.*

Winschiers-Theophilus, H., Zaman, T., Jensen, K. L., Rodil, K., & Yeo, A. W. (2013). *Mobile Technologies for Preservation of Indigenous Knowledge in Rural Communities.* Paper presented at the The Conference on Information Technology in Asia (CITA). doi:10.1109/CITA.2013.6637561

KEY TERMS AND DEFINITIONS

Bario: A Malaysian village located in the centre of the Kelabit Highlands in the northeast of Sarawak, very close to the international border with Indonesian Kalimantan, and 3280 feet above sea level.

Holistic: means system as a whole where all aspects of life are interconnected.

Long Lamai: A remote Penan village on the border of Kalimantan(Indonesia) and Sarawak (Malaysia).

OCAP: The principles of ownership, control, access and possession developed by First Nations to control the data collection processes in their communities.

Penan: The Penan are nomadic aboriginal people living in East Malaysia and Brunei.

TIE: Tacit, Implicit and Explicit forms of knowledge.

Section 3
Usability Engineering

Chapter 13
Usability Evaluation Methods:
A Systematic Review

Ana Isabel Martins
University of Aveiro, Portugal

Anabela G. Silva
University of Aveiro, Portugal

Alexandra Queirós
University of Aveiro, Portugal

Nelson Pacheco Rocha
University of Aveiro, Portugal

ABSTRACT

This chapter aims to identify, analyze, and classify the methodologies and methods described in the literature for the usability evaluation of systems and services based on information and communication technologies. The methodology used was a systematic review of the literature. The studies included in the analysis were classified into empirical and analytical methodologies (test, inquiry, controlled experiment, or inspection). A total of 2116 studies were included, of which 1308 were classified. In terms of results, the inquiry methodology was the most frequent in this review, followed by test, inspection, and finally, the controlled experiment methodology. A combination of methodologies is relatively common, especially the combination of test and inquiry methodologies, probably because they assess different but complementary aspects of usability contributing to a more comprehensive assessment.

INTRODUCTION

The Human Computer Interaction is a research area that results from the convergence of several disciplines, including cognitive science, software engineering and human factors engineering (Carroll, 2013). Research and practice in this area emerged in the early 80's of last century, originally integrated as a sub-specialty of computer science and, ever since, expanded on an ongoing basis, attracting professionals from many other disciplines, and incorporating diverse concepts and approaches (Carroll, 2013).

The research related with Human Computer Interaction, which seeks to minimize the effort of users and simultaneously to provide a wide range of functions, is being influenced by a broad set of trends arising from various technological developments, namely (Vanderheiden & Henry, 2001): increasing capacity of the communication infrastructures, extension of the wireless communications, multimedia integration, multimodality and mobility, increasing use of technologies

DOI: 10.4018/978-1-4666-6485-2.ch013

that enable the miniaturization of the terminal equipment, the growing importance of portable devices that combine multiple functions (*e.g.* calculus, telephone or internet access), increasing importance of services customization considering different systems and different contexts, gradual release of the screen and keyboard interactions, and advances in a broad range of knowledge areas (*e.g.* computational linguistics, artificial vision, artificial intelligence or speech recognition) that provide new interaction mechanisms.

All these technological developments have led to the recognition of human-computer interaction as an interdisciplinary scientific area (Carroll, 2013), within which the issues related to usability are of great importance in terms of research efforts.

In addition to this Introduction, the present paper is composed of more six sections: Usability, Usability Evaluation Methods, Methods, Results, Discussion, and Conclusion.

USABILITY

The concept of usability was originally articulated naively in the slogan 'easy to learn, easy to use' in the 80's of the last century. This term was often used to refer to the capability of a product to be easily used. This corresponds to the definition of usability as a software quality in ISO 9126-11: 'a set of attributes of software which bear on the effort needed for use and on the individual assessment of such use by a stated or implied set of users' (Carroll, 2013).

During the 90's, more sophisticated understandings of usability shifted from an all-or-nothing binary property to a continuum spanning of different extents of usability. Usability turned to be about supporting users in achieving their goals, and not only the user interaction characteristics (Cockton, 2013). According to ISO 9241-11, usability is the extent to which a system or service may be used by specific users in a given context of use, to achieve particular goals with efficiency and effectiveness, while promoting feelings of pleasure (Nielsen, 2003; ISO, 1999).

Current understanding of usability is thus different from the early days of HCI in the 80's. Usability now often subsumes qualities like fun, well-being, collective efficacy, aesthetic tension, enhanced creativity, support for human development, and many others. Usability is part of a broader concept, user experience (Nielsen & Norman, 2013), that, according to the definition of ISO 9241-210 (ISO, 2010), includes all the user's emotions, beliefs, preferences, perceptions, physical and psychological responses, behaviors and accomplishments that occur before, during and after the interaction.

Gualtieri (2009) argues that a good user experience should be useful - users must accomplish their goals; usable - users should be able to achieve the goals, performing tasks with minimal effort; desirable - should appeal the emotions of the users. User's desires are influenced by aspects such as image, language, aesthetics, fun and sophistication (these are the aspects that allow emotional involvement and make brands stand out from their competitors) (Gualtieri, 2009).

Even so, usability remains important. The value of the recent widening focus to user experience is that it places usability in context. Usability is no longer expected to establish its value in isolation, but is instead one of several complementary contributors to design quality (Cockton, 2013).

These recent focus on quality in use and user experience makes it clear that the design of interactive systems cannot just consider the features and attributes of the systems. Instead, the designers must focus on the interaction of users and software in specific settings. They cannot reason solely in terms of whether software is inherently usable or not, but instead they must consider what does or will happen when systems are used, whether successfully, unsuccessfully, or some mix of both. Once the designers focus on interaction, a wider view is inevitable, favoring a broad range of concerns over a narrow focus on software and hardware features (Cockton, 2013).

The standard ISO 9241-11, precursor of ISO 9241-210, distinguishes three usability factors:

- Effectiveness.
- Efficiency.
- Satisfaction.

These factors should be evaluated in a holistic manner that combines multifaceted parameters and criteria. However, in practical terms, the tendency is to evaluate, for each parameter, if the minimum thresholds are met. For example, a software product can be considered unusable in some operational contexts if users cannot perform the key tasks within an acceptable time interval (efficiency criterion) (Cockton, 2013).

The effectiveness criterion is related to the achievement degree of the intended objectives and increases the evaluation complexity.

Regarding satisfaction, it is important to consider that the use may be, objectively, efficient and effective, but cause uncomfortable experiences to users.

The standard ISO 25010 (ISO, 2011) has added two new factors to the standard ISO 9241-11:

- Absence of risk.
- Context coverage.

The absence of risk focuses on security issues of end-users, while context coverage is a broader concept which, in terms of usability, associates specific users and their goals to the context of use.

A very recent approach about usability, referred as PET design, which stands for Persuasion, Emotion and Trust, has its basis in a deep understanding of customer's subtle emotional triggers and employs a rigorous set of new research-based methods and techniques (Schaffer, 2009). This approach is being applied in web design and is based on the assumptions that user engagement rather than classic usability is what sets effective web design apart. Once a customer has entered a web site, it is important to create a sense of trust. Persuasive design is more qualitative, deep, and subtle than usability, since the thinking processes that guide our commercial choices are complex and emotional, not logical and linear (Schaffer, 2009).

The good usability have several benefits, such as: increased efficiency and productivity, reduced error rate and training requirements and improved acceptance (Bevan, Claridge & Petrie, 2005; Bevan, 1998). Furthermore, good usability has impact in disadvantaged costumers and users with special needs. In this respect, user centered design provides a framework for achieving accessibility and Design for All. The Design for All philosophy emphasizes the need to provide access to information systems for the broadest possible range of users, mainly the young and elderly, and people with impaired physical and visual capabilities (European Commission, 2006). Designing for All is developing for human diversity, social inclusion and equality. It enables all people to have equal opportunities to participate in all aspects of life in society. To accomplish this, everything that is developed, in particular, the environment, day to day life objects, culture and information, should be accessible and designed for everyone, regardless of their individual differences (Wegge & Zimmermann, 2007; Queirós, Alvarelhão, Silva, Teixeira & Rocha, 2013).

Despite of all the benefits described above, there are also barriers to usability. For large organizations, successful usability design requires technical and cultural changes and strategic commitment: usability must be a system development objective of all the involved stakeholders.

Given the change of paradigms associated with usability, translated by the evolution of standard ISO 9241-11 to the standard ISO 25010, a wide range of methods for a correct evaluation of the usability issues is necessary. The usability of a system is the result of a complex set of interactions of users with the system and the surrounding context, so it is impossible that a single method can address all the factors involved (Cockton, 2013).

USABILITY EVALUATION METHODS

Usability evaluation is an important part of the overall design of user interaction mechanisms, which consists of interactive cycles of design, prototyping and validation (Ivory & Hearst, 2001). Usually, the development process focuses on the adherence to technical specifications. This is one of the reasons why a significant number of systems are either partially used, misused, abused, not used at all or fail to gain broad acceptance (Bevan & Bruval, 2003). The introducing of user centered methods ensures that 'real products can be used by real people to achieve their tasks in real world (Bevan, 1998). Good usability allows reducing tasks execution times, errors or learning times, and improves user satisfaction.

Usability evaluation must be understood holistically in the context of a particular project and cannot be performed disaggregated from the functions that are intended to be supported. Ideally, usability evaluation must be present at all development stages, and must be iterative to enable a continuous evolution of the quality of results. The literature describes several methodologies and tools to ensure that usability issues are considered during the development process. The selection of these methodologies and tools depends on the development stage and available resources (Martin, Hanington & Hanington, 2012).

The evaluation may be performed in a laboratory, but since the context of use is important, it must be performed in the real context of use whenever possible (Marques & Nunes, 2012). There are methodologies that require data from users, while others rely on usability experts. Therefore, usability evaluation can be empirical (based on actual usage of data) or analytical (based on the examination of an interactive system and/ or potential interactions with it).

For the purpose of this systematic review and based on existing literature we propose that usability evaluation procedures are classified as follows:

- **Test methodologies:** Involve observing users while they perform predefined tasks (Nielsen, 1994a). Test methodologies aim to observe and measure the user interaction and consist of collecting mostly quantitative data from users (Afonso, Lima & Cota, 2013). They focus on people and their tasks, and seek empirical evidence about how to improve the user interaction (Martin, Hanington & Hanington, 2012). Usability testing usually involves systematic observations to determine how well participants can use the system or service being evaluated (Mitchell, 2007). The usability test is centered on what the user does, and not so much on what the user says, so it focuses mainly on the user behavior (Mitchell, 2007).

- **Inquiry methodologies:** Involve collecting qualitative data from users. Although the data collected is subjective, they provide valuable information on what the users want (Bevan & Bruval, 2003). Qualitative data, although subjective, may help to know what users actually want, and for that reason, survey methods are often used for evaluating usability, particularly, interviews and questionnaires or focus groups (Shneiderman, 1992). The interviews and questionnaires reflect the opinions of potential users and help to identify the strengths and weaknesses in terms of usability. In turn, a focus group is a group discussion on a particular topic, led by a moderator.

- **Controlled experiments methodologies:** Involve the application of the scientific method to test hypotheses with real users through the control of variables and use samples big enough to determine statistical significance. Although controlled experiments represent one of the usability evaluation methodologies less affected by bias, they are also the most difficult to implement due to the required number of participants and variables to control (Rubin & Chisnell, 2008).

- **Inspection methodologies:** Involve the participation of experts to assess the various aspects of the user interaction (Martin, Hanington & Hanington, 2012). Many inspection methods lend themselves to the inspection of user interface specifications that have not necessarily been implemented yet, which means that inspection can be performed early in the usability engineering lifecycle (Nielsen, 1994b, 1995a).

The first three types of usability evaluation methodologies are empirical (*i.e.* based on data collected from users) while the last one is analytical (*i.e.* based on expert's inspection).

Considering the importance of usability, an effort was made to characterize and quantify what has been recently done in terms of usability evaluation by conducting a systematic literature review.

A review is systematic if it is based on a clearly formulated question and follows well defined steps (Beverly & Edmunds-Otter, 2006):

- **Identification of relevant studies by systematically searching the literature:** Relevant sources of information should be selected in line with the systematic review topic and sensitive search strategy should be developed.
- **Selection of relevant studies that meet a priori inclusion criteria:** Before conducting the systematic review, a set of inclusion and exclusion criteria originating directly from the research question should be defined to guide the selection of references to be included in the review.

- **Appraisal of included studies' quality:** It informs on whether included studies have attempted to minimize bias and error in their design.
- **Extraction of key information from included studies:** It involves the identification and extraction of relevant information in line with the systematic review aims.
- **Summary, interpretation and presentation of results:** The extracted information must be synthetized and presented using tables or graphs.

It is the explicit and systematic approach that distinguishes systematic reviews from traditional reviews and commentaries. Systematic reviews have to follow a clearly defined protocol previously defined in line with their aims, in order to comprehensively identify and synthetize available literature on a specific topic. This allows for reproducibility and minimizes selection bias. They are valuable pieces of research as they synthetize and compare large amounts of research, making it quickly accessible for readers (Beverly & Edmunds-Otter, 2006).

In this paper, a systematic approach to the literature search was used. We followed the systematic literature review process described by Kitchenham (2004). This allowed us to verify if what is said in theory is supported in practice and to describe the current situation in terms of usability evaluation. Appraisal of included studies was not performed due to the high number of references.

The objective of this work is to identify, analyze and classify the methodologies and methods described in the literature for usability evaluation of both systems and services, based on information technologies. For the propose of this review, a system is defined as a set of interacting or interdependent components, and a service is one or more systems integrated in a well-structured organizational environment.

The following sections describe the methods used to conduct this systematic review and discuss the results obtained.

METHODS

A systematic review of the literature about usability evaluation published from 1st January 2010 until 31st December 2012 was undertaken. For each reference included in the review, the methodology(ies) and method(s) used to assess usability were identified and classified, whenever the study allowed such classification.

To conduct the present study, the following research question was formulated: What are the usability evaluation methodologies and methods being applied to the evaluation of systems or services based on information technologies?

After having identified these methodologies and methods, two additional research question were included: i) What is the relative weight between papers reporting on systems evaluation and papers reporting on services evaluation? and ii) Which kind of systems or services are being evaluated in terms of usability?

The following search terms were used: 'usability evaluation' or 'usability test' or 'usability testing' or 'user centered'. To limit the number of references, the search was restricted to the topic, which includes title, abstract, keywords and author fields.

Studies were sought using Web of Science Databases, because they index over 12,000 of the highest impact journals worldwide, including those of the Association for Computing Machinery - ACM Digital Library - and Institute of Electrical and Electronics Engineers - IEEE journals. The research was conducted on January 6, 2013.

The database search resulted in 2116 references, of those, 808 were excluded: 69 were duplicated, 171 did not have abstract and 568 were out of the research scope (Figure 1). All studies that use the term usability with a different meaning from that used in the information technologies field were excluded. Some studies associate usability to something to be consumed (*e.g.* the 'usability' of the water). A total of 1308 references were selected for a more detailed analysis. All studies included for a further analysis fit the following inclusion criteria: referencing a usability evaluation of a system or service based on information technologies or referencing tools and guidelines for usability evaluation.

Most papers that meet the inclusion criteria contain enough information to identify the usability evaluation methods used and were included in a category called: *evaluates - with information*.

Besides this, the following categories were considered:

- **Evaluates Without Information:** When the inclusion criterion is satisfied but there are no information about the methodology used for the usability evaluation (Böck, Siegert, Haase, Lange & Wendemuth, 2011; Debevc, Kosec & Holzinger, 2010; Dees, 2011; Tosi, Belli, Rinaldi & Tucci, 2012; Martín-Gutiérrez, Contero & Alcaniz, 2010).

- **No Assessment Information:** When an assessment was performed, but the authors do not explicitly state whether this assessment included a usability evaluation (Luna, Hall, Hilgers & Ge, 2010; Murphy-Hill & Black, 2010; Usui, Takano, Fukushima & Yairi, 2010; Sunyaev, Kaletsch & Krcmar, 2010; Shin, Lee, Shin & Lee, 2010).

- **No Evaluation:** When authors do not refer to a usability evaluation, for example, when they explain that it will take place in future work or when it is a conceptual paper, such as reviews (Freire, Arezes & Campos, 2012; Yamaoka & Tukuda, 2011; McCarthy & Swierenga, 2010; Mahatody, Sagar & Kolski, 2010; Smets, Abbing, Neerincx, Lindenberg & van Oostendorp, 2010).

Figure 1. Flow chart for the identification of related literature

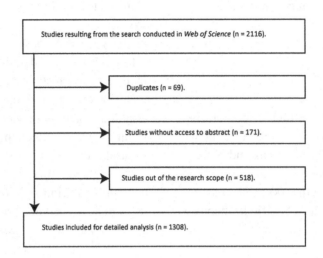

- **Tools:** This category is used to classify the studies that do not report on any evaluation but present tools and guidelines for usability evaluation and improvement of systems or services development (Elling, Lentz & de Jong, 2012; Weinhold, Oettl & Bekavac, 2011; Tamir & Mueller, 2010; Still & Morris, 2010; Olmsted-Hawala, Murphy, Hawala & Ashenfelter, 2010).

The diagram in Figure 2 illustrates the classification process of the studies included in this review.

Every time a usability evaluation was performed (categories: *Evaluates - with information* and *Evaluates - without information*) and information was available in the study, the object of the evaluation was registered and classified into two categories (system or service) depending on what was evaluated.

A data extraction form was designed to collect all the information needed to address the research questions and data synthesis. This form included: publication years, authors, titles, methodologies and methods used in the usability evaluation, what was evaluated and its categorization. Data analysis was performed using the statistical tool Microsoft Excel 2013.

RESULTS

In this section, we present the results of the studies selected for a detailed analysis totaling 1308 papers. Of these, the majority (621) indicates the methodology and methods used for the usability evaluation, 236 were classified as *Evaluates - without information*, 265 refer to an evaluation (however do not present information about an eventual usability evaluation) - *No assessment information*, 52 do not evaluate usability - *No evaluation* and 134 are *Tools* or *guidelines* for usability evaluation. Figure 3 illustrates the distribution of papers according to category.

Of the 621 studies indicating the usability evaluation methodologies applied, many used more than one methodology type, which justifies the following values: 591 studies involved evaluations with users (empirical methodologies) and 67 underwent evaluations involving experts (analytical methodologies).

Figure 2. Detailed analysis

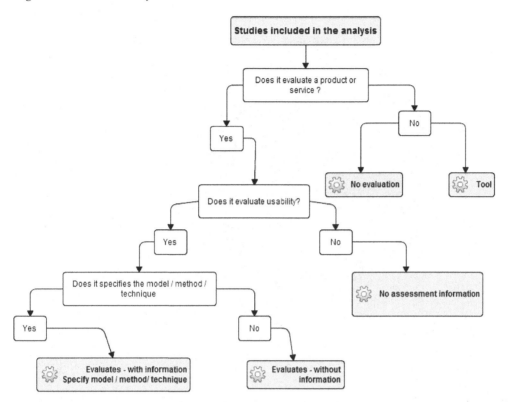

Additionally, in the analyzed empirical studies, 211 used test methods, 278 used inquiry methods and 3 used controlled experiments.

The review identified several test methods: rapid prototyping (mock up), performance evaluation, observation, think-aloud, remote usability testing and simulation. The test methods identified in this review are described below:

- Rapid prototyping is related to the use of a mockup or a low fidelity prototype (not implemented) to collect preliminary data about user interaction (Bernsen & Dybkjaer, 2009). Rapid prototyping is an economical method that can be quickly created and changed. Despite being caught in a preliminary stage of development, the information collected is valid and reliable (Bernsen & Dybkjaer, 2009). The unfinished aspect of a mock up can promote

criticism from users who feel more comfortable enumerating the disadvantages of a specific system or service in this phase comparing to an advanced stage of development (Bernsen & Dybkjaer, 2009).

- Performance evaluation is centered in the users and the tasks they perform, and it involves the collection of quantitative data. The participant's performances are evaluated by recording elements related to the execution of particular tasks (*e.g.* execution time, success/failure, or number of errors) (Nielsen, 1994a). The eye-tracking technique is an example of performance evaluation that registers the spot where the user is looking at the interface, and the movement of the eyes relative to the head, using an eye tracker (Marques & Nunes, 2012).

Figure 3. Studies distribution categories

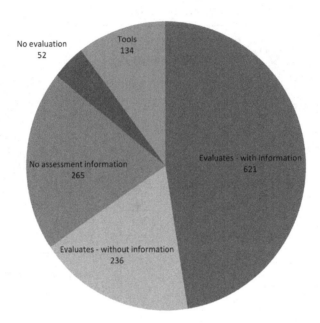

- Observation is a fundamental research method and consists of attentive visualization and systematic recording of a particular phenomenon, including people, artifacts, environments, behaviors and interactions (Martin, Hanington & Hanington, 2012). Observation can be direct, when the researcher is present during the task execution, or indirect, when the task is observed through other means, such as video recording. Methodologies based on observations are especially useful in the specification of user requirements to obtain information. They are also useful to study tasks and processes. The user's cooperation is essential, and the interpersonal skills of the observer are also important. Notes and recordings should be analyzed by the observer, which is a demanding and time-consuming process (Bevan & Bruval, 2003).
- Think-aloud requires participants to verbalize what they are doing and thinking

as they perform a specific task, revealing aspects of the user interaction that incites feelings of joy, confusion or frustration (Martin, Hanington & Hanington, 2012). Accordingly to think-aloud procedures, the users are invited to talk about what they see, do, think or feel as they interact with the system or service. This allows observers to collect information on how the user completes the task. Observers should record objectively what the user is saying, without trying to interpret their actions and words (Bevan & Bruval, 2003).

- Remote usability testing is a usability evaluation method where evaluators are separated in space and/or time from users. In a traditional usability evaluation, users are directly observed by evaluators, however, in a remote usability test, the communication networks act as a bridge between evaluators and users, leading to review the user's interaction in their natural conditions and environments. The assessment procedures can be synchronous (*e.g.* the use of videoconference and remote sharing applications) and asynchronous (*e.g.* subjective feedback about the user interaction or automatic collection of user data, such as number of clicks or critical incidents occurring during the interaction) (Castillo, 1997). This approach also facilitates the quick collection of feedback from users who are in remote areas with reduced overall costs.

- Simulation consists in reproducing real operations functionality as they evolve over time, in other words, using a simulator for a total or partial representation of a task to be replicated (Ziv, Wolpe, Small & Glick, 2003). Simulation based methods should be used at an early stage, when the system or service has not reached a state of stable development. Thus, it is possible to perform an assessment at an embry-

onic stage, so that the changes considered necessary are likely to be executed (Ai & Weng, 2008). To be effective the simulation technique should be conducted by a professional expert in the system or service being developed.

Regarding the test methodologies, the most frequent test method used in the studies included in this review was performance evaluation with 122 studies. Observation was used in 47 studies, followed by the think-aloud method with 38 studies. Both simulation and rapid prototyping were reported in 9 studies. Finally, 5 studies reported the use of remote usability testing. Figure 4 shows the distribution test methodologies used for usability evaluation.

The inquiry methods identified in this review were focus group, interview, questionnaire and diary study:

Figure 4. Test methods used

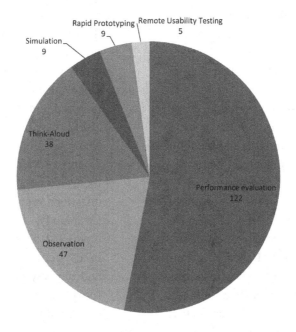

- Focus group requires collecting qualitative data. It involves a small number of people in an informal discussion group, focused on a specific subject (Wilkinson, 2003). A moderator introduces the topic and guides the discussion. The goal is to extract the participant's perceptions, feelings, attitudes and ideas about a given subject. This type of methods is often used in the idealization process of new products (Bevan & Bruval, 2003).

- Interview is a fundamental method in direct contact with the participants, to gather opinions, attitudes, perceptions and experiences (Martin, Hanington & Hanington, 2012). The interviews are usually conducted by an interviewer who dialogue with the participant. Because interviews have a one-to-one nature, errors and misunderstandings can be quickly identified and clarified (Bevan & Bruval, 2003).

- Questionnaire is a tool to collect self-registration information as characteristics, thoughts, feelings, perceptions, behaviors or attitudes, usually in a written form (Martin, Hanington & Hanington, 2012). A questionnaire has the advantage of being cheap, do not require test equipment, and the results reflect the user's opinions, namely about the strengths and weaknesses of the user interaction.

- Diary study is a non-intrusive field method in which the users are in a different location of the evaluators and can manage their own time and means of gathering information (Brandt, Weiss & Klemmer, 2007). The data are recorded in the moment that occurs, which reduces the risk of false information (Tomitsch, Singh & Javadian, 2010). Participants record specific events throughout the day. The data resulting from this collection can then be used to guide the implementation of clarification interviews. The diary study is normally used to understand how people carry out daily activities in order to guide the design of new products.

The questionnaire method was the most common in this systematic review with 194 studies, followed by the interview method with 77 studies. The focus group was reported in 30 studies and the least mentioned method was the diary study (2 studies). The graphic of the Figure 5 shows the distribution of studies classified according to inquiry methods.

As regards to the inspection methodologies, the methods identified in this review were: task analysis, cognitive walkthrough and heuristic evaluation.

- Task analysis means learning with the goals and habits of users (Bevan & Bruval, 2003) and, therefore, it should define what the user is engaged to do (actions and/or cognitive processes) to accomplish a task. The technique consists of an analysis of what the user should perform in terms of actions and cognitive processes to perform certain task. A detailed task analysis can be accomplished to understand a system and its information flow. Failure to implement this method increases the likelihood of costly problems in the development phase. Once the tasks are defined, the functions required to support these tasks can be precisely specified (Bevan & Bruval, 2003; Marques & Nunes, 2012).

- Cognitive walkthrough is the simulation of the user's cognitive behavior by answering questions regarding their cognitive model (Mahatody, Kolski & Sagar, 2009). In practice, it assesses whether the tasks order in a system reflects the cognitive processes and the way people think anticipating the 'next steps'. As a group, experts run a step by step process, setting a set of questions at each step. After identifying the issues that

Figure 5. Inquiry methods being used

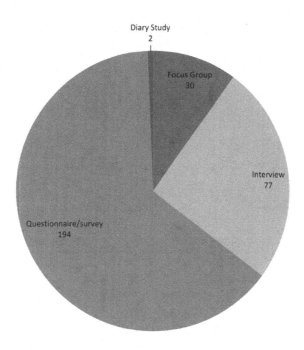

can be improved, experts gather this information in a report and then the software is redesigned to address the problems identified (Martin, Hanington & Hanington, 2012).

- Heuristic evaluation involves a small set of evaluators examining the user interaction through the utilization of recognized usability principles, the heuristics. According to Nielsen (1994a; 1995b) heuristic evaluation is relatively fast and cheap to implement.

A total of 60 studies were found that involved specialist's evaluation (inspection). In terms of methods, the heuristic evaluation method was the most frequent (53 studies), followed by the cognitive walkthrough and task analysis with 9 and 4 studies, respectively (see the graphic of Figure 6).

Finally, this systematic literature review found that numerous studies have used a combination

of several methods. Of the 211 studies that used test methods, 102 also used the inquiry methods and 19 used inspection methods. On the other end, of the 278 studies that used inquiry methods, 6 also used inspection methods. Furthermore, 9 studies used simultaneously the test, inspection and inquiry methods.

In this systematic review, the usability evaluation described in the majority of the studies (780, i.e. 98%) was related to systems such as, health information systems (Croll, 2010; Sadasivam, Delaughter, Crenshaw, Sobko, Williams, Coley, Ray, Ford, Allison & Houston, 2011; Viitanen, Hypponen, Laaveri, Vanska, Reponen & Winblad, 2011; Atack, Luke & Chien, 2008; Vera-Munoz, Arredondo, Peinado, Ottaviano, Paez & De Barrionuevo, 2011), speech recognition software (Derman, Arenovich & Strauss, 2010), Virtual Reality (VR) programs (Hall, Conboy-Hill & Taylor, 2011; Dores, Carvalho, Barbosa, Almeida, Guerreiro, Leitão, Sousa & Castro-Caldas, 2011),

Figure 6. Inspection methods used

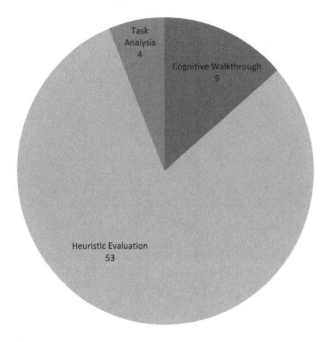

e-learning platforms (Oliveira, Oliveros, Pimentel & Queiroz-Neto, 2011; Skellas & Ioannidis, 2011; Granić & Ćukušić, 2011) simulators (Wentink, Mulder, Rietman & Veltink, 2011), computer games (Papaloukas, Patriarcheas & Xenos, 2011; Omar & Jaafar, 2011; Miller, Chang, Wang, Beier & Klisch, 2011), health websites (Ferron, Brunette, McHugo, Devitt, Martin & Drake, 2011; Atkinson, Saperstein, Desmond, Gold, Billing & Tian, 2009), e-government websites (Suzuki, Karashima & Nishiguchi, 2011) health devices such as pill reminders for older adults (Ansari, 2011), hearing devices (Tufts, Hamilton, Ucci & Rubas, 2011) and assistive devices (Sävenstedt, Meiland, Dröes & Moelaert, 2010) or mobile communication devices (Aryana, Boks & Navabi, 2011; Raita & Oulasvirta, 2011; Öztürk & Rızvanoğlu, 2011). Only 16 studies (2%) described a usability evaluation of services such as mobile-banking services (Kang, Lee & Lee, 2012; Zollet & Back, 2010), u-home services (Lee, Bahn, Rhiu, Yun & Choi, 2011), web portals (Hellmers, Thomaschewski, Holt & Wriedt, 2012), interactive services (Ost-

lund, Dahlbäck & Petersson, 2010; Sandberg & Andersson, 2011) or smart homes (Turner, 2011). Fifty one studies were not included in these two categories because information was not enough for us to understand the typology of what was evaluated.

DISCUSSION

This systematic review provides an overview of the usability evaluation methodologies and methods that have been used during the last years. This section summarizes the main findings of the systematic review and discusses its implications for research and practice as well as its limitations.

The analysis revealed that the empirical methodologies (which comprises test, inquiry and controlled experiment) are the most frequently used (as mentioned in the literature), which seems to confirm the recognition of the end-users role as a source of knowledge for usability evaluations.

Regarding the test methodologies, the most widely used method was the performance evaluation. It is a method that involves the collection of quantitative data. The reduced number of studies using controlled experiments identified in this systematic review might be explained by the fact that this methodology requires a large number of resources, both in terms of skills, logistics and sample size. The method of inquiry methodologies most frequently used was the questionnaire. This self-reported tool enables the collection of qualitative information such as characteristics, thoughts, feelings, perceptions, behaviors and attitudes from users.

The evaluation of systems or services is a complex task and the utilization of only one method may not allow an exhaustive usability evaluation. A large number of systems or services were evaluated using a combination of different usability evaluation methodologies and methods. This combination enables complementary results, which contribute to a more comprehensive evaluation of several features of the systems or services. The most frequent method combination found in this review was the use of test and inquiry methods, particularly performance evaluation and questionnaires. A possible explanation, is the fact that test methods are more objective, resulting normally in quantitative data (*e.g.* performance evaluations), and the inquiry methods are more subjective resulting normally in qualitative data (*e.g.* questionnaires). Thus, these methods seem to be complementary and the combination of both is likely to result in a more complete evaluation.

Martin, Hanington & Hanington, (2012) suggest that a combination of various methods for usability evaluation happens because methods are incompletely specified in order to be consistently applied. In addition, the different methods have different capabilities and limitations and provide different types of information, so that their combination is important. For this reason, it can be expected that the usability evaluation involves a combination of several methods (Martin, Hanington & Hanington, 2012).

Most of the literature included in this systematic review focused the usability evaluation of systems (98%). This seems to reveal that the development and evaluation is technology-oriented, addressing, in most cases, systems (or part of systems) and neglecting services that integrate one or more systems according to a well-defined organizational structure.

In summary, the main findings of this systematic review are:

- Empirical methodologies were the most frequently used for usability evaluation;
- For test methodologies, the most widely used method was performance evaluation;
- For inquiry methodologies, the most frequently used method was the questionnaire;
- The reduced number of studies using controlled experiments may be explained by the large number of resources required;
- A large number of systems or services were evaluated using a combination of different usability evaluation methodologies and methods. This combination enables complementary results;
- The most frequent method combination was test and inquiry methods, particularly performance evaluation and questionnaires.
- Most of the studies focused on the usability evaluation of systems which seems to reveal that the development and evaluation is technology-oriented.

Implications for Research and Practice

This review showed that a great number of studies about the usability evaluation of systems and services have been reported. Therefore, this paper might serve as a basis for future research of systems and services usability evaluation, as it contributes to the scientific community by providing an overview of the most used methodologies and methods over the last years.

An aspect to note is that a large number of studies (236) reported usability evaluations, but they do not refer how these evaluations were performed, which seems to indicate that some authors do not recognize the importance of describing the methodology used for the usability evaluation. As this is such an important aspect, it is recommended to always include this information in the study report.

It was also found that in many studies the term usability was used inconsistently, referring to something able to be consumed and not with the meaning that was considered in this review. This inconsistency is an indicator that a standardization of nomenclature is required. Nevertheless, taking into account that the majority of studies indicated the methodology and methods used to evaluate usability (621 studies), it may reveal that this is an important area recognized by professionals. The large number of studies classified as tools shows that creating and developing tools that facilitate usability evaluations and improvements is of great interest for the academic community.

Limitations of This Review

There are methods for usability evaluation that were not identified in this systematic review, probably because the total number of studies was not enough to cover all methods, or due to the limited number of years covered by the search. In addition, the search strategy used might not have been sensitive enough to identify studies that did not have usability evaluation as the main goal. This is probably the major limitation of this study. Furthermore, although a rigorous process of quality control has been implemented it is always possible some inaccuracy in data extraction and classification.

CONCLUSION

Although our findings may be indicative of the field, further reviews are needed to confirm the results obtained. Future work includes the extension of this review by including other sources. Furthermore, we intend to analyze the variability of methods used on usability evaluation over the years and for that we have to include other publications years on the systematic review.

Throughout this chapter, we described the concept of usability evaluation and exposed the results of a systematic literature review. This review aimed to identify, analyze, and classify the methodologies and methods described in the literature for usability evaluation of systems or services based on information technologies.

The systematic literature review performed consisted of classifying the empirical and analytical methodologies (test, inquiry, controlled experiment or inspection) and methods. A total of 2116 studies were included, of which 1308 were classified. The inquiry methodology was the most commonly used in the studies included in this review, followed by test and inspection methodologies and, finally, the controlled experiments. The methods combination is relatively frequent, especially the combination of test and inquiry methods, probably because it enables the collection of different types of information, thereby contributing to comprehensive evaluations.

Usability is a fundamental aspect to consider in the development cycle of systems or services that necessarily have to be framed by the characteristics of users, tasks to perform, and the surrounding context (social, organizational and physical) for which the development is intended.

Since the 80's of the last century, a bunch of new approaches for usability evaluation were developed. Once properly adjusted, configured and combined, they can provide valuable contributions for iterative development of interaction mechanisms. However, some gaps remain and a greater focus on usability evaluation in real contexts of use is needed. Without this effort, usability issues can be faced with disappointment, distrust, skepticism and lack of appreciation in some technological development environments.

Organizations are increasingly aware to the issue of usability, but the guidance about how to do usability tends to be technique-centered, concentrating on specific approaches for designing or evaluating systems (Bevan & Curson, 1999).

Cockton (2013) argues that in the future the usability evaluation will play a central role. Users will be an integral part of development teams and will be part of an approach "BIG - Balanced, Integrated and Generous". Usability must find their own place in interaction design as an essential part of the team, recognized and universally accepted (Cockton, 2013).

ACKNOWLEDGMENT

This work was supported by COMPETE (Sistema de Incentivos à Investigação e Desenvolvimento Tecnológico, Projetos de I&DT Empresas em co-promoção) and FEDER from the European Union, under QREN Living Usability Lab for Next Generation Networks, QREN AAL4ALL and QREN Smartphones for Seniors.

REFERENCES

Afonso, A. P., Lima, J. R., & Cota, M. P. (2013). Usability Assessment of Web Interfaces: User Testing. In *Proceedings of Information Systems and Technologies (CISTI),* (pp. 1-7). IEEE.

Ai, H., & Weng, F. (2008). User Simulation as Testing for Spoken Dialog Systems. In *Proceedings of the 9th SIGdial Workshop on Discourse and Dialogue* (pp. 164-171). Association for Computational Linguistics. doi:10.3115/1622064.1622097

Ansari, S. (2011). Designing Interactive Pill Reminders for Older Adults: A Formative Study. In Universal Access in Human-Computer Interaction. Users Diversity (pp. 121-130). Springer. doi:10.1007/978-3-642-21663-3_13

Aryana, B., Boks, C., & Navabi, A. (2011). Possibilities for Cultural Customization of Mobile Communication Devices: the Case of Iranian Mobile Users. In Human Centered Design (pp. 177-186). Springer. doi:10.1007/978-3-642-21753-1_21

Atack, L., Luke, R., & Chien, E. (2008). Evaluation of Patient Satisfaction with Tailored Online Patient Education Information. *Computers, Informatics, Nursing, 26*(5), 258–264. doi:10.1097/01.NCN.0000304838.52207.90 PMID:18769180

Atkinson, N. L., Saperstein, S. L., Desmond, S. M., Gold, R. S., Billing, A. S., & Tian, J. (2009). Rural eHealth Nutrition Education for Limited-Income Families: An Iterative and User-Centered Design Approach. *Journal of Medical Internet Research, 11*(2), e21. doi:10.2196/jmir.1148 PMID:19632974

Bernsen, N. O., & Dybkjær, L. (2009). *Multimodal Usability.* Springer.

Bevan, N. (1998). European Usability Support Centres: Support for a More Usable Information Society. In *Proceedings of TAP Annual Concertation Meeting.* European Commission.

Bevan, N., & Bruval, P. (2003). *Usability Net: Tools & Methods.* Retrieved July 14, 2013, from http://www.usabilitynet.org/tools/list.htm

Bevan, N., Claridge, N., & Petrie, H. (2005). Tenuta: Simplified Guidance for Usability and Accessibility. In *Proceedings of HCI International.* Lawrence Erlbaum Associates.

Bevan, N., & Curson, I. (1999). Planning and Implementing User-Centred Design. In Proceedings of CHI'99 Extended Abstracts on Human Factors in Computing Systems (pp. 137-138). ACM.

Beverly, C., & Edmunds-Otter, M. (2006). Systematic Reviews and Secondary Research. In K. Gerrish, & A. Lacey (Eds.), *The Research Process in Nursing* (pp. 316–334). Oxford, UK: Blackwell Publishing.

Böck, R., Siegert, I., Haase, M., Lange, J., & Wendemuth, A. (2011). ikannotate - A Tool for Labelling, Transcription, and Annotation of Emotionally Coloured Speech. In Affective Computing and Intelligent Interaction (pp. 25-34). Springer.

Brandt, J., Weiss, N., & Klemmer, S. R. (2007). txt 4 l8r: Lowering the Burden for Diary Studies under Mobile Conditions. In Proceedings of CHI'07 Extended Abstracts on Human Factors in Computing Systems (pp. 2303-2308). ACM.

Carroll, J. M. (2013). Human Computer Interaction. In M. Soegaard, & R. F. Dam (Eds.), *The Encyclopedia of Human-Computer Interaction* (2nd ed.). The Interaction Design Foundation.

Castillo, J. C. (1997). *The User-Reported Critical Incident Method for Remote Usability Evaluation* (Doctoral dissertation). Virginia Polytechnic Institute and State University.

Cockton, G. (2013). Usability Evaluation. In M. Soegaard, & R. F. Dam (Eds.), *The Encyclopedia of Human-Computer Interaction* (2nd ed.). The Interaction Design Foundation.

Croll, J. (2010). Testing for Usability is not Enough: Why Clinician Acceptance of Health Information Systems is also Crucial for Successful Implementation? In E-Health (pp. 49-60). Springer.

Debevc, M., Kosec, P., & Holzinger, A. (2010). E-learning Accessibility for the Deaf and Hard of Hearing-Practical Examples and Experiences. In HCI in Work and Learning, Life and Leisure (pp. 203-213). Springer. doi:10.1007/978-3-642-16607-5_13

Dees, W. (2011). Usability of Nomadic User Interfaces. In *Human-Computer Interaction. Towards Mobile and Intelligent Interaction Environments* (pp. 195–204). Springer. doi:10.1007/978-3-642-21616-9_22

Derman, Y. D., Arenovich, T., & Strauss, J. (2010). Speech Recognition Software and Electronic Psychiatric Progress Notes: Physicians' Ratings and Preferences. *BMC Medical Informatics and Decision Making*, *10*(1), 44. doi:10.1186/1472-6947-10-44 PMID:20738875

Dores, A. R., Carvalho, I. P., Barbosa, F., Almeida, I., Guerreiro, S., Leitão, M., et al. (2011). Serious Games: Are They Part of the Solution in the Domain of Cognitive Rehabilitation? In Serious Games Development and Applications (pp. 95-105). Springer.

Elling, S., Lentz, L., & de Jong, M. (2012). Combining Concurrent Think-Aloud Protocols and Eye-Tracking Observations: An Analysis of Verbalizations and Silences. *IEEE Transactions on Professional Communication*, *55*(3), 206–220. doi:10.1109/TPC.2012.2206190

European Commission. (2006). *The Build-for-All Reference Manual*. European Commission.

Ferron, J. C., Brunette, M. F., McHugo, G. J., Devitt, T. S., Martin, W. M., & Drake, R. E. (2011). Developing a Quit Smoking Website that is Usable by People with Severe Mental Illnesses. *Psychiatric Rehabilitation Journal*, *35*(2), 111–116. doi:10.2975/35.2.2011.111.116 PMID:22020840

Freire, L. L., Arezes, P. M., & Campos, J. C. (2012). A Literature Review about Usability Evaluation Methods for e-Learning Platforms. *Work (Reading, Mass.)*, *41*, 1038–1044. PMID:22316857

Granić, A., & Ćukušić, M. (2011). Usability Testing and Expert Inspections Complemented by Educational Evaluation: A Case Study of an e-Learning Platform. *Journal of Educational Technology & Society*, *14*(2).

Gualtieri, M. (2009). Best Practices. In *User Experience (UX)*. Forrester Research.

Hall, V., Conboy-Hill, S., & Taylor, D. (2011). Using Virtual Reality to Provide Health Care Information to People with Intellectual Disabilities: Acceptability, Usability, and Potential Utility. *Journal of Medical Internet Research*, *13*(4), e91. doi:10.2196/jmir.1917 PMID:22082765

Hellmers, J., Thomaschewski, J., Holt, E. M., & Wriedt, T. (2012). Usability Evaluation Methods for a Scientific Internet Information Portal. *Journal of Universal Computer Science*, *18*(10), 1308–1322.

ISO. (1999). *ISO 9241: Ergonomics of Human System Interaction Organization.* International Organization for Standardization.

ISO. (2010). *ISO 9241- 210: Ergonomics of Human System Interaction - Part 210: Human-Centred Design for Interactive Systems.* International Organization for Standardization.

ISO. (2011). *ISO 25010: Systems and Software Engineering - Systems and Software Quality Requirements and Evaluation (SQuaRE) - System and Software Quality Models.* International Organization for Standardization.

Ivory, M. Y., & Hearst, M. A. (2001). The State of the Art in Automating Usability Evaluation of User Interfaces. *ACM Computing Surveys*, *33*(4), 470–516. doi:10.1145/503112.503114

Kang, H., Lee, M. J., & Lee, J. K. (2012). Are You Still with Us? A Study of the Post-Adoption Determinants of Sustained Use of Mobile-Banking Services. *Journal of Organizational Computing and Electronic Commerce*, *22*(2), 132–159. doi:10.1080/10919392.2012.667710

Kitchenham, B. (2004). Procedures for Performing Systematic Reviews. *Keele University*, *33*, 2004.

Lee, J., Bahn, S., Rhiu, I., Yun, M. H., & Choi, H. (2011). An Evaluation Metric on Human-Service Interactivity of Ubiquitous Services. In D. Lin, & H. Chen (Eds.), *Ergonomics for All: Celebrating PPCOE's 20 Years of Excellence* (pp. 347–352). PPCOE. doi:10.1201/b10529-66

Luna, R., Hall, R., Hilgers, M., & Ge, L. (2010). GIS Learning Tool for Civil Engineers. *International Journal of Engineering Education*, *26*(1), 52.

Mahatody, T., Kolski, C., & Sagar, M. (2009). CWE: Assistance Environment for the Evaluation Operating a Set of Variations of the Cognitive Walkthrough Ergonomic Inspection Method. In Engineering Psychology and Cognitive Ergonomics (pp. 52-61). Springer.

Mahatody, T., Sagar, M., & Kolski, C. (2010). State of the Art on the Cognitive Walkthrough Method, its Variants and Evolutions. *Journal of Human–Computer Interaction*, *26*(8), 741–785. doi:10.1080/10447311003781409

Marques, S., & Nunes, I. (2012). Usability of Interfaces. In S. Marques, & I. Nunes (Eds.), *Industrial Engineering and Management: Ergonomics - A Systems Approach* (pp. 155–171). InTech.

Martin, B., Hanington, B., & Hanington, B. M. (2012). *Universal Methods of Design: 100 Ways to Research Complex Problems, Develop Innovative Ideas, and Design Effective Solutions.* Rockport Publishers.

Martín-Gutiérrez, J., Contero, M., & Alcañiz, M. (2010). Evaluating the Usability of an Augmented Reality Based Educational Application. In *Intelligent Tutoring Systems* (pp. 296–306). Springer. doi:10.1007/978-3-642-13388-6_34

McCarthy, J. E., & Swierenga, S. J. (2010). What We Know about Dyslexia and Web Accessibility: A Research Review. *Universal Access in the Information Society*, 9(2), 147–152. doi:10.1007/s10209-009-0160-5

Miller, L. M., Chang, C. I., Wang, S., Beier, M. E., & Klisch, Y. (2011). Learning and Motivational Impacts of a Multimedia Science Game. *Computers & Education*, 57(1), 1425–1433. doi:10.1016/j.compedu.2011.01.016

Mitchell, P. P. (2007). *A Step-by-Step Guide to Usability Testing*. iUniverse.

Murphy-Hill, E., & Black, A. P. (2010). An Interactive Ambient Visualization for Code Smells. In *Proceedings of the 5th International Symposium on Software Visualization* (pp. 5-14). ACM. doi:10.1145/1879211.1879216

Nielsen, J. (1994a). *Usability Engineering*. Elsevier.

Nielsen, J. (1994b). Usability Inspection Methods. In *Conference Companion on Human Factors in Computing Systems* (pp. 413–414). ACM. doi:10.1145/259963.260531

Nielsen, J. (1995a). *Summary of Usability Inspection Methods*. Retrieved November 17 2013, from http://www.nngroup.com/articles/summary-of-usability-inspection-methods/

Nielsen, J. (1995b). *How to Conduct a Heuristic Evaluation*. Retrieved November 18, 2013 from http://www.nngroup.com/articles/how-to-conduct-a-heuristic-evaluation/

Nielsen, J. (2003). *Usability 101: Introduction to Usability*. Retrieved December 16, 2013 from http://useit.com/alertbox/20030825.html

Nielsen, J., & Norman, D. (2013). *The Definition of User Experience*. Retrieved December 16, 2013 from http://www.nngroup.com/articles/definition-user-experience/

Oliveira, L. S., Oliveros, D. V., Pimentel, M., & Queiroz-Neto, J. P. (2011). Work in Progress - Alternative Interfaces for e-Learning Platforms Used in Remote Areas. In *Frontiers in Education Conference (FIE), 2011* (pp. T4C-1). IEEE.

Olmsted-Hawala, E. L., Murphy, E. D., Hawala, S., & Ashenfelter, K. T. (2010). Think-Aloud Protocols: a Comparison of Three Think-Aloud Protocols for Use in Testing Data-Dissemination Web Sites for Usability. In *Proceedings of the SIGCHI Conference on Human Factors in Computing Systems* (pp. 2381-2390). ACM. doi:10.1145/1753326.1753685

Omar, H. M., & Jaafar, A. (2011). Usability of Educational Computer Game (Usa_ECG): Applying Analytic Hierarchy Process. In *Visual Informatics: Sustaining Research and Innovations* (pp. 147-156). Springer.

Ostlund, M., Dahlbäck, N., & Petersson, G. I. (2010). 3D Visualization as a Communicative Aid in Pharmaceutical Advice-Giving over Distance. *Journal of Medical Internet Research*, 13(3), e50. doi:10.2196/jmir.1437 PMID:21771714

Öztürk, Ö., & Rızvanoğlu, K. (2011). How to Improve User Experience in Mobile Social Networking: A User-Centered Study with Turkish Mobile Social Network Site Users. In Design, User Experience, and Usability: Theory, Methods, Tools and Practice (pp. 521-530). Springer.

Papaloukas, S., Patriarcheas, K., & Xenos, M. (2011). Games' Usability and Learning - the Educational Videogame BeTheManager! In *Proceedings of the 5th European Conference on Games Based Learning* (pp. 449-456). ACPI.

Queirós, A., Alvarelhão, J., Silva, A., Teixeira, A., & Rocha, N. (2013). A Conceptual Framework for the Design and Development of AAL Services. In M. Cruz-Cunha, I. Miranda, & P. Gonçalves (Eds.), *Handbook of Research on ICTs for Human-Centered Healthcare and Social Care Services: Developments and Applications* (pp. 568–586). IGI Global. doi:10.4018/978-1-4666-3986-7.ch030

Raita, E., & Oulasvirta, A. (2011). Too Good to be Bad: Favorable Product Expectations Boost Subjective Usability Ratings. *Interacting with Computers*, *23*(4), 363–371. doi:10.1016/j.intcom.2011.04.002

Rubin, J., & Chisnell, D. (2008). *Handbook of Usability Testing: How to Plan, Design, and Conduct Effective Tests*. John Wiley & Sons.

Sadasivam, R. S., Delaughter, K., Crenshaw, K., Sobko, H. J., Williams, J. H., & Coley, H. L. et al. (2011). Development of an Interactive, Web-Delivered System to Increase Provider - Patient Engagement in Smoking Cessation. *Journal of Medical Internet Research*, *13*(4), e87. doi:10.2196/jmir.1721 PMID:22011394

Sandberg, K. W., & Andersson, H. (2011). Usability Evaluation of an Interactive Service on Mobile Phone. In *Ergonomics for all: Celebrating PPCOE's 20 Years of Excellence-Selected Papers of the Pan-Pacific Conference on Ergonomics, PPCOE 2010* (pp. 67-72). PPCOE. doi:10.1201/b10529-15

Sävenstedt, S., Meiland, F., Dröes, R. M., & Moelaert, F. (2010). Evaluation of Cognitive Prosthetics. In *Supporting People with Dementia Using Pervasive Health Technologies* (pp. 197–206). Springer. doi:10.1007/978-1-84882-551-2_13

Schaffer, E. (2009). Beyond Usability: Designing Web Sites for Persuasion, Emotion, and Trust. *UX matters*. Retrieved September 22, 2013 from http://www.uxmatters.com/mt/archives/2009/01/beyond-usability-designing-web-sites-for-persuasion-emotion-and-trust.php

Shin, Y. M., Lee, S. C., Shin, B., & Lee, H. G. (2010). Examining Influencing Factors of Post-Adoption Usage of Mobile Internet: Focus on the User Perception of Supplier-Side Attributes. *Information Systems Frontiers*, *12*(5), 595–606. doi:10.1007/s10796-009-9184-x

Shneiderman, B. (1992). *Designing the User Interface: Strategies for Effective Human-Computer Interaction* (Vol. 2). Addison-Wesley.

Skellas, A. I., & Ioannidis, G. S. (2011). Web-Design for Learning Primary School Science Using LMSs: Evaluating Specially Designed Task-Oriented Design Using Young Schoolchildren. In *Proceedings of 14th International Conference on Interactive Collaborative Learning (ICL)*, (pp. 313-318). IEEE. doi:10.1109/ICL.2011.6059597

Smets, N. J. J. M., Abbing, M. S., Neerincx, M. A., Lindenberg, J., & van Oostendorp, H. (2010). Game-Based Versus Storyboard-Based Evaluations of Crew Support Prototypes for Long Duration Missions. *Acta Astronautica*, *66*(5), 810–820. doi:10.1016/j.actaastro.2009.08.032

Still, B., & Morris, J. (2010). The Blank-Page Technique: Reinvigorating Paper Prototyping in Usability Testing. *IEEE Transactions on Professional Communication*, *53*(2), 144–157. doi:10.1109/TPC.2010.2046100

Sunyaev, A., Kaletsch, A., & Krcmar, H. (2010). Comparative Evaluation of Google Health API vs. Microsoft HealthVault API. In *Proceedings of Healthinf 2010: the 3rd International Conference on Health Informatics* (pp. 195-201). INSTICC.

Suzuki, K., Karashima, M., & Nishiguchi, H. (2011). A Study on the Time Estimation Measurement for Web Usability Evaluation. In Design, User Experience, and Usability: Theory, Methods, Tools and Practice (pp. 53-59). Springer. doi:10.1007/978-3-642-21708-1_7

Tamir, D. E., & Mueller, C. J. (2010). Pinpointing Usability Issues Using an Effort Based Framework. In *Proceedings of 2010 IEEE International Conference on Systems Man and Cybernetics (SMC)*, (pp. 931-938). IEEE. doi:10.1109/ICSMC.2010.5641883

Tomitsch, M., Singh, N., & Javadian, G. (2010). Using Diaries for Evaluating Interactive Products: the Relevance of Form and Context. In *Proceedings of the 22nd Conference of the Computer-Human Interaction Special Interest Group of Australia on Computer-Human Interaction*. ACM. doi:10.1145/1952222.1952266

Tosi, F., Belli, A., Rinaldi, A., & Tucci, G. (2012). The Intermodal Bike: Multi-Modal Integration of Cycling Mobility through Product and Process Innovations in Bicycle Design. *Work (Reading, Mass.)*, *41*, 1501–1506. PMID:22316928

Tufts, J. B., Hamilton, M. A., Ucci, A. J., & Rubas, J. (2011). Evaluation by Industrial Workers of Passive and Level-Dependent Hearing Protection Devices. *Noise & Health*, *13*(50), 26. doi:10.4103/1463-1741.73998 PMID:21173484

Turner, K. J. (2011). Flexible Management of Smart Homes. *Journal of Ambient Intelligence and Smart Environments*, *3*(2), 83–109.

Usui, K., Takano, M., Fukushima, Y., & Yairi, I. E. (2010). The Evaluation of Visually Impaired People's Ability of Defining the Object Location on Touch-Screen. In *Proceedings of the 12th International ACM Sigaccess Conference on Computers and Accessibility* (pp. 287-288). ACM. doi:10.1145/1878803.1878874

Vanderheiden, G. C., & Henry, S. L. (2001). Everyone Interfaces. In C. Stephanidis (Ed.), *User interfaces for All: Concepts, Methods, and Tools*. CRC Press.

Vera-Muñoz, C., Arredondo, M. T., Peinado, I., Ottaviano, M., Páez, J. M., & de Barrionuevo, A. D. (2011). Results of the Usability and Acceptance Evaluation of a Cardiac Rehabilitation System. In Human-Computer Interaction. Users and Applications (pp. 219-225). Springer. doi:10.1007/978-3-642-21619-0_28

Viitanen, J., Hyppönen, H., Lääveri, T., Vänskä, J., Reponen, J., & Winblad, I. (2011). National Questionnaire Study on Clinical ICT Systems Proofs: Physicians Suffer From Poor Usability. *International Journal of Medical Informatics*, *80*(10), 708–725. doi:10.1016/j.ijmedinf.2011.06.010 PMID:21784701

Wegge, K. P., & Zimmermann, D. (2007). Accessibility, Usability, Safety, Ergonomics: Concepts, Models, and Differences. In Universal Acess in Human Computer Interaction. Coping with Diversity (pp. 294-301). Springer.

Weinhold, T., Oettl, S., & Bekavac, B. (2011). Heuristics for the Evaluation of Library Online Catalogues. In *New Trends in Qualitative and Quantitative Methods in Libraries: Selected Papers Presented at the 2nd Qualitative and Quantitative Methods in Libraries - Proceedings of the International Conference on Qqml2010* (p. 425). World Scientific. doi:10.1142/9789814350303_0052

Wentink, E. C., Mulder, A., Rietman, J. S., & Veltink, P. H. (2011). Vibrotactile Stimulation of the Upper Leg: Effects of Location, Stimulation Method and Habituation. In *Proceedings of Engineering in Medicine and Biology Society, EMBC, 2011 Annual International Conference of the IEEE* (pp. 1668-1671). IEEE.

Wilkinson, S. (2003). *Focus Groups in Qualitative Psychology - A Practical Guide to Research Methods*. London: Sage Publications.

Yamaoka, T., & Tukuda, S. (2011). A Proposal of Simple Usability Evaluation Method and its Application. In D. Lin, & H. Chen (Eds.), *Ergonomics for All: Celebrating PPCOE's 20 Years of Excellence* (pp. 63–66). PPCOE. doi:10.1201/ b10529-14

Ziv, A., Wolpe, P. R., Small, S. D., & Glick, S. (2003). Simulation-Based Medical Education: An Ethical Imperative. *Academic Medicine*, *78*(8), 783–788. doi:10.1097/00001888-200308000-00006 PMID:12915366

Zollet, R., & Back, A. (2010). *Website Usability for Internet Banking. Institute of Information Management*. University of St Gallen.

ADDITIONAL READING

Albers, M., & Still, B. (Eds.). (2010). *Usability of Complex Information Systems: Evaluation of User Interaction*. CRC press. doi:10.1201/ EBK1439828946

Albert, W., & Tullis, T. (2013). *Measuring the User Experience: Collecting, Analyzing, and Presenting Usability Metrics*. Newnes.

Bernsen, N. O., & Dybkjaer, L. (2009). *Multimodal Usability*. Springer.

Caddick, R., & Cable, S. (2011). *Communicating the User Experience: A Practical Guide for Creating Useful Ux Documentation*. John Wiley & Sons.

De Sá, M., & Carriço, L. (2011). Designing and Evaluating Mobile Interaction: Challenges and Trends. *Foundations and Trends in Human-Computer Interaction*, *4*(3), 175–243. doi:10.1561/1100000025

Dix, A., Finlay, J., Abowd, G., & Beale, R. (2004). *Human-Computer Interaction* (3rd ed.). Prentice Hall.

George, C. A. (2008). *User-Centred Library Websites: Usability Evaluation Methods* (pp. 97–108). Chandos Publishing. doi:10.1016/B978-1-84334-359-2.50004-4

Jeffries, R., & Desurvire, H. (1992). Usability Testing vs. Heuristic Evaluation: Was there a Contest? *ACM SIGCHI Bulletin*, *24*(4), 39–41. doi:10.1145/142167.142179

Kumar, R. (2005). *Human Computer Interaction*. Firewall Media.

Mayhew, D. J. (1999). The Usability Engineering Lifecycle. In CHI'99 Extended Abstracts on Human Factors in Computing Systems (pp. 147-148). ACM.

Mitchell, P. P. (2007). *A Step-by-Step Guide to Usability Testing*. iUniverse.

Nielsen, J. (1994). *Usability Engineering*. Elsevier.

Preece, J., Rogers, Y., Sharp, H., Benyon, D., Holland, S., & Carey, T. (1994). *Human-Computer Interaction*. Addison-Wesley.

Soares, M. M., & Rebelo, F. (Eds.). (2012). *Advances in Usability Evaluation*. CRC Press.

KEY TERMS AND DEFINITIONS

Accessibility: Accessibility is a general term used to describe the degree to which a device, system, service, or environment is available and accessible to the most people possible.

Design for All: Design for All emerges from a development and construction perspective that can contribute to a full accessibility in society. Designing for All is developing for human diversity, social inclusion and equality. It enables all people to have equal opportunities to participate in all aspects of life in society. To accomplish this, everything that is developed, in particular, the environment, day to day life objects, culture and information, should be accessible and designed for everyone, regardless of their individual differences.

Research Methodology: A Research Methodology is a way to systematically solve the research problem. It consists in the various steps that are generally adopted by a researcher in studying his research problem along with the logic behind them. It is necessary for the researcher to know not only the research methods/techniques but also the methodology.

Research Methods: Research Methods may be understood as all those methods/techniques that are used for conduction of research. Research methods or techniques thus refer to the procedures the researchers use in performing research operations.

Service: Service is composed by one or more systems integrated in a well-structured organizational environment.

System: System is a set of interacting or interdependent components able to react to surrounding stimulus (inputs). Systematic Review – A Systematic Review is a standard procedure to identify and summarize the existing evidence in a specific area, increasing the probability of finding relevant literature, improving reproducibility and decreasing review bias.

Usability: Usability is the extent to which a system or service may be used by specific users in a given context of use, to achieve particular goals with efficiency and effectiveness, while promoting feelings of pleasure. Usability is a fundamental aspect to consider in the development cycle of systems or services that necessarily have to be framed by the characteristics of users, tasks to perform, and the surrounding context (social, organizational and physical).

User Centered Design: User Centered Design is a development approach of interactive systems that focus specifically on making systems usable. It is a multi-disciplinary activity that incorporates human factors ergonomics knowledge, involving human resources, skills, limitations and needs. It should focus on the users' characteristics and needs, and must be applied since the beginning of the development process, to create useful and easy to use applications.

Usability Controlled Experiments Methodologies: Usability Controlled Experiments Methodologies consist in the application of the scientific method to test hypotheses with real users through the control of variables and use samples big enough to determine statistical significance.

Usability Evaluation Method: A usability evaluation method identifies the processes, means or modes of data collection required to evaluate the usability of a system or service.

Usability Evaluation Methodology: Usability Evaluation Methodology is the systematization of the methods used to structure, plan and control the process of usability evaluation.

User Experience: User Experience encompasses all aspects of end-user interaction with the system or service. The first requirement for a great user experience is to respond exactly to user's specific needs, without confusing or discomfort. After that, the simplicity and elegance makes users happy to own and use the system or service.

Usability Inspection Methodologies: Usability Inspection Methodologies involve the participation of experts to assess the various aspects of the user interaction.

Usability Inquiry Methodologies: Usability Inquiry Methodologies the collecting of qualitative data from users in order to understand what they want.

Usability Test Methodologies: Usability Test Methodologies consist in the observation and measure of the user interaction and consist of collecting mostly quantitative data from users, while they perform predefined tasks in order to seek empirical evidence about how to improve the user interaction.

Chapter 14
Personas and Scenarios Based on Functioning and Health Conditions

Alexandra Queirós
University of Aveiro, Portugal

Anabela G. Silva
University of Aveiro, Portugal

Margarida Cerqueira
University of Aveiro, Portugal

Joaquim Alvarelhão
University of Aveiro, Portugal

Ana Isabel Martins
University of Aveiro, Portugal

Nelson Pacheco Rocha
University of Aveiro, Portugal

ABSTRACT

This chapter presents how the concepts of the International Classification of Functioning, Disability, and Health (ICF) can be used to optimize the role of personas and scenarios in the development and evaluation of Ambient Assisted Living (AAL) systems and services, especially in aspects related to human functioning and health conditions.

INTRODUCTION

The development of technological solutions with natural and effective user interaction mechanisms can facilitate the daily lives of older people, decrease isolation and info-exclusion, promote the ability to work, as well as independence and wellbeing. The ageing population, the increase in caregiver burden and the importance of living independently motivate the development of Ambient Assisted Living (AAL) systems and services (Cook & Das, 2007). AAL solutions must have

a broad range of intelligent functions in terms of user interaction, supported by usable and accessible interfaces with adaptive mechanisms (Cook & Das, 2007).

A recent systematic literature review (Queirós, Silva, Alvarelhão, Rocha & Teixeira, 2013) shows that usability and accessibility issues are not sufficiently considered within the AAL domain. Furthermore, AAL systems and services have complex interaction mechanisms, including explicit and implicit interactions, and multimodality is a fundamental aspect. Therefore, more discus-

DOI: 10.4018/978-1-4666-6485-2.ch014

sion is needed on the issues around usability and accessibility.

A close involvement of the end-users is crucial to improve usability and accessibility. However, this is less successful when the user population is heterogeneous and, for example, the involvement of older and disabled people introduces additional difficulties (Astell, Alm, Gowans, Ellis, Dye & Vaughan, 2009; Newell, Gregor, Morgan, Pullin & Macaulay, 2011). Moreover, procedures to identify requirements and collect evaluation data from older and disabled people are not straightforward and monitoring and interacting with them in their home environments, rather than in a workplace, have additional challenges (Goodman-Deane, Keith & Whitney, 2008; Zajicek, 2004).

Considering that potential end-users of AAL systems and services are older people, health conditions are important factors. Furthermore, AAL aims to increase the autonomy of older people, to assist in their day-to-day activities and, consequently, to improve their functioning and quality of life. Therefore, the use of systematic mechanisms to characterize issues related to functioning and health conditions and their impact in terms of quality of life should be a major concern.

This paper presents how the conceptual framework of the International Classification of Functioning, Disability and Health (ICF) (WHO, 2001) of the World Health Organization (WHO) can be used to optimize the role of personas and scenarios in the development of AAL solutions. Special attention is given to aspects related to human functioning and health conditions.

In addition to Introduction, the paper is composed of more five sections: Background, Related Work, Methods, Results and Discussion.

BACKGROUND

AAL is being considered one of the important concerns for applied engineering (Kleinberger, Becker, Ras, Holzinger & Müller, 2007) where safety, contextualization, transparency, accessi-

bility, usability and artificial intelligence play a major role. The general goal of AAL solutions is to apply the Ambient Intelligence (AmI) concepts and technologies to enable older adults, or other people with specific demands, to live longer in their natural environment. In technological terms, the AAL comprises a heterogeneous field of applications ranging from quite simple devices such as intelligent medication dispensers, bed sensors or falls detectors (Lombardi, Ferri, Rescio, Grassi & Malcovati, 2009) to complex systems such as the combine use of different technologies to predict user's affective and cognitive states (Kapoor, 2010; Leon, Clarke, Callaghan & Doctor, 2010).

The AAL concerns and developments are in line with the WHO active ageing framework (WHO, 2002). To overcome the pressures resulting from the demographic ageing, WHO argues that governments, international organizations and civil society should promote active ageing policies and programmes. Active ageing depends on a variety of influences or determinants that surround individuals, families and nations related with personal characteristics, culture and gender, but also with societal characteristics and infra-structures (*e.g.* physical environments, support services or social and economic contexts).

In terms of individual perspective, the three basic pillars of active ageing are (WHO, 2002):

- The full participation in socioeconomic, cultural, spiritual and civic affairs, according to basic human rights, capacities, needs and preferences.
- The access to the entire range of health and social services that address the needs and rights of the older adults.
- The protection, dignity and care in events that older adults are no longer able to support and protect themselves.

Therefore, the implementation of active ageing emphasizes the rights of people to equality of opportunity and treatment in all aspects of life as they grow older and also a positive thinking about enablement instead of disablement: a disabling perspective increases the needs of older people and leads to isolation and dependence, while an enabling perspective focuses on restoring functions and expanding the participation of the older adults in all aspects of society (WHO, 2002). AAL is an example of enablement instruments in accordance with the active ageing perspective. This is essential, considering the facts that as people age their quality of life (perception of the position in life in the context of the surrounding culture and value system) is largely determined by their ability to maintain autonomy (ability to control, cope with and make personal decisions about how one lives on a day-to-day basis) and independence (commonly understood as the ability to perform functions related to daily living with no and/or little help from others) (WHO, 2002).

Dependency is strongly related with the ability to perform Activities of Daily Living (ADL). The impossibility of performing basic ADL (*e.g.* personal hygiene, dressing and undressing, self feeding, functional transfers or ambulation) or instrumental ADL (*e.g.* housekeeping, taking medications as prescribed, managing money, shopping for groceries or clothing, use of telephone or other form of communication or transportation within the community) usually implies that the individual (although, in some circumstances, living alone) is in the border of dependency and needs help and support. It is clear that AAL applications can not supply these needs completely but they can mitigate the effects by means of specialized applications (*e.g.* an electronic commerce solution for shopping or a well-managed external housekeeping service) (PERSONA, 2008). AAL systems described in the literature are intended for use both indoor and outdoor in any environment or at home (Queirós *et al.*, 2013; Paterno, Santoro & Scorcia, 2010; Yao-Jen & Tsen-Yung, 2010). Some of them are being conceived to be used for independent living (Bell & Dourish, 2007) with the general aim of increasing the performance of older adults in a broad spectrum of activities: personal

care, self feeding (*e.g.* planning the weekly menu or nutritional adviser (Lazaro, Fides, Navarro & Guille, 2010), household management (Boll, Heuten, Meyer & Meis, 2010) taking medications as prescribed, ambulation (Krieg-Brückner, Röfer, Shi & Gersdorf, 2010) or shopping (Keegan, O'Hare & O'Grady, 2008). Additionally, with the objective of directly or indirectly improve the individual's quality of life AAL systems can contribute to the individual participation in society: social participation, extending professional life or entertainment. Finally, AAL systems can contribute to the reorientation in health systems (Botella, Garcia-Palacios, Baños & Quero, 2009) that are currently organized around acute, episodic experiences of disease, namely, by allowing the development of a broad range of services such as care prevention, care promotion or home-caregiver support, either by health professionals or by any formal or non-formal caregiver (Alcañiz, Botella, Baños, Zaragoza & Guixeres, 2009). The ultimate goals are to provide distance support (*e.g.* distance training (Plischke & Kohls, 2009) or telerehabilitation programs (Kairy, Lehoux, Vincent & Visintin, 2009)) or to provide the caregiver with accurate, up to date information (Dadlani, Sinitsyn, Fontijn & Markopoulos, 2011) so that the right care at the right time can be delivered (*e.g.* monitoring and controlling biological signs, behavior's or emotions (Fanucci, Pardini, Costalli, Dalmiani, Salinas, De La Higuera, Vukovic & Cicigoj, 2009; Fayn & Rubel, 2010)).

Other class of devices that are being included in AAL environments arose during the last years. Networked, ubiquitous robotic systems that convey data and physical actions (*e.g.* motion and forces) can pave the way to innovative products. Based on the analysis of the capabilities of various types of robots, it can be foreseen enormous possibilities to use their capacity to interact with humans within AAL applications (ISTAG, 2009). One of the main challenges concerning robotics is to humanize the robots. Published research (Koch, Jung, Wettach, Nemeth & Berns, 2008) conceptualizes robots as a part of an intelligent environment where the robot does not only offer its own features via natural speech interaction but also becomes an interface agent between users and smart environments.

Since an AAL environment comprises numerous ubiquitous devices and systems, effective development frameworks are required to mask the effects of heterogeneous physical devices, communication networks, intelligent components and applications. The development frameworks comprise suitable implementation architectures and development methodologies to enable efficient engineering, deployment, and run-time management of reconfigurable AAL systems (Berger, Dittmann, Caragiozidis, Mouratidis, Kavadias & Loupis, 2008; Stuikys & Damasevicius, 2007).

The AAL implementation architectures must deal with the complexity associated, in part, to the amount of different devices that need to be seamlessly integrated in a common and homogeneous environment, despite the fact of each device having its own characteristics (Carneiro, Novais, Costa, Gomes & Neves, 2009). Furthermore, they also must consider the availability of the devices and components needed for every intended service and must also know some other important characteristics about the services they are supporting (as the geographic location, the cost or the probable effects), so that when a specific services is suggested to particular users, the suggesting must correspond to the most adequate services to those specific situation. Finally, AAL architectures should present suitable solutions for safety (Coronato & De Pietro, 2010), security (Esquivel, Haya, García-Herranz & Alamán, 2009) and privacy (Un & Price, 2007), consider both the individual and the context, in order to provide the user with the adequate support.

In terms of architectures, different types of conceptualization can be found, namely multi-agent architectures with multiple control algorithms as agents for managing different tasks (Wang, Abdulla & Salcic, 2009), services oriented architectures, which allow developing software as services delivered and consumed on demand (Janse, Vink & Georgantas, 2008), or combination of both (Goumopoulos & Kameas, 2009).

The development of AAL systems requires appropriate user-centered design methodologies (Ahram, Karwowski & Amaba, 2010). Therefore, a key step in the development of the AAL paradigm is the availability of efficient development methodologies considering the definition of the requirements of different user's profiles (*e.g.* older adults, theirs relatives and theirs formal and informal care providers), different types of tasks and different usage contexts (Oberzaucher, Werner, Mairbock, Beck, Panek, Hlauschek & Zagler, 2009; Un & Price, 2007). This is crucial for ALL be able to correspond to its expectations.

The acceptance of the AAL paradigm is, obviously, closing related with the quality of the available services. The AAL paradigm has a wide scope application. It intends to provide applications to enable active aging at home, workplace and community, to contribute to the autonomy, independence and quality of life of older adults, to improve their participation in social activities and to reduce the costs of health services and social support services. This wide scope of the AAL paradigm put a strong pressure in the need of adequate development and evaluation methodologies (Connelly, Siek, Mulder, Neely, Stevenson & Kray, 2008). Furthermore, ethical and legal issues associated with the AAL must be considered (De Hert, Gutwirth, Moscibroda, Wright & Fuster, 2009; Lehikoinen, Lehikoinen & Huuskonen, 2008; Remmers, 2010).

RELATED WORK

User centred design (ISO, 2010) requires powerful tools to retrieve, visualize, analyse and communicate user needs and requirements (Guðjónsdóttir, 2010). Cooper (1999) proposed the personas and scenarios method to bridge this gap and to facilitate the understanding of user needs and desires throughout the whole system development process (Guðjónsdóttir, 2010; Miaskiewicz & Kozar, 2011). This method was significantly developed by several authors (Nielsen, 2004; Pruitt & Adlin, 2006) and it is considered by researchers and practitioners (Blomquist & Arvola, 2002; Cooper, 1999; Pruitt & Grudin, 2003; Sinha, 2003) that it might have potential to include end-user information during the systems development process (Rönkkö, 2005).

A persona is an archetype that should be a precise description of a hypothetical user (with a given name and a face) and his or her needs, goals and tasks (Blomquist & Arvola, 2002). On the other hand, scenarios are stories with settings, personas who have needs and goals and a sequence of events and tasks (Pruitt & Grudin, 2003). During the development process it is supposed that the persona's needs and goals will be achieved, which can contribute to offer the right product to the right person (Blomquist & Arvola, 2002).

Given the available methods, there are many alternatives that can be considered as a starting point for the definition of personas and scenarios: ethnographic studies, market research, usability studies, interviews, questionnaires, observational studies, focus groups, brainstorming, nominal groups or diaries.

The information gathered through these methods allows systematization for different persona's characteristics and the elaboration for different scenario's requirements. The definition of the personas implies the transformation of abstract concepts into a more objective and understandable framework (Faily & Fléchais, 2010; Marcengo, Guercio & Rapp, 2009; Mulder & Yaar, 2007; Pruitt & Grudin, 2003; Siegel, 2010; Wöckl, Yildizoglu, Buber, Aparicio, Kruijff & Tscheligi, 2012) (*i.e.* the information should be summed up to create different personas). Pruitt and Grudin (2003) propose the rigorous study of end users to create personas, linking them to foundational documents, which include data from the studies

used to inform the development of personas (data, key attributes or reference materials) (Matthews, Judge & Whittaker, 2012; Pruitt & Grudin, 2003).

Moreover, the information should be presented as if personas are real people (Long, 2009), what requires selecting and adding photos or drawings to support the textual information.

Each persona has several personal goals to achieve and the scenarios are written to show how involved personas could accomplish these goals using the system or service being developed (Cooper, 1999; Guðjónsdóttir, 2010; Pruitt & Adlin, 2006). Therefore, scenarios are beneficial to completing the personas. Particularly, scenarios can be used to build the stories of the intended users and how the system being developed assists them in their work or leisure activities (Guðjónsdóttir, 2010).

One of the important criticisms to the personas and scenarios method is the lack of research demonstrating its effectiveness (Guðjónsdóttir, 2010). The few research studies that have been conducted, namely related to the use of personas by small project teams in short, focused field studies (Cooper & Reimann, 2003; Matthews, Judge & Whittaker, 2012; Rönkkö, 2005), or sessions facilitated by the researchers (Chang, Lim & Stolterman, 2008; Dotan, Maiden, Lichtner & Germanovich, 2009; Nielsen, 2004), demonstrate that personas possess some advantages (Matthews, Judge & Whittaker, 2012). However, Blomquist & Arvola (2002) have conducted a twelve-week participant observation study using personas and showed that they never became a natural part of the project. Additionally, Rönkkö (2005) instructed three 17-member student design teams to use personas during their design processes and to communicate with a development team and found that the students were hesitant to replace the users with personas for design work. This study suggested that personas are primarily useful for communicating end-user characteristics and design decisions to developers (Matthews, Judge & Whittaker, 2012).

Nevertheless, during the last decade, the personas and scenarios method became increasingly popular for the development of a broad range of solutions (Guðjónsdóttir, 2010). This strong impact of personas and scenarios is due to the fact that the method helps to achieve several goals. First, since personas have names and often include visually rich information (*e.g.* photos or real-life characteristics of the end-users) and bring sociopolitical issues to discussion (each persona has a set of attributes, namely, gender, age, ethnicity, family or cohabitation arrangements, socio-economic background and work or home environment (Pruitt & Grudin, 2003) they can act as concrete representations of the needs and goals that the development process should meet (Blomquist & Arvola, 2002). Therefore, designers and developers can gain insights on end user's characteristics and have a more realistic idea about them without being influenced by personal biases (Blomquist & Arvola, 2002). Furthermore, personas help designers and developers to focus their attention sequentially on different kinds of users (Pruitt & Grudin, 2003), because the method helps to establish who it is (and consequently who is not) being developed for. This is important in the development process because focusing on personas the designers and developers can avoid the problem of invoking the 'elastic user' who can be bent and stretched to suit the needs of the invoker (Matthews, Judge & Whittaker, 2012).

Second, personas are means of communication, both within and outside the development team (Cooper, 1999; Cooper & Reimann, 2003; Matthews, Judge & Whittaker, 2012; Pruitt & Adlin, 2006; Pruitt & Grudin, 2003). Personas and scenarios can engage teams in thinking about users during the development process, making efficient decisions without inappropriate generalization, and communicating about users to various stakeholders (Cooper, 1999; Cooper & Reimann, 2003; Goodwin & Cooper, 2009; Matthews, Judge & Whittaker, 2012; Pruitt & Adlin, 2006; Pruitt & Grudin, 2003). The method seems

to provide an opportunity for all members of the project to focus on the same thing, as it did during critique meetings (Matthews, Judge & Whittaker, 2012). They are especially useful in aligning large development teams towards specific user issues, making decisions about requirements, and arguing for particular approaches easier (Matthews, Judge & Whittaker, 2012). A persona helps the developer to empathize with the users, to understand their behaviours and deeper needs, which means that it can act as a communication tool to build support for a chosen solution or more generally to advocate user needs (Matthews, Judge & Whittaker, 2012).

Finally, in later phases of the development process, the explicit needs, goals and experience that are expressed in the personas can also be useful tools when using empirical or analytical usability evaluation methods (Blomquist & Arvola, 2002). In particular, the scenarios developed to support the personas can be used in usability evaluations, where they can be the basis for writing test cases.

The literature shows that the personas and scenarios method is being applied in several areas, either related to simple interactions (*e.g.* web interaction) (Mulder & Yaar, 2007) or complex collaborative interactions (*e.g.* collaborative personas were used to develop reusable design tools for collaboration (Judge, Matthews & Whittaker, 2012)) and specific target users (*e.g.* children's (Antle, 2006) or teenagers (Horton, Read, Fitton, Toth & Little, 2012)). Concerning older and disabled people, there are personas that consider accessibility information (Pruitt & Grudin, 2003), while others are used to represent disabled people (Schulz & Fuglerud, 2012).

Significant research and development efforts are being made related to information technologies based systems and services for older people, where the usability is a major concern. The importance of following a user centred approach and the use of personas and scenarios are reported by various researchers (Budde, Stulp & Sancho-Pradel, 2008; Picking, Robinet, Grout, McGinn, Roy, Ellis & Oram, 2009; Rönkkö, 2005; Sellner, Tschelig,

Moser, Fuchsberger & Neureiter, 2012; Sinha, 2003). In particular Bernhard Wöckl *et al.* (2012) have developed a set of 36 senior personas covering a broad range of characteristics of European older adults. These personas include the discrimination of technological skills and health conditions, and are prepared to be re-used in the development of different information technologies based solutions, including AAL systems and services.

METHODS

Considering that potential end-users of AAL systems and services are older people, health conditions are important factors. Furthermore, AAL aims to increase the autonomy of older people, to assist their daily living activities, improving, therefore, their functioning and quality of life.

Thus, in terms of methodological approach, the personas and scenarios models proposed by Cooper (1999) (the research baseline) were modified, considering the fundamental concepts of the ICF, in order to highlight user's functioning and health conditions. As it was mentioned before, personas, despite being fictitious, must be precisely and accurately defined from detailed knowledge about the target population (Cooper, 1999). The details are important to promote a consistent view of potential end-users among all stakeholders, allowing a humanized perspective. Therefore, it is necessary to consider various aspects:

- The characteristics of the potential users of the system or service being developed and what roles they can play.
- The potential user's needs and behaviours, and how these may vary over time.
- The potential user's motivations and expectations in respect of the systems or services being developed.

In the development of AAL systems and services, scenarios typically describe how a given system or service can be used, in a given context and in a given period of time. They should provide the surrounding contexts that need to be explored, the identification of situations or events that might have an impact on personas and different types of requirements, namely information, actions, technological, interaction (*i.e.* what kind of precautions should be considered in the management of the interaction mechanisms that may vary according to the scenarios being considered), business or corporate requirements.

To determine what concepts should be used to enrich the personas and scenarios baseline, a revision of the ICF was performed.

The ICF offers a framework for conceptualizing functioning associated to health conditions (Peterson, 2005) and it considers that many factors affect and have influence on the individual's performance and thereby on the decisions made on what type of service is needed either delivered by care staff, relatives, aid appliances and technology.

In practice, there is not a large separation between the determination of a need, analysis, partial conclusion and decision. For this reason it can be difficult to systemize the information that can influence a decision; however, this systematization is important when the decisions have to be classified.

The ICF structure separates between the body, activities, participation and contextual factors (WHO, 2001) as part of the individual's functioning. Additionally, it considers the context (environmental factors and personal factors) as components that can enhance or limit the performance, depending on how the individual experiences limitations (*e.g.* due to possible weakness, illness and/or handicap).

Following there is a description of each of the ICF elements (WHO, 2001):

- **Activities:** Activities are the individual's recital of assignments and tasks. Difficulties with these activities are noted as activity limitations. Limitations are usually due to function depreciation of bodily functions but also due to environmental hindrances.

When the individual's ability to do activities is evaluated the consequences of function depreciation or environmental barriers become clear.

- **Participation:** Participation covers the individual's involvement in daily life and society. Difficulties in participation are classified as participation restrictions. The same way as activities limitations, the participation restrictions can be caused by weakness, illness and/or handicap but also due to environmental hindrances. There is also a restriction when the individual is not being able to do activities according to with his or her own norms of what is considered acceptable.

- **Body Functions and Structures:** The body's functions entail the individual's physiological functions and the body structures correspond to the human anatomical structures. ICF defines disability as any problem of the individual with his or her bodily functions. Physical functions depreciations can, in principle, have no consequences for the individual's ability to do activities, especially if there is a help aid that compensates a particular function depreciation (*e.g.* a individual with weak eyesight wearing glasses would not have a limitation; a individual with a missing leg with a prosthesis will be able to do activities).

- **Contextual Factors:** The contextual factors are the environmental and personal factors which either enhance or limit the individual's functioning. These factors are indirectly understood in the sections of evaluation of activities and participation; however, they are important to explain certain situations (*e.g.* two individuals with the same diagnosis or physical function depreciation may have different limitations when it comes to activities and participation). The environmental factors are the physical, social or attitudinal world ranging from the immediate to more general environment. The personal factors entail elements that make people different and unique, such as life style, education level, sex, race, life events or psychological characteristics.

Differences in mastering capacity are a possible explanation to why individuals with the same physical function depreciations do not have the same limitations when performing various activities. For example, when it is windy outside, some individuals will put up wind shelters, whilst others put up windmills. Dependently on whether one looks upon changes as strenuous or as a challenge which contain new options.

The ICF divides the environmental factors into five chapters: products and technology; natural environment and human-made changes to environment; support and relationships; attitudes; services, systems and policies. These factors can have a positive (*i.e.* be facilitators) or negative impact (*i.e.* be barriers) on the individual's performance as a member of society, on the individual's capacity to execute actions or tasks, or on the individual's body function or structure. When coding an environmental factor as a facilitator, issues such as the accessibility of the resource, and whether access is dependable or variable, of good or poor quality, should be considered.

The classification has individual items or codes defined within each chapter. The ICF contains 1,424 codes organized according to an alphanumeric system. Each code begins with a letter that corresponds to its component domain: b (Body Functions), s (Body Structures), d (Activities and Participation) or e (Environmental Factors). The letter is followed by between one and five numeric digits. Items are organized as a nested system so that users can telescope from broad to very detailed items depending upon the needs presented by particular applications of the ICF. The broadest descriptor of functioning is represented by the chapter (domain) in which the item appears. For example, chapter 5 of the Activities and Participation (d) component of the ICF is Self-care. The next level of coding is what the ICF refers to as the second level of detail or specification. These codes consist of the letter indicating the component domain (b, s, d, or e) followed by three numeric digits. The first numeric digit always corresponds to chapter in that component domain in which the code is found. Within the Self-care chapter, the code Dressing d540 represents the second level of detail.

The ICF Short Version consists of codes at the second level of detail (*i.e.* a letter plus three digits). In the full version of the ICF, more detailed codes with four digits (third level of detail) are found under most three-digit codes. In some cases, there are even more specific and detailed codes that contain five numeric digits (fourth level of detail). For example, in the full version of the ICF, the codes Taking off footwear d5403 and Choosing appropriate clothing d5404 are among the separate components or sub codes under Dressing d540 (Peterson, 2005).

The existence of a conceptual framework based on standardized concepts can provide a common language between strategic planners, technological innovators, care providers and users for the development of new services in general and, in particular, new AAL services.

The aforementioned ICF concepts can be used, within personas definition, to consider and structure aspects such as:

- The relevant aspects of health conditions that may constrain the systems or services use.
- The body's structures and functions.
- Activities and participation.
- Contextual factors, both environmental factors (including technological systems and services) and personal factors (*i.e.* what is normally considered in personas

definition, such as the specific life history, the individual lifestyle or the daily tasks).

Finally, since ICF considers that the individual's functioning results of his/her own health conditions interacting with his contextual factors (Alvarelhão, Silva, Martins, Queirós, Amaro, Rocha & Laíns, 2012), this dynamic interaction is important for scenario's definition. The description of a narrative of events or experienced situations by a persona (a persona can remain unchanged, but the scenario demands change in the use of systems and services) can be enriched by the identification, in a given situation, of the factors or of the positive or negative events (facilitators or barriers, according to ICF) that impact on activity and participation of personas. In the case of barriers, it might be relevant to take into account how often a factor hinders the person, whether the hindrance is great or small, or avoidable or not. It should also be kept in mind that an environmental factor can be a barrier either because of its presence (*e.g.* negative attitudes towards people) or its absence (*e.g.* the unavailability of a needed service).

RESULTS

The persona Emília Rodrigues (Table 1) was developed according to the principles proposed by Cooper (1999). When analysing the description of the persona, we can easily see that the personal history consists of a set of personal characteristics and description of some aspects of daily routine. In particular, some information appears described in various ways. This is the case of occupation that is referred in the topic Occupation and in the topic Personal History ("... especially in her household management"). On the other hand, the points related to health conditions are focused on an existing pathology. Finally, it is possible to state a negative point of view, as we can see by the discrimination of possible frustrations.

Table 1. Example of a persona

Persona Emília Rodrigues
Persona: Principal. Name: Emília Rodrigues. Age: 62 years old. Location: Coimbra. Technological Proficiency: Insufficient computer skills. Occupation: Housewife.
Personal History: Emília is married to Filipe Rodrigues and has one daughter, Júlia, already married. In the evening, she usually calls her daughter while preparing the dinner to chat a little bit. Sometimes she has difficulties in holding or manipulating the telephone handset due to an arthritic condition of her right superior limb. Furthermore, the telephone network is not reliable and sometimes she needs to repeat the call. Because Emília is right handed the arthritis impacts her life, especially in tasks related to the management of her household. She loves to do handcraft. In the past, she uses to spend hours making presents to her relatives and friends. Nowadays, it is much more difficult. She also suffers from diabetes. Because of this chronic disease, Emília needs a daily medication plan and frequent appointments with her General Practitioner. As she is a sick person she rarely leaves her house to meet relatives and friends.
Motivation: Emília would like to talk to her daughter in an easier way, while she is preparing the dinner, because at that time her daughter is available. She is also interested in something that could remind her to take her medication on time.
Frustrations: Although she had several tips from friends to remember to take her medication correctly, nothing works. She often forgets to take her medication on time.
Quote:

In the persona models proposed by the authors, there is a concern to identify additional groups of information:

- **Personal Factors:** Individual's life history and characteristics (*e.g.* she loves to do handcraft). Personal factors have consequences on the daily routine (*e.g.* "In the evening, she usually calls her daughter while preparing the dinner to chat a little bit").

- **Health Conditions:** Generic term for diseases (acute or chronic), disturbance, injuries or traumas. Health conditions should not be understood only as a disease, but also as specific features which are present in the persona, and that will restrain the use of the systems or services. It may also include other circumstances like stress, ageing, congenital abnormality or predisposition (*e.g.* Emília has mobility limitations in her right superior limb, due to an arthritic condition).

- **Activity Type:** Task execution or action of an individual (*e.g.* preparing the dinner).

- **Participation Type:** Involvement of the individual in a real life situation (*e.g.* to meet relatives and friends or household management).

- **Environmental Factors:** The physical, social or attitudinal world ranging from the immediate to the more general environment (*e.g.* the telephone network is not reliable and that implicates that sometimes Emília needs to repeat the call).

Therefore, instead of the heterogeneous personal history, the authors propose a clear distinction between personal factors and daily routine, because this information is considered essential in the context of AAL systems and services. On the other hand, the authors strongly suggest the use of a neutral perspective associated to the ICF (only those facts that determine the functioning or performance should be identified), which requires a careful description. For instance, instead of referring to "Since she is a sick person she rarely leave her house to meet relatives and friends" we should refer "she rarely leaves her house to meet relatives and friends", *i.e.* only neutral information. In this perspective, there can be no references to frustrations, but only abilities and personal factors.

In terms of health conditions, these should not appear associated to a deficiency in body structures or functions or to an existing pathology, but rather to a holistic perspective. Often a limitation in activities or a restriction in participation is due to health conditions, but they are also influenced by the context in which the activities or participation are held. The definition of a persona using ICF concepts should clarify what health conditions and context situations might interfere with the performance of the individual along with the description of his or her daily routine and participation types. Incidentally, the concept of participation appears as something innovative in the elaboration of personas, because it is more

complex than activity as it contains information related to a life event.

The modified version of the persona Emília Rodrigues (Table 2) includes personal factors that might influence the way she interacts with the systems and services: Emília has 62 years old, lives with her husband, has insufficient computer skills and is a housewife. According to this information the interaction may have to be simplified due to her limitations in terms of computer literacy.

The daily routine is also an important element for the definition of personas as it will constrain the use of the available systems and services. In the current example, Emília has the habit of calling her daughter while she is preparing the dinner. This means that preparing the dinner can interfere with the interaction with the telephone.

The health conditions are associated to relevant information that will impact the performance of some activities and participation. For example, Emília has diabetes and arthritis and these can interfere with the functions and interaction of systems and services. On the other hand, activities and participation turn out to be implicit in health

Table 2. Modified version of the persona Emília Rodrigues

Persona Emília Rodrigues
Name: Emília Rodrigues [Personal factor]. Age: 62 years old [Personal factor].
Emília lives in Coimbra with her husband Filipe Rodrigues. She is a housewife [Personal factor].
Emília does not know very well how to work with electronic devices [Personal factor]. She is right handed [Personal factor].
She loves to do handcraft [Personal factor].
She is diabetic and has arthritis in her right superior limb [Health conditions].
In the past, she uses to spend hours handcrafting presents to her relatives and friends [Activity type]. Nowadays, it is much more difficult.
Emília needs a daily medication plan and frequent appointments with her General Practitioner [Daily Routine].
Emília rarely leaves her house to meet relatives and friends [Participation type].
Emília has the habit of calling her daughter while she is preparing dinner [Participation type]. However, she has some difficulty in doing both activities at the same time due to her limitation in the right superior limb.
The telephone network is not reliable and, therefore, Emília needs sometimes to repeat the call [Environmental factor].
Emília would like to have a hand-free telephone to contact her daughter. Furthermore, she would like a system to help her to control the medication [Activity type].

conditions. For example, the regular surveillance of her chronic diseases has impact in her daily routine.

The case of participation is similar to activities since they may result from variations in health conditions and daily routine, or be identified as specific interests (*e.g.* Emília wants to take medication on time).

As mentioned before, the definition of scenarios should also consider all the existing information on the needs of the target users, in order to specify the functional requirements of the system or service being developed:

- **Problem Scenario:** Identification of the actual situation, events (positive or negative) that have impact on personas activities. For example, the voice interaction is a barrier in a noisy environment or the keyboard is big enough to facilitate the writing of a SMS.
- **Information Requirement:** Information units that the systems have to include. For example, in an email application the basic elements can be messages or contacts.
- **Functional Requirement:** Actions that the systems have to complete, information that the systems have to present, as well technological requirements, considering the relevance that may have in the system's performance. For example, the characteristics of a specific technology.

- **Interaction Requirement:** Detailed information about how the user interaction should be, which can vary according to the created scenario, even if there is no alteration in user's characteristics.
- **Other Requirement:** Business, corporative or customer requirements. For example, prices or installation conditions of a specific system or service.

When developing a scenario, such as the scenario of Table 3, the identification of the problem is an important issue because it situates the activity to be performed. For example, Emília usually calls her daughter while she is preparing the dinner, which is a difficult task due to the arthritic condition that causes her pain in the superior limb.

In this example, associated with the identification of the problem, there are some interaction requirements (*e.g.* hand-free telephone). Another identified problem was the need of a system to help her to control the medication. Therefore, Emília needs an easy to use medication alert system that should not interfere with her activities.

The model proposed by the authors can be also be used in personas that have more complex problems in their health conditions. In fact this model can be very useful to identify all the components that compromised the health conditions. This information can be very important for those who develop systems and services for older people, indicating clearly how the interaction and

Table 3. An illustrative example of a scenario for the persona Emília Rodrigues

Emília has diabetes and must take medication on time. Frequently, due to her daily tasks, she takes medication at wrong hours or even forgets to take it. This situation stresses her husband that is tired of being the "nurse" of Emília [Problem scenario].
Emília has to monitor her health conditions, so she needs frequent appointments with her General Practitioner. To visit the General Practitioner she has to take the train and has to check the train timetable [Problem scenario]. Ideally, there should be a service to help her control the appointments. There should also be a service to book the train tickets [Functionality requirements].
Emília has the habit of calling her daughter in the evening, while she is preparing the dinner, because at that time her daughter is available [Problem scenario]. However, since she cannot do everything with her left hand [Interaction requirement], the duration of the call is limited.

the design have to be implemented in order to improve its usability.

The persona Manuel Rocha (Table 4) illustrates how health conditions can be a source of valuable information for the developers. When a body structure is missing this can interfere with the interaction user (Manuel does not have an arm and this can interfere with activities that needs two hands, for instance click in three keys simultaneously). This fact will have repercussion in participation (Manuel stopped playing cards with his neighbours, which affect his social life). The body functions (insomnias or numbness) can lead to a disease and a possible prevention is the maintenance of physical activities. This kind of information can help to develop services to promote physical activities in consonance with daily routines (the numbness of Manuel suggests that he needs to realize more physical activities, but he does not want to miss the soup opera). Another important component that interferes with health conditions and the development of services are the ambient factors (Manuel has economic difficulties and, therefore, he cannot afford a smartphone acquisition).

In terms of model scenario it is important to understand if the requirements are changeable or unchangeable (for instance, the interaction require-

ment for Manuel is unchangeable, because it is related to the arm amputation). It is also important for the functionality requirement to understand what the real user needs (Manuel needs a service that allow him to send good quality images directly to his doctor) and for data requirement (the image must have a good resolution). Personas and scenarios should be used together, given that persona's description is used in scenarios and because some details of scenarios can be explained by persona's information (*e.g.* Manuel can't afford an expensive smartphone) (Table 5).

DISCUSSION

The proposed persona models can be used to define personas with complex health conditions and strong limitations in activities or restrictions in participation. In fact, they are useful to identify all the components related to functioning and not only health conditions. The information related to health conditions, body structures and functions, activity, participation and environmental factors (personal or contextual factors) is important for AAL systems and services designers and developers, in order to guide them through the development process. Furthermore, the proposed models

Table 4. Persona Manuel Rocha

Name: Manuel Rocha Age: 88 years old.
Manuel is a widower and lives in Crasto, Aveiro, where the access is very difficult due to street's bad conditions. He has economic difficulties.
He does a basic use of his cellular phone.
He likes to watch television, especially soups opera.
He had to amputate his left arm due to a bike accident. Manuel suffers from insomnias and numbness that limits his mobility. Recently a spot appeared in his left leg.
Manuel used to play card games with his neighbours every afternoon, but since the amputation he has a sedentary life, sitting all day to watch television or sleeping.
His daughter goes every day, around 06h30m PM, to his home to be with him, and to prepare the dinner and the lunch for the next day.
Manuel would like to walk

Table 5. An illustrative example of a scenario for the persona Manuel Rocha

Manuel amputated his left arm due to a byke accident [Interaction requirement]. This event caused some restrictions in his life, namely in his interpersonal relationships: he gave up the cards game with his neighbors. Manuel really misses the card game and would like to keep up his neighbors even if it was at distance. [Functionality requirement].
The card game was the only physical activity of Manuel (it implies go out, walk through the village, and the arms movement). Nowadays he has a sedentary life, sitting in the sofa and seeing television all the time. Whether by being much time sitting down or sleeping in the afternoon, he usually has insomnias during the night [Problem requirement]. Every day, his visit him for company and to prepare the dinner, as well the lunch for the next day.
Yesterday, he visited his General Practitioner, Dr. Mário. To solve Manuel insomnias problem without medication Dr. Mário suggested that Manuel´s daughter should call him [Functionality requirement] during the afternoon to avoid Manuel to snooze. She should also stimulate him with some games [Data requirement]. Dr. Mário also recommended that he should walk every day. Manuel didn't the idea because he doesn't want to miss his favorite soap operas [Functionality requirement].
Dr. Mário was concerned about the spot in Manuel left leg [Problem requirement]. To be able to follow this problem and to avoid the visit of Manuel to the health center, Dr. Mario suggested Manuel or his daughter to send him a spot's image weekly [Data requirement] to his institutional email [Functionality requirement]. The problem is that Manuel can't afford a smartphone [Other requirements].

are suitable to highlight the dynamic interaction between these factors. For instance, if a body structure or function is missing then there is an interference with the user interaction but also an impact in terms of activity and participation (*e.g.* since Emília has an arthritic condition, she has difficulties in using the telephone while preparing the dinner and this has an impact on the quality of her contacts with her daughter or on her capacity to do handcraft).

One of the concepts that emerge using ICF is a more comprehensive perspective. Although the full ICF terminology is not used (for instance, we do not refer that "Emília has limitation in d3600 Using telecommunication devices", we refer that "it is difficult for her to maintain long telephone conversations", which facilitates the application of the proposed models), the definition of health conditions, body structures and functions, activity and participation and contextual factors are relevant to understand the individual's conditions, routines and needs. This is essential for the personas definition and for the identification of different types of scenario's requirements.

Therefore, the personas and scenarios modified models proved to fulfil the research goals of this paper, *i.e.* to highlight aspects related to functioning and health conditions in the personas and scenarios definition.

One of the problems of the development of AAL systems and services is the difficulty of communication between users, care providers and technological professionals. Stakeholders with different backgrounds need a common language in order to make teamwork more efficient and effective. In this respect, the ICF conceptual framework can contribute for that common language.

A qualitative analysis was performed during the application of the modified personas and scenarios models in various research and development projects (Teixeira *et al.*, 2013a; Teixeira, Ferreira, Almeida, Rosa, Casimiro & Queirós, 2013b). From this qualitative analysis, which considered the opinions of all stakeholders involved in the development process, resulted three different opinions. First, it was clear that most of the health professionals were comfortable using ICF concepts and, moreover, those concepts help to increase their confidence both in the solutions being developed and in the other members of the multidisciplinary team. Second, those designers and developers that did not have experience in working with personas and scenarios easily accepted to apply the new model after the training sessions. Finally, some of the designers and developers experienced with personas and scenarios methodologies demonstrated a firm resistance to the new approach. However, this resistance decreased as the projects progressed. Therefore, the ICF a conceptual framework can be used to facilitate the understanding of the user needs and requirements.

CONCLUSION

The described personas and scenarios models are being used to develop applications on several projects, including telerehabilitation applications (Teixeira *et al.*, 2013a) multimodal applications and smart phone applications (Teixeira *et al.*, 2013b).The developed tools proved suitable for their purposes and are expected to be explored in future developments.

One of the problems of the development of AAL systems and services is the difficulty of communication between users, care providers and technological professionals. Stakeholders with different backgrounds need a common language in order to make teamwork more efficient and effective. The ICF conceptual framework can contribute to this goal. However, there is still a long way to go so that all persons involved in AAL development are able to share a common language and a set of common concepts.

ACKNOWLEDGMENT

This work was supported by COMPETE (Sistema de Incentivos à Investigação e Desenvolvimento Tecnológico, Projetos de I&DT Empresas em co-promoção) and FEDER from the European Union, under QREN Living Usability Lab for Next Generation Networks, QREN AAL4ALL and QREN Smartphones for Seniors.

REFERENCES

Ahram, T. Z., Karwowski, W., & Amaba, B. (2010). User-Centered Systems Engineering Approach to Design and Modeling of Smarter Products. *In Proceedings of System of Systems Engineering* (SoSE), (pp. 1-6). IEEE. doi:10.1109/SYSOSE.2010.5544041

Alcañiz, M., Botella, C., Baños, R. M., Zaragoza, I., & Guixeres, J. (2009). The Intelligent e-Therapy System: A New Paradigm for Telepsychology and Cybertherapy. *British Journal of Guidance & Counselling*, *37*(3), 287–296. doi:10.1080/03069880902957015

Alvarelhão, J., Silva, A., Martins, A., Queirós, A., Amaro, A., Rocha, N., & Laíns, J. (2012). Comparing the Content of Instruments Assessing Environmental Factors using the International Classification of Functioning, Disability and Health. *Journal of Rehabilitation Medicine*, *44*(1), 1–6. doi:10.2340/16501977-0905 PMID:22234318

Antle, A. (2006). Child-Personas: Fact or Fiction? In *Proceedings of the 6th Conference on Designing Interactive Systems* (pp. 22-30). ACM. doi:10.1145/1142405.1142411

Astell, A., Alm, N., Gowans, G., Ellis, M., Dye, R., & Vaughan, P. (2009). Involving Older People with Dementia and their Carers in Designing Computer Based Support Systems: Some Methodological Considerations. *Universal Access in the Information Society*, *8*(1), 49–58. doi:10.1007/s10209-008-0129-9

Bell, G., & Dourish, P. (2007). Yesterday's Tomorrows: Notes on Ubiquitous Computing's Dominant Vision. *Personal and Ubiquitous Computing*, *11*(2), 133–143. doi:10.1007/s00779-006-0071-x

Berger, M., Dittmann, L., Caragiozidis, M., Mouratidis, N., Kavadias, C., & Loupis, M. (2008). A Component-Based Software Architecture: Reconfigurable Software for Ambient Intelligent Networked Services Environments. In *Proceedings of Software and Data Technologies* (ICSOFT) (pp. 174-179). IEEE.

Blomquist, Å., & Arvola, M. (2002). Personas in Action: Ethnography in an Interaction Design Team. In *Proceedings of the 2nd Nordic Conference on Human-Computer Interaction* (pp. 197-200). ACM. doi:10.1145/572020.572044

Boll, S., Heuten, E., Meyer, M., & Meis, M. (2010). Development of a Multimodal Reminder System for Older Persons in their Residential Home. *Informatics for Health & Social Care*, 35(3-4), 104–124. doi:10.3109/17538157.2010.528651 PMID:21133767

Botella, C., Garcia-Palacios, A., Baños, R. M., & Quero, S. (2009). Cybertherapy: Advantages, Limitations, and Ethical Issues. *PsychNology Journal*, 7(1).

Budde, S. H., Stulp, F., & Sancho-Pradel, D. L. (2008). Using Persona Descriptions as a Communication Tool in Interdisciplinary System Design. *Gerontechnology (Valkenswaard)*, 7(2), 82. doi:10.4017/gt.2008.07.02.019.00

Carneiro, D., Novais, P., Costa, R., Gomes, P., & Neves, J. (2009). EMon: Embodied Monitorization. In Ambient Intelligence (pp. 133-142). Springer.

Chang, Y., Lim, Y., & Stolterman, E. (2008). Personas: From Theory to Practices. In *Proceedings of the 5th Nordic Conference on Human-Computer Interaction: Building Bridges* (pp. 439-442). ACM.

Connelly, K., Siek, K., Mulder, I., Neely, S., Stevenson, G., & Kray, C. (2008). Evaluating Pervasive and Ubiquitous Systems. *Pervasive Computing, IEEE*, 7(3), 85–88. doi:10.1109/MPRV.2008.47

Cook, D., & Das, S. (2007). How Smart are our Environments? An Updated Look at the State of the Art. *Pervasive and Mobile Computing*, 3(2), 53–73. doi:10.1016/j.pmcj.2006.12.001

Cooper, A. (1999). *The Inmates are Running the Asylum: Why High-Tech Products Drive us Crazy and How to Restore the Sanity*. Pearson Education. doi:10.1007/978-3-322-99786-9_1

Cooper, A., & Reimann, R. (2003). *About Face 2.0: The Essentials of Interaction Design*. John Wiley & Sons.

Coronato, A., & De Pietro, G. (2010). A Middleware Architecture for Safety Critical Ambient Intelligence Applications. In Proceedings of Smart Spaces and Next Generation Wired/Wireless Networking (pp. 26-37). Springer. doi:10.1007/978-3-642-14891-0_3

Dadlani, P., Sinitsyn, A., Fontijn, W., & Markopoulos, P. (2011). Aurama: Caregiver Awareness for Living Independently with an Augmented Picture Frame Display. *AI & Society*, 25(2), 233–245. doi:10.1007/s00146-009-0253-y

De Hert, P., Gutwirth, S., Moscibroda, A., Wright, D., & Fuster, G. (2009). Legal Safeguards for Privacy and Data Protection in Ambient Intelligence. *Personal and Ubiquitous Computing*, 13(6), 435–444. doi:10.1007/s00779-008-0211-6

Dotan, A., Maiden, N., Lichtner, V., & Germanovich, L. (2009). Designing with only Four People in Mind? A Case Study of Using Personas to Redesign a Work Integrated Learning Support System. In Human-Computer Interaction - INTERACT 2009 (pp. 497-509). Springer.

Esquivel, A., Haya, P., García-Herranz, M., & Alamán, X. (2009). Harnessing "Fair Trade" Metaphor as Privacy Control in Ambient Intelligent. In *Ambient Intelligence Perspectives: Selected Papers from the 1st International Ambient Intelligence Forum, 2008* (Vol. 1, p. 73). IOS Press.

Faily, S., & Fléchais, I. (2010). The Secret Lives of Assumptions: Developing and Refining Assumption Personas for Secure System Design. In Human-Centred Software Engineering (pp. 111-118). Springer.

Fanucci, L., Pardini, G., Costalli, F., Dalmiani, S., Salinas, J., & De La Higuera, J. et al. (2009). Health @ Home: A New Homecare Model for Patients with Chronic Heart Failure. *Assistive Technology from Adapted Equipment to Inclusive Environments: AAATE, 25,* 87.

Fayn, J., & Rubel, P. (2010). Toward a Personal Health Society in Cardiology. Information Technology in Biomedicine. *IEEE Transactions on, 14*(2), 401–409.

Goodman-Deane, J., Keith, S., & Whitney, G. (2008). HCI and the Older Population. In Proceedings of the 22nd British HCI Group Annual Conference on People and Computers: Culture, Creativity. *Interaction, 2,* 193–194.

Goodwin, K., & Cooper, A. (2009). *Designing for the Digital Age: How to Create Human-Centered Products and Services*. John Wiley & Sons.

Goumopoulos, C., & Kameas, A. (2009). A Service Oriented Architecture Combining Agents and Ontologies Towards Pervasive Adaptation. In *Intelligent Environments 2009: Proceedings of the 5th International Conference on Intelligent Environments* (*Vol. 2*, p. 228). IOS Press

Guðjónsdóttir, R. (2010). *Personas and Scenarios in Use*. Doctoral Thesis submitted to the Kungliga Tekniska Högskolan in fulfilment of the requirements for the Degree of Doctor in Human-Computer Interaction.

Horton, M., Read, J., Fitton, D., Toth, N., & Little, L. (2012). Too Cool at School - Understanding Cool Teenagers. *PsychNology Journal, 10*(2), 73–91.

ISO. (2010). *ISO 9241-210: Ergonomics of Human-System Interaction - Part 210: Human-Centred Design for Interactive Systems*. International Organization for Standardization.

ISTAG. (2009). *ICT Advisory Groups Report on Orientations for Work Programme 2011-2013*. European Commission.

Janse, M., Vink, P., & Georgantas, N. (2008). Amigo Architecture: Service Oriented Architecture for Intelligent Future In-Home Networks. In Constructing Ambient Intelligence (pp. 371-378). Springer.

Judge, T., Matthews, T., & Whittaker, S. (2012). Comparing Collaboration and Individual Personas for the Design and Evaluation of Collaboration Software. In *Proceedings of the 2012 ACM Annual Conference on Human Factors in Computing Systems* (pp. 1997-2000). ACM. doi:10.1145/2207676.2208344

Kairy, D., Lehoux, P., Vincent, C., & Visintin, M. (2009). A Systematic Review of Clinical Outcomes, Clinical Process, Healthcare Utilization and Costs Associated with Telerehabilitation. *Disability and Rehabilitation, 31*(6), 427–347. doi:10.1080/09638280802062553 PMID:18720118

Kapoor, A. (2010). New Frontiers in Machine Learning for Predictive User Modeling. In A. Hamid, R. López-Cózar, & J. C. Augusto (Eds.), *Human-Centric Interfaces for Ambient Intelligence* (pp. 374–392). Academic Press. doi:10.1016/B978-0-12-374708-2.00015-2

Keegan, S., O'Hare, G., & O'Grady, M. (2008). Easishop: Ambient Intelligence Assists Everyday Shopping. *Information Sciences, 178*(3), 588–611. doi:10.1016/j.ins.2007.08.027

Kleinberger, T., Becker, M., Ras, E., Holzinger, A., & Müller, P. (2007). Ambient Intelligence in Assisted Living: Enable Elderly People to Handle Future Interfaces. In Universal Access in Human-Computer Interaction: Ambient Interaction (pp. 103-112). Springer.

Koch, J., Jung, H., Wettach, J., Nemeth, G., & Berns, K. (2008). Dynamic Speech Interaction for Robotic Agents. In L. Suh, & M. Kim (Eds.), *Recent Progress in Robotics: Viable Robotic Service to Human* (pp. 303–315). Springer. doi:10.1007/978-3-540-76729-9_24

Krieg-Brückner, B., Röfer, T., Shi, H., & Gersdorf, B. (2010). Mobility Assistance in the Bremen Ambient Assisted Living Lab. GeroPsych. *The Journal of Gerontopsychology and Geriatric Psychiatry*, *23*(2), 121–130. doi:10.1024/1662-9647/a000009

Lazaro, J. P., Fides, A., Navarro, A., & Guille, S. (2010). Ambient Assisted Nutritional Advisor for Elderly People Living at Home. In *Proceedings of Engineering in Medicine and Biology Society* (EMBC), (pp. 198-203). IEEE. doi:10.1109/IEMBS.2010.5627945

Lehikoinen, J., Lehikoinen, J., & Huuskonen, P. (2008). Understanding Privacy Regulation in Ubicomp Interactions. *Personal and Ubiquitous Computing*, *12*(8), 543–553. doi:10.1007/s00779-007-0163-2

Leon, E., Clarke, G., Callaghan, V., & Doctor, F. (2010). Affect-Aware Behaviour Modelling and Control Inside an Intelligent Environment. *Pervasive and Mobile Computing*, *6*(5), 559–574. doi:10.1016/j.pmcj.2009.12.002

Lombardi, A., Ferri, M., Rescio, G., Grassi, M., & Malcovati, P. (2009). Wearable Wireless Accelerometer with Embedded Fall-Detection Logic for Multi-Sensor Ambient Assisted Living Applications. In Sensors, 2009 IEEE (pp. 1967-1970). IEEE. doi:10.1109/ICSENS.2009.5398327

Long, F. (2009). Real or Imaginary: The Effectiveness of Using Personas in Product Design. In *Proceedings of the Irish Ergonomics Society Annual Conference* (pp. 1-10). Academic Press.

Marcengo, A., Guercio, E., & Rapp, A. (2009). Personas Layering: A Cost Effective Model for Service Design in Medium-Long Term Telco Research Projects. In Human Centered Design (pp. 256-265). Springer. doi:10.1007/978-3-642-02806-9_30

Matthews, T., Judge, T., & Whittaker, S. (2012). How Do Designers and User Experience Professionals Actually Perceive and Use Personas. In *Proceedings of the SIGCHI Conference on Human Factors in Computing Systems* (pp. 1219-1228). ACM. doi:10.1145/2207676.2208573

Miaskiewicz, T., & Kozar, K. A. (2011). Personas and User-Centered Design: How Can Personas Benefit Product Design Processes? *Design Studies*, *32*(5), 417–430. doi:10.1016/j.destud.2011.03.003

Mulder, S., & Yaar, Z. (2007). *The User is Always Right: A Practical Guide to Creating and Using Personas for the Web*. New Riders.

Newell, A., Gregor, P., Morgan, M., Pullin, G., & Macaulay, C. (2011). User-Sensitive Inclusive Design. *Universal Access in the Information Society*, *10*(3), 235–243. doi:10.1007/s10209-010-0203-y

Nielsen, L. (2004). *Engaging Personas and Narrative Scenarios*. Handelshøjskolen.

Oberzaucher, J., Werner, K., Mairbock, H., Beck, C., Panek, P., Hlauschek, W., & Zagler, W. (2009). A Videophone Prototype System Evaluated by Elderly Users in the Living Lab Schwechat. In *HCI and Usability for e-Inclusion* (pp. 345–352). Springer. doi:10.1007/978-3-642-10308-7_24

Paterno, F., Santoro, C., & Scorcia, A. (2010). Ambient Intelligence for Supporting Task Continuity across Multiple Devices and Implementation Languages. *The Computer Journal, 53*(8), 1210–1228. doi:10.1093/comjnl/bxp014

PERSONA - PERceptive Spaces promoting iNdependent Aging. (2008). *Report Describing Values, Trends, User needs and Guidelines for Service Characteristics in the AAL Persona Context*. European Commission.

Peterson, D. B. (2005). International Classification of Functioning, Disability and Health: An Introduction for Rehabilitation Psychologists. *Rehabilitation Psychology, 50*(2), 105–112. doi:10.1037/0090-5550.50.2.105

Picking, R., Robinet, A., Grout, V., McGinn, J., Roy, A., Ellis, S., & Oram, D. (2009). A Case Study Using a Methodological Approach to Developing User Interfaces for Elderly and Disabled People. *The Computer Journal, 53*(6), 842–859. doi:10.1093/comjnl/bxp089

Plischke, H., & Kohls, N. (2009). Keep It Simple! Assisting Older People with Mental and Physical Training. In Universal Access in Human-Computer Interaction: Addressing Diversity (pp. 278-287). Springer. doi:10.1007/978-3-642-02707-9_32

Pruitt, J., & Adlin, T. (2006). *The Persona Lifecycle: Keeping People in Mind throughout the Product Design*. Morgan Kaufman.

Pruitt, J., & Grudin, J. (2003). Personas: Practice and Theory. In *Proceedings of the 2003 Conference on Designing for User Experiences* (pp. 1-15). ACM. doi:10.1145/997078.997089

Queirós, A., Silva, A., Alvarelhão, J., Rocha, N., & Teixeira, A. (2013). *Usability, Accessibility and Ambient Assisted Living: A Systematic Literature Review. International Journal of Universal Access in the Information Society.* doi::10.1007/s10209-013-0328-x

Remmers, H. (2010). Environments for Ageing, Assistive Technology and Self-Determination: Ethical Perspectives. *Informatics for Health & Social Care, 35*(3-4), 200–210. doi:10.3109/17538157.2010.528649 PMID:21133773

Rönkkö, K. (2005). An Empirical Study Demonstrating how Different Design Constraints, Project Organization, and Contexts Limited the Utility of Personas. In *Proceedings of the 38th Annual Hawaii International Conference* (p. 220a). IEEE.

Schulz, T., & Fuglerud, K. (2012). Creating Personas with Disabilities. In Computers Helping People with Special Needs (pp. 145-152). Springer.

Sellner, W., Tschelig, M., Moser, C., Fuchsberger, V., & Neureiter, K. (2012). Revisiting Personas: The Making-of for Special User Groups. In Proceedings of CHI'12 Extended Abstracts on Human Factors in Computing Systems (pp. 453-468). ACM.

Siegel, D. A. (2010). The Mystique of Numbers: Belief in Quantitative Approaches to Segmentation and Persona Development. In Proceedings of CHI'10 Extended Abstracts on Human Factors in Computing Systems (pp. 4721-4732). ACM.

Sinha, R. (2003). Persona Development for Information Rich Domains. In Proceedings of CHI'03 Extended Abstracts on Human Factors in Computing Systems (pp. 830-831). ACM.

Stuikys, V., & Damasevicius, R. (2007). Variability-Oriented Embedded Component Design for Ambient Intelligence. Information Technology and Control, Kaunas. *Technologija, 36*(1), 16–29.

Teixeira, A., Ferreira, F., Almeida, N., Rosa, A., Casimiro, J., & Queirós, A. (2013b). Multimodality and Adaptation for an Enhanced Mobile Medication Assistant for the Elderly. In *Proceedings of 3rd Workshop on Mobile Accessibility in Conference on Human Factors in Computing Systems*. ACM.

Teixeira, A., Pereira, C., Silva, M. O., Alvarelhão, J., Silva, A., Cerqueira, M., et al. (2013a). New Telerehabilitation Services for the Elderly. In I. Miranda & M. Cruz-Cunha (Eds.), Handbook of Research on ICTs for Healthcare and Social Services: Developments and Applications (pp. 109-132). IGI Global

Un, S., & Price, N. (2007). Bridging the Gap between Technological Possibilities and People: Involving People in the Early Phases of Technology Development. *Technological Forecasting and Social Change*, *74*(9), 1758–1772. doi:10.1016/j.techfore.2007.05.008

Wang, K., Abdulla, W., & Salcic, Z. (2009). Ambient Intelligence Platform Using Multi-Agent System and Mobile Ubiquitous Hardware. *Pervasive and Mobile Computing*, *5*(5), 558–573. doi:10.1016/j.pmcj.2009.06.003

WHO. (2001). *The International Classification of Functioning, Disability and Health (ICF)*. World Health Organization.

WHO. (2002). *Active Ageing: A Policy Framework*. World Health Organization.

Wöckl, B., Yildizoglu, U., Buber, I., Aparicio, D. B., Kruijff, E., & Tscheligi, M. (2012). Basic Senior Personas: A Representative Design Tool Covering the Spectrum of European Older Adults. In *Proceedings of the 14th International ACM SIGACCESS Conference on Computers and Accessibility* (pp. 25-32). ACM. doi:10.1145/2384916.2384922

Yao-Jen, C., & Tsen-Yung, W. (2010). Indoor Wayfinding Based On Wireless Sensor Networks For Individuals With Multiple Special Needs. *Cybernetics and Systems*, *41*(4), 317–333. doi:10.1080/01969721003778584

Zajicek, M. (2004). Successful and Available: Interface Design Exemplars for Older Users. *Interacting with Computers*, *16*(3), 411–430. doi:10.1016/j.intcom.2004.04.003

ADDITIONAL READING

Adlin, T., & Pruitt, J. (2010). *The Essential Persona Lifecycle: Your Guide to Building and Using Personas*. Morgan Kaufmann.

Augusto, J. C., Huch, M., Kameas, A., Maitland, J., & McCullagh, P. (Eds.). (2012). *Handbook of Ambient Assisted Living: Technology for Healthcare, Rehabilitation and Well-Being*. IOS Press.

Chong, N.-Y., & Mastrogiovanni, F. (2011). *Handbook of Research on Ambient Intelligence and Smart Environments: Trends and Perspectives*. IGI Global. doi:10.4018/978-1-61692-857-5

Cooper, A. (1999). *The Inmates are Running the Asylum: Why High-Tech Products Drive us Crazy and How to Restore the Sanity*. Pearson Education. doi:10.1007/978-3-322-99786-9_1

Cooper, A., Reimann, R., & Cronin, D. (2012). *About Face 3: the Essentials of Interaction Design*. John Wiley & Sons.

Peterson, D. B. (2005). International Classification of Functioning, Disability and Health: An Introduction for Rehabilitation Psychologists. *Rehabilitation Psychology*, *50*(2), 105–112. doi:10.1037/0090-5550.50.2.105

KEY TERMS AND DEFINITIONS

Accessibility: Accessibility is a general term used to describe the degree to which a product, device, service, or environment is available and accessible to the most people possible.

Active Ageing: A process of optimizing opportunities for health, participation and security, in order to enhance quality of life as people age.

Activities: Activities are the individual's recital of assignments and tasks.

Ambient Assisted Living: Ambient Assisted Living is a new paradigm that aims to apply technological solutions to increase the autonomy of older people, to assist in their day-do-day activities and, consequently, to improve their functioning, autonomy, independence and quality of life.

Body Functions and Structures: The body's functions entail the individual's physiological functions and the body structures correspond to the human anatomical structures.

Contextual Factors: The contextual factors are the environmental and personal factors which either enhance or limit the individual's functioning.

Functioning: Functioning encompasses all the body functions, activities and participation.

Health Conditions: Health conditions is a generic term for diseases (acute or chronic), disturbance, injuries or traumas. Health conditions should be understood as specific features that impacts in what a person does or can do in terms of actions, tasks or participation on areas of life according to his or her temporary or permanent disease or disorder.

Participation: Participation covers the individual's involvement in daily life and society.

Persona: A persona is an archetype that should be a precise description of a hypothetical user and his or her needs, goals and tasks.

Scenario: Scenarios is a story with settings, personas who have needs and goals and a sequence of events and tasks.

Usability: Usability is the extent to which a system or service may be used by specific users in a given context of use, to achieve particular goals with efficiency and effectiveness, while promoting feelings of pleasure. Usability is a fundamental aspect to consider in the development cycle of systems or services that necessarily have to be framed by the characteristics of users, tasks to perform, and the surrounding context (social, organizational and physical).

User Centred Design: User Centred Design is a development approach of interactive systems that focus specifically on making systems usable. It is a multi-disciplinary activity that incorporates human factors ergonomics knowledge, involving human resources, skills, limitations and needs. It should focus on the user's characteristics and needs, and must be applied since the beginning of the development process, to create useful and easy to use applications.

Chapter 15
Role of Usability in E–Learning System:
An Empirical Study of OWASP WebGoat

Muhammad Ahmad Amin
Bahria University, Pakistan

Saqib Saeed
University of Dammam, Saudi Arabia

ABSTRACT

Amongst open-source e-learning systems, WebGoat, a progression of OWASP, provides some room for teaching the penetration testing techniques. Yet, it is a major concern of its learners as to whether the WebGoat interface is user-friendly enough to help them acquaint themselves of the desired Web application security knowledge. This chapter encompasses a heuristic evaluation of this application to acquire the usability of contemporary version of WebGoat. In this context of evaluation, the in-house formal lab testing of WebGoat was conducted by the authors. The results highlight some important issues and usability problems that frequently pop-up in the contemporary version. The research results would be pivotal to the embedding of an operational as well as user-friendly interface for its future version.

INTRODUCTION

Amongst the principal attributes of quality, usability is the one that appraises user interfaces (Nielsen, 2012). Usability has five major quality components (learnability, efficiency, memorability, error and satisfaction) which play a vital role in assessing the user friendliness of any product (Nielsen, 2012). It is a matter of enhancing as well as maintaining the user productivity, meanwhile meeting the desired quality metrics (Nielsen,

2012). The term e-Learning system, a learning platform, expresses a wide range of information and communication technology (ICT) system used to deliver learning and teaching processes (Pecheanu et al. 2011). It reduces the training cost in terms of providing less travelling and accommodation, ultimately lowering teaching cost. Amongst a variety of e-Learning systems, OWASP WebGoat is the open source e-Learning system aiming at easing the facilitation of the penetration testing techniques. In this paper we explore

DOI: 10.4018/978-1-4666-6485-2.ch015

the usability issues in WebGoat, so that its future versions can improve on usability aspects.

This paper is structured as follows: Section 2 highlights the related work in the field of usability. Section 3 covers the methodology and is followed by empirical data in section 4. Section 5 wraps up the paper by a conclusion.

RELATED WORK

Several studies have discussed the importance and benefits of usability. Nielsen (1994) introduced the perception of web usability by affirming that creation of easy navigation and spontaneously structured web pages helps user to search the requisite information easily. Krug (2009) have chalked out that there are many design rules available to achieve the usability in web applications and successful implementation of web usage. Usability has been explored in different settings like health (cf. Hatzilygeroudis et al. 2007), e-government (cf. Saeed et al. 2013), education (cf. Oliveira et al. 2011) etc. Katsanos et al. (2012) professed that usability is mandatory to any academic software as well. According to them usability assessment of any pedagogical software comprises of an understandable requirement, preceding its incorporation into the academic realm. Kakasevski et al. (2008) highlighted the quick boost of ICT infrastructures these days. Every educational institution finds it indispensible to make use of internet as a pivot for an interactive system. The quest for the ultimate erudition has resulted in the progression of computing (Kakasevski et al., 2008). Floyd et al. (2012) have brought to light some e-Learning environments such as virtual universities, education portals, complete online courses and electronic course supplements that have been recently surfaced in the contemporary scenario. To accomplish a competitive scenario, a lot of universities are offering online degrees

and certificates solely depending on e-Learning systems. This pedagogical method is in a stark contrast to conventional pedagogical methodologies, though not substituting it entirely but expanding new horizons of knowledge to learners. Almarashdeh et al. (2011) have described that an e-Learning system is an e-environment that is used to sketch, execute and review a particular facilitating process. Generally, it offers gateways to create and deliver the syllabi, criticaly analyzing learner's performance and monitoring his interest. Trainers find it feasible to design courses and execute their pedagogical skills at the platform of various institutions. Georgiakakis et al. (2005) have declared that developing intricate frameworks for monitoring the e-Learning system in both educational and professional scenarios require tailoring. Al-Khalifa (2010) described consumer approval with e-Learning system using questionnaire method and suggested further usability studies to be pursued in order to assess an e-Learning system encompassing various usability evaluation techniques. Fogie (2003) has highlighted the need for learning web application security, as it is one of the major concern which ideally requires a safe infrastructure, where developers understand the new technologies as well as attacker learn how to exploit them. To accomplish this purpose OWASP (open web application security project) designed an open source e-Learning system WebGoat, offering an opportunity to web developers as well as professionals to understand web application security (Livshits, 2005). Fogie (2003) has pointed out, contrary to other learning environment encompassing security such as Found stone's Hackme series and Badstore, WebGoat was initially perceived merely to offer e-Learning environment for learning penetration testing techniques rather than focusing on the usability evaluation itself. In this paper we focus on usability evaluation of WebGoat (shown in figure 1), using heuristic evaluation.

Figure 1. Snapshot of OWASP WebGoat (adopt, after hosted on local machine)

Figure 2. Visibility of selected lesson category in WebGoat Application

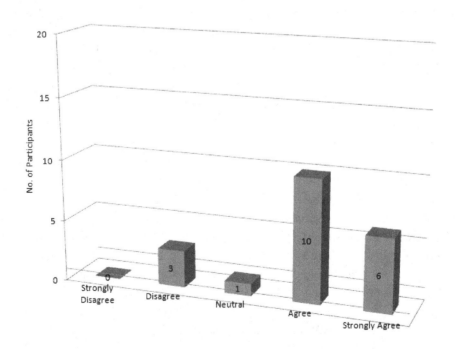

METHODOLOGY

A set of evaluation criteria was developed for each heuristic to be used as a checklist for the evaluation of the e-Learning system (cf. Chen & Macredie, 2005).The benefit of using a detailed checklist is to identify maximum number of usability problems. For the research mechanism, an open source e-Learning system WebGoat, a project of OWASP (Open web application security project) was selected to be evaluated. The evaluation was conducted through two sessions of formal in-house lab testing based on usability inspection (cf. Chen & Macredie, 2005).

EMPIRICAL STUDY

To comprehend the usability problems, we conducted a survey on the current version of an open source e-Learning system WebGoat, a progression of OWASP. For this research, we arranged two sessions of in-house formal lab testing each of which involving 10 participants with the work experiences in the range between 1 to 10 years approximately. Their education levels were MS / MCS / BCS and their ages were in the range of 22 to 40 years. The designations of respondents included Data Center Manager, Senior Software Manager, Software Consultant, Network Security Manager, Software Developer, Information Security Manager, Senior IS Officer, CEO, Software Security engineer, Cyber Security Officer, Project Manager, Security Analyst, Quality Analyst, Programmer, Software Engineer and IS Coordinator. The questions were categorized by Jakob Nielson's heuristics (cf. Nielsen, 1994a), (available in Appendix).

The visibility of system status in WebGoat is an important usability attribute. It is important as it helps learner to easily navigate through the selected lesson category. The responses showed that 10 out of the 20 participants agreed and 6 strongly agreed that WebGoat highlighted the selected lesson category, whereas 1 respondent remained neutral and 3 disagreed, as shown in Figure 2.

Availability of guidance about the remaining topics in currently selected lesson category in WebGoat is a necessary element to complete the lesson. According to our survey, 9 respondents of our participants agreed and 5 strongly agreed upon its availability. Whereas, 3 of the responses were neutral and 3 disagreed, as shown in Figure 3.

To display the progress bar while loading of any lesson is an important factor. It is important as learner may continuously know the remaining time for loading the lesson. In our survey, 8 of our participants disagreed whereas 8 strongly disagreed upon its availability in WebGoat. However, 3 of our respondents remained neutral and 1 agreed as shown in Figure 4.

WebGoat lessons are to be ordered according to the latest ranking of OWASP top ten vulnerabilities. It is important as the success of any e-Learning system is based on its contents revision. In our survey we found that 8 respondents did not agree that OWASP follows the latest contents whereas 3 of them strongly disagreed, 6 remained neutral and 3 agreed, as shown in Figure 5.

It is important to manage the menu and submenu of all categories of lessons in logical order to match the WebGoat to the real world learning scenario. In our survey 10 out of 20 participants agreed that WebGoat manages the menu and sub menu in logical order. However 1 respondent strongly agreed, 7 responded as neutral. 2 of them disagreed as shown in Figure 6.

We also asked about the availability of relevant input fields, according to the vulnerability lesson. In our survey, we got 13 out of 20 participants who agreed and 3 of them strongly agreed upon

Figure 3. Guidance about the remaining topics in current selected category

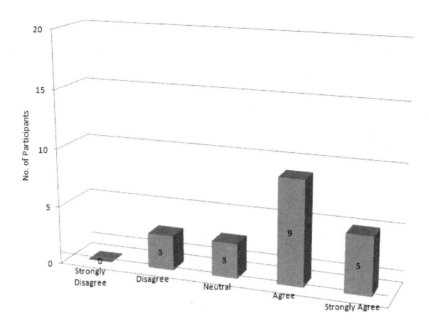

Figure 4. Display of progress bar during lesson loading

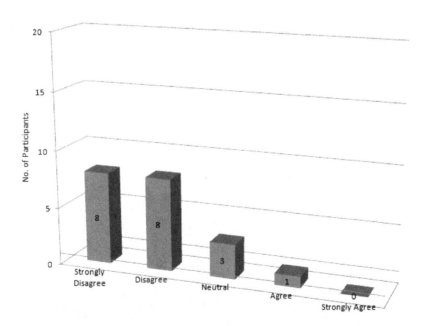

Figure 5. Order of lessons, according to latest ranking of vulnerabilities by OWASP

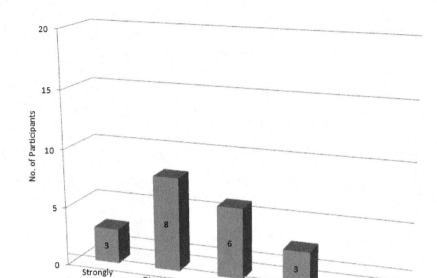

Figure 6. Logical ordered management of menu

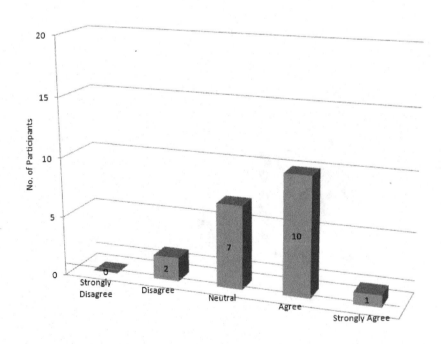

Figure 7. Availability of input field as per vulnerability lesson

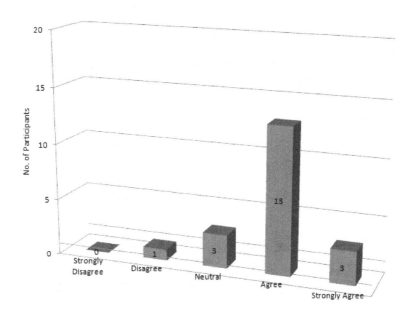

its availability in WebGoat. On the other hand, 3 of them were neutral and only 1 disagreed as shown in Figure 7.

Learner always like the support of hierarchical navigation. We got 10 responses out of 20 participants who agreed and 2 of them strongly agreed that WebGoat provided the freedom of easy navigation. However, 2 of them had neutral response. 5 disagreed and one was strongly disagreed as shown in Figure 8.

Facility to restart the lesson at any stage is an important feature in an e-learning system. It helps the learner to recap, if he felt any confusion. We got 7 responses out of 20 participants who agreed and 4 strongly agreed upon its availability in WebGoat but 2 were neutral, 5 disagreed and 2 strongly disagreed, as shown in Figure 9.

Option to change/customize the color theme of interface is also an important attribute of usability. It attracts the learner, and motivates them to get involved in lessons. In our survey, 14 responses out of 20 strongly disagreed and 5 disagreed upon

its availability in WebGoat. Only 1 respondent was neutral as shown in Figure 10.

The consistency between web pages of an e-learning system is very useful for quick learning of interface. It helps them to easily navigate between different web pages, as well. In our survey, 7 participants responded as agreed and 4 strongly agreed upon system consistency in WebGoat. However, 4 responded to be neutral, 3 disagreed and 2 strongly disagreed, as shown in Figure 11.

Scrollbars (horizontal/vertical) are important, for providing better navigation for viewing long contents. In our survey, 10 responses out of 20 agreed and 5 strongly agreed upon the availability of this important feature in WebGoat. However, 3 respondents were neutral and 2 disagreed, as shown in Figure 12.

Consistency in displaying the instructions/ guidance about the input field of the topic is also useful for better learnability. We got 7 responses out of 20 participants who agreed and 1 strongly agreed upon consistency element in WebGoat user interface. On the other hand 5 respondents were

Figure 8. Permitting multiple level navigational menus

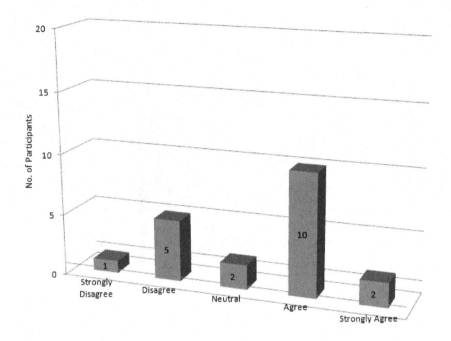

Figure 9. Freedom to restart the lesson

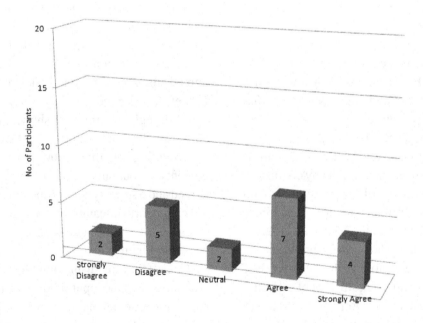

Figure 10. Customization of color theme

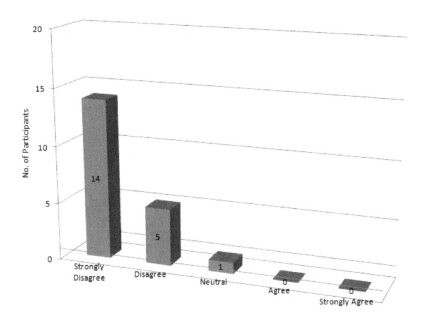

Figure 11. Consistency between all web pages

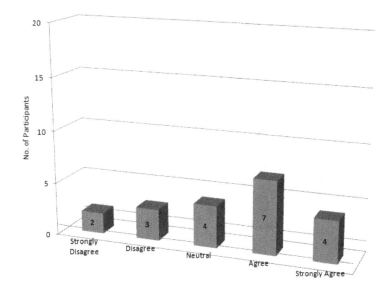

neutral, 4 disagreed and 3 strongly disagreed, as shown in Figure 13.

Providing default values in the input fields helps in the prevention of errors, which is an important usability attribute. In our survey, 14 participants out of 20 agreed and 1 strongly agreed upon its availability in WebGoat. Similarly 2 re-

Figure 12. Facility of horizontal / vertical scrollbars

Figure 13. Display of lesson instruction on consistent location

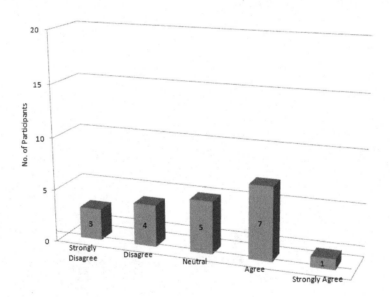

spondents were neutral and 3 strongly disagreed, as shown in Figure 14.

To place frequently used options in a convenient order is quite useful to enhance the efficiency of users to effectively respond in learning environ-ment. In our survey, 10 respondents out of 20 remained neutral. 7 disagreed, 2 agreed and only 1 strongly agreed that WebGoat has better placed frequently used options, as shown in Figure 15.

Figure 14. Availability of default values in lesson forms to prevent error

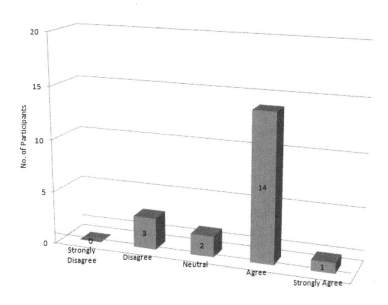

Figure 15. Order of options convenient for the learner

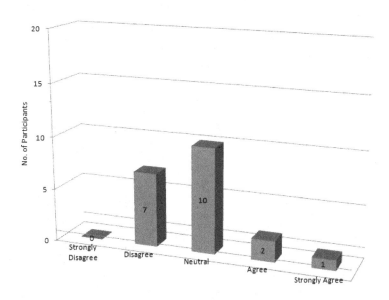

Displaying the logout option on the top of the screen is useful for learner to exit the system when required. In our survey, 10 participants out of 20 agreed and 3 strongly agreed that this feature is well placed in WebGoat. However, 2 respondents were neutral, 3 disagreed and 2 strongly disagreed, as shown in Figure 16.

It is a significant feature for the system to draw a mechanism that easily differentiates between highlighted and un-highlighted contents of the lesson.

Figure 16. Facilitate learner to Logout the system

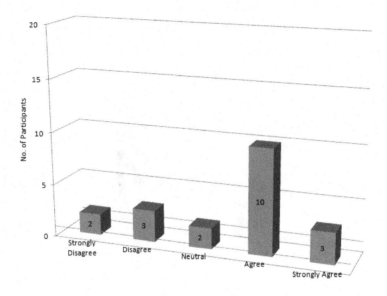

Figure 17. Mechanism to distinguish between emphasized and non-emphasized data

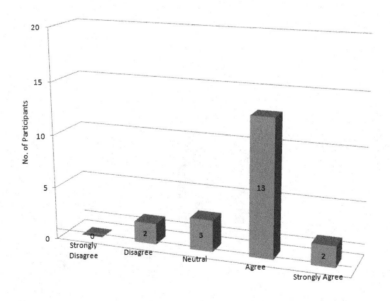

In our survey, 13 responses out of 20 participants agreed and 2 strongly agreed about its presence in WebGoat. However 3 respondents were neutral and 2 disagreed, as shown in Figure 17.

Segregation of topics into logically ordered groups help the learners to easily remember the read and unread portions of lessons. In our survey, we got 13 responses out 20 participants who agreed and 2 strongly agreed that the current

Figure 18. Logically ordered grouping of topics with lesson category

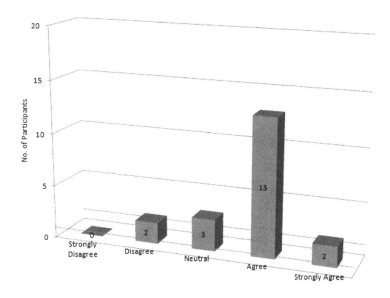

Figure 19. Visibility of prompts to learner

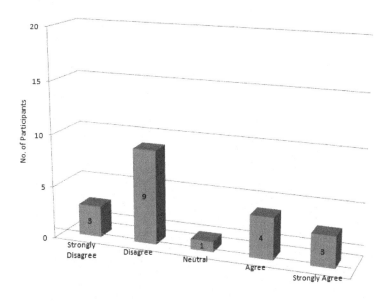

version of WebGoat supports this kind of segregation. However 3 respondents were neutral and 2 disagreed, as shown in Figure 18.

Learners always feel comfortable with the visibility of prompts, and it also helps in error prevention. In our survey, we got 9 responses out of 20 participants who disagreed and 3 strongly

Figure 20. Facility of session management to identify incomplete lesson

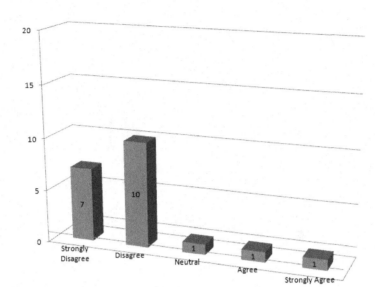

Figure 21. Availability of accelerators / shortcuts for experienced learner

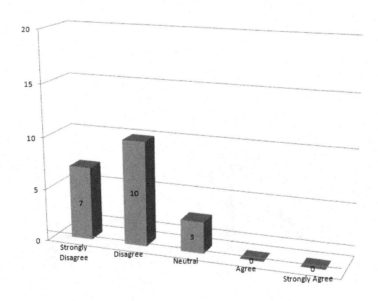

disagreed that the current version had bad visibility of prompts. However, 1 respondent was neutral 4 agreed and 3 strongly agreed, as shown in Figure 19.

Session management is an important feature of interactive systems. We got 10 responses who disagreed and 7 strongly disagreed that the current system did not maintain sessions. However

1 respondent was neutral, 1 agreed and 1 strongly agreed, as shown in Figure 20.

Availability of accelerators in the system is very useful for expert users. In our survey, 10 respondents disagreed, 7 strongly disagreed and three remained neutral about the availability of such features in WebGoat, as shown in Figure 21.

CONCLUSION

This paper discussed the usability of WebGoat, by applying Jakob Nielson's heuristics (cf. Nielsen, 1994a). This results highlight that although some feautres are well designed in WebGoat, however there is need to further improve the usability aspect. This study has highlighted some recommendations for the development of more user-friendly interface for WebGoat. The results of our study are recommendations for the open source developers and designers, who can rectify these weaknesses in future versions.

REFERENCES

Al-Khalifa, H. S. (2010). A first step in evaluating the usability of Jusur learning management system. In *Proceedings of the Third Annual Forum on E-Learning Excellence: Bringing Global Quality to Local Context*. Academic Press.

Almarashdeh, I. A., Sahari, N., & Mat Zin, N. A. (2011, July). Heuristic evaluation of distance learning management system interface. In *Proceedings of Electrical Engineering and Informatics (ICEEI)*, (pp. 1-6). IEEE. doi:10.1109/ICEEI.2011.6021542

Chen, S. Y., & Macredie, R. D. (2005). The assessment of usability of electronic shopping: A heuristic evaluation. *International Journal of Information Management*, 25(6), 516–532. doi:10.1016/j.ijinfomgt.2005.08.008

Floyd, C., Schultz, T., & Fulton, S., & the US Air Force Academy. (2012, June). Security Vulnerabilities in theopen source MoodleeLearning System. In *Proceedings of the 16th Colloquium for Information Systems Security Education*. Academic Press.

Fogie, S. (2003, May). *Practical Web Application Security with WebGoat - InformIT*. Retrieved from http://www.informit.com/guides/content.aspx?g=security&seqNum=344

Georgiakakis, P., Papasalouros, A., Retalis, S., Siassiakos, K., & Papaspyrou, N. (2005). Evaluating the usability of web-based learning management systems. *THEMES in Education*, 6(1), 45–59.

Hatzilygeroudis, I., Koutsojannis, C., & Papachristou, N. (2007, June). Evaluation of usability and assessment capabilities of an e-Learning System for Nursing Radiation Protection. In *Proceedings of Computer-Based Medical Systems*, (pp. 301-306). IEEE. doi:10.1109/CBMS.2007.47

Kakasevski, G., Mihajlov, M., Arsenovski, S., & Chungurski, S. (2008, June). Evaluating usability in learning management system Moodle. In *Proceedings of Information Technology Interfaces*, (pp. 613-618). IEEE. doi:10.1109/ITI.2008.4588480

Katsanos, C., Tselios, N., & Xenos, M. (2012, October). Perceived Usability Evaluation of Learning Management Systems: A First Step towards Standardization of the System Usability Scale in Greek. In *Proceedings of Informatics (PCI)*, (pp. 302-307). IEEE. doi:10.1109/PCi.2012.38

Krug, S. (2009). *Don't make me think: A common sense approach to web usability*. Pearson Education.

Livshits, V. B., & Lam, M. S. (2005, August). Finding security vulnerabilities in Java applications with static analysis. In *Proceedings of the 14th conference on USENIX Security Symposium* (*Vol. 14*, pp. 18-18). USENIX.

Nielsen, J. (1994, April). Enhancing the explanatory power of usability heuristics. In *Proceedings of the SIGCHI conference on Human Factors in Computing Systems* (pp. 152-158). ACM. doi:10.1145/259963.260333

Nielsen, J. (1994a, April). Usability inspection methods. In *Conference companion on Human factors in computing systems* (pp. 413–414). ACM. doi:10.1145/259963.260531

Nielsen, J. (2012, January). *Usability 101: Introduction to Usability*. Retrieved from http://www.nngroup.com/articles/usability-101introduction-to-usability/

Oliveira, L. S., Oliveros, D. V., da Graça Pimentel, M., & Queiroz-Neto, J. P. (2011, October). Work in progress—Alternative interfaces for e-learning platforms used in remote areas. In *Proceedings of Frontiers in Education Conference (FIE), 2011* (pp. T4C-1). IEEE.

Pecheanu, E., Stefanescu, D., Dumitriu, L., & Segal, C. (2011, April). Methods to evaluate open source learning platforms. In *Proceedings of Global Engineering Education Conference (EDUCON)*, (pp. 1152-1161). IEEE. doi:10.1109/EDUCON.2011.5773292

Saeed, S., Wahab, F., Cheema, S. A., & Ashraf, S. (2013). Role of Usability in E-Government and E-Commerce Portals: An Empirical Study of Pakistan. *Life Science Journal, 10*(1S).

ADDITIONAL READING

Ardito, C., De Marsico, M., Lanzilotti, R., Levialdi, S., Roselli, T., Rossano, V., & Tersigni, M. (2004, May). Usability of e-learning tools. In *Proceedings of the working conference on Advanced visual interfaces* (pp. 80-84). ACM. doi:10.1145/989863.989873

Chen, Y. C., Hwang, R. H., & Wang, C. Y. (2012). Development and evaluation of a Web 2.0 annotation system as a learning tool in an e-learning environment. *Computers & Education, 58*(4), 1094–1105. doi:10.1016/j.compedu.2011.12.017

Downey, S., Wentling, R. M., Wentling, T., & Wadsworth, A. (2005). The relationship between national culture and the usability of an e-learning system. *Human Resource Development International, 8*(1), 47–64. doi:10.1080/1367886042000338245

Drachsler, H., Pecceu, D., Arts, T., Hutten, E., Rutledge, L., Van Rosmalen, P., & Koper, R. (2010). ReMashed-An Usability Study of a Recommender System for Mash-Ups for Learning. *International Journal of Emerging Technologies in Learning*.

Dyckhoff, A. L., Zielke, D., Bültmann, M., Chatti, M. A., & Schroeder, U. (2012). Design and Implementation of a Learning Analytics Toolkit for Teachers. *Journal of Educational Technology & Society, 15*(3).

Freire, L. L., Arezes, P. M., & Campos, J. C. (2012). A literature review about usability evaluation methods for e-learning platforms. *Work (Reading, Mass.), 41*, 1038–1044. PMID:22316857

Govaerts, S., Verbert, K., Dahrendorf, D., Ullrich, C., Schmidt, M., Werkle, M., & Law, E. L. (2011). Towards responsive open learning environments: the ROLE interoperability framework. In *Towards Ubiquitous Learning* (pp. 125–138). Springer Berlin Heidelberg. doi:10.1007/978-3-642-23985-4_11

Hamtini, T. M., & Hudaib, A. A. (2012). Measuring E-Learning Web-Based Application Usability. *International Review on Computers & Software, 7*(1).

Hassanzadeh, A., Kanaani, F., & Elahi, S. (2012). A model for measuring e-learning systems success in universities. *Expert Systems with Applications, 39*(12), 10959–10966. doi:10.1016/j.eswa.2012.03.028

Huang, Y. M., Liang, T. H., Su, Y. N., & Chen, N. S. (2012). Empowering personalized learning with an interactive e-book learning system for elementary school students. *Educational Technology Research and Development, 60*(4), 703–722. doi:10.1007/s11423-012-9237-6

Hung, J. L. (2012). Trends of e-learning research from 2000 to 2008: Use of text mining and bibliometrics. *British Journal of Educational Technology, 43*(1), 5–16. doi:10.1111/j.1467-8535.2010.01144.x

Jochems, W., Koper, R., & Van Merrienboer, J. (Eds.). (2013). integrated e-learning: Implications for pedagogy, technology and organization. Routledge.

Kumar, S., Gankotiya, A. K., & Dutta, K. (2011, April). A comparative study of moodle with other e-learning systems. In *Electronics Computer Technology (ICECT), 2011 3rd International Conference on* (Vol. 5, pp. 414-418). IEEE. doi:10.1109/ICECTECH.2011.5942032

Moore, J. L., Dickson-Deane, C., & Galyen, K. (2011). E-Learning, online learning, and distance learning environments: Are they the same? *The Internet and Higher Education, 14*(2), 129–135. doi:10.1016/j.iheduc.2010.10.001

Padayachee, I., Kotze, P., & van Der Merwe, A. (2010). *ISO 9126 external systems quality characteristics, sub-characteristics and domain specific criteria for evaluating e-Learning systems*. South Africa: The Southern African Computer Lecturers' Association, University of Pretoria.

Pauli, J., & Engebretson, P. (2012). Filling Your Cyber Operations Training Toolbox. *Security & Privacy, IEEE, 10*(5), 71–74. doi:10.1109/MSP.2012.117

Rakoczi, G., & Pohl, M. (2012, July). Visualisation and analysis of multiuser gaze data: Eye tracking usability studies in the special context of e-learning. In *Advanced Learning Technologies (ICALT), 2012 IEEE 12th International Conference on* (pp. 738-739). IEEE.

Rennie, F., & Morrison, T. (2012). *E-learning and social networking handbook: Resources for higher education*. Routledge.

Saeed, S., & Amjad, A. (2013). Understanding Usability Issues of Pakistani University Websites. *Life Science Journal, 106s.*

Saeed, S., Jamshaid, I., & Sikander, S. (2012). Usability Evaluation of Hospital Websites in Pakistan. [IJTD]. *International Journal of Technology Diffusion, 3*(4), 29–35. doi:10.4018/jtd.2012100103

Saeed, S., Malik, I. A., & Wahab, F. (2013). Usability Evaluation of Pakistani Security Agencies Websites. [IJEP]. *International Journal of E-Politics, 4*(3), 57–69. doi:10.4018/jep.2013070105

Saeed, S., & Reddick, C. G. (2013). *Human-Centered System Design for Electronic Governance*. IGI Global USA. doi:10.4018/978-1-4666-3640-8

Saeed, S., & Rohde, M. (2010, May). Computer enabled social movements? Usage of a collaborative web platform within the European social forum. In *9th International Conference on the Design of Cooperative Systems* (pp. 245-264). doi:10.1007/978-1-84996-211-7_14

Shi, L., Al Qudah, D., Qaffas, A., & Cristea, A. I. (2013). Topolor: a social personalized adaptive e-learning system. In *User Modeling, Adaptation, and Personalization* (pp. 338-340). Springer Berlin Heidelberg. doi:10.1007/978-3-642-38844-6_32

Siegenthaler, E., Wurtz, P., & Groner, R. (2010). Improving the usability of E-book readers. *Journal of Usability Studies*, 6(1), 25–38.

Sonntag, M. (2013, September). Learning security through insecurity. In *e-Learning and e-Technologies in Education (ICEEE), 2013 Second International Conference on* (pp. 143-148). IEEE. doi:10.1109/ICeLeTE.2013.6644363

Sung, E., & Mayer, R. E. (2012). Affective impact of navigational and signaling aids to e-learning. *Computers in Human Behavior*, 28(2), 473–483. doi:10.1016/j.chb.2011.10.019

Yengin, I., Karahoca, A., & Karahoca, D. (2011). E-learning success model for instructors' satisfactions in perspective of interaction and usability outcomes. *Procedia Computer Science*, 3, 1396–1403. doi:10.1016/j.procs.2011.01.021

Zaharias, P., & Poylymenakou, A. (2009). Developing a usability evaluation method for e-learning applications: Beyond functional usability. *International Journal of Human-Computer Interaction*, 25(1), 75–98. doi:10.1080/10447310802546716

KEY TERMS AND DEFINITIONS

Interactive System: In computing, it pertains to the functional relationship offered and generated by the user via web interface. The course of action channelizes as soon as the system is put to command by the user, be it a software application or an automated machine.

OWASP: Open Web Application Security Project is a global NGO bent on bettering the security issues offered by any software.

Penetration Testing: It is a susceptibility evaluation that determines and brings to light the assailable frailties of software, whereas a penetration tests attempts encapsulating any violation or breach in a system or any illegitimate ingress/ trespass.

Usability Inspection: It is an argument for the set of techniques where an assessor examines a user interface. It can ideally be applied in the early stages of the development process by assessing the prototype of the system.

Usability: It is an excellence that evaluates facilitation of user interface as to how feasible it is for handling for a layman. It, also, pertains to the strategies adapted to better usability of the design processes.

User Interface: It is the perceptible part of an operating system through which a user handles a software. It modifies as to how commands are issued or as to how the information is displayed on the screen.

Vulnerability: It is the hubris, the fatal flaw that reduces a web application to nothing, if ever compromised at the hands of an intruder, thus giving way to cyber theft, bereaving it of all secure information and assets it comprises of.

Web Application Security: Primarily transact with impenetrable security of various websites and e-applications.

WebGoat: It is a craftily designed web application, purposely vulnerable, meant for imparting web application security lessons to the professional e-Learners. The lessons enable the users to practically learn to maneuver the superficial security breach offered by application via penetration testing. The application is a peripheral, pedagogical, realia offering its users with various hints and code for users' feasibility.

Compilation of References

Adams, J. C., & Webster, A. R. (2012). What do students learn about programming from game, music video, and storytelling projects? In *Proceedings of the 43rd ACM technical symposium on Computer Science Education* (pp. 643–648). New York: ACM. doi:10.1145/2157136.2157319

Adams, M. J., Tenney, Y. J., & Pew, R. W. (1995). Situation awareness and the cognitive management of complex systems. *Human Factors*, *37*(1), 85–104. doi:10.1518/001872095779049462

Afonso, A. P., Lima, J. R., & Cota, M. P. (2013). Usability Assessment of Web Interfaces: User Testing. In *Proceedings of Information Systems and Technologies (CISTI)*, (pp. 1-7). IEEE.

Agner, L. (2012). *Usability of journalism to tablets: A review of the interaction by gestures at a news app. In 12o ErgoDesign*. Natal, Brazil: USIHC.

Agrawal, A. (2002). Indigenous knowledge and the politics of classification. *International Social Science Journal*, *54*(173), 287–297. doi:10.1111/1468-2451.00382

Ahram, T. Z., Karwowski, W., & Amaba, B. (2010). User-Centered Systems Engineering Approach to Design and Modeling of Smarter Products. *In Proceedings of System of Systems Engineering* (SoSE), (pp. 1-6). IEEE. doi:10.1109/SYSOSE.2010.5544041

Ai, H., & Weng, F. (2008). User Simulation as Testing for Spoken Dialog Systems. In *Proceedings of the 9th SIGdial Workshop on Discourse and Dialogue* (pp. 164-171). Association for Computational Linguistics. doi:10.3115/1622064.1622097

Aikenhead, G., & Ogawa, M. (2007). Indigenous knowledge and science revisited. *Cultural Studies of Science Education*, *2*(3), 539–620. doi:10.1007/s11422-007-9067-8

Albinsson, P.-A. (2004). *Interacting with command and control systems: Tools for operators and designers*. Licentiate thesis (No. 1132). Linköping, Sweden: Linköping University.

Alcañiz, M., Botella, C., Baños, R. M., Zaragoza, I., & Guixeres, J. (2009). The Intelligent e-Therapy System: A New Paradigm for Telepsychology and Cybertherapy. *British Journal of Guidance & Counselling*, *37*(3), 287–296. doi:10.1080/03069880902957015

Alexander, C., Ishikawa, S., & Silverstein, M. (1977). *A pattern language: towns, buildings, construction*. Oxford, UK: Oxford University Press.

Alfredson, J. (2001). *Aspects of situational awareness and its measures in an aircraft simulation context*. Licentiate thesis (No. 865). Linköping, Sweden: Linköping University.

Alfredson, J. (2007). *Differences in situational awareness and how to manage them in development of complex systems*. Doctoral dissertation (No. 1132). Linköping, Sweden: Linköping University.

Alfredson, J., Angelborg-Thanderz, M., Danielsson, M., Farkin, B., Farmer, E., Hadley, B., et al. (1996). *Human awareness criteria* (Tech. Rep. No. VINTHEC-WP1-TR01). Amsterdam: National Aerospace Laboratory NLR.

Alfredson, J., & Andersson, R. (2012). Managing human factors in the development of fighter aircraft. In E. Abu-Taieh, A. El Sheikh, & M. Jafari (Eds.), *Technology Engineering and Management in Aviation: Advancements and Discoveries* (pp. 101–116). IGI Global.

Alfredson, J., Holmberg, J., Andersson, R., & Wikforss, M. (2011). Applied cognitive ergonomics design principles for fighter aircraft. In HarrisD. (Ed.) *Proceedings of the 9th International Conference on Engineering Psychology and Cognitive Ergonomics (EPCE 2011)* (pp. 473–483). Springer-Verlag. doi:10.1007/978-3-642-21741-8_50

Al-Khalifa, H. S. (2010). A first step in evaluating the usability of Jusur learning management system. In *Proceedings of the Third Annual Forum on E-Learning Excellence: Bringing Global Quality to Local Context.* Academic Press.

Almarashdeh, I. A., Sahari, N., & Mat Zin, N. A. (2011, July). Heuristic evaluation of distance learning management system interface. In *Proceedings of Electrical Engineering and Informatics (ICEEI),* (pp. 1-6). IEEE. doi:10.1109/ICEEI.2011.6021542

Alvarelhão, J., Silva, A., Martins, A., Queirós, A., Amaro, A., Rocha, N., & Laíns, J. (2012). Comparing the Content of Instruments Assessing Environmental Factors using the International Classification of Functioning, Disability and Health. *Journal of Rehabilitation Medicine, 44*(1), 1–6. doi:10.2340/16501977-0905 PMID:22234318

Annett, J. (2002). Subjective rating scales: Science or art? *Ergonomics, 45*(14), 966–987. doi:10.1080/00140130210166951 PMID:12569049

Ansari, S. (2011). Designing Interactive Pill Reminders for Older Adults: A Formative Study. In Universal Access in Human-Computer Interaction. Users Diversity (pp. 121-130). Springer. doi:10.1007/978-3-642-21663-3_13

Antle, A. (2006). Child-Personas: Fact or Fiction? In *Proceedings of the 6th Conference on Designing Interactive Systems* (pp. 22-30). ACM. doi:10.1145/1142405.1142411

Appleton, B. (1997). Patterns and software: Essential concepts and terminology. *Object Magazine Online, 3*(5), 20–25.

Arango, G. F. (1988). *Domain engineering for software reuse* (Doctoral dissertation). Retrieved from ProQuest Dissertations and Theses. (UMI No. 8827979).

Arruda, C., & Rossi, A. (2009). Creating the conditions for innovation. *Dom. The Journal of the Dom Cabral Foundation, 8,* 37–43.

Artman, H. (2000). Team situation assessment and information distribution. *Ergonomics, 43*(8), 1111–1128. doi:10.1080/00140130050084905 PMID:10975176

Aryana, B., Boks, C., & Navabi, A. (2011). Possibilities for Cultural Customization of Mobile Communication Devices: the Case of Iranian Mobile Users. In Human Centered Design (pp. 177-186). Springer. doi:10.1007/978-3-642-21753-1_21

Astell, A., Alm, N., Gowans, G., Ellis, M., Dye, R., & Vaughan, P. (2009). Involving Older People with Dementia and their Carers in Designing Computer Based Support Systems: Some Methodological Considerations. *Universal Access in the Information Society, 8*(1), 49–58. doi:10.1007/s10209-008-0129-9

Asundi, J., Kazman, R., & Klein, M. H. (2001). Economic Modeling of Software Architectures. *News at SEI.* Retrieved from Website: http://www.sei.cmu.edu/library/abstracts/news-at-sei/architect3q01.cfm

Atack, L., Luke, R., & Chien, E. (2008). Evaluation of Patient Satisfaction with Tailored Online Patient Education Information. *Computers, Informatics, Nursing, 26*(5), 258–264. doi:10.1097/01.NCN.0000304838.52207.90 PMID:18769180

Atkinson, N. L., Saperstein, S. L., Desmond, S. M., Gold, R. S., Billing, A. S., & Tian, J. (2009). Rural eHealth Nutrition Education for Limited-Income Families: An Iterative and User-Centered Design Approach. *Journal of Medical Internet Research, 11*(2), e21. doi:10.2196/jmir.1148 PMID:19632974

Aungst, S. G., & Wilson, D. T. (2005). A primer for navigating the shoals of applying wireless technology to marketing problems. *Journal of Business and Industrial Marketing, 20*(2), 59–69. doi:10.1108/08858620510583650

Avnet, M. S., & Weigel, A. L. (2013). The structural approach to shared knowledge: An application to engineering design teams. *Human Factors, 55*(3), 581–594. doi:10.1177/0018720812462388 PMID:23829032

Bannon, L. J. (1991). From Human Factors to Human Actors: The Role of Psychology and Human Computer Interaction Studies in System Design. In J. Greenbaum, & M. Kyng (Eds.), *Design At Work: Cooperative Design of Computer Systems* (pp. 25–44). Lawrence Erlbaum Associates, Inc. Publishers.

Barber, B. R. (1984). *Strong Democracy: Participatory Politics for a New Age.* Berkley, CA: University of California Press.

Barcelos, T. S., & Silveira, I. F. (2012). Teaching computational thinking in initial series. In *Proceedings of CLEI 2012.* Medellín: Centro Latinoamericano de Estudios en Informática.

Barcelos, T. S., Carvalho, T., Schimiguel, J., & Silveira, I. F. (2011). Análise comparativa de heurísticas para avaliação de jogos digitais. In *Proc. IHC+CLIHC 2011* (pp. 187–196). Pernambuco, Brazil: SBC.

Barchéus, F., & Mårtensson, L. (2006). Air traffic management and future technology: The views of the controllers. *Human Factors and Aerospace Safety, 6*(1), 1–16.

Bardin, L. (1977). *Content analysis.* Lisbon: Edições 70.

Barge, J. K. (1996). Leadership Skills and the Dialectics of Leadership in Group Decision Making. In *Communication and group decision making* (2nd ed., pp. 301–342). Thousand Oaks, CA: Sage Publications.

Barras, R. (1986). Towards a Theory of Innovation in Services. *Research Policy, 15*(4), 161–173. doi:10.1016/0048-7333(86)90012-0

Basili, V., Caldeira, G., & Rombach, H. D. (1994). Goal Question Metric Paradigm. In Encyclopedia of Software Engineering. John Wiley & Sons.

Bateson, A. G., Alexander, R. A., & Murphy, M. D. (1987). Cognitive processing differences between novice and expert computer programmers. *International Journal of Man-Machine Studies, 26*(6), 649–660. doi:10.1016/S0020-7373(87)80058-5

Bauerlein, M. (2011). *The digital divide: arguments for and against Facebook, Google, texting, and the age of social networking.* London: Penguin.

Bayliss, J. D., & Strout, S. (2006). Games as a "flavor" of CS1. *SIGCSE Bulletin, 38*(1), 500–504. doi:10.1145/1124706.1121498

Beaubouef, T. (2002). Why computer science students need math. *SIGCSE Bulletin, 34*(4), 57–59. doi:10.1145/820127.820166

Bellamy, C., & Taylor, J. A. (1998). *Governing in the Information Age.* Maidenhead, UK: Open University Press.

Bell, G., & Dourish, P. (2007). Yesterday's Tomorrows: Notes on Ubiquitous Computing's Dominant Vision. *Personal and Ubiquitous Computing, 11*(2), 133–143. doi:10.1007/s00779-006-0071-x

Bellifemine, F., Caire, G., & Greenwood, D. (2007). *Developing Multi-Agent Systems with JADE.* Chichester, UK: John Wiley & Sons. doi:10.1002/9780470058411

Berger, M., Dittmann, L., Caragiozidis, M., Mouratidis, N., Kavadias, C., & Loupis, M. (2008). A Component-Based Software Architecture: Reconfigurable Software for Ambient Intelligent Networked Services Environments. In *Proceedings of Software and Data Technologies* (ICSOFT) (pp. 174-179). IEEE.

Berkes, F. (2008). *Sacred ecology.* Routledge.

Berkowitz, S. D. (1982). *An introduction to structural analysis: The network approach to social research.* Toronto: Butterworth.

Bernsen, N. O., & Dybkjær, L. (2009). *Multimodal Usability.* Springer.

Bessant, J., & Tidd, J. (2009). *Innovation and Entrepreneurship.* Porto Alegre: Bookman.

Bevan, N., & Bruval, P. (2003). *Usability Net: Tools & Methods.* Retrieved July 14, 2013, from http://www.usabilitynet.org/tools/list.htm

Bevan, N., & Curson, I. (1999). Planning and Implementing User-Centred Design. In Proceedings of CHI'99 Extended Abstracts on Human Factors in Computing Systems (pp. 137-138). ACM.

Bevan, N., Claridge, N., & Petrie, H. (2005). Tenuta: Simplified Guidance for Usability and Accessibility. In *Proceedings of HCI International.* Lawrence Erlbaum Associates.

Bevan, N. (1998). European Usability Support Centres: Support for a More Usable Information Society. In *Proceedings of TAP Annual Concertation Meeting.* European Commission.

Beverly, C., & Edmunds-Otter, M. (2006). Systematic Reviews and Secondary Research. In K. Gerrish, & A. Lacey (Eds.), *The Research Process in Nursing* (pp. 316–334). Oxford, UK: Blackwell Publishing.

Bhatnagar, S. (2004). *E-Government: From Vision to Implementation*. New Delhi: Sage Publications.

Bicking, M., & Wimmer, M. A. (2010). Tools and Technologies in eParticipation: Insights from Project Evaluation. In F. De Cindio, A. Machintosh, & C. Peraboni (Eds.), *Online Deliberation:Proceedings of the Fourth International Conference* (pp. 75 – 86). OD2010.

Bimber, B. (1998). The Internet and Political Transformation: Populism, Community and Accelerated Pluralism. *Polity*, *31*(1), 133–160. doi:10.2307/3235370

Bishop, P., & Anderson, L. (2004). *E-Government to E-Democracy: 'High-Tech' Solutions to 'No Tech' Problems*. Paper presented to the Australian Electronic Governance Conference. Melbourne, Australia.

Blomquist, Å., & Arvola, M. (2002). Personas in Action: Ethnography in an Interaction Design Team. In *Proceedings of the 2nd Nordic Conference on Human-Computer Interaction* (pp. 197-200). ACM. doi:10.1145/572020.572044

Blumler, J. C., & Coleman, S. (2001). Realising Democracy Online: A Civic Commons in Cyberspace (IPPR Citizens Online Research Publication No.2). London, UK: IPPR.

Böck, R., Siegert, I., Haase, M., Lange, J., & Wendemuth, A. (2011). ikannotate - A Tool for Labelling, Transcription, and Annotation of Emotionally Coloured Speech. In Affective Computing and Intelligent Interaction (pp. 25-34). Springer.

Boehm, B. (1984). *Software Engineering Economics*. Englewood Cliffs, NJ: Prentice-Hall.

Boehm, B. W., & Sullivan, K. J. (2000). Software economics: A roadmap. In *Proceedings of the conference on The future of Software engineering* (pp. 319-343). ACM.

Boivie, I., Gulliksen, J., & Göransson, B. (2006). The lonesome cowboy: A study of the usability designer role in systems development. *Interacting with Computers*, *18*(4), 601–634. doi:10.1016/j.intcom.2005.10.003

Boll, S., Heuten, E., Meyer, M., & Meis, M. (2010). Development of a Multimodal Reminder System for Older Persons in their Residential Home. *Informatics for Health & Social Care*, *35*(3-4), 104–124. doi:10.3109/17538157.2010.528651 PMID:21133767

Borgatti, S. P., Everett, M. G., & Freeman, L. C. (2002). *Ucinet for Windows: Software for Social Network Analysis*. Cambridge, MA: Analytic Technologies.

Botella, C., Garcia-Palacios, A., Baños, R. M., & Quero, S. (2009). Cybertherapy: Advantages, Limitations, and Ethical Issues. *PsychNology Journal*, *7*(1).

Brambilla, F. R. (2009). Sales Force Automation (SFA) como ferramenta de vendas em aplicação do Customer Relationship Management (CRM). In SIMPOI. São Paulo, Brazil: Academic Press.

Brandon, D. P., & Hollingshead, A. B. (1999). Collaborative Learning and Computer-Supported Group. *Communication Education*, *48*(2), 1–19. doi:10.1080/03634529909379159

Brandt, J., Weiss, N., & Klemmer, S. R. (2007). txt 4 l8r: Lowering the Burden for Diary Studies under Mobile Conditions. In Proceedings of CHI'07 Extended Abstracts on Human Factors in Computing Systems (pp. 2303-2308). ACM.

Brasil. Ministério da Educação. (2002). *PCN+ Ensino Médio: Orientações Curriculares Complementares aos Parâmetros Curriculares Nacionais*. Brasília: MEC/SEB.

Brehmer, B., & Svenmarck, P. (1995). Distributed decision making in dynamic environments: Time scales and architectures of decision making. In J.-P. Caverni, M. Bar-Hillel, F. H. Barron, & H. Jungermann (Eds.), *Contributions to decision making - I* (pp. 155–174). Amsterdam: Elsevier.

Brown, J. M., Lindgaard, G., & Biddle, R. (2011). Collaborative Events and Shared Artifacts: Agile Interaction Designers and Developers Working Toward Common Aims. In *Proceedings of 2011 AGILE Conference*. IEEE. doi:10.1109/AGILE.2011.45

Brown, A. (1987). Metacognition, executive control, self regulation, and other more mysterious mechanisms. In F. E. Weinert, & R. H. Kluwe (Eds.), *Metacognition, motivation and understanding* (pp. 65–116). Hillsdale, NJ: Erlbaum.

Brown, A. W. (2012). *Enterprise software delivery: bringing agility and efficiency to the global software supply chain*. Boston, MA: Addison-Wesley.

Brown, D. (Ed.). (2012). *Agile user experience design: a practitioner's guide to making it work*. Oxford, UK: Newnes.

Brown, D. M. (2013). *Designing Together*. San Francisco, CA: New Riders Press.

Budde, S. H., Stulp, F., & Sancho-Pradel, D. L. (2008). Using Persona Descriptions as a Communication Tool in Interdisciplinary System Design. *Gerontechnology (Valkenswaard)*, *7*(2), 82. doi:10.4017/gt.2008.07.02.019.00

Burtis, A. T. (2009). Managing Indigenous Knowledge And Traditional Cultural Expressions: Is Technology The Solution? *Articles*, *33*, 10.

Bush, V. (1945). As we may think. *Atlantic Monthly*, *176*(1), 101–108.

Cajander, Å. (2010). *Usability - Who Cares? The Introduction of User-Centred Systems Design in Organisations*. Doctoral thesis, Uppsala University, Sweden. Uppsala: Acta Universitatis Upsaliensis.

Campbell, P. F., & McCabe, G. P. (1984). Predicting the success of freshmen in a computer science major. *Communications of the ACM*, *27*(11), 1108–1113. http://doi.acm.org/10.1145/1968.358288

Candell, O. (2009). *Development of Information Support Solutions for Complex Technical Systems using eMaintenance*. Doctoral dissertation. Luleå, Sweden: Luleå University of Technology.

Carayon, P., Hoonakker, P., & Smith, M. J. (2012). Human Factors in Organizational Design and Management. In G. Salvendy (Ed.), *Handbook of Human Factors and Ergonomics* – (4th ed., pp. 534–552). John Wiley and Sons. doi:10.1002/9781118131350.ch18

Carillo, K. & Okoli, chitu. (2008). The Open Source Movement: A Revolution In Software Development. *Journal of Computer Information Systems*, *49*(2), 1–9.

Carnegie Mellon University. (2013). *Alice - An educational software that teaches students computer programming in a 3D environment*. Retrieved August 15, 2013, from http://www.alice.org

Carneiro, D., Novais, P., Costa, R., Gomes, P., & Neves, J. (2009). EMon: Embodied Monitorization. In Ambient Intelligence (pp. 133-142). Springer.

Carr, N. (2004). *Does IT Matter? Information Technology and the Corrosion of Competitive Advantage*. Boston: Harvard Business School Press.

Carroll, N. (2012). *Service science: An empirical study on the socio-technical dynamics of public sector service network innovation*. (PhD Thesis). University of Limerick, Limerick, Ireland.

Carroll, N., Richardson, I., & Whelan, E. (2012). Service Science: Exploring Complex Agile Service Networks through Organisational Network Analysis. In Agile and Lean Service-Oriented Development: Foundations, Theory and Practice. Hershey, PA: IGI Global.

Carroll, J. M. (2013). Human Computer Interaction. In M. Soegaard, & R. F. Dam (Eds.), *The Encyclopedia of Human-Computer Interaction* (2nd ed.). The Interaction Design Foundation.

Carroll, N., Whelan, E., & Richardson, I. (2010). Applying social network analysis to discover service innovation within agile service networks. *Service Science*, *2*(4), 225–244. doi:10.1287/serv.2.4.225

Carter, L. (2006). Why students with an apparent aptitude for computer science don't choose to major in computer science. *SIGCSE Bulletin*, *38*(1), 27–31. doi:10.1145/1124706.1121352

Castillo, J. C. (1997). *The User-Reported Critical Incident Method for Remote Usability Evaluation* (Doctoral dissertation). Virginia Polytechnic Institute and State University.

Catinat, M., & Vedel, T. (2000). Public Policies for Digital Democracy. In K. L. Hacker, & J. van Dijk (Eds.), *Digital Democracy: Issues of Theory and Practice* (pp. 184–208). London: Sage Publications.

Chambres, P., Izaute, M., & Marescaux, P.-J. (Eds.). (2002). *Metacognition: Process, function and use*. Boston: Kluwer Academic Publishers. doi:10.1007/978-1-4615-1099-4

Chang, Y., Lim, Y., & Stolterman, E. (2008). Personas: From Theory to Practices. In *Proceedings of the 5th Nordic Conference on Human-Computer Interaction: Building Bridges* (pp. 439-442). ACM.

Charrier, G. (1974). Cog's ladder: a model of group development. In J. E. Jones (Ed.), *The 1974 Annual Handbook for Group Facilitators* (pp. 142–145). Hoboken, NJ: John Wiley & Sons.

Chase, W. G., & Simon, H. A. (1973). Perception in chess. *Cognitive Psychology*, *4*(1), 55–81. doi:10.1016/0010-0285(73)90004-2

Chengalur-Smith, S., & Sidorova, A. (2003). *Survival of open-source projects: A population ecology perspective.* Paper presented at the 24th International Conference of Information Systems. Atlanta, GA.

Chen, S. Y., Fan, J.-P., & Macredie, R. D. (2006). Navigation in hypermedia learning systems: Experts vs. novices. *Computers in Human Behavior*, *22*(2), 251–266. doi:10.1016/j.chb.2004.06.004

Chen, S. Y., & Macredie, R. D. (2005). The assessment of usability of electronic shopping: A heuristic evaluation. *International Journal of Information Management*, *25*(6), 516–532. doi:10.1016/j.ijinfomgt.2005.08.008

Chesbrough, H. (2004). *UC Berkeley, Open Innovation: Renewing Growth from Industrial R&D.* Paper presented at the 10th Annual Innovation Convergence. Minneapolis, MN.

Chesbrough, H. (2003). *Open Innovation: The New Imperative for Creating and Profiting from Technology.* Boston: Harvard Business School Press.

Chesbrough, H. (2011). Bringing Open Innovation to Services. *MIT Sloan Management Review*, *52*(2), 85–90.

Chesbrough, H. W. (2003). The era of open innovation. *MIT Sloan Management Review*, *44*(3), 35–41.

Chi, M. T. H., Feltovich, P. J., & Glaser, R. (1981). Categorization and representation of physics problems by experts and novices. *Cognitive Science*, *5*(2), 121–152. doi:10.1207/s15516709cog0502_2

Chun, S., Shulman, S., Sandoval, R., & Hovy, E. (2010). Government 2.0: Making Connections Between Citizens, Data and Government. *Information Polity Journal*, *15*(1-2), 1–9.

Clancy, M. J., & Linn, M. C. (1999). Patterns and pedagogy. *SIGCSE Bulletin*, *31*(1), 37–42. doi:10.1145/384266.299673

Cockton, G. (2013). Usability Evaluation. In M. Soegaard, & R. F. Dam (Eds.), *The Encyclopedia of Human-Computer Interaction* (2nd ed.). The Interaction Design Foundation.

Cohn, M. (2004). *User stories applied: for agile software development.* Boston, MA: Addison-Wesley.

Colazo, J. (2007). *Innovation success: An empirical study of software development projects in the context of the open source paradigm.* The University of Western Ontario.

Colazo, J., & Fang, Y. (2009). Impact of license choice on Open Source Software development activity. *Journal of the American Society for Information Science and Technology*, *60*(5), 997–1011. doi:10.1002/asi.21039

Coleman, S. (2011). The Wisdom of Which Crowd? On the Pathology of a Listening Government. *The Political Quarterly*, *82*(3), 355–364.

Coleman, S., & Gotze, J. (2001). *Bowling Together: Online Public Engagement in Policy Deliberation.* London: Hansard Society.

Coley, L. S., Lindemann, E., & Wagner, S. M. (2012). Tangible and intangible resource inequity in customer-supplier relationships. *Journal of Business and Industrial Marketing*, *27*(8), 611–622. doi:10.1108/08858621211273565

Colley, A., Banton, L., Down, J., & Pither, A. (1992). An Expert-Novice Comparison in Musical Composition. *Psychology of Music*, *20*(2), 124–137. doi:10.1177/0305735692202003

Conchúir, Ó. (2009). Benefits of global software development: Exploring the unexplored. *Software Process Improvement and Practice*, *14*(4), 201–212. doi:10.1002/spip.417

Connelly, K., Siek, K., Mulder, I., Neely, S., Stevenson, G., & Kray, C. (2008). Evaluating Pervasive and Ubiquitous Systems. *Pervasive Computing, IEEE*, *7*(3), 85–88. doi:10.1109/MPRV.2008.47

Cook, D., & Das, S. (2007). How Smart are our Environments? An Updated Look at the State of the Art. *Pervasive and Mobile Computing*, *3*(2), 53–73. doi:10.1016/j.pmcj.2006.12.001

Cooper, A. (1999). *The Inmates are Running the Asylum: Why High-Tech Products Drive us Crazy and How to Restore the Sanity.* Pearson Education. doi:10.1007/978-3-322-99786-9_1

Cooper, A., & Cronin, R. R. D. (2007). *About Face 3: The Essentials of Interaction Design.* Indianapolis, IN: John Wiley & Sons.

Cooper, A., & Reimann, R. (2003). *About Face 2.0: The Essentials of Interaction Design.* John Wiley & Sons.

Coplien, J. O., & Bjørnvig, G. (2011). *Lean architecture: for agile software development.* Hoboken, NJ: John Wiley & Sons.

Coronato, A., & De Pietro, G. (2010). A Middleware Architecture for Safety Critical Ambient Intelligence Applications. In Proceedings of Smart Spaces and Next Generation Wired/Wireless Networking (pp. 26-37). Springer. doi:10.1007/978-3-642-14891-0_3

Cossentino, M. (2005). From Requirements to Code with PASSI Methodology. In B. Henderson-Sellers, & P. Giorgini (Eds.), *Agent-Oriented Methodologies* (pp. 79–106). Hershey, PA: Idea Group Publishing; doi:10.4018/978-1-59140-581-8.ch004

Crenshaw, T. L., Chambers, E. W., Metcalf, H., & Thakkar, U. (2008). A case study of retention practices at the University of Illinois at Urbana-Champaign. In *Proc. SIGCSE 2008* (pp. 412–416). New York: ACM. doi:10.1145/1352135.1352276

Creswell, J. W., & Miller, D. L. (2000). Determining validity in qualitative inquiry. *Theory into Practice, 39*(3), 124–130. doi:10.1207/s15430421tip3903_2

Croll, J. (2010). Testing for Usability is not Enough: Why Clinician Acceptance of Health Information Systems is also Crucial for Successful Implementation? In E-Health (pp. 49-60). Springer.

Cross, R. L., & Parker, A. (2004). *The Hidden Power of Social Networks: Understanding how Work Really Gets Done in Organizations.* Boston, MA: Harvard Business School Press.

Crowston, K., Annabi, H., & Howison, J. (2003). *Defining open source software project success.* Paper presented at the 24th International Conference on Information Systems. Seattle, WA.

Crowston, K., Wei, K., & Howinson, J. & Wiggins, A. (2010). Free/Libre Open Source Software Development: What we know and what we do not know. Syracuse, NY: University School of Information Studies.

Crowston, K., Howison, J., & Annabi, H. (2006). Information systems success in free and open source software development: Theory and measures. *Software Process Improvement and Practice, 11*(2), 123–148. doi:10.1002/spip.259

Crowston, K., & Scozzi, B. (2002). Open source software projects as virtual organisations: Competency rallying for software development. *IEE Software Proceedings, 149*(1), 3–17. doi:10.1049/ip-sen:20020197

Crozier, M., & Friedberg, E. (1980). *Actors and Systems.* University of Chicago Press.

Cruickshank, P., Edelmann, N., & Smith, C. (2010). Signing an e-Petition as a Transition from Lurking to Participation. In H. J. Scholl, & M. Janssen (Eds.), *Electronic Government and Electronic Participation: Joint Proceedings of Ongoing Research and Projects of IFIP EGOV and IFIP ePart 2010* (pp. 275–282). Linz, Austria: Trauner Verlag.

Cunningham, W. (2006, August). Design principles of wiki: how can so little do so much? In *International Symposium on Wikis* (pp. 13-14), Odense, Denmark. doi:10.1145/1149453.1149459

Curtis, B., Hefley, B., & Miller, S. (2009). *People Capability Maturity Model (P-CMM) Version 2.0* (2nd ed., pp. 2009–TR-003). Pittsburgh, PA: Software Engineering Institute. CMU/SEI.

Czaja, S. J., & Nair, S. N. (2012). Human Factors Engineering and Systems Design. In G. Salvendy (Ed.), *Handbook of Human Factors and Ergonomics* (4th ed., pp. 38–56). John Wiley and Sons. doi:10.1002/9781118131350.ch2

Czarnecki, K., & Eisenecker, U. W. (2000). *Generative Programming: Methods, Tools, and Applications.* New York, NY: ACM Press/Addison-Wesley Publishing Co..

Dada, D. (2006). The Failure of E-Government in Developing Countries: A Literature Review. *The Electronic Journal on Information Systems in Developing Countries, 26*(7), 1–10.

Dadlani, P., Sinitsyn, A., Fontijn, W., & Markopoulos, P. (2011). Aurama: Caregiver Awareness for Living Independently with an Augmented Picture Frame Display. *AI & Society*, *25*(2), 233–245. doi:10.1007/s00146-009-0253-y

Daft, R. L. (2007). *Teoría y Diseño Organizacional (9ᵗʰ ed.)*. DF, México: Cengage Learning Editores.

Dalkir, K. (2005). *Knowledge management in theory and practice*. Burlington, MA: Elsevier Butterworth-Heinemann.

Darses, F., & Wolff, M. (2006). How do designers represent to themselves the users' needs? *Applied Ergonomics*, *37*(6), 757–764. doi:10.1016/j.apergo.2005.11.004 PMID:16442493

Davidsson, S., & Alm, H. (2014). *Context adaptable driver information – Or, what do whom need and want when?* Applied Cognitive Ergonomics.

Davis, B. (2009). *97 things every project manager should know: collective wisdom from the experts*. Sebastopol, CA: O'Reilly Media.

Davis, F. D., Bagozzi, R. P., & Warshaw, P. R. (1989). User Acceptance of Computer Technology: A Comparison of Two Theoretical Models. *Management Science*, *35*(8), 982–1003. doi:10.1287/mnsc.35.8.982

De Hert, P., Gutwirth, S., Moscibroda, A., Wright, D., & Fuster, G. (2009). Legal Safeguards for Privacy and Data Protection in Ambient Intelligence. *Personal and Ubiquitous Computing*, *13*(6), 435–444. doi:10.1007/s00779-008-0211-6

Debevc, M., Kosec, P., & Holzinger, A. (2010). E-learning Accessibility for the Deaf and Hard of Hearing-Practical Examples and Experiences. In HCI in Work and Learning, Life and Leisure (pp. 203-213). Springer. doi:10.1007/978-3-642-16607-5_13

Dees, W. (2011). Usability of Nomadic User Interfaces. In *Human-Computer Interaction. Towards Mobile and Intelligent Interaction Environments* (pp. 195–204). Springer. doi:10.1007/978-3-642-21616-9_22

Defense Science Board (2012). *The role of autonomy in DoD systems*. Washington, DC: Undersecretary of Defense.

Dekker, S. W. A. (1996). Cognitive complexity in management by exception: Deriving early human factors requirements for an envisioned air traffic management world. In D. Harris (Ed.), Engineering psychology and cognitive ergonomics, volume I: Transportation systems (pp. 201-210). Aldershot, UK: Ashgate.

Dekker, S. W. A. (2003). Illusions of explanation: A critical essay on error classification. *The International Journal of Aviation Psychology*, *13*(2), 95–106. doi:10.1207/S15327108IJAP1302_01

Dekker, S. W. A. (2005). *Ten questions about human error: A new view of human factors and systems safety*. Mahwah, NJ: Erlbaum.

Dekker, S. W. A. (2007). Doctors are more dangerous than gun owners: A rejoinder to error counting. *Human Factors*, *49*(2), 177–184. doi:10.1518/001872007X312423 PMID:17447661

Dekker, S. W. A., & Lützhöft, M. (2004). Correspondence, cognition and sensemaking: A radical empiricist view of situation awareness. In S. Banbury, & S. Tremblay (Eds.), *A cognitive approach to situation awareness: Theory and application* (pp. 22–41). Aldershot, UK: Ashgate.

Dekker, S. W. A., & Woods, D. D. (1999). Extracting data from the future: Assessment and certification of envisioned systems. In S. Dekker, & E. Hollnagel (Eds.), *Coping with computers in the cockpit* (pp. 131–143). Aldershot, UK: Ashgate.

DeLone, W. H., & McLean, E. R. (2003). The DeLone and McLean Model of Information Systems Success: A Ten-Year Update. *Journal of Management Information Systems*, *19*(4), 9–30.

Denner, J., Werner, L., & Ortiz, E. (2012). Computer games created by middle school girls: Can they be used to measure understanding of computer science concepts? *Computers & Education*, *58*(1), 240–249. doi:10.1016/j.compedu.2011.08.006

Denning, P., Horning, J., Parnas, D., & Weinstein, L. (2005). Wikipedia risks. *Communications of the ACM*, *48*(12), 152–152. doi:10.1145/1101779.1101804

Derman, Y. D., Arenovich, T., & Strauss, J. (2010). Speech Recognition Software and Electronic Psychiatric Progress Notes: Physicians' Ratings and Preferences. *BMC Medical Informatics and Decision Making, 10*(1), 44. doi:10.1186/1472-6947-10-44 PMID:20738875

Devedžić, V., & Milenković, S. A. R. (2011). Teaching agile software development: A case study. *Education. IEEE Transactions on, 54*(2), 273–278.

Dewey, J. (1916). *Democracy and Education.* Mineola, NY: Dover Publications, Inc.

di Gennaro, C., & Dutton, W. H. (2006). The Internet and the Public: Online and Offline Political Participation in the UK. *Parliamentary Affairs, 59*(2), 299–313. doi:10.1093/pa/gsl004

Díaz, O., & Puente, G. (2011, October). Wiki scaffolding: helping organizations to set up wikis. In *Proceedings of the 7th International Symposium on Wikis and Open Collaboration* (pp. 154-162). New York, NY: ACM. doi:10.1145/2038558.2038583

Dileo, J., Jacobs, T., & Deloach, S. (2002). Integrating Ontologies into Multi-Agent Systems Engineering. *Proceedings of 4th International Bi-Conference Workshop on Agent Oriented Information Systems (AOIS 2002).* Bologna, Italy.

Dores, A. R., Carvalho, I. P., Barbosa, F., Almeida, I., Guerreiro, S., Leitão, M., et al. (2011). Serious Games: Are They Part of the Solution in the Domain of Cognitive Rehabilitation? In Serious Games Development and Applications (pp. 95-105). Springer.

Dotan, A., Maiden, N., Lichtner, V., & Germanovich, L. (2009). Designing with only Four People in Mind? A Case Study of Using Personas to Redesign a Work Integrated Learning Support System. In Human-Computer Interaction - INTERACT 2009 (pp. 497-509). Springer.

Downs, A. (1964). *Inside Bureaucracy.* Boston: Little Brown.

Drumond, L., & Girardi, R. (2008). A Multi-agent Legal Recommender System. *Journal of Artificial Intelligence and Law, 16*(2), 175–207. doi:10.1007/s10506-008-9062-8

Dunn-Jensen, L. M. (2014). Groups Meet... Teams Improve: Building Teams That Learn. *Academy of Management Learning & Education, 13*(1), 151–153.

Dutton, W. H., & Peltu, M. (2007). *Reconfiguring Government Public Engagements: Enhancing the Communicative Power of Citizens* (Oxford Internet Institute Forum Discussion Paper No. 9). Oxford Internet Institute.

Dutton, W. H. (1992). The Ecology of Games Shaping Telecommunications Policy. *Communication Theory, 2*(4), 303–324. doi:10.1111/j.1468-2885.1992.tb00046.x

East, J. P., Thomas, S. R., Wallingford, E., Beck, W., & Drake, J. (1996). Pattern-based programming instruction. In *Proceedings of the ASEE Annual Conference and Exposition.* Washington, DC: ASEE.

Ebersbach, A., Adelung, A., Dueck, G., Glaser, M., Heigl, R., & Warta, A. (2008). *Wiki: web collaboration.* New York, NY: Springer.

Edwards, C., & Harwood, J. (2003). Social Identity in the Classroom: An Examination of Age Identification Between Students and Instructors. *Communication Education, 52*(1), 60–65. doi:10.1080/03634520302463

Efimova, L. A. (2009). *Passion at work: blogging practices of knowledge workers. Novay PhD Research Series, 24.* Enschede, The Netherlands: Novay.

Eggers, W. D. (2005). *Government 2.0: Using Technology to Improve Education, Cut Red Tape, Reduce Gridlock and Enhance Democracy.* Lanham, MD: Rowman and Littlefield Publishers Inc.

Eisenhardt, K. M. (1989). Building Theories from Case Study Research. *Academy of Management Review, 14*(4), 532–550.

Ek, Å. (2006). *Safety culture in sea and aviation transport.* Doctoral dissertation. Lund, Sweden: Lund University.

Elling, S., Lentz, L., & de Jong, M. (2012). Combining Concurrent Think-Aloud Protocols and Eye-Tracking Observations: An Analysis of Verbalizations and Silences. *IEEE Transactions on Professional Communication, 55*(3), 206–220. doi:10.1109/TPC.2012.2206190

Elliot, M., & Scacchi, W. (2008). Mobilization of software developers: The free software movement. *Information Technology & People*, *21*(1), 4–33. doi:10.1108/09593840810860315

Ellis, D. G., & Fisher, B. A. (1994). *Small Group Decision Making: Communication and the Group Process*. New York: McGraw-Hill.

Endsley, M. R. (1988). Situation awareness global assessment technique (SAGAT). In *Proceedings of the IEEE National Aerospace and Electronics Conference* (pp. 789-795). New York: IEEE.

Endsley, M. R. (1995a). Measurement of situation awareness in dynamic systems. *Human Factors*, *37*(1), 65–84. doi:10.1518/001872095779049499

Endsley, M. R. (1995b). Toward a theory of situation awareness in dynamic systems. *Human Factors*, *37*(1), 32–64. doi:10.1518/001872095779049543

Endsley, M. R. (2000). Direct measurement of situation awareness: Validity and use of SAGAT. In M. R. Endsley, & D. J. Garland (Eds.), *Situation awareness analysis and measurement* (pp. 147–173). Mahwah, NJ: Erlbaum.

Endsley, M. R., Bolstad, C. A., Jones, D. G., & Riley, J. M. (2003). Situation awareness oriented design: From user's cognitive requirements to creating effective supporting technologies. In *Proceedings of the Human Factors and Ergonomics Society 47th Annual Meeting* (pp. 268-272). Santa Monica, CA: Human Factors and Ergonomics Society.

Endsley, M. R., Bolté, B., & Jones, D. G. (2003). *Designing for situation awareness: An approach to user-centered design*. London: Taylor & Francis. doi:10.1201/9780203485088

Esquivel, A., Haya, P., García-Herranz, M., & Alamán, X. (2009). Harnessing "Fair Trade" Metaphor as Privacy Control in Ambient Intelligent. In *Ambient Intelligence Perspectives: Selected Papers from the 1st International Ambient Intelligence Forum, 2008* (Vol. 1, p. 73). IOS Press.

European Commission. (2006). *The Build-for-All Reference Manual*. European Commission.

Faily, S., & Fléchais, I. (2010). The Secret Lives of Assumptions: Developing and Refining Assumption Personas for Secure System Design. In Human-Centred Software Engineering (pp. 111-118). Springer.

Fällman, D. (2003). *In romance with the materials of mobile interaction: A phenomenological approach to the design of mobile information technology*. Doctoral dissertation. Umeå, Sweden: University of Umeå.

Fancott, T., Kamthan, P., & Shahmir, N. (2012). Implications of the Social Web Environment for User Story Education. *Electronic Journal of e-Learning*, *10*(1).

Fang, Y., & Neufeld, D. (2009). Understanding Sustained Participation in Open Source Software Projects. *Journal of Management Information Systems*, *25*(4), 9–50. doi:10.2753/MIS0742-1222250401

Fanucci, L., Pardini, G., Costalli, F., Dalmiani, S., Salinas, J., & De La Higuera, J. et al. (2009). Health @ Home: A New Homecare Model for Patients with Chronic Heart Failure. *Assistive Technology from Adapted Equipment to Inclusive Environments: AAATE*, *25*, 87.

Fayn, J., & Rubel, P. (2010). Toward a Personal Health Society in Cardiology. Information Technology in Biomedicine. *IEEE Transactions on*, *14*(2), 401–409.

Feigh, K. M., & Pritchett, A. R. (2014). Requirements for effective function allocation: A critical review. *Journal of Cognititve Engineering and Decision Making*, *8*(1), 23–32. doi:10.1177/1555343413490945

Feller, J. et al. (2005). *Perspectives on Free and Open Source Software*. Cambridge, MA: MIT Press.

Ferguson, R. (2006). *Digital Dialogues: Interim Report, December 2005 – August 2006*. London: The Hansard Society.

Ferreira, D., & da Silva, A. R. (2008, September). Wiki supported collaborative requirements engineering. In Proceedings of Wikis4SE 2008 Workshop. Porto, Portugal: Academic Press.

Ferron, J. C., Brunette, M. F., McHugo, G. J., Devitt, T. S., Martin, W. M., & Drake, R. E. (2011). Developing a Quit Smoking Website that is Usable by People with Severe Mental Illnesses. *Psychiatric Rehabilitation Journal*, *35*(2), 111–116. doi:10.2975/35.2.2011.111.116 PMID:22020840

Fichman, R. G., & Kemerer, C. F. (2012). Adoption of software engineering process innovations: The case of object-orientation. *Sloan Management Review*, *34*(2).

Fieldhouse, E., Tranmer, M., & Russel, A. (2007). Something about Young People or Something about Elections? Electoral Participation of Young People in Europe: Evidence from a Multilevel Analysis of the European Social Survey. *European Journal of Political Research*, *46*(6), 797–822. doi:10.1111/j.1475-6765.2007.00713.x

Firestone, W. A. (1989). Educational Policy as an Ecology of Games. *Educational Researcher*, *18*(7), 18–24. doi:10.2307/1177165

First Nations Centre. (2007). *OCAP: Ownership, Control, Access and Possession. Ottawa*, Canada: First Nations Information Governance Committee, Assembly of First Nations Ottawa.

Fishkin, J. S. (1995). *The Voice of the People: Public Opinion and Democracy*. New York: Yale University Press.

Fitzgerald, B. (2006). The transformation of open source software. *Management Information Systems Quarterly*, *30*(3), 587–598.

Flach, J. M. (1995). Maintaining situation awareness when stalking cognition in the wild. In D. J. Garland & M. R. Endsley (Eds.), *Proceedings of an International Conference on Experimental Analysis and Measurement of Situation Awareness* (pp. 25-34). Daytona Beach, FL: Embry-Riddle Aeronautical University Press.

Flavell, J. H. (1976). Metacognitive aspects of problem solving. In L. B. Resnick (Ed.), *The Nature of Intelligence* (pp. 231–235). Hillsdale, NJ: Erlbaum.

Floyd, C., Schultz, T., & Fulton, S., & the US Air Force Academy. (2012, June). Security Vulnerabilities in the open source Moodle eLearning System. In *Proceedings of the 16th Colloquium for Information Systems Security Education*. Academic Press.

Fogie, S. (2003, May). *Practical Web Application Security with WebGoat - InformIT*. Retrieved from http://www.informit.com/guides/content.aspx?g=security&seqNum=344

Francis, D., & Bessant, J. (2005). Targeting innovation and implications for capability development. *Technovation*, *25*(3), 171–183. doi:10.1016/j.technovation.2004.03.004

Franklin, D., Conrad, P., Boe, B., Nilsen, K., Hill, C., & Len, M., … Waite, R. (2013). Assessment of computer science learning in a scratch-based outreach program. In *Proceeding of the 44th ACM technical symposium on Computer science education* (pp. 371–376). New York, NY: ACM. doi:10.1145/2445196.2445304

Fredriksson, M. (2004). *Online engineering: On the nature of open computational systems*. Doctoral dissertation (No. 2004:05). Karlskrona, Sweden: Blekinge Institute of Technology.

Freeman, L. C. (1989). Social Networks and the Structure Experiment. In Research Methods in Social Network Analysis. George Mason University Press.

Freire, L. L., Arezes, P. M., & Campos, J. C. (2012). A Literature Review about Usability Evaluation Methods for e-Learning Platforms. *Work (Reading, Mass.)*, *41*, 1038–1044. PMID:22316857

Friedman-Hill, E. (2003). *Jess in action: rule-based systems in java*. Greenwich, UK: Manning Publications Co.

Friedman, T. L. (2006). *The world is flat*. New York: Penguin Books.

Frydenberg, M. (2008). Wikis as a tool for collaborative course management. *MERLOT Journal of Online Learning and Teaching*, *4*(2), 169–181.

Füller, J., & Matzler, K. (2007). Virtual Product experience and customer participation – A chance for customer-centered, really new products. *Technovation*, *27*(6-7), 378–387. doi:10.1016/j.technovation.2006.09.005

Gallouj, F., & Weinstein, O. (1997). Innovation in Services. *Research Policy*, *26*(4-5), 537–556. doi:10.1016/S0048-7333(97)00030-9

Galorath, D. D., & Evans, M. W. (2006). *Software sizing, estimation, and risk management: when performance is measured performance improves*. Boca Raton, FL: CRC Press. doi:10.1201/9781420013122

Gartner Research. (2011). *Ipad and Beyond: The Media Tablet in Business*. Retrieved August 10, 2012, from http://www.gartner.com/technology/research/ipad-media-tablet/

Gebauer, H., & Kowalkowski, C. (2012). Customer-focused and service-focused orientation in organizational structures. *Journal of Business and Industrial Marketing*, *27*(7), 527–537. doi:10.1108/08858621211257293

Gebauer, H., Ren, G., Valtakoski, A., & Reynoso, J. (2012). Service-driven manufacturing: Provision, evolution and financial impact of services in industrial firms. *Journal of Service Management*, *23*(1), 120–136. doi:10.1108/09564231211209005

Geoghegan, T. (2007). The Petition, the 'Prat' and the Political Ideal, *BBC News – Magazine: February 13, 2007*. Available at: http://news.bbc.co.uk/1/hi/magazine/6354735.stm

Georgiakakis, P., Papasalouros, A., Retalis, S., Siassiakos, K., & Papaspyrou, N. (2005). Evaluating the usability of web-based learning management systems. *THEMES in Education*, *6*(1), 45–59.

Ghosh, R., Glott, R., Krieger, B., & Robles, G. (2002). Free/Libre and Open Source Software: Survey and Study (Technical Report). Netherlands: International Institute of Infonomics, University of Maastricht. Retrieved from http://www.math.unipd.it/~bellio/FLOSS%20Final%20Report%20-%20Part%204%20-%20Survey%20of%20Developers.pdf

Ginat, D. (2004). On Novice Loop Boundaries and Range Conceptions. *Computer Science Education*, *14*(3), 165–181. doi:10.1080/0899340042000302709

Girardi, R. (1992). In O. Frameworks (Ed.), *Application Engineering: Putting Reuse to Work. Dennis Tsichritzis* (pp. 137–149). Geneva, Switzerland: University of Geneva.

Girardi, R., & Leite, A. (2008). A Knowledge-based Tool for Multi-Agent Domain Engineering. *Knowledge-Based Systems*, *21*(7), 604–611. doi:10.1016/j.knosys.2008.03.036

Girardi, R., & Leite, A. (2011). Knowledge Engineering Support for Agent-Oriented Software Reuse. In M. Ramachandran (Ed.), *Knowledge Engineering for Software Development Life Cycles: Support Technologies and Applications* (pp. 177–195). Hershey, PA: IGI Global; doi:10.4018/978-1-60960-509-4.ch010

Gnaniah, J., Yeo, A., Songan, P., Zen, H., & Hamid, K. A. (2004). *A Comparison on the Implementation Approaches for the e-Bario and e-Bedian Projects.* Paper presented at the 7th International Conference on Work With Computing Systems (WWCS). Kuala Lumpur.

Goetz, J. P., & LeCompte, M. D. (1984). *Ethnography and qualitative design in educational research.* Orlando, FL: Academic Press.

Golbeck, J. (2013). *Analyzing the social web.* Oxford, UK: Newnes.

Goma, H. (2005). *Designing Software Product Lines with UML: From Use Cases to pattern-based Software Architectures.* Boston, MA: Addison-Wesley. doi:10.1109/SEW.2005.5

Goodhart, M. (2007). Europe's Democratic Deficits through the Looking Glass: The European Union as a Challenge for Democracy. *Perspectives on Politics*, *5*(3), 567–584. doi:10.1017/S1537592707071551

Goodman-Deane, J., Keith, S., & Whitney, G. (2008). HCI and the Older Population. In Proceedings of the 22nd British HCI Group Annual Conference on People and Computers: Culture, Creativity. *Interaction*, *2*, 193–194.

Goodwin, K., & Cooper, A. (2009). *Designing for the Digital Age: How to Create Human-Centered Products and Services.* John Wiley & Sons.

Goumopoulos, C., & Kameas, A. (2009). A Service Oriented Architecture Combining Agents and Ontologies Towards Pervasive Adaptation. In *Intelligent Environments 2009:Proceedings of the 5th International Conference on Intelligent Environments* (Vol. 2, p. 228). IOS Press

Governor, J., Hinchcliffe, D., & Nickull, D. (2009). *Web 2.0 architectures: what entrepreneurs and information architects need to know.* Sebastopol, CA: O'Reilly Media.

Granić, A., & Ćukušić, M. (2011). Usability Testing and Expert Inspections Complemented by Educational Evaluation: A Case Study of an e-Learning Platform. *Journal of Educational Technology & Society*, *14*(2).

Grewal, R., Lilien, G. L., & Mallapragada, G. (2006). Location, location, location: How network embeddedness affects project success in open source systems. *Management Science*, *52*(7), 1043–1056. doi:10.1287/mnsc.1060.0550

Grove, S. J., Fisk, R. P., & Jonh, J. (2003). The future of services marketing: Forecasts from ten services experts. *Journal of Services Marketing*, *17*(2), 107–121. doi:10.1108/08876040310467899

Gruber, T. R. (1995). Toward Principles for the Design of Ontologies used for Knowledge Sharing. *International Journal of Human-Computer Studies*, *43*(5-6), 907–928. doi:10.1006/ijhc.1995.1081

Gualtieri, M. (2009). Best Practices. In *User Experience (UX)*. Forrester Research.

Guðjónsdóttir, R. (2010). *Personas and Scenarios in Use*. Doctoral Thesis submitted to the Kungliga Tekniska Högskolan in fulfilment of the requirements for the Degree of Doctor in Human-Computer Interaction.

Gulliksen, J., Boivie, I., & Göransson, B. (2006). Usability professionals: Current practices and future development. *Interacting with Computers*, *18*(4), 568–600. doi:10.1016/j.intcom.2005.10.005

Gutzwiller, R. S., & Clegg, B. A. (2013). The role of working memory in levels of situation awareness. *Journal of Cognitive Engineering and Decision Making*, *7*(2), 141–154. doi:10.1177/1555343412451749

Haberman, B., & Muller, O. (2008). *Teaching abstraction to novices: Pattern-based and ADT-based problem-solving processes*. IEEE. doi::10.1109/FIE.2008.4720415

Haenlein, M., & Kaplan, A. M. (2004). A Beginner's Guide to Partial Least Squares Analysis. *Understanding Statistics*, *3*(4), 283–297. doi:10.1207/s15328031us0304_4

Hall, B. L., Dei, G. J. S., & Rosenberg, D. G. (2000). *Indigenous knowledges in global contexts: Multiple readings of our world*. University of Toronto press.

Hall, V., Conboy-Hill, S., & Taylor, D. (2011). Using Virtual Reality to Provide Health Care Information to People with Intellectual Disabilities: Acceptability, Usability, and Potential Utility. *Journal of Medical Internet Research*, *13*(4), e91. doi:10.2196/jmir.1917 PMID:22082765

Handerson-Sellers, B., & Giorgini, P. (2005). *Agent-Oriented Methodologies*. Hershey, PA: IDEA Group Publishing. doi:10.4018/978-1-59140-581-8

Handley, H. A. H. (2014). A network model for human interoperability. *Human Factors*, *56*(2), 349–360. doi:10.1177/0018720813493640 PMID:24689253

Handley, H., & Smillie, R. (2008). Architecture framework human view: The NATO approach. *Systems Engineering*, *11*(2), 156–164. doi:10.1002/sys.20093

Hansen, M. (1999). The search-transfer problem: The role of weak ties in sharing knowledge across organization subunits. *Administrative Science Quarterly*, *44*(1), 82–111. doi:10.2307/2667032

Harris, R., Bala, P., Songan, P., Lien, E. K. G., & Trang, T. (2001). Challenges and opportunities in introducing information and communication technologies to the Kelabit community of North Central Borneo. *New Media & Society*, *3*(3), 270–295. doi:10.1177/14614440122226092

Harsu, M. (2002). *A Survey of Domain Engineering*. Tampere, Finland: Tampere University of Technology.

Hartman, B. O., & Secrist, G. E. (1991). Situational awareness is more than exceptional vision. *Aviation, Space, and Environmental Medicine*, *62*, 1084–1089. PMID:1741725

Hassan, N. R. (2009). Using Social Network Analysis to Measure IT-Enabled Business Process Performance. *Information Systems Management*, *26*(1), 61–76. doi:10.1080/10580530802557762

Hatzilygeroudis, I., Koutsojannis, C., & Papachristou, N. (2007, June). Evaluation of usability and assessment capabilities of an e-Learning System for Nursing Radiation Protection. In *Proceedings of Computer-Based Medical Systems*, (pp. 301-306). IEEE. doi:10.1109/CBMS.2007.47

Hawley, A. W. L., Sherry, E. E., & Johnson, C. J. (2004). A biologists' perspective on amalgamating traditional environmental knowledge and resource management. *British Columbia Journal of Ecosystems and Management*, *5*, 36–50.

Heeks, R. (2003). *Most eGovernment-for-Development Projects Fail: How Can the Risks be Reduced?* (i-Government Working Paper Series, Paper No. 14). Manchester, UK: IDPM.

Hellmers, J., Thomaschewski, J., Holt, E. M., & Wriedt, T. (2012). Usability Evaluation Methods for a Scientific Internet Information Portal. *Journal of Universal Computer Science*, *18*(10), 1308–1322.

Hernandez, C. C., Silva, L., Segura, R. A., Schimiguel, J., Ledon, M. F. P., Bezerra, L. N. M., & Silveira, I. F. (2010). Teaching Programming Principles through a Game Engine. *CLEI Electronic Journal*, 1–8.

Hester, A. J. (2010, May). Increasing collaborative knowledge management in your organization: characteristics of wiki technology and wiki users. In *Proceedings of the 2010 Special Interest Group on Management Information System's 48th annual conference on Computer personnel research on Computer personnel research* (pp. 158-164). New York, NY: ACM. doi:10.1145/1796900.1796961

Highsmith, J. (2009). *Agile project management: creating innovative products*. Upper Saddle River, NJ: Pearson Education.

Himanen, P. (2004). *La ética del hacker y el espíritu de la era de la información*. Barcelona: Destino libro.

Hirokawa, R. Y. (2003). Communication and Group Decision-Making Efficacy. In *Small Group Communication: Theory & Practice* (pp. 125–133). Los Angeles, CA: Rosbury Publishing Co.

Hirokawa, R. Y., & Poole, M. S. (1996). *Communication and Group Decision Making*. Thousand Oaks, CA: SAGE Publications.

Hix, D., & Hartson, H. (1993). Developing user interfaces: ensuring usability through product and process. New York: John Wiley & Sons, Inc.

Hoda, R., Noble, J., & Marshall, S. (2012). Documentation strategies on agile software development projects. *International Journal of Agile and Extreme Software Development*, *1*(1), 23–37. doi:10.1504/IJAESD.2012.048308

Hoff, J. (2006). The Shaping of Digital Political Communication – Creating e-Democracy in a Danish Municipality: Intentions and Realities. In H. K. Hansen, & J. Hoff (Eds.), *Digital Governance://Networked Societies. Creating Authority, Community and Identity in a Globalized World* (pp. 261–299). Copenhagen: Samfundslitteratur Press/NORDICOM.

Hohmann, L. (2006). *Innovation games: creating breakthrough products through collaborative play*. Upper Saddle River, NJ: Pearson Education.

Hollnagel, E., & Woods, D. D. (1983). Cognitive systems engineering: New wine in new bottles. *International Journal of Man-Machine Studies*, *18*(6), 583–600. doi:10.1016/S0020-7373(83)80034-0

Hollnagel, E., & Woods, D. D. (2005). *Joint cognitive systems: Foundations of cognitive systems engineering*. Boca Raton, FL: Taylor & Francis. doi:10.1201/9781420038194

Horton, M., Read, J., Fitton, D., Toth, N., & Little, L. (2012). Too Cool at School - Understanding Cool Teenagers. *PsychNology Journal*, *10*(2), 73–91.

HREOC. (2009). *Native Title Report 2008 Human Rights and Equal Opportunity Commission, Sydney*. Sydney: Native Title Unit Australian Human Rights Commission.

Hult, L., Irestig, M., & Lundberg, J. (2006). Design perspectives. *Human-Computer Interaction*, *21*(1), 5–48. doi:10.1207/s15327051hci2101_2

Humprey, W. (2000). *The personal software process (PSP)*. Pittsburgh, PA: Software Engineering Institute. CMU/SEI.

Humprey, W. (2009). *The Watts New? Collection: Columns by the SEI's Watts Humphrey*. Pittsburgh, PA: Software Engineering Institute. CMU/SEI.

IEEE. (2000). *Std 1471-2000, IEEE Recommended Practice for Architectural Description of Software Intensive Systems*. Retrieved from Website: http://standards.ieee.org/catalog/software4.html#1471-200

Ifm and IBM. (2008). *Succeeding through Service Innovation: A Service Perspective for Education, Research, Business and Government*. Cambridge, UK: University of Cambridge Institute for Manufacturing.

ISO. (1999). *ISO 9241: Ergonomics of Human System Interaction Organization*. International Organization for Standardization.

ISO. (2010). *ISO 9241- 210: Ergonomics of Human System Interaction - Part 210: Human-Centred Design for Interactive Systems*. International Organization for Standardization.

ISO. (2011). *ISO 25010: Systems and Software Engineering - Systems and Software Quality Requirements and Evaluation (SQuaRE) - System and Software Quality Models*. International Organization for Standardization.

ISTAG. (2009). *ICT Advisory Groups Report on Orientations for Work Programme 2011-2013*. European Commission.

Ivory, M. Y., & Hearst, M. A. (2001). The State of the Art in Automating Usability Evaluation of User Interfaces. *ACM Computing Surveys*, *33*(4), 470–516. doi:10.1145/503112.503114

Jacko, J. A., Yi, J. S., Sainfort, F., & McClellan, M. (2012). Human Factors and Ergonomic Methods. In G. Salvendy (Ed.), *Handbook of Human Factors and Ergonomics* – (4th ed., pp. 289–329). John Wiley and Sons. doi:10.1002/9781118131350.ch10

Janis, I. L. (1971). Groupthink. *Psychology Today*, *5*(6), 43–46.

Janse, M., Vink, P., & Georgantas, N. (2008). Amigo Architecture: Service Oriented Architecture for Intelligent Future In-Home Networks. In Constructing Ambient Intelligence (pp. 371-378). Springer.

Jansen, M., & Girardi, R. (2006). GENMADEM: A Methodology for Generative Multi-agent Domain Engineering. In MorisioMaurizio (Ed.), *Proceedings of the 9th International Conference on Software Reuse (LNCS)*, (Vol. 4039, pp. 399-402). New York, NY: Springer. doi:10.1007/11763864_32

Janssen, D., & Kies, R. (2004). Online Forums and Deliberative Democracy: Hypotheses, Variables and Methodologies. *e-Democracy Centre e-Working Papers No. 1*.

Jick, T. D. (1979). Mixing Qualitative and Quantitative Methods: Triangulation in Action. *Administrative Science Quarterly*, *24*(4), 602–611. doi:10.2307/2392366

Johnson, D., & Johnson, R. (1991). *Cooperative learning: Increasing college faculty instructional productivity*. Indianapolis, IN: Jossey-Bass.

Jones, D. G., & Endsley, M. R. (1996). Sources of situation awareness errors in aviation. *Aviation, Space, and Environmental Medicine*, *67*(6), 507–512. PMID:8827130

Jones, D. G., Endsley, M. R., Bolstad, M., & Estes, G. (2004). The designer's situation awareness toolkit: Support for user-centered design. In *Proceedings of the Human Factors Society 48th Annual Meeting* (pp. 653-657). Santa Monica, CA: Human Factors Society.

Jones, D. G., & Kaber, D. B. (2005). Situation awareness measurement and the situation awareness global assessment technique. In N. Stanton, A. Hedge, K. Brookhuis, E. Salas, & H. Hendrick (Eds.), *Handbook of human factors and ergonomics methods* (pp. 42.1–42.7). Boca Raton, FL: CRC Press.

Jones, K. (2002). Issues in the Teaching and Learning of Geometry. In *Aspects of Teaching Secondary Mathematics: perspectives on practice* (pp. 121–139). London: Routledge.

Judge, T., Matthews, T., & Whittaker, S. (2012). Comparing Collaboration and Individual Personas for the Design and Evaluation of Collaboration Software. In *Proceedings of the 2012 ACM Annual Conference on Human Factors in Computing Systems* (pp. 1997-2000). ACM. doi:10.1145/2207676.2208344

Juul, J. (2005). *Half-real: Video Games between Real Rules and Fictional Worlds*. MIT Press.

Kairy, D., Lehoux, P., Vincent, C., & Visintin, M. (2009). A Systematic Review of Clinical Outcomes, Clinical Process, Healthcare Utilization and Costs Associated with Telerehabilitation. *Disability and Rehabilitation*, *31*(6), 427–347. doi:10.1080/09638280802062553 PMID:18720118

Kakasevski, G., Mihajlov, M., Arsenovski, S., & Chungurski, S. (2008, June). Evaluating usability in learning management system Moodle. In *Proceedings of Information Technology Interfaces*, (pp. 613-618). IEEE. doi:10.1109/ITI.2008.4588480

Kamthan, P. (2013, May). On the role of wiki for managing knowledge in agile software development. In *Collaboration Technologies and Systems (CTS), 2013 International Conference on* (pp. 622-623). New York, NY: IEEE. doi:10.1109/CTS.2013.6567299

Kang, H., Lee, M. J., & Lee, J. K. (2012). Are You Still with Us? A Study of the Post-Adoption Determinants of Sustained Use of Mobile-Banking Services. *Journal of Organizational Computing and Electronic Commerce*, *22*(2), 132–159. doi:10.1080/10919392.2012.667710

Kapoor, A. (2010). New Frontiers in Machine Learning for Predictive User Modeling. In A. Hamid, R. López-Cózar, & J. C. Augusto (Eds.), *Human-Centric Interfaces for Ambient Intelligence* (pp. 374–392). Academic Press. doi:10.1016/B978-0-12-374708-2.00015-2

Kapuire, G. K., & Blake, E. (2011). *An attempt to merge local and technological paradigms in the digital representation of indigenous knowledge.* Paper presented at the Indigenous Knowledge Technology Conference 2011. Namibia.

Karwowski, W. (2012). The Discipline of Human Factors and Ergonomics. In G. Salvendy (Ed.), *Handbook of Human Factors and Ergonomics – (4th ed., pp. 3–37).* John Wiley and Sons. doi:10.1002/9781118131350.ch1

Katsanos, C., Tselios, N., & Xenos, M. (2012, October). Perceived Usability Evaluation of Learning Management Systems: A First Step towards Standardization of the System Usability Scale in Greek. In *Proceedings of Informatics (PCI),* (pp. 302-307). IEEE. doi:10.1109/PCi.2012.38

Keast, R., Mandell, M. P., Brown, K., & Woolcock, G. (2004). Network Structures: Working Differently and Changing Expectations. *Public Administration Review*, *64*(3), 363–371. doi:10.1111/j.1540-6210.2004.00380.x

Keegan, S., O'Hare, G., & O'Grady, M. (2008). Easishop: Ambient Intelligence Assists Everyday Shopping. *Information Sciences*, *178*(3), 588–611. doi:10.1016/j.ins.2007.08.027

Khatri, V., & Brown, C. V. (2010). Designing data governance. *Communications of the ACM*, *53*(1), 148–152. doi:10.1145/1629175.1629210

Kies, R., & Wojcik, S. (2010). European Web-Deliberation: Lessons from the European Citizens Consultation. In F. De Cindio, A. Machintosh, & C. Peraboni (Eds.), *Online Deliberation: Proceedings of the Fourth International Conference* (pp. 198 – 211). OD2010.

Kitchenham, B. (1996). *DESMET: A method for evaluating Software Engineering methods and tools* (Technical Report TR96-09). Department of Computer Science, University of Keele.

Kitchenham, B. (2004). Procedures for Performing Systematic Reviews. *Keele University*, *33*, 2004.

Kleinberger, T., Becker, M., Ras, E., Holzinger, A., & Müller, P. (2007). Ambient Intelligence in Assisted Living: Enable Elderly People to Handle Future Interfaces. In Universal Access in Human-Computer Interaction: Ambient Interaction (pp. 103-112). Springer.

Klein, G., Orasanu, J., Calderwood, R., & Zsambok, C. (Eds.). (1993). *Decision making in action: Models and methods.* Norwood, NJ: Ablex.

Knez, W. L., & Ham, D. J. (2006). A comparison of the effects of fatigue on subjective and objective assessment of situation awareness in cycling. *Journal of Sports Science & Medicine*, *5*(1), 89–96. PMID:24198685

Koch, J., Jung, H., Wettach, J., Nemeth, G., & Berns, K. (2008). Dynamic Speech Interaction for Robotic Agents. In L. Suh, & M. Kim (Eds.), *Recent Progress in Robotics: Viable Robotic Service to Human* (pp. 303–315). Springer. doi:10.1007/978-3-540-76729-9_24

Koch, S., & Schneider, G. (2002). Effort, co-operation and co-ordination in an open source software project: GNOME. *Information Systems Journal*, *12*(1), 27–42. doi:10.1046/j.1365-2575.2002.00110.x

Koppenjan, J., & Groenewegen, J. (2005). Istitutional design for complex technological systems. *International Journal of Technology. Policy and Management*, *5*(3), 40–257.

Kotler, P. (1993). *Administração de Marketing: análise, planejamento, implementação e controle.* São Paulo: Atlas.

Kramer, J. (2007). Is abstraction the key to computing? *Communications of the ACM*, *50*(4), 36–42. doi:10.1145/1232743.1232745

Krieg-Brückner, B., Röfer, T., Shi, H., & Gersdorf, B. (2010). Mobility Assistance in the Bremen Ambient Assisted Living Lab. GeroPsych. *The Journal of Gerontopsychology and Geriatric Psychiatry*, *23*(2), 121–130. doi:10.1024/1662-9647/a000009

Krug, S. (2009). *Don't make me think: A common sense approach to web usability*. Pearson Education.

Kuutti, K. (1996). Activity Theory as a Potential Framework for Human Computer Interaction Research. In B. A. Nardi (Ed.), Context and Consciousness: Activity Theory and Human Computer Interaction (pp. 17 – 44). Boston, MA: MIT Press.

Larkin, J., McDermott, J., Simon, D. P., & Simon, H. A. (1980). Expert and Novice Performance in Solving Physics Problems. *Science*, *208*(4450), 1335–1342. doi:10.1126/science.208.4450.1335 PMID:17775709

Larman, C., & Basili, V. R. (2003). Iterative and Incremental Development: A Brief History. *Computer*, *36*(6), 47–56. doi:10.1109/MC.2003.1204375

Lazaro, J. P., Fides, A., Navarro, A., & Guille, S. (2010). Ambient Assisted Nutritional Advisor for Elderly People Living at Home. In *Proceedings of Engineering in Medicine and Biology Society* (EMBC), (pp. 198-203). IEEE. doi:10.1109/IEMBS.2010.5627945

Learmonth, M. (1997). *Giving It All Away*. Available at: http://metroactive.com /papers/metro/05.08.97/cover/linus-9719.html

Lee, I., Martin, F., Denner, J., Coulter, B., Allan, W., & Erickson, J. et al. (2011). Computational thinking for youth in practice. *ACM Inroads*, *2*(1), 32–37. doi:10.1145/1929887.1929902

Lee, J., Bahn, S., Rhiu, I., Yun, M. H., & Choi, H. (2011). An Evaluation Metric on Human-Service Interactivity of Ubiquitous Services. In D. Lin, & H. Chen (Eds.), *Ergonomics for All: Celebrating PPCOE's 20 Years of Excellence* (pp. 347–352). PPCOE. doi:10.1201/b10529-66

Lee, M. J., & McLoughlin, C. (2011). *Web 2.0-based e-learning: applying social informatics for tertiary teaching*. Hershey, PA: Information Science Reference.

Lehikoinen, J., Lehikoinen, J., & Huuskonen, P. (2008). Understanding Privacy Regulation in Ubicomp Interactions. *Personal and Ubiquitous Computing*, *12*(8), 543–553. doi:10.1007/s00779-007-0163-2

Leite, A., & Girardi, R. (2009). A Process for Multi-Agent Domain and Application Engineering: the Domain Analysis and Application Requirements Engineering Phases. In *Proceedings of the 11th International Conference on Enterprise Information Systems (ICEIS'09)*. Milan, Italy: INSTICC.

Leite, A., Girardi, R., & Cavalcante, U. (2008). An Ontology for Multi-Agent Domain and Application Engineering. In *Proceedings of the 2008 IEEE International Conference on Information Reuse and Integration (IEEE IRI-08)*. Piscataway, NJ: IEEE Press. doi:10.1109/IRI.2008.4583012

Leite, A., Girardi, R., & Cavalcante, U. (2008). MAAEM: A Multi-agent Application Engineering Methodology. In *Proceedings of the 20th International Conference on Software Engineering and Knowledge Engineering (SEKE'08)*. Skokie, IL: Knowledge Systems Institute.

Leon, E., Clarke, G., Callaghan, V., & Doctor, F. (2010). Affect-Aware Behaviour Modelling and Control Inside an Intelligent Environment. *Pervasive and Mobile Computing*, *6*(5), 559–574. doi:10.1016/j.pmcj.2009.12.002

Lettl, C., Herstatt, C., & Gemuenden, H. G. (2006). Learning from users for radical innovation. *International Journal of Technology Management*, *33*(1), 25. doi:10.1504/IJTM.2006.008190

Leuf, B., & Cunningham, W. (2001). *The wiki way: quick collaboration on the web*. Boston, MA: Addison-Wesley.

Leutenegger, S. T. (2006). A CS1 to CS2 bridge class using 2D game programming. *Journal of Computing Sciences in Colleges*, *21*(5), 76–83.

Lewis, A. (1982). *The Psychology of Taxation*. Oxford, UK: Martin Robertson & Company.

Lichacz, F. M. J., Cain, B., & Patel, S. (2003). Calibration of confidence in situation awareness queries. In *Proceedings of the Human Factors and Ergonomics Society 47th Annual Meeting* (pp. 222-226). Santa Monica, CA: Human Factors and Ergonomics Society. doi:10.1177/154193120304700147

Lichacz, F. M. J., & Farrell, P. S. E. (2005). The calibration of situation awareness and confidence within a multinational operational net assessment. *Military Psychology*, *17*(4), 247–268. doi:10.1207/s15327876mp1704_1

Linux Foundation. (n.d.). *About Us*. Retrieved January 5, 2011 from: http://www.linuxfoundation.org/about

Lister, R., Simon, B., Thompson, E., Whalley, J. L., & Prasad, C. (2006). Not seeing the forest for the trees: novice programmers and the SOLO taxonomy. In *Proceedings of the 11th annual SIGCSE conference on Innovation and technology in computer science education* (pp. 118–122). New York, NY: ACM. doi:10.1145/1140124.1140157

Liu, X. (2008). *Design architecture, developer networks and performance of open source software projects*. Boston: Boston University.

Livshits, V. B., & Lam, M. S. (2005, August). Finding security vulnerabilities in Java applications with static analysis. In *Proceedings of the 14th conference on USENIX Security Symposium* (*Vol. 14*, pp. 18-18). USENIX.

Lohmann, S., Dietzold, S., Heim, P., & Heino, N. (2009, March). A Web Platform for Social Requirements Engineering. In *Software Engineering* (Vol. 150, pp. 309–315). Workshops.

Lombardi, A., Ferri, M., Rescio, G., Grassi, M., & Malcovati, P. (2009). Wearable Wireless Accelerometer with Embedded Fall-Detection Logic for Multi-Sensor Ambient Assisted Living Applications. In Sensors, 2009 IEEE (pp. 1967-1970). IEEE. doi:10.1109/ICSENS.2009.5398327

Long, F. (2009). Real or Imaginary: The Effectiveness of Using Personas in Product Design. In *Proceedings of the Irish Ergonomics Society Annual Conference* (pp. 1-10). Academic Press.

Long, J. (2004). *Understanding the creation and adoption of information technology innovations: The case of Open Source software development and the diffusion of mobile commerce*. The University of Texas at Austin.

Long, J. (2006). Understanding the Role of Core Developers in Open Source Software Development. *Journal of Information, Information Technology, and Organizations*, *1*, 75–85.

Loshin, P. (2005). Something for Everyone! Open Source Isn't Just For Linux Users. *Computer Power User*, *5*(5), 66–71.

Loukis, E., & Wimmer, M. A. (2010). Analysing Different Models of Structured Electronic Consultation on Legislation Under Formation. In F. De Cindio, A. Macintosh, & C. Peraboni (Eds.), *Online Deliberation: Proceedings of the Fourth International Conference* (pp. 14 – 26). OD2010.

Louridas, P. (2006). Using wikis in software development. *Software, IEEE*, *23*(2), 88–91. doi:10.1109/MS.2006.62

Luna, R., Hall, R., Hilgers, M., & Ge, L. (2010). GIS Learning Tool for Civil Engineers. *International Journal of Engineering Education*, *26*(1), 52.

Macchi, M., & Oviedo, G. (2008). *Indigenous and traditional peoples and climate change: Issues Paper*. International Union for Conservation of Nature.

Macintosh, A., Malina, A., & Farrell, S. (2002). Digital Democracy through Electronic Petitioning. In W. J. McIver Jr, & A. K. Elmagarmid (Eds.), *Advances in Digital Government: Technology, Human Factors and Policy* (pp. 137–162). Dordrecht: Kluwer Academic Publishing. doi:10.1007/0-306-47374-7_8

Mader, S. (2008). *Wikipatterns: a practical guide to improving productivity and collaboration in your organization*. Hoboken, NJ: John Wiley & Sons.

Mahatody, T., Kolski, C., & Sagar, M. (2009). CWE: Assistance Environment for the Evaluation Operating a Set of Variations of the Cognitive Walkthrough Ergonomic Inspection Method. In Engineering Psychology and Cognitive Ergonomics (pp. 52-61). Springer.

Mahatody, T., Sagar, M., & Kolski, C. (2010). State of the Art on the Cognitive Walkthrough Method, its Variants and Evolutions. *Journal of Human–Computer Interaction*, *26*(8), 741–785. doi:10.1080/10447311003781409

Mahnic, V. (2012). A capstone course on agile software development using Scrum. *Education. IEEE Transactions on*, *55*(1), 99–106.

Malan, D. J., & Leitner, H. H. (2007). Scratch for budding computer scientists. *SIGCSE Bulletin*, *39*(1), 223–227. doi:10.1145/1227504.1227388

Maloney, J. H., Peppler, K., Kafai, Y., Resnick, M., & Rusk, N. (2008). Programming by choice: urban youth learning programming with scratch. In *Proceedings of the 39th SIGCSE technical symposium on Computer science education* (pp. 367–371). New York, NY: ACM. doi:10.1145/1352135.1352260

Marcengo, A., Guercio, E., & Rapp, A. (2009). Personas Layering: A Cost Effective Model for Service Design in Medium-Long Term Telco Research Projects. In Human Centered Design (pp. 256-265). Springer. doi:10.1007/978-3-642-02806-9_30

Marelli, A. (2000). *Introducción al análisis y desarrollo de modelos de competencias*. Montevideo: Boletín Cinterfor/OIT. N° 149.

Mariano, R. (2008). *Development of a Family of Recommender Systems based on the Semantic Web Technology and its Reuse on the Recommendation of Legal Tax Information Items*. (Unpublished Master's dissertation). Federal University of Maranhão, Brazil.

Mariano, R., Girardi, R., Leite, A., Drumond, L., & Maranhão, D. (2008). A Case Study on Domain Analysis of Semantic Web Multi-agent Recommender Systems. *Proceedings 3th International Conference on Software and Data Technologies (ICSOFT'08)*. New York, NY: SciTePress.

Marques, S., & Nunes, I. (2012). Usability of Interfaces. In S. Marques, & I. Nunes (Eds.), *Industrial Engineering and Management: Ergonomics - A Systems Approach* (pp. 155–171). InTech.

Marsden, P. V. (2005). Recent Developments in Network Measurement. In P. J. Carrington, J. Scott, & S. Wasserman (Eds.), *Models and methods in social network analysis* (pp. 8–30). New York: Cambridge University Press. doi:10.1017/CBO9780511811395.002

Martín, N., Martín, V., & Trevilla, C. (2009). *Influencia de la motivación intrínseca y extrínseca sobre la transmisión de conocimiento: El caso de una organización sin fines de lucro*. CIRIEC-España, revista de economía pública, social y cooperativa.

Martin, B., Hanington, B., & Hanington, B. M. (2012). *Universal Methods of Design: 100 Ways to Research Complex Problems, Develop Innovative Ideas, and Design Effective Solutions*. Rockport Publishers.

Martín-Gutiérrez, J., Contero, M., & Alcañiz, M. (2010). Evaluating the Usability of an Augmented Reality Based Educational Application. In *Intelligent Tutoring Systems* (pp. 296–306). Springer. doi:10.1007/978-3-642-13388-6_34

Mathias, E. (1996). *Recording and Using Indigenous Knowledge: A Manual*. International Institute for Rural Reconstruction, Silang, Cavite, Philippines.

Matthews, T., Judge, T., & Whittaker, S. (2012). How Do Designers and User Experience Professionals Actually Perceive and Use Personas. In *Proceedings of the SIGCHI Conference on Human Factors in Computing Systems* (pp. 1219-1228). ACM. doi:10.1145/2207676.2208573

Mayer, R. C., Davis, J. H., & Schoorman, F. D. (1995). An Integrative Model of Organization Trust. *Academy of Management Review*, *20*(3), 709–734.

Mazzocchi, F. (2009). *Analyzing Knowledge as Part of a Cultural Framework: The Case of Traditional Ecological Knowledge* (Vol. 36). Academic Press.

McCarthy, J. E., & Swierenga, S. J. (2010). What We Know about Dyslexia and Web Accessibility: A Research Review. *Universal Access in the Information Society*, *9*(2), 147–152. doi:10.1007/s10209-009-0160-5

Mcgrath, J. E. (1991). Time, Interaction, and Performance (TIP): A Theory of Groups. *Small Group Research*, *22*(2), 147–174. doi:10.1177/1046496491222001

McGregor, D. (2004). Coming full circle: Indigenous knowledge, environment, and our future. *American Indian Quarterly*, *28*(3/4), 385–410. doi:10.1353/aiq.2004.0101

McGuinness, B. (1995). Situational awareness measurement in cockpit evaluation trials. In Situation Awareness: Limitations and Enhancement in the Aviation Environment (AGARD-CP-575, pp. 7.1-7.8). Neuilly-Sur-Seine, France: NATO Research and Technology Organization.

McGuinness, B. (2004). Quantitative analysis of situational awareness (QUASA): Applying signal detection theory to true/false probes and self-ratings. In *Proceedings of 9th International Command and Control Research and Technology Symposium* (pp. 159-178). Washington, DC: US Department of Defence Command and Control Research Program.

McGuinness, M. (2008). *Creative Management for Creative Teams, Business Coaching and Creative Business.* Retrieved from: http://media.lateralaction.com/creative-management.pdf

McHugh, O., Conboy, K., & Lang, M. (2012). Agile Practices: The Impact on Trust in Software Project Teams. *IEEE Software, 29*(3), 71–76. doi:10.1109/MS.2011.118

McKeithen, K. B., Reitman, J. S., Rueter, H. H., & Hirtle, S. C. (1981). Knowledge organization and skill differences in computer programmers. *Cognitive Psychology, 13*(3), 307–325. doi:10.1016/0010-0285(81)90012-8

Means, B., Salas, E., Crandall, B., & Jacobs, T. O. (1993). Training decision makers for the real world. In G. A. Klein, J. Orasanu, R. Calderwood, & C. E. Zsambok (Eds.), *Decision making in action: Models and methods* (pp. 306–326). Norwood, NJ: Ablex.

Merril, D. (2002). A Pebble-in-the-Pond Model For Instructional Design. *Performance Improvement, 41*(7), 41–46. doi:10.1002/pfi.4140410709

Miaskiewicz, T., & Kozar, K. A. (2011). Personas and User-Centered Design: How Can Personas Benefit Product Design Processes? *Design Studies, 32*(5), 417–430. doi:10.1016/j.destud.2011.03.003

Microsoft Research. (2014). *Kodu Game Lab Community.* Retrieved January 16, 2014, from http://www.kodugamelab.com/

Midha, V. (2007). *Antecedent to the success of open source software.* The University of North Carolina at Greensboro.

Midha, V. et al. (2010). Improving Open Source Software Maintenance. *Journal of Computer Information Systems, 50*(3), 81–90.

Miller, G. A. (1956). The magical number seven, plus or minus two: Some limits on our capacity for processing information. *Psychological Review, 63*(2), 81–97. doi:10.1037/h0043158 PMID:13310704

Miller, L. M., Chang, C. I., Wang, S., Beier, M. E., & Klisch, Y. (2011). Learning and Motivational Impacts of a Multimedia Science Game. *Computers & Education, 57*(1), 1425–1433. doi:10.1016/j.compedu.2011.01.016

Minocha, S., Petre, M., & Roberts, D. (2008). Using wikis to simulate distributed requirements development in a software engineering course. *International Journal of Engineering Education, 24*(4), 689–704.

MIT Media Lab & the Lifelong Kindergarten Group. (2012). Scratch. *Scratch.* Retrieved April 27, 2012, from http://scratch.mit.edu

Mitchell, P. P. (2007). *A Step-by-Step Guide to Usability Testing.* iUniverse.

Mockus, A., Fielding, R. T., & Herbsleb, J. D. (2002). Two case studies of open source software development: Apache and Mozilla. *ACM Transactions on Software Engineering and Methodology, 11*(3), 309–346. doi:10.1145/567793.567795

Montuschi, L. (2004). *Ética y razonamiento moral, Dilemas morales y comportamiento ético en las organizaciones.* Buenos Aires: Serie Documentos de Trabajo Universidad del CEMA. Retrieved from http://www.ucema.edu.ar/publicaciones/download/documentos/219.pdf

Moody, G. (2002). *Rebel code: Linux and the open source revolution.* London: Penguin.

Moreira, M. (2013). *Being agile: your roadmap to successful adoption of agile.* New York, NY: Apress. doi:10.1007/978-1-4302-5840-7

Mozilla Foundation. (2011). *The Mozilla Foundation.* Retrieved from http://www.mozilla.org/foundation/

Mulder, S., & Yaar, Z. (2007). *The User is Always Right: A Practical Guide to Creating and Using Personas for the Web.* New Riders.

Mulgund, S., Rinkus, G., Illgen, C., Zacharias, G., & Friskie, J. (1997). OLIPSA: On-line intelligent processor for situation assessment. In K. Garner (Ed.), *Second Annual Symposium and Exhibition on Situational Awareness in the Tactical Air Environment.* Patuxent River, MD: Naval Air Warfare Center Aircraft Division.

Muller, O., Haberman, B., & Averbuch, H. (2004). (An almost) pedagogical pattern for pattern-based problem-solving instruction. *ACM SIGCSE Bulletin, 36*(3), 102. doi:10.1145/1026487.1008025

Muratet, M., Torguet, P., Jessel, J.-P., & Viallet, F. (2009). Towards a serious game to help students learn computer programming. *International Journal of Computer Games Technology*, 3:1–3:12. doi:10.1155/2009/470590

Murphy-Hill, E., & Black, A. P. (2010). An Interactive Ambient Visualization for Code Smells. In *Proceedings of the 5th International Symposium on Software Visualization* (pp. 5-14). ACM. doi:10.1145/1879211.1879216

Myerson, R. B. (1991). Game Theory: Analysis of Conflict. Harvard University Press.

Mylopoulos, J., Castro, J., & Kolp, M. (2013). The Evolution of Tropos. In J. Bubenko, J. Krogstie, O. Pastor, B. Pernici, C. Rolland, & A. Sølvberg (Eds.), *Seminal Contributions to Information Systems Engineering* (pp. 281–287). New York, NY: Springer; doi:10.1007/978-3-642-36926-1_22

Nakamura, J., & Csikszentmihalyi, M. (2009). Flow theory and research. In *Oxford Handbook of Positive Psychology* (2nd ed., pp. 195–206). Oxford, UK: Oxford University Press.

Nakashima, D., & Roué, M. (2002). Indigenous knowledge, peoples and sustainable practice. Encyclopedia of Global Environmental Change, 5, 314-324.

National Institute of Urban Affairs. (2004). *Reforming the Property Tax System (Research Study Series no. 94)*. New Delhi: NIUA Press.

Neisser, U. (1976). *Cognition and reality principles and implications of cognitive psychology*. San Francisco: Freeman.

Netcraft. (2007, February). *Web Server Survey*. Available at: http://news.netcraft.com/archives/web_server_survey. Html

Newell, A., Gregor, P., Morgan, M., Pullin, G., & Macaulay, C. (2011). User-Sensitive Inclusive Design. *Universal Access in the Information Society*, 10(3), 235–243. doi:10.1007/s10209-010-0203-y

Newton, E., & Girardi, R. (2007) PROPOST: A knowledge-based tool for supporting Project Portfolio Management. *Proceedings of the International Conference on Systems Engineering and Modeling (ICSEM 2007)*. Piscataway, NJ: IEEE Press doi:10.1109/ICSEM.2007.373328

Ngidang, D. (2005). Deconstruction and reconstruction of Native Customary Land tenure in Sarawak. 東南アジア研究, *43*(1), 47-75.

Ngulube, P. (2002). Managing and preserving indigenous knowledge in the knowledge management era: challenges and opportunities for information professionals. *Information Development, 18*(2), 95-102.

Nielsen, J. (1995a). *Summary of Usability Inspection Methods*. Retrieved November 17 2013, from http://www.nngroup.com/articles/summary-of-usability-inspection-methods/

Nielsen, J. (1995b). *How to Conduct a Heuristic Evaluation*. Retrieved November 18, 2013 from http://www.nngroup.com/articles/how-to-conduct-a-heuristic-evaluation/

Nielsen, J. (2003). *Usability 101: Introduction to Usability*. Retrieved December 16, 2013 from http://useit.com/alertbox/20030825.html

Nielsen, J. (2012, January). *Usability 101: Introduction to Usability*. Retrieved from http://www.nngroup.com/articles/usability-101introduction-to-usability/

Nielsen, J., & Norman, D. (2013). *The Definition of User Experience*. Retrieved December 16, 2013 from http://www.nngroup.com/articles/definition-user-experience/

Nielsen, J. (1994, April). Enhancing the explanatory power of usability heuristics. In *Proceedings of the SIGCHI conference on Human Factors in Computing Systems* (pp. 152-158). ACM. doi:10.1145/259963.260333

Nielsen, J. (1994a). *Usability Engineering*. Elsevier.

Nielsen, J. (1994b). Usability Inspection Methods. In *Conference Companion on Human Factors in Computing Systems* (pp. 413–414). ACM. doi:10.1145/259963.260531

Nielsen, J., & Molich, R. (1990). Heuristic evaluation of user interfaces. In *CHI '90: Proceedings of the SIGCHI conference on Human factors in computing systems* (pp. 249–256). New York: ACM. http://doi.acm.org/10.1145/97243.97281

Nielsen, L. (2004). *Engaging Personas and Narrative Scenarios*. Handelshøjskolen.

Norman, D. A. (2013). *The design of everyday things: revised and expanded edition.* New York, NY: Basic Books.

Nunes, I., Kulesza, U., Nunes, C., & Lucena, C. A. (2009). A Domain Engineering Process for Developing Multi-Agent Systems Product Lines. In *Proceedings of the 8th International Conference of Autonomous Agents and Multi-agent Systems(AAMAS'12).* Liverpool, England: IFAAMAS.

O'Reilly, T. (2005). What is web 2.0: design patterns and business models for the next generation of software. Sebastopol, CA: O'Reilly Network.

O'Sullivan, M. D. (2012). *Wikipedia: A New Community of Practice?* London: Ashgate Publishing.

Oberzaucher, J., Werner, K., Mairbock, H., Beck, C., Panek, P., Hlauschek, W., & Zagler, W. (2009). A Videophone Prototype System Evaluated by Elderly Users in the Living Lab Schwechat. In *HCI and Usability for e-Inclusion* (pp. 345–352). Springer. doi:10.1007/978-3-642-10308-7_24

Object Management Group. (2013). *Software Process Engineering Metamodel Specification.* Needham, MA: OMG Press.

Odell, J., Parunak, H. V., & Bauer, B. (2000). Extending UML for Agents. In *Proceedings of the Agent-Oriented Information Systems Workshop at the 17th National Conference on Artificial Intelligence (AAI'00).* Palo Alto, CA: AAAI Press.

Oliveira, L. S., Oliveros, D. V., da Graça Pimentel, M., & Queiroz-Neto, J. P. (2011, October). Work in progress— Alternative interfaces for e-learning platforms used in remote areas. In *Proceedings of Frontiers in Education Conference (FIE), 2011* (pp. T4C-1). IEEE.

Olmsted-Hawala, E. L., Murphy, E. D., Hawala, S., & Ashenfelter, K. T. (2010). Think-Aloud Protocols: a Comparison of Three Think-Aloud Protocols for Use in Testing Data-Dissemination Web Sites for Usability. In *Proceedings of the SIGCHI Conference on Human Factors in Computing Systems* (pp. 2381-2390). ACM. doi:10.1145/1753326.1753685

Omar, H. M., & Jaafar, A. (2011). Usability of Educational Computer Game (Usa_ECG): Applying Analytic Hierarchy Process. In Visual Informatics: Sustaining Research and Innovations (pp. 147-156). Springer.

Onetti, V. (2011). *La Evaluación, Innovación y experiencias educativas.* ISSN 1988-6047, 39. Retrieved February 2011 from: http://www.csi-csif.es/andalucia/modules/mod_ense/revista/pdf/Numero_39/VANESSA_ONETTI_ONETTI_1.pdf

Open Source Initiative. (2005). Available at http://www.opensource.org

Oppenneer, M. (2008). *A Value Sensitive Design Approach to Indigenous Knowledge Management Systems.* Retrieved 11 Oct, 2012, from http://www.ethnosproject.org/site/wp-trackback.php?p=71

Ostlund, M., Dahlbäck, N., & Petersson, G. I. (2010). 3D Visualization as a Communicative Aid in Pharmaceutical Advice-Giving over Distance. *Journal of Medical Internet Research, 13*(3), e50. doi:10.2196/jmir.1437 PMID:21771714

Öztürk, Ö., & Rızvanoğlu, K. (2011). How to Improve User Experience in Mobile Social Networking: A User-Centered Study with Turkish Mobile Social Network Site Users. In Design, User Experience, and Usability: Theory, Methods, Tools and Practice (pp. 521-530). Springer.

Papaloukas, S., Patriarcheas, K., & Xenos, M. (2011). Games' Usability and Learning - the Educational Videogame BeTheManager! In *Proceedings of the 5th European Conference on Games Based Learning* (pp. 449-456). ACPI.

Papantonopoulos, S. (2004). How system designers think: A study of design thinking in human factors engineering. *Ergonomics, 47*(14), 1528–1548. doi:10.1080/00140130412331290916 PMID:15697068

Paterno, F., Santoro, C., & Scorcia, A. (2010). Ambient Intelligence for Supporting Task Continuity across Multiple Devices and Implementation Languages. *The Computer Journal, 53*(8), 1210–1228. doi:10.1093/comjnl/bxp014

Paulson, J. W., Succi, G., & Eberlein, A. (2004). An Empirical Study of Open-Source and Closed-Source Software Products. *IEEE Transactions on Software Engineering, 30*(4), 246–256. doi:10.1109/TSE.2004.1274044

Pecheanu, E., Stefanescu, D., Dumitriu, L., & Segal, C. (2011, April). Methods to evaluate open source learning platforms. In *Proceedings ofGlobal Engineering Education Conference (EDUCON)*, (pp. 1152-1161). IEEE. doi:10.1109/EDUCON.2011.5773292

Peppler, K., & Kafai, Y. (2009). Gaming Fluencies: Pathways into Participatory Culture in a Community Design Studio. *International Journal of Learning and Media*, *1*(4), 45–58. doi:10.1162/ijlm_a_00032

Pérez, M., Domínguez, K., Mendoza, L., & Grimán, A. (2006). *Human Perspective in System Development Quality*.Acapulco, México: AMCIS.

Perez, M., Grimán, A., Mendoza, L., & Rojas, T. (2004). A Systemic Methodological Framework for IS Research. New York: *AMCIS*.

Perini, A., & Susi, A. (2004). Developing Tools for Agent-Oriented Visual Modeling. In G. Lindemann, J. Denzinger, I. J. Timm, & R. Unland (Eds.), *Multi-agent System Technologies*. . New York, NY: Springer. doi:10.1007/978-3-540-30082-3_13

Perkins, D. N. (1989). Reasoning as it is and could be: An empirical perspective. In D. M. Topping, D. C. Crowell, & V. N. Kobayashi (Eds.), *The 3ʳᵈ International Conference on Thinking* (pp. 175-194). Hillsdale, NJ: Erlbaum.

Perkins, T. K. (2006, June). *Knowledge: the core problem of project failure. CrossTalk*.

PERSONA - PERceptive Spaces promoting iNdependent Aging. (2008). *Report Describing Values, Trends, User needs and Guidelines for Service Characteristics in the AAL Persona Context*. European Commission.

Peterson, D. B. (2005). International Classification of Functioning, Disability and Health: An Introduction for Rehabilitation Psychologists.*Rehabilitation Psychology*, *50*(2), 105–112. doi:10.1037/0090-5550.50.2.105

Phuwanartnurak, A. J. (2009, May). Interdisciplinary collaboration through wikis in software development. In *Wikis for Software Engineering, 2009. WIKIS4SE'09. ICSE Workshop on* (pp. 82-90). New York, NY: IEEE. doi:10.1109/WIKIS4SE.2009.5070000

Piccoli, G., & Ives, B. (2003). Trust and the Unintended Effects of Behavior Control in Virtual Teams. *Management Information Systems Quarterly*, *27*(3), 365–395.

Picking, R., Robinet, A., Grout, V., McGinn, J., Roy, A., Ellis, S., & Oram, D. (2009). A Case Study Using a Methodological Approach to Developing User Interfaces for Elderly and Disabled People. *The Computer Journal*, *53*(6), 842–859. doi:10.1093/comjnl/bxp089

Pinna, S., Mauri, S., Lorrai, P., Marchesi, M., & Serra, N. (2003). XPSwiki: an agile tool supporting the planning game. In *Extreme Programming and Agile Processes in Software Engineering* (pp. 104–113). New York, NY: Springer. doi:10.1007/3-540-44870-5_14

Plischke, H., & Kohls, N. (2009). Keep It Simple! Assisting Older People with Mental and Physical Training. In Universal Access in Human-Computer Interaction: Addressing Diversity (pp. 278-287). Springer. doi:10.1007/978-3-642-02707-9_32

Pohl, K., Bockle, G., & Linden, F. (2005). *Software Product Line Engineering: Foundations, Principles and Techniques*. New York, NY: Springer. doi:10.1007/3-540-28901-1

Polya, G. (2004). *How to solve it: a new aspect of mathematical method*. Princeton, NJ: Princeton University Press.

Poole, M. S. (1996). Group communication and the structuring process. In Small Group Communication: Theory & Practice (7th ed., pp. 85–95). Madison, WI: Brown & Benchmark.

Poole, M. S., & DeSanctis, G. (1989). *Use of Group Decision Support Systems as an Appropriation Process*. Paper presented at the System Sciences. Kailua-Kona, HI.

Poole, M. S., & Roth, J. (1989). Decision Development in Small Groups V Test of a Contingency Model. *Human Communication Research*, *15*(4), 549–589. doi:10.1111/j.1468-2958.1989.tb00199.x

Postmes, T., Spears, R., & Cihangir, S. (2001). Quality of Decision Making and Group Norms. *Journal of Personality and Social Psychology*, *80*(6), 918–930. doi:10.1037/0022-3514.80.6.918 PMID:11414374

Postmes, T., Spears, R., Lee, A. T., & Novak, R. J. (2005). Individuality and Social Influence in Groups: Inductive and Deductive Routes to Group Identity. *Journal of Personality and Social Psychology*, *89*(5), 747–763. doi:10.1037/0022-3514.89.5.747 PMID:16351366

Prensky, M. (2004). *Digital Game-Based Learning.* Washington, DC: McGraw-Hill Pub. Co.

Pressman, R. (2006). *Ingeniería del Software, Un enfoque práctico. 6ª edición.* DF, México: McGrawHill.

Pritchett, A. R., Kim, S. Y., & Feigh, K. M. (2014a). Measuring human-automation function allocation. *Journal of Cognititve Engineering and Decision Making, 8*(1), 52–77. doi:10.1177/1555343413490166

Pritchett, A. R., Kim, S. Y., & Feigh, K. M. (2014b). Modeling human-automation function allocation. *Journal of Cognititve Engineering and Decision Making, 8*(1), 33–51. doi:10.1177/1555343413490944

Proctor, R. W., & Dutta, A. (1995). *Skill acquisition and human performance.* London: SAGE.

Proctor, R. W., & Vu, K.-P. L. (2012). Selection and Control of Action. In G. Salvendy (Ed.), *Handbook of Human Factors and Ergonomics* (4th ed., pp. 95–116). John Wiley and Sons. doi:10.1002/9781118131350.ch4

Pruitt, J., & Adlin, T. (2006). *The Persona Lifecycle: Keeping People in Mind throughout the Product Design.* Morgan Kaufman.

Pruitt, J., & Grudin, J. (2003). Personas: Practice and Theory. In *Proceedings of the 2003 Conference on Designing for User Experiences* (pp. 1-15). ACM. doi:10.1145/997078.997089

Queirós, A., Alvarelhão, J., Silva, A., Teixeira, A., & Rocha, N. (2013). A Conceptual Framework for the Design and Development of AAL Services. In M. Cruz-Cunha, I. Miranda, & P. Gonçalves (Eds.), *Handbook of Research on ICTs for Human-Centered Healthcare and Social Care Services: Developments and Applications* (pp. 568–586). IGI Global. doi:10.4018/978-1-4666-3986-7.ch030

Queirós, A., Silva, A., Alvarelhão, J., Rocha, N., & Teixeira, A. (2013). *Usability, Accessibility and Ambient Assisted Living: A Systematic Literature Review. International Journal of Universal Access in the Information Society.* doi::10.1007/s10209-013-0328-x

Qureshi, I., & Fang, Y. (2011). Socialization in Open Source Software Projects: A Growth Mixture Modeling Approach. *Organizational Research Methods, 14*(1), 208–238. doi:10.1177/1094428110375002

Raita, E., & Oulasvirta, A. (2011). Too Good to be Bad: Favorable Product Expectations Boost Subjective Usability Ratings. *Interacting with Computers, 23*(4), 363–371. doi:10.1016/j.intcom.2011.04.002

Ramírez, Y. (2004). El perfil de competencias y la evaluación cualitativa del aprendizaje en la I y II etapas de educación básica. *Educere, 8*(25), 159–166.

Rankin, A., Lundberg, J., Woltjer, R., Rollenhagen, C., & Hollnagel, E. (2014). Resilience in everyday operations: A framework for analyzing adaptations in high-risk work. *Journal of Cognititve Engineering and Decision Making, 8*(1), 78–97. doi:10.1177/1555343413498753

Ras, E., Rech, J., & Weber, S. (2009). Investigating the suitability of web X.Y. features for software engineering-towards an empirical survey. In *Software Engineering* (pp. 285–296). Workshops.

Rasmussen, J. (1983). Skills, rules, and knowledge: Signals, signs, and symbols, and other distinction in human performance models. *IEEE Transactions on Systems, Man, and Cybernetics, 13*(3), 257–266. doi:10.1109/TSMC.1983.6313160

Rasmussen, J. (1986). *Information processing and human-machine interaction: An approach to cognitive engineering.* New York: North-Holland.

Raymond, E. S. (2001). *The Cathedral and the Bazaar: Musings on Linux and Open Sourceby an Accidental Revolutionary* (Rev. ed.). Sebastopol, CA: O'Reilly.

Reagle, J. M. (2010). *Good faith collaboration: The culture of Wikipedia.* Cambridge, MA: MIT Press.

Reason, J. (1988). Cognitive aids in process environments: Prostheses or tools? In E. Hollnagel, G. Mancini, & D. D. Woods (Eds.), *Cognitive engineering in complex dynamic worlds* (pp. 7–14). London: Academic Press.

Reason, J. (1990). *Human error.* Cambridge, UK: Cambridge University Press. doi:10.1017/CBO9781139062367

Reason, J. (1997). *Managing the risks of organizational accidents.* Aldershot, UK: Ashgate.

Rehman, R. U. (2006). *Factors that contribute to open source software project success.* (Master thesis). Carleton University.

Remmers, H. (2010). Environments for Ageing, Assistive Technology and Self-Determination: Ethical Perspectives. *Informatics for Health & Social Care*, *35*(3-4), 200–210. doi:10.3109/17538157.2010.528649 PMID:21133773

Rettich, K. (2011, October). Using the wiki to deliver paperless software documentation. In *Professional Communication Conference (IPCC), 2011 IEEE International* (pp. 1-8). New York, NY: IEEE. doi:10.1109/IPCC.2011.6087219

Rizvi, M., Humphries, T., Major, D., Jones, M., & Lauzun, H. (2011). A CS0 course using Scratch. *Journal of Computing Sciences in Colleges*, *26*(3), 19–27.

Rönkkö, K. (2005). An Empirical Study Demonstrating how Different Design Constraints, Project Organization, and Contexts Limited the Utility of Personas. In *Proceedings of the 38th Annual Hawaii International Conference* (p. 220a). IEEE.

Rosander, M., Stiwne, D., & Granstrom, K. (1998). "Bipolar groupthink": Assessing groupthink tendencies in authentic work groups. *Scandinavian Journal of Psychology*, *39*(2), 81–92. doi:10.1111/1467-9450.00060 PMID:9676161

Rossi, A. (2009). *The open innovation as a source of value creation for organizations*. Retrieved August 15, 2010, from http://www.fdc.org.br/pt/pesquisa/inovacao/Documents/artigos_blog/inovacao_aberta.pdf

Rothfuss, G. J. A. (2002). *A Framework for Open Source Projects*. (M.S. Thesis). University of Zurich.

Rubalcaba, L., Michel, S., Sundbo, J., Brow, S., & Reynoso, J. (2012). Shaping, organizing, and rethinking service innovation: A multidimesional framework. *Journal of Service Management*, *23*(5), 696–715. doi:10.1108/09564231211269847

Rubin, J., & Chisnell, D. (2008). *Handbook of Usability Testing: How to Plan, Design, and Conduct Effective Tests*. John Wiley & Sons.

Russel, S., & Norvig, P. (2009). *Artificial Intelligence: A Modern Approach* (3rd ed.). Upper Saddle River, NJ: Prentice-Hall.

Ryzhkova, N. (2009). *The contribution of the user innovation methods to open innovation*. Blekinge, Sweden: Blekinge Institute of Technology.

Sadasivam, R. S., Delaughter, K., Crenshaw, K., Sobko, H. J., Williams, J. H., & Coley, H. L. et al. (2011). Development of an Interactive, Web-Delivered System to Increase Provider - Patient Engagement in Smoking Cessation. *Journal of Medical Internet Research*, *13*(4), e87. doi:10.2196/jmir.1721 PMID:22011394

Saeed, S., Wahab, F., Cheema, S. A., & Ashraf, S. (2013). Role of Usability in E-Government and E-Commerce Portals: An Empirical Study of Pakistan. *Life Science Journal, 10*(1S).

Salen, K. (2007). Gaming literacies: A game design study in action. *Journal of Educational Multimedia and Hypermedia*, *16*(3), 301–322.

Salo, J. (2012). The role of mobile technology in a buyer-supplier relationship: A case study from the steel industry. *Journal of Business and Industrial Marketing*, *27*(7), 554–563. doi:10.1108/08858621211257329

Salvendy, G. (2012). *Handbook of Human Factors and Ergonomics* (4th ed.). John Wiley and Sons. doi:10.1002/9781118131350

Sandberg, K. W., & Andersson, H. (2011). Usability Evaluation of an Interactive Service on Mobile Phone. In *Ergonomics for all: Celebrating PPCOE's 20 Years of Excellence-Selected Papers of the Pan-Pacific Conference on Ergonomics, PPCOE 2010* (pp. 67-72). PPCOE. doi:10.1201/b10529-15

Santander, V. F. A., & Castro, J. F. B. (2002). Deriving Use Cases from Organizational Modeling. In *Proceedings of IEEE Int. Conf. Requirements Eng.* doi:10.1109/ICRE.2002.1048503

Sato, S.K. (2011). The advertising aesthetic innovation: Smartphones and tablets. *Thought and Reality Magazine, 26* (3).

Sävenstedt, S., Meiland, F., Dröes, R. M., & Moelaert, F. (2010). Evaluation of Cognitive Prosthetics. In *Supporting People with Dementia Using Pervasive Health Technologies* (pp. 197–206). Springer. doi:10.1007/978-1-84882-551-2_13

Schadler, T. (2004). *Open Source Moves into the Mainstream*. Cambridge, MA: Forrester Research.

Schaffer, E. (2009). Beyond Usability: Designing Web Sites for Persuasion, Emotion, and Trust. *UX matters*. Retrieved September 22, 2013 from http://www.uxmatters.com/mt/archives/2009/01/beyond-usability-designing-web-sites-for-persuasion-emotion-and-trust.php

Scharpf, F. W. (1997). *Games Real Actors Play: Actor-Centered Institutionalism in Policy Research*. Oxford, UK: Westview Press.

Schermelleh-Engel, K., Moosbrugger, H., & Müller, H. (2003). Evaluating the Fit of Structural Equation Models: Tests of Significance and Descriptive Goodness-of-Fit Measures. *Methods of Psychological Research*, *8*(2), 23–74.

Schneider, K. (2009). *Experience and knowledge management in software engineering* (pp. 99–109). New York, NY: Springer. doi:10.1007/978-3-540-95880-2_4

Schön, D., & Bennett, J. (1996). Reflective conversations with materials. In T. Winograd, J. Bennett, L. De Young, & B. Hartfield (Eds.), *Bringing design to software*. New York: ACM Press.

Schulz, T., & Fuglerud, K. (2012). Creating Personas with Disabilities. In Computers Helping People with Special Needs (pp. 145-152). Springer.

Schummer, T., & Lukosch, S. (2007). *Patterns for computer-mediated interaction* (Vol. 11). Hoboken, NJ: John Wiley & Sons.

Schweik, C., & Semenov, A. (2003). The Institutional Design of Open Source Programming: Implications for Addressing Complex Public Policy and Management Problems. *First Monday*, *8*(1). doi:10.5210/fm.v8i1.1019

Scott, J. (1991). *Social Network Analysis: A Handbook*. London: Sage.

Seibold, D. R. (1979). Making Meetings More Successful: Plans, Formats, and Procedures for Group Problem-Solving. *Journal of Business Communication*, *16*(4), 3–20. doi:10.1177/002194367901600401

Sellner, W., Tschelig, M., Moser, C., Fuchsberger, V., & Neureiter, K. (2012). Revisiting Personas: The Making-of for Special User Groups. In Proceedings of CHI'12 Extended Abstracts on Human Factors in Computing Systems (pp. 453-468). ACM.

Sen, R. (2007). A Strategic Analysis of Competition Between Open Source and Proprietary Software. *Journal of Management Information Systems*, *24*(1), 233–257. doi:10.2753/MIS0742-1222240107

Settle, A. (2011). Computational thinking in a game design course. In *Proceedings of the 2011 conference on Information technology education* (pp. 61–66). New York, NY: ACM. doi:10.1145/2047594.2047612

Shin, Y. M., Lee, S. C., Shin, B., & Lee, H. G. (2010). Examining Influencing Factors of Post-Adoption Usage of Mobile Internet: Focus on the User Perception of Supplier-Side Attributes. *Information Systems Frontiers*, *12*(5), 595–606. doi:10.1007/s10796-009-9184-x

Shneiderman, B. (1976). Exploratory experiments in programmer behavior. *International Journal of Computer & Information Sciences*, *5*(2), 123–143. doi:10.1007/BF00975629

Shneiderman, B. (1992). *Designing the User Interface: Strategies for Effective Human-Computer Interaction* (Vol. 2). Addison-Wesley.

Shneiderman, B. (2000). Creating creativity: User interfaces for supporting innovation. *ACM Transactions on Computer-Human Interaction*, *7*(1), 114–138. doi:10.1145/344949.345077

Shneiderman, B., & Mayer, R. (1979). Syntactic/semantic interactions in programmer behavior: A model and experimental results. *International Journal of Computer & Information Sciences*, *8*(3), 219–238. doi:10.1007/BF00977789

Shujun, L., & Kokar, M. (2013). Agent Communication Language. In I. Mohammed, & S. Mohamad (Eds.), *Flexible Adaptation in Cognitive Radios* (pp. 37–44). New York, NY: Springer.

Siegel, D. A. (2010). The Mystique of Numbers: Belief in Quantitative Approaches to Segmentation and Persona Development. In Proceedings of CHI'10 Extended Abstracts on Human Factors in Computing Systems (pp. 4721-4732). ACM.

Siew, S.-T., Yeo, A. W., & Zaman, T. (2013). *Participatory Action Research in Software Development: Indigenous Knowledge Management Systems Case Study. In Human-Computer Interaction. Human-Centred Design Approaches, Methods, Tools, and Environments* (pp. 470–479). Berlin: Springer.

Sillitti, A., & Succi, G. (2005). Requirements engineering for agile methods. In *Engineering and Managing Software Requirements* (pp. 309–326). New York, NY: Springer. doi:10.1007/3-540-28244-0_14

Silva, C., Castro, J., Tedesco, P., Araújo, J., Moreira, A., & Mylopoulos, J. (2006). Improving the Architectural Detailed Design of Multi-Agent Systems: The Tropos Case. In *Proceedings of the 5th International Workshop on Software Engineering for Large Scale Systems (SELMAS'06)*. New York, NY: ACM Press.

Silva, V., & Lucena, C. (2007). Modeling Multi-Agent Systems. *Communications of the ACM, 50*(5), 103–108. doi:10.1145/1230819.1241671

Simons, R. (2005). *Levers of organization design: How managers use accountability systems for greater performance and commitment.* Boston: Harvard Business School Press.

Singer, G. (2002). *Methods for validating cockpit design: The best tool for the task.* Doctoral dissertation. Stockholm: Royal Institute of Technology.

Sinha, R. (2003). Persona Development for Information Rich Domains. In Proceedings of CHI'03 Extended Abstracts on Human Factors in Computing Systems (pp. 830-831). ACM.

Skellas, A. I., & Ioannidis, G. S. (2011). Web-Design for Learning Primary School Science Using LMSs: Evaluating Specially Designed Task-Oriented Design Using Young Schoolchildren. In *Proceedings of 14th International Conference on Interactive Collaborative Learning (ICL)*, (pp. 313-318). IEEE. doi:10.1109/ICL.2011.6059597

Smets, N. J. J. M., Abbing, M. S., Neerincx, M. A., Lindenberg, J., & van Oostendorp, H. (2010). Game-Based Versus Storyboard-Based Evaluations of Crew Support Prototypes for Long Duration Missions. *Acta Astronautica, 66*(5), 810–820. doi:10.1016/j.actaastro.2009.08.032

Šmite, D., Moe, N. B., & Ågerfalk, P. J. (2010). *Agility across time and space: implementing agile methods in global software projects.* New York, NY: Springer. doi:10.1007/978-3-642-12442-6

Šmite, D., Wohlin, C., Gorschek, T., & Feldt, R. (2010). Empirical evidence in global software engineering: A systematic review. *Empirical Software Engineering, 15*(1), 91–118. doi:10.1007/s10664-009-9123-y

Smith, K., & Hancock, P. A. (1995). Situation awareness is adaptive, externally directed consciousness. *Human Factors, 37*(1), 137–148. doi:10.1518/001872095779049444

Sneddon, A., Mearns, K., & Flin, R. (2006). Situation awareness and safety in offshore drill crews. *Cognition Technology and Work, 8*(4), 255–267. doi:10.1007/s10111-006-0040-1

Soares, S., Deutsch, T., Hanna, S., & Malik, P. (2012). *Big Data Governance: A Framework to Assess Maturity. IBM Data Magazine.*

Software Engineering Institute (SEI). (2010). *Team Software Process.* Retrieved from http://www.sei.cmu.edu/tsp/

Sohn, Y. W., & Doane, S. M. (2004). Memory processes of flight situation awareness: Interactive roles of working memory capacity, long-term working memory, and expertise. *Human Factors, 46*(3), 461–475. doi:10.1518/hfes.46.3.461.50392 PMID:15573546

Soloway, E., Bonar, J., & Ehrlich, K. (1982). What do novices know about programming? In *Directions in Human-Computer Interaction* (pp. 87–122). New York: Ablex.

Sommerville, I. (2005). *Ingeniería del Software.* Madrid: Pearson Educación.

Sosa, J. (2005). *Perspectiva Humana en la Calidad Sistémica de los Sistemas de Información.* (Master Degree Thesis). Universidad Simón Bolívar, Venezuela.

Souza, P. R. de A., & Dias, L. R. (2012). Kodu Game Labs: Estimulando o Raciocínio Lógico através de Jogos. In *Anais do 23º Simpósio Brasileiro de Informática na Educação.* Rio de Janeiro: SBC. Retrieved from http://br-ie.org/pub/index.php/sbie/article/view/1733

Spohrer, J., & Maglio, P. P. (2009). Service Science: Toward a Smarter Planet. In Service Engineering. Wiley.

Spohrer, J., Maglio, P. P., Bailey, J., & Gruhl, D. (2007). Steps Toward a Science of Service Systems. *IEEE Computer*, *40*(1), 71–77. doi:10.1109/MC.2007.33

Stallman, R. M. (2004). *Software libre para una sociedad libre*. Madrid: Traficantes de Sueños.

Stanton, N. A., Stewart, R., Harris, D., Houghton, R. J., Baber, C., & McMaster, R. et al. (2006). Distributed situation awareness in dynamic systems: Theoretical development and application of an ergonomics methodology. *Ergonomics*, *49*(12-13), 1288–1311. doi:10.1080/00140130600612762 PMID:17008257

Star, S. L., & Griesemer, J. R. (1989). Institutional ecology, 'translations' and boundary objects: Amateurs and professionals in Berkeley's museum of vertebrate zoology, 1907-39. *Social Studies of Science*, *19*(3), 387–420. doi:10.1177/030631289019003001

Stewart, K. J., Ammeter, A. P., & Maruping, L. M. (2006). Impacts of License Choice and Organizational Sponsorship on User Interest and Development Activity in Open Source Software Projects. *Information Systems Research*, *17*(2), 126–144. doi:10.1287/isre.1060.0082

Stewart, K. J., & Gosain, S. (2006). The impact of ideology on effectiveness in open source software development teams. *Management Information Systems Quarterly*, *30*(2), 291–314.

Still, B., & Morris, J. (2010). The Blank-Page Technique: Reinvigorating Paper Prototyping in Usability Testing. *IEEE Transactions on Professional Communication*, *53*(2), 144–157. doi:10.1109/TPC.2010.2046100

Stolee, K. T., & Fristoe, T. (2011). Expressing computer science concepts through Kodu game lab. In *Proceedings of the 42nd ACM technical symposium on Computer science education* (pp. 99–104). New York: ACM. doi:10.1145/1953163.1953197

Strategy Analytcs. (2012). *Apple iPad Captures 68 Percent Share of 25 Million Global Tablet Shipments in Q2 2012*. Retrieved August 10, 2012, from http://blogs. strategyanalytics.com/TTS/post/2012/07/25/Apple-iPad-Captures-68-Percent-Share-of-25-Million-Global-Tablet-Shipments-in-Q2-2012.aspx

Stuikys, V., & Damasevicius, R. (2007). Variability-Oriented Embedded Component Design for Ambient Intelligence. Information Technology and Control, Kaunas. *Technologija*, *36*(1), 16–29.

Subramaniam, C., Sen, R., & Nelson, M. L. (2009). Determinants of open source software project success: A longitudinal study. *Decision Support Systems*, *46*(2), 576–585. doi:10.1016/j.dss.2008.10.005

Sundbo, S. (1997). Management Innovation in Services. *Service Industries Journal*, *17*(3), 432–455. doi:10.1080/02642069700000028

Sunyaev, A., Kaletsch, A., & Krcmar, H. (2010). Comparative Evaluation of Google Health API vs. Microsoft HealthVault API. In *Proceedings of Healthinf 2010: the 3rd International Conference on Health Informatics* (pp. 195-201). INSTICC.

Suzuki, K., Karashima, M., & Nishiguchi, H. (2011). A Study on the Time Estimation Measurement for Web Usability Evaluation. In Design, User Experience, and Usability: Theory, Methods, Tools and Practice (pp. 53-59). Springer. doi:10.1007/978-3-642-21708-1_7

Tabaka, J. (2006). *Collaboration explained: facilitation skills for software project leaders*. Upper Saddle River, NJ: Pearson Education.

Taina, J. (2011). Good, Bad, and Beautiful Software-In Search of Green Software Quality Factors. *CEPIS UPGRADE*, *12*(4), 22–27.

Tajfel, H., & Turner, J. C. (1986). The Social Identity Theory of Intergroup Behavior. In *Psychology of Intergroup Relations* (pp. 1–19). Chicago: Nelson-Hall Publishers.

Tamburri, D. A., Lago, P., & van Vliet, H. (2013). Uncovering latent social communities in software development. *Software, IEEE*, *30*(1), 29–36. doi:10.1109/MS.2012.170

Tamir, D. E., & Mueller, C. J. (2010). Pinpointing Usability Issues Using an Effort Based Framework. In *Proceedings of 2010 IEEE International Conference on Systems Man and Cybernetics (SMC)*, (pp. 931-938). IEEE. doi:10.1109/ICSMC.2010.5641883

Tapscott, D., & Williams, A. D. (2008). *Wikinomics: how mass collaboration changes everything*. London: Penguin.

Taylor, G. S., Reinerman-Jones, L. E., Szalma, J. L., Mouloua, M., & Hancock, P. A. (2013). What to automate: Addressing the multidimensionality of cognitive resources through systems design. *Journal of Cognitive Engineering and Decision Making*, 7(4), 311–329. doi:10.1177/1555343413495396

Teixeira, A., Ferreira, F., Almeida, N., Rosa, A., Casimiro, J., & Queirós, A. (2013b). Multimodality and Adaptation for an Enhanced Mobile Medication Assistant for the Elderly. In *Proceedings of 3rd Workshop on Mobile Accessibility in Conference on Human Factors in Computing Systems*. ACM.

Teixeira, A., Pereira, C., Silva, M. O., Alvarelhão, J., Silva, A., Cerqueira, M., et al. (2013a). New Telerehabilitation Services for the Elderly. In I. Miranda & M. Cruz-Cunha (Eds.), Handbook of Research on ICTs for Healthcare and Social Services: Developments and Applications (pp. 109-132). IGI Global

The CSTA Standards Task Force. (2011). *CSTA K-12 Computer Science Standards*. New York: ACM Computer Science Teachers Association. Retrieved from http://csta.acm.org/Curriculum/sub/CurrFiles/CSTA_K-12_CSS.pdf

Thomas, G. (2006). *The DGI data governance framework*. Orlando, FL: The Data Governance Institute.

Thomas, J. C., Kellogg, W. A., & Erickson, T. (2001). The knowledge management puzzle: Human and social factors in knowledge management. *IBM Systems Journal*, 40(4), 863–884. doi:10.1147/sj.404.0863

Thomassen, J., & Schmitt, H. (1999). Introduction: Political Representation and Legitimacy in the European Union. In H. Schmitt, & J. Thomassen (Eds.), *Political Representation and Legitimacy in the European Union* (pp. 3–21). Oxford, UK: Oxford University Press. doi:10.1093/0198296614.003.0001

Tichy, N. M., Tushman, M. L., & Frombrun, C. (1979). Social Network Analysis for Organizations. *Academy of Management Review*, 4, 507–519.

Tirole, J., & Lerner, J. (2002). Some Simple Economics of Open Source. *The Journal of Industrial Economics*, 50(2), 197–234.

Tirole, J., & Lerner, J. (2005). The Scope of Open Source Licensing. *Journal of Law Economics and Organization*, 21(1), 20–56. doi:10.1093/jleo/ewi002

Tomitsch, M., Singh, N., & Javadian, G. (2010). Using Diaries for Evaluating Interactive Products: the Relevance of Form and Context. In *Proceedings of the 22nd Conference of the Computer-Human Interaction Special Interest Group of Australia on Computer-Human Interaction*. ACM. doi:10.1145/1952222.1952266

Tosi, F., Belli, A., Rinaldi, A., & Tucci, G. (2012). The Intermodal Bike: Multi-Modal Integration of Cycling Mobility through Product and Process Innovations in Bicycle Design. *Work (Reading, Mass.)*, 41, 1501–1506. PMID:22316928

Tretyak, O., & Sloev, I. (2013). Customer flow: Evaluating the long-term impact of marketing on value creation. *Journal of Business and Industrial Marketing*, 28(3), 221–228. doi:10.1108/08858621311302877

Triandis, H. C. (1995). *Individualism & Collectivism*. Boulder, CO: Westview Press.

Tuckman, B. W. (1965). Developmental sequence in small groups. *Psychological Bulletin*, 63(6), 384–399. doi:10.1037/h0022100 PMID:14314073

Tuckman, B. W., & Jensen, M. A. C. (1977). Stages of Small-Group Development Revisited. *Group & Organization Management*, 2(4), 419–427. doi:10.1177/105960117700200404

Tufts, J. B., Hamilton, M. A., Ucci, A. J., & Rubas, J. (2011). Evaluation by Industrial Workers of Passive and Level-Dependent Hearing Protection Devices. *Noise & Health*, 13(50), 26. doi:10.4103/1463-1741.73998 PMID:21173484

Turner, K. J. (2011). Flexible Management of Smart Homes. *Journal of Ambient Intelligence and Smart Environments*, 3(2), 83–109.

Uchida, S. et al. (2005). Software analysis by code clones in open source software. *Journal of Computer Information Systems*, 45(3), 1–11.

Un, S., & Price, N. (2007). Bridging the Gap between Technological Possibilities and People: Involving People in the Early Phases of Technology Development. *Technological Forecasting and Social Change, 74*(9), 1758–1772. doi:10.1016/j.techfore.2007.05.008

Usui, K., Takano, M., Fukushima, Y., & Yairi, I. E. (2010). The Evaluation of Visually Impaired People's Ability of Defining the Object Location on Touch-Screen. In *Proceedings of the 12th International ACM Sigaccess Conference on Computers and Accessibility* (pp. 287-288). ACM. doi:10.1145/1878803.1878874

Vanderheiden, G. C., & Henry, S. L. (2001). Everyone Interfaces. In C. Stephanidis (Ed.), *User interfaces for All: Concepts, Methods, and Tools*. CRC Press.

Vedel, T. (1989). Télématique et configurations d'acteurs: Une perspective européenne. *Reseaux, 7*(37), 9–28.

Velden, M. V. D. (2010). *Design for the contact zone*. Paper presented at the Seventh International Conference on Cultural Attitudes Towards Communications and Technology. Vancouver, Canada.

Velden, M. V. D. (2002). Knowledge facts, knowledge fiction: The role of ICTs in knowledge management for development. *Journal of International Development, 14*(1), 25–37. doi:10.1002/jid.862

Venkatesh, V., Morris, M. G., Davis, G. B., & Davis, F. D. (2003). User acceptance of information technology: Toward a unified view. *Management Information Systems Quarterly, 27*(3).

Vera-Muñoz, C., Arredondo, M. T., Peinado, I., Ottaviano, M., Páez, J. M., & de Barrionuevo, A. D. (2011). Results of the Usability and Acceptance Evaluation of a Cardiac Rehabilitation System. In Human-Computer Interaction. Users and Applications (pp. 219-225). Springer. doi:10.1007/978-3-642-21619-0_28

Viitanen, J., Hyppönen, H., Lääveri, T., Vänskä, J., Reponen, J., & Winblad, I. (2011). National Questionnaire Study on Clinical ICT Systems Proofs: Physicians Suffer From Poor Usability. *International Journal of Medical Informatics, 80*(10), 708–725. doi:10.1016/j.ijmedinf.2011.06.010 PMID:21784701

Virkar, S. (2011). *The Politics of Implementing e-Government for Development: The Ecology of Games Shaping Property Tax Administration in Bangalore City*. (Unpublished Doctoral Thesis). Oxford, UK: University of Oxford

Virkar, S. (2011). *The Politics of Implementing e-Government for Development: The Ecology of Games Shaping Property Tax Administration in Bangalore City*. (Unpublished Doctoral Thesis). University of Oxford, Oxford, UK.

Virkar, S. (2013a). Designing and Implementing e-Government Projects: Actors, Influences, and Fields of Play. In S. Saeed & C. G. Reddick (Eds.), Human-Centered Design for Electronic Government. Hershey, PA: IGI Global.

Virkar, S. (2013c). Re-engaging the Public in the Digital Age: e-Consultation Initiatives in the Government 2.0 Landscape. In Encyclopedia of Information Science and Technology (3rd ed.). Hershey, PA: IGI Global.

Virkar, S. (2007). *(Dis) Connected Citizenship? Exploring Barriers to eConsultation in Europe. Report to the European Commission for the The Breaking Barriers to eGovernment: Overcoming Obstacles to Improving European Public Services*. Project.

Virkar, S. (2013b). What's in a Game? The Politics of Shaping Property Tax Administration in Bangalore, India. In J. Bishop, & A. M. G. Solo (Eds.), *Politics in the Information Age*. London: Springer Inc.

Vygotsky, L. S. (1978). Zone of Proximal Development. In *Mind in society: The development of higher psychological processes* (pp. 52–91). Oxford, UK: Harvard University Press.

Walker, G. H., Stanton, N. A., & Young, M. S. (2006). The ironies of vehicle feedback in car design. *Ergonomics, 49*(2), 161–179. doi:10.1080/00140130500448085 PMID:16484143

Waltz, E., & Llinas, J. (1990). *Multisensor data fusion*. Norwood, MA: Artech House.

Wang, A. Y. (1994). Pride and Prejudice in High School Gang Members. *Adolescence*, *29*(114), 279–291. Retrieved from http://web.a.ebscohost.com.ezproxy.lib.utah.edu/ehost/detail?sid=b9dfc377-8d27-4165-8dd9-ca51192b63c0%40sessionmgr4001&vid=2&hid=4101&bdata=JnNpdGU9ZWhvc3QtbGl2ZQ%3d%3d#db=s3h&AN=9408150252 PMID:8085481

Wang, K., Abdulla, W., & Salcic, Z. (2009). Ambient Intelligence Platform Using Multi-Agent System and Mobile Ubiquitous Hardware. *Pervasive and Mobile Computing*, *5*(5), 558–573. doi:10.1016/j.pmcj.2009.06.003

Wasserman, A. I. (2010). Software Engineering Issues for Mobile Application Development. *FoSER*, *2010*(November), 7–8.

Wasserman, S., & Faust, K. (1994). *Social network analysis: Methods and applications*. Cambridge, UK: Cambridge University Press. doi:10.1017/CBO9780511815478

Wasserman, S., Scott, J., & Carrington, P. J. (2005). Introduction. In P. J. Carrington, J. Scott, & S. Wasserman (Eds.), *Models and methods in social network analysis* (pp. 1–7). New York: Cambridge University Press. doi:10.1017/CBO9780511811395.001

Waters, A. J., Gobet, F., & Leyden, G. (2002). Visuospatial abilities of chess players. *British Journal of Psychology*, *93*(4), 557–565. doi:10.1348/000712602761381402 PMID:12519534

Watts, D. J. (2004). The "New" Science of Networks. *Annual Review of Sociology*, *30*(1), 243–270. doi:10.1146/annurev.soc.30.020404.104342

Watts, D. J., & Strogatz, S. H. (1998). Collective Dynamics of 'Small-World' Networks. *Nature*, *393*(6684), 440–442. doi:10.1038/30918 PMID:9623998

Wegge, K. P., & Zimmermann, D. (2007). Accessibility, Usability, Safety, Ergonomics: Concepts, Models, and Differences. In Universal Acess in Human Computer Interaction. Coping with Diversity (pp. 294-301). Springer.

Weinhold, T., Oettl, S., & Bekavac, B. (2011). Heuristics for the Evaluation of Library Online Catalogues. In *New Trends in Qualitative and Quantitative Methods in Libraries: Selected Papers Presented at the 2nd Qualitative and Quantitative Methods in Libraries - Proceedings of the International Conference on Qqml2010* (p. 425). World Scientific. doi:10.1142/9789814350303_0052

Weiser, M., & Shertz, J. (1983). Programming problem representation in novice and expert programmers. *International Journal of Man-Machine Studies*, *19*(4), 391–398. doi:10.1016/S0020-7373(83)80061-3

Wellman, B., & Berkowitz, S. D. (1988). *Social Structures: A Network Approach*. Greenwich, CT: JAI Press.

Wenger, E. (1998). *Communities of Practice*. Cambridge, UK: Cambridge University Press. doi:10.1017/CBO9780511803932

Wenger, E., McDermott, R., & Snyder, W. (2002). *Cultivating Communities of Practice*. Boston, MA: Harvard Business School Press.

Wentink, E. C., Mulder, A., Rietman, J. S., & Veltink, P. H. (2011). Vibrotactile Stimulation of the Upper Leg: Effects of Location, Stimulation Method and Habituation. In *Proceedings of Engineering in Medicine and Biology Society, EMBC, 2011 Annual International Conference of the IEEE* (pp. 1668-1671). IEEE.

West, D. A. (2004). E-government and the Transformation of Service Delivery and Citizen Attitudes. *Public Administration Review*, *64*(1), 15–27. doi:10.1111/j.1540-6210.2004.00343.x

White, L. J., & Cohen, E. I. (1980). A domain strategy for computer program testing. *IEEE Transactions on Software Engineering*, *6*(3), 247–257. doi:10.1109/TSE.1980.234486

Whitworth, E. (2008). Experience Report: The Social Nature of Agile Teams (pp. 429–435). In *Proceedings of Agile 2008 Conference*. IEEE. doi:10.1109/Agile.2008.53

Whitworth, E., & Biddle, R. (2007). *The Social Nature of Agile Teams*. Paper presented at the AGILE. Washington, DC.

WHO. (2001). *The International Classification of Functioning, Disability and Health (ICF)*. World Health Organization.

WHO. (2002). *Active Ageing: A Policy Framework*. World Health Organization.

Wilkinson, S. (2003). *Focus Groups in Qualitative Psychology - A Practical Guide to Research Methods*. London: Sage Publications.

Wilson, B. C., & Shrock, S. (2001). Contributing to success in an introductory computer science course: a study of twelve factors. In *Proceedings of the thirty-second SIGCSE technical symposium on Computer Science Education* (pp. 184–188). New York: ACM. doi:10.1145/364447.364581

Winschiers-Theophilus, H., Jensen, K., & Rodil, K. (2012). *Locally situated digital representation of indigenous knowledge*. Paper presented at the Cultural Attitudes Towards Technology and Communication. Australia.

Wöckl, B., Yildizoglu, U., Buber, I., Aparicio, D. B., Kruijff, E., & Tscheligi, M. (2012). Basic Senior Personas: A Representative Design Tool Covering the Spectrum of European Older Adults. In *Proceedings of the 14th International ACM SIGACCESS Conference on Computers and Accessibility* (pp. 25-32). ACM. doi:10.1145/2384916.2384922

Woltjer, R. (2009). *Functional modeling of constraint management in aviation safety and command and control*. Doctoral dissertation (No.1249). Linköping, Sweden: Linköping University.

Woods, D. D., & Dekker, S. W. A. (2001). Anticipating the effects of technology change: A new era of dynamics for ergonomics. *Theoretical Issues in Ergonomics Science*, *1*(3), 272–282. doi:10.1080/14639220110037452

Woods, D. D., & Hollnagel, E. (2006). *Joint cognitive systems: Patterns in cognitive systems engineering*. Boca Raton, FL: Taylor & Francis. doi:10.1201/9781420005684

Wooldridge, M., Jennings, N. R., & Kinny, D. (2000). The Gaia Methodology for Agent-Oriented Analysis and Design. *Journal of Autonomous Agents and Multi-Agent Systems*, *3*(3), 285–312. doi:10.1023/A:1010071910869

Xu, B., Xu, Y., & Lin, Z. (2011). A Study of Open Source Software Development from Control Perspective. University of Nebraska.

Yamaoka, T., & Tukuda, S. (2011). A Proposal of Simple Usability Evaluation Method and its Application. In D. Lin, & H. Chen (Eds.), *Ergonomics for All: Celebrating PPCOE's 20 Years of Excellence* (pp. 63–66). PPCOE. doi:10.1201/b10529-14

Yao-Jen, C., & Tsen-Yung, W. (2010). Indoor Wayfinding Based On Wireless Sensor Networks For Individuals With Multiple Special Needs. *Cybernetics and Systems*, *41*(4), 317–333. doi:10.1080/01969721003778584

Yeo, A. W., Zaman, T., & Kulathuramaiyer, N. (2013). Indigenous Knowledge Management in the Kelabit community in Eastern Malaysia: Insights and reflections for contemporary KM design. *International Journal of Sociotechnology and Knowledge Development*, *5*(1), 23–36. doi:10.4018/jskd.2013010103

Yin, R. K. (2005). Case study: Planning and methods (3rd ed.). Porto Alegre: Bookman.

Yin, R. K. (2003). *Case Study Research: Design and Methods (vol. 5)*. London: Sage Publications.

YoYo Games, Ltd. (2014). *GameMaker: Studio*. Retrieved January 16, 2014, from https://www.yoyogames.com/studio

Yu, E. (1997). Towards Modelling and Reasoning Support for Early-Phase Requirement Engineering. In *Proceedings of IEEE Int. Symp. Requirements Eng.* (pp. 226-235). IEEE. doi:10.1109/ISRE.1997.566873

Yu, E. (2009). Social Modeling and i. In A. T. Borgida, V. Chaudhri, P. Giorgini, & E. S. Yu (Eds.), *Conceptual Modeling: Foundations and Applications - Essays in Honor of John Mylopoulos (LNCS)* (Vol. 5600). Springer.

Yu, E., Giorgini, P., Maiden, N., & Mylopoulos, J. (2011). *Social Modeling for Requirements Engineering*. Cambridge, MA: MIT Press.

Zacharias, G. L., Miao, A. X., Illgen, C. X., Yara, J. M., & Siouris, G. M. (1996). SAMPLE: Situation awareness model for pilot in-the-loop evaluation. In *Proceedings of the First Annual Symposium on Situational Awareness in the Tactical Air Environment*. Patuxent River, MD: Naval Air Warfare Center Aircraft Division.

Zajicek, M. (2004). Successful and Available: Interface Design Exemplars for Older Users. *Interacting with Computers*, *16*(3), 411–430. doi:10.1016/j.intcom.2004.04.003

Zaman, T., Yeo, A. W., & Kulathuramaiyer, N. (2011a). *Harnessing community's creative expression and indigenous wisdom to create value*. Paper presented at the Indigenous Knowledge Technology Conference 2011 (IKTC2011): Embracing Indigenous Knowledge Systems in a New Technology Design Paradigm. Windhoek, Namibia.

Zaman, T., Yeo, A. W., & Kulathuramaiyer, N. (2011b). *Indigenous Knowledge Governance Framework (IKGF): A holistic model for indigenous knowledge management*. Paper presented at the Second International Conference on User Science and Engineering (i-USEr2011) Doctoral Consortium. Kualalumpur.

Zaman, T., Yeo, A. W., & Kulathuramaiyer, N. (2013). Augmenting Indigenous Knowledge Management with Information and Communication Technology. *International Journal of Services Technology and Management, 19*(1/2/3), 12.

Zambonelli, F., Jennings, N., & Wooldridge, M. (2003). Developing multi-agent systems: The Gaia methodology. *ACM Transactions on Software Engineering and Methodology, 12*(3), 317–370. doi:10.1145/958961.958963

Zent, S. (2009). *A genealogy of scientific representations of indigenous knowledge. In Landscape, process, and power: Re-evaluating traditional environmental knowledge. Studies in environmental anthropology and ethnobiology* (pp. 19–67). Oxford, UK: Berghan Books.

Zhao, J. L., Hsu, C., Jain, H. K., Spohrer, J. C., & Tanniru, M. (2008). ICIS 2007 panel report: bridging service computing and service management: How MIS contributes to service orientation. *Communications of the Association for Information Systems, 22*, 413–428.

Ziv, A., Wolpe, P. R., Small, S. D., & Glick, S. (2003). Simulation-Based Medical Education: An Ethical Imperative. *Academic Medicine, 78*(8), 783–788. doi:10.1097/00001888-200308000-00006 PMID:12915366

Zollet, R., & Back, A. (2010). *Website Usability for Internet Banking. Institute of Information Management*. University of St Gallen.

About the Contributors

Saqib Saeed is an assistant professor at University of Dammam, Saudi Arabia. He has a PhD in Information Systems from the University of Siegen, Germany, and a Master's degree in Software Technology from Stuttgart University of Applied Sciences, Germany. Dr. Saeed is also a certified software quality engineer from the American Society for Quality. He is a member of advisory boards of several international journals besides being guest editor of several special issues. Dr. Saeed's research interests lie in the areas of human-centered computing, computer supported cooperative work, empirical software engineering, and ICT4D, and he has more than 50 publications to his credit.

Imran Sarwar Bajwa is an Assistant Professor of Computer Science at The Islamia University of Bahawalpur, Pakistan. He has worked on various research projects in University of Birmingham, UK (2009-2012) and University of Coimbra, Portugal (2006-2007). His research interests are Natural Language Processing, Automated Software Modelling, Enterprise Computing, and Image Processing.

Zaigham Mahmood is a researcher and author. He has an MSc in Mathematics, MSc in Computer Science, and PhD in Modelling of Phase Equilibria. Dr. Mahmood is a Senior Technology Consultant at Debesis Education UK, a researcher at the University of Derby UK, and Professor Extraordinaire at the North West University in South Africa. He is, currently, also a Foreign Professor at NUST and IIU in Islamabad Pakistan. Professor Mahmood has published over 100 articles in international journals and conference proceedings in addition to seven books on cloud computing and reference texts on e-government. He is also the Editor-in-Chief of the *Journal of E-Government Studies and Best Practices* and Series Editor-in-Chief of the IGI book series on A*dvances in Electronic Government, Digital Divide, and Regional Development (AEGDDRD)*. Professor Mahmood is an active researcher; he also serves as editorial board member of several journals, books, and conferences; guest editor for journal special issues; organiser and chair of conference tracks and workshops; and keynote speaker at conferences.

* * *

Jens Alfredson is since 2006 and in an earlier period from 1996-2001, employed by Saab, developing and evaluating novel presentations for fighter aircraft displays. He received a MSc in Industrial Ergonomics from Luleå University of Technology in 1995. He received a PhD in Human-Machine Interaction from Linköping University of Technology in 2007. Since 1999, he is certificated as an Authorized European Ergonomist, EurErg (CREE). He has previously (2001-2006) worked as a researcher at the department of Man-System-Interaction, Swedish Defense Research Agency.

José Joaquim Alvarelhão is Assistant of the Health Sciences School of the University of Aveiro. He received is BSc degree in Occupational Therapy in 1989, and his MSc degree in Public Health in 2010 from University of Porto. He is currently member of Direction Board of the Health Sciences School of the University of Aveiro. He also is member of the Executive committee of the International Cerebral Palsy Society and the Head of the Scientific Council of the Cerebral Palsy Portuguese Federation. His current research interests include human functionality, ambient assisted living services and disability issues. He has been involved in various European and national funded research projects, has more than twenty research publications distributed by books, book chapters, journals and proceedings of international conferences.

Muhammad Ahmad Amin has, for a very long time, worked as a Team Lead in the department of Software Development in both the public & private sector, and still is affiliated currently with various projects of public sector in Pakistan. He received his MCS degree from University of Arid Agriculture, Rawalpindi, Pakistan, in 2001 and MS in Software Engineering from Bahria University, Islamabad, Pakistan, in 2014. His current research interests are usability evaluation of open-source e-Learning and m-Learning systems.

Thiago Schumacher Barcelos earned his degree in Computer Science at Universidade de São Paulo (1999). He has a Master's degree in Computer Science (Area: Human-Computer Interaction) also by Universidade de São Paulo (2002). Thiago is currently a PhD candidate at Universidade Cruzeiro do Sul in the area of Science and Mathematics Teaching. He is also a researcher and lecturer at Instituto Federal de Educação, Ciência e Tecnologia de São Paulo. His current research areas are: ICT for Education, Human-Computer Interaction and Software Engineering.

Noel Carroll works in the field of Knowledge Management at the University of Limerick, Ireland. He previously worked as a postdoctoral researcher at Dublin City University in Cloud Computing. Noels research is currently focused on developing service analytics and methods, which support the assessment of service ecosystems. He completed his PhD at Lero – the Irish Software Engineering Research Centre, University of Limerick, which focuses on the emerging discipline of Service Science. His research explores methods to examine the socio-technical dynamics of complex service systems. The research examines Service Science initiatives and identifies methods to investigate the value of IT across service networks. He is particularly interested in applying social network analysis and actor-network theory to examine the socio-technical influence of IT on service dynamics. He also holds a Master's (research) in Business and a Degree (Hons) in Information Systems Management. His research activities cover a wide scope from Service Science, Software Engineering, Cloud Computing, and Education.

Zulaima Chiquín born in Venezuela, she studied for her BCompSc degree at the Central University of Venezuela (2002), she studied her degree from Antonio José of Sucre University in Attitudes facilitative of the teacher (2007). She obtained her MSc degree from "Simon Bolivar" University in Systems Engineering (2013). During these studies, she worked as a teaching at the University of Simón Bolívar on the Computer Engineering. She has served as teachers in the Antonio Jose de Sucre university of the vicerectorate Luis Caballero Mejias (2006-2009). Since 2008 she has been carrying out research in the fields of e-learning, Free/Libre Open Source software and software quality.

Laura B. Dahl is a doctoral candidate in Communication at the University of Utah. Her primary research and teaching focus has involved communication behaviors among and between design and development teams for Websites and software. She worked for 15 years in the Web development industry as a developer and database manager. Her research interests continue to grow into studying the communication aspects of design teams that either promote or discourage successful completion of software and Web projects.

Nelson Pacheco da Rocha is Full Professor of the University of Aveiro. He received his BSc degree in Electronics and Telecommunications Engineering in 1983 and his PhD in Electronics Engineering in 1992, from the University of Aveiro. He was the Head of Health Sciences School (2001-2011) and Pro-Rector of the University of Aveiro (2005-2010). Since 2001, he is the Head of the Health Sciences Department of the University of Aveiro. His current research interests include the application of information and communications technologies to healthcare and social services, the secondary use of electronic health records, and the interconnection of human functionality and ambient assisted living services. He has been involved in various European and national funded research projects, has supervised several PhD and MSc students and has a patent and more than one hundred research publications distributed by books, book chapters, international journals and proceedings of international conferences.

Margarida de Melo Cerqueira is Adjunct Professor in Health Sciences School of the University of Aveiro. She received her BSc degree in Educational Sciences in 1999, from University of Coimbra, and her MSc degree in Information Management in 2003 and his PhD in Health Sciences in 2010, from the University of Aveiro. Her current research interests includes social and educational gerontology, active ageing, the application of information and communications technologies to healthcare and social services, and the interconnection of human functionality and ambient assisted living services. She has some research publications distributed by books, international journals and proceedings of international conferences.

Kenyer Domínguez is a Integral Time Professor at Simón Bolívar University, Venezuela. He obtained his degree from Simón Bolívar University in Computer Engineering (2002) and he completed his MSc degree from Simón Bolívar University in System Engineering (2006). Since 2002, he has been carrying out research in the fields of Information Systems, Free/Libre Open Source software, and software quality.

Amir Hossein Ghapanchi is a tenured faculty member at the School of Information and Communication Technology, Griffith University, Australia. Dr Ghapanchi is a section editor for Australasian Journal of Information System, and an associate editor for *International Journal of Enterprise Information Systems* and *International Journal of Strategic Decision Sciences*. Amir has published over 50 referred publications including 40 journal articles in prestigious information systems and management journals such as *Information and Organization*, *Journal of the Association for Information Science and Technology* (JASIST), *Electronic Markets*, *Journal of Medical Internet Research*, *Journal of Computer and System Sciences*, *International Journal of Project Management*, *Journal of Systems and Software*, and *International Journal of Information Management*. Amir has been in receipt of several internal/external research and L&T grants.

Rosario Girardi earned her PhD (Computer Science) from University of Geneva, Switzerland in 1996 and her Master's of Computer Science from UFRGS, Brazil in 1991. She served as Engineer (Computer Science) at UdelaR, Uruguay in 1982 and as Lawyer at OAB, Brazil in 2012. She is an Associate Professor (Computer Science Department) at Federal University of Maranhão. She acts as lecturer, researcher, and advisor on the Graduate course in Electric Engineering (Computer Science area) and on the Undergraduate course in Computer Science. Her specialization areas are: Artificial Intelligence, Legal Computing, Software Engineering, and Information Engineering. Since 2001, she coordinates research projects with support of the CNPq and CAPES federal funding agencies and receives a CNPq research productivity grant since 2008. Dr. Girardi has orientated more than 100 final degree, research works, and teaching apprenticeships at the graduate and undergraduate level. She has produced more than 100 publications in books, book chapters, journals, and proceedings of events related with her research activities. She has been participating as member of program committees, lecturer and moderator in several national and international events related with her specialties. More information can be found at http://buscatextual. cnpq.br/buscatextual/visualizacv.do?id=K4707610E5.

Pankaj Kamthan has degrees in mathematics, mathematics education, and computer science. His teaching and research interests include agile methodologies, conceptual modeling, requirements engineering, software engineering education, and software quality. He has been teaching in academia and industry for the past two decades. He has taught over 20 courses in undergraduate and graduate programs and is an avid user of information technology in his courses. He has been a technical editor, participated in standards development, and served on program committees of conferences and editorial boards of journals related to e-learning, information technology, and resource management. He has authored over 75 scholarly publications.

Narayanan Kulathuramaiyer is senior research fellow of the Institute of Social Informatics and Technological Innovations and currently a Professor of Computer Science at the Faculty of Computer Science and Information Technology, Universiti Malaysia Sarawak (UNIMAS).

Adriana Leite earned her Master's of Electric Engineering (Computer Science area) from Federal University of Maranhão, UFMA, Brazil in 2009, her Especialist in Systems Analysis and Design from the Federal University of Maranhão in 2006, and her Undergraduate in Computer Technology from University Center of Maranhão in 2004. She has experience in Computer Science, focusing on Software Engineering, acting on the following subjects: Agent Architectures, Software Reuse, Domain Engineering, Application Engineering and Ontologies. More information can be found at http://lattes.cnpq. br/6606037022631240.

Ana Isabel Martins is a researcher at the Institute of Electronics and Telematics Engineering of Aveiro. She received her BSc degree in Gerontology in 2009 at the Health Sciences School of University of Aveiro and her MSc degree in Gerontology at the Health Sciences Department of the University of Aveiro in 2010. Currently, she is a PhD student in Health Sciences and Technology in the same department. She has been researching in the areas of use and commercialization of assistive products, assessment of human functioning and environmental factors using the International Classification of Functioning Disability and Health, and more recently, the evaluation of Ambient Assisted Living products and services in a Living Lab approach.

Sergio Ricardo Mazini obtained his bachelor degree in Information Systems (FATEB, 1996), postgraduate in Analysis, Development, and Project Management Systems (UNILINS, 2000), and he is master in Production Engineering (São Paulo State University – UNESP, 2011). He acts as Professor of Business Administration and Information Systems courses. He acts, also, as a consultant and systems analyst at Orion Management Solutions. He has experience in business consulting, business management, production engineering, development of information systems, innovation management, knowledge management, and enterprise portals.

Edumilis Méndez is a Associate Lecturer at Simón Bolívar University, Venezuela. She´s Systems Engineer (1999) and obtained her MSc degree from Simón Bolívar University in System Engineering (2004). Since 2003, she has been carrying out research in the fields of software project management, software development methodologies, software testing, and software quality.

Luis E. Mendoza is a Titular Lecturer at Simón Bolívar University, Venezuela. He completed his MSc degree from Simón Bolívar University in System Engineering (2000) and his PhD degree from University of Granada, Spain, in Advanced Methods and Techniques for Software Development (2011). Since 1999, he has been carrying out research in the fields of business process modeling and verification, systems integration, software development methodologies, and software quality.

Alexandra Queirós is Coordinator Professor of the Health Sciences School of the University of Aveiro. She received her BSc degree in Information and Communication Technologies in 1998, her MSc degree in Information Management in 2001, and her PhD in Health Technologies in 2006 from the University of Aveiro. She is currently member of the Scientific Council of the University of Aveiro. Her current research interests include human functionality, ambient assisted living services, and the application of information and communications technologies to healthcare and social care services. She has been involved in various European and national funded research projects, has supervised several MSc students, and has more than 40 research publications distributed by books, book chapters, journals, and proceedings of international conferences.

Anabela Gonçalves Silva is Assistant Professor at the Health School, Aveiro University. She received her BSc degree in Physiotherapy in 1999 and took her PhD at the Center for Pain Research in 2009 at Leeds Metropolitan University. She worked as a physiotherapist at several clinics and rehabilitation centers and lectures at Aveiro's University since 2001. Her current research interests include human functioning and disability and how they are affected by pain and environmental factors, methodologies of assessment related to pain and function, the interconnection of human functioning and ambient assisted living services and neck pain. She had a PhD scholarship from the Foundation of Science and Technology, has supervised several MSc students, and has several publications in International journals and conference proceedings.

Ismar Frango Silveira earned his degree in Mathematics-Informatics at Universidade Federal de Juiz de Fora (1994), Master of Science (Area: Computer Graphics) by the Instituto Tecnológico de Aeronáutica (1997), and his PhD in Electrical Engineering by Universidade de São Paulo (2003). He is currently Professor at Universidade Presbiteriana Mackenzie and Universidade Cruzeiro do Sul, both in São Paulo, Brazil. His research concentrates on Digital Games, Learning Objects, Collaborative Virtual Environments, and ICT for Education in general.

Roberto Muñoz Soto earned his degree in Informatics Engineering at Universidad de Valparaíso (UV), Chile. He has a Master's degree in Informatics Engineering (Area: Human-Computer Interaction) by the Pontificia Universidad Catolica de Valparaíso, Chile (2012). He is currently a full-time professor at Universidad de Valparaíso, and his research concentrates on Human-Computer Interaction and ICT for Education.

Shefali Virkar is postdoctoral researcher at the University of Oxford (UK) currently reading for a DPhil in Politics. Her doctoral research seeks to explore the growing use of Information and Communication Technologies (ICTs) to promote better governance in the developing world, with special focus on the political and institutional impacts of ICTs on local public administration reform in India. Shefali holds an MA in Globalisation, Governance, and Development from the University of Warwick, UK. Her Master's thesis analysed the concept of the Digital Divide in a globalising world, its impact developing countries, and the ensuing policy implications. At Oxford, Shefali is a member of Keble College.

Alvin W. Yeo is the Director of the Institute of Social Informatics and Technological Innovations and an Associate Professor at the Faculty of Computer Science and Information Technology Innovations, Universiti Malaysia Sarawak (UNIMAS).

Tariq Zaman earned his PhD from the Faculty of Computer Science and Information Technology, Univeristi Malaysia Sarawak, Malaysia and currently works as postdoctoral research fellow in the Institute of Social Informatics and Technological Innovations Universiti Malaysia Sarawak (UNIMAS).

Index

A

Accessibility 35, 224, 252, 272, 274-275, 279, 281, 293
Active Ageing 275-276, 293
Actor Goals and Motivations 41, 89
Actor Perceptions 41, 76, 89
Affordance 190
Agile Methodology 174-176, 179, 190
Alpha Development Status 102
Ambient Assisted Living 274, 293
Analogy 141-142, 145-146, 164, 171-172
Architectural Design 195, 197-199, 204-206, 213, 218
Artifact 179, 183, 190

B

Bario 237, 240, 242, 245, 248
Beta Development Status 102
Body Functions and Structures 294
Breakout 147, 152, 154-156, 162-163, 171
Business Intelligence 49, 64
Busy Wait Loop 160, 171

C

Co-Evaluation 219, 222-224, 234-235
Collaboration 47, 99, 104-105, 107, 113, 117, 126, 177, 182, 222-223, 237, 240, 279
Complex Systems 118-119, 123, 128-134, 140, 275
Computer Integrated Manufacturing 64
Contextual Factors 280, 282, 286-287, 294
Country Context Gap 41, 89

D

Decision Making 25, 64, 107-108, 111-112, 117, 119, 126, 128, 130, 133, 192
Design-Actuality Gap 42, 76-77, 86, 90

Design-Actuality Gap Model or Framework 42, 90
Design for All 252, 272
Design-Use Process 118, 127-132, 134, 140
Detailed Design 193, 195, 198-199, 206, 213, 218
Digital Catalog 44, 54, 56, 64
Digital Native 191
Domain and Application Engineering 193-194, 211, 218

E

E-Administration 24, 42, 90
Ecology of Games 70, 74-77
E-Consultation 25, 27-32, 34, 42, 90
E-Democracy 24-26, 28, 33, 35, 42, 90
E-Engagement 24-25, 28, 42, 90
E-Governance 24, 28, 32, 42, 90
E-Government 24, 26, 28, 32, 42, 67-73, 75-77, 82-83, 86-87, 90, 262, 296
Enterprise Resource Planning 64
e-petition 33
E-Services 24, 42, 90
eToro 244
Evaluation 42, 66, 90, 112-113, 127, 133, 141, 143-144, 147, 150, 153, 158-159, 194, 219-224, 226-228, 230, 232-235, 250-257, 259-265, 272, 274-275, 277, 279, 295-296, 298, 312
E-Voting 24, 28, 42, 90

F

FLOSS 96, 219-221, 223-226, 228, 232, 234, 236
FLOSS Communities 236
FLOSS Foundations 236
FP&IC 244
Free Open Source Software (FLOSS) 236
Function Allocation 130-131, 140

Software Design 87, 108-109, 117, 143, 145, 218
Software Engineering 44-45, 55-56, 164, 173-174, 176-179, 185, 192-193, 211, 225, 228, 250
software platform design 68
Software Process 178, 195, 214, 220-221
Software Quality 97-99, 221, 236, 251
Software Reuse 218
Sprite 146, 154, 156-163, 172
Stable Development Status 102
Systemic Quality 219-220, 236

T

Tablet 49, 51, 53-56, 65-66
Technological Variables 43, 91
TIE 242, 248
Total Failure 43, 77, 91

U

Usability Controlled Experiments Methodologies 272
Usability Evaluation Methodology 272
Usability Inquiry Methodologies 273
Usability Inspection Methodologies 273, 298, 312
Usability Test Methodologies 273
Use Case 191
User Centered Design 252, 272, 277, 294

User Experience 104, 113, 128, 150, 152, 175, 178, 185, 191, 251, 272
User Interface 143, 179, 195, 197, 200-202, 204-205, 207-208, 210, 301, 312
User Story 178, 191

V

Vulnerability 298, 301, 312

W

Web Application Security 295-296, 298, 312
WebGoat 295-298, 301, 303-307, 309, 312
Wiki 173-174, 176-186, 191